Multinational Enterprises and Trade Policy

Multinational Enterprises and Trade Policy

The Selected Scientific Papers of Alan M. Rugman
Volume Two

Alan M. Rugman

*Professor of International Business, Faculty of Management,
University of Toronto, Canada*

Edward Elgar
Cheltenham, UK • Brookfield, US

Published by
Edward Elgar Publishing Limited
8 Lansdown Place
Cheltenham
Glos GL50 2HU
UK

Edward Elgar Publishing Company
Old Post Road
Brookfield
Vermont 05036
US

A catalogue record for this book is available from the British Library

ISBN 1 85898 408 4

Printed in Great Britain by Galliard (Printers) Ltd, Great Yarmouth

Contents

PART III   THE DOUBLE DIAMOND FRAMEWORK

PART IV   FREE TRADE AND NAFTA

Acknowledgments

The publishers wish to thank the following who have kindly given permission for the use of copyright material.

1   Alan M. Rugman. 'The Role of Multinational Enterprises in U.S.–Canadian Economic Relations' *Columbia Journal of World Business*, **XXI** (2) (Summer 1986), 15–27. Copyright 1986. *Columbia Journal of World Business*. Reprinted with permission.

2   Alan M. Rugman. 'Research and Development by Multinational and Domestic Firms in Canada' *Canadian Public Policy*, **VII** (4) (Autumn 1981), 604–16. Reprinted by permission of the publisher.

3   Alan M. Rugman and Alain Verbeke. 'Multinational Corporate Strategy and the Canada–U.S. Free Trade Agreement' *Management International Review*, **30** (3) (Summer 1990), 253–66. Reprinted by permission of the publisher.

4   Michael Gestrin and Alan M. Rugman. 'The Strategic Response of Multinational Enterprises to NAFTA' *Columbia Journal of World Business*, **28** (4) (Winter 1993), 18–29. Copyright 1993. *Columbia Journal of World Business*. Reprinted with permission.

5   Alan M. Rugman and Alain Verbeke. 'Multinational Enterprise and National Economic Policy' in Peter J. Buckley and Mark Casson (eds), *Multinational Enterprises in the World Economy: Essays in Honour of John H. Dunning* (Aldershot, UK: Edward Elgar, 1993), 194–211. Reprinted by permission of the publisher.

6   Lee T. Brown, Alan M. Rugman and Alain Verbeke. 'Japanese Joint Ventures with Western Multinationals: Synthesising the Economic and Cultural Explanations of Failure' *Asia Pacific Journal of Management*, **6** (2) (April 1989), 225–42. Reprinted by permission of the publisher.

7   Alan M. Rugman and Alain Verbeke. 'Strategic Management and Trade Policy' *Journal of International Economic Studies*, (3) (Tokyo: Institute of Comparative Economic Studies, Hosei University, March 1989), 139–52. Reprinted by permission of the publisher.

8   Alan M. Rugman and Alain Verbeke. 'Mintzberg's Intended and Emergent Corporate Strategies and Trade Policy' *Canadian Journal of Administrative Sciences*, **8** (3) (September 1991), 200–208. Reprinted by permission of the publisher.

9   Alan M. Rugman and Michael V. Gestrin. 'U.S. Trade Laws as Barriers to Globalisation' *The World Economy*, **14** (3) (September 1991), 335–52. Reprinted by permission of Blackwell Publishers.

10   Alan Rugman and Michael Gestrin. 'E.C. Anti-dumping Laws as a Barrier to Trade' *European Management Journal*, **9** (4) (December 1991), 475–82. Reprinted by permission of Blackwell Publishers.

11   Alan M. Rugman and Alain Verbeke. 'Trade Policy in the Asia–Pacific Region: A

U.S.–Japan Comparison' *Journal of Business Administration*, **17** (1–2) (1987–8), 89–107. Reprinted by permission of the publisher.

12   Alan M. Rugman and Alain Verbeke. 'Strategic Trade Policy is Not Good Strategy' *Hitotsubashi Journal of Commerce and Management*, **25** (1) (December 1990), 75–97. Reprinted by permission of the publisher.

13   Sidney J. Gray and Alan M. Rugman. 'Does the United States Have a Deficit with Japan in Foreign Direct Investment?' *Transnational Corporations*, **3** (2) (August 1994), 127–37. Reprinted by permission of the United Nations Publication Board.

14   Alan M. Rugman and Alain Verbeke. 'Europe 1992 and Competitive Strategies for North American Firms' *Business Horizons*, **34** (6) (November–December 1991), 76–81. Reprinted by permission of the publisher.

15   Alan M. Rugman. 'Diamond in the Rough' *Business Quarterly*, **55** (3), 61–4. Reprinted with permission of *Business Quarterly*, published by the Western Business School, The University of Western Ontario, London, Canada, Winter 1991.

16   Alan M. Rugman and Joseph R. D'Cruz. 'The "Double Diamond" Model of International Competitiveness: The Canadian Experience' *Management International Review*, **33** (2) (1993), 17–39. Reprinted by permission of the publisher.

17   Alan M. Rugman. 'Porter Takes the Wrong Turn' *Business Quarterly*, **56** (3), 59–64. Reprinted with permission of *Business Quarterly*, published by the Western Business School, The University of Western Ontario, London, Canada, Winter 1992.

18   Alan M. Rugman and Alain Verbeke. 'How to Operationalize Porter's Diamond of International Competitiveness' *The International Executive*, **35** (4) (July–August 1993), 283–99. Copyright 1993, Wiley-Liss Inc., Wiley & Sons, Inc. Reprinted by permission of the publisher.

19   Alan M. Rugman. 'Environmental Regulations and International Competitiveness: Strategies for Canada's Forest Products Industry' *The International Executive* **37** (5) (September–October 1995), 451–65. Copyright 1995, Wiley-Liss, Inc., Wiley & Sons, Inc. Reprinted by permission of the publisher.

20   Alan M. Rugman, Alain Verbeke and Stephen Luxmore. 'Corporate Strategy and the Free Trade Agreement: Adjustment by Canadian Multinational Enterprises' *Canadian Journal of Regional Science*, **XIII** (2–3) (Summer–Autumn 1990). Reprinted by permission of the publisher.

21   Alan M. Rugman and Andrew Anderson. 'The Canada–U.S. Free Trade Agreement and Canada's Agri-Food Industries' *Northeastern Journal of Agriculture and Resource Economics*, **19** (2) (October 1990), 70–79. Reprinted by permission of the publisher.

22   Alan M. Rugman and Mark A.A. Warner. 'Foreign Ownership, Free Trade and the Canadian Energy Sector' *Journal of Energy and Development*, **14** (1) (Autumn 1988), 1–18. Copyright 1990 by the International Research Center for Energy and Economic Development. Reprinted by permission of the publisher.

23   Alan M. Rugman. 'A Canadian Perspective on NAFTA' *The International Executive*, **36** (1) (January–February 1994), 33–54. Copyright 1994, Wiley-Liss, Inc., Wiley & Sons, Inc. Reprinted by permission of the publisher.

24   Michael Gestrin and Alan M. Rugman. 'The North American Free Trade Agreement and Foreign Direct Investment' *Transnational Corporations*, **3** (1) (February 1994), 77–95. Reprinted by permission of the United Nations Publication Board.

25   Mark A.A. Warner and Alan M. Rugman. 'Competitiveness: An Emerging Strategy of Discrimination in U.S. Antitrust and R&D Policy?' *Law and Policy in International Business*, **25** (3) (Spring), 945–82. © 1994 & Georgetown University. Reprinted with the permission of the publisher.

Introduction

In this Introduction I continue on from Volume 1 and briefly review the key contribution of each article to the literature of international business. I reconsider the intellectual, institutional and personal context within which each article originated. This process provides an historical overview of these articles over the last 20 years, a period in which the reputation of the field of international business has increased within the academic profession and policy community. The Introduction also offers me the privilege of acknowledging debts of gratitude to my co-authors, collaborators and sponsors.

Volume 2 of my selected papers on policy builds upon the theoretical contributions of Volume 1. Thus, Part I of this book deals with the application of internalization theory to business–government relations, including applications to Canada–US free trade and to Asia; Part II deals with the 'theory of shelter', i.e., the manner in which the administration of trade policies can be captured by domestic interest groups so that the policies are applied as a discriminatory entry barrier against foreign firms. Part III looks at applications of the 'double diamond' framework of international competitiveness, including an unusual treatment of environmental regulations. Part IV is a set of papers examining the trade and investment implications of the North American Free Trade Agreement (NAFTA) and its impact on competitiveness. Throughout the four parts, the critical role of the multinational enterprise (MNE) is emphasized so this book can be viewed as an applied set of papers built upon the theoretical foundations of the theory of the MNE.

Part I

Part I is a set of six papers in which the theoretical principles of Volume 1, on internalization theory, are applied to trade and investment policy issues. The first few papers do this in a US–Canada context; the last paper in Part I considers applications to cultural factors and opportunism in an Asian context; the fifth paper offers a general framework for the analysis of government–multinational enterprise relations, in which national responsiveness strategy is included along with globalization strategies.

For help at a critical stage of my career in making the transition from theoretical to policy work I am especially grateful to my current colleague, A.E. Safarian. When I began my work on Canadian trade and investment issues while still at the University of Winnipeg, I was somewhat isolated from the leading thinkers in these areas except through their published work. While completing my book on *Multinationals in Canada* in 1980, I sent it to Ed Safarian for his comments and requested that he consider writing a foreword. Although at that time we had never met, he replied with extensive and detailed comments which greatly improved the book. Ed also contributed a wonderful foreword, placing my book 'in the context of intellectual thought in Canada and elsewhere' on the subject of the regulation of multinational enterprises. Ed has continued to give me good advice and when I joined the University of Toronto he helped to broaden my horizons by introducing me to a more diverse intellectual community at Massey College, an affiliation which has perhaps been the most rewarding of my life.

The use of Canada as a laboratory for social science experiments on the regulation of foreign direct investment (FDI) is highly appropriate for two reasons. First, Canada has a large amount of (mainly US) foreign ownership – as much as 40 per cent of its manufacturing sector at certain times. Second, more recently Canada has developed its own MNEs and recorded an unusually large share of FDI in the United States. Chapter 1 was prepared while I was on sabbatical leave at the Center for International Affairs at Harvard University in 1984–5. It represents a strong statement of the efficiency aspects of MNEs and it views MNEs as agents for the economic integration of the United States and Canada. It is of some interest that the second of my three conclusions was wrong. Due to the size asymmetry of the US–Canada economic relationship, I predicted that the United States would continue to deal with Canada on a multilateral basis, whereas within two years the United States agreed to Canada's agenda of a bilateral free trade agreement.

As another dimension of the efficiency aspects of MNEs, I had earlier used internalization theory to analyze explicitly the performance of US subsidiaries in Canada and their contribution to Canadian economic development. In Chapter 2, I relate this empirical work on the research and development (R&D) done by US subsidiaries to the largely protectionist literature in Canada advocating an independent science and technology (S&T) policy. I show that US subsidiaries are an integral part of the Canadian economic system and that the R&D contribution, in particular, is on a par with Canadian firms. This confirms an earlier finding to the same effect by Ed Safarian. The source of some of the most misinformed analysis of Canadian S&T policy and technology transfer by foreign-owned firms was the Science Council of Canada. This institution was abolished by the federal conservative government in 1992, just as it was beginning to balance its studies with a less nationalist line, due to the influence of its last chair, Dr Geraldine Kenney-Wallace, now a colleague of mine at Massey College.

In policy applications of internalization theory the most useful framework is one where the firm-specific advantages (FSAs) can be related to the relevant host or home country advantages (CSAs). The FSA–CSA framework also captures the key elements of Dunning's eclectic theory (as shown in Chapter 5, below). One of the most powerful applications of the FSA–CSA framework has been to determine the response of MNEs to the institutional fabric of the Canada–U.S. Free Trade Agreement (FTA), and NAFTA. In Chapter 3, Alain Verbeke and I apply this framework to the FTA. In Chapter 4, Michael Gestrin and I apply it to NAFTA. These analyses provide similar results; the 50 largest MNEs which account for over 70 per cent of the US–Canadian trade and over 80 per cent of FDI have corporate strategies in place to take advantage of the FTA and/or NAFTA. I have found that this framework is useful in teaching and is also accepted by senior executives involved in strategic planning. While the FTA was being negotiated over the 1986–8 period, I served as the only academic member of Canada's International Trade Advisory Committee. The other members were the CEOs of these large MNEs, and a few presidents of several smaller companies. I learned a great deal about corporate strategy and business–government relationships from this experience, and in subsequent work I have attempted to make my analytical work relevant and of practical value to both business executives and government officials.

In order to develop a consensus that the FSA–CSA matrix is a general framework for the analysis of corporate strategy and government policy, Alain Verbeke and I incorporate Dunning's eclectic model into it in Chapter 5. We then use the same FSA–CSA framework to incorporate the Doz and Bartlett and Ghoshal work on national responsiveness, creating the concept of 'location-bound FSAs' to do this. In earlier work extending corporate strategy into an international dimension, all FSAs were assumed to be 'non-location bound'. For example, Porter's cost, differentiation and focus strategies are all non-location bound. This paper is a powerful tool to integrate the literature in the allegedly different sub-fields of international business and international management. As was argued in theory papers in Volume 1, there is no real difference between these approaches since the management of the MNE is the common link. Thus, the large volume of John Dunning's work on MNEs and government policy is of direct relevance to all scholars in international business and/or international management.

With internalization theory being solidly embedded in transaction cost analysis, it is important to move beyond the economics-driven regulatory issues of trade and investment agreements towards related disciplines. The recent work on organizational learning, the resource-based view of the firm, and on business networks, has taken transaction cost analysis into areas of culture and organizational behaviour (OB). In Chapter 6, co-authored with Lee Brown, a doctoral candidate in OB, and Alain Verbeke, we review the literature on joint ventures between Asian and Western MNEs. We relate the economic aspects of compatibility of the FSAs of the joint venture partners to mechanisms which control opportunistic behaviour. Following this we re-analyse relevant literature on joint ventures to determine when scholars have explained joint venture failure due solely to either economic or cultural incompatibility, or due to a combination of both.

Part II

Part II consists of eight papers, four of them co-authored with Alain Verbeke of Brussels University. In these, Alain and I develop the theory of shelter and apply it to issues in US–Canadian trade policy, and also to US–Japanese trade policy. All of these papers were completed at the University of Toronto, where I was recruited in 1987 to head the international business activities of the Faculty of Management. Many of the papers in Volume 2 come out of research projects funded by the Research Programme of the Ontario Centre for International Business (OCIB). The OCIB was a joint venture between the management and law faculties of the University of Toronto and York University, and also involved the business school at Wilfrid Laurier University. It was financed by a five-year grant from the Province of Ontario over the 1988–93 period. I was the Research Director of the OCIB over the lifetime of the grant and was responsible for introducing a peer refereeing system and related administrative activities to allocate about one million dollars in research projects over that period. Over one hundred research working papers were produced by the management and law programme, with most subsequently being published in refereed journals or in books, including those in several volumes of my edited *Research in Global Strategic Management* series. Part of the funding for OCIB also provided for visits of prominent scholars, such as

Dr Alain Verbeke. I am grateful to him for his conceptual insight and original thinking which greatly improved my research.

The analytical framework of Chapter 7 is so strong that I use it on a regular basis in my courses in international business. As one of the first influential papers in the new sub-field of international political economy, it brings together not just elements of politics, economics and law but also the strategic management decisions of the MNE. There are two matrices: one for corporate strategy and one for government policy (in particular, trade policy). Their interaction provides a rich framework of cases in which it can be demonstrated unambiguously that only non-efficiency-based firms need to pursue the 'fourth generic' of shelter-based strategies in the non-market environment. Such firms then interact with the 'technical track' of US trade bureaucracy to transform the administration of US unfair trade laws into discriminatory barriers to entry against rival foreign firms. The protectionist US firms seeking shelter capture (or influence strongly) what should be an independent technical track and return it to the political sphere of influence. The application of this model to the Canadian softwood lumber case is particularly useful; as late as February 1996, the US coalition for fair trade in lumber succeeded in forcing Canadian provincial governments to impose export quotas in order to avoid the threat of another biased countervailing-duty case.

Some of my colleages in strategic management have been slow to take on board some of the international political economy aspects of the theory of shelter. Therefore, Alain Verbeke and I deliberately chose to rework our shelter concepts in terms of Henry Mintzberg's famous distinction between intended and emergent strategy. In Chapter 8 we are able to demonstrate in a convincing manner that the process by which US trade remedy law is administered leads to the emergent strategy of protection for domestic firms, which is a realized non-competitive strategy for US firms involved in this process. We again use the softwood lumber example, plus a summary of the fresh Atlantic groundfish case, as illustrations of emergent strategies.

While the focus of the previous two papers is the problem of Canadian resource-based firms losing access to a large triad market, the opposite side of corporate strategy needs to be examined. Thus, in Chapter 9 (co-authored with Michael Gestrin), we concentrate on the use of US trade remedy laws from the perspective of US firms seeking shelter. What we find is the paradox of the protectionist US steel industry being the biggest user of countervailing-duty and anti-dumping measures whereas the equally protectionist US textiles and apparel sectors are the lowest users. The latter sectors secure shelter by other means, such as through the GATT's multi-fibre agreement and discriminatory rules of origin, both of these being achieved through well-known lobbying. What is of concern is the more subtle lobbying of sectors such as steel and chemicals which have changed the administration of the technical track of unfair trade barriers into a similar protectionist quagmire.

Chapter 10, also co-authored with Michael Gestrin, provides data to show that the Europeans are just as bad as the Americans in the abusive use of trade remedy laws, in this case anti-dumping laws. These are also subject to capture by protectionist Europeans firms; indeed the Brussels bureaucracy is even worse than the US one, since European decisions do not even follow a transparent process where foreign firms can gain legal standing and launch appeals. European steel, chemicals and electronics firms have all used anti-dumping laws as trade barriers against more efficient foreign rivals, especially Asian firms. The power of triad areas, such as the European Union and the United States, to deny access to their markets of the more efficient products from other triad partners, but particularly from smaller, open trading economies, is one of the most troubling issues of international trade policy. The potential and actual efficiency gains of comparative advantage continue to be threatened by this new form of disguised (or contingent) protectionism.

Japan is the third part of the triad and it is not neglected in these studies of trade policy. In Chapter 11 (co-authored with Alain Verbeke) we show that Japan has pursued a non-free trade strategy and that its internal competitive structure has been such that this strategy was successful. In contrast, the United States is schizophrenic enough to believe that it has been pursuing free trade, whereas in reality it too has been following a non-free trade strategy. The main problem in the United States is that this is an unanticipated, or emergent, strategy and that the US internal political structure is inconsistent with its policy objectives. The three matrices in this paper provide a useful classification of the US and Japanese cases. I have found these to be useful in teaching and this paper has been reproduced by others in books of readings.

Strategic trade policy is one of the biggest frauds perpetuated by economists or policy makers. The trivial mathematical nature of the Brander and Spencer cases has been widely misunderstood, indeed misrepresented, by advocates of US industrial policy. In Chapter 12 (again co-authored with Alain Verbeke) we revisit the Brander and Spencer rationale for rent-seeking behaviour in strategic trade policy using the Krugman payoff matrix. We do not quibble with the assumed numbers showing that a subsidized sector can earn rents from a first mover advantage in a strategic game. We make a more powerful point. We demonstrate that the implementation structure of the US economic and political system is inconsistent with strategic trade policy. Lobbies in the United States will distort subsidies into non-efficiency and protectionist uses. There is ample evidence of such an 'administrative heritage' in US government policy making, in contrast to the Japanese system which has an efficiency-based strategic trade policy. Unfortunately this paper has not received the attention it deserves and US trade and industrial policy is still shelter-based.

Another area where policy makers are misled by casual research is on the subject of the alleged US deficit in foreign direct investment with Japan. In Chapter 13, along with Sid Gray, I recalculate the relative stocks of Japanese FDI in the United States compared to US FDI in Japan. The Department of Commerce figures show four times as much Japanese FDI in the United States as US FDI in Japan (the Japanese FDI flow numbers, which do not measure stocks accurately, actually show a ratio of 18 to 1). Our paper demonstrates that the stocks are approximately equal, once they are recalculated at current stock market values (not at historical book value) and at current exchange rates. I have found that policy makers, and even some of my academic colleagues, tend to advocate corrective and interventionist strategies even when there is no sound empirical foundation for their concern. While good data on FDI are difficult to come by, there is no excuse for such poor methodology and the misuse of data in policy analysis.

The single European market has been the subject of numerous studies, many of which argue that an integrated European market will allow consolidation of European firms so that they can better pursue 'natural' strategies of cost leadership, differentiation and focus. In a globalized system, European integration should develop European-based champions. How do non-European firms react? In Chapter 14 Alain Verbeke and I show that North American firms have two basic strategies. First, the subsidiaries of North American firms in Europe can behave as 'insiders' and take advantage of the changes in European integration. Second, the 'outsiders' will find access more difficult and may need to switch from exporting to foreign direct investment or consider strategies of national responsiveness. In addition, the North American subsidiaries of European firms will be affected by rationalization pressures versus new investment opportunities. The actual response, of course, depends upon careful analysis of individual firm and industry cases. We do this elsewhere, in a series of papers in Volume 3 of my *Research in Global Strategic Management* (1993).

Part III

The five papers in Part III develop a framework to analyse international competitiveness. All of these papers use Canadian examples but the work is relevant for the many other smaller, open, trading economies whose competitiveness depends on having access to triad markets. In many ways the key distinction necessary in work on international competitiveness is that between firms based in the triad (of the United States, the EU and Japan) versus non-triad firms. There is a fundamental asymmetry in strategy-making for these two sets of firms. The ones from smaller non-triad nations cannot develop successful global strategies (except in small niches) until they gain access to at least one of the triad markets. For Canadian firms, this is the United States; for Korean firms both the United States and Japan, etc. Canada is one-tenth the size of the US market and its large MNEs need to be players there. In contrast, a US MNE can develop successful strategies in the huge US home market and then go abroad. A US domestic strategy could easily become a successful global strategy. If a US firm blows it in Canada, it only loses one-tenth of its potential sales. But if a Canadian firm does not succeed in the United States, it loses its chance to be a global business. This concept of size asymmetry and its relevance for international business strategy has been largely ignored in the strategy literature. In particular, it has been ignored by the most prominent scholar in the field, Michael Porter.

The appearance of Michael Porter's book, *The Competitive Advantage of Nations*, with its 'diamond' framework set new terms of reference for analysis of international competitiveness. Chapter 15 is a critical review of Porter's book, written immediately after its publication and before efforts were made by his consulting firm, Monitor, to apply the framework to Canada. I express doubts about Porter's old-fashioned treatment of inbound FDI (which he dismisses as a source of competitive advantage) and his naive understanding of Canadian-owned MNEs (which he treats as purely resource-based, whereas they have value-added marketing advantages, as discussed in Chapter 13 of Volume 1). In more general terms, I argue that the home-based diamond is not a realistic framework for analysis of the competitiveness of small, open, trading economies (like Canada) which need access to a triad market to develop global identities. This is an argument for a 'double diamond' model.

Chapter 16, one of my most cited and influential articles reproduced in several books of readings, is an exposition of the double diamond model. This paper is co-authored with my Toronto strategy colleague, Joe D'Cruz, and was first developed in the second Kodak Canada study, *Fast Forward*, we produced in 1991. We are grateful to Kodak Canada's president, Ron Morrison, for his support of our work and for the administration of the distribution of the three Kodak studies. Over 25,000 copies of this particular publication were requested and it became extremely influential with business leaders, government officials, and teachers. This article appeared in a special issue of *Management International Review* devoted to applications of the Porter diamond model to smaller, open economies. The double diamond concept is an important extension of Porter's seminal work in this field.

I had more difficulty writing Chapter 17 than any other in my academic career. It is a revised version of a commentary on the Porter/Monitor consulting study of Canadian competitiveness. This commentary was requested by the lead sponsor, the Business Council on National Issues, and it did not appreciate hearing that the million dollar study by Porter's consulting firm was a waste of money. Unfortunately Porter's team was unable to take on board any of these well-intentioned criticisms and they explicitly rejected the double diamond framework in a response to this article. Indeed, Michael Porter has consistently refused to consider any modification of his framework for smaller countries seeking triad market access. There now exists a substantial scholarly literature extending and adapting the diamond framework. Both the single diamond and the double diamond framework have been tested across a variety of countries, including New Zealand, Australia, Austria, South Korea, Sweden and others. Since these inevitably support the double diamond model rather than the single diamond it is somewhat puzzling that Michael Porter continues to disregard the now substantive body of work which refutes his core contribution to the field of international competitiveness. In academic life there is a thin line to walk between scholarship and consulting. It is disappointing to me that Michael Porter has failed to engage in a scholarly debate about the merits of the double diamond as a general framework for analysis of international competitiveness.

The key intellectual problem in using Porter's diamond framework is the appropriate unit of analysis. In earlier work, Porter takes the industry as the locus of competitive advantage and conducts empirical work on strategic groups. Yet in international business, the relevant unit of analysis is the MNE, i.e., strategic decisions are made at firm level. Thus a resource-based theory of the firm, with a focus on managerial resources and firm-specific advantages, is the standard for analysis. In Chapter 18, co-authored with Alain Verbeke, five levels of analysis are considered: local; regional; national; foreign; and global. These are related to the four endogenous and two exogenous variables in Porter's home diamond model, yielding 30 potentially relevant cases. To make Porter's model at all relevant for managers as a decision making tool, we use a SWOT analysis to classify the potential strategic opportunities. This approach succeeds in incorporating some key aspects of international business into the otherwise sterile and ethnocentric Porter home-country diamond framework.

The final chapter (Chapter 19) in Part III takes issue with a policy recommendation by Porter to the effect that government can induce firm-level competitive advantages by enacting stringent environmental standards. While this may be true for large triad economies it is wrong for smaller countries which need access to a triad market. If a smaller nation passes tight environmental standards it will not help its firms in larger markets; indeed, it may hinder them. Instead, environmental regulations in the larger host market are the relevant benchmarks for firms from non-triad nations. This paper also extends the concept of 'shelter' (discussed in Part II above) to environmental regulations. I demonstrate that a domestic industry can usually benefit at the expense of a foreign rival when environmental laws are used as discriminatory entry barriers.

Part IV

The extent to which trade policy has now become investment policy is the theme of the six papers in Part IV. All six papers examine the strategic decisions of MNEs and smaller firms as they accommodate themselves to the new legal and institutional environment of so-called 'free trade' agreements. In fact, both the Canada–US Free Trade Agreement (FTA) of 1989 and the North American Free Trade Agreement (NAFTA) of 1994 are as much about investment issues as trade ones. In both agreements, tariffs are abolished and many non-tariff barriers to trade are eliminated or at least reduced. However, the major portions of both trade agreements actually deal with investment issues. Both the FTA and NAFTA enshrine the principle of national treatment and right of establishment for all business enterprises in each of the member states. There are negotiated lists of sectors and regulations not subject to national treatment, especially in NAFTA; this has a major implication for analysis of how companies adjust to the FTA and NAFTA. In general, most of the computable general equilibrium models used by economists to calculate the impact of such trade agreements lead to misleading conclusions since they can only capture the static tariff-elimination effects and not the more important dynamic investment-related effects. While the latter are indeed difficult to quantify, they should not be ignored. All of these six papers attempt to examine the broader picture of corporate adjustment to trade agreements, often on a case by case or sectoral basis. Such work is difficult to undertake since the findings are inevitably case or sector specific. But a combination of such studies can yield some general insights into the adjustment process by MNEs to free trade.

Chapter 20 is a summary of research undertaken by my doctoral student, Stephen Luxmore, using a conceptual framework developed by Alain Verbeke and myself. The framework is a variant of the FSA–CSA matrix discussed above in Part II for Chapters 3 and 4 of this book. However, while those chapters were conducted at industry or sector level, this one is at firm level, indeed, at the strategic business unit (SBU) level within the four MNEs examined. Based on personal interviews with senior managers and corporate information publicly available, we are able to position the SBUs in the modified FSA–CSA matrix and make reasonable interpretations of the strategic changes undergone by the MNEs. The four MNEs studied are: John Labatt; Noranda; Northern Telecom; and Nova. It is concluded that three of the four MNEs were well positioned before the FTA and the impact of the FTA was largely neutral.

Chapter 21 is co-authored with Andrew Anderson. I am very grateful to Andrew for his help over the 1989–92 period, first as a research assistant and ultimately as a colleague at the Ontario Centre for International Business at the University of Toronto. Many of our papers investigated the impact of the FTA on the administration of US unfair trade laws, and the new dispute settlement panels to review countervailing duty (CVD) and anti-dumping (AD) cases under the terms of the FTA. Some of this work is reported here, in connection with the adjustment by the agricultural sector to the FTA. There have been numerous CVD and AD cases in this sector. The MNEs in the food processing sector were adversely affected by the exemption of Canada's supply management programmes for the FTA, and there was a general retrenchment to low cost US sources of supply in the dairy and feather sectors. Other areas, especially pork and fish, were very much affected by rulings of the dispute settlement panels. In all cases, investment decisions were altered by the FTA.

The energy sector in Canada was largely developed by US capital and is still mostly foreign-owned. The FTA changed the institutional fabric for this sector. In effect, in the FTA, Canada agreed to end potential discriminatory treatment of US energy MNEs in Canada, as had occurred under the Trudeau government in the 1980–81 period when the infamous National Energy Program led to a net divestment from Canada in 1980–85 of over $15 billion (Cdn.) – the largest sectoral outflow of FDI in history. In Chapter 22, co-authored with Mark Warner, I examine changes in the extent of foreign ownership in the Canadian energy sector in response to Canadian regulatory policies. It is concluded that the FTA will stabilize foreign investment in the energy sector by reducing the risk of future unanticipated discriminatory regulations.

In many ways, Chapter 23 synthesizes my current views on the MNE and public policy. I use the triad data and this matrix on a regular basis with both MBA students and managers in executive programmes. This permits me to develop discussion and insights into the nature of triad power, the NAFTA, and corporate strategies for adjustment to NAFTA. The original paper was developed for an inaugural lecture as a visiting professor at Western Washington University. I am indebted to Dean Dennis Murphy for the invitation to conduct research on US–Canadian relations and for the opportunity to talk to American business people about Canadian issues. There are now more than a dozen Canadian studies centres in the United States, partly funded by the Government of Canada, and it has been a privilege for me to speak at many of them on different aspects of the FTA and NAFTA.

The investment provisions of NAFTA are profound enough to be worthy of careful study. In Chapter 24 Michael Gestrin and I review the legal, political, economic and strategic management contexts of the NAFTA investment provisions, including the large number of reservations from national treatment. We also consider investment-related trade measures in NAFTA, especially rules of origin (which have a major impact in the auto sector). Michael Gestrin and I have argued elsewhere that the investment provisions of NAFTA could be used as a prototype for the multilateral agreement on investment (MAI) being developed at the OECD over the 1995–7 period. The national treatment principle, with reservations for potentially vulnerable sectors, reflects the current economic realities of FDI by MNEs while retaining a large amount of political sovereignty for the nation state.

One of the unfinished items of business in the investment provisions of NAFTA is the US exemption from national treatment for reasons of national security. This is a loose term which can be corrupted by the US Congress into a potentially broad set of discriminatory measures. In the final chapter (Chapter 25), co-authored with lawyer Mark Warner, we report on such an attempt by US protectionists to abuse the national security loophole. At one stage in 1994, both the House and Senate had passed different versions of a US Competitiveness Act which had the impact of discriminating against the subsidiaries of Canadian MNEs in the United States, despite the provisions of NAFTA. While this legislation eventually failed to pass, it is highly likely that in a future Congress new legislation will be put forward to regulate and restrict FDI on the grounds of national security. Scholars of international business must remain vigilant in order to expose such protectionist measures in the future.

Personal Acknowledgments

In addition to my co-authors mentioned above, I would like to thank the numerous people who have supported my research over the last two decades.

First, I am grateful for the dedication and efficiency of my two principal secretaries: Pat Zwicker at Dalhousie University over the 1980–86 period, and Amy Ho at the University of Toronto over the 1989–95 period.

A group of excellent research assistants helped me in my research. At Dalhousie, the more prominent ones were: John McIlveen, Andrew Anderson, Jocelyn Bennett, Kathy Richardson, and Sheila Douglas. At Toronto, Andrew Anderson was my leading research associate and collaborator for the 1989–92 period. Others making significant contributions were Michael Gestrin, Tom Boddez, Bill Mohri, Mike Scott and Sam He.

In preparing these two books for publication, I am extremely grateful to my assistant, Hilary Buttrick, for her insights and hard work.

As inspirations for my research career I am grateful to my former teachers, especially Harry G. Johnson and Edith Penrose at London University and Herbert Grubel, my doctoral supervisor at Simon Fraser University. I have interacted with three colleagues who are exceptional original thinkers: Mark Casson, Ian H. Giddy, and Alain Verbeke. The person closest to being a mentor for me is John Dunning and I appreciate the high standards that he sets. At Toronto, my work has been helped enormously by the insight and collegiality of Ed Safarian and Joe D'Cruz. Other colleagues who have helped to improve the quality of my work include my collaborators in writing such as Don Lecraw, Lorraine Eden, Richard Hodgetts, Laurence Booth, Andrew Anderson, Michael Gestrin, Mark Warner and others whose contributions are mentioned in the specific papers reproduced in these two volumes.

I am also grateful to my students over the last 25 years, many of whom have asked good and incisive questions that have demanded improved thinking and new research to meet their high standards. The most rewarding aspect of a professor's life is the opportunity to meld research and teaching on a daily basis while interacting with highly intelligent colleagues and students.

I am also appreciative of the help provided by senior managers whose strategies and competitiveness I have studied and to research officers and government officials who have provided financial help for this research work. I am also grateful to enlightened university administrators who have organized time for me to conduct this research.

Finally, but most important, the research achievements recorded here could never have occurred without the support and inspiration of my family. Helen, my wife for 25 years, was the first person to proofread my work as she celebrated with me the news of the forthcoming publication of my first article in a refereed academic journal in 1974. The celebration of our silver wedding anniversary in July 1995 coincided with the contract to publish these 50 selected papers. Without Helen's unstinting love and support, this work could never have been produced. My son Andrew is another source of inspiration. As I see Andrew prosper in overcoming his disabilities he sets high standards for personal achievement and love that I can only admire and hope to match one day in the future.

Alan M. Rugman
Toronto

PART I

APPLICATIONS OF INTERNALIZATION THEORY TO GOVERNMENT POLICY

The Role of Multinational Enterprises in US-Canadian Economic Relations

Alan M. Rugman

This paper discusses the role that Multinational Enterprises play in the Canadian economy. The author demonstrates that US and Canadian multinationals rely upon different sources of strength for their success. These country specific and firm specific advantages are outlined. Finally, policy recommendations which take these advantages into account are made.

THE FOCUS OF this paper is an examination of the ways in which multinational enterprises influence economic and political relationships between the United States and Canada. The issue of foreign ownership of the Canadian economy by US multinationals, and the converse issue of Canadian investment in the United States, is examined.

In Part I of the paper the behavior of US subsidiaries in Canada is analyzed, with particular reference to their contribution to Canada's research and development (R&D) and exporting objectives. In Part II of the paper the performance of Canadian-owned multinationals is dis-

cussed. In particular, the recent role of Canadian investment in the United States is considered as a complement to the more traditional influence of the US multinationals in Canada. Case studies of the largest Canadian multinationals are reported and the findings generalized within the framework of the modern theories of foreign direct investment and strategic management. Implications for US and Canadian trade and investment policies are drawn out.

A final section deals with some of the policy implications of this two-way multinational activity in North America. One conclusion drawn is that Canada should not be too concerned about following a high-technology strategy for its industrial development. Instead, it is found that Canada's abundant resources are a source of strength for its multinationals and that the activities of both

US and Canadian multinationals are efficient in the use of these resources.

THE BEHAVIOR OF US SUBSIDIARIES IN CANADA

This section of the paper first presents in summary form details of the primary characteristics of the Canadian subsidiaries of the largest US-based multinational enterprises (MNEs) operating in Canada. Data are reported on the sales, R&D to sales ratio, exports to sales ratio and financial performance of each of the 22 largest US subsidiaries. These data are used to interpret some theoretical propositions about why the parent MNE chose to enter the Canadian market by foreign direct investment (FDI) rather than alternative modes of entry. The nature of subsidiary performance is also discussed and related to the behavior of

Dr. Rugman is a Professor and Director of the Centre for International Business Studies, Dalhousie University, Nova Scotia. Last year he was Visiting Scholar at the Center for International Affairs, Harvard University.

US parent MNEs and Canadian based MNEs. Also discussed is the manner in which recent Canadian policy towards FDI has evolved and drawn reactions from US MNEs as they have adjusted to changes in the environmental parameters imposed by Canadian federal and provincial governments.

The second major theme of the first part of this paper investigates the implications for trade and investments of two critical aspects of the behavior of US subsidiaries. These are: the degree to which R&D can be decentralized by US parents to their Canadian subsidiaries, and the contribution made by such subsidiaries to Canadian exports. Reference is made to issues of public policy concerning, first, work on Canada's proposed world mandate policy and its potential effect on parent-subsidiary relationships, and, second, evidence of the export performance of subsidiaries, and the reasons for their surprisingly good export performance.

Identification and Size of the Largest US Subsidiaries in Canada

The significance of FDI in Canada is well known. The overall Canadian economy is now approximately 22 percent foreign-owned. Certain sectors of the economy have a far greater foreign participation than this, notably fuels at 70 percent and manufacturing at 55 percent. The latest *Financial Post* list of the 500 largest corporations in Canada includes 222 foreign-owned firms, which is 44 percent of the total. American (US) FDI accounts for the great majority of such FDI in Canada.

The 22 largest US-owned Canadian subsidiaries are reported in Table 1. They are ranked in decreasing order of size, as measured by 1982 sales in Canada. The largest, General Motors of Canada, ranks at number two on the Financial Post 500 list for 1982. The twenty-second, Westinghouse Canada, ranks at number 104. Given the heavy concentration of foreign ownership in fuels and manufacturing, it is not surprising to see seven and nine firms in these categories respectively.

In Canada there is a popular yardstick that everything is 10 percent of the size of its American counterpart. Thus, it is not unexpected that the mean percentage contribution to parent company sales by Canadian subsidiaries is nearly 10 percent (shown in the last column of Table 1). Individual subsidiary contributions to parent sales range from 29.5 percent (Chrysler) to 1.7 percent (Mobil and Chevron).

Evidence on the Performance of US Subsidiaries in Canada

The financial performance of the Canadian subsidiaries and their US parents over the last decade is reported in summary form in Table 2. The conventional measure of performance used is the return on equity

(ROE). Return is defined as the net income after taxes while equity is the year-end value of stockholders' equity. The standard deviation about the mean of the 10 year ROE is used as a proxy measure for risk. When interpreting these results it is useful to keep in perspective the finding in Rugman (1980, 1981, 1983), and by others, that the profits of MNEs average around a 12 to 14 percent ROE and that there is no significant difference in either the earnings of MNEs and the uninational firms of similar size, or between the ROE of parent MNEs and their subsidiaries.

In 12 of the 22 cases the subsidiary's ROE exceeds that of the parent although generally at greater risk. Thus, the mean ROE of both subsidiaries (at 14 percent) and parents (at 13.4 percent) is not sig-

TABLE 1

Size of 22 Large Canadian Subsidiaries of US Multinationals

Subsidiary	Parent	1982 Sales (US $000's) Subsidiary	Parent	Subsidiary to Parent Sales (%)
GM	GM	7,752	60,026	12.9
Imperial	Exxon	6,981	97,173	7.2
Ford	Ford	5,942	37,067	16.0
Texaco	Texaco	3,862	46,986	8.2
Gulf	Gulf	3,792	28,427	13.3
Chrysler	Chrysler	2,962	10,045	29.5
Safeway	Safeway	2,673	17,633	15.2
Simpson Sears	S. Roebuck	2,541	30,020	8.5
IBM	IBM	1,785	34,364	5.2
Woolworth	Woolworth	1,353	6,590	20.5
CGE	GE	1,324	26,500	5.0
Suncor	Sun	1,250	15,519	8.1
ACT	GTE	1,139	12,066	9.4
Mobil	Mobil	1,005	59,946	1.7
Amoco	Standard (Ind.)	981	28,073	3.5
Dow	Dow	872	10,618	8.2
DuPont	DuPont	794	33,331	7.5
K-Mart	K-Mart	765	16,772	4.6
I. Harvester	I. Harvester	712	4,725	15.1
P and G	P and G	670	11,994	5.6
Chevron	Standard (Ca.)	580	34,362	1.7
Westinghouse	W.E.	573	9,745	5.9
MEAN				9.67

Sources: Financial Post, "The Financial Post 500", Annual.

Fortune, "The Fortune 500 Largest US Industrial Corporations", May Issues, 1974-83.

Financial Post Survey of Industrials.

Canadian Business, "The Canadian Business 500", July 1980.
Corporate Annual Reports.

nificantly different. But the standard deviation for all 22 subsidiaries is 5.88 percent compared to that of the parent MNEs at 3.87 percent. Thus, on average, the subsidiaries appear to have marginally higher returns than their parents but the variability of returns, or risk, is substantially higher. Similar results, but for earlier time periods, and especially for MNEs in the petroleum and mineral resource industries, were reported in Rugman (1979, 1980).

While the level of profits is the same, why is the mean standard deviation of the subsidiaries more than 50 percent greater than that of their parents? The answer probably lies in the relatively smaller size of the Canadian economy in which all firms experience more risk than firms operating in the larger and more diversified US economy. It also partly reflects the degree of multinationality of the parent MNEs, who are active in more foreign markets than the subsidiaries. The benefits of international diversification, where offsetting national covariances tend to stabilize returns, were demonstrated for these US MNEs in Rugman (1979).

The data in Table 2 also help to dispel another popular misconception about the power of MNEs. It is sometimes argued that the parent MNEs can use transfer prices to squeeze the profits of their Canadian subsidiaries. If this were being done then it would result in the Canadian ROE being lower than that of their parent ROE. However, because the mean ROEs are roughly equivalent, such an argument cannot be supported. For further evidence on the lack of transfer pricing in the Canadian petroleum industry, see Rugman (1985).

Evidence on R&D and Exports by Canadian Subsidiaries

The 1970s were characterized by increasing government regulation of the Canadian economy. In the area of FDI much of the nationalistic case for regulation of foreign ownership has been summarized, if not embellished, by the Gray Report (1972). More recently, policy instruments such as the National Energy Policy

TABLE 2

Performance of 22 Large Canadian Subsidiaries of US Multinationals

1973-1982

Subsidiary	ROE-Sub.		ROE-Parent	
	Mean	S.D.	Mean	S.D.
GM	20.1	12.85	12.0	8.11
Imperial	16.1	4.62	16.8	3.28
Ford	8.1	8.74	8.6	7.40
Texaco	17.9	9.25	13.5	4.53
Gulf	15.6	3.38	12.5	2.57
Chrysler	4.6	5.86	3.1	5.29
Safeway	13.8	1.55	13.3	2.47
Simpson Sears	10.5	3.22	10.7	2.04
IBM	22.7	2.95	19.9	2.06
Woolworth	11.6[1]	2.37	8.8	3.81
CGE	11.2	1.96	17.2	2.51
Suncor	10.7	9.93	14.6	4.09
ACT	5.0[2]	1.65	12.9	1.92
Mobil	24.7	5.06	15.0	4.52
Amoco	18.0	6.70	16.2	2.49
Dow	16.0	9.75	18.5	5.62
DuPont	9.8	9.80	12.7	3.70
K-Mart	10.2	3.85	14.3	3.75
I Harvester	14.5	9.87	7.4	5.85
P and G	19.0	6.84	17.1	1.06
Chevron	13.2[3]	5.59	15.1	3.63
Westinghouse	14.5	3.47	10.5	4.47
MEAN	14.0	5.88	13.21	3.87

Sources: Financial Post, "The Financial Post 500", Annual.

Fortune, "The Fortune 500 Largest US Industrial Corporations", May Issues, 1974-83.

Financial Post Survey of Industrials.

Canadian Business, "The Canadian Business 500", July 1980.
Corporate Annual Reports.

(NEP) and the Foreign Investment Review Agency (FIRA) have been used to increase the domestic ownership of the economy. In the context of government support for R&D a world product mandate (WPM) policy has been advocated by the Science Council of Canada (1980). Under this policy only subsidiaries which have a WPM are to receive R&D grants, whereas present research policy does not discriminate in this manner. With a WPM the subsidiary of an MNE acquires full responsibility for the development, production and marketing of a single product line on a worldwide scale.

The Science Council of Canada views increased R&D as the primary means to increase technological exports. The advanced nations of the world are moving to specialize in more research intensive goods, leaving the production of standardized product lines to newly industrialized nations such as the flying dragons of South East Asia. Canada, as an advanced nation, is apparently not making the high-technology transition as rapidly as the others. Indeed, R&D expenditure in Canada is less than one percent of GNP, compared to well over two percent for the United States and most European countries. But the Science Council, by recommending policies to encourage WPMs, are assigning the blame for the relatively low level of R&D in Canada to foreign subsidiaries, whereas it is not clear that this is the source of the problem, or even that there is a problem of a lack of R&D in Canada.

For Canada to join the high-technology race would imply the creation of a new country-specific advantage. Canada's current country-specific advantages are in the exploration, processing and marketing of raw materials and resources. Only in isolated cases has Canada enjoyed preeminence in a particular technological field. The movement of scarce resources to high-technology industries may be at the expense of Canada's country-specific advantages at a time when considerable improvements in efficiency of resource-based industries are required to meet expanding global competition.

The underlying objective of the promotion of WPMs by selective R&D subsidiaries is to decentralize R&D from parent MNEs to Canadian subsidiaries, but this faces many problems at the MNE level, see Poynter and Rugman (1982) and Rugman and Bennett (1982). These studies concluded that most parent MNEs would be unwilling to compromise their internal organizational structure by moving towards the decentralization required for WPMs. Thus, the two primary benefits sought by the WPM policy, increased R&D expenditures and more technologically based exports, are both doomed to failure. In any case, the WPM policy is not based on a sound assessment of the R&D performance of subsidiaries, which is just as good, if not better, than domestic Canadian firms. For the 22 largest US subsidiaries in Canada the evidence on R&D is now examined, as is the export performance of their subsidiaries.

Data on R&D expenditure and export sales are presented in Table 3 for 18 of the 22 subsidiaries. Data for Woolworth, Anglo Canadian Telephone, Simpsons-Sears, and K-Mart Canada were not available, so these four US subsidiaries were excluded. Contrary to the popular criticism that foreign ownership worsens Canada's trade position, it can be observed that exports by the subsidiaries exceed those of the parents at 29.5 percent and 10.2 percent respectively. It should also be noted that the largest US subsidiaries in Canada are not dominated by resource extraction firms, which might have been expect-

ed to supply their parents. Instead, most of the subsidiaries use parent firm-specific advantages in technology, knowledge and other areas to transfer technology to Canadian consumers, so exporting is a bonus. The export performance of this group of subsidiaries is similar to that of the largest Canadian-owned MNEs, identified later. The mean export to sales percentage for these Canadian firms is 28.8, roughly the same as the export performance of the subsidiaries.

The mean R&D to sales percentages in Table 3 confirm that subsidiaries undertake less R&D than their parents at 0.8 and 2.25 percent respectively. Less R&D in the subsidiaries is to be expected given that the initial reasons for FDI in Canada are either horizontal integration to service the Canadian market from

within, thereby avoiding tariff and non-tariff barriers or vertical integration to seek resources unobtainable or less attractive in the last country. Compounding these reasons is the proprietary nature of R&D knowledge held by the parent firm which risks dissipation of any firm-specific advantage in technology when it decentralizes its R&D function. Despite this risk foreign subsidiaries in Canada contribute to the level of R&D performed in this country.

Some evidence suggests that the R&D performance of subsidiaries is no less than Canadian-owned firms and is often better. Data at the firm level are limited and most of the comparative studies have been at the industry (rather than firm) level (see Caves et al. (1982). Safarian (1968) did not find any difference in R&D

TABLE 3

Research and Export Performance of Canadian Subsidiaries
(Percent)

Canadian Subsidiary (percent owned)	R&D to Sales[2]		Exports to Sales[3]	
	Sub	Parent	Sub	Parent
General Motors of Canada (100)	0.25	3.47	65.6	25.0[1]
Imperial Oil (74)	0.65	0.53	na	74.0[1]
Ford Motor of Canada (92)	na	4.30	na	49.0[1]
Texaco Canada (90)	0.37	2.33	na	0.0
Gulf Canada (75)	1.27	0.55	na	38.0[1]
Chrysler Canada (100)	na	2.60	na	20.0[1]
Canada Safeway (96)	na	na	4.0[1]	na
IBM Canada (100)	1.23	5.73	30.7	6.0
Canadian General Electric (92)	1.53	2.97	na	13.0
Suncor (75)	0.45	0.30	19.7	26.0[1]
Mobil Oil Canada (91)	0.35	0.30	na	65.0[1]
Amoco (100)	na	4.67	na	18.0[1]
Dow Chemical Canada (100)	1.00	3.10	20.1	49.0[1]
DuPont of Canada (75)	0.90	3.20	18.4	12.0
International Harvester Canada (100)	na	3.37	43.0[1]	6.0
Proctor and Gamble (100)	na	2.17	na	32.0[1]
Chevron Canada (100)	na	3.33	na	53.0[1]
Westinghouse Canada (95)	na	2.30	22.2	14.0
	0.80	2.25[4]	29.5[5]	10.2[5]

Notes:
1. Foreign Sales to Total Sales.
2. Subsidiary R&D is mean R&D for 1979-82. Parent Company R&D is the mean R&D for 1979-81.
3. Figure shown is for the most recent available period: 1980, 81 or 82.
4. Mean shown is for those ten parent companies for which a comparative subsidiary figure is available. The actual mean for 17 parents is 2.66.
5. Mean export sales only, foreign to total sales excluded from computation.

Sources: **Financial Post**, March 12, 1983 and November 28, 1981 (R&D). Corporate Annual Reports.

between resident and non-resident firms in his survey. Rugman (1981), confirmed this but also found that subsidiaries did better than other Canadian firms; the mean R&D to sales percentages for groups of the largest 12 parents, subsidiaries and domestic firms were 3.12, 2.07 and 1.19 respectively. To expand on this work the R&D to sales ratio for 13 Canadian MNEs was calculated for the same time period reported in Table 3. The mean R&D of these Canadian-owned firms is 0.94, which is not significantly different from the mean R&D of the 10 subsidiaries. If Northern Telecon, Canada's largest R&D establishment, is omitted, the mean falls to 0.44.

The ratio of R&D expenditures to sales for an expanded list of US subsidiaries is given in Table 4. Eleven new subsidiaries are added to the list of ten in Table 3 for which information on R&D was available. All firms are listed in the *Financial Post's* leading R&D spenders in Canada, so the higher mean R&D to sales percentage of 1.73 is to be expected, versus 0.80 in Table 3. It is interesting to note that the *Financial Post's* total sample of leading R&D spenders includes eight government controlled firms, 22 private Canadian-owned firms, and 21 foreign subsidiaries.

Table 4 reveals the trends in R&D expenditures over recent years. Of the 18 subsidiaries for which data are listed, nine are increasing their R&D, six are maintaining their R&D at stable levels, two are fluctuating and only one is in decline. Thus, one-half of the subsidiaries are increasing their R&D expenditures while another third are maintaining theirs. It is ironic that the WPM initiative is occurring at a time when these subsidiaries are already achieving the Science Council's (misplaced) objective of increased R&D in Canada!

Canadian Policy Towards US MNEs

As discussed at greater length in Rugman (1980), and confirmed here, the high degree of FDI in Canada has not resulted in an unsatisfactory economic performance by the subsidiaries themselves. In terms of pro-

fitability, R&D capacity and exporting, foreign subsidiaries of US MNEs perform as well as domestic Canadian firms. FDI in Canada can be largely attributed to two factors; government-imposed market imperfections such as tariffs, and the nature of the Canadian country-specific advantage. Since Confederation, to protect manufacturing (and now high-tech industries), Canada has erected tariff and non-tariff barriers to imports. US MNEs, with close proximity to Canadian markets, have usually regarded Canada as one of the earliest foreign markets to enter, due to the perceived low information costs of exporting to a neighboring country. As MNEs vied for market shares in import-competing sectors in

Canada, some found it necessary to keep down their costs by avoiding the Canadian tariff. Thus, they switched to Canadian production by FDI. The tariff, while attempting to encourage and protect domestically-owned industry actually fostered FDI in Canada by these types of horizontally integrated MNEs.

The second major reason for FDI in Canada is to exploit the country's advantages in raw materials and resources. Vertical integration has been a factor since resource-based MNEs need to acquire control over raw material inputs in order to reduce interruptions in supply, operate capital intensive plants at as near to full capacity as possible, and ensure

TABLE 4

R & D to Sales Percentages for Selected Canadian Subsidiaries of US Multinationals

	Parent Co.[3] Mean	Sub. Mean	1982	1979	1980	1981	Trend
General Motors	3.47	0.25	0.3	0.2	na	na	Stable[2]
Imperial Oil	0.53	0.65	0.6	0.7	0.7	0.6	Stable
Texaco	2.33	0.37	na	0.5	0.4	0.2	Rising
Gulf	0.55	1.27	na	1.6	1.1	1.1	Rising
IBM	5.73	1.23	1.6	1.2	1.1	1.0	Rising
CGE	2.97	1.53	1.1	1.6	1.9	1.5	Fluctuating
Suncor	0.30	0.45	0.4	0.5	na	na	NA
Mobil	0.30	0.35	0.2	0.5	na	na	NA
Dow Chemical	3.10	1.00	1.0	1.0	1.0	1.0	Stable
DuPont	3.20	0.90	1.2	0.9	0.7	0.8	Rising
Pratt and Whitney[1]	5.93	16.10	21.6	14.6	12.1	15.9	Rising
NCR	na	6.78	8.7	7.3	6.0	5.1	Rising
Control Data	na	6.08	5.2	5.7	6.3	7.1	Decline
Honeywell	6.17	1.43	2.7	2.0	0.8	0.2	Rising
Xerox	5.17	1.43	1.4	1.3	1.5	1.5	Stable
Litton[1]	1.73	4.10	5.8	2.4	4.1	na	Fluctuating
Fiberglass	na	1.68	2.0	1.6	1.6	1.5	Rising
General Foods	1.37	1.00	1.0	1.0	1.0	1.0	Stable
Johnson & Johnson	4.87	3.20	3.2	3.2	na	na	NA
Sheritt Gordon	na	1.53	1.8	1.7	1.3	1.3	Rising
Ingersoll Rand	na	0.80	1.2	0.4	na	na	NA
Union Carbide	1.90	0.30	na	0.4	0.3	0.2	Stable
MEAN[4]	2.76	1.73					

Notes:
1. Firm has a world product mandate.
2. Defined as: Fluctuating less than 0.2 percentage points.
3. 1979-1981.
4. Excludes Pratt and Whitney as unrepresentative of the sample in general.
5. na — Not Available.
6. NA — Not Applicable, insufficient data available to indicate a trend.

Sources: Financial Post, March 12, 1983.
   Financial Post, November 28, 1981
   Corporate Annual Reports.

orderly marketing of narrow product lines.

The nature of horizontal and vertical integration by MNEs in Canada has been fostered by inappropriate Canadian policies. Horizontally integrated MNEs can be discouraged by removal of tariff and non-tariff barriers. Then, the US-based MNEs would export rather than engage in FDI in Canada. Of course, such trade liberalization could now lead to major short-run adjustment problems, especially of unemployment and factor reallocation, particularly in Southern Ontario. However, one hundred years of inefficiency is no recommendation for another century of myopic Canadian trade policy.

Vertically integrated MNEs can be discouraged by the development of Canadian-based MNEs. If Canada encourages the development of its own MNEs, which build upon its country-specific advantages in resources, energy and services, then they will act as rivals to US-based MNEs. By building upon Canada's natural country-specific advantages both trade and investments will be encouraged and promoted. This is the topic to which attention is now directed.

THE BEHAVIOR OF CANADIAN MULTINATIONALS IN THE UNITED STATES

The second half of this paper has as its focus an interesting, perhaps unique, set of MNEs based in a small, open economy, Canada. The structure and performance of the largest Canadian industrial MNEs is analyzed and from this research the special firm-specific advantages of each of the MNEs are identified.

It is discovered that the great majority of the Canadian MNEs have firm-specific advantages in the production, distribution and trading of resource based products. Indeed, only two of the MNEs possess the knowledge or technology based firm-specific advantages of the typical US, European or Japanese MNEs. Thus, the Canadian firm-specific advantages are related to the country-specific advantage of Canada in resources. Yet, since these MNEs are engaged in foreign direct investment

(FDI), rather than exporting or licensing, it is apparent that significant environmental constraints determine FDI as the foreign entry mode. The manner in which the country-specific advantages are internalized by the Canadian MNEs is studied in this paper, as are the implications for strategic planning of these MNEs in a world of increasing global competition.

The theoretical background for this work comes from a combination of two areas of analysis of the corporate enterprise. First, the work of Rugman (1980, 1981) on the theory of internalization is used as a basis for identification of the firm-specific advantages of each MNE. In this prior work it has been shown that each MNE has internalized, i.e., secured property rights over, a special differential advantage. Frequently this is in the form of a knowledge advantage (based on R&D expenditures which have generated a technological edge), but it may also occur as a result of marketing advantages, as in the possession of a well-established and respected distribution network, or even in more intangible aspects of the skills of the company management. The second strand of theory used is the work by Michael Porter (1980) on competitive analysis, which is readily applicable in an international dimension. Here his emphasis on entry and exit barriers and the analysis of competitive forces as they influence the strategic planning of the corporation is applied in a global context.

In Porter's model the firm needs to assess the environment in which it operates, especially the industry or industries in which it competes. Competition in the industry depends on five competitive forces; rivalry among existing firms, the threat of new entrants, the threat of substitution, and the bargaining power of both suppliers and buyers. The goal of competitive analysis is to assess the strength of such competitive forces in order to determine the best strategy to adopt.

Insight as to the strength of each force is available through analysis of entry and exit barriers in the industry. The key entry barriers are: scale

economies whereby existing firms enjoy production and cost advantages over new entrants; product differentiation as rivals must break the barrier of existing brand loyalties; huge capital requirements involved in entering a new industry; switching costs necessary to change suppliers; access to distribution channels where established firms already have control of the distributors; and government regulation which may bar entry or impose licensing requirements on a new firm.

Exit barriers include: the existence of equipment which is of such a highly technical nature that it has low marketability; fixed costs associated with settlements of contractual arrangements with workers and low productivity once it is known that liquidation will take place; strategic barriers if the business is fundamental to the firm's strategy and image; information barriers where the absence of clear and accurate information makes it impossible to assess performance; emotional barriers associated with managerial pride in the company and the fear of loss of status; and government influence which may prevent a firm from exiting in order to preserve jobs or for other social reasons.

Identification of Canadian Multinationals

The 25 largest Canadian-owned companies are reported in Table 5. The firms are an inclusive set from the 1982 *Fortune International 500*, a listing of the world's largest non-US industrial firms. Nine foreign-owned subsidiaries also made the *Fortune* list but are excluded from Table 5. To identify the Canadian MNEs a MNE is defined as a firm with a foreign operating subsidiary in at least one foreign country and a minimum foreign total sales ratio (F/T) of 20 percent. These criteria reduced the set of firms in Table 1 to a group of 16 MNEs, as shown in Table 6.

Canadian Pacific, the largest industrial corporation in Canada, is deleted since it is a holding company. Instead, one of its subsidiaries, AMCA International is included. AMCA (formerly Dominion Bridge) is the largest multinational subsidiary of Canadian Pacific and its sales are large enough to have it included on the *Fortune* listing were it not a subsidiary. AMCA is a diversified MNE engaged in manufacturing, engineering and construction.

The 16 Canadian MNEs are almost all resource based. The industrial mix is as follows: pulp and paper—4; mining and metal manufacturing—3; beverages—3 and six other single industry categories. The special cases include: NOVA, a petroleum resource MNE; Massey-Ferguson, the farm machinery manufacturer; Moore, the world's largest producer of business forms; Genstar, a vertically integrated construction materials and mining resource MNE; and AMCA, the steel related equipment manufacturer specializing in resource extraction and processing equipment. The only non-resource based Canadian MNE is Northern Telecom. It is the second largest manufacturer of telecommunications equipment in North America and is widely considered to have the most advanced digital telephone switching equipment available.

In terms of sales, the Canadian MNEs are smaller than their US (and European) counterparts. The average size (from Table 6, converted to US dollars) is $1,752 billion. The largest 50 US and European MNEs by contrast have average sales of $16 and $12.4 billion respectively (Rugman 1983).

The financial performance of the Canadian MNEs, as measured by the return-on-equity (ROE) over the last ten years, is 12.8 percent compared to 14.3 and 8.5 for the largest 50 US and European MNEs respectively. The ROE for European MNEs is biased downward by the significant presence of state-owned enterprises, see Rugman (1983). The risk of these returns as proxied by one standard deviation (SD) is 5.3, 3.6 and 5.2 respectively for Canadian, US and European MNEs. In short, the Canadian MNEs earn comparable returns to US MNEs but at greater risk, while earning higher returns at the same risk level relative to European MNEs.

TABLE 5

The 24 Largest Canadian-Owned Companies — 1982

Fortune Rank	Firm Name	1982 Sales (billions Cdn. dollars)¹
36	Canadian Pacific	12.288
102	Alcan Alumium	5.729
145	Canada Development Corp.	4.001
165	NOVA, An Alberta Corp.	3.501
172	Petro-Canada	3.329
191	Hiram-Walker Resources	3.085
198	Northern Telecom	3.035
201	Canada Packers	3.019
208	Dome Petroleum	2.929
211	International Thomson	2.879
219	Noranda Mines	2.793
239	Massey Ferguson	2.539
255	Seagram	2.364
261	Moore	2.279
289	Stelco	2.020
311	John Labatt	1.864
315	MacMillan Bloedel	1.843
331	Genstar	1.761
339	Domtar	1.686
351	Abitibi-Price	1.635
365	Molson	1.578
377	Inco	1.525
389	Dofasco	1.485
398	Consolidated-Bathhurst	1.424

¹Converted from US dollars at $1.2337 Cdn.: US.

Source: "The Fortune International 500", **Fortune**, August 22, 1983.

Firm-Specific Advantages of Canadian Multinationals

The special nature of the firm specific advantage of Canadian MNEs is that it is usually based upon Canada's country-specific advantage in resources. As a relatively small nation of 25 million people spread out across one of the largest land masses in the world, Canada has an abundance of resources, ranging from timber, minerals, and fish to energy sources based on hydro-electric power, oil and natural gas. Traditionally, Canada has been able to market its resources by exports, especially to its close neighbor, the United States. The interesting question is why does Canada now need to service foreign markets by FDI rather than by exporting? There are two answers to this question.

First, there are "natural" market imperfections which make it necessary for firms to retain knowledge about their firm-specific advantage within the network of the MNE rather than risk its dissipation on open markets. This by now classic transaction cost explanation of the need for internalization is, however, somewhat weak in the Canadian context since relatively few Canadian MNEs have a firm-specific advantage in production know-how. Indeed, only Northern Telecom has the typical knowledge-based firm-specific advantage of most of the US, European, and Japanese MNEs. Yet, when the concept of internalization is extended to include control over the marketing function, as well as over production, then it becomes clearer that many of the Canadian MNEs benefit from such control. The brand name products marketed by Seagram and other beverage-based MNEs, the long-established clients of the pulp and paper MNEs and the distribution network of Massey-Ferguson, all serve to illustrate the critical value of internal ownership of the marketing function.

Second, there are "unnatural" mar-

TABLE 6

The 16 Largest Canadian Industrial Multinationals

Firm	Average Sales 1978-1982 (billions)	F/T	S/T	1973-1982 ROE	S.I.
Alcan	5.169	na[2]	77	11.5	7.7
Seagram	2.991	92	92	10.4	2.8
Massey-Ferguson	2.688	93	93	6.5	6.5
Noranda	2.578	60	28	13.1	8.6
Hiram Walker	2.565	na	47	11.7	2.5
Northern Telecom	2.214	61	48	14.9	5.8
MacMillan Bloedel	2.135	88[1]	39[1]	8.9	7.6
Moore	1.991	90	90	17.3	1.9
NOVA	1.990	na	34	12.1	2.2
Inco	1.636	82	42	9.7	7.6
Genstar	1.584	na	52	14.4	5.6
Domtar	1.568	29[1]	8[1]	12.6	7.5
Abitibi-Price	1.505	66	14	13.4	5.5
AMCA	1.403	na	78	15.8	2.8
Consolidated-Bathurst	1.323	54	20	16.6	7.7
Molson	1.235	na	27	15.5	2.1
Mean	2.161	72	49	12.8	5.3

[1] 1981

[2] not available

Source: Corporate Annual Reports

Notes:
    a) F/T is defined as the rate of foreign (F) to total (T) sales
       S/T is defined as the rate of sales by subsidiaries (S) to total sales
       (The difference between F and S is exports (E) from the home country nation
    b) ROE is the mean return on equity, i.e. the ratio of net income after tax and before
       extraordinary items divided by the average net worth (value of shareholder's equity)
    c) S.D. means standard deviation

ket imperfections, that is, regulations and controls imposed by governments. These serve to increase the cost of exporting. Sometimes exports from Canada are restricted, as when there are tariffs. Since tariffs on resource imports, especially by the United States, are minimal, it is necessary to look to non-tariff barriers to understand why trading is being replaced by FDI. In recent years a veritable galaxy of federal, state and municipal regulations have arisen, often for good reasons of their own, to protect domestic workers and industries threatened by international competition. To break down these barriers to trade, Canadian firms have turned to FDI to substitute for exporting.

Together, the natural and unnatural market imperfections have acted as a strong incentive for Can-

adian MNEs to develop and replace exporting. In the process, the Canadian firms have often become more sophisticated in their international operations, and more aware of the need for strategic planning in the face of rivalry from powerful global competitors.

The special characteristics of each key MNE, or group of Canadian MNEs, is now examined and their firm-specific advantages are identified in the next section as entry and exit barriers. Table 7 is a summary of the firm-specific advantages of the largest 16 Canadian MNEs, arranged by industry group. Following this there is a section in which the nature of the firm-specific advantage is related to the organizational structure and strategic planning of each of these MNEs.

Entry and Exit Barriers of Canadian Multinationals

i) Canadian Pulp and Paper Multinationals

The ability of the largest Canadian forest products companies to internalize Canada's country-specific advantage in timber resources is a major reason why these firms are competitive in domestic and global markets. The majority of Canada's timber resources are owned by the provincial governments. Generally, Canadian forest product companies control and manage these timber resources on the basis of long-term leases from provincial governments. These leases, and a feeling of nationalism, provide Canadian pulp and paper MNEs with a sufficient supply of secure resources to compete in global markets. While the leases themselves are not formal entry barriers to foreign competition, the Canadian system is sufficiently different from that of the United States to deter foreign competition for Canada's timber resource. US rivals are used to a market system and private ownership of the forest.

Canadian pulp and paper MNEs also benefit from vertical integration. This facilitates the development of manufacturing and marketing expertise, most notably in the production and marketing of newsprint. These advantages enable Canadian MNEs to compete effectively in foreign markets, especially in the vital nearby US market. The Canadian firms have established long-standing relationships with major customers which act as switching barriers to entry for rivals. Recently, to avoid environmental and political risks, they have entered into joint ventures with purchasers (newspaper companies) which further helps to strengthen the degree of vertical integration.

An important exit barrier for the largest Canadian pulp and paper MNEs is the specialized assets which they control, again the most important of which is the vast timber reserves of Canada. Furthermore, many of their production facilities are highly capital-intensive and these specialized investments also represent significant entry and exit barriers. A final exit

TABLE 7

Firm-Specific Advantages of Canadian MNEs

Firm	Firm-Specific Advantage
Abitibi-Price	World leader in newsprint sales; timberland leases; good and long-standing customer relationships.
Consolidated-Bathurst	Experience in the production, management and marketing of diversified pulp and paper products; vertical integration; timberland leases.
Domtar	Product diversification; long-term leases and holdings of natural resources.
MacMillan Bloedel	Access to and control over high quality coastal timber; vertical integration.
Seagram	Internationally recognized brand name products; marketing; network of affiliated dealers.
Hiram Walker	Internationally recognized brand name products; well-established marketing relationships with agents; ownership of oil and gas resources.
Molson	Brand names in beverage production; marketing expertise; product diversification.
Alcan	Vertical integration; ownership of cheap hydroelectric power.
Inco	Quality, location and size of propriety mineral holdings; experience and market knowledge; cheap hydroelectric power.
Noranda	Ownership of mineral resources; product diversification; vertical integration.
Massey-Ferguson	World-wide distribution, sales and service network; well-known standardized products.
AMCA (Dominion Bridge)	Experience and expertise in the design, engineering and marketing of resource-related equipment; product diversification; vertical integration.
Genstar	Vertical integration in construction; diversification.
NOVA	Provincial monopoly over gas transmission; expertise and experience; vertical integration; financial strength.
Northern Telecom	R&D technology in digital telephone switching equipment using semi-conductors; aggressive world-wide marketing; efficient production; protected home market with Bell Canada.
Moore	Marketing network; innovative and adaptive to changing technology in office support systems; corporate culture; financial strength.

barrier is the dependence of many of these firms on the US market. Once the pulp and paper firms establish production facilities in the United States the scale of the US operations tends to lock the firms into this market. Since the US market is ten times the size of that in Canada, a Canadian MNE finds investment in the United States to be a larger entry and exit barrier than would a US firm investing in the relatively smaller Canadian market.

ii) Liquor and Beer Multinationals

In the liquor industry, where scale economies, capital requirements and government regulations are relatively insignificant barriers to entry, Seagram and Hiram Walker have used strong firm-specific advantages to restrict competition. Potential rivals may have only limited difficulty in financing entry into the industry and subsequently achieving scale economies in production, especially if they are able to acquire an established operation. However, rivals are unable to compete effectively without access to distribution channels.

Seagram and Hiram Walker have both established extensive networks of distributors, agents and affiliates which enable the firms to maintain market shares and respond quickly to changing opportunities. Control over these networks amounts to a tremendous entry barrier to potential and existing rivals. It also creates high switching costs. Internationally recognized brand names facilitate product differentiation and are instrumental in retaining loyalty in the distribution network.

Both MNEs have also attempted portfolio diversification strategies. Recent activities on the part of Hiram Walker to diversify into oil and gas and lessen its dependence on liquor are evidence of relatively low exit barriers. Hiram Walker has gone as far as to contract out many of its distilling and aging operations in the United States. The move is also evidence of confidence in its brand reputation and distribution networks. Hiram Walker has thus used its liquor operations as a cash cow to finance diversification into oil (Home Oil) and gas (Consumers' Gas).

Seagram, although also diversifying (particularly into DuPont), continues to concentrate on its liquor businesses as a result of strong strategic and emotional exit barriers. The liquor business is fundamental to the firm's strategy and image because Seagram attempts to be the world leader in most brands. The long-standing Bronfman family association also reinforces the commitment of the company of the business. Management at Hiram Walker, on the other hand, does not have such a strong commitment to the liquor business.

Molson's firm-specific advantage in marketing experience and expertise has resulted in a high entry barrier in that its brand names are well-differentiated and enjoy high market acceptance. This is a strong barrier in the nature and competitive brewing industry. Through brand diversification Molson has enhanced its already significant barriers to entry. Potential rivals would have to make a major capital investment, not only to achieve the economies of scale enjoyed by Molson, but also to enter the many regional markets because government regulation prohibits the interprovincial sale of beer. With established facilities in each of the regional markets, Molson has been able to distribute its brands nationally and effectively shield itself from new national competition.

Like the liquor multinationals, Molson faces significant exit barriers. Strategic and emotional barriers are the key deterrents to exiting. While government, social interests and specialized assets are normally exit barriers, the competitive nature of the industry would render the assets marketable and stifle government and social objections as few jobs would be lost.

iii) Mining Multinationals

An increasing level of world competition in the 1970s and early 1980s is partial evidence of a storage of effective barriers to entry in world mineral resource markets. In the past, most Canadian mining multinationals have enjoyed a competitive advantage as a result of economies of scale and ownership of the mineral resource. The small size of the domestic market necessitates global competition for these firms. The capital intensity of the business, the immense size of the required investment and lack of known resource deposits were at one time sufficient entry barriers. However, the discovery and subsequent development of rich ore deposits in third world nations has helped to erode these barriers. Government sponsorship and state ownership in such countries have all but eliminated capital costs and scale economies as barriers for rivals in such nations.

The increase in worldwide productive capacity has led to an oversupply of both ores and processed products. The increase in the availability of raw materials and smelted metals means that potential entrants no longer face huge capital investments which were once necessary in order to achieve scale economies in extraction and smelting. New rivals may now proceed directly into fabrication where competition is now at an intense level with cost and efficiency the key factors.

Canadian mining MNEs retain some competitive advantages, however, and their firm-specific advantages have resulted in new entry barriers. Vertical integration in extraction, processing and marketing yields a cost advantage. The firm-specific advantages of Alcan, Inco and Noranda in experience and expertise in extraction and processing also help to promote cost efficiency. New rivals initially lack such knowledge. Vertical integration through the ownership of natural resources also ensures stable supplies, thereby reducing the bargaining power of suppliers and reliance on the cyclical primary and speculative secondary markets.

Through extension to the marketing function, vertical integration in mining helps to stabilize demand and reduces the bargaining power of buyers. It also creates a barrier by closing markets to rivals and creating switching costs. The related firm-specific advantages in marketing experience and market knowledge help to close distribution channels. Switching costs are created as the Canadian firms benefit from long-standing relation-

ships and long-term contracts with customers.

An important firm-specific advantage and barrier to entry is inexpensive hydroelectric power, particularly for Alcan and, to a lesser extent, Inco. Smelting and processing are energy intense. Thus, through ownership of the hydroelectric generating facilities and access to relatively cheap Canadian energy, Canadian mining MNEs enjoy a significant cost advantage independent of scale.

These barriers have not been very effective in barring competition from plastic, carbon fibre, and new alloy substitutes. Nor have they been purchased on the open market. Consequently, Alcan, Inco, and Noranda have all intensified R&D for product and market development. They have also expanded fabrication and concentration on market niches in order to combat substitute competition.

While entry barriers are only moderately high, exit barriers are very strong. The presence of specialized assets, coupled with overcapacity in the industry, reduces the firm's value and marketability. There are also high fixed costs associated with liquidation as well as government and social barriers since these firms are the key employers in many regions of Canada. Strategic exit barriers and emotional barriers are also powerful.

iv) Other Multinationals
Massey-Ferguson

Massey-Ferguson at one time benefited from firm-specific advantages in the efficient production of tractors and combines. In recent years the absence of technological innovation in farm machinery, coupled with relatively low entry barriers in this mature and competitive industry, have forced Massey-Ferguson to rely on its well-established international marketing and distribution network. Today this is still its main firm-specific advantage. The standardization of farm machinery products has resulted in little product differentiation and brand loyalty. Consequently, there are low switching costs as many distributors carry the lines of many manufacturers. Capital requirements and scale economies are not necessarily restrictive, especially to an established company diversifying into farm machinery by concentrating on a market niche.

Massey-Ferguson's marketing and distribution network creates switching costs and prevents new rivals from gaining access to the distribution network. Toyota was forced to join with Massey-Ferguson in order to market and distribute a line of small tractors. This firm-specific advantage also reduces the bargaining power of buyers. Exit barriers are quite significant; otherwise Massey-Ferguson might well have left the business during its crisis years early in the 1980s. While the presence of specialized assets may have been partly responsible for this decision, strategic, emotional, social and government exit barriers were also important.

AMCA and Genstar

AMCA and Genstar are each involved in several industries. However, they have differentiated themselves because they are two of only a few firms who can complete turnkey commercial and industrial projects. They also have firm-specific advantages in design and engineering expertise and vertical integration in all aspects of a project. Thus, rivals are faced with high switching costs, huge capital requirements and scale economies in attempting to compete with them. Vertical integration reduces the bargaining power of both suppliers and buyers and rivalry from both potential entrants and established competitors. AMCA and Genstar face high exit barriers in the ownership of specialized assets, the high fixed costs of liquidation and strategic and emotional barriers.

NOVA

NOVA's first important firm-specific advantage was its government-granted monopoly over gas transmission in the province of Alberta. NOVA used the related experience, expertise, and cash flows to expand its transmission business and to diversify into petrochemicals and petroleum. Vertical integration in all three of its main businesses reduces the bargaining power of buyers and suppliers and

ensures stability of markets and supplies. NOVA faces strong exit barriers, particularly provincial legislation which specifically outlines its authorized businesses. Strategic exit barriers are also present along with highly specialized assets.

Northern Telecom

Nortel's firm-specific advantage is based upon R&D expenditures of 10 percent of sales. This has led to proprietary technology in digital telephone switching equipment. It is dependent upon one major product line (and its variants) for most of its revenues, but is still able to expand sales into new markets as the product line has not yet matured. There are few entry barriers in the industry, thus firm-specific advantages must be guarded from potential dissipation. Recent regulations in both Canada and the United States have created an opportunity for new competition. There are many firms presently engaged in telecommunications silicon chip technology and a new discovery by a rival could quickly destroy Nortel's technological advantage. Furthermore, many high-tech firms possess both the financial strength and the ability to achieve the necessary scale economies once the technology is acquired.

Northern Telecom has other firm-specific advantages which help deter competition. Its aggressive world-wide marketing creates switching costs and differentiates its product. Its association with Bell Canada helps to protect its home market from competition. Nortel also creates switching costs in that it sells a total system, whereas new and existing rivals are often unable to do so. Due to the shortage of significantly high entry barriers, Nortel needs to continue to expand its product lines and diversify into other areas of information processing and communications. Exit barriers are significant while the Canadian and Ontario governments take pride in promoting high-tech firms.

Moore

Moore's primary firm-specific advantage is its extensive world-wide marketing network. This allows it to

monitor and respond to the changing needs of business and the latest innovations in office systems. Thus, Moore is both innovative and adaptive. Moore has used its firm-specific advantage to create strong entry barriers for anyone wishing to compete on a global basis. The strength of these barriers is evidenced by an absence of global competition.

Rivals are faced with large capital requirements in trying to emulate Moore's distribution network and corporate culture. Moore also has vast financial resources capable of withstanding or initiating intense price and/or marketing and service competition. Market knowledge and customer service have differentiated Moore's products and services and created switching costs for rivals. The main exit barriers confronting Moore are strategic and emotional. However, these barriers lose most of their impact as a result of the limited scope of global competition.

Lessons for Management and Policy

In today's world of increasing global competition, large US, European and Japanese multinationals compete aggressively for market share and profits in every corner of the world. The battles are fought over product lines that shift quickly as the tides of technological innovation ebb and flow between rival corporations. Yet, Canadian multinationals have been surprisingly successful global competitors despite the intensity of competition and the relatively small size of the open Canadian economy. In this paper, analysis of the 16 largest Canadian multinationals suggests a variety of reasons for this success. Three important implications for the strategic management of international business in Canada are generated.

First, successful multinationals need not be in the traditional US, Japanese and European mold, i.e. with advantages in proprietary knowledge and the embodiment of high technology. The Canadian pulp and paper, mining and liquor multinationals are non-traditional, yet successful multinationals. Furthermore, Moore Corporation is an example of a Canadian firm which developed firm-specific advantages to complement high technology rather than to rely upon it, as did Northern Telecom. Competitive analysis can lead to strategies which foster the growth of Canadian multinationals, whereas participation in high-tech industries by itself need not guarantee success.

Second, Canadian multinationals demonstrate that the firm-specific advantage of the multinational can be in marketing and experience. The efficient marketing of resource-based product lines is the primary strength of many Canadian MNEs. Seagram, Moore, and Massey-Ferguson are examples of the critical importance of marketing and distribution. Each has an extensive distribution network which gives it a distinct advantage over its competitors. In Massey-Ferguson's case, it is one of the few advantages which the firm continues to enjoy. These relationships help to reduce the environmental costs, especially the political risk, which is part and parcel of any foreign involvement. Effective distribution networks, market knowledge, and experience result in favorable barriers to entry and the reduction of competitive forces. Switching costs, product differentiation, and control of the distribution channels are effective even when cost, scale, and government barriers do not exist.

Third, the firm-specific advantages of Canadian multinationals often build upon Canada's country-specific advantages. The firms either own mineral deposits, have established long-term leases for timber rights, or own energy resources which are cheap and abundant relative to foreign rivals. In short, Canadian multinationals have internalized Canada's country-specific advantages in resources, which in turn leads to special firm-specific advantages. The only non-resource based Canadian multinationals in the top 16 are Northern Telecom and Moore. Firm-specific advantages which build upon country-specific advantages can form formidable barriers to entry. Such firm-specific advantages give Canadian multinationals access not only to important sources of raw materials, but also to cheap Canadian hydroelectric

power. Nationalism can also be of importance since favored Canadian firms may receive preferential access to the resource from the responsible governments. Canadian multinationals also benefit from links with provincial governments which reduce information costs and political risk.

The Canadian MNEs studied in this paper provide a lesson for strategic managers and policy makers. They demonstrate the success of managerial strategies aimed at the marketing end of business rather than at the production end. Canadian MNEs are successful because they build on the resource strength of their own nation but process and distribute product lines in an aggressive manner on a world-wide basis. The Canadian MNEs are examples of the fallacy of over-reliance on technological strength alone. Resource-based MNEs are just as good, if not better, than high tech MNEs.

THE AGE OF EFFICIENCY: POLICY IMPLICATIONS OF MULTINATIONAL ACTIVITY

The policy implications of this study are straightforward (perhaps deceptively so). Broadly speaking, the focal point is the proposition that multinational enterprises are efficient organizations for the transmission of goods and services between the United States and Canada, and vice versa. While this concept of economic efficiency naturally has implications for social, cultural, and political value systems and philosophies, this paper has confined its attention to the purely economic aspects of the US-Canadian relationship, since this is the only area in which the author feels competent to generalize the research findings. What, then, are the economic implications of multinationals for US-Canadian relations? There are three issues to be placed upon the agenda.

First, the symmetry between exports and foreign direct investment. Basically a nation can choose to have its domestic markets serviced under conditions of free trade or, if protective forces are erected, then FDI will substitute for trade. In the former case many US firms will prewill remain some MNEs which need

fer to export to Canada, but there to set up subsidiaries in Canada to reduce transaction costs and other natural market imperfections. In general, liberalization of US-Canadian trade relations will cause a switch from FDI towards trade, and this movement should be welfare increasing after short-run adjustment costs are overcome.

Second, the asymmetry between US driven FDI in Canada, and Canadian FDI in the United States. The former is ten times as large as the latter. This means that US foreign ownership of the Canadian economy is a much bigger political issue in Canada than is Canadian FDI in the United States. Indeed, whereas FDI in Canada is now about 20 percent of GNP (down from 27 percent in 1971), in the United States total FDI is only three percent, with Canadian FDI being only 0.4 percent, see Rugman (1986). Furthermore, the United States seems happy to keep US-Canadian foreign policy, including trade and investment relations, on the back burner. The US relationship with Canada is perceived in the United States as basically a stable one and of secondary interest to its concerns with more powerful nations. On the other hand, Canada's relationship with the United States is the dominant factor in Canadian foreign policy, and is likely to remain so. This implies that Canada will often make bilateral trade and investment proposals, whereas the United States will prefer to deal with Canada on a multilateral basis.

Third, the focus of this paper has been upon the efficiency aspects of multinational enterprises. Efficiency should be given a higher profile in discussions of the US-Canadian relationship. There are too many interest groups active in both nations for the good of the nations as a whole. The welfare of consumers is too often sacrificed for the protection of selected groups of producers and workers. Policy makers must always be on guard against the pleading of such special interests. The flag of efficiency, though tattered and torn, remains the best beacon in the darkness of the real world of second best policies.

REFERENCES

Annual Reports, various

Canadian Business, "The Canadian Business 500", July 1980.

Caves, Richard E., Porter, Michael E. and Spence, Michael, *Competition in the Open Economy* (Cambridge, MA: Harvard University Press, 1982).

Financial Post Survey of Industrials

Financial Post, March 12, 1983 and November 28, 1981.

Financial Post, "The Financial Post 500", Annual.

Fortune, "The Fortune 500 Largest US Industrial Corporations", May Issues, 1974-83.

Gray, Herb, *Foreign Direct Investment In Canada* (Ottawa: Information Canada, 1972).

Litvak, L.A., and Maule, C.J., *The Canadian Multinationals* (Toronto: Butterworth and Company, 1981).

Porter, Michael E., *Competitive Strategy: Techniques for Analyzing Industries and Competitors* (New York: Free Press, Macmillan Publishers, 1980, pp. 54-61).

Poynter, Thomas A. and Rugman, Alan M., "World Product Mandates: How Will Multinationals Respond?", *Business Quarterly* (Fall, 1982).

Rugman, Alan M., *International Diversification and the Multinational Enterprise* (Lexington: D.C. Heath, 1979).

Rugman, Alan M., Multinationals in Canada: *Theory, Performance and Economic Impact* (Boston: Martinus Nijhoff, 1980).

Rugman, Alan M., *Inside the Multinationals: The Economics of Internal Markets* (New York: Columbia University Press, 1981).

Rugman, Alan M., "The Comparative Performance of US and European Multinational Enterprises, 1970-79" *Management International Review* (23:2, 1983, pp. 4-14).

Rugman, Alan M., "Canadian Foreign Direct Investment in the United States", in Peter H. Gray (editor), *Uncle Sam as Host* (Greenwich, Conn: JAI Press, 1986).

Rugman, Alan M., "Transfer Pricing in the Canadian Petroleum Industry," in Alan M. Rugman and Lorraine Eden, *Multinationals and Transfer Pricing* (London: Croom Helm and New York: St. Martin's Press, 1984, pp. 173-192).

Rugman, Alan M. and Bennett, Jocelyn, "Technology Transfer and World Product Mandating," *Columbia Journal of World Business* (Winter, 1982, pp. 58-62).

Safarian, A.E., *Foreign Ownership of Canadian Industry* (Toronto: McGraw-Hill, 1966, 2nd Edition, Toronto: University of Toronto Press, 1973).

Science Council of Canada, *Multinationals and Industrial Strategy: The Role of World Product Mandaes* (Science Council of Canada: Ottawa, 1980).

Stopford, John M., *The World Directory of Multinational Enterprises 1982-83* (London: Macmillan Publishers, 1982).

Research and Development by Multinational and Domestic Firms in Canada

ALAN M. RUGMAN*/Centre for International Business Studies,
Dalhousie University

This paper presents both theoretical and empirical support for the proposition that less R & D is done in the branch plants of multinational enterprises in Canada than in either the parent multinationals, or in independent Canadian firms of similar size to the subsidiaries. The theory of internalization predicts that the multinational enterprise will concentrate its initial and ongoing R & D in the parent firm. It does this to protect its knowledge advantage from the risk of dissipation and it uses an internal market to control and monitor the use of its firm specific advantage. The empirical work surveyed, and new studies reported, support this interpretation of its global strategy.

Cet article apporte une base théorique et empirique à l'appui du fait que l'on effectuerait moins de Recherche et Développement dans les succursales des entreprises multinationales que dans les multinationales elles-mêmes, ou dans les compagnies canadiennes indépendantes de même importance que les succursales. La théorie de l'internalisation avance que l'entreprise multinationale, tant initialement que par la suite, concentrera la recherche et le développement au niveau de la maison-mère. Cela arrive parce qu'elle désire protéger de la dispersion ses avantages au plan des connaissances. En outre, elle compte utiliser le marché interne pour contrôler et suivre attentivement l'utilisation des avantages spécifiques à sa succursale. Or, ce choix stratégique global est, en fait, corroboré par le travail empirique et par les nouvelles études que nous avons recensées.

INTRODUCTION

An essential element of Canada's industrial strategy is to increase the amount of Research and Development (R & D) expenditures. The proposed target is to have R & D at 1.5 per cent of GNP, up from the under 1 per cent level of recent years, but still below the current US level of 2.5 per cent. To promote R & D in Canada the federal government, and some of their provincial counterparts, offer both incentive grants and associated industrial policies which are perceived as helpful to technological development. A recent proposal is to encourage the use of world product mandates by the subsidiaries of foreign based (mainly US) multinationals in Canada.

The major objective of this paper is to analyse the contribution that such foreign owned

* Research for this paper was supported by a Fellowship from the Tenth Associates' Workshop in Business Research of the School of Business Adminsitration, University of Western Ontario, Summer 1980. Although they may still not agree with the final product, several colleagues have provided stimulating comments on previous drafts, namely: Judith Alexander, Harold Crookell, Don Daly, Dennis DeMelto, John Dunning, Ed Safarian and several anonymous referees.

firms can make to the growth of R & D expenditures in Canada relative to indigenous firms. A secondary objective is to question some of the doubtful premises of the protectionist elements of Canada's industrial strategy, especially the perceived desire to achieve greater technological sovereignty. The paper proceeds in the next section to review the modern theory of the multinational enterprise (MNE) so that it can be related to the issue of technology transfer to Canada. Following this there is a critical review of recent work on the determinants of R & D in Canada by foreign and domestic firms. Finally some empirical work is summarized in which the relative expenditures on R & D are examined for three groups of firms; parent MNE's, their subsidiaries in Canada and independent Canadian firms.

INTERNALIZATION AS THE MODERN THEORY OF THE MNE

It has been demonstrated by Buckley and Casson (1976), Dunning (1977, 1979) and Rugman (1980, 1981) that the activities of MNEs are explained by the theory of internalization. It is now becoming recognized by many scholars as the modern theory of foreign direct investment. It presents a systematic method for the MNEs to evaluate the relative importance of country specific factors (production functions) and firm specific factors (such as knowledge, technological 'know-how', management ability, or some other 'core skill') when they make the foreign investment decision. It can be used to explain the methods by which MNEs choose to service foreign markets, namely the choice over time between exporting, foreign direct investment or licensing, since the MNEs consider the relative net benefits of each modality.

The theory of internalization can be applied in a Canadian context to the specific issue of technology transfer in Canada. It offers similar predictions to those of Caves (1974) about the branch plant nature of Canadian subsidiaries, but makes these predictions more explicit. Internalization theory helps to explain why there is very little indigenous R & D in Canada, why the MNE has a propensity to prefer foreign direct investment to licensing and why the technology of a host nation such as Canada lags behind that of the United States, Japan and Europe.

The theory of internalization is utilized here to explain the nature of the transfer of technology to Canada by (mainly US) MNEs and to examine the issue of Canadian public support for R & D by MNEs versus independent Canadian firms. Internalization theory states that the internal market of the MNE is a mechanism which is used to monitor the use of its unique firm specific advantage (in knowledge or some other asset monopolized by the firm). Internalization is often a superior device to contractual arrangements such as licensing or joint ventures, since, from the viewpoint of the MNE, the risk of dissipation of its firm specific advantage is minimized when control of the asset is guaranteed via the organization of an internal market.

One prediction of internalization theory is that the MNE will use foreign direct investment (i.e., production by wholly controlled subsidiaries) to minimize the risk of dissipation of its firm specific advantage in knowledge (broadly defined to include technology and/or management skills). Typically this is best achieved by establishing subsidiaries which are 'miniature replicas' of the parent, but which are sufficiently efficient to overcome the additional costs of operating in a foreign business environment. These subsidiaries secure a greater worldwide market for the products of the MNE. Clearly little innovative capacity is to be expected in such subsidiaries.

The MNE is not in busines to transfer technology to Canada or to otherwise intervene in its affairs *per se*, but it is here to make profits over time, a market test which requires the cautious use of resources and technology by the firm. We shall see that the lack of technological independence by Canada is not the fault of the MNE but is determined by inappropriate Canadian industrial and science policy.

It was first recognized by Hymer (1976) that the MNE is an organization which exists in a world of market imperfections. Indeed, Hymer and Kindleberger (1969), both demonstrate that 'natural' imperfections in the goods or factor markets will generate MNE activity. Therefore it is obvious that internalization, which is a response to such externalities as the pricing of proprietary information, knowledge and intangible management skills occurs when its benefits outweigh the costs. Yet it is an error to confine internalization to these market imperfections alone. Indeed there is no reason why internalization is a theory of *international* production in such a case. To add the missing dimension we need to accept the point that multinational enterprises embody within themselves firm specific advantages which can be maintained only by foreign direct investment (FDI), rather than by such alternative modalities of servicing foreign markets as exporting or licensing. Thus internalization hypothesizes that FDI is superior to these other modes because of its lower relative cost. Exporting is also denied by tariffs and licensing faces the risk of dissipation of the firm specific advantage.

A second point is that market imperfections may well be created by government regulations and controls. Internalization is a response to such 'unnatural' market imperfections. Again, recognition of these elements makes internalization into a theory of the multinational enterprise (rather than a domestic firm). Yet the organization of an internal market is not a free good. Williamson (1975) and others, following on the seminal work of Coase (1937) have recognized the costs of co-ordination of an administrative fiat. These costs of control increase the greater the autonomy of the overseas subsidiaries. In particular, there is a risk to the firm's monopolistic advantage by excessive decentralization.

Centralized control of R & D is an implication of this modern version of the theory of the MNE. Unless the R & D is centralized in the parent its firm specific advantage is at risk. The MNE prefers to control the rate of use of its knowledge advantage, and it is afraid of dissipation. Fischer and Behrman (1979) recently studied the centralization of the management of foreign based R & D of 35 US and 18 European MNEs. They found that the more successful MNEs followed a centralized R & D strategy, which implies that the internal advantage of the MNE in knowledge or technology is better allocated on a worldwide basis when the MNE follows a centralized corporate plan. The centralized firms have superior communication and control systems. It has been shown also by Williamson (1975) that the internal markets of a firm are responsive to conditions of imperfect information and that firms are hierarchical and centralized. The resource allocation processes that are internalized are those which are not efficiently carried out in a decentralized manner, such as financial management and control of R & D (the source of the firm specific advantage to the MNE).

It is the linkage of country specific and firm specific advantages that distinguishes internalization theory from either the theory of trade or the theory of the firm. The MNE is the only organization to arbitrage the imperfections of both international and domestic markets. In the context of this paper it can be argued that the R & D expenditures of branch plants within the United States would be less than those of the parent firm, for the same reasons that R & D expenditures of branch plants in Canada are lower than those of the US parent. Yet this observation, correct so far as it goes, is limited to a firm specific (theory of the firm) focus. By using internalization theory we can see that country specific factors are also relevant; i.e., the fact that the US is technologically better endowed than Canada. This means that the MNE reflects the hue of its home nation's comparative advantage (in knowledge) as it proceeds to make a worldwide market to exploit its advantage in technology. As discussed earlier, these interrelationships between ownership (firm) specific advantage and country (location) specific advantage have also been recognized in the work of Dunning (1977, 1979) as the crucial elements in a modern theory of the MNE.

The firm specific advantages of the MNE are characterized by strengths in advertising, marketing, raising capital, risk diversification (see Rugman, 1979), management skills and so on, besides their good R & D performance. There are synergistic and agglomerative effects at work in the internal market of the MNE. The R & D function demonstrates scale economies, fixed costs and indivisibilities; few of these being available to (generally smaller) Canadian firms. In a Canadian context it is important to note first, that branch plants of the MNEs will do less R & D than their parents; and, second, that much of Canadian manufacturing industry is foreign owned. The combination of these two events serves to reduce the amount of R & D in Canada from what it would otherwise have been, *ceteris paribus*. Only if foreign owned firms are removed from the picture will Canada have an amount of R & D consistent with its country specific capability in the area of technology generation. It should be noted that this argument denies the role of MNEs as vehicles for the transfer of technology; indeed, internalization theory says that MNEs prefer to protect their knowledge advantage by an internal market rather than by contractual arrangements such as licensing.

INTERNALIZATION AND THE TRANSFER OF TECHNOLOGY TO CANADA

As a small, open economy Canada enjoys one of the highest standards of living in the world. Yet many nationalist groups have questioned the lack of technological independence and have sought to relate this perceived problem to the high degree of foreign ownership of the majority of the Canadian manufacturing and resource sectors. It is well known that the ratio of R & D expenditures to GNP for Canada is under 1 per cent, but it is over 2 per cent for the United States (in 1975 the actual percentages were 1.0 and 2.4, respectively). While, in percentage terms, Canada does only half the R & D of the United States most European nations also have a higher percentage; tending more towards 2 than 1. Historically the US percentage has been close to 3. Canada, therefore, has one of the lowest percentages of R & D expenditures to GNP for all advanced nations. Furthermore, the ratio has fallen from an average of 1.2 in the sixties and there appears to be little hope of raising it to the target level of 1.5 in the foreseeable future.

It has been advocated by the Science Council of Canada (1979, 1980) and by various nationalist groups that Canada should seek to increase the ratio of R & D to GNP. In terms of welfare economics it is, of course, not clear that there is anything suboptimal about the current ratio of R & D to sales. How do we know what is an 'appropriate' ratio? Do we also have socially suboptimal advertising or defence policies, as our expenditures on these items are also low relative to other nations? Of course, it is immediately apparent that sectoral policy targets can conflict with overall global welfare maximization. The apparent public policy rationalization for setting a target level of R & D to sales is a naive growth model which links technology to outward shifts of the aggregate production function; a theory which neglects problems of substitution and other changes over time.

One currently fashionable method of increasing Canada's technology is to pursue a 'world product mandate' under which Canadian based multinational firms would generate technology at home for future export abroad. The viability of such a policy of self-sufficiency in technology is considered here as an implication of the analysis of technology transfer. The objective of the production of technology is also related to the objective of consumption and income generation for the nation as a whole.

The Science Council of Canada (1979) and two of their most influential researchers, Britton and Gilmour (1978), have advanced a strategy of technological independence for Canada. They advocate such a nationalistic policy since they believe that there is insufficient transfer of technology to Canada from the multinational enterprises which dominate the nation. Nor is there an attractive climate for indigenous innovation in an economy with truncated firms, high production costs, low relative productivity and excessive concentration.

The preference of the Science Council for technological sovereignty has been roundly criticized by Daly (1979a) and Safarian (1979). Using basic economic analysis these authors demonstrate that there are internal inconsistencies in the Science Council's analysis. They also find that a nationalist science policy (like the tariff) is inefficient. They conclude that government intervention along the lines proposed by the Science Council would not be successful in sustaining Canadian technological development. This paper extends the analysis of Daly and Safarian by placing greater attention upon the modern theory of the multinational enterprise, so that an implication of internalization theory can be tested by examination of the relative amounts of R & D undertaken by multinationals versus domestic firms in Canada.

The relationship between R & D, degree of foreign control of manufacturing industry and implications for technological export activity has been studied by Safarian (1966), Globerman (1973) and most recently by Bones (1980). Safarian (1966) could not find any difference in R & D expenditures between resident and non-resident firms. His results, based on his survey of foreign owned firms in the Canadian economy in the early 1960s, are reported in Chapter 6 of his now classic study. The sample and survey response method of Safarian does not lend itself readily to econometric investigation so his findings cannot be regarded as definitive.

In his analysis of Statistics Canada industry level data Bones finds that most R & D in Canada is done by multinational firms. In 1975 more than 80 per cent of R & D by all Canadian industries took place in seven manufacturing industries, namely: aircraft and parts, electrical products, petroleum, machinery, chemicals, primary metals and paper. In these seven research-intensive manufacturing industries there occurs the highest degree of foreign ownership. The percentage of foreign control of industry sales (shown in parentheses) is: aircraft and parts (82.7), electrical (65.6), petroleum (96.0), machinery (67.5), chemicals (82.9), primary metals (17.1) and paper (43.6).

Thus it can be confirmed that the great bulk of R & D generated in Canada takes place in the manufacturing industries which experience the highest degree of foreign control. But when we translate this finding to a firm level analysis does it imply that the subsidiaries of (mainly US) multinational firms active in Canada are responsible for original R & D or does it mean they are conduits for the innovations of the parent multinational? Until Canadian policy towards R & D starts from the premise that multinational firms dominate the R & D components of the manufacturing sector of the economy and that their activities are explained by internalization theory it is unlikely that the source of technology transfer to Canada can be identified.

R. Frankl (1979) finds a strong positive relationship between R & D intensity in Canadian industries and their US counterparts. There is also a significant negative relationship between the degree of foreign control and the difference between US and Canadian R & D intensities. Frankl suggests that the parent multinational enjoys scale economies in R & D, and also benefits from indivisibilities in R & D. The Canadian subsidiary experiences truncation of its R & D capacity. She also suggests that the results support the hypothesis that there are greater barriers to technology flow between independent firms than between affiliates. The regressions from which these results emerge were run on a data base for 110 Canadian manufacturing industries and their US counterparts for 1972.

The overall result of the Frankl study is that R & D intensity in Canadian industry is lower than that in the United States. This poor performance (from the viewpoint of the host nation) is due almost entirely to the extensive foreign control of Canadian industry. Frankl's study thereby confirms a prediction of internalization theory which states that innovation occurs in the home nation rather than in the host nation. She argues that R & D expenditures in Canada would almost double if the R & D in Canadian subsidiaries of multinationals were of the same proportion as R & D expenditures by their parent firms.

To summarize, these two recent studies tend to support this current application of internalization theory in a Canadian context. They confirm that, while foreign owned firms in Canada produce most of the nation's R & D, these subsidiaries undertake less R & D than the parent firms of the multinationals. There is mixed evidence as to whether independent Canadian firms do as little R & D as the subsidiaries after allowing for their smaller size, but this is a point of secondary importance to the major finding of the authors that there is inadequate R & D in subsidiaries of multinational firms.

Of course, this raises the basic question as to how we are to interpret an 'inadequate' amount of R & D. While a target level of R & D can be set by policy makers the achievement of such an arbitrary number will raise a host of complex issues. These touch on the relative net benefits of importing technology versus adapting it; scale economies in R & D; the goals of national development and industrial strategy; and so on. This paper demonstrates that such complex issues of national policy need to be distinguished analytically from the R & D pricing and investment decisions of the MNE, since such firm level decisions are made independently and follow the premises of internalization theory.

Using this basis the relationship between technology generation in Canada and the extent of multinational activity in Canadian manufacturing industry can be studied in more detail. It has been shown in Rugman (1981) that the MNEs have a global strategy in the use of their R & D but that its production is done at head office in typical MNEs. They seek to preserve the knowledge asset of each firm by the process of internalization. Thus it can be hypothesized that little innovation, ongoing, or worthwhile, R & D is likely to be undertaken in Canada by foreign owned firms, and conversely, that independent Canadian owned firms will do relatively more R & D.

If an infant technology argument is being made then the best way to do it is by direct subsidies to Canadian owned firms, rather than by the continuation of the current policy which fails to discriminate between multinational and domestic firms. On the other hand, if it is cheaper to adapt and use foreign technology, as suggested by Daly and Globerman (1976), then multinationals should be encouraged, but there is no need for the infant technology argument to be used as well, since it conflicts with the reasons for multinationality. The overriding concern for public policy should be for efficiency rather than a misconceived attempt to achieve technological independence in an integrated world.

The paper now proceeds to examine the recent empirical literature on the determinants of Research and Development in Canada. This literature is found to offer an inadequate explanation of the motivation for technology transfer to Canada, which takes place at the firm level, rather than at the national level as assumed in the econometric work reviewed here. It is found that an appropriate test of the theory of internalization requires a firm level analysis of relative expenditures on R & D by parent, subsidiary and independent Canadian firms.

THE DETERMINANTS OF R & D IN CANADA

In more recent work on the economic variables that influence R & D in Canada it is found that the amount of grants for R & D from the federal government is important. Indeed this is often the only significant independent variable in econometric studies of the determinants of R & D in Canada. Globerman (1973) at industry level, Howe and McFetridge (1976) at firm level for the electrical industry, Hewitt (1980b) at firm level also for the electrical industry, and Alexander (1980) at industry level have all found government-financed R & D to be a significant variable positively related to the amount of R & D actually undertaken in Canada.

One reason for this may be the pervasive role of MNEs in Canada. They have received a greater share of grants for R & D than have Canadian firms, see Daly and Globerman (1976). As the subsidiary is linked to its parent MNE, by the internal market, it has expert marketing and management skills available to it. Therfore, the subsidiary of an MNE can probably use a given R & D grant 'better' than a Canadian firm which lacks these tie ins. By better is meant that more sales will result from a R & D grant. Yet it is not at all clear that the subsidiary really needed the R & D grant to stimulate such synergy. Nor is it clear that these R & D grants do anything more than distort the pricing decisions of the MNE.

At firm level, R & D to sales is positively related to size (of firm), and to concentration ratio, see Scherer (1970). Also the larger firms in Canada tend to secure more patents relative to smaller firms, see McFetridge and Weatherley (1977). At industry level there is a weaker relationship between size and R & D expenditures. Indeed, technological progressiveness is sometimes not related in a significant manner to sales, see Alexander (1980) and Hewitt (1980a), although Howe and McFetridge (1976) do find sales variables are significant in the linear determination of absolute R & D expenditures for three industry groups. The disparities are not really very surprising, since industry level data aggregates the firm level effects, such that size washes out as a variable affecting R & D. Orr (1974) shows that concentration ratios are related to tariffs and other barriers to entry. In turn, some authors find concentration and/or tariffs related to profitability and degree of foreign ownership, see Rosenbluth (1970), Bloch (1974), Eastman and Stykolt (1967) and Shapiro (1980). These findings are stronger using firm level data, but they also tend to hold across industries.

D.J. Daly, (1979b) and elsewhere, has examined the basic point that there are economies of scale in R & D. Scale economies permit the high fixed costs and overheads of R & D to be spread over larger runs. Unfortunately, in Canada the small size of the economy and the effects of protection mean that short runs are characteristic of industry. Daly argues that this helps explain why both Canadian and foreign owned companies undertake relatively little R & D in Canada. A related point is that scale economies in R & D will lead to greater centralization of the R & D function in the MNEs active in Canada. Once again we find an argument against world product mandating; the lack of scale economies in technology works against such mandates for most MNEs.

D.C. MacCharles (1981) has examined the costs of either producing knowledge independently (as is the case for Canadian owned firms) or purchasing R & D from the parent (as is the case for the subsidiary of an MNE). Using data on Canadian and US owned firms within the same industry groups MacCharles finds that the costs of knowledge acquisition are higher for independent Canadian than for US owned subsidiaries, especially for groupings of smaller firms. He also finds that the smaller Canadian owned firms are relatively inefficient in their use of R & D, since they have low levels of value added per worker despite spending relatively more on R & D than foreign owned firms of similar size. The work of MacCharles is consistent with internalization theory, especially with the premise that the synergistic effects of R & D are not available to small independent Canadian firms.

The interdependencies among the key variables affecting the structure of Canadian industry preclude the development of a theory based on casual relationships. Instead all of the following variables are interrelated in some positive manner: tariffs; foreign ownership; size; concentration; R & D; profitability; and growth rate.

Many empirical studies, by generations of Canadian economists, have examined sub-sets of these variables, with somewhat ambiguous results. If anything, these studies identify a positive relationship amongst the seven variables, although there are possible offsetting partial influences between any two variables. It is clear that there are omitted variables in these studies; here I suggest that the omissions lie at the firm level and that further work on the motivation of foreign direct investment by the MNEs may yield a better analysis of the determinants of R & D in Canada.

The less than satisfactory outcome of the existing detailed econometric studies of the determinants of R & D in Canada is the result of a fundamental misconception. The authors attempt to identify the significant variables determining R & D, where the dependent variable is viewed from a national perspective. Instead the very point of internalization theory is that R & D is determined within the multinational firm. Therefore a firm level analysis is required rather than the economy wide ones which have been undertaken so far.

The existing studies fall down since they are at an aggregate level and they have to straddle the artificial constraints of national boundaries. The macro level studies attempt to identify (from the viewpoint of Canada alone) the impact of R & D expenditure of grants by the Canadian government. Yet internalization theory predicts that decisions on R & D in Canadian subsidiaries are not made within a Canadian context at all but depend on the global investment strategy of the MNEs. Therefore aggregative, national studies fail to test for that part of R & D which is generated by foreign owned firms in Canada. Studies of variables which implicitly assume the autonomy of a nation state are not too helpful when the host nation's manufacturing sector is dominated by multinational firms. Studies of technological intensity (as proxied by the ratio of R & D to sales), however, must be conceived and performed within the context of a firm level analysis.

This paper has advanced the hypothesis that the level of R & D in Canada is explained better by what happens in the headquarters of an American multinational firm than by any list of variables drawn from the Canadian economy. The R & D undertaken by subsidiaries of US multinationals operating in Canada is predicated on the global strategy of that multinational enterprise. The actions of the Canadian federal and provincial governments to promote R & D in the nation will enter into the decision making set of the multinational enterprise only on its periphery.

The subsidies for R & D are of little importance to the initial R & D decision of the multinational firm, but such exogenous factors may affect its internal decisions regarding ongoing and future firm level R & D expenditures. Yet due to the uncertainties of host government policy towards R & D subsidization, the multinational firm would be foolish to become locked into a dependence on such host government support. Therefore the multinational will discount all such risky technological subsidies and will, in general, make its foreign investment decision according to the guidelines of internalization theory, as indicated earlier.

Conversely, the expenditures of the Canadian government for R & D will be of great importance to independent Canadian firms. The subsidies will act as an incentive to private industry in Canada and, all other things equal, should generate greater domestic technological innovations. This distinction between foreign and domestic owned firms is basic to Canadian industrial organization since the motivation of the two sets of firms is different. The remainder of this paper reports on a simple test of the basic implications of internalization theory in a Canadian context.

612 / Alan M. Rugman

RELATIVE EXPENDITURES ON R & D BY MULTINATIONAL AND
DOMESTIC FIRMS IN CANADA

The relative expenditures on R & D by three groups of corporations operating in Canada are
now examined. The groups are: the parent firms (US based multinational enterprises); the
Canadian subsidiaries of the multinationals; and a group of independent Canadian owned
firms of approximately similar size to the subsidiaries. Due to the absence of published data
on the R & D performed by subsidiaries a limited sample of firms is studied.

The basic hypothesis examined is that the R & D undertaken by subsidiaries is less than
that of independent Canadian firms. The lack of R & D in subsidiaries is explained by the
theory of internalization which states that subsidiaries exist to extend abroad the firm specific advantage of the parent firm. The multinational enterprises choose to regulate the use
of their advantages through an internal market when the net benefits of such internalization
exceed those of possible alternative methods of servicing foreign markets, such as exporting
(denied by tariffs) or licensing (denied by the risk of dissipation of the firm specific advantage).

There are no published data on the R & D undertaken by subsidiaries of multinational
firms operating in Canada. Given these constraints the information used in this project came
from a survey of R & D expenditures for 1977 made by the *Financial Post* and reported in
the issue of June 10th 1978. It covered thirty-five corporations active in R & D in Canada, in
the private sector, as identified by a directory of research establishments compiled by the
Ministry of State for Science and Technology (MOSST). The survey excluded R & D undertaken by Crown corporations, public utilities, and private firms in the areas of tar sands and
atomic energy. R & D is defined as 'all costs associated with the search for, and discovery of,
new knowledge that may be useful in developing new products, services, processes or techniques, or that might significantly improve existing products or processes.' Excluded are costs
of routine product improvement or seasonal changes of style, market research and testing,
quality control and legal costs to protect patents.

I divided the thirty-five firms from the survey initially into two groups; independent
Canadian firms and subsidiaries of multinational enterprises. Data were then gathered from
other published sources on the sales, profits (defined as net income after taxes), and for the
subsidiaries, percentage of foreign ownership. Next the parent firms of the subsidiaries were
identified, to form a third group; namely the parent multinationals. The R & D, profits and
sales of these parents were then found from published sources such as the *Fortune* Directory
of the largest 1,000 corporations, annual reports, etc. The full results of this study are available in Rugman (1981), and are summarized below:

TABLE 1   R & D expenditures as a per cent of sales for groups of 12 firms in 1977

US parents	Canadian subsidiaries	Independent Canadian
3.12	2.07	1.19

TABLE 2   R & D expenditures as a per cent of profits for groups of 12 firms in 1977

US parents	Canadian subsidiaries	Independent Canadian
60.27	41.43	29.78

The limited availability of data on the firm level R & D in Canada prevents sampling according to industry characteristics. Thus one of the weaker parts of this study is its neglect of the research intensity of some industry groups compared to others. Fortunately, as reported earlier, other investigators of R & D have pitched their studies at industry level, for example, Frankl (1979), Globerman (1973) and Hewitt (1980a). The present work complements these other studies but it cannot address itself to precisely the same question as they do.

I found that the mean size of the parents is about ten times that of their subsidiaries. Yet mean R & D expenditures of the parents are twenty times those of their subsidiaries. The independent Canadian firms have mean sales that are 50 per cent greater than mean sales of subsidiaries. But their absolute mean expenditures on R & D are also 50 per cent greater than those of the subsidiaries. The ratios of R & D to sales reported in the table above present a more complicated picture. For 9 of the 12 firms the ratio is greater for the parent than in its Canadian subsidiary. The mean ratio of R & D to sales for the sample of 12 parent firms is 3.12. This is well above the all industry composite for all US manufacturing industry over the 1975–1979 period (which averages 1.9). Consistent with the implications of internalization theory the mean R & D to sales ratio for the 12 subsidiaries is 2.07, that is, lower than the ratio of the parent firms. The 12 independent Canadian firms have a mean ratio of R & D sales of 1.19 which is lower than that of both the subsidiaries and the parents.

In a statistical analysis, in which the means for R & D to sales (for the samples of 12 firms) are tested for significant differences it is found that there are no significant differences between the respective means of the three samples, i.e., between 3.12, 2.07 and 1.19 on an F test (where the F ratio is 2.28) or between the subsidiaries and parents on a t test. Yet there is a significant difference between parent multinationals and independents on a t test. There is no significant difference between the mean of the R & D to sales ratio of the parent firms (3.12) and that of the corresponding Canadian subsidiaries (2.07). The calculated t-ratio (1.01) for the data of these two groups is less than the critical value for t for a two-tailed test at the 5 per cent confidence level. Similarly there is no significant difference between the means for the subsidiary and independent Canadian firms as the t-ratio is here also less than 2. Yet there is a significant difference between the mean of the R & D to sales ratio of the parent firms (3.12) and of the independent Canadian owned firms (1.19). The calculated t-ratio (2.77) for these sets of firms is greater than the critical value for a two-tailed test at the 5 per cent level.

Data on the ratio of R & D to profits, reported in the table, are much the same as those presented above. The absolute and mean profits of the parent firms are almost ten times those of their subsidiaries, but the profits of independent Canadian firms are 50 per cent greater than those of foreign controlled subsidiaries. The mean ratio of R & D to profits varies by sample groups, at 60.27 for parents; 41.43 for their subsidiaries; and 29.78 for independent Canadian firms. These means are not significantly different. In all three cases (parent-subsidiary, parent-Canadian, and subsidiary-Canadian) the calculated t-ratios, 0.739, 1.625 and 0.690 respectively, are less than the critical t statistic at the 5 per cent confidence level. The F ratio (0.91) is also less than the critical value required at the 5 per cent level.

CONCLUSIONS

This paper presented both theoretical and empirical support for the proposition that less R & D is done in the branch plants of multinational enterprises in Canada than in either their parent MNEs, or in independent Canadian firms of similar size. The theory of internalization predicts that the MNE will concentrate its R & D in the parent and conduct only a limited amount of truly innovative research in its offshore subsidiaries. The MNE seeks to protect its knowledge advantage by running an internal market to control the use of its R & D and avoid the risk of dissipation of its firm specific advantage.

The results of the statistical analysis of R & D expenditures at the firm level reported in

614 / Alan M. Rugman

the tables reveal that more R & D is done in the parent multinationals than in their Canadian subsidiaries, as predicted by internalization theory. In 9 of the 12 cases the R & D to sales ratio of the parent firm exceeds that of its subsidiary. Yet the statistical support for the hypothesis that the mean ratio of R & D to sales is less for the sample of subsidiaries than for their parent firms is weak since the difference in means is not significant. Neither is there statistical support for the proposition that independent Canadian firms do more (or less) R & D than foreign owned manufacturing firms operating in Canada. The same findings apply to the ratio of R & D undertaken by parent US multinationals than by independent Canadian firms. This may be interpreted as offering some support for the importance of country specific factors in providing a technological base for R & D. It is thus an indirect measure of support for a prediction of internalization theory, namely that more innovations occur in the nation of the parent firm, rather than in the nation of the subsidiary.

The ambiguous nature of some of these results is probably due to the inadequate nature of the samples. These were constructed according to data availability and are not fully representative of the characteristics of the population of parent, subsidiary and independent Canadian firms. There is also a possibility that the firms included in the subsidiary and independent samples are not fully representative of the Canadian economy, or its technological variation across industries. Until there are better data suitable for testing, it is necessary to exercise suitable caution in the use of these results. While the results can be improved with some manipulation, I have chosen not to do so since there is sufficient support for my basic premise about the relative lack of R & D in subsidiaries. I believe that this innovative methodology can be used to conduct more detailed tests when more firm level data on R & D become publicly available. Further attempts at verification or refutation of the implications of internalization theory for R & D in Canada will then become more feasible.

With the exceptions noted by the Science Council of Canda (1980) study of four successful world product mandates there is abundant theoretical and empirical support for the observation that innovations and ongoing R & D expenditures are centralized in the home nation of the multinational enterprise. The diffusion of technology to host nations such as Canada takes place as a byproduct of the strategic choice of the multinational enterprise, in which it generally prefers to retain control over its firm specific advantage in knowledge. Thus it uses the safer route of subsidiary production compared to the risky method of licensing, where there is a risk of dissipation of the firm specific advantage.

The preference of the typical multinational for internalization and control of its technology will make it very difficult for a host nation to alter the internal prices of the firm; indeed such attempts are likely to distort prices. The continuation of present Canadian science policies and non-discriminatory grants to both domestic and multinational firms is in conflict with the premises of internalization theory. It is necessary to consider more efficient alternatives. These include either direct subsidies for independent Canadian firms, that is discrimination against foreign owned firms, or the removal of market imperfections (such as tariffs) that have encouraged multinational activity in Canada in the first place. Since there is a possibility that a strategy of technological discrimination against foreign owned firms may invite retaliation abroad, it is apparent that the second alternative is more efficient.

REFERENCES

Alexander, Judith A. (1980) 'Research and Development Activity in Domestic and Foreign Controlled Industries,' mimeo, Centre for International Business Studies, Dalhousie University, Discussion Paper in International Business, No.4.

Bloch, Harry (1974) 'Prices, Costs, and Profits in Canadian Manufacturing: The Influence of Tariffs and Concentration,' *Canadian Journal of Economics*, November, VIII:4:564–610.

Bones, Herman P. (1980) 'Are Foreign Subsidiaries More Innovative?' *Foreign Investment Review*, Spring, 3:2:20–23.

Britton, John. H. and James M. Gilmour (1978) *The Weakest Link – A Technological Perspective on Canadian Industrial Underdevelopment* (Ottawa: Science Council of Canada)

Buckley, Peter and Mark Casson (1976) *The Future of the Multinational Enterprise* (London: Macmillan)

Caves, Richard E. (1974) 'The Causes of Direct Investment: Foreign Firms, Shares in Canadian and UK Manufacturing Industries,' *Review of Economics and Statistics*, 56:279–293.

Coase, Ronald H. (1937) 'The Nature of the Firm,' *Economica*, November, 4:386–405.

Daly, Donald J. (1979a) 'Weak Links in 'The Weakest Link',' *Canadian Public Policy – Analyse de Politiques*, Summer, V:3:307–317.

—— (1979b) 'Canada's Comparative Advantage,' Discussion Paper No. 135 (Ottawa: Economic Council of Canada)·

Daly, D.J. and S. Globerman (1976) *Tariff and Science Policies: Applications of a Model of Nationalism* (Toronto: University of Toronto Press)

Dunning, John H. (1977) 'Trade, Location of Economic Activity and the MNE: A Search for an Eclectic Approach,' in *The International Allocation of Economic Activity*, edited by Bertil Ohlin *et al.* (London: Macmillan)

—— (1979) 'Explaining Changing Patterns of International Production: In Defense of the Eclectic Theory,' *Oxford Bulletin of Economics and Statistics*, 4:269–296.

Eastman, Harry C. and S. Stykolt (1967) *The Tariff and Competition in Canada* (Toronto: Macmillan)

Fischer, William A. and Jack N. Behrman (1979) 'The Co-ordination of Foreign R and D Activities by Transnational Corporations,' *Journal of International Business Studies*, Winter, 10:28–35.

Frankl, Roslyn (1979) 'A Cross Section Analysis of Research and Development Intensity in Canadian Industries with Particular Reference to Foreign Control,' mimeo, Canada, Industry, Trade and Commerce, Economic Policy and Analysis Division.

Globerman, S. (1973) 'Market Structure and R and D in Canadian Manufacturing Industries,' *Quarterly Review of Economics and Business*, 13:2:59–67.

Hewitt, Gary K. (1980a) 'Research and Development Performed Abroad by U.S. Manufacturing Multinationals,' *Kyklos*, June, 33:2:308–327.

—— (1980b) 'Research and Development Performed in Canada by American Manufacturing Multinationals,' mimeo, Centre for International Business Studies, Dalhousie University, Discussion Paper in International Business, No.3.

Howe, J.D. and D.G. McFetridge (1976) 'Determinants of R and D Expenditures,' *Canadian Journal of Economics*, February, IX:1:57–71.

Hymer, Stephen H. (1976) *The International Operations of National Firms: A Study of Direct Foreign Investment* (Cambridge, Mass.: M.I.T. Press)

Kindleberger, Charles P. (1969) *American Business Abroad: Six Lectures on Direct Investment* (New York: Yale University Press)

MacCharles. Don C. (1981) *The Performance of Direct Investment in the Manufacturing Sector* (Saint John: University of New Brunswick)

616 / Alan M. Rugman

McFetridge, D.G. (1977) *Government Support of Scientific Research and Development: An Economic Analysis* (Toronto: University of Toronto Press)

McFetridge, D.G. and L.J. Weatherley (1977) *Notes on the Economics of Large Firm Size.* Study No. 20, Royal Commission on Corporate Concentration (Ottawa)

Orr, Dale (1974) 'The Determinants of Entry: A Study of the Canadian Manufacturing Industries,' *Review of Economics and Statistics*, February, LVI:1:58–66.

Rosenbluth, Gideon (1970) 'The Relation Between Foreign Control and Concentration in Canadian Industry,' *Canadian Journal of Economics*, February, III:1:14–38.

Rugman, Alan M.   (1979) *International Diversification and the Multinational Enterprise* (Lexington and Toronto: D.C. Heath)

—— (1980) *Multinationals in Canada: Theory, Performance and Economic Impact* (Boston: Martinus Nijhoff)

—— (1981) *Inside the Multinationals: The Economics of Internal Markets* (London: Croom Helm and New York: Columbia University Press)

Safarian, A.E. (1966) *Foreign Ownership of Canadian Industry* (Toronto: McGraw-Hill)

—— (1979) 'Foreign Ownership and Industrial Behaviour,' *Canadian Public Policy – Analyse de Politiques*, Summer, V:3:318–335.

Science Council of Canada (1979) *Forging the Links: A Technology Policy for Canada* (Ottawa: Science Council of Canada)

—— (1980) *Multinationals and Industrial Strategy: The Role of World Product Mandates* (Ottawa: Science Council of Canada)

Scherer, F.M. (1970) *Industrial Market Structure and Economic Performance* (Chicago: Rand-McNally)

Shapiro, Daniel M. (1980) *Foreign and Domestic Firms in Canada* (Toronto: Butterworths)

Williamson, Oliver E. (1975) *Markets and Hierarchies: Analysis and Antitrust Implications* (New York: Free Press; Macmillan)

mir vol. 30, 1990/3, pp. 253–266

mir
Management
International Review
© Gabler Verlag 1990

Alan M. Rugman/Alain Verbeke

Multinational Corporate Strategy and the Canada-U.S. Free Trade Agreement

Abstract

■ In Canada there are two sets of multinationals (MNEs): U.S. subsidiaries in Canada and Canadian-owned MNEs, the latter operating mainly in the United States. Their strategic planning is affected by environmental changes in international trade and investment policies.

■ This article develops a new model to analyze and predict the changes in competitive strategies undertaken by the two sets of MNEs in response to the Canada-U.S. Free Trade Agreement.

Key Words

■ Adjustment to the Canada-U.S. Free Trade Agreement is largely determined by the chief executive officers of some 50 large MNEs. The competitive strategies of these Canadian-based MNE are examined here.

Authors

Alan M. Rugman, Professor of International Business at the University of Toronto and Research Director of Ontario Centre for International Business, Toronto, Ontario, Canada.
Alain Verbeke, Assistant Professor of International Business at the University of Toronto, Toronto, Ontario, Canada.

Manuscript received June 1989.

Alan M. Rugman/Alain Verbeke

Introduction

The Canada-U.S. Free Trade Agreement concluded on January 2nd, 1988 implies a major environmental change for the Canadian operations of multinational enterprises (MNEs), see Canada (1988). This elimination of trade barriers may lead to a shift in strategy by these firms, as internalization theory, see Rugman (1981), predicts that changes in government regulations may alter the competitive advantages derived from operating in particular markets. In addition, these same MNEs, whether Canadian or foreign-owned, account for about 70 percent of all bilateral trade, see MacCharles (1987), so that they will bear a substantial portion of the adjustment costs resulting from free trade. In this article, we consider the process of strategic adjustment by these firms to bilateral trade liberalization.

We demonstrate that strategic adjustment by MNEs depends upon the nature of their firm-specific advantages (FSAs), country-specific advantages (CSAs) and on their existing competitive strategies. A framework is developed to assess the competitive position of these MNEs and it is used to predict their adjustment to the Agreement. Next, we apply this framework to the set of U.S. subsidiaries operating in Canada and to the indigenous Canadian MNEs. Finally these predictions are related to recent surveys undertaken by one of the authors.

Sources of Competitive Advantage

In order to interpret the impact of the Canada-U.S. Free Trade Agreement on the strategies of MNEs, we need an analytical framework that can incorporate factors particular to the firm as well as to the country. The model generated in this section of the paper weds the competitive strategy literature of Porter (1980, 1986) to the internalization theory of Rugman [1981] and Dunning and Rugman (1985), see also Rugman, Lecraw and Booth (1985).

Internalization theory argues that a firm's potential competitiveness depends upon its firm-specific advantages (FSAs). These FSAs refer to the core skills and know-how of a company, i.e., its distinctive competencies. The use of such FSAs within the context of a corporation constitutes a first source of competitive advantage, whether cost or differentiation based. FSAs, of course, only create the *potential* for actual competitive advantage in the market place. Only through the effective formulation and implementation of competitive strategies can FSAs be translated into cost or differentiation advantages. FSAs are thus the key source for obtaining competitive advantages in the market place. However, the potential competitive advantages which can be achieved also depend upon country-specific advantages (CSAs) facing the firm. The CSAs represent country characteristics that may give the firm an edge (strong CSA) or a disadvantage (weak CSA) vis-à-vis foreign rivals. Thus, tariff and non-tariff barriers to trade may constitute a CSA for protected firms in the domestic market.

It is through the use of competitive strategies that firms turn these FSAs and CSAs into actual competitive advantages in the market place. Building on the available pool of CSAs and FSAs, the firm makes decisions about the optimal global configuration and coordination along its value-added chain (operations, marketing, R & D, and logistics). In fact, the skill in making these decisions may in itself constitute a strong managerial FSA. A previous model of CSAs and FSAs was developed in Rugman and Verbeke (1988). It has also been found that most Canadian MNEs have strong resource based CSAs and differentiation enhancing FSAs, see Rugman and McIlveen (1985) and Rugman and Warner (1988). Their models have demonstrated that it is possible to move up a value-added chain, building upon strong resource based CSAs.

A Model of Competitive Strategies in Global Industries

Recognizing that there are different strategic avenues to success, it is useful to distinguish between Canadian firms based on the relative strengths of their CSAs and FSAs, see Figure 1.

This allows the classification of firms in global industries, according to their competitive strategies. Global industries are defined here as industries characterized by strong international competition and intra-industry trade. In this matrix, "strength" is a relative notion. A strong FSA means that the company has the potential to erect sustainable entry barriers against foreign rivals, so as to secure its product market domain. A strong CSA reflects the potential to be competitive against international rivals, but its source lies outside the firm (e.g. cheap and abundant labor, efficiency of the capital market, high quality human capital, abundant natural resources, government shelter).

The competitive strategy matrix for global industries is amenable to the generic competitive strategy work by Porter (1986). He demonstrates that firms in global industries can pursue strategies of global cost leadership, global differentiation and focus. The focus strategy itself consists of three possible options. First, there is global segmentation (focus A) whereby the firm pursues cost leadership or differentiation in many geographic markets but only in a selected

Alan M. Rugman/Alain Verbeke

Figure 1. Competitive Strategies in Global Industries

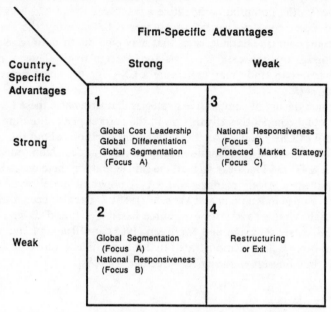

number of market segments. Second, a firm may follow a national responsiveness (focus B) strategy, whereby cost leadership or differentiation is targeted in a limited number of market segments, but only in one (or a few) geographic market(s). Finally, a protected market (focus C) strategy can be pursued. With this strategy, the firm's domain is primarily based in one country, but the segment scope may be very large. A competitive advantage is gained against global rivals as a result of government shelter. Here, the firm's main competitive advantage is not cost or differentiation based, but results from government intervention imposing artificial costs on foreign rivals. Hence, this strategy could be referred to as the "fourth generic" in the spirit of Boddewyn (1986). Cell 1 firms generally can follow any of the three generic strategies described above. If they choose a focus strategy, however, it will likely be a global segmentation (focus A) strategy. With their international competitive advantage they will be able to penetrate many foreign markets with all product lines that share strong FSAs and CSAs.

Firms in cell 2 will mostly confine themselves to some form of focus if they are faced with global competitors benefiting from strong CSAs. The relative disadvantage of such operations can only be compensated by reducing their geographic or segment scope, i.e., by developing some form of specialization in order to beat their rivals that benefit from strong FSAs and CSAs simultaneously. An alternative is of course to shift operations completely toward countries characterized by strong CSAs, but this is not always possible in cases of high exit barriers, foreign governments' discriminatory policies in favor of domestic firms and in cases where exports and foreign direct investment are imperfect substitutes. We should recognize, however, that conceptually it is possible for strong FSAs to largely compensate for the existence of weak CSAs, see Rugman and Verbeke (1988), thus allowing the pursuit of global cost leadership or differentiation.

Cell 3 firms are generally confined to a more limited geographic market domain except when producing a largely generic product, where FSAs have become unimportant (e.g., in cases where the products are in a late stage in the product life cycle, and where production FSAs, such as the possession of intangible skills, are less important than the CSAs of location and energy costs). MNEs in this quadrant generally follow focus strategies of national responsiveness or protected markets. Analogous to cell 2, the possibility exists that strong CSAs could compensate for the absence of strong FSAs in order to compete on world markets.

Cell 4 firms represent inefficient, foundering companies lacking any strong CSAs or FSAs. These firms, therefore, should be preparing to restructure or exit. Here we should recognize that, if the firm in question is a subsidiary, effective restructuring may be accomplished by, for example, transferring new FSAs of the parent company to the subsidiary, thus shifting it to quadrant 2.

In the discussion above, each MNE was considered as a homogenous entity, consisting of a single strategic business unit (SBU). For example, a position in cell 1 would imply that all operations – in cases of concentrated as well as dispersed configuration – would be characterized by strong CSAs. In practice, of course, a distinction needs to be made between the different SBUs composing the MNE.

In this context, we should also emphasize that in the discussion below the term "SBU" will not be used to indicate all of the MNEs operations, but only its Canadian operations, which may be affected by free trade. Thus, global differentiation, cost-leadership or segmentation in cell 1 reflect the existence of: (a) world product mandates or globally rationalized Canadian affiliates of foreign MNEs; and (b) the domestic operations of Canadian MNEs characterized by such strategies. Similar comments hold for the focus strategies pursued in cell 2 and 3 of Figure 1. A national responsiveness or protected market strategy means that the Canadian operations of an SBU are engaged in this mode of behavior, which does not necessarily always reflect the strategy of the SBU in all geographic markets.

For example, one SBU, which benefits from strong FSAs and CSAs in its home country, may be forced, say as a result of export restrictions, to set up a small, relatively inefficient operation in a host country. This strategy of national

Alan M. Rugman/Alain Verbeke

responsiveness may be extremely successful since the new operation will now benefit from location in the host country as the domestic, sheltered producers. However, in an international context, the operation's FSAs may be weak, as its scale may be highly cost inefficient. Finally, restructuring and exit in cell 4 again only refer to the Canadian operations of an SBU, and not necessarily to the SBU as a whole.

With free trade, changes in CSAs may lead to changes in the entry barriers associated with a particular operation of an MNE. Following Porter (1980), these entry barriers can be grouped as: economies of scale, capital requirements, switching costs, access to distribution channels, cost disadvantages independent of scale, and government policy. By affecting entry barriers, free trade may shift SBUs to a different quadrant of Figure 1, thus requiring MNEs to adjust their competitive strategy. Conceptually, twelve different shifts could result from bilateral trade liberalization (e.g., shifts from cell 1 to cell 2, 3, and 4; shifts from cell 2 to cell 1, 3, and 4, etc.). In our view, four of these cases are especially relevant.

In the first two cases, free trade, when it implies the abolition of government protection, leads SBUs to shift on the vertical axis of Figure 1. Strong CSAs may suddenly be turned into weak CSAs if government protection was an important source of competitive advantage. Here, the elimination of this entry barrier may severely affect the product market domain of the firm. What does this conceptual shift in Figure 1 mean in practice? There are two possibilities. Firms may shift from cell 1 to cell 2 or from cell 3 to cell 4. A shift to cell 2 implies that the SBU may have to reconsider the segment scope of its Canadian operations. The elimination of trade barriers will force it to restructure, typically in the direction of higher specialization and a narrower product market domain. A movement towards cell 4 implies that an SBU, whose competitive advantages were based on government shelter, now becomes subject to market forces, which may initiate exit or force restructuring of the Canadian operations.

In the third and fourth case, trade liberalization generates a shift on the horizontal axis, especially from cell 3 to cell 1, namely if it allows SBUs to take advantage of increased market opportunities, thus stimulating the development of new FSAs. For example, free trade may lead SBUs to benefit from scale economies and learning curve effects, thus strengthening their distinctive competence in reducing costs. Here, a shift is generated from the right hand side to the left hand side of Figure 1. This shift demonstrates that FSAs and CSAs are inter-related: The strengthening of the FSAs of Canadian operations results from the abolition of shelter (strong CSAs) which benefited foreign, in this case U.S., rivals.

An Application to Canada-U.S. Free Trade

The competitive strategy framework developed above allows us to conceptualize adjustment decisions in response to bilateral trade liberalization. We shall first study adjustment by Canadian-owned MNEs and, second, adjustment by U.S. subsidiaries in Canada. Much of the previous work on economic adjustment has focused on the macroeconomic effects of scale economies and productivity gains, see Baldwin and Gorecki (1986), Harris and Cox (1984) and Daly and MacCharles (1986). Although these factors are clearly important, strategic management decisions by firms are the basic source of any adjustment to freer trade.

As tariffs and non-tariff barriers are reduced and trade discipline is restored, many of the short-run, fragmented production processes in Canada may become inefficient (shift from top half to lower half of Figure 1). Thus, much of the adjustment will take place within industries and within firms as opposed to between industries, see Wonnacott (1987). MacCharles (1987) has also emphasized this intra-firm adjustment. Lipsey and York (1988) report that this was the experience among MNEs in the formation of the European Economic Community (EEC). In addition, trade liberalization may provide an incentive for SBUs to specialize their production and to increase their scale, so that their products are produced for a much larger market (a shift from quadrant 3 to quadrant 1).

Adjustment by Canadian Multinationals

The largest 22 Canadian public industrial MNEs have been identified in Rugman and McIlveen (1985) and Rugman (1988a). These 22 firms are: Alcan, Northern Telecom, Seagram, John Labatt, Gulf Canada, Noranda, Moore, Abitibi-Price, Nova, MacMillan Bloedel, Domtar, Molson, Consolidated-Bathurst, Ivaco, Varity, AMCA International, Inco, Cominco, Falconbridge, Bombardier, Canfor, and Magna International. These firms are already very active internationally. The five year average ratio of foreign to total sales is 67 percent and 42 percent of their assets are located outside Canada, see Rugman (1988a).

This international orientation has exposed these firms to the exigencies of operating in the global economy. Two factors have led them to develop restructuring strategies to deal with the new highly competitive global economy: 1) the harshness of the 1981–1982 recession on resource-based firms, see Rugman and Warner (1988); and 2) the rise of U.S. "administered protection", broadly defined as the use of countervail, anti-dumping duties and safeguard actions to protect inefficient firms, see Rugman (1988c) and Rugman and Anderson (1987).

Alan M. Rugman/Alain Verbeke

To understand the strategic decisions made by these firms in adjusting to this new trading environment, we will analyze them in their industry groups and position them in Figure 1, based upon extensive and ongoing process analysis of their core skills, see Rugman and McIlveen (1985) and Rugman (1988a). These 22 megafirms can be divided according to their principal operations into minerals, pulp and paper, distilleries, high-technology, oil and gas, and manufacturing.

The megafirms in the mineral sector are Alcan, Noranda, Inco, Cominco and Falconbridge. These firms enjoy strong CSAs in their access to Canada's abundant raw materials and proximity to the U.S. market. These advantages have been internalized into FSAs of vertical integration. In addition, most of these firms have developed skills in the production and marketing of at least one mineral. Due to the recession and the decline in the world mineral prices, they have tended to emphasize global segmentation strategies, focusing upon low costs. In addition, they have tried to move up the value-added chain in processing and manufacturing. These mature resource-based firms have traditionally been situated in cell 1, but their low financial performance, excluding Alcan, would tend to position them closer to the third quadrant, which implies an erosion of their FSAs.

The pulp and paper sector is populated by mature firms operating within cells 1 and 3. Abitibi-Price, Domtar, and Consolidated-Bathurst are cell 1 firms following primarily low cost segmentation strategies but expanding their product lines to markets other than their core areas. Some have expanded into other industries such as Domtar into chemicals, Abitibi-Price into up-scale papers and Consolidated-Bathurst into packaging. While MacMillan Bloedel and Canfor are following similar strategies, their consistently poorer competitive performance situates them perhaps closer to cell 3, where they attempt to compete on costs in the low end of the market (in terms of value added).

As with the minerals megafirms, these firms benefit from CSAs in access to Canadian natural resources. They have managed to develop FSAs of a vertically integrated production structure through long term contracts providing access to forests. The firms in this sector will benefit from the dispute settlement procedures of the Free Trade Agreement, see Rugman (1988b). This should insulate these Canadian producers from the abuses of U.S. administered protection, see Rugman and Porteous (1988). Thus, in terms of our framework they will move to the left of the horizontal axis of Figure 1; secure access to the U.S. market will allow them to develop new FSAs, especially in the area of cost competitiveness.

The distillery and brewery sector consists of John Labatt, Molson Industries and Seagram. These firms have FSAs in marketing their alcohol-based products. Provincial sales and production laws represent a CSA in protection. However, in the case of Molson and Labatt these must be balanced against the inefficient production scale (a weak FSA) forced on the industry, because of interprovincial barriers to trade (leading to the establishment of cost inefficient breweries in the different Canadian provinces). This inefficiency in manufacturing is only partly compensated for by marketing strengths and brand names, although the latter have permitted some degree of international expansion for Molson and Labatt brewery products. For these products, the two latter firms are largely situated closer to cell 3 then cell 1 and pursue a mixture of national responsiveness and protected market strategies. Thus, Molson and Labatt rely heavily on government shelter. As they operate in a mature industry, each is diversifying. Labatt derives greater revenue from its agri-food SBUs and has been integrating across the U.S. border. Molson has diversified into chemicals and retail merchandising. These SBUs account for over half of the firm's profits. Free trade will have little or no impact on the strategies of these firms. As a result of extensive lobbying activities, Labatt succeeded in exempting the beer industry from the free trade agreement, thus allowing this firm to maintain its protected market strategy and preventing a shift from quadrant 3 to quadrant 4. As for Seagram, it has also diversified into up-scale premium products. Its strategic equity link (22 percent ownership) to DuPont Chemicals has provided the source of capital for this diversification. Most of its operations are already located abroad and its Canadian operations rely primarily upon strong marketing FSAs. Hence, no effect of trade liberalization is anticipated.

Two non-traditional Canadian megafirms are represented by the high-technology innovators Northern Telecom and Moore. The FSAs upon which these firms rely are R & D, marketing, and service adaptability. The CSAs upon which they have built include proximity to the U.S. market and, in the case of Nortel, some government support (merely complementing its strong FSAs). Nortel is a cell 1 firm benefiting from its link to Bell, and its research unit Bell Northern. Moore is a cell 2 firm following a global segmentation strategy. Its emphasis on customization has made its FSAs dominate its CSAs. Both of these firms are well diversified along geographic and product lines, although Northern Telecom is now limiting its segment scope to increase competitiveness. Bilateral trade liberalization will enhance their competitive strengths, through easier access to the U.S. market, thus shifting them even further to the left hand side of Figure 1.

The two megafirms in the oil and gas sector are Nova and Gulf Canada Resources. After a period of reorganization, following its purchase from Chevron by Olympia and York, Gulf now operates as an exploration company. It has sought to diversify geographically into South East Asia to build on its core FSAs. Nova has diversified into other product areas such as petro-chemicals and telecommunications. Both are cell 1 firms situated to benefit from trade liberalization, as a result of stronger market opportunities in the U.S. from which the different SBUs' primary segmentation strategies will profit. The manufacturing sector consists of five firms in mature industries: Ivaco, Amca,

Alan M. Rugman/Alain Verbeke

Varity, Magna and Bombardier. The FSAs possessed by these firms consist primarily of marketing skills associated with brand names with a reputation for quality. Nevertheless, cost and price concerns have recently dominated the strategies of these firms. However, some, like Ivaco in steel products and Magna in automotive parts, have managed to move up a value-added chain to service product and geographic market niches.

Amca and Varity are undergoing major restructuring of their operations, dropping core product lines and seeking new ones, such as auto parts and engines for Varity. Especially Varity (previously Massey Ferguson) had moved to the far right of the horizontal axis of Figure 1 and is now attempting to develop new distinctive competition. Bombardier and Magna are successful cell 2 firms emphasizing segmentation strategies based upon marketing FSAs. Ivaco, a world leader in several steel and wire products following a differentiation strategy, is situated in cell 1. Trade liberalization will not adversely affect any of these three firms.

Adjustment by U.S. Subsidiaries in Canada

Canadian industrial policy dating from John A. Macdonald's National Policy has recognized that a protective tariff attracts foreign investment across the border. In the past century foreign manufacturers built plants in Canada to circumvent its high tariffs. As a result, foreign subsidiaries account for over 40 percent of assets in the manufacturing sector, see MacCharles (1987). Today the U.S. share of all foreign investment in Canada is around 76 percent, see Rugman (1987). Recently U.S. foreign ownership has been falling; as of 1986 it is only 18 percent of all non-financial corporations, see Statistics Canada (1988).

This section of the article predicts the possible actions of these key U.S. subsidiaries in responding to bilateral trade liberalization. The 13 largest U.S. industrial subsidiaries in Canada are: G.M. of Canada, Ford of Canada, Chrysler Canada, Imperial Oil, IBM Canada, Texaco Canada, Mobil Oil Canada, Canadian General Electric, Dow Chemical Canada, Amoco Canada, Du Pont Canada, Suncor Canada and Procter & Gamble. These 13 firms can also be positioned according to their FSAs and CSAs and their competitive strategies. However, in doing so it is necessary to distinguish between different types of U.S. subsidiaries.

Export performance data presented in Rugman (1988a) call into question the view that these firms operate solely as tariff factories as suggested by Baranson (1985). Branch plants whose presence is due solely to the existence of trade barriers, such as tariffs, and which produce on an inefficient scale according to international standards, will always move to cell 4 after trade liberalization. However, even in this case, the availability of strong FSAs of the parent,

Multinational Corporate Strategy

which can easily be transferred to the subsidiary, may merely lead to reorganization in Canada. In other words, in the short run, such branch plants may move from cell 3 to cell 4, but restructuring guided by the parent may initiate a shift toward quadrant 2 in the long run, typically through granting world product mandates or engaging in global rationalization. Today no causal link exists between tariff protection and foreign ownership; many of these subsidiaries are not just tariff factories relying primarily upon a protected market strategy.

D'Cruz (1986) and D'Cruz and Fleck (1987) have argued that six types of subsidiaries must be distinguished. These range from the importers and local service firms serving Canada only, to satellites and branch plants serving North America and globally rationalized and world product mandates serving a world market.

With trade liberalization, the importers and local service firms will remain intact, as will the globally rationalized and world product mandates. These firms have different levels of managerial autonomy, however they have an economic rationale beyond tariffs, namely to secure the Canadian domestic market through a strategy of national responsiveness in cell 3. The branch plants and satellite operations will more than likely either have to move on to become globally rationalized or obtain world product mandates, see Crookell (1987). In our framework, these subsidiaries would shift from cell 3 to cell 4, because of the elimination of tariff protection. The transfer of FSAs from the parent could then, however, lead to a shift toward quadrant 2. Clearly the process of moving towards global rationalization or obtaining a world product mandate will not be easy. World product mandates will have to be earned by the subsidiary; they will not be routinely granted by the parent. Only where strong CSAs in Canada potentially complement such FSAs will the latter be transferred to the Canadian subsidiary. This would then imply a shift from cell 4 to cell 1, and not cell 2. Only in the case of high exit barriers or distinctive advantages of locating in Canada would such a move be considered by the parent company.

In practice most of the largest subsidiaries of U.S. MNEs are situated in cell 1. Many of these firms have already begun product diversification to meet the new competitive global trading regime. For example, DuPont Canada has publicized the reduction of its segment scope to improve productivity and to obtain economies of scale, see Newall (1988). Interestingly, even with these scale increases they have found that their production flexibility to produce smaller runs has helped them to compete in the United States, even against their parent company.

The cell 1 firms are led by the "Big Three" automobile producers: General Motors, Ford and Chrysler. These firms benefit from the 1965 Canada-U.S. Auto Pact which established a managed trade arrangement for autos and auto parts. Other cell 1 firms building on CSAs particular to Canada and the market-

Alan M. Rugman/Alain Verbeke

ing and production FSAs of their parents are the oil and gas companies: Imperial Oil, Texaco, Mobil Oil, Amoco and Suncor. IBM Canada is also a cell 1 firm. Its parent company has chosen a pattern of international operation that emphasizes local marketing and global rationalization of production.

This set of U.S. subsidiaries also contains firms positioned in cell 3. Canadian General Electric (CGE) has already begun to gear up to compete globally by producing inputs for MNEs in Canada doing business abroad. In addition CGE has also allied itself to global markets by acting as a part of a network of the globally rationalized General Electric system. This process has necessitated rationalization of some operations to specialize in certain product lines. With these changes, CGE should move out of cell 3 and into cell 1. The existing strategy of national responsiveness is being replaced by a more global approach. Dow Chemical Canada also is located in cell 3 based on its weak market performance, which indicates weak managerial FSAs. To move to cell 1, the subsidiary will have to improve on these.

Procter & Gamble is a cell 3 firm. The CSAs upon which it builds are access to pulp and paper companies to reduce packaging costs as well as other primary products which are vital inputs into its production process. The firm also builds on its parent's strong FSAs in marketing and established brand names, but the tariff protection forces an inefficient production scale on its operations and this implies a weak FSA in Canada. As tariffs are reduced, intra-firm trade should increase and some rationalization should occur across the border, thus allowing the subsidiary to shift towards quadrant 1. Procter & Gamble has estimated that brands accounting for 45 percent of its volume can be manufactured in Canada at a cost less than or equal to that in the United States; see Gove (1988). Some other firms such as Quaker Oats Limited with food processing operations will suffer from the maintenance of agricultural marketing boards raising input prices. These firms, which are faced with suppliers pursuing protected market strategies, will have to restructure to become more globally competitive, or will end up moving to cell 4. Bilateral trade liberalization will prevent them from pursuing protected market strategies themselves.

To summarize, studies for the Economic Council of Canada by Don McFeteridge found that foreign-owned subsidiaries adjusted their operations in response to past trade liberalization in the same manner as Canadian firms; see ECC (1988a, 1988b). A key conclusion of these studies is that trade liberalization has been associated with the retention rather than the flight of U.S.-owned firms. This implies shifts toward the left-hand side of Figure 1 as a result of the transfer of new FSAs from the parent company.

Multinational Corporate Strategy

Surveys and Conclusions

The model and analysis in this paper is supported by surveys of these key Canadian MNEs and U.S. subsidiaries. In April 1987, a survey of the Chief Executive Officers of these firms was conducted. The results are reported in Rugman (1988 a). A second survey was conducted in the Spring of 1988 on the Canadian megafirms. The single most important finding of these surveys is that trade liberalization is welcomed by these firms. Seventy-five percent of these megafirms indicated that a Canada-U.S. free trade agreement would be beneficial to them. The basis of support for free trade is rooted in the prevailing belief that the status quo is one of increasing protection in the United States. Sixty-three percent indicated that the status quo did not benefit them.

On the question of adjustment to a bilateral trade agreement 31 percent expected to face adjustment costs. However, 80 percent of the Canadian firms and 94 percent of the U.S. firms indicate that adjustment assistance would not be required. These results have been confirmed by recent studies by several consulting firms after the signing of the Agreement; see Coopers and Lybrand (1988) and Thorne Ernst & Whinney (1988). In the Rugman surveys, seventy-five percent of the MNEs indicated that they would not close plants in Canada because of the Agreement. In fact, 50 percent forecasted that their investment in Canada would increase between 10 and 20 percent after five years of a free trade agreement, thus reflecting restructuring efforts to induce shifts toward the left of Figure 1.

This paper has presented a framework to assess the competitive strategies of firms and to analyze their adjustment to the Canada-U.S. Free Trade Agreement. Conceptual and empirical evidence suggest that adjustment is already underway. Both the Canadian MNEs and the U.S. subsidiaries have adapted their competitive strategies to the competitive global trading regime.

References

Baldwin, John and Paul Gorecki (1986) *The Role of Scale in Canada-U.S. Productivity Differences in the Manufacturing Sector*. Toronto: University of Toronto Press.

Baranson, Jack (1985) "Assessment of Likely Impact of a U.S.-Canadian Free Trade Agreement upon the Behaviour of U.S. Industrial Subsidiaries in Canada". Toronto: Ministry of Industry, Trade and Technology, Province of Ontario.

Boddewyn, Jean J. (1986) "International political strategy: A fourth 'generic' strategy?" Paper presented at the annual meeting of the Academy of International Business, London, November.

Canada (1988) *The Canada-U.S. Free Trade Agreement: An Economic Assessment*. Ottawa: Department of Finance.

Coopers and Lybrand (1988) *Implications for Free Trade and Canadian Corporate Strategies*. Toronto: The Coopers and Lybrand Consulting Group.

Crookell, Harold (1987) "Managing Canadian Subsidiaries in a Free Trade Environment". *Sloan Management Review* Fall: 71–76.

Daly, Donald and Donald MacCharles (1986) *Canadian Manufactured Exports: Constraints and Opportunities*. Halifax: The Institute for Research on Public Policy.

Alan M. Rugman/Alain Verbeke

D'Cruz, Joseph (1986) "Strategic Management of Subsidiaries" in Hamid Etemad and Louise Seguin Dulude (eds.) *Managing the Multinational Subsidiary.* London: Croom Helm.

D'Cruz, Joe and James Fleck (1987) *Yankee Canadians in the Global Economy.* London: National Centre for Management Research and Development, University of Western Ontario.

Dunning, John and Alan Rugman (1985) "The Contribution of Hymer's Dissertation to the Theory of Foreign Direct Investment". *American Economic Review* 75:2 (May): 228–232.

Economic Council of Canada (1988a) *Managing Adjustment: Policies for Trade-Sensitive Industries* Ottawa.

Economic Council of Canada (1988b) *Venturing Forth: An Assessment of the Canada-U.S. Trade Agreement* Ottawa.

Gove, Tom (1988) "Procter and Gamble Corporate Statement on the Canada-U.S. Free Trade Agreement" by the Manager of Management Systems and Distribution.

Harris, Richard and David Cox (1984) *Trade, Industrial Policy and Canadian Manufacturing.* Toronto: Ontario Economic Council.

Lipsey, Richard and Robert York (1988) *Evaluating the Free Trade Deal: A Guided Tour Through the Canada-U.S. Free Trade Agreement.* Toronto: C. D. Howe Institute.

MacCharles, Donald (1987) *Trade Among Multinationals: Intra-Industry Trade and National Competitiveness.* London: Croom Helm.

Newall, Ted (1988) "Stepping Out from Behind the Tariff Wall in Earle Gray (ed.) *Free Trade: Free Canada.* Woodville: Canadian Speeches.

Porter, Michael (1980) *Competitive Strategy: Techniques for Analyzing Industries and Competitors.* New York: Macmillan.

Porter, Michael (ed.) (1986) *Competition in Global Industries.* Boston: Harvard Business School Press.

Rugman, Alan M. (1981) *Inside the Multinationals: The Economics of Internal Markets.* New York: Columbia University Press.

Rugman, Alan M. (1987) *Outward Bound: Canadian Direct Investment in the United States.* Toronto: C. D. Howe Institute.

Rugman, Alan M. (1988a) *Trade Liberalization and International Investment.* Economic Council of Canada Discussion Paper 347.

Rugman, Alan M. (1988b) "The Free Trade Agreement and the Global Economy". *Business Quarterly* 53:1, Summer.

Rugman, Alan M. (1988c) "A Canadian Perspective on U.S. Administered Protection and the Free Trade Agreement". *Maine Law Review* 40:2, 305–324.

Rugman, Alan M. and Andrew Anderson (1987) *Administered Protection in America.* London: Croom Helm and New York: Methuen.

Rugman, Alan M., Donald J. Lecraw and Laurence D. Booth (1985) *International Business: Firm and Environment.* New York and Toronto: McGraw-Hill Book Co.

Rugman, Alan M. and John McIlveen (1985) *Megafirms: Strategies for Canada's Multinationals.* Toronto: Methuen.

Rugman, Alan M. and Samuel D. Porteous (1988) "The Softwood Lumber Decision of 1986: Broadening the Nature of U.S.-Administered Protection", *Review of International Business Law* 2:1 (April): 35–58.

Rugman, Alan M. and Alain Verbeke (1988) "Strategic Responses to Free Trade" in Maureen Farrow and Alan M. Rugman (1988) *Business Strategies and Free Trade.* Toronto: C. D. Howe Institute.

Rugman, Alan M. and Mark Warner (1988) "Corporate Responses to Free Trade: Strategies for Canada's Multinationals". National Centre for Management Research and Development Discussion Paper 88-10, May.

Statistics Canada (1988) *Canada's International Investment Position* (1985) 67–202. Ottawa: Ministry of Supply and Services.

Thorne, Ernst and Whinney (1988) *Canada-U.S. Free Trade Agreement: A Survey of North American Business Leaders.*

Wonnacott, Paul (1987) *The Canada-United States: The Quest for Free Trade.* Washington: The Institute for International Economics.

4

*Alan M. Rugman
and Michael Gestrin*

The Strategic Response of Multinational Enterprises to NAFTA

*The North American Free Trade Agreement
(NAFTA) incorporates both market liberalizing and
market closing measures. For example, the apparel
provisions of NAFTA will relieve Mexico of
burdensome quotas in the North American market
but will impose ultrastrict rules of origin upon the
industry. Rugman and Gestrin develop a framework that explains paradoxes such as this one by
distinguishing between measures that prompt
production at the national level versus the regional
level. Although their analysis only considers a few
significant industries, their framework illuminates
the agreement's impact upon virtually any sector
of the North American economy.*

The North American Free Trade Agreement (NAFTA) will have far-reaching implications for corporate decision-makers in North America. In particular, NAFTA will affect foreign direct investment (FDI) in the three signatories, impact the corporate strategies of multinational enterprises (MNEs) before and after the deal"s ratification, and force strategic adjustment of industries most affected by the agreement. In order to understand the impact of the NAFTA upon these areas, we first need to understand the investment-related sections of the agreement and their mix of trade liberalizing and protectionist elements.

The NAFTA will enhance the investment environment in three ways: It will open up the Mexican economy to Canadian and U.S. investors, it will provide enhanced security for all FDI in the NAFTA area and it will make the discriminatory measures that each of the signatories has chosen to maintain more transparent.[1] Yet the NAFTA also has many protectionist investment-related measures, particularly the rules of origin (especially as they apply to the automotive and textile and apparel sectors) and the lists of exemptions from national treatment.

The changes which the NAFTA brings to the North American investment regime will affect the corporate strategies of MNEs and thereby international and intraregional investment patterns. However, most of the large MNEs have already undertaken strategies to benefit from the NAFTA and to offset any potential negative impacts; for large MNEs the impact of the NAFTA is likely to be neutral. However, we do find that the NAFTA will give rise to increases in inward FDI for Mexico and that it will cause more corporate restructuring for "outsiders' than for firms already operating within North America.

The Strategic Behavior of MNEs and the NAFTA

Economic relations among the three NAFTA signatories are dominated by the activities of MNEs. As strategic actors, MNEs both react to changes in their environment and act to shape this environment to their advantage. Conventional (neoclassical) economic analysis tends to characterize environmental change as exogenous to the decision-making processes of firms. This type of analysis, however, overlooks two advantages particular to MNEs.

The first advantage relates to MNEs' ability to internalize portions of their value-added chains. Through internalization, the MNE maximizes the strategic benefits of the combination of Firm Specific Advantages (FSAs) held by the firm and Country Specific Advantages (CSAs) characterizing the national economies in which the firm operates. FSAs are defined as the competitive strengths of the company. These can be either production-based (cost or innovation advantages) or marketing-based (customization advantages). CSAs are initially defined as the natural factor endowments of a nation—basically the variables in its aggregate production function. However, CSAs can be influenced, indeed changed, by government policies.

The second advantage enjoyed by most MNEs is the capacity to change the environment in which they operate. More specifically, through the lobbying efforts of various industries

Alan M. Rugman is Professor of International Business in the Faculty of Management at the University of Toronto. In the past he has been a visiting professor at Columbia Business School, London Business School and Harvard University. During his current sabbatical leave he has been a visiting professor at UCLA and the Sloan School of Management, MIT. He has been a senior advisor to the Government of Canada on the Free Trade Agreement and NAFTA.

Michael Gestrin is a Policy Analyst at the Faculty of Management at the University of Toronto where he has obtained degrees in Economics and published (with Professor Rugman) on such topics as U.S. administered protection, foreign investment and NAFTA.

Reprint: 28418

the NAFTA has come to reflect the interests of MNEs in North America. The agreement therefore establishes NAFTA-based CSAs (advantages with respect to competitors based in the other NAFTA signatories) and NAFTA-based Region Specific Advantages (RSAs – advantages with respect to competitors based outside the NAFTA area). The implications of these two characteristics of MNEs, namely: 1) their ability to internalize and 2) their capacity to change the environment in which they operate, need to be considered.

The Organizational Responses of MNEs to the NAFTA

The process of strategic planning follows a pattern in which the competitive strengths of the corporation are constantly reassessed in light of new information about the domestic and international environments within which the firm operates. Such environmental changes include trade liberalization measures such as the NAFTA. Internalization theory serves to explain and predict how MNEs will react to environmental change. At the heart of this theory is the idea that markets and hierarchical structures (firms) are alternatives. Internalization allows a multinational enterprise to establish and maintain better proprietary control over its FSAs so that the economic rents associated with these do not accrue to other firms.[2] (See inset: The Theory of Internalization and the MNE)

Profitability, growth, market share and any other goals pursued by MNEs may also depend upon the ability of an MNE to internalize CSAs. CSAs, as mentioned above, are generally viewed as the variables of

the aggregate production function, and their value to particular firms will depend upon their quality, quantity and cost relative to substitute factors in other countries.[3] However, CSAs also include tariffs, non-tariff barriers and other government barriers to trade, including regulations on foreign direct investment (factors which are not commonly included in the neoclassical aggregate production function). To the extent that such measures favor domestic firms, these firms can be said to benefit from shelter-based CSAs.[4]

Internalization theory therefore predicts that the overall welfare impact of bilateral trade liberalization will be positive. Its main effects will be to reduce transaction costs associated with trade and to create more certainty for investment decisions. In cases where foreign direct investment and exports are complements, bilateral trade liberalization should increase the level of both.[5] The substitution of exports for FDI can be expected in cases where tariffs and regulations on trade are the main rationale for engaging in FDI and where exit barriers are low; under these conditions adjustment costs of relocating production activities will also be low. A largely neutral response in terms of FDI flows results when the activities of MNEs are strongly motivated by strategic considerations other than the desire to obviate tariff barriers. Documented examples of such common MNE behavior include the "exchange of threats" strategy identified by Graham[6] and the "window on R&D" behavior identified in the technology literature.[7]

Two important points have been raised in the above analysis. First, the theory of the MNE and a large body

of empirical work has shown that the organizational structures of MNEs are shaped by a multitude of factors reflecting the complexity and high degree of imperfection (oligopolistic market structures, lack of information, the partially excludable and nonrival nature of knowledge and technological know-how, etc.) of international markets. Put differently, the liberalizing measures of the NAFTA (many of which are phased in over 10 years) will only have an impact upon the investment patterns of MNEs where the activities of particular firms were originally and primarily motivated by high transaction costs in trade associated with the protectionist measures now being liberalized. In this regard, since the agreement leaves the investment and trade regimes of Canada and the United States more or less the same and liberalizes many sectors of the Mexican economy, internalization theory predicts that MNEs will not be motivated, as a group, to react strongly to the NAFTA in Canada or the United States, but may shift some resources from other low-cost economies to Mexico. This investment diversion is due to the fact that, under the NAFTA, Mexico will enjoy the freest access to the U.S. economy of any developing country.

Second, since MNEs are strategic actors, it can be assumed that all MNEs likely to be affected by the NAFTA will already have gauged the likelihood of the agreement coming into effect and will have anticipated this possibility in their strategic decision making.[8] Furthermore, it must be remembered that Mexico undertook to liberalize its economy unilaterally beginning in the mid-1980s and that the U.S.-Canadian trade and in-

The Theory of Internalization and the MNE

The new explanation of the activities of multinational firms makes use of the theory of internalization. Internalization is the managerial process by which property rights are obtained by the multinational enterprise (MNE), i.e., it gains ownership of a know-how advantage and it uses the internal hierarchical structure of the organization to prevent dissipation of this firm-specific advantage.

The modern theory of foreign direct investment (FDI) places emphasis upon the firm-specific advantages enjoyed by the MNE, and it implies that the theory of FDI is really a theory of the MNE. Firm-specific advantages can be obtained in several ways: scale economies, managerial expertise, a technological or knowledge advantage, monopoly, product differentiation, financial strength, or production, distribution, or marketing advantages. Such firm-specific advantages encourage the MNE to seek worldwide markets through the process of FDI.

The theory of internalization also suggests that a firm considers explicitly the relative costs of servicing foreign markets in one of three ways. First, the firm may simply wish to export to foreign markets. Second, the firm may engage in FDI; that is, set up an overseas subsidiary to produce for a local market. Third, a firm may wish to license to a possible host country producer. The method of servicing a foreign market may change over time, as the various costs associated with each of these strategies changes.

In short, new foreign activities typically have three stages: 1) exporting; 2) FDI; and 3) licensing. The condition for successful licensing, namely that foreign markets are fully segmented and that dissipation of firm-specific advantages can be avoided, are unlikely to be realized in practice, so licensing occurs only at a late stage of maturity of the product cycle. These three stages in servicing a foreign market over time are almost the reverse of the process of internationalization, which is the process of going abroad slowly through: 1) licensing; 2) exporting; 3) establishment of local warehouses and direct local sales; 4) local assembly and packing; 5) formation of a joint venture; and 6) FDI.

In terms of NAFTA, the theory of internalization provides important insights into the strategic management decisions of MNEs. Due to the institutional complexity, and the balancing of trade liberalization with protectionist measures, it is highly unlikely that under NAFTA the current business practices of MNEs already active in North America will be altered in any significant manner. Even before NAFTA most MNEs had already organized their activities across the three national borders to take advantage of relative factor costs and to prevent dissipation of their firm-specific advantages. The new institutional provisions of NAFTA will reinforce the economic logic of the existing degree of transborder integration already underway in North America. The NAFTA reflects the agenda of the MNEs and it will not remove the rationale for internalization. Only the future deepening of NAFTA and unambiguous "free trade" would eliminate the need for FDI and/or licensing, and permit MNEs to engage in exporting alone.

Source: Alan M. Rugman, "A New Theory of the Multinational Enterprise: Internationalization Versus Internalization," *Columbia Journal of World Business* 15, No. 1 (Spring 1980): 23-29.

vestment relationship is already, under the terms of the Canada-U.S. Free Trade Agreement (FTA) of 1989, the largest between any two countries in the world.[9] In many respects, the NAFTA is a reflection and a continuation of the process of economic liberalization which has characterized relations between the three NAFTA signatories since the mid-1980s and which has been driven by the activities of MNEs. It is therefore wrong to characterize MNEs as reactive entities which will suddenly and dramatically respond to the political and legislative act of ratifying the agreement. Rather, MNEs have been basing their long-term strategies upon the underlying forces and processes that will have been underway for a decade by the time the agreement comes into effect and that ultimately made the NAFTA politically viable.

The theory of MNEs suggests that the NAFTA will not bring about substantial movements of capital either in or out of the United States and Canada but will likely bring about some investment and trade diversion from some less developed countries (LDCs) to Mexico. Previous experience in the case of the FTA provides support for the view that most MNEs are motivated by a complex "basket" of factors such that the mild (and gradual) liberalization measures of agreements like the FTA and the NAFTA are not sufficient to warrant large scale organizational readjustments.

The Impact of NAFTA upon Country Specific and Region Specific Advantages

Conceptually, any industry can be analyzed in terms of whether or not it benefits from strong CSAs and whether or not the industry itself has strong or weak FSAs. A "strong" CSA or FSA is defined here as an advantage sufficient to ensure competitiveness with respect to foreign rivals.

Chart 1 presents a way of classifying industries in terms of the strengths of their CSAs and FSAs.[10]

International competitiveness is assured whenever FSAs and CSAs are strong simultaneously (quadrant 1). If CSAs are weak, however, FSAs will have to compensate if the industry in question is to compete with global rivals (quadrant 2). A similar situation arises when an industry suffers from weak FSAs; then only through strong CSAs can an internationally competitive position be maintained (quadrant 3). Finally, for industries where both CSAs and FSAs are lacking, competing internationally with efficient foreign rivals becomes virtually impossi-

Chart 1

The Competitive Advantage Matrix

Firm Specific Advantages

		Strong	Weak
Country and Region Specific Advantages	**Strong**	**1** Both FSAs and CSAs/RSAs are strong. International competitiveness is assured.	**3** FSAs are weak. Strong CSAs and RSAs are therefore necessary to maintain an internationally competitive position.
	Weak	**2** CSAs and RSAs are weak. FSAs are required for industry to compete with global rivals.	**4** Both FSAs and CSAs are weak. Competing internationally with foreign rivals is impossible.

ble (quadrant 4).

An example may make this clearer. The Canadian forest products industry is not particularly strong in terms of its FSAs, but it does enjoy a compensating CSA in terms of an abundance of trees. More generally, well endowed natural resource sectors are often located in quadrant 3 because an overwhelming CSA can limit international competition and hence reduce the main impetus for developing strong FSAs. This dynamic constitutes the flip side of Porter's observation that, within the context of the home country diamond framework, a weak area of the economy can turn into a competitive advantage if this weakness impels other segments of the economy to continuously strive for competitive advantage.[11] Another group of industries that commonly locate in quadrant 3 are those whose strong CSAs derive from government protection or favoritism of one form or another. Among the industries often included in this quadrant are sunset and sunrise industries (which vary from economy to economy).

Trade and investment liberalizing agreements such as the NAFTA can affect both CSAs and FSAs. Trade liberalization has an impact upon FSAs through its dynamic effects – by encouraging a more open and competitive economic environment, the NAFTA will force firms to develop strong FSAs. The NAFTA, however, has a more immediate (and usually protectionist) impact upon CSAs. This is due to such factors as the agreement's effect upon tariffs, rules of origin, dispute settlement mechanisms, etc.

Four possibilities arise with regards to the NAFTA's impact upon CSAs: 1) that the agreement weakens an indus-try's CSAs by removing protective measures vis-a-vis competitors in other NAFTA signatories; 2) that the agreement weakens an industry's CSAs by removing protective measures vis-a-vis competitors based outside the NAFTA region – in this case we refer to a reduction of Region Specific Advantages (RSAs); 3) that the agreement strengthens an industry's CSAs with respect to competitors based in other NAFTA signatories; and 4) that the agreement strengthens an industry's RSAs with respect to competitors based outside the NAFTA region.

The reader should note that while, conceptually, CSAs and RSAs are the same thing, a distinction needs to be made to capture some of the dynamics behind the negotiation of trade and investment agreements such as the NAFTA. First of all, depending upon the size and extent to which an MNE has internalized operations across borders in North America, it will have a preference for NAFTA-based RSAs over NAFTA-based CSAs. The reason for this is that NAFTA-based CSAs do not confer any particular advantage to the "regional" firm and, in fact, are likely to raise transaction costs for the MNE. "National" firms (or champions), on the other hand, have not internalized aspects of their operations across borders, and thus prefer CSAs to RSAs. The generalization which emerges from these observations is that firms will always seek to enhance their competitive position by establishing CSAs (or RSAs) which offer the closest fit (in a geographic sense) to match the scope of their operations.

Another reason for drawing the distinction between CSAs and RSAs is that, to the extent that an agreement such as the NAFTA affects one or the other, we can roughly gauge to what extent the agreement will affect investment patterns among the NAFTA signatories versus the extent to which it will affect investment patterns between the NAFTA region and the rest of the world. What our subsequent analysis will reveal is that, in terms of evaluating the impact of the NAFTA, the areas in which investment patterns are most likely to experience considerable change are those in which firms or industries have weak FSAs and the NAFTA does not supply these with either the CSAs or RSAs necessary for their continued commercial viability. These concepts (CSAs, RSAs, FSAs) are extremely useful in analyzing both the structure of the operations of various industries in North America as well as the extent to which the interests of MNEs are reflected in the NAFTA.

To summarize, the theory of the MNE outlined above allows us to make the following two predictions: 1) MNEs (with strong FSAs) that have already adapted to an integrated North American market will seek, through lobbying efforts, to further liberalize trade and strengthen their RSAs; 2) MNEs (and domestic or noninternationalized firms in each of the markets) that have not internalized their operations across the three markets will seek protectionism through NAFTA to strengthen their CSAs with respect to competitors based in the other NAFTA markets.

The NAFTA's Impact upon Specific Industries

Based on the logic of Chart 1, we are now able to analyze the impact of the NAFTA upon the key industries in each of the NAFTA signatories. Our analysis will focus upon the agreement's impact along the vertical axis – the axis that pertains to CSAs and RSAs. Recall that quadrant 4 of the matrix, reflecting weak CSAs/RSAs and FSAs, is the one quadrant that foreshadows drastic change (which can take the form of either restructuring or exit). The other three quadrants, on the other hand, represent situations in which the investments of MNEs are financially viable and, while in isolated cases drastic changes based upon strategic considerations are possible, in the aggregate these three quadrants will be relatively passive in terms of investment flows.

By applying Chart 1 to the main industrial sectors of each NAFTA signatory we are able to identify areas in each of the three economies likely to be dramatically affected by the implementation of the NAFTA.[12] We begin our analysis in Chart 2 with a consideration of the NAFTA's impact upon the CSA position of key industries in each of the NAFTA signatories. Subsequently, in Chart 3, we consider the NAFTA's impact upon RSAs.

The NAFTA and Country Specific Advantages

Chart 2 places various industries from the three NAFTA signatories in the CSA-based competitive advantage matrix. Since we are only concerned with the specific impact of the NAFTA upon various economic sectors, the vertical axis specifies CSAs that have been either strengthened or weakened by the agreement. In other words, only industries whose CSAs have changed as a result of the NAFTA have been included in the chart.

In quadrant 1 we find industries which are both strong in terms of their FSAs and their NAFTA-based CSAs. This combination is somewhat counterintuitive since the literature on CSAs and FSAs unambiguously identifies artificial CSAs (the type of CSAs generated by government) as a threat to the long-term potential for maintaining strong FSAs.[13] The reason for this is that artificial, shelter-based CSAs shield domestic producers from international competition which is ultimately an essential ingredient

Chart 2

The Impact of the NAFTA upon Country Specific Advantages

Firm Specific Advantages

		Strong	Weak
Country Specific Advantages	**Strengthened by NAFTA**	**1** **United States** High technology related to defense; some energy. **Canada** Some energy. **Mexico** None.	**3** **United States** Maritime; cabotage; steel; agriculture; textiles. **Canada** Culture; agriculture. **Mexico** Energy; telecom. services; natural resources.
	Weakened by NAFTA	**2** **United States** None. **Canada** Apparel. **Mexico** None.	**4** **United States** Apparel; citrus products; roses; household appliances. **Canada** Textiles; household appliances; steel; beer. **Mexico** Most manufacturing.

for developing strong FSAs. Not surprisingly, then, the industries that find themselves in quadrant 1 are generally characterized by "political" features that have motivated government to establish barriers to foreign competition even though, at least from a business perspective, this protection isn't needed.

The most significant sectors included in quadrant 1 are the high technology sectors related to defense in the United States and some areas of the energy sectors in the United States and Canada (especially uranium, again for security reasons). Mexico also has security concerns, and has placed severe restrictions upon foreign investment in its energy and natural resource sectors in the NAFTA; however, these industries are not characterized by strong FSAs, and therefore do not appear in quadrant 1. Indeed, Mexico has no industries listed in quadrant 1. While, as discussed previously, quadrant 1 does not imply potentially disruptive changes in investment patterns, of concern is the likely effect of continued (and potentially expanded) protection for the U.S. high technology sector upon FSAs.[14]

Quadrant 3 contains the industries that are popularly known as the "sacred cows" of each of the signatories. These industries or sectors are generally characterized by some form of strong leverage or clout in domestic political circles. The "sacred cows" of the United States and Canada are not affected by the NAFTA. In the United States, the maritime sector, cabotage in all forms of transportation, steel, and many agricultural products benefit from protection under the terms of the NAFTA. In Canada, the best known sector receiving protection un-

der the NAFTA is the cultural sector. As in the United States, several subsectors of the agricultural sector are also protected (by marketing boards in Canada), namely dairy, poultry and eggs. The areas in Mexico that are characterized by weak FSAs and protection under the NAFTA are those found in Mexico's Annex 3 Constitutional reservations.[15] The most significant of these cover most of the energy sector (coal being one of the few areas liberalized), telecommunications services (which in many respects mirrors Canada's cultural reservations), and control over natural resources. It is expected, given the extent to which Mexico's FSAs are weak in some of these sectors, especially in energy, that strong NAFTA-based CSAs could have the effect of retarding Mexico's economic progress due to the creation of bottlenecks in critical areas.

Quadrant 2 is almost empty reflecting, interestingly, the fact that the NAFTA, on the whole, has not made North America a more dynamic and competitive environment for firms that already enjoy strong FSAs. The one exception we have included (and there doubtless exist several notable others that we have omitted) is in the Canadian apparel industry. The reason that this sector has had its NAFTA-based CSAs reduced pertains to the effect of the agreement upon this sector's main input – textiles. By considerably tightening the content rules for textiles and apparel, Canadian apparel producers, which have enjoyed strong design-based FSAs, will have a harder time sourcing high quality, inexpensive textiles outside of the NAFTA area.

Finally, quadrant 4 lists sectors that will experience the most signifi-

cant change as a result of the NAFTA. In the United States, these include the apparel sector, various agricultural products in which Mexico enjoys a comparative advantage and household appliances. In Canada, the sectors that will have to undergo considerable adjustments to the NAFTA include household appliances, steel and beer. (The impact on these sectors is a carryover from the FTA.) The Canadian steel sector has a weak CSA by omission since the FTA and the NAFTA could not address the problems associated with the abuse by U.S. firms of American trade law. The problems for the Canadian beer industry were brought upon itself as it lobbied for an exemption from national treatment in the FTA; now it is caught in trade law actions. The household appliances sectors of the United States and Canada will both suffer from increased competition from Mexico.

The most striking feature of quadrant 4 is the inclusion, for Mexico, of its entire manufacturing sector. After decades of import substitution policies and protectionism, Mexican manufacturing, in the aggregate, suffers from extremely weak FSAs. Under the terms of the NAFTA, however, all tariff protection for the manufacturing sector will be eliminated during the agreement's 10 year phase-out period. Most tariff protection, in fact, will disappear during the first five years of the agreement coming into effect.

Compared with the quadrant 4 lists of Canada and the United States, Mexico will clearly bear the brunt of adjustment costs (and consequent efficiency-based opportunities) associated with the NAFTA. Indeed, while adjustment to increased international competition has been focused on the sunset industries in the United States and Canada, the Mexican economy is pursuing a wholesale restructuring of its economy in anticipation of NAFTA at a pace that has rarely been matched in the history of economic reform.

A final comment on Chart 2 serves as a starting point for our consideration of the NAFTA's impact on RSAs. Chart 2 does not include several key sectors of the North American economy, especially autos and auto parts. The reason for this is that during the 1980s and early 1990s most MNEs have been pursuing regionalization strategies aimed at rationalizing, through strategic internalization, the organization of their value-added chains across national boundaries. Indeed, as argued earlier, these large firms have explicitly sought to avoid the development of NAFTA-based CSAs since these can only lead to higher transaction costs for both the internalized as well as the international market transactions of these firms.

The NAFTA and Region Specific Advantages

Chart 3 is the same as Chart 2 except that the vertical axis now concerns the strengthening or weakening of Region Specific Advantages (RSAs) by the NAFTA. Conceptually, the main difference between the industries placed in Charts 2 and 3 is that those located in the former are characterized (predominantly) by uni-national corporate structures while those in the latter have already adopted a regional outlook. The industries listed in Chart 3 perceive a North American border in their strategic planning and

Chart 3

The Impact of the NAFTA upon Region Specific Advantages

Firm Specific Advantages

		Strong	Weak
Region Specific Advantages	**Strengthened by NAFTA**	**1** **United States** Chemicals; computers; trucking; energy; petrochemicals; agriculture; electronics. **Canada** Chemicals; energy; some forest products. **Mexico** Electronics; apparel.	**3** **United States** Autos; auto parts. **Canada** Autos, auto parts. **Mexico** TV tubes.
	Weakened by NAFTA	**2** **United States** None. **Canada** None. **Mexico** None.	**4** **United States** None. **Canada** None. **Mexico** None.

largely ignore the national boundaries that separate the three NAFTA signatories. An example is the Canadian-owned telecommunications company, Northern Telecom, which already considers the U.S.-Canadian market as a fully integrated one, as do most other large Canadian MNEs.[16]

The interpretation of Chart 3 is the same as that for Chart 2. Quadrants 1-3 are largely neutral in terms of their implications for investment patterns, while quadrant 4 implies that considerable readjustment for the sectors listed is essential. The only difference in this regard is that the investment flows under consideration in Chart 3 are those between the NAFTA area and the rest of the world.

The first striking feature of Chart 3 is the fact that, on the vertical axis, quadrants 2 and 4, representing weak NAFTA-based RSAs, are empty. This reflects a profound feature of MNE activity – international production by large MNEs is undergoing a process of regionalization along triad lines, not a process of globalization. If particular industries had achieved a high level of integration of value-added activities at the global level, they would view RSAs in the same negative light as regionally integrated firms view CSAs. No industries, however, have sought, either in the main text of the NAFTA, or in the lists of reservations, to eliminate or phase out NAFTA-based RSAs in order to lower transaction costs between NAFTA-based and non-NAFTA based operations.

Quadrant 1 of Chart 3 lists industries that enjoy both strong FSAs and strong NAFTA-based RSAs. Unlike the list of industries in quadrant 1 of Chart 2, however, the list in quadrant 1 of Chart 3 is much more "mainstream" in its composition. Recall that strong NAFTA-based CSAs are generally only conferred upon industries that are characterized by some sort of "political" attributes that are independent of their competitiveness. Sectors related to national security therefore dominated quadrant 1 of the NAFTA-based CSA matrix.

A subtle difference between NAFTA-based CSAs and RSAs underlies this apparent discrepancy. As discussed, a strong NAFTA-based CSA usually takes the form of discriminatory measures that favor domestic over foreign producers. RSAs are based upon similar preferential treatment being offered at a regional level. RSAs, however, usually involve the opening of a particular sector in one NAFTA signatory, in which RSAs are strong. RSAs have been strengthened under these conditions since the MNEs with strong FSAs now have better access to a larger basket of productive resources, relative to non-NAFTA competitors.

In theory, the same dynamic can take place at the national level. For example, if the NAFTA had served to lower interprovincial trade barriers in Canada, then quadrant 1 of Chart 2 would contain some Canadian industries unrelated to national security issues. Their NAFTA-based CSAs would have become stronger not through extra protection but through a NAFTA-induced rationalization of production at the national level, which in turn would give rise to efficiency gains relative to foreign competitors. What quadrant 1 indicates, therefore, is that the chemicals (including pharmaceuticals), computers, trucking, petrochemicals, energy, electronics goods and several agricultural sectors in the United States stand to gain strong RSAs as a result of the NAFTA through an opening of these sectors in Mexico to American investment.

Non-NAFTA-based investors will also enjoy better access to these areas, but in many ways U.S. investors will still enjoy preferential treatment relative to "outsiders." Furthermore, even if U.S. investors did not get preferential treatment relative to "outsiders," their RSAs would still be made stronger since Mexico represents an improvement of the organization of the regional operations of U.S. MNEs. "Outsiders" making investments in Mexico with a view to serving the North American market will remain at a disadvantage in terms of having to deal with the higher transaction costs associated with the NAFTA's tight rules of origin.

Canada also stands to gain from the preferential opening of the Mexican market in the areas of chemicals, energy and some forest products. The two industries in which Mexico is expected to enjoy substantial gains are certain electronics goods and apparel. In both cases, invest-

ment diversion from low cost producers is expected.[17] These industries provide good examples of the different ways in which the NAFTA can create RSAs.

Impact of NAFTA on Electronics, Apparel and Autos.

In the electronics sector, strong RSAs are created by the elimination of duty drawback programs in Mexico. For example, before the NAFTA, television tubes could be imported by Mexican television manufacturers duty-free for the production of televisions subsequently exported to the United States at preferential rates. After the NAFTA, a tariff of 15% will apply to imported tubes; only televisions with regionally produced tubes will have duty-free access into the U.S. market, and all televisions with non-regionally produced tubes will be subject to a 5% tariff into the United States.[18] Therefore, North American tube producers have been granted protection on a regional, not a national basis. In essence, the new rules for the electronics industry treat this sector as if North America were already a unified and integrated market.

Turning to the apparel industry, we find a similar situation. The NAFTA will serve to bring down the barriers to trade among the NAFTA signatories in apparel products. In other words, Mexico will no longer be subject to Multi-Fibre Arrangement quotas in the North American market. However, extremely tight rules of origin, combined with the fact that all other major low cost apparel producers will still be subject to their MFA quota agreements, provide for a stark contrast between the almost complete trade and investment liberalization within the NAFTA area and the much tighter protection of this sector on a regional basis.

In both of the above examples, the NAFTA-based RSAs are likely to speed up regional integration. American television producers will invest in additional tube production capacity since relative regional tariff structures created by the NAFTA erode Asian competitiveness. Investment in apparel production facilities is likely to increase in Mexico as restrictions upon Mexican exports to the North American market are lifted while regional trade restrictions remain in force.

The most economically significant industry to benefit from RSAs in the NAFTA is the automotive industry. This industry is located in quadrant 3 of Chart 3. Relative to Japanese and some European producers, this sector in North America suffers from weak FSAs (although these have been improving lately). Strong RSAs under the NAFTA will derive from tightened rules of origin (for automobiles, light trucks, and their engines and transmissions a regional value content requirement of 62.5% is required), the introduction of a protectionist "tracing" formula to determine value added, and explicit distinctions between incumbents and new producers for purposes of granting preferences to the former.[19]

As with the electronics and apparel industries, the tightened rules of origin for autos are meant to encourage more regional production at the expense of nonregional producers. The tracing requirement serves the same function by eliminating the problem of "roll-up."[20] Roll-up occurs when an intermediate product contains

nonregionally produced inputs but is treated as 100% originating when it is introduced at the next stage of assembly. Tracing overcomes this problem by requiring manufacturers to keep track of all materials used in production that are not produced regionally. Tracing effectively serves to further tighten the regional content requirement of production since more nonoriginating products will count against the "originating" status that allows a given product to enter the NAFTA markets duty free. Finally, the NAFTA auto provisions grant benefits to "incumbents' in Canada and Mexico by allowing these producers to continue to benefit from duty drawback and deferral programs, whereas new producers will not be allowed to import inputs duty free or at reduced rates.

Conclusion

An understanding of the relationship between MNEs and the institutional environment in which they operate is essential to an understanding of what the impact of the NAFTA will be upon North American investment patterns. By applying internalization theory and by extending the concept of CSAs to a regional level of analysis (RSAs) we conclude that the impact of the NAFTA upon investment patterns in Canada and the United States will be mainly neutral, while Mexico will benefit from considerable investment diversion away from other LDCs.

By eliminating the majority of Mexico's administrative CSAs, thereby integrating the Mexican, U.S. and Canadian economies, the NAFTA has moved the North American market in a global direction. By establishing a

new and expansive level of protectionism in the form of RSAs, the NAFTA reminds us that globalization is not yet a reality.

The paradoxical nature of the NAFTA in terms of its propensity to at once apply liberalizing and discriminatory measures to the same industry is explained by the introduction of a new "administrative" level to the North American trade and investment regime. Corporate decision-makers need to be cognizant of the ways in which the NAFTA shapes the "playing fields" upon which international competitive battles will be waged. In sum, the NAFTA will give rise to a more competitive, highly integrated North American market. However, the agreement suggests that regionalism, and not globalism, is the relevant benchmark for corporate strategy.

This article is based on Chapter 8 in Alan M. Rugman, ed., Foreign Investment and North American Free Trade *(Columbia, SC: University of South Carolina Press, 1994).*

Notes

1 For a more detailed discussion see Alan M. Rugman and Michael Gestrin, "The Investment Provisions of NAFTA" in Steven Globerman and Michael Walker (eds.), *Assessing NAFTA: A Trinational Analysis* (Vancouver, BC: The Fraser Institute, 1993) 271-292.

2 Alan M. Rugman, "A New Theory of the Multinational Enterprise: Internationalization Versus Internalization," *Columbia Journal of World Business* 15, No. 1 (Spring 1980): 23-29; and Alan M. Rugman, *Inside the Multinationals: The Economics of Internal Markets* (New York: Columbia University Press, 1981).

3 Alan M. Rugman, Donald Lecraw and Laurence Booth, *International Business: Firm and Environment* (New York: McGraw-Hill, 1985).

4 For an explanation of the theory of shelter see Alan M. Rugman and Alain Verbeke, *Global Corporate Strategy and Trade Policy* (London and New York: Routledge, 1990), especially Chapters 1-4.

5 A. E. Safarian, "The Relationship Between Trade Agreements and International Direct Investment," in David W. Conklin and Thomas A. Courchene (eds.), *Canadian Trade at a Crossroads: Options for New International Agreements* (Toronto: Ontario Economic Council, 1985); and A.E. Safarian, *Multinational Enterprise and Public Policy* (Aldershot, U.K. and Brookfield, Vermont: Edward Elgar, 1993).

6 E.M. Graham, "Oligopolistic Imitation and European Direct Investment in the United States," D.B.A. Dissertation, Harvard University, 1975.

7 John H. Dunning, *Multinational Enterprises and the Global Economy* (Addison-Wesley Publishers, 1993), Chapters 11 and 12; and Organization for Economic Cooperation and Development, The Technology/Economy Programme, *Technology and the Economy: The Key Relationships* (Paris: OECD, 1992).

8 A similar point was made in Alan M. Rugman, *Multinationals and Canada-United States Free Trade* (Columbia: University of South Carolina Press, 1990).

9 Alan M. Rugman, "The Role of Multinational Enterprises in U.S.-Canadian Economic Relations," *Columbia Journal of World Business* 21, No. 2 (Summer 1986): 15-27.

10 For a more detailed discussion of this matrix, and its relationship to the literature in international business, see Alan M. Rugman and Alain Verbeke, *Global Corporate Strategy and Trade Policy* (London and New York: Routledge, 1990), especially Chapter 5.

11 Michael E. Porter, *The Competitive Advantage of Nations* (New York: The Free Press, 1990). Of course, it is not at all clear that the Porter diamond framework is relevant for Canadian business strategy, due to its inability to handle foreign ownership, asymmetries in trade relations between small, open economies like Canada and triad ones like the United States, and the high degree of integration of the Canadian and U.S. economies due to the FTA. See: Alan M. Rugman and Joseph R. D'Cruz "The 'Double Diamond' Model of International Competitiveness: The Canadian Experience," *Management International Review* 33, Special Issue 2 (1993): 17-40; and Alan M. Rugman and Alain Verbeke, "How to Operationalize Porter's Diamond of International Competitiveness," *The International Executive* 33, No. 4 (July/August 1993): 283-299.

12 A similar analysis, using a related framework, was undertaken with respect to the FTA by Alan M. Rugman and Alain Verbeke, "Multinational Corporate Strategy and the Canada-U.S. Free Trade Agreement," *Management International Review* 30, No. 3 (1990): 253-266; and Alan M. Rugman, Alain Verbeke and Stephen Luxmore, "Corporate Strategy and the Free Trade Agreement: Adjustment by Canadian Multinational Enterprises," *Canadian Journal of Regional Science* 13, Nos. 2/3 (Summer-Autumn, 1990): 307-330.

13 Alan M. Rugman and Michael Gestrin, "U.S. Trade Laws as Barriers to Globalization," *World Economy* 14, No. 3 (1991): 335-352.

14 For a more detailed discussion of these issues, see E.M. Graham, "Foreign Direct Investment in the United States and U.S. Interests," *Science*, Volume 254, December 20, 1991, 1740-1745; and E.M. Graham and Michael E. Ebert, "Foreign Direct Investment and U.S. National Security: Fixing Exon-Florio," *World Economy*, Volume 14, 1991: 245-268.

15 For more details on the organization of the reservations, see Gary Clyde Hufbauer and Jeffrey J. Schott, *NAFTA: An Assessment* (Washington, DC: Institute for International Economics, February 1993); and Michael Gestrin and Alan M. Rugman, "The NAFTA's Impact on the North American Investment Regime," *Commentary*, No. 42 (Toronto: C. D. Howe Institute, March 1993).

16 For analysis of the strategies of Canadian-owned multinational enterprises see Alan M. Rugman and John McIlveen, *Megafirms: Strategies for Canada's Multinationals* (Toronto: Methuen, 1995); Alan M. Rugman and Mark Warner, "Strategies for the Canadian Multinationals," in Alan M. Rugman (ed.), *International Business in Canada* (Toronto: Prentice Hall, 1989), 200-229.

17 United States, *Potential Impact on the U.S. Economy and Selected Industries of the North American Free-Trade Agreement* (Washington, DC: U.S. International Trade Commission, Publication 2596, January 1993).

18 Ibid.

19 For an excellent analysis of the rules of origin in the NAFTA applied to the auto sector, see: Jon R. Johnson, "NAFTA and the Trade in Automotive Goods," in Steven Globerman and Michael Walker (eds.) *Assessing NAFTA: A Trinational Analysis* (Vancouver, BC: The Fraser Institute), 87-129.

20 Ibid.

5

Excerpt from Peter J. Buckley and Mark Casson (eds), *Multinational Enterprises in the World Economy: Essays in Honour of John H. Dunning* (Aldershot, UK: Edward Elgar, 1993)

11. Multinational Enterprise and National Economic Policy

Alan M. Rugman and Alain Verbeke

11.1. INTRODUCTION

In this chapter the three elements of John Dunning's eclectic paradigm are operationalized into two key elements for strategic management; firm-specific advantages (FSAs) and country-specific advantages (CSAs). A model is developed to capture the interactive nature of FSAs and CSAs as they determine international competitiveness. This approach permits us to build upon some of the recurrent themes of John Dunning's research into the relationships between multinational enterprises (MNEs) and nation states. One of these has been the nature of government regulation of the MNE and the extent to which it may affect MNE efficiency and national competitiveness.

We re-examine this economic relationship between FSAs and CSAs in terms of the strategic management concepts of globalization (economic integration) and national responsiveness (sovereignty). We extend previous work in this area by management scholars by introducing the concepts of non-location-bound FSAs (which internalize globalization efficiencies) and location-bound FSAs (which capture elements of national responsiveness). We examine the administrative heritage of groups of triad-based MNEs in order to detect the nature of their sustainable competitive advantages. We find that the different combinations of non-location-bound FSAs and location-bound FSAs held by MNEs are the basis for the development of sustainable national policies for international competitiveness. In contrast 'shelter'-based national policies, such as trade protectionism, are usually not sources of national competitive advantage.

As examples, we examine the nature of business-government interaction in the formulation and implementation of the Canada-US Free Trade Agreement. We find that this institutionalized change in national economic policies was determined in an interactive manner with the relevant MNEs, and that these MNEs are now developing both location-bound and non-location-bound FSAs. Further, the nature of these FSAs helps to

Figure 11.1.   The competitive advantage matrix

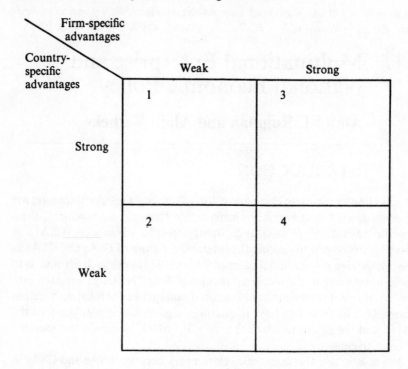

improve the international competitiveness of the home country of the MNEs. We conclude that John Dunning's pioneering work in this area has laid a solid foundation for analysis of the MNE and national economic policy.

11.2.   DUNNING AND MULTINATIONAL CORPORATE STRATEGY

Corporate strategic management in an MNE is a process of making decisions and taking actions that have a substantial influence on the firm's survival, profitability and growth. The main factors influencing an MNE's strategy and international competitive positioning are compatible with ownership (O), location (L) and internalization (I) advantages, as embodied in the eclectic, or OLI paradigm developed by Dunning (1981a, 1988a). For strategic management purposes Dunning's framework can be rephrased in terms of Figure 11.1.

In Figure 11.1 following Rugman (1981, 1990), ownership advantages are included as FSAs, whereas location advantages are designated as CSAs. In this model, the MNE as a whole, its different strategic business units, national operations or product lines, can be positioned according to the relative strength of their FSAs and CSAs. The model takes into account the prior, simultaneous, or the subsequent choice of a particular mode of operation (for example, exports, internal production, licensing or joint venture activity).

Dunning himself (1981a, p. 113) has already related the interactions among the three elements of the OLI paradigm and three structural determinants, that is those specific to particular countries, to particular types of activities (or industries) and to particular firms or industries. It is apparent that country factors may influence ownership advantages, and that a firm's strategy and its organizational knowledge may partly determine the attractiveness of particular locations for the development of specific activities.

Dunning's framework, however, is primarily aimed at explaining the observed behaviour of MNEs, without explicitly leading to concrete implications for the strategic management of individual firms. In contrast, in our framework, the different structural variables are translated as the strength or weakness of a particular MNE's set of ownership and location advantages affecting the firm's capabilities in obtaining a favourable competitive position and performance.

FSAs are defined as the possession of a unique body of knowledge or a special skill by a firm, which generates a cost-reducing or differentiation-enhancing capability. CSAs, if defined broadly, result from specific 'environmental', 'system' and 'policy' characteristics of the nation in which MNEs operate, as described by Dunning (1988b). These FSAs (largely intangible assets) and CSAs (largely immobile resources) constitute the basis for a cost or differentiation advantage in the market-place, that is, for firm-level entry barriers against competition. However, both FSAs and CSAs can be 'strong' or 'weak' in comparison to rival companies. In this sense their relative impact can be positive, (strong, FSA or CSA), namely as the basis for cost or differentiative advantages, or negative (weak FSA or CSA), namely when providing an insufficient basis for a cost or differentiation advantage.

Corporate strategic management involves the constant reassessment of FSAs and CSAs in light of new information about the domestic and international environments within which the firm operates. In Rugman (1988) FSAs are considered as managerial-decision variables. In contrast, CSAs are regarded as environmental parameters, which are largely exogenous for the firm. However, here we will also consider government-induced CSAs, for example through trade and industrial policies.

More specifically, this chapter extends this FSA-CSA framework in two ways. These are of specific relevance to the interaction between strategies of MNEs and government trade and industrial policies. First, it will be shown that a distinction needs to be made between location-bound and non-location-bound FSAs as core sources for a firm's competitiveness. Secondly, it will be argued that government-imposed CSAs are not always exogenous parameters for MNEs, but may sometimes be influenced by firms. From a strategic management perspective, MNEs may develop both location-bound and non-location-bound FSAs in government relations to improve their competitiveness, or they may try to use government as a tool to obtain shelter from foreign competition.

Our approach is consistent with Buckley (1990). He makes the useful point that internalization theory explains the growth of the firm relative to markets whereas competitive advantage is based on an advantage relative to another firm. This is precisely the point that we are making, with the additional insight that, while FSAs can result from both approaches, there exist a set of FSAs specifically developed by business-government interaction. When these are shelter-based FSAs, they can benefit domestic firms and MNEs at the expense of foreign firms relying on exports.

11.3.   LOCATION-BOUND AND NON-LOCATION-BOUND FIRM-SPECIFIC ADVANTAGES

Dunning (1988b) has argued that an MNE may posses two types of knowledge. First, knowledge of asset creation and usage (innovation and efficiency improving ability in different functional areas). Secondly, knowledge of organizing economic activity (the ability to choose, design and operate the optimal institutional form for the development of value added activities). The core characteristic of such knowledge is that it needs to be created by the firm. In our view, however, building upon Bartlett and Ghoshal (1989), both types of knowledge can be non-location bound or location bound. Non-location-bound FSAs reflect capabilities of 'integration', whereas location-bound FSAs reflect capabilities of 'national responsiveness'.

International integration at the firm level can take three forms in terms of the configuration and co-ordination of the firm's activities. First, there can be a concentration of particular activities in specific countries to obtain economies of scale. In this case, integration reflects a centralized configuration of the firm's core assets.

Secondly, integration can take the form of transfer of know-how across borders, thus creating economies of scope. Here, integration refers to a dispersion of the firm's asset configuration, combined with a specific type of international co-ordination of activities: the transfer and subsequent use of know-how abroad, thus creating 'standards' in terms of work content and processes, outputs, skills or norms. This requires the use of similar manufacturing processes on the production side, the use of identical brand names in marketing, the standardization of skill requirements to perform specific activities, and the sharing of a common corporate culture across borders.

Thirdly, integration may refer to the exploitation of national differences (due to a firm-level response to a nation's comparative advantage). Here, the firm is again characterized by a dispersed configuration of assets. Co-ordination is achieved by linking the dispersed assets of the firm so that it can make optimal use of imperfections in the markets for production factors, intermediate outputs and final products. Exploitation of national differences on the input side typically requires substantial intra-firm trade.

In each of these three cases the firm uses core skills, or FSAs, to be competitive abroad. The economies of scale, economies of scope, or benefits from the exploitation of national differences, result from the firm's proprietary know-how. This know-how is used across borders, that is know-how can be 'non-location bound'. For example, economies of scale become relevant in an international context only when the manufactured products embody characteristics which make the product competitive abroad. Economies of scope can only be reaped if the know-how being transferred gives the firm a competitive edge *vis-à-vis* foreign rivals. Benefits of exploiting national differences only arise if the firm possesses necessary co-ordination skills to take advantage of market imperfections in the international arena.

In contrast, a focus on national responsiveness is the opposite of integration; it means that the international expansion of a firm needs to be accompanied by the development of specific capabilities in the various countries where the company will operate. The firm's asset configuration may be centralized or dispersed, but the profitability and growth of its operations in the different countries will largely depend on its ability to adapt to local circumstances, both in terms of market demands and government regulation. In other words, location-bound FSAs need to be developed when know-how becomes of crucial importance in specific geographical areas and it cannot be used outside the area.

The core theoretical premise of this chapter, building on Rugman and Verbeke (1990a), is that the present global environment requires firms to develop dual sets of FSAs. These are the non-location-bound FSAs, required to reap economies of integration, plus location-bound FSAs, required to successfully adapt to location-specific requirements. This is consistent with Dunning's (1988b, p. 260) view on the 'schizophrenic nature of international economic relations,' whereby requirements for integration and national responsiveness need to be met simultaneously. In practice, given industry-wide environmental opportunities for integration, and requirements for national responsiveness, firms respond in different ways. The 'administrative heritage' of any firm (see Bartlett, 1986) may substantially influence its emphasis on either location-bound or non-location-bound elements.

The analysis above is represented in Figure 11.2. Location-bound FSAs are shown on the horizontal axis and non-location-bound FSAs on the vertical axis; both have weak and strong dimensions. Quadrant 1 reflects the case whereby the possession of non-location-bound FSAs is of prime importance to the firm's international competitive position. Here the firm will be able to achieve a satisfactory economic performance only if economies of scale, and/or economies of scope, and/or benefits of exploiting national differences, can be captured on an international scale.

Figure 11.2.   Firm-specific sources of international competitive advantage in global industries

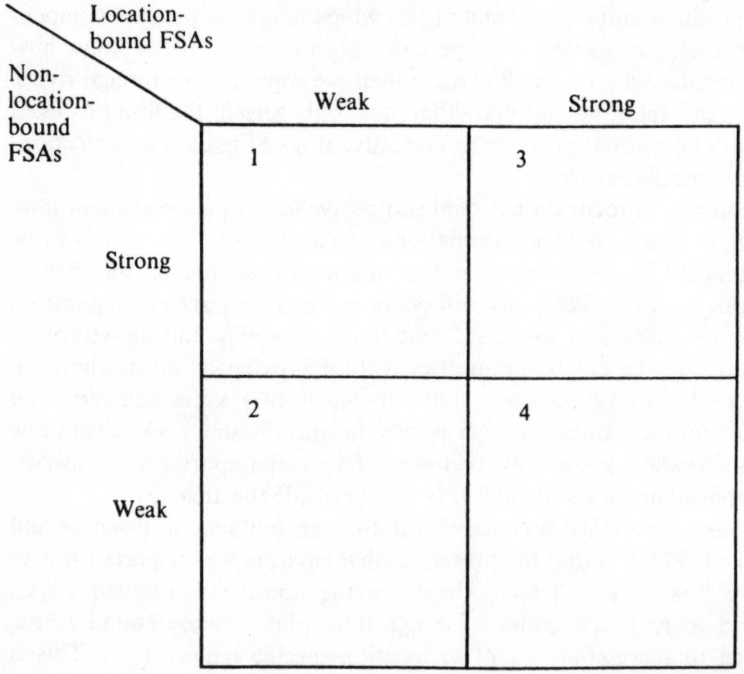

In the literature, examples of the emphasis on economies of scale can be found in Levitt (1983) and Leontiades (1984). The importance of scope economies is apparent in most of the economics-driven internalization theory literature, recently synthesized by Dunning (1988a). It can also be found in the strategic management literature (for example Hamel and Prahalad, 1985). Finally, the importance of exploiting national differences has been analysed by Kogut (1985). The possibilities and internal contradictions associated with developing the three types of integration economies simultaneously have been described in Ghoshal (1987) and Bartlett and Ghoshal (1989).

Quadrant 2 of Figure 11.2 is a situation whereby neither location-bound nor non-location-bound firm-specific advantages constitute sources of international competitive performance of a firm. This quadrant reflects the existence of firms with little potential for international competitive advantage against global competitors, or a uninational firm engaged in strategies of national responsiveness. Such firms face only three alternatives: (i) internal restructuring through the development of new FSAs, (ii) a form of alliance implying the external acquisition of FSAs, or (iii) exit.

Quadrant 3 indicates the existence of firms which have developed both location-bound and non-location-bound FSAs as sources of international competitive advantage. These firms have a distinctive competitive edge compared with global rivals that have focused exclusively on the development of non-location-bound FSAs and have neglected to adapt specific functional activities (for example, marketing) to local circumstances. On the other hand, these firms rely on a mix of benefits related to scale, scope and exploitation of national differences, all of which are non-location bound.

Quadrant 4 contains firms where location-bound FSAs constitute a firm's core source of competitive advantage against firms that rely more on non-location-bound FSAs. Typically, these are uninational firms or MNEs which have focused on the development of location-bound FSAs in their dispersed operations.

To an extent, scale, scope and exploitation of national differences may sometimes merely constitute different perspectives of the same capability of an MNE. For example, concentrated large-scale manufacturing of particular products may be useless without dispersed marketing operations sharing the same skills and brand name, and without location of the production capacity in particular countries to exploit international market imperfections. The creation of economies of scope may require a firm to be a minimum size in order to allow replication and the establishment of different operations in several countries. Finally, the exploitation of national differences may again require a minimum scale to successfully disperse the different activities in the value chain over several countries. It also requires economies of scope, especially as regards the effective transfer of common managerial skills and internal 'infrastructure' capabilities to allow the successful international co-ordination of the firm's activities.

It is critical to note that there is a major difference between a strategy of exploitation of national differences and a strategy of national responsiveness. In the former case, a firm takes advantage of international market imperfections to improve its economic performance. This opportunity occurs due to the comparative advantage of nations and the resulting differences in the price and quality of factor inputs. It may also exist on the output side. For example, an export promotion programme in a host country, or the existence of a leading market for absorbing new products, can lead an MNE to benefit from exploiting these CSAs. These are internalized into FSAs and can thus be used across borders (that is in a non-location-bound fashion).

In contrast, national responsiveness requires that a firm adapts itself to local circumstances. A firm then forgoes the benefits of integration because of the requirement to tailor its activities to host-country needs (see Doz, 1986). A strategy of national responsiveness does not permit the firm to gain benefits outside of the country in which the adaptation process takes place. No CSA is internalized into non-location-bound FSAs that can be used across borders. Only in the long run, and especially when related to organizational learning and innovation, can location-bound FSAs be turned into non-location-bound FSAs through, for example, the process of locally leveraged or globally linked innovations (Rugman and Verbeke, 1990a). However, the occurrence of such an innovation process itself is conditional upon the prior existence of non-location-bound FSAs. These require shared co-ordination mechanisms among the different units involved, with economies of scope. In short, national responsiveness needs a dispersed configuration of activities combined with low international co-ordination. It is the opposite of a strategy of integration.

11.4. FIRM-SPECIFIC ADVANTAGES AND GOVERNMENT REGULATION

When dealing with governments in areas such as local content requirements, product pricing, ownership, transfer pricing and so on, MNEs may choose to develop an FSA in government relations. It may be location-bound or non-location bound. The empirical work of Mahini and Wells (1986) and Mahini (1987), which investigates government relations in thirteen large US MNEs, demonstrates the relevance of this difference.[1]

According to Mahini and Wells (1986), the present trend toward global competition is inducing more firms to move towards a centralized or co-ordinated approach. The latter approach, based on a combination of location-bound and non-location-bound FSAs, is consistent with Rugman and Verbeke (1990a, 1991), who analyse the dual requirements of simultaneously attempting to reap benefits of integration and national responsiveness. Using the terminology of Mahini and Wells (1986) the 'policy approach' does not appear to be relevant in an era of global competition; most MNEs no longer have a truly monopolistic advantage. The 'diffuse strategy' is not optimal either, as it does not really recognize the need to create company-specific knowledge to cope with governments. In addition, even if know-how in government relations is developed, it is of a purely location-bound nature, usable only in a particular national operation.

This literature on MNE-government relations suggests that FSAs may need to be developed to influence regulation. There are distinct strategies followed by MNEs in negotiations with government agencies. There are several ways to develop such FSAs, which will involve a mixture of location-bound and non-location-bound characteristics.

Neither the eclectic model of Dunning (1981a, 1988a), nor traditional internalization theory fully assess the impact of government regulations on the behaviour of MNEs (see, for example, Buckley and Casson, 1976; Hennart, 1982, 1986, 1989; Rugman, 1981, and Grosse 1985). Most of the authors model trade-policy restrictions, such as tariff and non-tariff barriers, as exogenously imposed, unnatural market imperfections. MNEs deal with them in a similar fashion to natural market imperfections (for example, the public goods nature of knowledge), which may require the substitution of FDI for exports. This analysis needs to be modified when its assumptions are not operative. There are three cases to consider.

First, in traditional analysis it is assumed that MNEs consider government trade-policy regulation as a given environmental parameter that cannot be influenced. In reality, business may interact with government and thereby affect trade policies. Baldwin (1986) synthesizes a body of empirical evidence which demonstrates the public-choice nature of inter-action between firms and government trade agencies in the United States. In the context of MNEs, several authors, such as Gladwin and Walter (1980), Rutenberg (1982, especially Chapter 4), Poynter (1985), Doz (1986), Grosse and Kujawa (1988), and Boddewyn (1988), have also suggested that strong interrelationships may exist between strategic management in MNEs and government policies.[2]

Secondly, traditionally it is assumed that protectionist trade and industrial policy do not influence the MNE's product-market domain, nor its market share in host countries, since foreign direct investment (local (FDI) production) can substitute for exports (home production and trade). This suggests that trade protectionism for the most part would not affect the MNE's competitive position. Yet in reality, the existence of intra-firm trade and global sourcing indicates that trade and investment flows generated by MNEs are often complements or imperfect substitutes (see Rugman, 1990). Hence if protectionism hinders intra-firm trade, it may strongly influence an MNE's competitiveness. In this case, MNEs may need to develop a location-bound FSA in government relations in order to benefit from government-induced CSAs. These CSAs in turn may then be a prerequisite for the subsequent exploitation of non-location-bound FSAs.

Thirdly, *ceteris paribus*, MNEs will always prefer less protection to more protection, as increased unnatural market imperfections imply higher transaction costs associated with exporting, one of the modes of servicing foreign markets.

However, two elements may stimulate MNEs to have a preference for maintaining protection in the form of trade barriers. An MNE's set of FSAs may have been eroded over time so that protection allows some shelter from foreign exports. In addition, an MNE's production operations in host countries may become obsolete if their scale was designed to serve only a small market. The abolition of protection could thus lead to increased competition from efficient exporters. Moreover, as Eaton and Lipsey (1981) indicate, the managers of subsidiaries located in host countries may themselves oppose the elimination of trade barriers, as freer imports could mean the closure of their operations in the face of low exit barriers.

11.5.   TRADE POLICY PREFERENCES OF MULTINATIONAL ENTERPRISE

In more general terms, and using Figure 11.1, it can be demonstrated that the erection and preservation of trade barriers may constitute a significant country- or (location-) specific advantage for the operations of an MNE in a particular country. As a result, the competitive strength of such sheltered operations could be severely affected if trade barriers were abolished, shifting the position of a particular operation of the MNE from the upper

Figure 11.3.   MNE preferences for trade policy measures

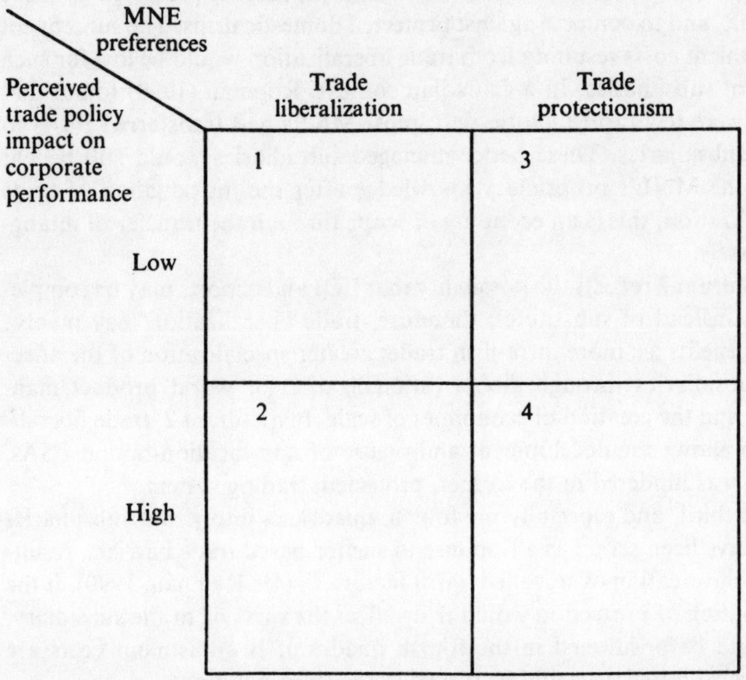

MNE preferences	Trade liberalization	Trade protectionism
Perceived trade policy impact on corporate performance		
Low	1	3
High	2	4

to the lower side of the CSA axis. An integrated MNE can, of course, be in several of these quadrants at once; its overall reaction depends on a balanced analysis of the potential impacts and preferences of a trade policy change.

Once it is recognized that MNEs are not indifferent to possible changes in the government regulation of trade, and may benefit from maintaining protectionism, four types of preferences of firms can be distinguished, as represented in Figure 11.3.

The horizontal axis of Figure 11.3 reflects the preference of MNEs for trade liberalization or protectionism. The vertical axis captures the degree to which the preferred set of trade policies is perceived to affect the firm's competitiveness. With trade liberalization, the perceived 'benefits' to firms positioned in quadrants 1 and 2 should be calculated relative to the *status quo*; for firms located in quadrants 3 and 4, the 'costs'.

The first quadrant reflects the benefits of trade liberalization for MNEs. Its impact on an MNE's competitive position is low, as these subsidiaries are not 'tariff factories' (which are in quadrant 4), but efficient subsidiaries using some of the MNE's FSAs. The MNE's proprietary know-how allowed it to set up efficient subsidiaries in the market protected by trade barriers, and to compete against protected domestic firms. The subsequent adjustment costs resulting from trade liberalization would be low for such efficient subsidiaries. In a Canadian context, Rugman (1990) found that there were few tariff factories left; most MNEs had transferred FSAs to their subsidiaries. These better managed subsidiaries would still benefit from the MNE's proprietary knowledge after the introduction of trade liberalization; this is an economy of scope through the transfer of intangible assets.

Quadrant 2 reflects the possibility that FDI and exports may be complements instead of substitutes; therefore, trade liberalization may involve such benefits as: more intra-firm trade; greater specialization of the affected subsidiaries through global rationalization or world product mandates; and the creation of economies of scale. In quadrant 2, trade liberalization allows the development and/or use of non-location-bound FSAs, which was hindered in the former, protected, trading system.

The third, and especially the fourth, quadrants imply that subsidiaries may have been set up as a response to shelter-based trade barriers, resulting in the creation of so-called 'tariff factories', (see Rugman, 1990). If the elimination of protection would truly affect the survival of the subsidiary, it would be positioned in the fourth quadrant. If adjustment costs are relatively limited, it would be placed in the third quadrant.

Although these subsidiaries benefit from the FSAs of the parent (technological know-how, credit rating, and so on), they may have to produce at a less than optimal scale (see Eastman and Stykolt, 1967). Moreover, trade barriers may lead subsidiaries to produce an excessively diversified product mix, resulting in high unit costs because of the limited volume produced (Harris, 1985, 1987; and the Macdonald Commission (see Canada, 1985)). The sunk costs incurred as a result of setting up inefficient plants may then lead to an 'emerging' preference, in the spirit of Mintzberg and McHugh (1985), in favour of maintaining existing protection.

Our basic thesis is that MNEs located on the left hand side of Figure 11.3, especially in quadrant 2, may want to develop location-bound FSAs in government relations in order to improve their cost-reducing or differentiation-enhancing ability. In contrast, firms on the right hand side, in particular the tariff factories of quadrant 4 of Figure 11.3, do not develop FSAs in government relations. Their core objective is to obtain or keep a government-induced CSA, which imposes artificial costs on foreign rivals without improving their company-specific capabilities to compete internationally.

11.6.   CORPORATE STRATEGY AND GOVERNMENT TRADE POLICY

Building upon the analysis in the previous sections, two distinctive strategies can be used in order to influence government trade-policy measures. The first strategy includes the development of FSAs in government relations, to improve the mix of benefits of integration and national responsiveness accruing to the firm, as compared to rival firms. Here, MNEs may choose to develop a particular mix of location-bound or non-location-bound FSAs to deal with public agencies. The core result of a successful strategy in this area should be an improvement of the firm's cost-reducing or differentiation-enhancing capabilities as compared to a situation whereby government policy would have been considered as an exogenous parameter. The effective use of an FSA in government relations leads to an improvement in the competitive ability of the firm.

In contrast, the second strategy aims at influencing government policy by attempting to reduce artificially the competitive ability of rivals, without improving the cost-reducing or differentiation-enhancing capability of the firm itself.[3]

Here, four issues need to be considered. First, business firms may try to lobby for the erection of trade barriers in order to 'compensate' for similar protection given by foreign governments to their domestic companies. It may not always be clear whether firms see this 'compensation' as a second best solution when a free trading system is made impossible because of government regulation, or as a tool to prevent foreign firms turning their FSAs into actual cost or differentiative advantages. It is hypothesized here, building upon the comparative costs models of Lavergne (1981) and Ray (1981), that the intent of managers on this issue can be predicted.

As a basis of this prediction, the firm-level entry barriers benefiting the company relative to rival companies, after the introduction of the measures lobbied for, should be compared with the entry barriers in the case in which all government-imposed support mechanisms were eliminated (including government support favourable to rival firms). If the former are much higher than the latter, the probability of shelter-based behaviour will be very high. Thus, the demand for shelter by firms depends upon the perceived gap between entry barriers benefiting the firm before, and after, the introduction of shelter. This 'Darwinian' approach is consistent with the empirical work of authors such as Pugel and Walter (1985) and Milner (1988). The supply of shelter by government will then depend upon the ability of the firm's management to create a perception by relevant public agencies that the performance gap should be closed. This 'marketing

effort' may build upon national goals, especially in the area of distributional considerations or private goals of relevant politicians and bureaucrats
(for example, the contribution of shelter to vote- or budget-maximizing;
see Rugman and Anderson, 1987 and Rugman and Verbeke, 1990b).

Secondly, government support may sometimes be given without any
efforts exerted by firms to receive such help (for example, for equity or
voting considerations). The implementation of government-imposed
market imperfections such as tariffs, quotas and production subsidies
should then not be regarded as the result of shelter-based firm behaviour.
In this case it is the government which creates artificial costs for foreign
competitors. This may then lead to an emerging strategy based on shelter
(see Rugman and Verbeke, 1991).

Thirdly, the time frame is important. The need to develop strong FSAs
(infant industry argument) or the need to adapt to unexpected environmental changes (for example, exchange rate stability which threatens the
successful exploitation of FSAs), may lead firms to lobby for protection.
As long as their prime intent is not to gain long-run (indefinite) shelter,
they would not be subject to the danger associated with shelter-based
advantages, namely the creation of X-inefficiency, in the spirit of Leibenstein (1976) and Bergsman (1974). This raises the possibility of a secondary shelter-based strategy in the short term, as a complement to a long-run
efficiency-driven strategy, with cost-reducing and differentiation-enhancing goals.

Fourthly, some firms, especially MNEs, which operate in several
markets, may attempt to improve their cost-reducing or differentiation-
enhancing capabilities and also attempt to obtain shelter simultaneously.
For example, in small markets where the competitive subsidiaries are
restricted, they could attempt to raise trade barriers against more efficient
foreign exporters. In this context, it should be recognized that shelter is
only a relevant concept in cases where a minimum degree of micro-
efficiency, based on FSAs, is already achieved. Thus, a firm may attempt
to acquire shelter *vis-à-vis* foreign competitors, while simultaneously competing on the basis of its FSAs against rival companies in the domestic
market.[4]

In the next section we shall consider the possibility that MNEs may
have a preference toward the creation (or non-elimination) of shelter
against rival firms through government trade measures, using the example
of the Canada-US Free Trade Agreement (FTA).

11.7.   MNEs AND THE CANADA-US FREE TRADE AGREEMENT

Two issues arise once it is accepted that MNEs are not indifferent to trade barriers or changes in trade regulation. First, trade and investment may be complements for firms which favour the elimination of trade barriers and which develop FSAs in government relations to achieve this. Secondly, the elimination of trade barriers may severely affect the competitive position of firms which favour the *status quo*, thus providing an incentive to seek shelter. In this section some evidence is reviewed about these two cases, based upon the impact of the Canada-US Free Trade Agreement on the operations of Canadian MNEs and the Canadian subsidiaries of US MNEs.

Safarian (1985) has examined the issue of whether or not investment is a substitute for, or a complement to trade. He considered the potential effects of the FTA on the activities of multinational enterprises. Safarian indicates that tariff barriers, which provided the initial rationale for the location of subsidiaries in Canada, are no longer a major CSA for most MNEs operating in Canada. The removal of trade barriers should allow Canadian manufacturing to develop new non-location-bound FSAs by rationalizing; that is, scaling-up and specializing in fewer product lines. Both Canadian and US multinationals will still invest in the other country to capture and maintain their markets. Both trade and investment between Canada and the United States will increase (that is, complementing each other rather than substituting for one another). Burgess (1986) also finds that exporting and establishing branch plants are complements, not substitutes.

Such analysis suggests that a number of both Canadian and US multinationals would be positioned in quadrant 2 of Figure 11.3. The FTA would be of benefit to them, but it would also force them to engage in substantial strategic changes. There are incentives for firms to create location-bound FSAs in government relations, primarily to be able to develop and exploit non-location-bound FSAs in production. The existence of intra-firm trade (see MacCharles (1985, 1987) and Rugman, 1990) suggests that North American intra-firm trade would expand after the FTA in the form of an increase in both final and intermediate products. Finally, it has been argued by economists such as Safarian (1985), Wolf (1989) and Crookell (1990) that the FTA will generate incentives for US subsidiaries in Canada to expand production because of world product mandates. Whether this would actually be realized has been a matter of controversy (see Rugman and Bennett, 1982; and Poynter and Rugman, 1982). It does indicate, however, a strong potential impact from the removal of protectionist barriers on the affected firms' corporate strategies, especially in terms of allowing the creation and use of new non-location-bound FSAs.

Quadrant 4 is the situation for tariff factories. D'Cruz and Fleck (1988) found that a number of branch plants and subsidiaries of US multinationals will indeed be severely affected by the elimination of trade barriers. These 'miniature replicas' of their US parents build upon the government-induced CSAs of trade protectionism. The tariff factories lack economies of scale and would face only two alternatives after the removal of such shelter; exit or commence global rationalization. The latter requires specialization in a narrow product domain to achieve economies of scale. Such scenarios would occur, according to these authors, in the food processing and grocery products industries. These firms may then have an incentive to lobby so as to maintain shelter, especially the managers of subsidiaries and even at the expense of corporate goals.

To test empirically the theoretical predictions above, Rugman (1990) surveyed the corporate strategic response to trade liberalization of the 21 largest Canadian multinationals and the 22 largest US subsidiaries in Canada. This was done to obtain data on the viewpoint of senior management as to their trade policy preferences and to ascertain the expected costs and benefits of the FTA on their corporations. Rugman found that the overwhelming majority of US subsidiaries and Canadian MNEs are in favour of the FTA. With respect to the complementarity of trade and investment, 50 and 70 per cent of the Canadian and US firms respectively expect their investment in Canada to increase between 10 and 20 per cent in response to trade liberalization. Furthermore, none of the firms indicate that they would replace FDI by exporting.

These responses are consistent with the framework developed in the previous sections. Rugman and Anderson (1987) have demonstrated that the *status quo* in Canada-US trade relations is one of increasing 'administered' protection. Many US firms are able to obtain shelter by appealing to their government's 'technical' bodies which are responsible for implementing US trade policy. This strategy, corresponding to quadrant 4 of Figure 11.3, gives these firms an artificial advantage over their foreign rivals. Since trade and investment are complements, foreign rivals cannot negate such artificial costs by direct investment in the United States. Hence, the Canadian firms have largely adopted strategies in quadrant 2 of Figure 11.3 in order to eliminate the shelter-based competitive advantage of some US firms. This complementarity of trade and investment also accounts for the US subsidiaries' strategic preferences for decreasing trade barriers.

An analysis of actual strategies developed by firms located in Canada toward the Canadian government and their impact on the trade negotiations in the 1986–1987 period, has been performed in Rugman and Anderson (1987, Chapter 5) and Rugman and Verbeke (1990b). These studies demonstrate that a large majority of Canadian business, both multinationals and small firms, developed an FSA in government relations. They are able to influence government through the establishment of institutional structures such as the International Trade Advisory Committee (ITAC) and the Sectoral Advisory Groups for International Trade (SAGITs).

In terms of the model, the FTA provides these firms with the means to reduce the impact of trade protectionism sought by US rivals. In other words, the FSA in government relations created by Canadian firms allowed them to participate in the design of a new set of CSAs, which were required to develop and exploit new non-location-bound FSAs. The bilateral trade dispute settlement mechanism allows the legal review of trade policy decisions made by US trade law bodies (see Anderson and Rugman 1990). It has led to a new, lower standard of deference being shown by the binational panels, than at the US Court of International Trade. This has led to the reversal of several US trade law decisions involving Canada, such as the red raspberries and pork cases. This process should help to ensure that US firms obtain a shelter-based advantage only when the competitive position of Canadian rivals is also based on shelter and not on the efficient development and use of FSAs.

11.8.   CONCLUSIONS

This chapter builds upon the strategic principle that MNEs need to develop strong FSAs to be competitive on a global scale. The FSAs can be both location-bound and non-location bound. In addition, some CSAs constitute a second source of competitive advantage, if they can be turned into FSAs. Three main conclusions follow from the analysis presented here.

First, government-imposed CSAs may constitute an endogenous parameter for the management of an MNE. In order to influence government on a continuing basis, an FSA in government relations should be developed. Such an FSA will improve the cost-reducing or differentiation-enhancing capability of a firm. The FSA in government relations should then lead to a more attractive set of CSAs of benefit to the firm.

Secondly, government can also be used as a tool to obtain shelter. In this case, firms artificially prevent (foreign) competitors from exploiting or developing their FSAs. In other words, rival companies are prevented from using their cost-reducing or differentiation-enhancing capabilities as a result of government-imposed barriers. Hence, the firm triggering the erection of trade barriers does not really have an FSA in government relations, as its lobbying efforts do not improve its cost-reducing or differentiation-enhancing potential.

Thirdly, in the specific area of trade policy, MNEs may develop location-bound FSAs in government relations; these create a new set of CSAs (environmental characteristics stemming from trade liberalization). These CSAs are a prerequisite for the development and exploitation of non-location-bound FSAs, fostering the global competitiveness of both the firms and the affected nations.

NOTES

1. These firms include Atlantic Richfield, Conoco, Cummins Engine, Eli Lilly, Exxon, Ford Motor, Gulf Oil, IBM, International Harvester, ITT, Mobil, Socal and Xerox.
2. This issue is largely neglected in Porter's (1990) work on the competitive advantage of nations, where little attention is devoted to multinational activity and the interactions between MNEs and governments (see Dunning, 1990a and Rugman, 1991).
3. This chapter is not concerned with the social efficiency consequences of the two types of strategies. Even strategies aiming at enhancing a firm's cost-reducing or differentiation-enhancing capabilities through the development of new FSAs, may be welfare-reducing (see Dunning and Rugman, 1985). In addition, strategies that aim at developing new FSAs, or using them more effectively, may partly build upon (short term) government protectionism, as suggested by the strategic trade-policy literature (see Rugman and Verbeke, 1990b for an in-depth discussion).
4. The importance of shelter-based strategies is largely neglected in the strategic management literature, where cost leadership, differentiation and focus are considered to be the 'three generic' strategies that can be pursued by firms. In Rugman and Verbeke (1990b), however, it is demonstrated that the truly generic strategies of firms are the efficiency-driven ones, building upon FSAs, and the shelter-based ones. In this context, it should be emphasized that Porter's (1986) 'protected market strategy' does not fit in his own framework of three generic strategies.

6

ASIA PACIFIC JOURNAL OF MANAGEMENT   VOL. 6, NO. 2 : 225-242

Japanese Joint Ventures With Western Multinationals: Synthesising the Economic and Cultural Explanations of Failure

Lee T. Brown, Alan M. Rugman, and Alain Verbeke*

Many research studies have been done to explain the reasons for the tensions and failures observed in joint ventures between Japanese and Western multinational enterprises. These studies have identified, with various degrees of sophistication, the existence of cultural differences as a primary determinant of failure. Alternative explanations focus upon a transaction cost approach, emphasising opportunism and the danger of cheating in such strategic alliances. This paper synthesises the literature through the development of a new conceptual framework. This framework, which distinguishes between economic and cultural reasons for failure, provides a new lens to view the literature. It is demonstrated that the simple view of cultural incompatibility needs to be replaced by an awareness of the combined impact of cultural and economic forces on the viability of joint ventures between Japanese and Western firms.

JAPANESE AND WESTERN JOINT VENTURE PARTNERS

Since the 1960s, joint ventures between firms of two different nationalities have increased dramatically, particularly between horizontally-related firms (Hergert and Morris, 1988; Harrigan, 1988). American and European multinational enterprises (MNEs) have begun to link up with Japanese firms for joint ventures in the non-Japanese partner's home country, a significant departure from the previous trend, in which most transnational cooperative ventures with a Japanese partner were based in Japan. Japanese firms are now seeking information about circumvention of protectionist measures, knowledge of the local culture, and the access to distribution channels.

* Lee T. Brown is a doctoral candidate in the Faculty of Management at the University of Toronto. Alan M. Rugman is Royal Bank Visiting Professor at the University of Alberta and Professor of International Business at the University of Toronto. Alain Verbeke is Assistant Professor of International Business at the University of Toronto. Helpful comments have been received from Nancy Adler, Mark Casson, Martin Evans, Tom Roehl, Mark Warner and Ken Watson.

Japanese Joint Ventures: Brown, Rugman and Verbeke

Recently, complaints have been voiced that Japanese firms do not behave ethically in cooperative arrangements. They "plan ahead to increase the benefits they extract from an alliance across the 'collaborative membrane', leaving the European or American partner in a worse strategic position" (Contractor and Lorange, 1988, summarising Hamel, Doz and Prahalad, 1986). In any attempt to assess the validity of the complaints against Japanese joint venture partners, a very salient issue must be considered. Due to the dramatic improvement of the Japanese economy since World War II, Japanese business has become surrounded by myths in the West. Portrayed alternately as brilliant and disciplined or underhanded and dishonest, Japanese firms have come to be looked on as either the potential saviours of sagging Western economies, or as a powerful menace. Commentators on Japanese-Western relationships have painted Japanese firms as either smarter than their venture partners, or as intentionally unethical. Rarely, if at all, has the argument been made that a mixture of economic and cultural factors may be responsible for the lack of satisfaction with Japanese firms as joint venture partners, and that some of these contextual factors may be alterable. This is the perspective that will be explored in this paper.

Specifically, several questions will be addressed: Do Japanese firms usurp competitive advantages from their joint venture partners more than firms of other nationalities? Might certain types of joint ventures be more likely to provoke suspicion among participants than others? How much might cultural differences contribute to the perception of cheating, and can these differences be overcome? To help answer these questions, a model will be developed to distinguish economics-based (transaction cost-related) from culture-based explanations of joint venture failure. This model will be applied to analyse and synthesise the growing literature in this area. In the literature on strategic alliances, the term "joint venture" is sometimes used to refer to a specific ownership structure, while at other times it is used more generally to mean any form of strategic partnership which is neither completely arm's-length nor completely internalised. For the purposes of this paper, the second, more general definition is used.

A TRANSACTION COST PERSPECTIVE OF JOINT VENTURE FAILURE

Internalisation theory, as developed by Rugman (1981, 1985) lays out the conditions under which production and exchange are arranged within the international markets of a multinational enterprise. The main thrust of this theory is the analysis of the transaction costs associated with each activity when penetrating a foreign market. The theory can easily be extended to explain the choice of joint ventures as an entry mode to serve foreign markets.

The transaction cost rationale for choosing cooperative ventures over wholly -owned subsidiaries is described in Beamish's (1988) extension to Rugman's

ASIA PACIFIC JOURNAL OF MANAGEMENT   VOL. 6, NO. 2

(1981) internalisation explanation of MNEs. Under certain conditions, transaction costs associated with joint ventures will be lower than that of wholly-owned subsidiaries. Buckley and Casson (1988) developed a similar transaction cost-based theory of cooperation in international business. The conditions for such ventures to be successful relate to the absence of opportunistic behaviour (in the spirit of Williamson, 1985) by the coalition partners, and their ability to econo-mise on bounded rationality through the joint venture. In our view, joint ventures should be preferred if the two partners possess firm specific advantages (FSAs) which complement each other.

The concept of FSA refers to a company's proprietary know-how in terms of unique skills that reduce costs or differentiate products. Only if the FSAs of the partners are compatible will that cooperation lead to additional cost-reducing or differentiation- enhancing potential. In this instance, an international joint venture makes economic sense, when compared to other entry modes. Contractor and Lorange (1988, pp. 9-10) detail the strategic contributions that joint ventures can make to increase revenues and decrease costs for their sponsors.

In addition, from a transaction cost perspective, the benefits of using the partner's FSAs must be weighed against the costs associated with managing the joint venture, and the risk of dissipation of the corporation's own FSAs.

Joint ventures will only succeed if efficient safeguards can be introduced against opportunistic behaviour. This is to prevent one partner from acquiring the FSA of the other partner and terminating the venture, or using the FSA at the expenses of the initial owner. Hence, an efficient reward and control system must be introduced that correctly reflects the contribution of each firm in the venture. Beamish (1988) demonstrates that there are limits to the relative efficiency gains provided by joint ventures. These gains are subject to the risk of dissipation of proprietary knowledge if some of the partners engage in "cheating" behaviour.

On the basis of the analysis made above, Exhibit 1 can be constructed. The horizontal axis measures the compatibility of the FSAs of the firms involved. This compatibility can be weak or strong. An activity should be transferred to a joint venture only if it can be done more efficiently by the partners together, i.e., when synergistic effects occur from complementary FSAs. The vertical axis reflects the possibility of introducing safeguards against opportunistic behaviour. They are either inefficient or efficient. Such safeguards include structural arrangements to regulate the contribution and the flow of benefits to each firm participating in the venture. In practice this may imply the rights of each partner to veto certain decisions, a particular representation of each partner in the management structure governing the joint venture, and the use of specific planning procedures.

In quadrant 1, the FSAs of the partners are not compatible, i.e., they do not lead to synergistic effects. There are inefficient safeguards against cheating. Each

Japanese Joint Ventures: Brown, Rugman and Verbeke

EXHIBIT 1

Transaction Cost-Related Causes of
Joint Venture Failure

Compatibility of FSAs
Weak   Strong

	Weak	Strong
Inefficient	1	3
Efficient	2	4

Safeguards
Against
Cheating

partner could pursue its own interests at the expenses of the other. Failure to honour the contracted obligations or any informal obligations may lead to the failure of the joint venture. Respecting informal understandings is as important for success as abiding by formal undertakings (Williamson, 1985).

Quadrant 2 captures the case where sufficient safeguards could be introduced against cheating, but where no joint benefits could be generated because the FSAs of the firms involved do not complement each other.

The third quadrant identifies a bad governance structure as the main cause of joint venture failure. Here the venture will not succeed in spite of the strong compatibility of the FSAs of the different partners. The incentive to cheat arises from participant's perceptions of the benefits available from cheating. Participants will be motivated to cheat if they cannot punish each other through recourse to legal channels or more direct methods, or if participants do not share in the residual risks of the venture. Since the existence of benefits associated with cheating is the key to motivating opportunistic behaviour, firms with an established reputation for always carrying out reprisals in response to cheating, provide their partners with the strongest incentives to abstain from opportunistic behaviour. Thus, foregoing short-term gains in order to develop a reputation for reciprocating forbearance is an investment that allows firms to save on future transac-

ASIA PACIFIC JOURNAL OF MANAGEMENT   VOL. 6, NO. 2

tion costs. In other words, some firms may develop a special skill in the efficient management of joint ventures. This FSA then reduces the need for extensive structural safeguards. Limited bureaucratic control systems suffice to create an efficient safeguard against opportunism. In this particular case, the two axes of Exhibit 1 are interrelated. An FSA in the management of joint ventures increases the compatibility of the two partners and also limits the requirements for achieving an efficient safeguard structure.

The relationship between FSA compatibility and efficient safeguards is dynamic. It is possible that a low initial level of mutual forbearance can be transformed into a high degree of trust, thus reducing the required structural safeguards to avoid cheating. The joint venture then moves to quadrant 4, where a transaction cost framework would normally predict cooperative arrangements to be successful.

Such a view of joint ventures is largely based upon Western concepts of legal institutions and bureaucratic control to enforce internal relationships, although it does recognise the importance of trust. It may or may not explain Japanese thinking. The transaction cost framework presented here is already an advance upon the type of framework used by Porter (1980). He stresses the competitive potential of all business relationships, and devises strategies for gaining the competitive advantage. By contrast, Buckley and Casson (1988) emphasise the gains from cooperation and the mechanisms for maintaining balanced power in order to reduce the incentives to cheat, thereby husbanding the potential benefits of the cooperative relationship. The costs of cooperation arise from the risk of opportunistic behaviour in a context of vulnerability. In terms of creating only a limited number of explicit safeguards, the greater the trust, the more vulnerability is acceptable.

In practice, joint ventures located in quadrant 4 may still fail because of transaction costs resulting from uncertainty and bounded rationality. For example, one partner may not realise during the negotiations how much it will contribute to the joint venture (and to the other partner), and thus may not demand adequate compensation. One partner may not be aware of the potential value of its proprietary knowledge until the other partner has appropriated it. One partner may be more skilled at learning and making use of the other partner's skills and resources. Control over various kinds of access may be lost.

Each of these scenarios involves the dissipation of an FSA without adequate compensation. Due to the prevalence of transfers of intangible sources of wealth, the potential for incorrectly estimating the costs and benefits of the joint venture is very high, in spite of efficient safeguards against cheating. This constitutes a major problem if one participant believes the ratio of its contribution to his returns to be lower than the other participant's. If the costs and benefits are

Japanese Joint Ventures: Brown, Rugman and Verbeke

incorrectly estimated by one participant but not the other, the participant who feels inadequately compensated may be motivated to dissolve the relationship or to cheat in spite of a safeguard structure which was agreed upon. Thus, the gains from forbearance may never be realised due to the difficulty of generating suffi-cient knowledge to exercise informed decisions. In this case, the venture shifts back to quadrant 3.

In our view, however, the bounded rationality problem as a cause of joint venture failure in quadrant 4 is only a secondary issue. In the next section we shall argue that culture-related elements are the main cause of failure for joint ventures in quadrant 4 of Exhibit 1.

We shall now attempt to explain failed ventures between Japanese and Western partners using Exhibit 1, leaving the culture issue aside, for the moment. In the 1960s and 1970s, entry into the Japanese market via direct investment became necessary in order to compete with Japanese rivals in their protected home market. Such investments enabled foreign firms to force their Japanese competi-tors to redirect more resources to maintaining market share in the home market. This defensive type of foreign investment was a strategic move, which would benefit the company as a whole even if the Japanese branch was not a big money -maker (Hladik, 1985, p. 28). However, because of entry barriers into the Japanese market, a Japanese partner became necessary. Western firms had a greater ten-dency to enter into joint ventures with Japanese partners, even when the risk of dissipation of the company's FSAs was high. Thus, it was not at all surprising that such joint ventures would result in complaints from the Western partner that its FSAs had been usurped.

Any form of entry into a foreign market incurs the risk of dissipation of replicable FSAs (Rugman, 1981, 1985; Beamish, 1988). Joint ventures entail a high risk of dissipation of replicable FSAs because the partners need to exchange information in order to make the partnership work. This risk is tolerable only if the returns from the venture are sufficient to compensate for any advantage lost through the sharing of the FSA. If a firm's survival rests solely on a limited set of easily replicable FSAs, the risk of FSA dissipation through the venture is ex-tremely great. The returns are then highly unlikely to compensate for the eventual failure of the company due to the loss of its competitive advantage. This would position most failed ventures described above in quadrant 3 of Exhibit 1. Insuffi-cient resources were devoted to the creation of an efficient safeguard structure.

In addition, there are a class of failed joint ventures in quadrant 1. Here the Western partner is less able to make use of the benefits provided by the Japanese partner. This is particularly likely in joint ventures between small, entrepreneurial, technology companies in the West, and large Japanese industrial concerns. Hull, Slowinski, Wharton and Azumi (1988) find that Japanese corporations are now offering to reengineer, manufacture, and sell the product inventions of small U.S. high-tech firms in the Asian market. In exchange, the small high-tech firms receive money and process technology to help them manufacture for the U.S. market. This presents two potential problems.

First, the entrepreneurial firm is unlikely to have either the capital to set up its own manufacturing facilities, or the know-how to make full use of the process engineering knowledge available from the Japanese corporation. Second, the Japanese firm is able to begin to export into the U.S. market the very product obtained from the technology entrepreneur. With an ability to use manufacturing learning curve effects, the Japanese import can undercut the price of the domestically produced product, even though the domestic producer had access to the Japanese partner's process technology. In such cases, it is the simultaneous occurrence of incompatible FSAs (from the perspective of the small firm) and the inefficiency of the safeguard structure which leads to failure.

THE INCOMPATIBILITY OF SOCIETAL VALUES: THE SIMPLE VIEW

In contrast to the recent development of economics-based thinking about Western-Japanese joint venture failure, the difference between Japanese and Western cultures has become a popular catch-all explanation for such difficulties. Despite the number of books and articles which attempt to interpret Japanese culture (and business practices) for foreigners, it appears that the implications of the differences cannot be fully appreciated without being experienced (Eason, 1986).

What these cultural differences mean and how they should be handled cover a wide spectrum. At one extreme, Reich and Mankin (1986) and Wolf (1983) take the view that Japanese culture is simply not conducive to good business relations. They argue that, coordinated by the Ministry of International Trade and Industry, Japanese firms use (by Western standards) unethical practices such as cartels, collusion and dumping to dominate world trade. Joint ventures place what remaining competitive advantages Western firms have left at the ready disposal of power-hungry Japanese partners.

According to Wolf (1983) and de Mente (1968), the Japanese simultaneously feel superior to other races and insecure about their future. Japan's lack of natural resources and usable land mass and its inability to impose its will militarily during World War II seem to have had a deep psychological effect, and have created a feeling that security for the future will be found only through economic power. Ohmae (1985) points out that, just as the West has fears about the economic intentions of Japan, the Japanese believe that German companies are intending to destroy the Japanese chemical industry through massive R & D

Japanese Joint Ventures: Brown, Rugman and Verbeke

investments and cost competitiveness, and that the Americans are corrupting the Japanese with fast food.

According to this simple view, the West fears Japan because it has gone so quickly from disaster to economic dominance. Having been caught napping in the automobile, semiconductor, and consumer electronics markets, Western companies have come to believe that the Japanese are a supremely clever, and possibly evil, competitive force that cannot be overcome. Writings such as Wolf's (1983) and Reich and Mankin's (1986) are too simplistic although both authors base their contentions on evidence, such as the Hitachi espionage, and documented instances of product copying.

At the other end of the spectrum are writers who claim that joint ventures between Japanese and Western firms fail because Western firms are too culture-bound, insensitive to the nuances of Japanese business practices, and entrenched in their own bad management practices. In a study of Western-Japanese joint ventures within Japan, Pucik (1988, p. 488) states:

> The reason for low performance could often be traced to the poor organizational capability of the Western partner to manage and control the cooperative relationship. This deficiency demonstrated itself in a number of forms ranging from ignorance about or misreading of the strategic intentions of their Japanese partner, to disagreements about the implementation of daily business decisions. In particular, the Western firms observed did not pay sufficient attention to the competitive aspects of the joint venture relationship and were not prepared for the possibility of changes in the relative power of their Japanese partners over time.

It can be argued that these reasons for failure can easily be given a transaction cost based interpretation, related to incompatible FSAs and inefficient safeguards. The issue of culture is crucial here. The first source of joint venture failure is not the absence of sufficient safeguards or weak compatibility of FSAs, but the culturally-related inability of Western firms to introduce an efficient governance structure, and to reap the benefits of using the Japanese partners' FSAs.

Two interesting implications arise from Pucik's analysis: One, the assumption that the Western partner should have had control over the relationship, and two, that competitive behaviour was to be expected within the relationship which the Western partner should have guarded against. Using the Buckley and Casson (1988) framework, however, it could be argued that efficient safeguards do not imply that one partner has full control in a cooperative relationship. If the ventures began with a perceived power asymmetry in favour of the Western partner, it seems likely that the Western partner, perhaps inadvertently, behaved in a way that was viewed as cheating by the Japanese partner. Given the Japanese tendency toward circumlocution and avoidance of unpleasantness in communications

ASIA PACIFIC JOURNAL OF MANAGEMENT   VOL. 6, NO. 2

(Wright, 1979; De Mente, 1968, 1972; Wolf, 1983), the Western partner might not become aware of the Japanese partner's dissatisfaction. Since cheating by one partner reduces or removes the incentive for the other partner to refrain from cheating, it is expected that the Japanese partner would cheat once power shifted in its favour. In any case, the main reason for joint venture failure is the low compatibility of societal values, rather than the absence of efficient structural safeguards or a low compatibility of FSAs.

Falling between the two extremes are writers who take the position that problems arising from cultural differences are very great, but can be overcome by good management on both sides. De Mente (1968, 1972) finds aspects of Japanese culture which simply cannot be reconciled with American management practice. De Mente characterises American management practice as revolving around a code of ethics, while Japanese management is dominated by a code of manners. The ideal of American business is outstanding achievement without resorting to deception or foul play. In Japan, the ideals are form, etiquette and "face"– values which have become deeply ingrained due to centuries of attention to such matters.

While American employees strive for outstanding personal achievement, Japanese employees are concerned with collective achievement, fitting in, and being inconspicuous. While, to an American "sincerity" means lack of pretense or deceit, to a Japanese it means not doing anything that would cause anyone to lose face. Basic values such as truth, honesty and fairness mean entirely different things to the Japanese than they do to Westerners.

There are numerous other differences between Japanese and Western firms that make joint ventures difficult. Again, due to diverging societal values, Japanese firms emphasise long-term growth over short-term profit, while Western firms must give equal if not greater attention to short-term results (Wright, 1979). These opposing views are fostered by the differences in financial markets and legal environments between Japan and many Western nations. Individuals are expected to subordinate themselves to the group to a far greater degree in Japan, and as a result, team loyalty and consensus is much greater and more highly valued (Lorsch, 1987). In spite of the length of time that Western firms have been conducting business in Japan, and the number of books and articles that stress the profound differences between Japanese and Western cultures, and interpret Japanese culture for Westerners, it appears that Western firms still do not spend adequate time in learning about Japan and Japanese business practice before making a decision on the best way to move into the Japanese market (Eason, 1986).

Japanese Joint Ventures: Brown, Rugman and Verbeke

THE INCOMPATIBILITY OF SOCIETAL VALUES:
MORE COMPLEX VIEWS

The possibility exists that the emphasis on cultural differences reviewed so far is exaggerated and even misplaced. Problems of understanding and adapting to local culture always exist whenever a firm moves into a market in a nation where it has not done business before. Since U.S. companies that form international coalitions tend to be larger and more experienced than U.S. companies that do not (Ghemawat, Porter and Rawlinson, 1986), many of the companies that form joint ventures with Japanese firms have had experiences in international ventures. It can therefore be assumed that they have at least some awareness of the problems of managing transnational relationships. Thus, for culture to be a major factor behind the problems between partners in Japanese-Western joint ventures, the differences between Japanese and Western cultures would have to be greater than the differences among Western cultures.

There is some evidence to support this contention. Hofstede (1980) has found major differences in four different dimensions of culture among employees of one firm at branches in forty countries. The dimensions used were power distance, uncertainty avoidance, individualism, and masculinity. When the scores of English-speaking countries such as Canada, the United States, and Great Britain are compared with Japan's, it was seen that the average scores on each of the four indices for the English-speaking countries are clustered, with none of the differences between the scores being statistically significant. In contrast, the difference in the scores between Japan and these English-speaking countries are statistically significant for all but the power distance index. In fact, for the masculinity index, Japan had the highest score, while the English-speaking countries did not differ significantly from the mean. Conversely, on the individuality index, the United States had the highest score while Japan did not differ significantly from the mean.

The implication that can be drawn from Hofstede's analysis is that with regard to these four dimensions of culture relevant for business practice, Japan is significantly different from Western countries, with the difference between Japan and the United States being the most. Although Western nations differ among themselves, the differences are, for the most part, not as great as the differences between these countries and Japan. On these grounds, joint ventures with Japanese firms will generally be more difficult to manage than international joint ventures between Western nations.

In contrast, McMillan (1984) takes the view that the key to the great success of the Japanese has simply been good management practice, and that many of their practices are applicable in any country. This view seems to have

ASIA PACIFIC JOURNAL OF MANAGEMENT   VOL. 6, NO. 2

some merit. If McMillan is correct, one reason for the recent upsurge in joint ventures between Japanese and American firms within the United States may be that American firms are finally attempting to find out what Japanese practices can be used to their advantage. They may also be aimed at learning how to work with Japanese partners so that they can jointly participate in ventures elsewhere in the world.

The work by Westney (1988) supports McMillan's view. She argues that U.S. firms often suffer from the "not-invented-here" syndrome. This syndrome implies that insufficient resources are allocated to scan the environment for innovations and actively adapt them. In contrast, Japanese firms consider environmental scanning and reverse engineering as important functions, and are more apt to commercialise available technology despite making relatively few major discoveries. In addition, the Japanese realised early in the 20th century that they had fallen behind the rest of the world in economic and technological progress, and became keenly aware of the need to catch up. Thus, adopting outside methods and technology and adapting them to fit the new environment has greater historical legitimacy in Japan than elsewhere.

The implication for joint ventures is that many Japanese firms have developed a culturally determined FSA in well-honed learning skills and the willingness to absorb useful ideas from foreign venture partners. Westney (1988) finds that one of the factors that has facilitated Japanese management of cooperative relationships is the practice of sending employees on temporary assignments outside the firm as part of their career development. Although this is done in some Western multinationals as well, most managers are reluctant to be away from head office for too long because of the risk of being forgotten. This routine movement of employees among Japanese firms trains key personnel to cope with new situations, such as joint ventures, and absorb whatever information they can. This gives the Japanese a seemingly unfair advantage in joint ventures with Western partners; the Western partner may not be aware of how much information it is making available to the Japanese partner, and may be shocked at some point to discover that much more of its proprietary knowledge has been transferred to the partner than had been foreseen.

Given the cost of creating proprietary knowledge, and its intangible nature, unexpected transfers of knowledge may cause the disadvantaged partner to accuse the other partner of cheating. Alternatively, Western firms, having a more adversarial view of strategic alliances, could view the Japanese partner's superior ability to make use of the experience and knowledge gained in the joint venture as cheating.

Japanese Joint Ventures: Brown, Rugman and Verbeke

THE INCOMPATIBILITY OF CORPORATE CULTURES

In the previous section, we argued that significant cultural differences between Japan and Western countries create conflict in business arrangements of all kinds between their firms. However, by viewing culture in a unitary fashion, some important distinctions were overlooked. In reality, culture related problems that occur in many joint ventures consist of two elements: incompatibility of ambient cultures (the culture of the nation as a whole) and, incompatibility of organisational cultures.

Joint venture problems arising from a weak compatibility in organisational culture can be attributed to differences in ambient cultures. The distinction between the two is important because organisational cultures are more open and responsive to intentional change than are ambient cultures. Another important consideration that arises from distinguishing between ambient and organisational cultures is that all Japanese firms are not alike, any more than all Western firms are, and that choosing the right joint venture partner is an important issue. For example, Harrigan (1988, p. 67) claims that General Motors' values are more similar to those of its venture partner, Toyota, than to Ford's values. Such strong compatibility of organisational culture make it easier for issues of strategy to be worked out. Here, it should be recognised that a successful joint venture does not necessarily require similar values. In fact, value-differences used in a collaborative fashion may lead to culture based synergies.

It is not surprising that problems arise when joint ventures were created to gain access to the Japanese market. Western firms neglected to spend sufficient resources to fully investigate a number of joint venture partners before choosing one. Since Japanese negotiators are often not forthright or candid, Western managers have trouble reading the signals. Hence, the probability that a number of organisational mismatches result is high. More recently, the fear and awe of the Japanese miracle have become factors that motivate Western firms to enter into joint ventures. In taking this action, they hope to co-opt an actual or potential competitor and reduce the threat posed by the Japanese. This led to a number of hastily-formed joint venture arrangements between incompatible partners in terms of corporate culture.

A study by Harrigan (1988) examined how differences between sponsoring firms (that is, the joint venture partners) might affect the efficiency of the strategic alliance. The majority (57.2 percent) of the joint ventures in the study were between pairs of U.S. firms, but the next-largest category of partner pairs was Japanese-U.S., which accounted for 14.4 percent of the sample. Harrigan found that 58.9 percent of ventures between the pairs of U.S. partners were judged to be unsuccessful by one or both companies. This result demonstrates that ventures between Japanese and Western firms are not always more problematic than those between two Western firms.

ASIA PACIFIC JOURNAL OF MANAGEMENT   VOL. 6, NO. 2

Dissatisfaction on the part of one or both joint venture partners is a common phenomenon; in our view it is current Western thinking about Japan that makes Japanese-Western joint ventures stand out from the rest.

Harrigan found that Japanese sponsors occurred most frequently in industries like automobiles, communications equipment, computer and peripheral equipment, metals fabrication, pharmaceuticals, precision controls and robotics, steel, and videotape recorders and videodisc players. Automobiles, metals fabrication and pharmaceuticals had higher than 50 percent success rates. In automobiles, none of the ventures were between two U.S. firms, suggesting that, in this industry at least, homogenous societal values are certainly not a critical factor in the creation of joint ventures. In communications equipment, computers and peripherals, metal fabrication and pharmaceuticals, the ventures were less likely to be successful if both sponsors were U.S. firms than when one or both sponsors were not. This finding is particularly striking as metal fabrication and pharmaceuticals were two of the industries that had the greatest relative levels of success. Clearly, transnational ventures are not more prone to failure in all industries. It also appears from this empirical research that the compatibility of organisational cultures is more important than similarity of national origin.

LINKING ECONOMIC AND CULTURAL EXPLANATIONS FOR
JOINT VENTURE FAILURE

The recent upswing in joint ventures between Japanese and Western firms probably stems from the desire to co-opt what each side sees as a threatening force. This hypothesis is consistent with the findings of Hergert and Morris (1988) and Harrigan (1988). They show that most joint ventures formed since 1975 are between competitors or potential competitors, rather than vertically-linked firms. The problem engendered by using a joint venture to co-opt a competitor is that, while the joint venture lessens competition in some or all markets, it opens each side to risks of dissipation of proprietary knowledge.

Several of the cultural practices discussed previously suggest that, particularly in Japanese-Western joint ventures, each side will overestimate the likelihood of cheating by the other partner in the near future, thus reducing the expected stream of benefits from cooperation. For example, Japanese managers believe contracts are an indication of distrust (Eason, 1986). Westerners, in contrast, feel that the unwillingness to sign and abide by contracts is an indication of dishonourable intent. The Japanese believe the straightforwardness of Westerners is rude and probably masks deceit. Westerners believe the Japanese inability to come to the point quickly denotes trickery, and find their negotiating tactics underhanded. In short, each side places a moral value on certain kinds of behaviour, and sees the other side's behaviour as immoral. The ill-feeling this engenders undoubtedly

Japanese Joint Ventures: Brown, Rugman and Verbeke

predisposes members of both sides of the agreement to interpret the problems that would occur even between joint ventures of partners of the same nationality, as intentional deception.

Buckley and Casson (1988) point out that the discontinuation of forbearance by one partner in an agreement seriously impairs the other partner's incentive to continue to forbear. This means that culture related misunderstandings that lead to false attributions of cheating will lead to genuine attempts to cheat. They have also argued that an inefficient safeguard structure, in terms of not eliminating excessive power imbalances between the partners incite the weaker partner to cheat out of fear of the stronger partner doing so first. Because the weaker partner is less able to punish the stronger partner, the weaker partner assumes that the stronger partner will use its superior power to unfair advantage, simply because it can do so with impunity.

In the context of Japan-Western joint ventures each firm often perceives itself as the weak partner due to dealing so closely with a powerful competitor whose nature is not fully understood. The likelihood of cheating increases dramatically. Hence, differences in ambient cultures, and organisational cultures may lead to a web of fear and mistrust that increase both actual cheating and perceptions of cheating in joint ventures between Japanese and Western firms.

The opportunisitic behaviour, discussed in the transaction cost perspective of joint venture failure, triggered by culturally determined expectations of the partner's behaviour implies that economics and culture based explanations of joint venture failure cannot be unbundled in practice and should be investigated simultaneously. This conclusion is also in accordance with the observation made earlier that many Japanese firms have a culturally determined FSA in absorbing knowledge through joint ventures. It is paradoxical that such an FSA diminishes the overall compatibility of the FSAs of the partners and requires a more elaborate safeguard structure to regulate the flow of benefits accruing to each of them.

A MATRIX OF ECONOMIC AND CULTURAL DIFFERENCES

In order to classify the existing literature, the matrix in Exhibit 2 combines cultural and economic (transaction cost related) reasons for joint venture failure. On the vertical axis, weak economic compatibility is identified as a possible reason for failure. This may occur even if the firms have FSAs that complement each other. For example, some degree of failure is anticipated when firms are positioned in quadrant 3 of Exhibit 1, where an inefficient governance structure has been introduced to implement the joint venture.

EXHIBIT 2

Japanese-Western Joint Venture Outcomes

Cultural Compatibility

		Strong	Weak
Economic Compatibility	**Strong**	1 Succeed 4, 12	3 Probably Fail 5, 6, 7, 13, 15, 17, 19, 20, 25, 26
	Weak	2 Probably Succeed 2, 3, 8, 10, 11, 18, 21, 22	4 Fail 1, 9, 14, 16, 24

The horizontal axis treats cultural incompatibility in a similar fashion. When there are strong perceptions of cultural incompatibility, there is a high probability that the joint venture will fail. Exhibit 2 also allows us to analyse the simultaneous impact of economic and cultural elements on the viability of joint ventures. In quadrant 1, there is a strong possibility that the joint venture will succeed since there is strong economic and cultural compatibility.

The more subtle quadrants are the intermediate cases. In quadrant 2, there is a strong cultural compatibility but a weak economic one. This implies that transaction cost related reasons for possible joint venture failure, need to be understood by the joint venture partners in order for it to succeed. There is every reason to believe that Japanese and Western firms can analyse issues such as opportunism and work towards the success of joint ventures in quadrant 2 through the implementation of efficient safeguards, thus shifting the venture to quadrant 1.

However, in quadrant 3, weak cultural compatibility combined with strong economic compatiability will probably lead to the failure of such a joint venture, because of the impact of culturally determined perceptions on actual opportunistic behaviour. It is much more difficult for the partners to recognise the nature and effect of cultural differences than it is to recognise problems solely related to economic compatibility. The perception of cultural incompatibility is clouded by subjectivity on the part of the participants, whereas problems of economic com-

Japanese Joint Ventures: Brown, Rugman and Verbeke

patibility can be analysed more objectively. Therefore, it is predicted that quadrant 3 joint ventures will probably fail whereas quadrant 2 ones may still be successful.

The literature reviewed in this paper can now be summarised using this matrix. The article numbers from the reference list are used to indicate the primary focus of the key argument (implicit or explicit) in each contribution made to explain joint venture failure. For example, the writers stressing transaction cost reasons for failure, such as Buckley and Casson and Harrigan, are positioned in quadrant 2. Writers emphasising cultural differences as sufficient reasons for failure, such as de Mente, Pucik, and Wright, are in quadrant 3. Finally, writers emphasising both economic and cultural factors, such as Hamel, Doz and Prahalad, McMillan, and Westney, are in quadrant 4.

As mentioned earlier, it may be extremely difficult in practice to unbundle economic and cultural reasons for failure, but this should not prevent researchers from attempting to identify the prime source of failure (locating the venture in quadrant 2 or 3) and recognising that the interaction between economic and cultural elements may lead the venture to shift to quadrant 4.

MAKING JOINT VENTURES SUCCEED

Hamel, Doz and Prahalad (1986) suggest that the problem of cheating by Japanese joint venture partners should be dealt with by limiting ventures to short-term arrangements. Several of the factors discussed in this paper suggest that this solution will not work. First, Japanese manager appear to be more comfortable with long-term relationship. Short-term arrangements therefore may arouse negative feelings. Second, a short-term arrangement is apt to have low status within the Japanese parent, which means that the best personnel will not be sent to operate it (Puchik, 1988). Third, a short-term arrangement usually carries with it a smaller stream of potential benefits than a long-term arrangement. This being so, neither side will be as motivated to forbear because the immediate benefits from cheating may match or exceed the expected benefits of cooperation. For this reason, short-term arrangements are far more likely to evoke competition than cooperation.

In order for joint ventures between Japanese and Western firms to succeed, it will be necessary to improve management's information about their partners. This requires mutual understanding of each other's economic and cultural philosophies and practices, (Adler and Doktor, 1986). Acquiring such knowledge, let alone understanding it well enough to embed it into the organisational structures of the two sets of multinational enterprises, will be a major challenge. One step towards success would be to advance management perceptions beyond a recogni-

ASIA PACIFIC JOURNAL OF MANAGEMENT   VOL. 6, NO. 2

tion of simplistic country-specific factors towards a more detailed understanding of the precise nature of each other's corporate culture.

REFERENCES

Adler, N. J. and Doktor, R. in collaboration with S. G. Redding (1986), "From the Atlantic to the Pacific century: Cross-cultural Management Reviewed", *Journal of Management,* 12 (2), pp. 295 – 318.

Beamish, P. W. (1988), "Equity Joint Ventures and the Theory of the Multinational Enterprise", Chapter 7 of *Multinational Joint Ventures in Developing Countries,* London: Routledge.

Buckley, P.J. and Casson, M. (1988), "A Theory of Cooperation in International Business", *Management International Review,* 28, Special Issue, pp. 19 – 38

Contractor, F. and Lorange, P. (1988), "Competition vs. Cooperation: a Benefit-cost Framework for Choosing Between Fully-owned Investments and Cooperative Relationships", *Management International Review,* 28, Special Issue, pp. 5 – 18.

de mente, Boys (1968), *Japanese Manners and Ethics in Business,* Tokyo: East Asia Publishing Co.

_____ , (1972), *How To Do Business in Japan,* Los Angeles: Centre for International Business.

Eason, Harry (1986), "In Japan, Make Haste Slowly", *Nations's Business,* May, p. 48.

Ghemawat, P. Porter, M.E. and Rawlinson, R.A. (1986), "Patterns of International Coalition Activity", in Porter, M.E. (ed.), *Competition in Global Industries.* Boston: Harvard Business School Press.

Hamel, G., Doz, Y. and Prahalad, C. (1986), *Strategic Partnerships; Success or Surrender?* Paper presented at the Rutgers/Wharton Colloquium on Cooperative Strategies in International Business, October.

Harrigan, K. R. (1988), "Strategic Alliances and Partner Asymmetries", *Management International Review,* 28, Special Issue, pp. 53 – 72

Hergert, M. and Morris, D. (1988), "Trends in Collaborative Agreements", in F. Contractor and P. Lorange (eds.), *Cooperative Strategies in International Business,* Lexington, MA: Lexington Books.

Hladik, K. J. (1985), *International Joint Ventures,* Lexington, MA: Lexington Books.

Hofstede, G. (1980), *Culture's Consequences: International Differences in Work-Related Values,* Beverly Hills: Sage.

Japanese Joint Ventures: Brown, Rugman and Verbeke

Hull, F., Slowinski, G., Wharton, R. and Azumi, K. (1988), "Strategic Partnerships Between Technological Entrepreneurs in the United States and Large Corporations in Japan and the United States", in F. Contractor and P. Lorange (eds.), *Cooperative Strategies in International Business*. Lexington, MA: Lexington Books.

Lrosch, J. (1987), "Baseball and Besuboru: a Metaphor for U.S.-Japanese Misunderstanding", *Speaking of Japan,* Nov. 1, pp. 15 – 20.

McMillan, C. J. (1984), *The Japanese Industrial System,* Berlin: Walter de Gruyter.

Ohmae, K. (1985), *Triad Power*, New York: The Free Press.

Porter, M. E. (1980), *Competitive Strategy*, New York: The Free Press.

Pucik, V. (1988), "Strategic Alliances with the Japanese: Implications for Human Resource Management", in F. Contractor and P. Lorange (eds.), *Cooperative Strategies in International Business*, Lexington, MA: Lexington Books.

Reich, R. B., and Mankin, E.D. (1986), "Joint Ventures with Japan Give Away Out Future", *Harvard Business Review*, March – April, pp. 78 – 86.

Rugman, A. M. (1981), *Inside the Multinationals: The Economics of Internal Markets,* New York: Columbia University Press.

_____ , (1985), "Internalization is Still a General Theory of Foreign Direct Investment", *Weltwirtschaftliches Archiv,* September, pp. 570 – 575.

Williamson, O. E. (1985), "The Economic Institutions of Capitalism", New York: The Free Press.

Westney, E. (1988), "Domestic and Foreign Learning Curves in Managing International Cooperative Strategies", in F. Contractor and P. Lorange (eds.), *Cooperative Strategies in International Business,* Lexington, MA: Lexington Books.

Wolf, M. (1983), "The Japanese Conspiracy", New York: Empire Books.

Wright, R. W. (1979), "Joint Venture Problems in Japan", *Columbia Journal of World Business,* 14 (1), pp. 25 – 31.

PART II

STRATEGIC TRADE POLICY AND SHELTER THEORY

[7]

Journal of International Economic Studies (1989) No. 3, 139–152
© 1989 The Institute of Comparative Economic Studies. Hosei University

STRATEGIC MANAGEMENT AND TRADE POLICY

Alan M. Rugman* and Alain Verbeke**

*Professor of International Business, University of Toronto
** Visiting Research Fellow, Centre for International Business Studies, Dalhousie University

In this article a new framework is developed to analyze and assess strategies of business firms towards their environment. It is argued that four basic options are available to strategic planners as guiding mechanisms for firm behavior. The nature of the strategies developed (efficiency or non-efficiency-related) and the channels used to pursue these strategies (market environment or non-market environment) constitute the two variables used to classify firm behavior. The fourth option, pursuing non-efficiency strategies through positioning the firm in its non-market environment, is analyzed in depth in relation to government trade policies. Emphasis is put on the interactions between firms engaging in the fourth option and government which pursues economic objectives through the use of a 'technical track' (bureaucracy). It is shown that business firms can generate unintended trade policy outputs through influencing government, hence generating an ineffective trade policy. This situation is illustrated by the 'Softwood Lumber Case', whereby U.S. business firms have used the technical track to induce trade policy measures which are in contradiction with U.S. trade policy objectives.

1. Introduction

At the frontier between economics, political science and management there is a new business literature being developed which addresses the issue of how a firm interacts with government policy makers. This literature has its roots in the industrial organization side of economics, the area of conflict resolution and lobbying activities in political science and the concepts of strategic planning in management. The ideas from this literature have a useful application in the world of international business, particularly in the case of trade policy.

Critical in this new literature is analysis of the manner in which the strategic planners of the firm react to environmental charges, such as new directions in government policy. Porter (1980 and 1985) has developed a paradigm of three generic strategies which capture the essentials of the firm's competitive strategies. These strategies are: cost competition, product differentiation and focus. All of these are basically efficiency strategies subject to exogeneous policy induced environmental constraints.

In this article we take these principles of strategic management and apply them to trade policy. Today many companies are using the policy measures of their government as a type of competitive strategy, what Boddewyn (1986) calls the "fourth generic". While Boddewyn discusses the international political strategy of multinational enterprises, in this article we focus upon one particular type of political action, namely trade policy, as it can be used by managers of both international and import competing firms. We have in mind, for example, the use of countervailing duty and anti-dumping trade remedy laws and procedures now enacted by most

Alan M. RUGMAN and Alain VERBEKE

industrialized countries following adoption in 1979 of the FATT subsidies code. In particular, we consider the use by American firms of the procedures available under the U.S. trade law process. It has been demonstrated by Rugman and Anderson (1987), for example, that between 1979 and 1986 over 50 separate actions were brought by U.S. producers against rival Canadian traders.

The major contribution of this paper is our focus upon the interactive nature of trade policy formulation and implementation. We argue that the strategic planners of the firm not only react to (exogeneous) trade policy measures but actively lobby and interact with government bureaucrats and politicians as a means of endogenizing the political process to their own advantage. In this manner trade policy moves from the realm of the neutral state and the technical administration of democratically determined laws and procedures, towards a more commercial and self-serving set of competitive entry barriers. This process serves to give some firms a competitive advantage in the short-run. However, due to the nature of such non-tariff barriers to trade (which, by definition, protect uncompetitive firms and industries at the expense of consumers and the long-run national interest) there is a problem facing the strategic planners of the firm. Their short-run success at achieving an entry barrier by protection usually results in the perpetuation or development of inefficiencies which can erode the long-run competitive edge of the firm.

2. Strategies of Business Firms

The strategies of business firms can be efficiency or non-efficiency oriented. We define efficiency strategies as all strategies that aim at achieving survival, profit and growth through (a) the provision of cheaper and/or better products and services to the firm's customer than those of potential competitors and (b) transaction cost minimizing behavior for the firm.

The competitive strengths of the firm flow from firm specific advantages and/or country specific advantages. Rugman (1981, 1986) develops such a model for multi-national enterprises where firm specific advantages (FSAs) are controlled by the firm and the country specific advantages (CSAs) are exogeneously determined by principles of comparative advantage.

Non-efficiency strategies can be defined as all strategies aimed at achieving survival, profit and growth or any other set of objectives through (a) other means than the provision of cheaper and/or better products and services to the firm's customers as compared with competitors, and (b) non-transaction cost minimizing behavior.

In cases where a non-efficiency strategy is pursued, a firm will only be able to achieve survival, profit and growth as a result of shelter from competitive pressures. One method to shelter the firm is through the development of strategies to secure trade barriers against rival (foreign) companies. Another method is by forming a cartel, a form of "natural" shelter, in contrast to the trade protection. which is a form of "unnatural" shelter, in the spirit of Rugman (1981). It could evne seek to eliminate competition altogether. by obtaining a monopoly.

Another possibility is that a set of objectives other than survival. profit and growth is being pursued. Examples include company compliance with public policy objectives of maintaining high (inefficient) employment levels, sustaining declining industries or the exporting sector, and increasing income levels in underdeveloped

STRATEGIC MANAGEMENT AND TRADE POLICY

regions. In such cases the achievement of low costs or uniqueness of the products and services provided may be unimportant for the firms involved.

The strategic planners can use two 'channels' to implement their strategies, namely, by positioning the firm in its market environment (coping with market forces) or by positioning the firm in its non-market environment (coping with non-market forces). The non-market environment consists of government(s) and pressure groups.

Recognizing these disparate strategies, to be pursued by the strategic planners of business firms and the channels used to achieve them, four basic options can be distinguished, as shown in Diagram 1.

3. The Four Options for Strategic Planners

Diagram 1 identifies the four basic options that can be considered for selection by the strategic planners. An important point is that policy makers in business firms may actually maximize their utility by pursuing non-efficiency strategies; from their point of view the third and fourth option may be rational action alternatives, especially in the short run.

Option 1: The strategic planners can opt to pursue efficiency strategies through positioning the firm in its market environment. Economic theory describes and analyzes such behavior. Well known examples are the three generic strategies of Porter (1980), namely cost leadership, differentiation and focus, and the transaction cost theory of Williamson (1975), (1985), whereby firms internalize to respond to market imperfections and transaction costs. In both cases economics-based strategies are developed to cope with competitors, providers of inputs and buyers of outputs. Porter also discusses strategies towards so called substitutes and potential entrants. In his framework a firm can and should obtain competitive advantages as a result of pursuing efficiency strategies. The cost-leadership strategy is a self-evident example of efficiency. seeking through the process of price competition to develop the potential to earn rents. The differentiation and focus strategies also have the same efficiency implication. In these cases identical goods and services (including all characteristics of the goods and services) cannot be provided. by rival producers. to the customers at similar price levels. Again this leads to entry barriers and the chance to earn rents. It is our contention that all business firms should strive to be successful in this first option. to the extent that existing competitive advantages inevitably turn out to be of a short-run nature. ultimately eroded by the gale of competitive forces. especially given the high degree of interdependence in today's global economy.

Option 2: The firm's policy makers can still pursue economic efficiency, but their strategies emphasize the issue of coping with non-market forces. Recent theories which analyze such strategies include the discussion by Doz (1986) and Mahini and Wells (1986), of the behavior of multinational enterprises towards sovereign host country governments. In order to achieve their objectives such firms have to comply with, or are influenced by government regulation and intervention. Firms may also be involved in bargaining with governments, or in exercising corporate social responsibility to meld private sector economic objectives into public sector social and political values. It is self-evident that options 1 and 2 go together

STRATEGIC MANAGEMENT AND TRADE POLICY

well. and it will depend on the characteristics of the firm's transactions which option will dominate. For example. if nearly all sales are made to government-controlled customers. as is sometimes the case with aircraft. telecommunications equipment and electrical power systems. the second option may be extremely important for the firms involved. Similarly, government procurement, defence and other public sector activities will require that firms operate according to the second option.

Option 3: The strategic planners can be pursuing non-efficiency strategies even when positioning the firm in its market environment. The choice of this option can often be observed in declining industries, whereby x-inefficient firms (Leibenstein. 1976) themselves (rather than governments) try to limit competitive pressures through cartel or other collusive agreements.

It should be emphasised that the third option is an unstable one, especially in global industries where cartels and monopolies are inevitably eroded. Unless the firms choosing this option are granted permanent protection by government. in which case they simultaneously engage in the fourth option. they will be forced in the long run to shift to the first option or to exit.

It is probable that firms attempt to shift to the third option only because they have been unsuccessful in the first two options. They have become firms whose survival, profit and growth are endangered. In this case they often cease to pursue strategies of low cost and uniqueness of products and services. They attempt to engage in strategies to restrict competition. for example backward integration to limit the access of efficiency seeking competitors to raw materials. Another common tactic is to head to the seats of political power and argue for government protection in order to maintain employment and output in the face of "unfair" (subsidized) foreign competition. This puts the firm into the fourth option.

In empirical investigations it may become very difficult to distinguish transaction cost minimizing behavior (low cost objective, first option) from the use of asset-power to close markets (elimination of efficiency-seeking competitors by firms engaging in the third option). Dunning and Rugman (1985) have explored this distinction for multinational enterprises. An evaluation on a case by case basis may then be necessary to establish whether firms are pursuing the first or the third option.

Option 4: Finally, the strategic planners can pursue non-efficiency strategies through positioning the firm in its non-market environment. This option includes requesting and influencing governments to raise barriers against competition or to receive subsidies and other advantages. Examples would be attempts to seek tariff or non-tariff protection and public subsidies for sunset industries. Recently, Porter (1986) has recognized the existence of such protected market strategies in global industries. but he has not performed an in-depth analysis of the resulting relationships between firms and government. It is clear that this option. as well as the third option. invariably diminishes social welfare and efficiency although both strategies may be viable for the firm.

In practical situations. problems may arise when trying to make a distinction between the second and fourth option. There are a number of situations whereby efficiency seeking firms need to interact with governments. Such government intervention can then lead to a decrease of costs for the firm. Examples are: the alloca-

STRATEGIC MANAGEMENT AND TRADE POLICY

tion of subsidies and special tax concessions and other advantages to multinationals that set up a subsidiary in a host country; the provision of health and welfare services which help raise the value of human capital; public insurance for business transactions; the use of diplomatic representation in foreign countries for purposes of export promotion; and the use of special public assistance development and infrastructure projects.

All of these events require the firm to develop strategies toward government. All can result in a decline of transaction costs for the firm. In contrast, the fourth option is designed to shelter the firm through government intervention and protection. This (inefficient) process serves to increase transaction costs for competitors without doing anything to substantially reduce the transaction costs for the protected firm(s). Thus the fourth option is only a short run pallative for the long run ills of the firm.

From this perspective only in-depth process analyses of firm behavior can allow a clear distinction to be made between actions aimed at reducing transaction costs and actions where the prime objective is to raise these costs for competitors. In practice it is not easy to determine if the award to one firm by the government of monopolistic rights to develop a scarce resource, as a result of lobbying activities, should be interpreted as an attempt to reduce transaction costs for the firm or to raise transaction costs for (potential) competitors: in both cases entry barriers are generated for competitors.

Once a business firm engages in the second or fourth option it becomes important to influence trade policy, as it determines to a large extent the level of transaction costs for foreign competitors. Trade policy is also of major importance for determining the level of transaction costs for the business firm when penetrating foreign markets. The second option consists of using trade policy in order to decrease transaction costs for the firm, while the fourth option is primarily aimed at increasing relative transaction costs for competitors.

4. Trade Policy Formulation

The trade policy objectives of government are broad and may include both economic and non-economic objectives. Economic objectives are concerned with creating and maintaining national wealth and with its distribution, attributes which have so far been the focus of the discussion. Non-economic objectives relate to the government's provision of defence and security; cultural and political autonomy; social programs; and related aspects of sovereignty.

National trade policy objectives can be identified by analyzing policy documents and policy statements. Regardless of the objectives pursued, two structural instruments can be used to carry out trade policy, namely a political track, which is directly and formally accountable to political constituencies, and a technical track (or bureaucracy). In terms of a trade policy formulation Finger et. al. (1982) have made such a distinction between the political track in the United States (where the President and Congress are involved) and the technical track (where the U.S. International Trade Commission and the Department of Commerce administer U.S. trade laws in a supposedly non political manner).

Alan M. RUGMAN and Alain VERBEKE

It will be apparent that this distinction assumes that Congress acts as a broker for various regional and sectoral interests, generating trade laws which are somehow in the national interest of the United States. Only if trade laws formulation can be somehow removed from political lobbying does it make sense to have a technical track. using economics-based criteria and legal procedures to implement such a policy. Unfortunately, it is in practice difficult to realize this distinction, as documented by Baldwin (1986), Lenway (1983) and Rugman and Anderson (1987).

A further problem is that the public choice literature in economics suggests that politicians act out of self-interest, for example to maximize the probabilities of being re-elected. The work by Buchanan and Tullock (1962) Tullock (1965, Niskanen (1971), Breton (1974), Mueller (1979) and others in this field yields many examples of self-serving behavior by both politicians and bureaucrats. This calls into question the basic integrity of a brokerage function by the political system, and the ability of the technical track to administer laws and procedures, without becoming subject to outside influences. For the moment these problems will be placed on hold and the distinction between the political track and a workable technical track will be made.

Four options are available to government when formulating trade policy. These require choosing between economic or non-economic objectives and choosing the structural instruments to attain these objectives. These four options are represented in Diagram 2.

Three problems exist with respect to pursuing national economic objectives (the first and second option).

First. even in the presence of clear economic objectives, the actual activities of subsystems in the political and technical track may completely deviate from them. The resulting ineffectiveness of trade policy will not necessarily be currected because society has other criteria than merely trade policy criteria on its agenda. In other words. ineffective policies may be pursued because they generate high yields to specific pressure groups while their costs are spread over all taxpayers and consumers. Examples of such protectionist policies whereby pressure groups generate tariff barriers are given in Ethier (1983) and Baldwin (1986). Society at large does not have access to sufficient information to perform an objective assessment of trade policy activities. nor does it possess clear yardsticks to assess the impact of trade policy.

Second the political track in turn cannot be expected to eliminate ineffectiveness in all circumstances. By definition it is subject to the pressure of political constituencies. whereby some constituencies may have more power to influence behavior of the political track than others as demonstrated by Lindblom (1977) and Olson (1965). especially if its members are primarily guided by vote maximizing considerations (Arnold (1981). Mayhew (1974)). An application of this to trade policy can be found in Caves (1976). In this case the pursuit of non-economic objectives may well dominate actual trade policy activities. in spite of the existence of economic objectives for trade policy. So why are economic objectives formulated in the first place? The main reason is that policy formulation and implementation are distinct activities.

Policy formulation is a process which in many cases is not heavily influenced by specific pressure groups, except in the authorization stage (voting of a law), but even then the influence of specific groups is primarily restricted to generating positive or negative votes from the subsystems in the political track. In addition, specific pressure groups are less concerned with general policy objectives than with concrete policy measures (implementation stage), which they may then still try to influence, especially since the implications of trade policy objectives will not always be clear to them. Finally, in a dynamic perspective, the possibility cannot be excluded that specific pressure groups (such as policy makers in a declining industry) arise when general trade policy objectives already exist. In this case it may be much easier to influence the implementation of trade policy than to change its formulation.

The authority of the political track over the technical track can sometimes be extremely limited, namely when neither extensive cultural controls nor structural controls can be exerted on behavior and only outputs can be controlled. Even then, the political track will often not be able to monitor all attributes of the technical track's outputs (which is a problem of comparative ignorance), so that the latter will be able to engage in discretionary behavior (Lindsay, 1976) (Brown and Jackson, 1982).

Finally, the political track, being guided to a large extent by vote maximizing considerations, may want to use the technical track as a 'lightning conductor'. If the political track wishes to avoid being put under continuous pressure by specific constituencies that demand "non-economic" trade policy measures, then a meaningful alternative consists of completely delegating the implementation of trade policy to a public body that does not formally depend on a specific 'clientele'. As a result, the political track can avoid taking decisions with an uncertain outcome in terms of gaining or losing votes.

Third, the technical track, in cases where it is charged with implementing trade policy, may not, in practice, be able to pursue official trade policy objectives. Its activities can only be monitored in a very limited way by the political track, so that bureau managers may, to a large extent, pursue their own objectives. Further, it may be put under pressure by the political track to perform activities which are conflicting with formal trade policy objectives. Finally, it may be influenced by its 'clientele'. Although the technical track is not directly accountable to political sonstituencies, it may well engage in collusive behavior with specific pressure groups, as when it seeks to preserve its members' positions and budgets. Such behavior can be expected if the technical track is used by the political track as a lightning conductor and pressure groups have easy access to it.

Although the political track may choose the first and second option, or a combination of both in its policy formulation, the actual implementation of trade policy may deviate from that which could be expected on the basis of rational trade policy objectives. A distinction should thus be made between intended and unintended policy outputs, whereby the former are in accordance with the national trade policy objectives, while the latter are not. A trade policy can be called "effective" if only intended policy outputs are observed. Ineffectiveness will appear whenever the outputs of some activities are unintended.

Finally, particular attention should be paid to the activities of the technical track, precisely because it is not formally responsible to political constituencies. In

Alan M. RUGMAN and Alain VERBEKE

practice it may primarily serve the needs of specific pressure groups. It is then important to establish whether a high sensitivity to clientele needs is consistent with national trade policy objectives or not.

5. Influencing Trade Policy: The Softwood Lumber Case

On the basis of the analysis performed in the previous sections, we can now examine the strategies of business firms aimed at influencing government trade policies. An important question to be answered is whether firms pursue the second or the fourth option (outlined in Diagram 1). If the formulation of trade policy by government is assumed to be given at a specific point in time (Diagram 2), then an analysis can be made of the influence of business firms on the activities of the political and technical track, in terms of generating intended or unintended policy outputs. Particular attention must be paid to influence exerted on the technical track that leads to the creation of unintended policy outputs. Policy improving measures should be taken if firms engaged in the fourth option generate high unintended policy outputs through influencing the activities of the technical track. In that case business firms guided by non-efficiency strategies help in creating and sustaining ineffective trade policies.

In this section we shall be concerned with the case where government is supposed to pursue economic trade policy objectives (formulation stage), but whereby some ineffectiveness can be observed in the implementation stage. This occurs when business firms engaged in the fourth option (Diagram 1) try to generate unintended trade policy activities and outputs and when the behavior of the political and technical track is partly guided by non-economic considerations.

As an example of the failure of the technical track and the politicization of U.S. trade policy leading to unintended and ineffective policy outcomes it is worthwhile to briefly review the softwood lumber countervailing duty cases of 1983 and 1986. In both cases the U.S. lumber industry, mainly in the Northwestern Pacific states alleged that rival Canadian producers were receiving government subsidies (in the form of low provincial stumpage rates) in the production of timber, giving them an unfair cost advantage. Consequently the U.S. industry requested that countervailing duties be imposed to offset the alleged degrees of subsidization.

Since under U.S. trade law the importance of countervailing duties requires purely technical track investigations, there is no room for the President or Congress to be formally involved in the procedures. The U.S. International Trade Commission (ITC) investigates and votes on material injury while the Commerce Department undertakes a separate investigation to determine the nature and amount of the subsidy, and the extent of the countervailing duty to be levied on future imports of the product. In 1983 the ITC voted material injury, as it now tends to do in the great majority of cases brought before it. However, Commerce determined that the Canadian provinces (which own the timber) set their stumpage rates in such a manner that they were "generally available" to all users of timber products, that is, there was no direct export subsidy to the softwood lumber industry.

Therefore the 1983 case was lost on technical grounds and that should have been the end of the matter. However, the U.S. lumber industry kept the issue alive by

STRATEGIC MANAGEMENT AND TRADE POLICY

lobbying in Congress and various bills were presented which would have allowed the United States to challenge the resource pricing policies of sovereign foreign governments. In particular. the Gibbons bill of 1986 contained provisions which would have imposed tariffs to offset the alleged subsidies received by West Coast Canadian lumber producers.

In mid 1986 a second countervailing duty action against Canadian softwood lumber was introduced. Again the ITC voted material injury but this time the Commerce Department. for the first-time. apparently bowed to political pressure from the U.S. industry and in its preliminary decision in October it reversed its 1983 ruling on general availability. In doing so the principle of general availability. a basic tenet of the GATT Subsidies Code (used as the rationale for U.S. trade law). was violated and a dangerous precedent was created which could affect the internal resource pricing policies of sovereign governments.

In order to avoid the second and final stage of the Commerce Department ruling. the Canadian federal government (in accord with the provinces and industries involved) reached a political compromise with the U.S. administration. whereby Canada agreed to impose an export tax equivalent to the fifteen percent countervail duty ruled by Commerce in its October report. This accommodation raised a political storm in Canada and it threatened, for a time. to disrupt the bilateral negotiations for a comprehensive free trade area.

Within the context of this article the softwood lumber case yields the following insights into the process of trade policy formulation and implementation.

First, in Diagram 1, the U.S. lumber industry is adopting the fourth option. using the non-market environment to pursue a non-efficiency strategy. It might be argued by some economists that the use of countervailing duties to offset a foreign subsidy is actually an efficiency-based strategy. This assumes that the foreign subsidy is purely a technical distortion and that domestic producers are otherwise operating efficiently. Unfortunately the picture is more clouded than this: in particular, a failure of the U.S. technical track procedures is that none of the subsidies being received by the U.S. producers are even investigated. The technical track is a one-eyed jack.

Second. in terms of Diagram 2. policy formulation of the U.S. administration. and even of Congress. involves mainly economic objectives. Many documents state that the United States is a free trade nation and that it supports the objectives of GATT in liberalizing trade. The United States has also adopted a technical track process to implement its trade policy, so it believes itself to be in quadrant 2.

Third, it is apparent that the actual implementation of U.S. trade policy generates high unintended policy outputs by the technical track (although some observers still believe this is not the case). It could then be argued that the degree of import restraints would have been much higher in the absence of GATT (Lenway. 1983). but there have been. in practice. unintended non-economic policy outcomes from the technical track procedures. The ITC and Commerce Department have both deviated from the technical track in the administration of trade law actions against Canada in recent years. In particular. proper economic analysis is not used by the ITC in voting material injury. This was demonstrated in the fresh Atlantic groundfish case of 1986 when injury was voted despite statistically insignificant question-

Alan M. RUGMAN and Alain VERBEKE

naire data and invalid analysis, as shown in Chapter 4 of Rugman and Anderson (1987).

Finally, it should be emphasized that the tendency of U.S. trade policy to be characterized by unintended policy outcomes is due to an excessive responsiveness to pressure groups. The softwood lumber case is a classic example of the abuse of the technical track because of its responsiveness to clientele needs. Yet it is not in the long-run interests of business firms to seek the protection of the fourth option of Diagram 1. Hence, it is now necessary to reform the administration of U.S. trade policy so that the present ineffective decision structure is eliminated and implementation of U.S. policy conforms with quadrant 2 of Diagram 2.

The lessons of the softwood lumber case are as follows. First, the U.S. technica. track has now become politicized in both the decisions of the ITC and now in the Commerce Department. It has long been recognized that the ITC was mainly influenced by Congress (which is very responsive to pressure groups) but the fact that the Commerce Department is part of the executive branch brought some balance to the technical track. Now it is apparent that Congress has control of the execution of U.S. trade policy and uses the technical track as a rationale to implement inefficient policy measures. Second, it has been demonstrated that U.S. industries can achieve protection through the technical track procedures, even when problems arise for bilateral economic relations. Unintended policy outcomes abound.

This is neither effective, nor is it in the long-run interests of either U.S. protected industries or the nation itself. The failure of the U.S. technical track is also a major problem for the trading partners of the United States. It is a situation where there are no winners and a process which is the problem, not the solution to "freer" U.S. – World trade.

6. Conclusions

It has been demonstrated here that strategic management in business firms interacts strongly with government policy, especially in the international business area, where trade policy was used as an example of their interrelationship. It is our contention that any analysis of strategic management activities towards government should make a distinction between behavior guided by efficiency and non-effieicney strategies. Influencing trade policy may be extremely important for business firms, as it helps to determine the level of transaction costs they and their rivals face when operating in an international environment. Distinguishing efficiency from non-efficiency seeking behavior is crucial, since, in spite of clear economic trade policy objectives, firms engaged in 'the fourth option' may generate unintended trade policy outputs. They do this by abusing the political and/or technical track, especially when the latter becomes susceptible to clientele needs. From the point of view of the strategic planners of a firm the fourth option may be a rational short term action alternative, but the result of this process is the generation of ineffective trade policies which can only be corrected through institutional reforms.

Diagram 1

THE CORPORATE STRATEGY MATRIX

Corporate Strategies

	Efficiency	Non-Efficiency
Market Environment	1	3
Non-market Environment	2	4

Channels to Achieve Strageties

Alan M. RUGMAN and Alain VERBEKE

Diagram 2

FORMULATION OF TRADE POLICY

Government Objectives

		Economic	Non-Economic
Political Track		1	3
Technical Track		2	4

Government's Structural Instruments to carry out trade policy

STRATEGIC MANAGEMENT AND TRADE POLICY

References

Arnold, D.S., "Legislators, Bureaucrats and Locational Decisions," *Public Choice*, 37:7 (1981): 107-132.

Baldwin Richard E., *The Political Economy of U.S. Import Policy* (Cambridge Mass.: MTT Press, 1985).

Boddewyn, Jean J., "International Political Strategy: A Fourth Generic Strategy?". Unpublished paper. Baruch College, City University of New York: 1986.

Breton, Albert, *The Economic Theory of Representative Government* (Chicago, Ill: Aldine, 1974).

Brown, C.V. and P.M. Jackson, *Public Sector Economics* (Oxford: Martin Robertson, 1982).

Buchanan, James M. and Gordon Tullock. *The Calculus of Consent* (Ann Arbor, Mich.: University of Michigan Press, 1962).

Caves Richard E., "Economic Models of Political Choice: Canada's Tariff Structure", *Canadian Journal of Economics*. 9:2 (May 1976): 278-300.

Doz, Yves L., *Strategic Management in Multinational Companies* (Oxford: Pergamon Press, 1985).

Dunning, John H. and Alan M. Rugman. "The Influence of Hymer's Dissertation on the Theory of Foreign Direct Investment," *American Economic Review*. 75:2 (May 1985): 228-232.

Ethier Wilfred. *Modern International Economics* (New York: Norton, 1983).

Finger, J.M., H. Keith Hall and Douglas Nelson. "The Political Economy of Administered Protection," *American Economic Review*. 72:3 (June 1982): 452-456.

Leibenstein, Harvey. *Beyond Economic Man* Cambridge, Mass.: Harvard University Press, 1976).

Lenway, Stefanie A., "The Impact of American Business on International Trade Policy," *Research in Corporate Social Performance and Policy*, Vol. 5 (Greenwich, Conn: JAI Press, 1983).

Lindblom, Charles E., Politics and Markets. *The World's Political-Economic Systems* (New York: Basic Books, 1977).

Lindsay, Cotton. "A Theory of Government Enterprise." *Journal of Political Economy* 84:5 (October 1976): 1067-1078.

Mahini, Amir and Louis T. Wells Jr. "Government Relations in the Global Firm", in Michael E. Porter. *Competition in Global Industries* (Cambridge, Mass.: Harvard Business School Press, 1986): 297-314.

Mayhew, D., *Congress: The Electoral Connection* (New Haven: Yale University Press, 1974).

Mueller, Dennis. *Public Choice* (Cambridge: Cambridge University Press, 1979).

Niskanen, W., *Bureaucracy and Representative Government* (Chicago, Ill.: Aldine Atherton, 1971).

Olson, Mancur. *The Logic of Collective Action. Public Goods and the Theory of Groups* (Cambridge-Mass.: Harvard University Press, 1965).

Porter, Michael E., *Competitive Strategy: Techniques for Analyzing Industries and Competitors* (New York: The Free Press MacMillan, 1980).

Alan M. RUGMAN and Alain VERBEKE

Porter, Michael E., *Competitive Advantage: Creating and Sustaining Superior Performance* (New York: The Free Press MacMillan, 1985).

Porter, Michael E. (ed.) *Competition in Global Industries* (Cambridge, Mass.: Harvard Business School Press 1986).

Rugman, Alan M., *Inside the Multinatinals* (London: Croom Helm and New York: Columbia University Press, 1981).

Rugman, Alan M. and Andrew Anderson, *Administered Protection in America*. (London: Croom Helm and New York: Methuen, 1987).

Rugman, Alan M., "National Strategies for International Competitiveness," *Issues in North American Trade and Finance, North American Economics and Finance Association*. Proceedings, 6th International Congress (Montreal, 1986): 315-326.

Tullock, Gordon, *The Politics of Bureaucracy* (Washington D.C., Public Affairs Press, 1965).

Williamson, Oliver E., *Markets and Hierarchies: Analysis and Antitrust Implications* (New York: The Free Press MacMillan, 1975).

Williamson, Oliver E., *The Economic Institutions of Capitalism* (New York: The Free Press MacMillan, 1985).

Mintzberg's Intended and Emergent Corporate Strategies and Trade Policy

ALAN M. RUGMAN
ALAIN VERBEKE
University of Toronto

Abstract
Earlier work by Mintzberg has distinguished between intended and emergent strategies. This work is extended in an international dimension and a new analytical framework is developed to assess the interactions between firms and government in the formulation and implementation of trade policy. The concept of "shelter" is introduced and analyzed. The model is applied to recent developments in U.S.-Canadian trade policy, especially the rise of U.S. "administered" protection as a type of strategy pursued by U.S. firms to erect entry barriers against foreign rivals.

Résumé
Mintzberg a fait une distinction entre les stratégies intentionnelles et les stratégies émergentes. Les résultats de ses recherches sont étendues ici en leur donnant une dimension internationale et un nouvel encadrement conceptuel est développé afin de pouvoir évaluer les interactions entre les entreprises et les pouvoirs publics dans le domaine de la formulation et réalisation de la politique commerciale. Le concept "d'abri artificiel" ("shelter") est introduit et analysé. Le modèle conceptuel est appliqué aux développements récents dans les échanges commerciaux bilatéraux, entre les États-Unis et le Canada, en particulier la montée du protectionnisme administratif aux États-Unis, qui est utilisé par certaines firmes Américaines comme un type de stratégie afin d'ériger des barrières d'entrée contre les concurrents étrangers.

The focus of this article is the manner in which firms influence national trade policies. The analysis presented differs in four ways from the usual treatment of trade policy in the literature on international strategic management.

First, public policy is regarded as a device through which the relative competitive position of different rivals can be altered. Hence, policy measures such as changes in trade barriers are not considered merely as exogenous factors, but as variables which firms can influence.[1]

Second, the concept of non-competitive strategy is introduced to describe corporate behaviour aimed at creating shelter. Shelter is defined as a government imposed entry barrier (such as tariff protection) which substitutes for the conventional entry barriers recognized in industrial economics theory. A crucial distinction is made between the use of government as (a) a tool to reduce costs and differentiate products and (b) a means of acquiring shelter to substitute for the firm's lack of capability to reduce cost or differentiate products. As explained in the next section of this article, only the latter constitutes a non-competitive strategy.[2]

Third, it will be shown that the demand for shelter very often is not an intended strategy of managers but constitutes

an emergent strategy, resulting from a firm's interactions with public agencies in the area of trade policy. In this context, the paradigm developed by Mintzberg et al. (1976), Mintzberg and McHugh (1985), and Mintzberg and Waters (1985) on the difference between intended and emergent strategies will be extended to model the interaction between firms and government.

Fourth, as public policy can be influenced by business firms, we argue that realized trade policies of governments often contain an important emergent component. In this context, firm behaviour may not only hinder the realization of intended trade policies of government but, if the actual trade policy structure can be influenced, there may not even be any linkage remaining between a government's intended trade policy and its actual realized strategy. The relevance of the new conceptual framework is demonstrated through an application to the issue of U.S. administered protection and recent U.S.-Canadian trade policy and corporate strategy.

Non-Competitive Strategies and Shelter

In this article, the view is taken that firms can adopt either a competitive strategy or a non-competitive strategy when coping with government. In the former case, government regulation is considered by firms as one of the forces driving industry competition. Here, firms attempt to improve or sus-

Address all correspondence to Alan M. Rugman, Ontario Centre for International Business, Faculty of Management, University of Toronto, 246 Bloor St. West, Toronto, Ontario M5S 1V4.

tain their economic performance (financial performance and/or market share) through strategic actions building upon their firm-specific advantages.[3] These are the corporation's distinctive competencies, i.e., skills and know-how with potential cost-reducing or differentiation-enhancing impacts.

Government policy is used as a tool to improve the corporation's distinctive competences (e.g., lobbying for subsidies to create new differentiation potential) or to improve the realization of the firms's strategy (e.g., using a country's defense ministry to improve the firm's differentiation effectiveness when selling arms abroad).[4] In this case, government policy could be considered as a complement to the corporation's present distinctive competences. The main intent of the firm's management is to create a superior performance through reducing costs or differentiating production. Such behaviour may lead to the erection of entry barriers for rival firms, but the main sources of the firm's competitiveness remain its distinctive competences. It is even possible for a firm to have a firm-specific advantage in its dealings with governments, thus improving its potential to reduce costs or differentiate products.[5]

In contrast, when engaging in a non-competitive strategy, the firm obtains shelter to substitute for cost-reducing or differentiation-enhancing capability. For example, government regulation can be used to prevent (potential) competitors from turning their distinctive competences into actual cost or differentiation advantages in the market place. Examples include tariffs and non-tariff barriers to trade.[6] This type of strategy clearly falls outside of Porter's (1980) and (1985) conventional analysis of competitive strategy.

It is our contention, based upon empirical research by such trade economists as Lavergne (1981), Pugel and Walter (1985), and Ray (1981), that the use of this non-competitive strategy against foreign rivals occurs primarily when firms need government shelter as a substitute for the lack of strong firm-specific advantages with cost-reducing or differentiation-enhancing potential. This will occur primarily when firms face strong import competition, do not benefit from easy access to foreign markets (through possessing production operations abroad), and have a low level of diversification. High diversification implies that a firm can adjust its product mix more easily than a specialized firm, when faced with strong import competition. Hence, it has an advantage of risk pooling. In addition, it could be argued that conflicts among different strategic business units in one firm will lead to a dominant position of the units with the strongest distinctive competences (Pugel & Walter, 1985). The reason for this situation is that the units opposed to developing a non-competitive strategy are likely to include those product areas on which the firm hopes to build its future growth.

The two alternatives described above, namely the use of government trade policy as a tool to complement the firm's distinctive competences or as a device to create shelter, have not yet been clearly identified in the strategy literature. For example, Porter (1986), in his discussion of global competition, only recognizes the existence of "protected market strategies," whereby comparatively inefficient firms secure survival through government trade protectionism. The case

whereby firms interact with government in the same way as they cope with the other forces driving industry competition is, however, not discussed. The latter mode of behavior would include, for example, the case whereby comparatively efficient firms lobby to eliminate trade barriers (Rugman & Anderson, 1987c; Rugman & Verbeke, 1989). It also includes the case whereby business-government relations improve a firm's international competitive position through state support that is selective and limited in time (Rugman & Verbeke, 1990a). However, two elements need to be recognized.

First, attempts to use government as a complement of the firm's distinctive competences may sometimes fail. Second, even if government is used as a tool to substitute for a company's firm-specific advantage, this may still be successful if shelter is used only in the short run and if the company's intent is to develop competitive strategies over a longer time period. This may occur when infant industry and old industry programmes are implemented effectively. See Rugman and Verbeke (1990a, 1990b) for a detailed analysis.

Emerging Corporate Strategies and Trade Policy

In contrast to existing models of the impact of business firms on trade policy, it is important to distinguish between intended and emerging patterns in both corporate behaviour and government trade policy, following Mintzberg and Waters (1985).

The institutional structure, within which trade policy is conducted, may stimulate firms to engage in a non-competitive strategy. The importance of organizational structure for the realization of intended strategies in firms has been recognized by several authors. See, for example, Bartlett (1986), Bower (1970), Burgelman and Sayles (1986), Mintzberg (1978, 1983, 1989), and Williamson (1985). It is our contention that similar conclusions will hold for strategies in government agencies (Peters, 1985; Sabatier, 1988).

The starting point of our framework is that a firm may "impose" an emergent strategy on government agencies, which is made possible through an institutional structure very receptive to clientele needs. Moreover, the firm's strategy may contain an important emergent component itself, if such behaviour is stimulated by the institutional structure within which trade policy is implemented.

The ideas above can be rephrased in terms of the conceptual framework developed by Mintzberg and Waters (1985). The formation of government policies mostly results from complex interactions among a multitude of actors (Allison, 1971). Nevertheless, there is often a clear distinction between the policy makers who formulate trade policy and those who implement it. Hence, "unconnected" strategies may develop, whereby an unadapted organizational structure allows specific public agencies to pursue objectives which are in contradiction to national trade policy formulation.

In other words, if policy formulation has the form of a mixed "umbrella" and "process" strategy whereby the political track (e.g., Congress) attempts to guide the strategy of the technical track (public bureaucracy) through merely defining legal boundaries (umbrella part of strategy) and elements of the institutional structure (process part of the strategy), an emergent trade policy may develop if specific trade policy implementing agencies are loosely coupled with trade policy formulators. The umbrella part of the political track's strategy aims at providing a set of rules within which the technical track may operate relatively freely. The process part of the strategy implies that the political track does not need to be involved in day-to-day decisions on specific cases, but decides upon the structure of the decision process cases need to go through before a final decision is reached. Thus, the unconnected trade policy behaviour of a technical track may directly contradict the mixed umbrella-process strategy of the political track.

It is not suggested here that the technical track in trade policy implementation consists merely of self-interested individuals, but that mixed motives, not all related to national trade policy objectives, may well guide their behaviour.[7] Thus, in terms of implementation structure, it is important to assess the technical track's "sensitivity" to clientele needs. This is extremely important as high sensitivity may possibly become a major source of unintended policy outcomes, ones that are in conflict with the intended national trade policy.

In addition, the existence of such an unadapted trade policy structure may stimulate firms to develop strategies aimed at using unconnected trade policies to their own advantage. In more concrete terms, this may imply that public agencies, which take a protectionist stand in trade policy and continuously favour inefficient domestic producers at the expense of their comparatively more efficient foreign rivals, may stimulate other domestic firms to engage in a non-competitive strategy.

Finally, unconnected strategies of public agencies themselves may then lead to the development of further inconsistencies between the intended policy of trade policy formulators and the institutional structure and legal boundaries meant to facilitate trade policy implementation. This will occur if trade policy implementing agencies may also affect the functioning of the structure and the legal boundaries within which they operate. This will be demonstrated in the next section, using the example of administered protection in the United States.

The essence of the conceptual framework developed above is captured in Figure 1 which represents the new view of strategy, extending the theory described in Mintzberg (1978), Mintzberg et al. (1976), Mintzberg and McHugh (1985), and Mintzberg and Waters (1985). Figure 2 extends this thinking to trade policy.

The New View of Trade Policy

Figure 1 demonstrates four points. First, any intended pattern in a stream of actions can only be realized in complex organizations through an appropriate organizational structure, e.g., Mintzberg's (1978, 1989) contingency approach to designing effective organizational configurations. This is represented by arrows 1 and 2b.

Second, although "structure" may be a major tool to "translate" intentions into actions, structure may sometimes hinder the realization of intentions. This is the problem of "administrative heritage" discussed by Bartlett (1986) and "inertia" as developed by Verbeke (1988). (See arrows 1 and 2a).

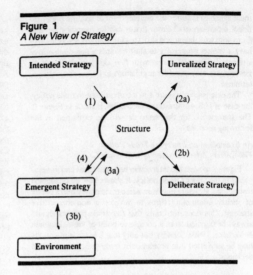

Figure 1
A New View of Strategy

Intended Strategy / Unrealized Strategy / (1) / (2a) / Structure / (4) / (2b) / (3a) / Emergent Strategy / Deliberate Strategy / (3b) / Environment

Third, the institutional structure of an organization may be influenced by "emergent" patterns of behaviour. For example, "unconnected" strategies of public agencies in the realm of trade policy can lead to the implementation of ineffective coordination and control systems (arrow 3a). In addition, structural changes may follow from "ad hoc" reactions to environmental pressures ("imposed" strategies: arrow 3b).

Fourth, structure may do two things. First, it may put boundaries on the extent to which emergent strategies have a chance of succeeding. An organization's administrative heritage may thus limit the possibilities for emergent strategies to be implemented. Second, it may stimulate the creation of emergent strategies. Such emergent strategies may either contribute to the organization's ultimate goals, or subvert its goals (Rugman & Verbeke, 1990a, 1990b).

In the context of trade policy, Figure 1 is of great use when analyzing the interactions between business firms and government. Three major points can be noted.

First, business firms may have intended strategies aimed at influencing government policy. An emergent strategy on the part of government with respect to trade policy is generated (arrows 3a and 3b) leading to unintended policy outcomes (arrow 2b) and the non-realization of trade policy goals (arrow 2a). The government's intended and realized strategies are completely different.

Second, a trade policy structure which permits emergent policies to develop (arrow 4) may stimulate business firms to develop a non-competitive strategy. This occurs especially if the implementation structure is very sensitive to pressure groups.

Third, the issue of how a corporation's organizational structure may affect a shift of behaviour from a competitive to a non-competitive strategy is not dealt with in this article, but a large body of literature demonstrates that influencing government agencies requires the development of specific organizational arrangements.[8] From that it can be hypothesized that firms with well developed skills in public affairs activities may have a greater propensity to shift towards a non-competitive strategy. In contrast, firms with few skills in dealing with government may consider regulations to be exogenously determined.

The extension of Figure 1 to a current issue in trade policy, the case of U.S. administered protection, is made in Figure 2. The framework for this analysis will be explained in the following sections.

An Example of an Emerging Trade Policy:
The Current Administration of U.S. Trade Law

Figure 2 models the interaction between firms and governments in the area of trade policy. It shows how an unadapted institutional structure may turn a free trade policy into a policy of shelter, stimulating firms to develop a non-competitive strategy. This does not imply that free trade policies should always be pursued from a normative point of view (Rugman & Verbeke, 1990a, 1990b), but only that free trade intentions may be subverted into protectionist trade policy actions and decisions.

This section demonstrates how a number of American firms have an intended strategy of creating trade barriers for foreign exporters through engaging in a non-competitive strategy. We draw upon extensive research related to administered protection, especially two examples analyzed in greater depth in Rugman and Anderson (1987b) and Rugman and Porteous (1988). Case studies involving Canada and the United States are considered. The first is an examination of the 1985-1986 countervail action on "Fresh Atlantic Groundfish from Canada," which resulted in a 5.82% duty. This study focuses on the role of the International Trade Commission (ITC). The second case study examines the 1986 "Softwood Lumber from Canada" countervail case, particularly those areas of the case which were the responsibility of the International Trade Administration (ITA) at the Department of Commerce. This case resulted in a 15% export tax being imposed by the Canadian government.

These cases are representative examples of over 50 Canada-U.S. trade remedy law investigations over the 1980-1987 period. For further discussion and evidence, see Rugman (1986a) and Rugman and Anderson (1987a). The present system of administered protection can be regarded as an example of political market failure, since specific interest groups stimulate the implementation of unconnected protec-

Figure 2
Intended and Emergent Corporate Strategies and Trade Policies

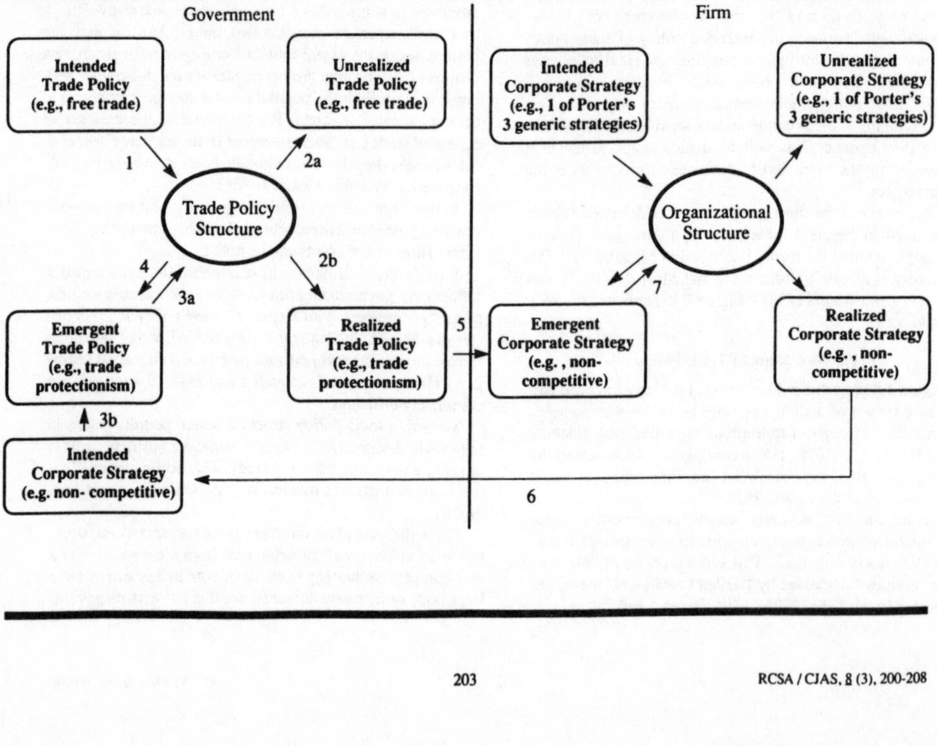

tionist policies which profit only themselves and are in contradiction with the U.S. intended policy of free trade.

Trade policy implementation was first delegated to a technical track by Congress in 1934, in order to shift the responsibility for trade policy measures to a forum in which no interest group bias would exist in favor of protectionism. In this sense, Congress insulated itself against its own tendency to subvert national free trade goals, which most members of Congress have supported over the last half century (Destler, 1986; Finger et al., 1982). In other words, an institutional structure was designed to facilitate the U.S. intended trade policy and prevent Congress from developing emergent policies of protectionism when pressured by interest groups (arrows 1 and 2b in Figure 1).

However, it was concluded by Rugman and Anderson (1987b), after a careful analysis of the decision making activities by the technical track in the Atlantic Groundfish case, that the rulings of "material" injury were a reaction to political pressure and were not based on the principles of comparative advantage. American business firms, pursuing a non-competitive strategy, were able to subvert intended U.S. free trade policy goals and develop an emergent policy of trade protectionism (arrows 3b and 3a). This process contrasts with statements which can be found in many other official U.S. government policy documents to the effect that the United States has an intended strategy of free trade.[9] For example, the United States adopted the "rules" of the General Agreement on Tariffs and Trade (GATT) at the Tokyo Round on subsidies and countervailing duties (Subsidies Code) and the 1967 GATT code on anti-dumping duties (which was revised to include similar rules as the Subsidies Code). These require an objective economic analysis for the test of "material injury" to the domestic industry in countervail and anti-dumping cases.

The GATT rules state that a causal link must be established between the subsidized imports and the alleged material injury. Yet Rugman and Anderson (1987b) found that the ITC did not establish this link at all when ruling on the Atlantic Groundfish case. Moreover, they concluded that the ITC reached its decision of material injury on inconclusive evidence and a superficial analysis of the economic factors it was supposed to consider. In fact, the ITC determination resulted from inefficient U.S. fishing companies with weak firm-specific advantages seeking shelter from competitors (arrow 3b). The resulting duty imposed against Canadian imports demonstrated that these firms had enough bargaining strength to influence decision making by the technical track and to impose an emergent technical track strategy of protectionism.

While the ITC was the agency with a problem in the first case, the ITA suddenly reversed its decision in the 1986 Canadian Softwood Lumber case, examined by Rugman and Porteous (1988). The ITA in this case broadened the definition of countervailable subsidy and narrowed that of general availability, threatening resource-based exports to the United States. A final negative countervailing duty determination was decided by the ITA on an identical Canadian Softwood Lumber case in 1983, but in 1986 the earlier ruling on general availability was reversed, leading to an affirmative preliminary countervailing duty determination. In 1983 the ITA found that

Canadian stumpage programs were available in Canada regardless of the industry or enterprise of the recipient and that any limitation on the industries actually using stumpage resulted only from the inherent characteristics of this natural resource.

The origin of the change in the ITA's approach can be traced to a decision by the U.S. Court of International Trade in October 1985 on a related appeal, the Cabot case. In that case, the Cabot Corporation, a U.S producer of carbon black, requested a review of a decision by the ITA dealing with the Mexican government's provision of carbon black feedstock and natural gas to two Mexican producers of carbon black. The ITA had ruled in 1983 that the government-set prices did not constitute a countervailable subsidy. The court decided, however, that the nominal general availability of benefits was not as important as the de facto benefits accruing to specific firms or industries. This decision was the basis of the surprising and politicized ITA 1986 ruling on softwood lumber, as detailed in Rugman and Porteous (1988) and in Percy and Yoder (1987).

The New View of Strategy and U.S. Trade Policy

The lessons of these two cases, within the context of the theoretical framework developed in this article, are as follows. First, in terms of Figure 2, the U.S. fishing and lumber industries are pursuing a non-competitive strategy towards trade policy (arrow 3b). Their prime purpose is to create shelter as a substitute for cost-reducing or differentiation-enhancing capability. In more general terms, it could be argued that their intended strategy is to create an emergent policy on the part of U.S. public agencies in favour of protectionism. This is possible because of the institutional structure of U.S. trade policy, which is very sensitive to clientele goals (arrow 4). The end result is that the intended U.S. free trade policy becomes unrealized while the realized trade policy is of a sheltering, non-free trade type (arrows 2a and 2b).

Second, the ineffective U.S. trade policy structure and the realized U.S. trade policy, characterized by strong unintended policy outcomes, pushes a growing number of weaker firms away from pursuing cost- or differentiation-based advantages (intended strategies) toward an emerging strategy of shelter (arrow 5). Why bother with pursuing a competitive strategy, as suggested, for example, by Porter (1980), if survival, profitability and growth can be obtained through protection (shelter-based)? In a dynamic perspective, this may then become a firm's intended strategy (arrow 6). This may even influence a firm's organizational structure. For example, departments may be set up and substantial managerial time may be devoted to lobbying for shelter (arrow 7).

Two puzzles exist: First, why do firms engaging in one of Porter's traditional strategies, or consumers affected by protectionism, not oppose protection? The main reason for this situation, following Olson (1965), is the fact that benefits of protection accrue to a small number of firms, while imposing only diffuse costs on most export industries or the general taxpayer and consumers.

Second, can the technical track through which trade policy is conducted really be considered as responsible for an "emergent" trade policy of protectionism, when Congress, i.e., the main trade policy formulating institution, is now, itself, in favour of increasing protectionism?[10] Congress has traditionally delegated the responsibilities of trade policy formulation and negotiation to the President but recently it has gradually regained its powers to make trade policy. The perceived lack of trust in the President to protect American interests, primarily business interests, obviously has an effect on agencies which administer trade law. Thus the technical track cannot be devoid of political or other interests (Finger et al., 1982). Although the technical track trade policy implementation structure was designed to prevent particular groups of politicians in Congress from developing emergent strategies of protectionism, in favour of pressure groups, it does not work that way. That is, the problem is more with implementation then formulation.

The impression may exist that, in general, the impact of specific pressure groups on policy implementation is low, as all cases undergo a formal, bureaucratic two-track procedure aimed at preventing emergent policies of protectionism. While it has long been recognized that the ITC is influenced by the short-run goals of members of Congress, the ITA brought some balance to the technical track in the past, especially since foreign policy goals have often determined its behaviour towards trade policy (Bauer, Pool & Dexter, 1972). Moreover, it has been argued that the GATT reinforced the agencies of the executive branch in favor of free international trade (Lenway, 1985). The softwood lumber decision of 1986 is a bad precedent for U.S. trade policy, since it raises the prospect of future decisions determined by pressure groups and the non-realization of the U.S. intended trade policy.[11]

Although the Canadian government avoided a final determination from the ITA in the softwood lumber case by self-imposing a 15% export tax on softwood lumber, the validity of the court decision in the Cabot case was not affected. The main problem with the administration of U.S. trade law is that cases in which a negative countervailable subsidy determination is decided can be brought back to the technical track over and over again, until an affirmative determination is granted. This affirmative ruling can then be used as a precedent for other cases in other industries, so that an increase in the development of non-competitive strategies can be predicted. For a review of the evidence, see Rugman and Anderson (1987a).

The United States now has a trade policy implementation structure whereby any industry, or even a single firm engaged in a non-competitive strategy, can trigger protectionist measures at negligible monetary costs. This also implies that it has become extremely difficult in the United States to draw the line between domestic policy concerns (e.g., maintaining employment in declining industries) and international trade policy objectives. In this way, the United States is now engaged on a path of increasing protectionist trade policy measures to shelter domestic producers from global competition. For detailed analysis, see Rugman and Verbeke (1989, 1990a).[12]

In the future the United States may reinforce this type of retail protection (i.e., the use of countervail and anti-dump actions) by adding wholesale protectionism in the form of the "super 301" and related measures (Cass, 1989). The explicit

and public use of 301 measures, governed by Congressional pressures, will then reinforce the less visible and more implicit protectionist strategy embodied in the use of countervail and anti-dumping measures. In a number of cases, business firms may of course attempt to use U.S. trade policy as a complement to their FSAs, for example when multinational enterprises are oriented toward opening foreign market to gain market share. Our view is, however, that the present institutional structure for conducting trade policy is not able to discriminate between the demand for trade assistance from firms engaging in a competitive strategy and firms seeking shelter. This was demonstrated in Rugman and Verbeke (1990b).

Conclusions

In this article, a new framework was developed to gain conceptual insights into the interrelations between corporate strategies and government trade policy. It was shown that the pressure exerted on government by firms engaging in a non-competitive strategy may constitute an important problem in a country with free trade goals like the United States. This will occur if the implementation structure is very sensitive to clientele demands. This implies, in Mintzberg's terminology, that the intended trade policy goals may be subverted and unintended (ineffective) policy outcomes generated.

It was demonstrated, through the use of two Canadian case studies, that the present system of administered protection in the United States corresponds to the framework of this model. It is concluded that U.S. trade policy has deviated from its intended strategy and that the emergent strategy has led to many unforeseen repercussions for strategic planners and governments. Firms and industries engaging in a non-competitive strategy are able to exert influence on government to realize shelter through trade barriers against foreign competition. This imposes an emergent strategy of protectionism on the United States.

References

Allison, G. T. (1985). *Essence of decision: Explaining the Cuban missile crisis.* Boston, MA: Little Brown.

Baldwin, E. (1985). *The political economy of U.S. import policy.* Cambridge, MA: M.I.T. Press.

Bartlett, C. (1986). Building and managing the transnational: The new organizational challenge. In M. E. Porter (Ed.), *Competition in global industries* (pp. 367-401). Boston, MA: Harvard Business School Press.

Bauer, R. A.; De Sola Pool, I., & Dexter, L. A. (1972). *American business and public policy: The politics of foreign trade.* Chicago: Aldine-Atherton.

Boddewyn, J. J. (1986, November). *International political strategy: A fourth 'generic' strategy?* Paper presented at the annual meeting of the Academy of International Business, London.

Bower, J. L. (1970). *Managing the resource allocation process.* Boston, MA: Harvard Business School, Division of Research.

Buchanan, J., Tollison, R., & Tullock, G. (1980). *Toward a theory of the rent-seeking society.* College Station: Texas A & M University Press.

Burgelman, R. A., & Sayles, L. (1986). *Inside corporate innovation: Strategy, structure, and managerial skills.* New York: The Free Press.

Cass, R. A. (1989). Economics in the administration of U.S. international trade law. (Research Working Paper No. 16). Toronto: Ontario Centre for International Business, Research Programme, University of Toronto.

Destler, I. M. (1986). *American trade politics: System under stress.* Washington, DC: Institute for International Economics, and New York: The Twentieth Century Fund.

Dickie, R. B. (1984). Influence of public affairs offices on corporate planning and of corporations on government policy. *Strategic Management Journal, 5,* 15-34.

Dunning, H., & Rugman, A. M. (1985). The influence of Hymer's dissertation on the theory of foreign direct investment. *American Economic Review, 75* (2), 228-232.

Etzioni, A. (1985). The political economy of imperfect competition. *Journal of Public Policy*, 5(2), 169-186.

Finger, J. M., Hall, H. K., & Nelson, D. R. (1982). The political economy of administered protection. *American Economic Review*, 72(3), 452-456.

Jackson, J. H., & Davey, W. J. (1986). *Legal problems of international economic relations: Cases, materials and text on the national and international regulation of transnational economic relations.* (American Case Work Series). St. Paul, MN: West.

Jackson, P. M. (1983). *The political economy of bureaucracy.* New Jersey: Barnes and Noble.

Kamani, A. (1984). Generic competitive strategies: An analytical approach. *Strategic Management Journal*, 5, 367-380.

Krueger, A. O. (1974). The political economy of the rent-seeking society. *American Economic Review*, 64, 291-303.

Lavergne, R. P. (1981). *The political economy of U.S. tariffs.* Unpublished doctoral dissertation, University of Toronto.

Lenway, S. A. (1985). *The politics of U.S. international trade law.* Boston, MA: Pitman.

Marcus, A. A., Kaufman, A. M., & Beam D. R., (Eds.) (1987). *Business strategy and public policy.* Westport, CT: Greenwood Press.

Mintzberg, H. (1978). Patterns in strategy formulation. *Management Science*, 24, 934-948.

Mintzberg, H. (1983). *Power in and around organizations.* Englewood Cliffs, NJ: Prentice-Hall.

Mintzberg, H. (1989). Beyond Configuration. In *Mintzberg on management: Inside our strange world of organization.* Mimeo, McGill University. New York: The Free Press.

Mintzberg, H., & McHugh, A. (1985). Strategy formulation in an adhocracy. *Administrative Science Quarterly*, 30 (2), 160-197.

Mintzberg, H., Raisinghani, H. D., & Theoret, A. (1976). The structure of unstructured decision-processes. *Administrative Science Quarterly*, 246-275.

Mintzberg, H., & Waters, J. (1985). Of strategies, deliberate and emergent. *Strategic Management Journal*, 6, 257-271.

Olson, M. (1965). *The logic of collective action: Public goods and the theory of groups.* Cambridge, MA: Harvard University Press.

Percy, M. B., & Yoder, C. (1987). *The softwood lumber dispute and Canada-U.S. trade in natural resources.* Halifax: Institute for Research on Public Policy.

Peters, B. G. (1985). The structure and organization of government: Concepts and issues. *Journal of Public Policy*, 5(1), 107-120.

Porteous, S., & Rugman, A.M. (1989). Canadian unfair trade laws and corporate strategy. *Review of International Business Law*, 3 (3), 237-270.

Porter, M. E. (1980.) *Competitive strategy: Techniques for analyzing industries and competitors.* New York: Macmillan.

Porter, M. E. (1986). *Competition in global industries.* Boston, MA: Harvard Business School Press.

Pugel, T.A., & Walter, I. (1985). U.S. corporate interests and the political economy of trade policy. *Review of Economics and Statistics*, 67, 465-473.

Ray, E.J. (1981). The determinants of tariff and nontariff trade restrictions in the United States. *Journal of Political Economy*, 89(1), 105-121.

Rugman, A. M. (1986a). U.S. protectionism and Canadian trade policy. *Journal of World Trade Law*, 20(4), 363-380.

Rugman, A. M. (1986b). New theories of the multinational enterprise: An assessment of internalization theory. *Bulletin of Economic Research*, 38(2), 101-118.

Rugman, A. M., & Anderson, A. D. M. (1987a). *Administered protection in America.* London: Croom Helm/ Routledge, and New York: St. Martin's Press.

Rugman, A. M., & Anderson, A. D. M. (1987b). A fishy business: The abuse of American trade law in the Atlantic Groundfish Case of 1985-1986. *Canadian Public Policy*, XII(2), 152-164.

Rugman, A. M., & Anderson, A. D. M. (1987c). Business and trade policy: The structure of Canada's new private sector advisory system. *Canadian Journal of Administrative Sciences*, 4(4), 367-380.

Rugman, A. M., & Porteous, S. (1988). The softwood lumber decision of 1986: Broadening the nature of U.S. administered protection. *Review of International Business Law*, 2(1), 35-58.

Rugman, A. M., & Verbeke, A. (1989). Strategic management and trade policy. *Journal of International Economic Studies*, 3, 135-152.

Rugman, A. M., & Verbeke, A. (1990a). *Global corporate strategy and trade policy.* London and New York: Routledge.

Rugman, A. M., & Verbeke, A. (1990b). Strategic trade policy is not good strategy. *Hitotsubashi Journal of Commerce and Management*, 25 (1), 75-97.

Sabatier, B. G. (1986). Top-down and bottom-up approaches to implementation research. *Journal of Public Policy*, 6(1), 21-48.

Tullock, G. (1967). The welfare costs of tariffs, monopolies and theft. *Western Economic Review*, 5, 224-232.

United States. (1989a, May 25). "Hills says purpose of 301 Actions is to expand trade." Statement by United States trade representative Carla Hills. Story: *GS4020525.*

United States. (1989b, May 25). Office of the United States trade representative, "Super 301" Trade Liberalization Priorities (3920), Fact Sheet. Story *GS4010525.*

Van Den Broeck, J. (Ed.) (1988). *Public choice.* Boston, MA: Kluwer Academic Publishers.

Verbeke, A. (1988). The managerial analysis of public infrastructure investment policies. In J. Van Den Broeck (Ed.), *Public choice.* Boston, MA: Kluwer Academic Publishers.

Verbeke, A., & Porteous, S. (1990). The strategic management of export controls. *Canadian Journal of Administrative Sciences*, 7 (3), 10-18.

Williamson, O. E. (1985). *The economic institutions of capitalism.* New York: The Free Press.

Winham, G. (1987). *International trade and the Tokyo round negotiation.* Lawrenceville, NJ: Princeton University Press.

Notes

1. A large body of literature obviously exists on the ways in which firms influence government. A synthesis of the strategic management literature in this area can be found in Marcus et al. (1987). An overview of the conceptual models used in the international economics and trade policy literature can be found in Baldwin (1985) and Lenway (1985). The influence exerted by firms on public agencies in the area of international trade and investment policy has not been well developed in the international business literature. An analysis of the limited academic work on this issue as well as an overview of research questions is developed by Boddewyn (1986). A new work which develops these issues further is by Rugman and Verbeke (1990a).

2. The concept of non-competitive strategy contrasts sharply with the traditional view of competitive strategy. In the latter case, a firm attempts to gain a competitive advantage in the market place through cost reduction or product differentiation, thereby creating entry barriers such as scale economies, cost advantage independent of scale, supplies switching costs, control our distribution channels, etc. This is consistent with industrial economic theory. These entry barriers basically result from the company's firm-specific advantages and its ability to provide cheap or differentiated products to the customer, as compared with (potential) competitors. In contrast, a non-competitive strategy leads to shelter in order to substitute for cost reducing or differentiation enhancing capability. This may occur when tariff and non-tariff barriers are created against foreign rivals.

3. The concept of firm-specific advantage, a type of distinctive competence, has been well developed in the international business literature, especially in internalization theory. Firm-specific advantages primarily relate to proprietary knowledge. As a result of the public goods nature of this knowledge and the absence of a well-functioning system of property rights, especially in the international context, the need to protect the company's firm-specific advantages is a major element in determining the scope and the size of the firm. See Dunning and Rugman (1985) and Rugman (1986b). The nature of the firm's proprietary knowledge (e.g., its "location" in specific segments of the value chain) determines the capacity of the company to gain a cost based competitive

advantage and/or a differentiation based competitive advantage.

4. In our view a firm can use competitive strategy to attempt to obtain a cost and differentiation advantage simultaneously. Hence, the use of government may improve the competitiveness of a company in terms of both cost and differentiation potential at the same time, in the spirit of Karnani (1984). In this context, cost competitiveness could even be considered as one specific type of differentiation.

5. The concept of firm-specific advantage in government relations is developed in Verbeke and Porteous (1990). They provide a specific application to the strategic management of export control regulations. It is demonstrated that development of long term relationships with public agencies may give specific firms a substantial cost or differentiation advantage, in contrast to rival firms that consider export controls as a completely exogenous parameter, beyond their managerial control. In this article we do not distinguish between firm behaviour and industry behaviour vis-a-vis government. Excellent overviews of the parameters determining a firm's choice in influencing government policy individually, or through collaboration with other firms, can be found in Etzioni (1985) and Marcus et al. (1987).

6. It could be argued, in accordance with the literature on rent-seeking (e.g., Buchanan, Tollison & Tullock, 1980; Krueger, 1974; Tullock, 1967), that shelter can only be acquired at a cost. In that sense, it would not be different from conventional entry barriers as described in industrial economics theory, as the company which benefits from government intervention has borne high costs itself to obtain shelter. In our view, however, obtaining shelter is comparatively inexpensive. It can be highly effective in cost/benefit terms, as compared to competitive advantages resulting from a competitive strategy. Even if creation of government shelter involves some costs, these may be unrelated to the resulting costs imposed on foreign competitors as a result of shelter. The question that arises is why all firms do not pursue such non-competitive strategies. There are two main reasons for this. First, firms benefiting from strong firm specific advantages will mostly not attempt to gain shelter, as similar strategies by foreign competitors could adversely affect them. Hence, only a limited number of firms pursue a shelter-based strategy. Second, to the extent that the creation of shelter requires high visibility in the political area, this could undermine the firm's claim that it represents legitimate interests. In other words, there is some risk that the benefits of shelter will be accompanied by conditions and restrictions imposed on the firm by public policy makers.

7. Excellent overviews of the literature on the goals pursued by bureaucrats and politicians can be found in

Jackson (1983) and Van Den Broeck (1988).

8. Analyses of the evidence in this area can be found in Dickie (1984) and Marcus et al. (1987).

9. While it is beyond the realm of this paper to examine the entire process of U.S. trade policy formulation, it is critical to understand that U.S. trade policy is fractured due to the divisions in power between the U.S. Congress and the Executive Branch. In general, trade policy formulation in the United States is often expressed in very liberal terms by members of the executive branch. Lenway (1985) indicates that certain agencies within the executive branch always support the liberalization of trade - Treasury, State, and the Office of the Special Trade Representative. Other agencies can be less supportive. These include, at times, Commerce and Labor. In contrast, in recent years Congress has been protectionist, but it, too, can be fractured in where it wants to go with trade policy. Previous Congressional uncertainty·in trade policy formulation left the President with the responsibility for trade negotiations. See Winham (1987). Other analysis of the formation of U.S. trade policy making can be found in Destler (1986), Baldwin (1985), and Jackson and Davey (1986). In all events, for the purposes of this analysis, we do not believe that it is unreasonable to assume that the United States, or at least the vast body of people in that country, believe the United States to be pursuing "free trade" objectives.

10. In 1988 the U.S. Congress twice voted for a protectionist trade bill. The first time it was vetoed by President Reagan, but in the later part of 1988 it was passed by both branches of government. This 1988 Trade Act contains provisions for the new "super 301" measures which have been initiated against Japan and other nations with a trade surplus with the United States (United States, 1989b). Although the United States argues that the new trade law measures are designed to eliminate significant trade barriers and trade-distorting practices, through multilateral and bilateral negotiations (United States, 1989a), such recent trade actions by the Congress are widely regarded as protectionist measures.

11. While the focus of this article is the use of administered protection by U.S. corporations, especially against Canadian traders, it should be noted that Canadian firms also use trade remedy laws. Rather than countervail, which is rarely used, Canadian firms frequently bring anti-dumping actions, sometimes on a repeated basis, against importers. The entire set of Canadian trade remedy law actions, over the 1980-1987 period, is reviewed and analyzed in Porteous and Rugman (1989). The strategic use of trade remedy laws on a bilateral basis does not, however, work in Canada, since it is only one tenth the size of the Unites States. Thus, on average, a countervail or anti-dumping action will only cause a U.S. competitor to lose, at most, one tenth of its market.

In contrast, a Canadian firm can lose access to a market potentially ten times as large as its domestic one when a U.S. competitor wins a trade law case.

12. The number of countervailing duty (CVD) and anti-dumping (AD) actions in the United States has fallen off slightly in the last two years, but they are still used to an extensive degree. The number of U.S. actions initiated, by year, is as follows:

Year	CVD	AD
1980	40	37
1981	7	15
1982	75	50
1983	35	40
1984	22	46
1985	60	61
1986	1	63
1987	11	41
1988	13	31
Total	304	384

The data are from annual reports of the General Agreement on Tariffs and Trade (GATT) in Geneva. The 304 CVD actions by the United States represents 61% of all CVDs in the world over this period. The only other nation using CVDs is Chile with 28% of the total (but only one of these was ever affirmed). The 384 U.S. AD actions represent 31% of all ADs in the world. Other nations using AD trade law include Australia with 25% of the total, Canada with 23%, and the European Community with 19%. These data do not indicate the value of goods being affected by such trade remedy law actions. However, the impact can be substantial. For example, in 1986 the value of Canadian exports to the United States subject to trade remedy law cases was over $6.2 billion, or about 7% of all its exports to the United States. See Rugman and Anderson (1987a). Given that one third of U.S.-Canadian trade is auto products covered by a special agreement, and that there are other areas such as energy trade, where the use of trade remedy law is precluded, it becomes apparent that a substantial portion of bilateral trade open to CVD and AD action is already affected by them. For further discussion see Rugman and Anderson (1987a).

[9]

US Trade Laws as Barriers to Globalisation

Alan M. Rugman and Michael V. Gestrin

1. INTRODUCTION

THE world economy is moving towards a system of 'triad'-based competition in which large multinational enterprises from the United States, the EC and Japan battle for global market shares and profits. By 1990 the world's largest 500 industrial corporations accounted for over $5 trillion in annual sales and collectively employed over 25 million people. (*Fortune*, 1991) Of these 500 firms, 164 were based in the United States, 130 in the EC and 111 in Japan, a total of 405 from these triad powers. These firms operate across borders and their globalisation strategies dominate the world's major industries such as autos, consumer electronics, chemicals, oil, food processing, computers, etc., see Ohmae (1990).

Access to at least one, if not two, of these triad markets has become a necessary condition for success in a globalised industry. Some smaller nations, such as Canada, have attempted to secure market access by institutional arrangement and formal linkages such as the Canada-US Free Trade Agreement. Yet the nature of competitive rivalry by firms in the triad leads them to seek to erect barriers to entry against rival firms, or firms from non-triad areas. In this paper, we explore one of these methods; the use of domestic unfair trade law procedures as a strategic weapon to keep our foreign rival firms. The general case of corporate strategy and the use of trade policy as a 'shelter' strategy has been developed by Rugman and Verbeke (1990). In this paper, specific attention

ALAN M. RUGMAN is Professor of International Business and MICHAEL V. GESTIN is a Research Assistant, both at the Ontario Centre for International Business, University of Toronto, Ontario, Canada. Research for this paper was partially supported by Title VI from the Center for International Business Education and Research at the University of Southern California. A previous version of the paper was presented at the Fourth IBEAR Research Conference on 'The Globalization of American Firms' at the University of Southern California, Los Angeles, June 20-21, 1991. Helpful comments were received from Alain Verbeke and Andrew Anderson of the University of Toronto and from a referee.

336   A. M. RUGMAN AND M. V. GESTRIN

is focused upon the nature of US trade remedy law and the influence of US corporations on the administration of the US technical track of countervailing duty and anti-dumping measures. It is argued that recourse to technical track protectionism may be rational, on occasion, for the individual US firm, but that it is inefficient from the viewpoint of the US economy and world economic system. Data are presented to analyse the nature and extent of the use of the US technical track in the 1980s.

The more specific theme of the paper is that, in order to survive globally, US firms need to develop sustainable competitive advantages. These are usually based upon proprietary firm-specific advantages (FSAs) in technology, management or marketing skills. The sources of the FSAs can often be found within a nation's home country 'diamond' of international competitiveness, to use Porter's terminology, see Porter (1990). They can be turned into competition-based entry barriers, which can be classified according to whether they are cost-reducing or differentiation-enhancing (Porter, 1980), through the use of competitive strategies. Such strategies are ultimately efficiency-based and capable of increasing national economic welfare.

In addition, US firms can also pursue strategies which involve the use of national policies and laws to erect shelter-based (discriminatory) entry barriers against foreign, rival firms. These actions do not generate sustainable competitive advantages and they are inefficient and welfare-reducing. These actions are called 'shelter' seeking strategies. They can best be explained by an examination of the political structure of the United States as it affects trade policy formulation and implementation, see Rugman and Verbeke (1990).

2. SHELTER AS A NEW FORM OF US PROTECTIONISM

The US Congress is designed to reflect regional and special interests. It is subject to extensive and intensive lobbying by both domestic and foreign interest groups. Recent research has established the thesis that the administration of US trade remedy laws (countervailing duty and anti-dumping actions) has been captured by a domestic clientele group seeking shelter, see Rugman and Verbeke (1990). Under this process, the test of 'material injury' due to allegedly subsidised or dumped imports is determined more by political considerations than by scientific economics, see Rugman (1988b). The high success rate of US plaintiffs in these cases implies a form of 'administered protection,' i.e. the erection of a shelter-based non-tariff barrier to entry against foreign firms in the same industry, see Rugman and Anderson (1987). The importance of this new type of protectionism is illustrated by the fact that US firms have well over 90 per cent of all the world's countervail actions, for evidence see Anderson and Rugman (1990).

Shelter-based strategies can be directed toward the 'technical track' or the 'political track', see Finger et al. (1982). The political track is defined here as directly involving the government and official diplomatic channels between countries. Pursuance of a technical track shelter strategy involves the use of the available bureaucratic and legal mechanisms to raise entry barriers against competitors. These mechanisms include countervailing duties (CVD), anti-dumping duties (AD), and safeguard actions. The 'political track' directly involves the government and the use of official diplomatic channels in order to improve the position of domestic firms vis-à-vis their competitors. Typical examples of political track protectionism in the United States include Voluntary Export Restraints (VERs), such as those in imports of autos, steel, and semiconductors. Another example, although not specific to the United States, is the institutionalised protectionism for textile and clothing products inherent in the Multi-Fibre Arrangement.

While the development of FSAs in technology, management or marketing skills bears costs which will be discounted by each firm against future anticipated returns from improvements in these areas, the same logic does not apply to shelter-based entry barriers. This is because shelter-based entry barriers are not needed by a firm using efficiency-based cost-reducing or differentiation-enhancing advantages. Shelter strategies do not develop sustainable FSAs. In fact, they can serve to undermine them.

The competitiveness of a firm or industry is determined by its strategic use of cost-reducing and differentiation-enhancing FSAs. For an industry which does not enjoy great cost-reducing or differentiation-enhancing potential, shelter-based entry barriers will serve to secure a share of the domestic (protected) market which it would not otherwise enjoy. However, for an industry which does enjoy cost-reducing and/or differentiation-enhancing potential, shelter-based entry barriers are not necessary and will serve to eventually limit it to a share of the domestic (protected) market, excluding it from the share of the global market which its 'natural' competitive advantages would otherwise permit.

In other words, the development of shelter-based entry barriers is not to be treated like any other input. The creation of real barriers is not subject to the type of cost-benefit analysis which guides firms in their allocation of resources to create competition-based entry barriers. Rather, the creation of shelter should be viewed as a second-best strategy, the pursuit of which is dependent upon a firm or industry's lack of capabilities to establish competition-based entry barriers. For an illustration of the relationship between these two types of corporate strategy, see Figure 1 (adapted from Rugman and Verbeke, 1991).

By pursuing shelter, US firms effectively turn their backs on globalisation. They use the political system to postpone the economic adjustments and changes required to generate sustainable competitive advantages. A strong protectionist culture in the United States continues to attempt to rationalise these shelter-

A. M. RUGMAN AND M. V. GESTRIN

based strategies. In contrast, in small, open trading economies (such as Canada) this protectionist mindset is being abandoned, leaving firms in such nations better placed to take advantage of the opportunities for globalisation. Thus Canada was more concerned to achieve redress against the perceived abuse of US trade law actions, than was the United States, during negotiations for the Canada-US Free Trade Agreement, see Rugman (1988a).

FIGURE 1
Relationship Between Types of Corporate Strategy

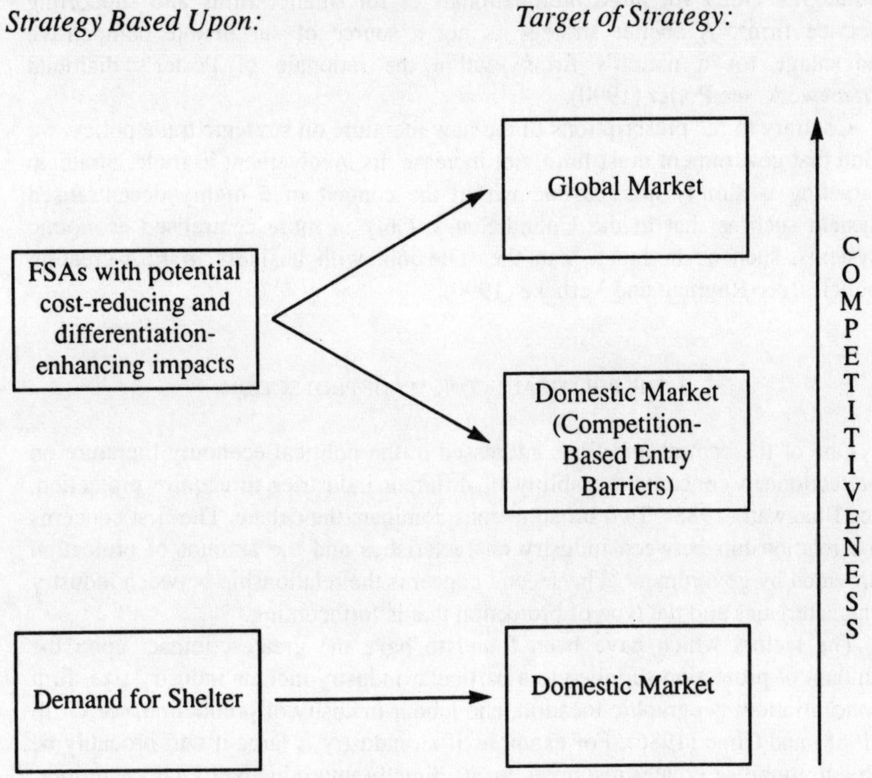

Strategy Based Upon: *Target of Strategy:*

Shelter-based strategies also suffer from the 'tragedy of the commons.' For each individual domestic firm with weak competitive advantages, the pursuance of shelter-based entry barriers reflects rational behaviour. The manager who chooses not to graze upon the protectionist pastures offered by government and bureaucracy will lose out in the short-run to competitors who do take advantage of such opportunities. Yet when other firms in the 'triad' pursue shelter-based entry barriers, the process of globalisation is impeded, and competitiveness is ultimately diminished, see Ostry (1990), and Rugman (1990).

In this study we will consider what factors influence the decision of firms to pursue shelter-based strategies, especially the factors which have encouraged firms to turn increasingly to the technical track as part of their overall shelter-seeking strategy. We find that the continued pursuit of discriminatory shelter-based strategies constitutes a form of slow economic suicide for US firms. While such strategies may seem rational from the perspective of the individual firm, the cumulative effects for the US economy will be to impede successful globalisation. With shelter there is no development of sustainable FSA-based strategies, either for large multinationals or for smaller firms and supporting service firms. A shelter strategy is not a source of sustainable competitive advantage for a nation's firms, within the rationale of Porter's diamond framework, see Porter (1990).

Contrary to the prescriptions of the new literature on strategic trade policy, we find that government must limit, not increase, its involvement in trade. Strategic targeting is simply not feasible within the context of a highly decentralised system such as that in the United States. Only in more centralised economic systems, such as in Japan, can the state join with business in FSA-creating policies, see Rugman and Verbeke (1990).

3. THE POLITICAL ECONOMY OF PROTECTION

One of the central questions addressed in the political economy literature on protectionism concerns the ability of different industries to acquire protection, see Bhagwati (1988). Two broad themes dominate the debate. The first concerns the relationship between industry characteristics and the amount of protection provided by government. The second concerns the relationship between industry characteristics and the type of protection that is forthcoming.

The factors which have been found to have the greatest impact upon the amount of protection supplied to a particular industry include industry size, firm concentration, geographic location, and labour intensity of production, see Grilli (1988) and Cline (1986). For example, if an industry is large it will probably be able to mobilise greater resources for its directly unproductive (DUP) activities. Conversely, if it is highly dispersed at the level of the firm, higher organisational costs and the free-rider problem are thought to hamper its lobby efforts.

The effect of industry characteristics upon the type of protection adopted are less well documented in the literature. Generally, however, it is believed that while most industries have had to content themselves with the protection offered by the technical track (AD and CVD), a few particularly powerful industries have been able to establish political track protectionist arrangements for themselves. In other words, up to a certain 'critical mass' of lobbying power all industries can affect the levels of protection they receive within the confines of the technical track, but beyond this point only a few large ones can push for a much broader set of protectionist instruments to choose from.

As mentioned above, industries which have won political track protection include autos, steel, electronics, and textiles and clothing, see Ostry (1990). These industries are believed to opt for protectionist instruments beyond AD and CVD because the products involved have characteristics which mitigate against the effectiveness of the technical track. The textile and clothing industry is a case in point. AD and CVD were considered to provide insufficient protection to this industry for three main reasons.

The first was that textiles and clothing are highly undifferentiated. This allows for easy trans-shipment. Trans-shipment involves the exporting of products from one country to another via a third. By doing so, an exporter can avoid AD measures, which are supposed to target particular industries in particular countries, and CVDs, which are supposed to target products from particular countries.

The second reason for the ineffectiveness of the technical track consists in the low start-up costs and small recoupment period which characterise textile and clothing production, see Bhagwati (1988). This characteristic of textile and clothing production makes this industry highly mobile, and hence, difficult to target with relatively precise trade instruments like AD and CVDs.

A third characteristic of textiles and apparel production which complicates protectionist policies is mutability. An example would be the conversion of a jacket upon which a duty is imposed into a vest and sleeves, upon which there are no duties, with a view to having the jacket reassembled in the importing country.

The iron and steel industries, on the other hand, are examples of cases in which the technical track has been effective. This is due to the high costs associated with the transportation of this industry's two main inputs, iron ore and coal, both of which are characterised by extremely high weight to value ratios. Furthermore, the physical capital for this industry is expensive and heavy, requiring extremely high start-up costs and long recoupment periods. As such, this industry has been easily targeted by AD and CVD. Later these were reinforced by the VER quotas. In this case, VERs and technical track instruments such as AD and CVD are complements, not substitutes. The technical track is used by politically powerful industries with weak FSAs to pressure the government to negotiate VERs. Another example of this type of complementarity can be found in the American auto industry's bid for protection from Japanese competitors in the early 1980s (see Lenway, 1983, for a detailed analysis of this case), and more recently in the case of vans from Japan.

Implicit in much of the political economy literature on protection is the view that protection can be conceptualised as a commodity which is produced by the government and demanded by industry. (See for example Bhagwati, 1988, and for a much earlier account, Breton, 1964). The price of protection for industry consists of the various costs associated with acquiring it; legal fees, the costs of maintaining a strong lobby, etc. The cost to the government of producing protection, on the other hand, consists of: the potential loss of votes due to higher consumer prices; the potential loss of international authority where protectionist policies damage legitimacy; the financial and bureaucratic costs of operating a system in which the treatment of goods in trade is highly differentiated, etc. Conversely, the cost of not producing protection is embodied in the loss of political support which accompanies high levels of unemployment.

Models of the market for protection such as this have served to underpin a number of empirical studies. Cline (1986), for example, in his study of the textiles, steel and automobile industries in the United States, found that the two factors with the most explanatory power for the distribution of protection were the size of a given industry's labour force and the level (not the rate) of import penetration. In addition, Cline's study suggests that even when an industry's size warrants protection, it might not be protected to the extent that it normally would be if the industry supplies inputs to an even larger industry, see Cline (1986), p. 214.

A more general earlier study by Takacs (1981) attempts to identify factors which are associated with both protectionist pressure and actual protection. The factors which she identifies as contributing the most to protectionist pressure include: the merchandise trade balance; import penetration; a 'demonstration' effect, defined as the success rate for petitions in the previous year; and legislative dummies, which serve to identify the effects of key trade acts. Specifically, Takacs tests for the effects of the trade Expansion Act of 1962, and the Trade Act of 1974. The first of these had a negative impact upon the number of petitions filed (protectionist pressure) while the second had a positive impact. The factors which she identifies as contributing to actual protection are the size of the trade deficit and the degree of import penetration. However, in contrast to her findings concerning the factors found to be most significant with regard to the number of petitions filed, Takacs suggests that the rate of capacity utilisation and the employment rate do not have a bearing upon actual levels of protection, see Takacs (1981, p.691).

Another significant factor which has been identified as shaping trading patterns consists of the threat of protection. This is the 'harassment thesis.' What it suggests is that the option of a firm or industry to file a trade complaint acts as an impediment to trade because foreign producers must incorporate this additional risk into their cost functions. The costs associated with the threat of

A. M. RUGMAN AND M. V. GESTRIN

protection increase both with the probability that such a case would be launched as well as with the actual costs associated with such a case. One study on the effects of harassment, for example, found that the threat of protection influences foreign pricing decisions. Foreign producers tend to raise prices to avoid charges of dumping, see Herander and Schwartz (1984, p.78).

TABLE 1
US AD and CVD Cases 1980-88

SITC Code	Description	Number of AD Cases	Number of CVD Cases	Number of All Cases
0–1	Food, live animals, beverages, tobacco	14	53	67
2	Crude materials, inedible, except fuels	20	4	24
3	Mineral fuels, lubricants, etc.	1	1	2
4	Animal and vegetable oils, fats, waxes	3	0	3
5	Chemicals and related products, n.e.s.	48	44	92
6.5	Textile, yarn, fabrics, etc.	8	11	19
6.7	Iron and steel	162	181	343
6.8	Non-ferrous metals	14	4	18
7	Machinery and transport equipment	81	8	89
8.4	Apparel and clothing	0	0	0
6 and 8*	Other manufactured goods	66	23	89
	All Products Listed	417	329	746

*This category includes sub-categories of sections 6 and 8. From section 6 these include manufactures of leather (6.1), rubber (6.2), cork and wood (6.3), paper and paperboard (6.4), non-metallic minerals (6.6), and manufactures of metals n.e.s. (6.9). From section 8 are included prefabricated buildings (8.1), furniture (8.2), travel goods (8.3), footwear (8.5), scientific instruments (8.7), photographic equipment (8.8), and miscellaneous manufactured goods (8.9).
Sources: United Nations Statistical Office, Standard International Trade Classification Revision 3 (1986), and International Trade Commission, various documents.

The predominant theme of this section is that a multitude of factors shape the effectiveness with which firms can successfully pursue shelter-based strategies. The key point emphasised in the preceding section was that firms will only pursue such strategies in the absence of strong FSAs. What it is important to realise, therefore, is that the factors identified in the several studies cited above, such as size of the labour force, firm concentration, and other factors such as unionisation levels, are not the determining factors for firms in their calculations of whether or not to pursue shelter-based strategies. Instead, this decision is influenced in the first instance by the firm or industry's endowment of FSAs. Industry and firm characteristics such as size of the labour force, etc., only determine how successful a shelter-based strategy will be once the decision to pursue such a strategy has been made. It is an industry's competitiveness which determines whether or not it will attempt to use technical track protection in a strategic manner — not its ability to secure protection (refer back to Figure 1).

4. ADMINISTERED PROTECTION BY SECTOR

Table 1 identifies the 746 AD and CVD cases, by industry, bought by US firms between 1980 and 1988. The total number of AD cases for this period was 417. CVD cases were slightly less numerous at 329. The objective of Table 1 is to help identify how many cases were launched by each of the major eleven sectors of the US economy. The majority of the total cases resulted in preliminary affirmative determinations of injury by the ITC, while the share of final affirmative cases was 24 per cent.

The product groups used in this analysis are based upon the divisions established by the one digit sections of the SITC Revision 3. Table 2 summarises the differences between these categories both in terms of the value of imports and the relative share of imports accounted for by each category. 'Machinery and transport equipment' is the largest category by this measure, reflecting the contribution of automobiles. The next largest category is 'mineral fuels, lubricants, etc.,' which reflects the considerable dependence of the United States upon foreign sources of energy. The remaining categories account for relatively smaller and more evenly distributed shares of total imports.

TABLE 2
US Total Imports by SITC Category 1980-87

SITC Code	Description	Value (US billion $)	Share of Imports (%)
0–1	Food, live animals, beverages, tobacco	132.8	6.88
2	Crude materials, inedible, except fuels	67.2	3.48
3	Mineral fuels, lubricants, etc.	417.5	21.62
4	Animal and vegetable oils, fats, waxes	3.8	0.20
5	Chemicals and related products, n.e.s.	77	3.99
6.5	Textile, yarn, fabrics, etc.	25.8	1.34
6.7	Iron and steel	65.1	3.37
6.8	Non-ferrous metals	43.9	2.27
7	Machinery and transport equipment	717.2	37.14
8.4	Apparel and clothing	73.8	3.82
6 and 8	Other manufactured goods	306.8	15.89
	All Products Listed	1930.9	100.00

Source: United Nations Statistical Office, International Trade Statistics Yearbook (1985, 1987).

The implication of these differences to a sectoral analysis of AD and CVD is that we cannot simply use the number of cases in each category as an indication of the incidence of the use of these instruments. The development of a common denominator is required before a comparison of these sectors in terms of the incidence of the use of AD and CVD can be attempted.

Since our concern is with the incidence of the technical track actions upon foreign competitors, the value of imports is used to weight each sector. Table 3

A. M. RUGMAN AND M. V. GESTRIN

TABLE 3
Number of Cases Weighted by Value of Imports

SITC Code	Description	1 All Cases	2 Share of Total Cases (%)	3 Value of Imports (US$ billion $)	4 Share of Imports (%)	5 Share of Cases/ Share of Imports (2/4)	6 Number of Cases/ Value of Imports* (1/3)
0–1	Food, live animals, beverages, tobacco	67	9.07	132.8	6.88	1.32	5.05
2	Crude materials, inedible, except fuels	24	3.25	67.2	3.48	0.93	3.57
3	Mineral fuels, lubricants, etc.	2	0.27	417.5	21.62	0.01	0.05
4	Animal and vegetable oils, fats, waxes	3	0.41	3.8	0.20	2.06	7.89
5	Chemicals and related products, n.e.s.	92	12.45	77	3.99	3.12	11.95
6.5	Textile, yarn, fabrics, etc.	19	2.57	25.8	1.34	1.92	7.36
6.7	Iron and steel	343	46.41	65.1	3.37	13.77	52.69
6.8	Non-ferrous metals	18	2.44	43.9	2.27	1.07	4.10
7	Machinery and transport equipment	89	12.04	717.2	37.14	0.32	1.24
8.4	Apparel and clothing	0	0.00	73.8	3.82	0.00	0.00
6 and 8	Other manufactured goods	89	12.04	306.8	15.89	0.76	2.90
	All Products Listed	746	100.95	1930.9	100.00	1.01	3.86

Average Per Category: 8.80

*The units used in the calculation of this column are number of cases for each US$10 billion worth of imports. Note that the import data cover the period 1980-86, while the case data cover the period 1980-87. This, however, does not affect the purpose of the weighting procedure, which is to supply a common denominator across the eleven sectors.

The figures which have been outlined in the last column indicate the broad SITC categories in which the weighted number of cases exceeds the weighted average for each category (8.80). The 'Share of Imports' column is calculated only on imports covered by this table.

Sources: United Nations Statistical Office, International Trade Statistics Yearbook (1985, 1987), and International Trade Commission, various documents.

therefore combines Tables 1 and 2 to provide a weighted measure of the number
of AD and CVD cases in each SITC category. The last column of Table 3 is expressed in terms of the number of cases per US$10 billion of imports to the US.

The average number of cases in each category for each $10 billion worth in
imports in this category is 8.80. As the last column of Table 3 indicates, only
two of the eleven category groups exceeds this average. The group with by far
the highest weighted ratio is iron and steel, with 52.69 cases per $10 billion
worth of iron and steel imports. The next highest category consists in chemicals
and their related products. Chemicals averaged 11.95 AD and CVD cases per
$10 billion of imports of these products from 1980 to 1988. The other nine
category groups were all below the average number of weighted cases per
category, indicating the extent to which the iron and steel industries dominated
the technical track during this period.

Table 4 extends the analysis by breaking down the weighted number of cases
in each category according to the number of AD cases. Iron and steel is
characterised as having the highest number-of-cases/value-of-imports ratio.
However, the animal and vegetable products sector has the second highest
concentration of AD cases. Chemicals rank third, with 6.23 cases per $10 billion
of chemical product imports. The average number of AD cases per $10 billion in
imports is 4.79.

TABLE 4
AD Cases Weighted by Value of Imports

SITC Code	Description	Number of AD Cases	Value of Imports (US billion $)	Number of AD Cases/ Value of Imports
0–1	Food, live animals, beverages, tobacco	14	132.8	1.05
2	Crude materials, inedible, except fuels	20	67.2	2.98
3	Mineral fuels, lubricants, etc.	1	417.5	0.02
4	Animal and vegetable oils, fats, waxes	3	3.8	7.89
5	Chemicals and related products, n.e.s.	48	77	6.23
6.5	Textile, yarn, fabrics, etc.	8	25.8	3.10
6.7	Iron and steel	162	65.1	24.88
6.8	Non-ferrous metals	14	43.9	3.19
7	Machinery and transport equipment	81	717.2	1.13
8.4	Apparel and clothing	0	73.8	0.00
6 and 8*	Other manufactured goods	66	306.8	2.15
	All Products Listed	417	1930.9	2.16

Average Per Category: 4.79

Notes: The figures which have been outlined in the last column indicate the broad SITC categories in which
the weighted number of AD cases exceeds the weighted average for each category (4.79). The last column is
expressed as the number of cases per US$10 billion worth of imports.
Sources: United Nations Statistical Office, International Trade Statistics Yearbook (1985, 1987).

Table 5 repeats the exercise for CVD cases. The sector with the dubious distinction of practising the most active shelter-based CVD policy is again iron and

steel, with 27.80 weighted cases. Two other sectors rank above the average number of weighted cases per category; the chemicals sector ranks second, textiles rank third, and the 'food, live animals, beverages and tobacco' sector ranks fourth. The average number of CVD cases per $10 billion in imports is 4.01.

5. INTERPRETING THE EMPIRICAL RESULTS

The findings in Tables 5 and 6 can be summarised as follows. First, in terms of the concentration of use of these instruments for the period under consideration, the iron and steel industries far outrank any other sectors. In the use of AD, iron and steel outranked the next most frequent user (animal and vegetable oils, according to the measure used in this analysis) by 215 per cent. In the use of CVD, iron and steel were even more dominant, outranking chemicals and related products by 478 per cent.

TABLE 5
CVD Cases Weighted by Value of Imports

SITC Code	Description	Number of CVD Cases	Value of Imports (US billion $)	Number of CVD Cases/ Value of Imports
0–1	Food, live animals, beverages, tobacco	53	132.8	3.99
2	Crude materials, inedible, except fuels	4	67.2	0.60
3	Mineral fuels, lubricants, etc.	1	417.5	0.02
4	Animal and vegetable oils, fats, waxes	0	3.8	0.00
5	Chemicals and related products, n.e.s.	44	77	5.71
6.5	Textile, yarn, fabrics, etc.	11	25.8	4.26
6.7	Iron and steel	181	65.1	27.80
6.8	Non-ferrous metals	4	43.9	0.91
7	Machinery and transport equipment	8	717.2	0.11
8.4	Apparel and clothing	0	73.8	0.00
6	Other manufactured goods	23	306.8	0.75
	All Products Listed	329	1930.9	1.70

Average Per Category: 4.01

Notes: The figures which have been outlined in the last column indicate the broad SITC categories in which the weighted number of CVD cases exceeds the weighted average for each category (4.01). The last column is expressed as the number of cases per US$10 billion worth of imports.
Sources: United Nations Statistical Office, International Trade Statistics Yearbook (1985, 1987).

Second, the use of AD was slightly more concentrated than the use of CVD. The standard deviation around the mean for AD cases was 7.1, whereas for CVD cases the standard deviation was approximately 8.1. This again reflects the degree to which iron and steel dominate the use of CVDs relative to other sectors of the economy. The use of AD is clearly more continuous across sectors. Three groups of users can be identified; first, as already mentioned, iron and steel dominates; second, two categories, 'animal and vegetable oils, fats, and waxes' and 'chemicals and related products, n.e.s.' represent another high-frequency user group; third, an intermediate group of users, all of whom average more than one case per $10 billion of imports, follows; fourth, the infrequent and non-users (less than one case per $10 billion of imports) include 'mineral fuels, lubricants, etc.' 'and apparel and clothing.' In contrast, using these same distinctions, the infrequent and non-users of CVDs are much more numerous, representing seven of the eleven category groups.

Third, Tables 3, 4 and 5 also emphasise that the use of protectionist instruments is very sector specific, and that the various sectors of the American economy display clear preference patterns in terms of the instruments most frequently used. Some sectors such as iron and steel have a history of using both the technical and the political tracks to develop shelter-based advantages. There may be a 'demonstration' effect as firms in one industry see others using these laws (particularly anti-dumping) and copy them. In contrast, the apparel and clothing industry, which also has a long history of pursuing shelter-based strategies, used neither AD nor CVD from 1980 to 1988. And yet other sectors display clear preferences for particular instruments from the 'menu' of technical track options. The 'food, live animals, beverages and tobacco' sector, for example, only ranks ninth out of eleven in its use of AD. However, it ranks fourth in its use of CVD, perhaps reflecting the current international disagreement over government subsidisation of agriculture.

TABLE 6
Rank of SITC Sectors by Import Weighted Number of Cases

SITC Code	Description	Ranking of Incidence of AD and CVD*	Ranking of Incidence of AD*	Ranking of Incidence of CVD*
6.7	Iron and steel	1	1	1
5	Chemicals and related products, n.e.s.	2	3	2
4	Animal and vegetable oils, fats, waxes	3	2	11
6.5	Textile, yarn, fabrics, etc.	4	5	3
0–1	Food, live animals, beverages, tobacco	5	9	4
6.8	Non-ferrous metals	6	4	5
2	Crude materials, inedible, except fuels	7	6	7
6 and 8	Other manufactured goods	8	7	6
7	Machinery and transport equipment	9	8	8
3	Mineral fuels, lubricants, etc.	10	10	9
8.4	Apparel and clothing	11	11	10

Source: Derived from Tables 3, 4 and 5.
*As weighted by imports. See previous tables.

Table 6 summarises the findings from Tables 3, 4 and 5 by ranking each product category according to the weighted number of cases for each category for AD and CVD combined. Each category is also ranked separately according to the incidence of AD and CVD cases. What the table suggests is that the choice by firms of the type of instruments used in pursuing a shelter-based strategy is sensitive to a multitude of factors, ranging from product characteristics, to industry size, to the availability of alternative sources of protection. It is for this reason that two of the most protectionist sectors of the American economy, 'iron and steel' and 'apparel and clothing' find themselves at opposite ends of this list.

6. RECENT EVOLUTION OF THE TECHNICAL TRACK

In 1985, the Trade Agreements Program of the Reagan administration outlined a new three pronged trade strategy, partly to supplement the post-War cornerstone of US trade policy, the multilateral GATT system. While multilateralism through the GATT would continue to play a role under the Trade Agreements Program, this role would be diminished. The two other trade policy directions included establishing bilateral Free Trade Agreements (FTAs), and expanding the role of the use of Section 301 of the 1974 Trade Act against unfair trade practices. Therefore, as Ostry puts it, 'Despite the continuing support for the Uruguay Round, neither the United States government nor the business community accepts any longer the preservation and strengthening of liberal multilateral trade as a single, overriding objective.' (Ostry, 1990, p. 30)

The primary significance of these developments to American firms is that the traditional distinction in US trade policy between political and technical track trade policy has become increasingly blurred. Indeed in the Annual Report of the President of the United States on the Trade Agreements Program for 1984-1985, a more active role for the government in the administration of US trade policy and of the technical track is described.

Underlying this heightened government role in administering trade policy is the growing perception in Congress that foreign governments are subsidising foreign companies and that US companies cannot compete on a level playing field. The effect of these developments has been to make the administration of trade policy somewhat more reflective of Congressional pressures and more sympathetic to US industry concerns, and for the United States Trade Representative's Office to become, 'the negotiating "combat" agency for trade issues,' (Grinols, 1989, p. 508). In other words, a strong linkage has been established between US domestic business interests and the administration of US trade policy. This new process seems to fall mid-way between the use of the technical track assigned to bureaucratic agencies and the political process of negotiating voluntary export restraints and other politically motivated trade policy goals, see Ostry (1990, p. 29).

The effectiveness of this intermediate system in providing shelter to US industry has been further bolstered with the Omnibus Trade and Competitiveness Act of 1988 (OTCA), which introduced the 'super' 301 and '301 Special' provisions. While the OTCA amendments themselves have not increased the likelihood that AD or CVD investigations under the technical track will end in findings of unfair trade practices, the OTCA has served to reinforce the influence of US industry on the administration of US trade policy. A major focus of the OTCA has been to target '"priority" countries and practices' (Grinols, 1989, p. 505). This clause has been interpreted, in practice, as one aimed mainly at Japan's bilateral trade balance with the United States. It has led to the US-Japan Structural Impediments Initiatives of 1990. The key criterion, which has already become important towards determining 'priority', has been the bilateral balance of payments on the current account with trading partners.

Another important aspect of the OCTA to firms pursuing discriminatory shelter is that it gives the Department of Commerce unprecedented discretionary powers (still subject to judicial review) to take retaliatory action against exporters suspected of practising 'circumvention.' This practice is described as consisting of avoiding AD and CVDs by producing in third countries, making minor changes and relocating the assembly of parts to either third countries or the importer itself (Ostry, 1990, p. 43). Other amendments in the OCTA, however, could be interpreted as likely to reduce the number of affirmative findings, the most notable example being the 'negligible imports' exception to cumulation. Indeed, to date the 1988 US OCTA has not led to an increase in US protection based on 301 measures. Only two petitions under Section 301 have been imposed (semiconductors and Brazilian pharmaceutical patent laws) but both measures have since been removed.

In summary, the formulation and administration of US trade policy has experienced considerable changes since 1985. These have tightened enforcement of technical track rules and facilitated their use and application (for a more detailed analysis see Rugman and Verbeke, 1989). The US Trade Agreements Program of 1985, itself served to blur the lines between the technical and political track paths to protection. Whereas the technical track traditionally served to deflect protectionist pressures away from politicians, the government's decision to break this 'barrier' by becoming a 'player' in the process meant that the firms would now be able to increase shelter by drawing the government directly into their own trade disputes. The 1988 US OCTA reinforced this trend by making government a potential partner of US industry in sectoral bilateral trade disputes; the full extent of this involvement, especially in the use of the Super 301, remains to be seen. Yet, already, parts of the new strategy have had an effect. From 1985 to 1988, the US government threatened to self-initiate cases 26 times against ten of its trading partners. In 18 of these instances, the mere threat was sufficient to extract concessions and the cases in question were never launched, see Ostry (1990, p. 28).

The period from 1985 to 1988 therefore confirmed the rapid evolution of US trade law procedures into an even more viable source of shelter for US industry. While the real burst of US technical track protectionism was, of course, in the 1982-83 period, especially in the case of the steel industry, the more recent developments have the potential to increase shelter type strategies, which will not position US firms to do well in a world of global competition. For example, although the US steel industry has rationalised and developed some efficient 'mini mills' it is still reliant on VERs and is basically dependent upon subsidies, see Anderson and Rugman (1989).

It should also be noted that the pursuance of shelter-based strategies has repercussions beyond the particular firms and industries pursuing such strategies. No sector of an economy exists in a vacuum. Forward, backward, and final demand linkages create a net of interwoven economic relationships throughout the economy. Therefore, while no attempt has been made in the present study to incorporate the implications of these linkages to the present trend of increased use of the technical track by American industry, this is clearly an important area for future research.

A concern is the effect of shelter-based strategies upon the service sectors. All products, including tradeables, embody the inputs of services. To the extent that firms in an economy are able to resist the process of economic globalisation through shelter-based strategies, they will impose similar distortions upon the services sector, which responds in its economic decision-making to developments in its upstream markets. Given the growing importance of the services sector in international trade this is a particularly significant aspect of the interaction between shelter-based strategies and economic linkages.

7. CONCLUSIONS

In this paper we have argued five interrelated points. First, it has been shown that corporate economic performance is the outcome of a combination of two types of corporate strategy. On the one hand, corporations can seek to develop FSAs which are either cost-reducing or differentiation-enhancing. If successful, such a strategy leads to competition-based entry barriers. On the other hand, corporations can seek to establish shelter-based entry barriers.

Second, we have argued that the pursuit of shelter-based entry barriers slows the process of globalisation. One reason for this is that the pursuit of directly unproductive activities diverts considerable resources away from activities which aim at cost-reduction and differentiation-enhancement. Another important reason is that by limiting imports, the cornerstone of the globalisation process, competition, is also limited.

Third, we have argued that the US economy suffers from a structural impediment to globalisation. This impediment arises out of a political system which is highly decentralised and thus sensitive to pressures from various lobby groups. Given, as we have said, that it is perfectly rational from the individual firm's perspective to pursue a shelter-based strategy as part of its overall corporate strategy (if it cannot produce competition-based entry-barriers), then the onus of responsibility for limiting the use of these strategies is not upon the firm but upon government.

Fourth, we have shown, using data on AD and CVD cases, in conjunction with import data, how the use of the technical track is distributed among major sectors of the US economy. What these data show is that some sectors, especially 'iron and steel,' have been much more active than others in their use of this track.

Finally, we have highlighted some recent developments in the evolution of US trade policy law and procedures which suggest that US trade policy has more shelter-based attributes. Particularly disturbing has been the US government's increasing willingness to become directly involved in trade disputes to bolster the technical track. This is disturbing because the technical track has traditionally served the purpose of protecting the politically sensitive executive branch in US politics from all but the most powerful lobbies — those which have been able to 'jump' from the technical to the political track. Now the executive, including the president, will be exposed to protectionist pressures from a much wider cross-section of US corporate society. Furthermore, some industries have shown signs of successfully using the technical track to pressure government to move more forcefully on their behalf on the political track. The 'iron and steel' sector is a case in point — by 'overloading' the technical track, it has pushed government to act on the political track. See USITC, 1989, for an overview of this case.

In sum, the increasingly political nature of the US trade policy threatens the globalisation of the US economy in two ways. First, it gives traditional political track actors (autos, semiconductors, iron and steel, etc.) one more lever with which to exercise a shelter-based strategy. Second, it gives smaller players an opportunity to pursue shelter through these new trade law procedures where before they might not have done so because the relevant political actors could not be brought 'on side.' Crucial to limiting the negative effects of both the technical and political tracks upon continued globalisation will be more research on the effects of these instruments upon corporate competitiveness.

REFERENCES

Anderson, A. and A. M. Rugman (1989), 'Subsidies in the US Steel Industry: A New Conceptual Framework and Literature Review,' *Journal of World Trade*, 23 (6), 59-83.

352   A. M. RUGMAN AND M. V. GESTRIN

Anderson, A. and A. M. Rugman (1990), 'Country-Factor Bias in the Administration of Antidumping and Countervailing Duty Cases,' 147-177 in M. Trebilcock and R. C. York (eds.), *Fair Exchange: Reforming Trade Remedy Laws* (Toronto: C.D. Howe Institute).

Bhagwati, J. N. (1988), *Protectionism* (Cambridge, Mass. MIT Press).

Breton, A. (1964), 'The Economics of Nationalism,' *Journal of Political Economy* 72 (4), 376-86.

Cline, W. R. (1986), 'US Trade and Industrial Policy: The Experience of Textiles, Steel, and Automobiles,' in P. R. Krugman (ed). *Strategic Trade Policy and the New International Economics* (MIT Press, Cambridge, Mass.).

Finger, J. M., H. K. Hall and D. R. Nelson (1982), 'The Political Economy of Administered Protection,' *American Economic Review* 72 (3), 452-66.

Fortune (1991), 'The Fortune Global 500' (July 29).

Grilli, E. (1988), 'Macro-economic Determinants of Trade Protection,' *The World Economy*, 11, 313-326.

Grinols, Earl L. (1989), 'Procedural Protectionism: The American Trade Bill and the New Interventionist Mode,' *Weltwirtschaftliches Archiv*, 125 (3), 501-522.

Herander, M. G. and J. B. Schwartz (1984), 'An Empirical Test of the Impact of the Threat of US Trade Policy: The Case of Antidumping Duties,' *Southern Economic Journal*, 51, 59-79.

Lenway, S. (1983), 'The Impact of American Business on International Trade Policy,' in L. E. Preston, *Research in Corporate Social Performance and Policy*, 5, 27-58.

Ohmae, K. (1990), *The Borderless World: Power and Strategy in the International Economy* (New York: Harper Business).

Ostry, S. (1990), *Governments and Corporations in a Shrinking World: Trade and Innovation Policies in the United States, Europe and Japan* (New York, Council on Foreign Relations).

Porter, M. E. (1980) *Competitive Strategy: Techniques for Analyzing Industries and Competitors* (New York: The Free Press, Macmillan).

Porter, M. E. (1990), *The Competitive Advantage of Nations* (New York: Free Press, Macmillan).

Rugman, A. M. (1988a), 'The Free Trade Agreement and the Global Economy,' *Business Quarterly* 53, 1 (Summer), 13-20.

Rugman, A. M. (1988b), 'A Canadian Perspective on US Administered Protection and the Free Trade Agreement,' *Maine Law Review* (September), 305-324.

Rugman, A. M. (1990), *Multinationals and Canada-United States Free Trade* (Columbia: University of South Carolina Press).

Rugman, A. M. and A. Anderson (1987), *Administered Protection in America* (New York: Methuen; London: Croom Helm/Routledge).

Rugman, A. M. and A. Verbeke (1989), 'Mintzberg's Intended and Emergent Corporate Strategies and Trade Policy,' Ontario Centre for International Business, Research Programme, Working Paper Series, 20, September 1989, to be published in *The Canadian Journal of Administrative Sciences* 8:3 (1991).

Rugman, A. M. and A. Verbeke (1990), *Global Corporate Strategy and Trade Policy* (London; New York: Routledge).

Rugman, A. M. and A. Verbeke (1991), 'Trade Barriers and Corporate Strategy in International Companies — The Canadian Experience,' *Long Range Planning* (June), 66-72.

Takacs, W. E. (1981), 'Pressures for Protectionism: An Empirical Analysis,' *Economic Enquiry*, 19, 687-693.

United States International Trade Commission (1989), *The Effects of the Steel Voluntary Restraint Agreements on US Steel-Consuming Industries*, Report to the Subcommittee on Ways and Means on Investigation No. 332-270 Under Section 332 of the Tariff Act of 1930, USITC Publication 2182 (May).

EC Anti-Dumping Laws as a Barrier to Trade

ALAN RUGMAN, *Professor of international Business, University of Toronto;* **MICHAEL GESTRIN,** *Doctoral Candidate, University of Toronto*

Anti-dumping (AD) laws in the EC are intended to establish 'fairness' between trading partners. But there are negative effects, in particular, firms with weak firm specific advantages can shelter behind AD laws; they can even follow shelter-based strategies and lobby for protection.

Alan Rugman and Michael Gestrin explain how shelter can be used as a management strategy, and how AD laws have grown up in the EC since 1979 to affect sectors of industry and geographic regions. They conclude by pointing out that a shelter-based strategy by a strong firm can undermine the very competitive pressures in its home market that made it internationally competitive in the first place.

Introduction

Dumping is acknowledged to be a potentially damaging practice in international trade. However, an analysis of the EC's use of its anti-dumping laws since 1980 reveals that these have given rise to problems much more serious than the dumping which they were supposed to discourage. By supplying weak firms with an opportunity to shelter themselves from foreign competition, the repeated use of anti-dumping laws threatens to constrain competitive forces and to retard globalization for the EC as a whole. As such, the anti-dumping laws have already contributed to a system of corporate welfare in sectors such as chemicals and iron and steel, with strong indications that the EC's electronics manufacturers are next in line.

In this paper, we consider the performance of the European Community's anti-dumping policies during the eleven-year period from 1980 to 1991. More specifically, we will consider whether the EC's anti-dumping (AD) codes have served to preserve fairness in trade between the EC and its trading partners. We will also identify trends in the use of the AD laws which are suggestive of future developments in this critical area of policy for managers.

The EC AD Laws and Globalization

Within the context of Europe's ongoing economic integration, and more generally, the increasingly globalized economic environment within which business must operate, European managers will be called upon to formulate strategies appropriate to this set of extraordinary circumstances. Firms will have to adapt quickly or become victims of capitalism's 'creative destruction.'

Unfortunately, where firms find themselves unable to develop sustainable competitive advantages, based upon firm-specific advantages (FSAs) in technology, management, and/or marketing skills, they are likely to resort to shelter-based strategies, aimed not at enhanced performance to meet the demands of globalization but at limiting globalization to meet their felt need for protection. A firm or industry which suffers from weak FSAs is dependent upon shelter-based strategies to secure for itself a share of the (protected) domestic market which it would not otherwise enjoy (Rugman and Verbeke, 1990 and Rugman and Gestrin, 1991).

Shelter-based business strategy is the conceptual counterpart to free trade. Just as the economic integration of Europe is expected to give rise to both static and dynamic gains (Cecchini, 1988), an avoidance of economic integration and globalization through protection will give rise to static and dynamic losses. The static losses accrue mainly to society in the form of higher prices and poorer selection. Dynamic losses accrue to protected industries as well as society since restrictions upon foreign competition will, in the medium to long term, give rise to corporate atrophy and eventual exit.

From the perspective of the firm, a protectionist strategy will appear eminently sensible in the absence of strong FSAs. If such a firm is able to protect itself from international competition, and hence extend its production run long enough to capitalize the original investment, it will obviously do so. From the perspective of society, however, such an extension constitutes a form of corporate welfare, as well as the diversion of scarce capital from potentially productive to unquestionably non-productive uses.

The significance of the AD laws within this context is that they present a window of opportunity to firms with weak or non-existent FSAs. There exists a powerful rationale for the existence of rules and mechanisms to guard against the damage which dumping may cause under certain circumstances; another danger is that firms will capture these laws and incorporate them into discriminatory strategies to compensate for weak or non-existent FSAs. (For a more thorough discussion of the theory of 'capture', refer to Rugman and Verbeke, 1990). The capture of American AD and anti-subsidy instruments has already been well documented (see, for example, Rugman and Anderson, 1987). We now move to a more detailed explanation of the concept of shelter, especially as it has been used as a management strategy.

The Strategy of Shelter

Before considering the historical record of the EC's use of its AD laws it is important to understand how such laws are now part of the strategic management of firms and industries. This has been developed at length by Rugman and Verbeke (1990) in an analysis of global firms and trade policy, and by Rugman and Gestrin (1991) in the context of US trade policy. The kind of performance a firm with strong FSAs will enjoy depends upon whether it pursues a competition-based or a shelter-based strategy. FSAs encompass the cumulation of technological, managerial and marketing skills which

give a firm its competitive edge. Shelter is a form of protection from market forces, usually a government-based barrier to entry, a discriminatory barrier against rival foreign firms.

In Figure 1, it is clear that firms with strong FSAs can focus solely upon competition-based strategies and fully exploit whatever advantages they enjoy in terms of technology, management and/or marketing skills. By doing so, their performance will be optimized both in the domestic as well as the global market.

Figure 1 also suggests the effects upon performance for a firm or industry with strong FSAs when pursuing a shelter-based strategy. In its domestic market, a shelter-based strategy serves to limit competition, and hence, the very forces which gave rise to strong FSAs in the first place. In the global market, a shelter-based strategy increases the likelihood that foreign producers who have been discriminated against will retaliate with their own market-closing activities. In other words, for firms with strong FSAs, there are no advantages to pursuing shelter-based strategies.

Figure 2 repeats the analysis of Figure 1 for firms with weak FSAs. For these firms, only one option is available

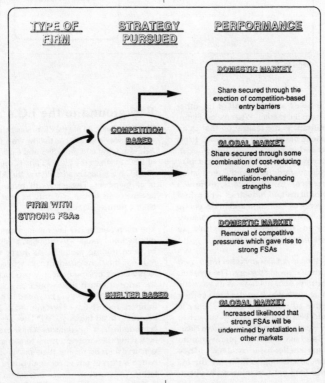

TYPE OF FIRM — **STRATEGY PURSUED** — **PERFORMANCE**

COMPETITION BASED

DOMESTIC MARKET
Share secured through the erection of competition-based entry barriers

GLOBAL MARKET
Share secured through some combination of cost-reducing and/or differentiation-enhancing strengths

FIRM WITH STRONG FSAs

SHELTER BASED

DOMESTIC MARKET
Removal of competitive pressures which gave rise to strong FSAs

GLOBAL MARKET
Increased likelihood that strong FSAs will be undermined by retaliation in other markets

Figure 1

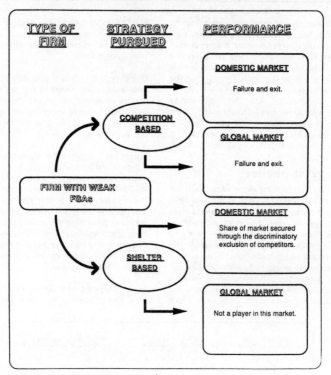

Figure 2

— to pursue shelter-based strategies. All of the other options lead to exit from the market. What makes Figure 2 all the more significant is the realization that in an economic environment based upon capitalism, firms such as those described in Figure 2 will always exist. Indeed, in such an environment failure and exit play an instrumental role towards constantly motivating change and improvement. In other words, there will always be a group of firms and industries which find themselves on the verge of extinction and in desperate search of economic elixirs. The EC's AD laws have unfortunately proven themselves susceptible to exploitation by these firms and industries.

Anti-dumping legislation is not like any other input used by firms in their formulation of strategy. The creation of discriminatory barriers does not have as its basis the kind of cost–benefit analysis which guides firms in their pursuit of competitive advantages. Rather, shelter is pursued as a second best strategy, largely subject to availability. In other words, and as Figure 2 makes clear, firms with weak FSAs have no other options than to pursue discriminatory shelter-based strategies. They form a *de facto* lobby, attempting to influence the EC bureaucracy and their national governments, to obtain protection.

Background to the EC's AD Laws

The EC's basic AD legislation was ratified in 1979.[1] As such, it was roughly consistent with the GATT's new Anti-dumping and Subsidies and Countervailing Codes of 1980, to which the EC is a Party (Commission, 1983:2). The EC bureaucracy administers the AD laws on behalf of all members. These laws therefore cannot be used against firms in the EC, only against firms exporting from countries outside the EC.

The main role of AD laws is to maintain 'fairness' in international trade — to establish a 'level playing field' between trading partners. As such, the laws aim to redress situations of unfairness when they occur due to predatory pricing or selling products abroad below the price at which they would be sold in the 'home' market. The AD laws are intended to protect firms and industries which have been injured as a result of unfair practices. In addition, the AD laws are used to punish firms, industries, or countries which use unfair practices by forcing these foreign firms to pay an anti-dumping penalty, thereby raising their prices in the importing nation's market (an effect analytically equivalent to a tariff). The purpose of such retaliation is to discourage dumping and subsidization (Jackson, 1989: 217). This latter role of the AD codes — to punish unfair trading behaviour — has become increasingly important over time, especially in the United States. (See for example USTR, 1991: 87–93).

> ### The EC has used AD laws to maintain 'fairness' between trading partners

Three main actors are involved in the administration of the EC AD codes. These are the Commission, the Council of Ministers, and the Advisory Committee. Of these, the Commission is the most powerful actor. Its duties include the initiation of proceedings, the termination of cases, the imposition of provisional duties, the acceptance of undertakings, and the recommendation of final measures to the Council for ratification. The Advisory Council consists of one representative from each member country — usually high ranking public servants. This body usually defers to the Commission. The Council of Ministers is the most politicized of the three bodies. Each state is represented by one Minister. The distribution of votes, however, is weighted unevenly among the representatives. Consequently, the final passage of bills is based upon a system of 'qualified majority' (Vermulst, 1987: 195–200).

Most trade complaints are launched by trade associations representing Community industries. Complaints are directed to the Commission which must then decide whether or not to launch an official investigation. This decision is based upon information supplied by the complainant in a standardized questionnaire, as well as any additional information which the Commissioin may collect during an informal initial investigation. The Commission will proceed with an investigation if it considers that there is 'sufficient evidence' of both unfair trade practices and injury to domestic producers. It is not clear, however, what constitutes 'sufficient evidence' since this initial stage of the process is secretive. Generally, the decision whether or not to initiate an investigation is made within six weeks of receipt of the complaint. If it is deemed that there is 'sufficient evidence,' the Commission will publish an initiation notice in the Office Journal (C series). After such a notice is published, interested parties on either side of the case have thirty days to submit their views to the Commission before the investigation actually begins (Vermulst, 1987: 201–203).

Investigations are six to twelve months long, and conclude with either a positive or negative finding of dumping. In the case of a negative finding the case is finished. On the other hand, if significant levels of dumping are found, the proceeding continues with a view to determining how much injury has been caused, and hence, what penalty should be imposed. Other nations, such as Canada and the United States, have similar AD procedures, but they are more transparent,

with publication of the decisions and procedures of the investigating authorities (see Rugman and Anderson, 1987, for details). The opaque nature of EC decisions is a powerful barrier facing foreign firms.

The AD cases can end in three possible ways. First, they may be terminated without the imposition of any type of remedial measures where either dumping margins have been insignificant or where injury has not occurred. Second, they may lead to the imposition of duties against dumped imports. According to the EC AD law, the calculation of these should be based upon the degree to which the dumping has caused injury, and not merely upon dumping margins. Under this rule, AD duties will usually be lower than if the dumping margins are calculated by simply subtracting the price at which the imported product is allegedly dumped from the price received by the exporting company in its domestic market (see Hindley (1988) for a more detailed account). This is because injury usually only begins to occur once the dumping exceeds a certain critical volume. Third, investigations may be resolved through the negotiation of either price or quantity undertakings. Undertakings are negotiated agreements between the importing country and the exporter. Most undertakings negotiated by the EC with its trading partners have been of the 'price' variety, where exporters to the European market have undertaken not to sell their products below a certain negotiated price.

Historical Patterns in the EC's Use of AD Laws

In this analysis we will consider the EC's use of its AD laws from three perspectives: first, the use of AD legislation over time; second, the use of AD legislation across sectors; and third, the use of AD legislation by the EC across geographic regions during the period 1980 to 1990.

The data include AD investigations as well as reviews of investigations. The rationale for including reviews of investigations in the analysis is that the rules which dictate their use, as well as the data, suggest that they are being used in a discriminatory fashion by firms. Many reviews are more analogous to independent investigations insofar as they can be used to cumulate the protective effects of AD duties. For example, the 1985 hardboard investigation targeted Argentina, Portugal, Switzerland, and Yugoslavia. When this apparently did not supply the domestic European hardboard producers with enough protection, they subsequently launched a review of earlier hardboard cases, launched in 1978, 1979, and 1982. Therefore, in the 1988 review, Brazil, Czechoslovakia, Poland, Romania, Sweden, and the USSR were targeted. In this situation, the review should clearly be treated as a separate case since it seeks to build upon the protection sought in the 1985 case (see review C165, 24.6.88, p. 2, for details).

Table 1   EC AD investigations and reviews by year (1980–1990)

Year	Number of AD investigations	Number of AD reviews	Total number of AD cases
1980	25	3	28
1981	47	17	64
1982	55	23	78
1983	36	10	46
1984	48	7	55
1985	36	19	55
1986	24	15	39
1987	42	5	47
1988	39	29	68
1989	26	17	43
1990	43	25	68
Totals	421	170	591

Sources: Commission of the European Communities, First through Ninth Annual Reports of the Commission on the Community's Anti-Dumping and Anti-Subsidy Activities (1982–1991).

Evolution of the EC's Use of AD over Time

Table 1 presents data on the number of investigations and reviews in each year for the period 1980 to 1990. Hereafter, as in this table, 'cases' will refer to investigations plus reviews. Over the entire period in question, 421 investigations and 170 reviews have been launched, for a total of 591 cases. The most striking feature of this table is the total absence of any discernible pattern over time in the use of this legislation. The mean is approximately 54, and the standard deviation around this mean is approximately 15.

Evolution of the EC's Use of AD across Sectors

The apparent randomness in the EC's use of AD legislation begins to break down once the data are analyzed in greater detail. Table 2 aggregates investigations, reviews, and cases over time but gives a sectoral breakdown of the data. The sectors used correspond to the United Nations Standard International Trade Classification (Revision 3) one- and two-digit commodity sectors. The data indicate that cases have been highly concentrated in four main sectors. These are 'chemicals and related products', 'other manufactured goods', 'machinery and transport equipment', and 'iron and steel'. These are the sectors which have been relatively active in pursuing protection through AD legislation. That this skewed distribution does not simply reflect discrepancies in the relative economic size of these sectors is indicated by the insignificant incidence of cases in such important economic sectors as 'mineral fuels, lubricants, etc.' (no cases), 'food, live animals, beverages, tobacco' (5 cases), and the textile and clothing sector (9 cases).

Evolution of the EC's Use of AD across Regions

Table 3 considers the EC's use of AD legislation from another important perspective. This table breaks the data down according to which geographic regions the EC targeted with AD during the period under review. As with the sectoral breakdown of the data, another strong pattern in the use of AD legislation emerges. The largest single share of cases, approximately 40 per cent, has been directed towards the COMECON countries. The next highest share, approximately 15 per cent,

Table 2   EC AD investigations and reviews by sector (1980–1990)

SITC Code	Description	Number of AD investigations	Number of AD reviews	Total number of AD cases
0–1	Food, live animals, beverages, tobacco	5	0	5
2	Crude materials, inedible, except fuels	38	17	55
3	Mineral fuels, lubricants, etc.	0	0	0
4	Animal and vegetable oils, fats, waxes	0	0	0
5	Chemicals and related products, n.e.s.	161	63	224
6.5	Textile yarn, fabrics, etc.	9	0	9
6.7	Iron and steel	49	18	67
6.8	Non-ferrous metals	18	5	23
7	Machinery and transport equipment	67	24	91
8.4	Apparel and clothing	0	0	0
6 and 8*	Other manufactured goods	74	43	117
	All Products Listed	421	170	591

* This category includes sub-sections of sections 6 and 8. From section 6 these include 6.1 (manufacturers of leather), 6.2 (rubber), 6.3 (cork and wood), 6.4 (paper and paperboard), 6.6 (non-metallic minerals), and 6.9 (manufactures of metals n.e.s.). From section 8, sub-sections 8.1 (prefabricated buildings), 8.2 (furniture), 8.3 (travel goods), 8.5 (footwear), 8.7 (scientific instruments), 8.8 (photographic equipment), and 8.9 (miscellaneous manufactured goods) are included.

Sources: Commission of the European Communities, First through Ninth Annual Reports of the Commission on the Community's Anti-Dumping and Anti-Subsidy Activities (1982–1991).

EC ANTI-DUMPING LAWS AS A BARRIER TO TRADE

Table 3   Regional incidence of AD cases launched by the EC (1980–1990)

Targeted country	Number of AD investigations	Number of AD reviews	Total number of AD cases
Japan	36	12	48
Asian NICs and Asean*	52	9	61
North America**	32	24	56
Africa	10	4	14
Latin /Central America***	37	13	50
Asian Socialist Countries†	31	8	39
Comecon Countries††	160	72	232
Other†††	63	28	91
Totals	421	170	591

* Includes cases against Malaysia, Singapore, S. Korea, Taiwan, Thailand, Hong Kong, Indonesia, and Macao.
** Includes cases against the United States and Canada.
*** Includes cases against Brazil, the Dominican Republic, Puerto Rico, Argentina, Venezuela, Surinam, Mexico, and Trinidad and Tobago.
† Includes cases against China and North Korea.
†† Includes cases against the USSR, Hungary, Bulgaria, Czechoslovakia, East Germany, Poland, Romania, Yugoslavia, and Albania.
††† Includes cases against Spain, Sweden, the Virgin Islands, Australia, Austria, Iceland, Israel, Norway, Turkey, Portugal, Switzerland, Kuwait, Libya, Finland, and India.

Source: Commission of the European Communities, First through Ninth Reports of the Commission on the Community's Anti-Dumping and Anti-Subsidy Activities (1982–1991).

Table 4   Regional share of cases by year (per cent)

Targeted country	1980	1981	1982	1983	1984	1985	1986	1987	1988	1989	1990	Totals
Japan	4	2	4	9	9	11	3	23	7	14	7	8
Asian NICs and Asean	14	2	1	9	2	7	10	21	21	16	16	10
North America	36	11	19	9	9	0	13	6	1	9	3	9
Africa	0	0	4	4	2	0	3	4	3	0	4	2
Latin /Central America	18	0	9	4	2	15	10	11	6	7	16	8
Socialist Block East	4	3	6	7	4	2	5	4	15	12	9	7
Socialist Block West	11	75	35	43	55	45	41	21	35	30	24	39
Other	14	8	22	15	18	20	15	9	12	12	21	15
Totals*	100	100	100	100	100	100	100	100	100	100	100	100

* Some columns do not actually add up to 100 due to rounding in the calculation of these figures.

Source: Commission of the European Communities, First through Ninth Reports of the Commission on the Community's Anti-Dumping and Anti-Subsidy Activities (1982–1991).

belongs to a group called 'other', which consists mainly of non-EC member European countries. All of the other regions on this list each account for less than ten per cent of total cases.

Table 4 extends the analysis from Table 3 by considering the cross-sectional evolution of the incidence of AD cases over both time and regions. The figures in the bottom row are the total numbers of cases per year, while the figures in the far right column are the total number of cases per country. Here, another pattern begins to emerge.

Although the COMECON countries were the most frequently targeted of any group during the period under review, their share of cases in each year is declining. Conversely, cases against Japan, the Asian NICs and the ASEAN countries have been steadily increasing during the period under consideration. Rival firms in these new competitors have been hurt by AD actions. For all of these countries the average number of cases per year over the period 1980–1990 is eighteen. From 1987 onwards, the number of cases per year for this region is consistently higher, averaging approximately 31 per year. Interestingly, EC AD cases against North America also appear to be on the decline.

Sectoral and Regional Biases

In this section we examine the extent to which the EC AD laws have displayed a tendency to be subject to capture by firms and industries seeking discriminatory protection. A considerable body of academic literature has attempted to deal with this issue and the intricacies of the use of the EC's AD instruments. (See, for example, Rugman and Verbeke (1990), Messerlin (1990),

Ostry (1990), and Stegeman (1990), who have all made contributions to our understanding of EC AD practices.)

Strong sectoral biases and clear patterns in the regional evolution of the use of AD laws suggest that the administration of the EC's AD laws leads to protection and shelter for the clientèle group. Indeed, it is interesting to note that sectorally, most AD cases originate from the chemicals and pharmaceuticals sectors, which have historically been among the most subsidized and protected sectors in Europe (*The Economist*, 8–14 June, 1991, 12–18). Furthermore, the regional patterns in the use of AD observed above correlate closely with problems in the EC's electronics industries, since it is exports of these products from the Pacific Basin which have given rise to substantial balance of trade deficits in this area. The EC's $25bn trade deficit with Japan will, at the very least, grease the AD wheels where exports from this country are concerned (*The Economist*, 8–14 June, 1991, 20).

The EC's strong bias in its targeting of COMECON exports highlights how technical aspects of AD legislation can significantly influence the outcomes of AD cases. The Commission is mandated to make its determination in an investigation based upon the 'best information available'. (Vermulst 1987: 207). If an exporter targeted in a case either does not supply information, or supplies information which, for whatever reason, is suspect, the Commission will base its decision primarily upon whatever other information has been supplied. Given that this other information has been predominantly supplied by the domestic complainant, bias in favour of the complainant will always exist under these circumstances. The COMECON producers have been disadvantaged on two counts where the 'best information available' rule is concerned. First, they have all been under one form or another of unwieldy and unresponsive state control. Second, the deficiencies in the accounting practices of COMECON producers are well documented and these would certainly undermine a defendant's case before the Commission. This is just one of many technical factors which, although not necessarily discriminatory in and of itself, could facilitate discriminatory behaviour.

Conclusions and Implications for Strategic Management

It would be overstating the case to suggest that abuse and discrimination runs rampant in the use of the EC AD mechanisms. However, the problems identified in this paper deserve attention. These problems fall under two categories: direct discriminatory effects and secondary discriminatory effects.

Direct discriminatory effects arise from the actual impact of AD cases upon trade. At first it may appear that the direct effects are not significant since only 0.6 per cent of the EC's total imports were affected by AD investigations in 1989 (Commission, 1991: 66). However, it should again be recalled that the use of AD legislation

is distributed very unevenly across sectors, with the highest concentration in the chemical sector, and indications of growing concentration in the high technology sectors. For example, the share of EC imports from Japan which is affected by AD measures is 3.5 per cent (Commission, 1991: 66). This is almost six times as high as the overall incidence of AD measures against imports from all sources.

This last point brings us to the issue of the secondary discriminatory effects of the EC AD laws. These effects are numerous. The first concerns the impact upon trade of the mere existence of these laws and the threat that European firms and industries might use them. (Herander and Schwarts, (19??), for example, have found that the US AD law has had a distortionary impact upon the pricing behaviour of exporters to the US market.) The second concerns the apparent tendency for the AD laws to give rise to government sponsored cartels (Messerlin, 1990). The EC's preference to see cases resolved through undertakings has necessitated rules which allow firms and industries to cooperate beyond what would be permissible under the Community's anti-collusion legislation (Stegemann, 1990). The third secondary effect concerns the uncertainty to which the AD laws have given rise. This paper has only touched upon a small number of the many factors which seem to dictate the changes in the type of patterns in the use of the EC AD laws which Tables 1 to 4 reported. What these highlight is the uncertainty faced by foreign producers and investors. Furthermore, much of this uncertainty results from the secrecy which surrounds the investigation and review processes. With such a concentration of powers over the entire process in one body, (i.e. the Commission), the likelihood that political pressures will come to influence the bureaucratic process is increased.

In sum, the EC AD laws are doubled-edged. They are needed to provide protection from a potential real threat — dumping — but their presence invites the development of another — the capture and use of these instruments by firms and industries with weak FSAs. Firms will always make use of any instruments available to them to further their economic survival. What managers and businesses must realize is that while protection through the use of AD buys time for the weak and dying firm or industry, it has the opposite effect upon an industry which does have the means to compete in an increasingly globalized environment. By lessening competition in its own home market, the strong firm essentially removes the kinds of pressure which gave rise to its strong FSAs in the first place.

Acknowledgements

The authors acknowledge helpful comments from Andrew Anderson in writing this paper.

Note

1   Council Regulation (EEC) No. 3017/79 of 20 December

EC ANTI-DUMPING LAWS AS A BARRIER TO TRADE

1979 on protection against dumped or subsidized imports from countries not members of the European Economic Community, and Commission Recommendation No. 3018/79/ECSC of 21 December 1979 on protection against dumped or subsidized imports from countries not members of the European Steel Community.

Bibliography

Cecchini, Paolo, *The European Challenge 1992: The Benefits of a Single Market*, The Commission of the European Communities, 1988.

Commission of the European Communities, *First Annual Report of the Commission of the European Communities on the Community's Anti-dumping and Anti-subsidy Activities*, Brussels, 28 September 1983, (COM (83) 519 Final /2). The second through ninth annual reports are coded, respectively, as follows; COM(84) 721 final, COM(86) 308 final, COM(87) 178 final, COM(88) 92 final, COM(89) 106 final, COM(90) 229 final, SEC(91) 92 final.

The Economist, '1992: Second Thoughts: A Survey of Business in Europe', 8–14 June, 1991.

Herander, Mark G. and J. Brad Schwartz, 'An Empirical Test of the Impact of the Threat of US Trade Policy: The Case of Antidumping Duties', *Southern Economic Journal*, 19?? 51: 59–79.

Hindley, Brian, 'Dumping and the Far East Trade of the European Community', *The World Economy*, 11:4, December 1988: 445–64.

Jackson, John H., *The World Trading System: Law and Policy of International Economic Relations*, The MIT Press, 1989.

Messerlin, Patrick A., 'Anti-Dumping Regulations or Procartel Law? The EC Chemical Cases', *The World Economy*, 13:4, December 1990: 465–92.

Ostry, Sylvia, *Governments and Corporations in a Shrinking World: Trade and Innovation Policies in the United States, Europe and Japan*, Council on Foreign Relations, New York, N.Y., 1990.

Rugman, Alan M. and Andrew S.M. Anderson, *Administered Protection in America*, Croom Helm/Routledge, London and New York, 1987.

Rugman, Alan M. and Michael Gestrin, 'US Trade Laws as Barriers to Globalization', paper presented at the Fourth IBEAR Research Conference on 'The Globalization of American Firms' at the University of Southern California, Loss Angeles, 20–21 June, 1991.

Rugman, Alan M. and Alain Verbeke, *Global Corporate Strategy and Trade Policy*, Croom Helm/Routledge, London and New York, 1990.

Stegemann, Klaus, 'EC Anti-Dumping Policy: Are Price Undertakings a Legal Substitute for Illegal Price Fixing?' *Weltwirtschaftliches Archiv*, 126:2, 1990: 268–298.

United States Trade Representative, *1991 Trade Policy Agenda and 1990 Annual Report of the President of the United States on the Trade Agreements Program*, Office of the United States Trade Representative, Washington, D.C., 1991.

Vermulst, Edwin A., *Antidumping Law and Practice in the United States and the European Communities: A Comparative Analysis*, Elsevier Science Publishers B.V., 1987.

Excerpt from *Journal of Business Administration*, **17** (1–2) (1987/8)

3

TRADE POLICY IN THE ASIA-PACIFIC REGION: A U.S.-JAPAN COMPARISON

Alan M. Rugman and Alain Verbeke*

INTRODUCTION

The methods by which nations can shape industrial policy have been at the forefront of recent work on Asia-Pacific relations. The economic success of Japan in the postwar period has led many other nations to attempt to emulate its perceived policy of state support for industry and trade. Even in the United States, influential voices have articulated the need for a new view of international economic policy; one in which the United States uses its size to turn the terms of trade in its favor by the use of import protection and export subsidies.

In this paper we develop a new conceptual framework to contrast Japanese and American attempts to formulate and implement such trade-oriented industrial policies. We demonstrate that the Japanese have been successful in reshaping their comparative advantage by the use of effective administrative structures at the national level. We find evidence of a policy structure which enhances the successful implementation of Japanese industrial strategies, as centralized policy choices are possible. In the United States, however, we have observed the recent escalation of decentralized administered protection, rather than the implementation of efficient national trade policies. The nature and extent of this new type of U.S. administered protection is considered and the failure of U.S. structure and trade

---

*The authors are, respectively, Professor of International Business, Faculty of Management, University of Toronto, and Visiting Research Fellow, Dalhousie University.

strategy is contrasted with the Japanese experience.

Examples and case histories are used, such as American attempts to protect the steel, textile, agricultural, and semiconductor industries and the Japanese policies to promote exports of autos, consumer electronics and related high technology products. The existence of transaction costs in the execution of U.S. trade policy in these areas is noted and contrasted with the methods by which Japan has dealt with the costs of policy administration. Implications are drawn out for both trade policy and the strategic planning of corporations. Finally, the interaction of such business-government relations is examined and lessons are drawn out for the formulation of trade policy in other countries of the Asia-Pacific region.

THE ASSESSMENT OF INTERNATIONAL TRADE STRATEGIES

The new theoretical framework developed in this paper allows us to compare U.S. and Japanese trade policies and to contrast their distinctive characteristics. Figure 1 is a conceptual assessment of the international trade strategies of governments according to their free trade or non-free trade orientation and the perceived degree of their success. The horizontal axis deals with the nature of trade strategy and the vertical axis with the "perceived" outcomes of these strategies.

A free-trade strategy means that government policy is to have the international flows in goods and services determined by the economic principles of comparative advantage. In this situation, the nation's "natural" country specific advantages (CSAs) will influence trade patterns. The CSAs capture the factor endowments of a nation, basically the variables in its aggregate production function (Rugman, 1981).

With a non-free trade orientation, the government shapes comparative advantage in its favor, or at least attempts to do so. It can do this by shifting its terms of trade (if it is a large country like Japan or the United States). In this case, unnatural market imperfections are created in favor of national firms, which gives them a competitive edge vis-à-vis foreign rivals (Rugman and Verbeke, 1987a). To some extent, every country in the world grants certain trading advantages to domestic firms. Methods include special export financing arrangements, tax rebates, preferential government procurement, and so on.

In Figure 1 it is the degree of government support that matters. The main question is whether government has a central policy to guide

JBA, Vol. 17 - No. 1 and 2, 87/88   *91*

FIGURE 1

ASSESSING INTERNATIONAL TRADE STRATEGIES

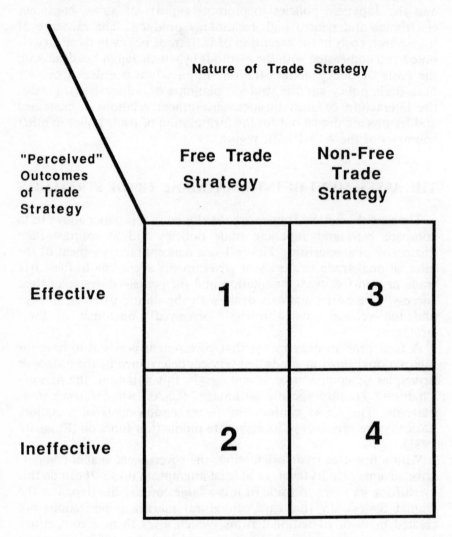

Nature of Trade Strategy

"Perceived" Outcomes of Trade Strategy	Free Trade Strategy	Non-Free Trade Strategy
Effective	1	3
Ineffective	2	4

and direct international trade or to let the market system determine trade flows. Turning to the vertical axis, the issue of policy effectiveness is a complex one. The concept of effectiveness used here is the perception of trade policy success, which is a normative assessment. This approach can be contrasted to the narrower concept of economic efficiency whereby, from a global perspective, a free trade environment is always the most efficient (first best). Also in terms of economic efficiency, from a national perspective, it may be efficient to pursue a non-free trade strategy in particular cases, such as (a) the monopoly tariff case; (b) the externalities and market imperfections case; (c) the infant industry protection case; (d) the profit shifting case; and, (e) the "compensating for unnatural market imperfections" case. However, in the next section it will be argued that even from a national perspective, such non-free trade strategies will only be efficient if specific conditions are fulfilled.

THE U.S. TRADE DEFICIT

The trade balance of a country is often used to assess the effectiveness of a nation's trade policy (McCraw, 1986). If the American and Japanese trade balances (with all nations), and their bilateral balances are used as a proxy for the success of the trade strategies of the United States and Japan, it would then appear that Japan has developed an enormous competitive advantage vis-à-vis the United States, as shown in Tables 1 and 2.

McCraw (1986) and his colleagues at the Harvard Business School have argued that Tables 1 and 2 suggest that the United States, which consistently had a trade surplus before 1971, but accumulated high trade deficits in the recent past, now has an ineffective trade strategy. In contrast, the Japanese surpluses indicate a highly effective trade strategy which has allowed Japanese firms to develop into global competitors to penetrate foreign markets through exports.

The U.S. trade balance is actually influenced by many factors, including tax policies, government spending, social and industrial policies, and macroeconomic factors, all of which constitute the elements in a nation's set of CSAs. Moreover, the strength of the firm specific advantages (FSAs) of the companies located in the nation and their choices of entry mode in foreign countries also have a profound influence on the trade balance, as does industry structure in general.

Internalization theory suggests that unnatural market imperfections in other nations, such as tariff and non-tariff barriers, will increase the relative benefits associated with foreign direct investment, as compared with exports (Rugman, 1981). While such effects

Table 1

AMERICAN AND JAPANESE TRADE BALANCES
(with all nations)

	(Billions of U.S. $)	
	U.S.	Japan
1975	2.2	-2.0
1980	- 36.2	-10.9
1981	- 39.6	8.6
1982	- 42.6	6.9
1983	- 69.4	20.6
1984	-123.3	33.5
1985	-143.8	39.6

Source: McCraw, 1986, p.31.

Table 2

AMERICAN TRADE DEFICIT WITH JAPAN

	(Billions of U.S. $)
1975	- 1.6
1980	- 10.4
1981	- 15.8
1982	- 17.0
1983	- 21.1
1984	- 37.0
1985	- 40.7

Source: McCraw, 1986, p.33.

may influence a nation's trade balance, they can hardly be considered to represent "bad" trade policy. International trade policy strategies alone do not constitute the main determining factor in explaining how trade deficits or surpluses evolve over time, although they may directly influence the export performance of domestic firms and/or the volume of imports from other countries.

Moreover, a nation's trade balance is only one element in its balance of payments. A trade deficit can be compensated by a surplus on the capital account, because of large short- or long-term investment opportunities. Then the trade deficit should not be regarded as the result of an inappropriate trade policy; instead it may reflect macro-economic factors such as changes in currency valuations and real interest rates. Hence, if a non-free trade strategy is implemented as a response to the perceived ineffectiveness of a free trade strategy signalled by a trade deficit, the result may well be greater economic inefficiency not only from a global point of view, but also from a national one.

Indeed, it has been demonstrated by Lawrence and Litan (1987) that the U.S. trade deficits merely result from the macroeconomic imbalance between American spending and production, which itself is caused by the government deficit ranging between $150 billion and $200 billion. Moreover, the Japanese "portion" of the U.S. trade deficit has not increased substantially between 1981 and 1985, so that Japanese non-free trade strategies in favor of domestic firms cannot be held responsible for the rising import volume of the United States.

A CLASSIFICATION OF NON-FREE TRADE STRATEGIES

Figure 2 is used to suggest that two broad types of non-free trade strategies exist, depending upon their "FSA-developing" or "sheltering" orientation. An FSA-developing non-free trade strategy has as its prime long run purpose to strengthen the FSAs of the firms involved and to maintain or improve their competitive position vis-à-vis foreign rivals on the basis of their economic efficiency. In contrast, a sheltering strategy does not aim at stimulating the development of strong FSAs; protection against foreign rivals is granted. This is done first where shelter in itself is the ultimate objective (perhaps as a response to lobbying pressures) and, second, when the satisfaction of social goals (such as maintaining inefficient employment levels in declining industries) is of major importance.

Two types of "tools" can be used to implement either of these non-free trade strategies: import restricting tools and export promoting ones. Both types may be complementary components of a nation's trade strategy. Moreover, short-term import restricting measures may well have long-term export promoting consequences if

FIGURE 2

A CLASSIFICATION OF NON-FREE TRADE STRATEGIES

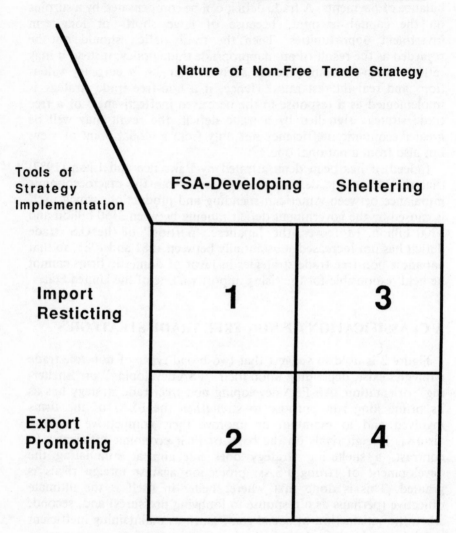

Nature of Non-Free Trade Strategy

Tools of
Strategy
Implementation

	FSA-Developing	Sheltering
Import Resticting	1	3
Export Promoting	2	4

domestic firms are able to develop strong FSAs in the absence of foreign competition in the domestic market. This leads to the issue of whether non-free trade strategies are efficient from the national point of view.

Sheltering strategies are always inefficient in the long run. They result from the pursuit of non-economic objectives and the influence exerted by specific pressure groups on government, reflecting the sensitivity of government decision-makers to the demands of clientele groups. High sensitivity to such groups can be explained by the utility maximizing considerations of politicians and bureaucrats (Rugman and Verbeke, 1987b).

In contrast, FSA-developing strategies may be efficient if the long-term benefits of government intervention are higher than their short-term costs. Such strategies are often difficult to implement successfully. In the infant industry case, a fast-growing internal market and active competition between domestic firms are some of the requirements for achieving economic efficiency (Brander, 1987; and Doz, 1986).

In the profit shifting case (Brander and Spencer, 1985; and Brander 1986, 1987), subsidies and other advantages may be granted by government to domestic firms to generate strategic effects (such as deterring entry by potential foreign competitors) or dynamic scale economies (learning curve effects). International competition is required to stimulate cost efficiency and innovative behavior of the domestic firms.

Efficient FSA-developing strategies are characterized by selectivity in the choice of firms and industries to which advantages will be granted. Moreover, a policy structure must exist, suitable to implement government strategies, without being dominated by the narrow interests of pressure groups. These two elements are especially important in the case of compensating for unnatural market imperfections. Here, a government which may be in favor of free trade can adopt a non-free trade strategy, because of unnatural market imperfections, such as trade barriers or export subsidies, imposed by foreign nations. As a result, domestic industries face unfair competition from the treasuries of foreign governments. Through countervailing actions, such as trade remedy laws, this unfair competition can be restricted (Hufbauer and Erb, 1985).

The efficient implementation of such trade remedy laws then requires a policy structure able to discriminate between domestic firms seeking government intervention on the basis of economic efficiency grounds and those merely interested in acquiring shelter. If advantages are granted to domestic firms, the chances of achieving long run economic efficiency may be increased by imposing performance requirements (such as productivity improvements) and by making government intervention self-liquidating.

FIGURE 3

THE POTENTIAL EFFECTIVENESS OF NON-FREE TRADE STRATEGIES

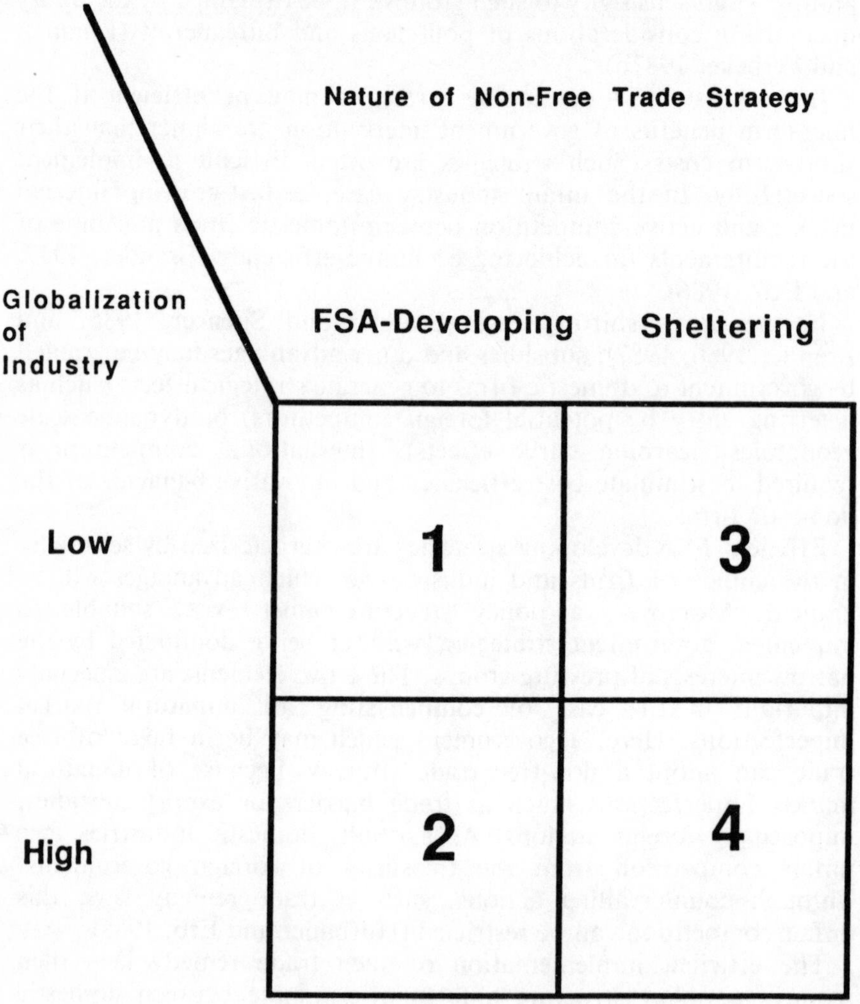

Nature of Non-Free Trade Strategy

Globalization of Industry	FSA-Developing	Sheltering
Low	1	3
High	2	4

Figure 3 is useful in predicting the potential (in)effectiveness of FSA-developing and sheltering strategies, based upon the degree of globalization of the affected industries. It is hypothesized that an FSA-developing strategy may potentially have positive long run trade balance effects, irrespective of the level of globalization of industries. A lower level of global competition will obviously increase potential effectiveness, since domestic firms will not be confronted with global competitors in the international environment, after having developed strong FSAs. In contrast, a sheltering strategy, which is always inefficient, can only be "effective" in the long run, as measured by the trade balance, in the absence of global compe..tion.

There are six main reasons why such a strategy is bound to fail in the long run, in the presence of global competition. First, if the main competitive advantage of a firm is neither based on overall cost competitiveness, product differentiation or focus (Porter, 1980) but on protection, the development of additional inefficiency in resource allocation and production can be expected, in the spirit of Leibenstein (1976), as the firm will be (partly) sheltered from pressures exerted by market forces. This implies that, in the long run, the chances of competing successfully in the international environment with global competitors are reduced. This can lead to negative trade balance effects, in contrast to the case in which government measures would help the firm to develop its FSAs.

Second, if government only grants shelter to firms on the condition that they will comply with social objectives such as maintaining high (inefficient) employment levels and production capacities or increasing income levels in underdeveloped regions, then a new source of micro-economic inefficiency will be created, again with negative long run trade balance effects.

Third, if inefficiency in resource allocation and production becomes too high as compared with foreign competitors, the shelter provided by governmental protection mechanisms may still be insufficient to guarantee the survival of the firm in the long run, especially if a large part of its production is exported. In this case, exit may become inevitable.

Fourth, the advantages granted by government may depend upon precarious political circumstances such as foreign policy options. The termination of those advantages could then jeopardize the firm's survival and lead to exit, especially if these advantages constituted the firm's main source of strength vis-à-vis foreign competition.

Fifth, if trade barriers are imposed on foreign competitors, this may result in retaliation by foreign governments with negative trade balance outcomes.

Sixth, if the products of sheltered industries (e.g., steel) are themselves used in downstream global industries (e.g., automobiles), then the international competitiveness and trade balance performance of the processing industry may be negatively affected. This is especially true if shelter is provided through trade barriers against cheap foreign imports.

U.S. TRADE POLICY

In this section, the recent evolution of American and Japanese trade policies will be contrasted using the theoretical framework developed above. The United States has traditionally pursued a free trade strategy. Trade policy implementation was delegated to a technical track by Congress in 1934, in order to shift the responsibility for trade policy measures to a forum in which no interest bias would exist in favor of protectionism. In this sense, Congress insulated itself from its own tendency to subvert national free trade goals to which most members of Congress agreed (Destler, 1986; and Finger et al., 1982). The 1934 Reciprocal Trade Act allowed the Executive Branch of government to negotiate reciprocal tariff reductions up to 50 percent of existing levels with other nations.

After World War II, the U.S. free trade strategy became even more predominant. Two major principles of trade strategy were formulated. The first one suggested that international political interests should dominate trade issues. The second one implied that free trade would, in the long run, generate the most effective economic results for the U.S. (Quadrant 1 of Figure 1).

There were a number of "exceptions" to this strategy. First, all presidents since Eisenhower have protected industries with high lobbying power such as textiles, steel, and footwear. In these cases, sheltering strategies were implemented using import restricting tools. Secondly, limited export-promoting incentives were provided to U.S. firms, such as American Export-Import Bank financing and tax advantages. These partly compensated for sometimes much larger incentives granted by other nations to their firms. In these cases, FSA-developing strategies were used.

Within the executive branch, however, the possibilities of implementing sheltering strategies were limited, as protectionist views in one department (such as Commerce or Labor) would be confronted with the free trade preferences of other departments (usually Treasury and State). The leading role performed by the United States in the past seven GATT rounds demonstrates, however, that an overall executive branch preference existed for free trade and for the elimination of international trade barriers.

Today, trade policy is again the prerogative of Congress. The perception by Congress that free trade strategies resulted in major negative effects for a number of U.S. industries affected by international rivalry (a perceived shift from Quadrant 1 to Quadrant 2 in Figure 1) led to the quasi-protectionist Trade Acts of 1974, 1979, and 1984 (an intended shift to Quadrant 3 in Figure 1).

The 1974 act introduced a number of specific non-free trade elements in U.S. trade law. First, it increased the power of the International Trade Commission vis-à-vis the President, who has traditionally been in favor of free trade because of broader international diplomatic and political objectives. Second, Congress limited the power of the President to reduce non-tariff barriers, as each such agreement required a majority vote of Congress.

The Trade Act of 1979 and the Trade and Tariff Act of 1984 were designed to substantially change the implementation of U.S. trade policy. In both cases the intent of Congress was to move towards Quadrant 3 of Figure 1, to allow American producers to be protected against alleged illegal dumping and foreign export subsidies. Hence, it was argued that unnatural market imperfections introduced by foreign nations should be "corrected" through the use of an American non-free trade strategy in severely affected sectors. The 1979 Trade Act shifted power to administer dumping and countervailing duty cases from the liberal Treasury Department to the Commerce Department. The act also contained restrictions limiting the power of the executive branch in trade policy implementation. The 1984 Act also encouraged the President to engage in retaliation against unfair foreign competition, and the International Trade Commission was asked by Congress to use broader criteria when determining the eligibility of an industry for import relief.

The three consecutive changes in U.S. trade policy, as described above, shifted part of the power to implement trade policy from the executive branch to private industry and labor organizations, as it became much easier to demand the implementation of protectionist measures. However, some observers such as Yoffie (1986, p.44) would suggest that the intended shift towards Quadrant 3 is nothing more than a "secondary" strategy, as free trade goals would still guide U.S. trade policy in many areas. Such a view can be documented by the fact that Presidents Ford, Carter, and Reagan have rejected the same percentage of "escape clause" and other general petitions as former presidents, although the number of industries filing petitions for import relief went up from 40 in 1977 to almost 200 in 1984.

In reality, a major shift is presently going on from a free trade strategy towards a non-free trade strategy. Today any U.S. firm or industry can file a petition against alleged unfair foreign imports, and try to obtain countervailing actions. Moreover, the criteria for determining what constitutes a countervailing foreign subsidy have been broadened as a result of the softwood lumber case of October 1986 (Rugman and Porteous, 1988). As a result, it will become much easier for U.S. firms with weak FSAs to raise the transaction costs for their foreign competitors through the use of U.S. administered protection.

Figure 2 identifies the characteristics of the current U.S. non-free trade strategy. The present protectionist strategy of the United States, as reflected in the institutional framework available to U.S. producers to petition against alleged "unfair" imports, is not a "secondary" strategy at all. This would only be implemented in cases of unfair foreign competition when the "primary" free trade strategy led to undesirable outcomes for the nation.

If the present non-free trade strategy were really a secondary strategy, its orientation would be FSA-developing. In that case, alleged foreign subsidies and dumping practices would be compared with "advantages" given to U.S. producers. Moreover, it would require selectivity in granting protection, whereby the U.S. government would discriminate between industries and firms that will remain or become internationally competitive in the long run and those that have no future in a more global environment. In this case, the temporary imposition of a CSA (such as protection against unfair imports) would build upon the FSAs of the firms involved or allow them to develop strong FSAs (Quadrants 1 and 2 of Figure 2). In the case of a sheltering strategy, however, regulations imposed by government in favor of domestic firms may merely compensate for the absence of strong FSAs.

The non-free trade strategy as developed by the United States has a sheltering orientation without any effort at serious selectivity. This was discussed in Rugman and Verbeke (1987c), where two countervailing actions against Canadian imports were studied (the Fresh Atlantic Groundfish case and the Softwood Lumber case). Moreover, little has been done to provide special assistance to facilitate American exports, as the United States has provided few tax advantages, little preferential export financing, and only a small number of export subsidies for non-agricultural and non-defense exports. The present emphasis on sheltering through the use of import restricting policy tools (Quadrant 3 of Figure 2) raises questions as to its economic efficiency and potential effectiveness to improve the U.S. trade balance in the long run. This issue can be clarified through the use of Figure 3.

Porter (1986) has observed an increased globalization across industries. In this case, the overall position of the United States in Figure 3 is located in the fourth quadrant. In terms of Figure 1, this would imply that the United States is now shifting to the fourth quadrant, instead of the third quadrant. Although jobs may be saved temporarily in such industries as steel and lumber, at a high cost for the general taxpayer (Ohmae, 1987), the trade balance effectiveness of such measures is questionable. Lawrence and Litan (1987) found that of 16 major U.S. industries receiving shelter since 1950, only one (the bicycle industry) was characterized by expansion after the elimination of protection. This research is consistent with our theoretical framework.

JAPANESE TRADE POLICY

In contrast to the United States, a non-free trade strategy has been successfully implemented in Japan after World War II (Quadrant 3 of Figure 1). In particular, the import of manufactured goods was severely restricted. The Japanese government used an elaborate set of tariffs and non-tariff barriers to limit foreign imports. A policy of selective granting of import licenses was used by the Ministry of International Trade and Industry (MITI) for raw materials. This non-free trade strategy primarily served long-term FSA-developing purposes (with some exceptions such as the sheltering strategy in the rice sector), with a gradual elimination of import restrictions.

One of the major industries selected for large scale development by MITI after World War II was the steel industry. A so-called "industrial rationalization" strategy was implemented in order to assure the development of strong FSAs in the protected steel firms (McCraw and O'Brien, 1986). Productivity improvements in the different firms became the main criterion used by MITI to allocate capacity expansion "rights." Such an FSA-developing strategy was, of course, conducive to the creation of a strong internationally competitive steel industry, since it stimulated intense domestic competition.

Similarly, Japanese industrial policies in the automobile sector were more "market promotional" than sheltering oriented (Doz, 1986; and Tyson 1987). The automobile industry case also demonstrates that MITI could not engage in autonomous central planning. In 1961 MITI made a proposal to organize passenger car manufacturers into three specialized groups (regular passenger cars, minicars and specialty cars), in order to improve scale economies. This proposal was rejected by the industry and domestic competition continued.

In other industries, MITI often set target dates when limitations on foreign competition would be abolished. In this way, Japanese firms were stimulated to adopt the most recent technological innovations so as to improve their competitiveness against foreign rivals after the elimination of Japanese trade barriers. Hence, import restrictions were merely a tool to encourage the development of strong FSAs, especially in manufacturing industries where dynamic scale economies were a prerequisite for international competitiveness.

During the 1970s and 1980s many of the previously dominant import restricting tools of the non-free trade strategy have been eliminated. Although non-tariff trade barriers still exist in many sectors, the average tariffs on industrial and mining products entering Japan were lower than American tariffs in 1982 and quantitative restrictions on imports existed for only five manufactured products (Yoffie, 1986, p.46). The Japanese government has also selectively eliminated import barriers faster than most other developed countries for products in which it chose not to engage in FSA-developing strategies.

As to export promoting tools, these have also been reduced as compared with the 1950s and 1960s, when numerous advantages were granted to Japanese firms with international activities. These included tax advantages, preferential financing, export insurance through MITI, and commercial bank credits at low interest rates. While export incentives remain extremely important, all special tax advantages had shifted to domestic projects by 1975 as the government perceived the existing FSAs of Japanese firms to be strong enough to compete internationally.

A related element is that this FSA-developing strategy could be successfully implemented only as a result of centralized coordination and choice, especially by MITI, which coordinated Japanese trade strategy in the post-war period. Japanese trade strategy forms an integrated part of an FSA-developing industrial policy (Morici, 1984). MITI does not engage in centralized strategic trade planning but has a close working relationship with private business (through groups such as Keidanren) and other ministries such as the Ministry of Finance. Selectivity in protection is possible because "advantages" will only be given to specific firms and industries after extensive consultation with the private sector's industrial and trade organizations.

This structure is completely different from the U.S. situation, whereby direct lobbying by individual firms or specific interest groups is much stronger (Ouchi, 1984). In Figures 2 and 3, Japanese industries are situated in the first and second quadrants with FSA-developing strategies, which explains the overall effectiveness of Japanese trade policy. The rise of the Japanese computer and semiconductor industry after 1955 is perhaps the classic example of an FSA-developing strategy. Here, infant industry protection has led to the development of strong internationally competitive firms (Ouchi, 1984). In generalizing about Japanese trade policy, Abegglen and Stalk (1985) have emphasized that, in most cases, no national champions are picked out by government; it is the marketplace that determines the "winning" and "losing" firms.

TRADE POLICY FOR THE NICs

The lessons for other Pacific Basin nations from the models developed here are to beware of the difficulties of policy implementation. The newly industrialized countries (NICs) like South Korea, Taiwan, Hong Kong, and Singapore are relatively small open trading economies. They do not have the large internal markets of either Japan or the United States, so a policy of export promotion is required. However, due to the new U.S. policy of administered protection, direct export subsidies and infant industry protection by the NICs are dangerous policies to pursue. Therefore the NICs must accept the discipline of operating a free trade strategy in Quadrant 1 of Figure 1, and be careful not to become trapped with the ineffective trade policy outcome of Quadrant 2. Another Pacific country, Canada, has been in pursuit of these types of open trade strategies in recent years.

The NICs can achieve their trade objectives, like Canada, by operating in Quadrant 2 of Figure 2; namely, an FSA-developing export promotion strategy. Then if their exports are in global industries, they will be equipped to survive in Quadrant 2 of Figure 3. All of this is easier said than done; but the implementation of successful trade strategies for the smaller partners in the Asia-Pacific region must always come as a result of understanding the policies of the two giants, Japan and the United States.

CONCLUSIONS AND NORMATIVE IMPLICATIONS

What are the normative implications of the above analysis for the United States? The first implication is that the U.S. trade balance is not a good indicator of economic efficiency. Hence, the United States should not attempt to redesign its policy towards a non-free trade strategy. The administrative heritage of public policy structures and private sector views on the role of government is not conducive to the successful implementation of a Japanese-style, centrally coordinated, non-free trade strategy. Instead, selectivity is required, in the sense that a non-free trade strategy should only be conducted where it is clear that free trade policies have failed (perhaps because of protectionism of other countries). A non-free trade strategy should remain a secondary strategy and, if it is pursued, it should be a micro-efficiency oriented one. Protection should not be granted to industries whose survival may become completely dependent upon shelter.

The main problem associated with the present system of U.S. decentralized administrative protection is that it provides shelter. It does not permit discrimination between protecting potential growth sectors and sunset industries that face an inevitable decline because of weakening FSAs. The escalating number of countervailing duty and anti-dumping cases suggests that a non-free trade strategy has become the new trade strategy of the United States. In turn, these non-tariff barriers to trade which are preventing foreign entry to the U.S. market would explain the enormous influx of foreign direct investment into the United States.

REFERENCES

Abegglen, James C., and George Stalk, Jr., (1985) *Kaisha. The Japanese Company* (New York: Basic Books).

Brander, James A., (1986) "Rationales for Strategic Trade and Industrial Policy," in Paul Krugman, (ed.), *Strategic Trade Policy and the New International Economics* (Cambridge, Mass.: MIT Press), pp. 23-46.

Brander, James A., (1987) "Shaping Comparative Advantage: Trade Policy, Industrial Policy and Economic Performance," in Richard G. Lipsey and

Wendy Dobson, (eds.), *Shaping Comparative Advantage* (Toronto: C.D. Howe Institute), pp. 1-56.

Brander, James A., and Barbara J. Spencer, (1985) "Export Subsidies and International Market Share Rivalry," *Journal of International Economics*, 18, pp. 83-100.

Destler, I.M., (1986) *American Trade Politics: System Under Stress* (Washington D.C.: Institute for International Economics).

Doz, Yves L., (1986) "Government Policies and Global Industries," in Michael E. Porter, (ed.), *Competition in Global Industries* (Boston, Mass.: Harvard Business School Press).

Finger, J.M., H. Keith Hall, and Douglas Nelson, (1982) "The Political Economy of Administered Protection," *American Economic Review* 72:3 June, pp. 452-456.

Hufbauer, Gary, and Joanna Erb, (1985) *Subsidies in International Trade* (Cambridge, Mass.: MIT Press).

Lawrence, Robert Z., and Robert E. Litan, (1987) "Why Protectionism Doesn't Pay," *Harvard Business Review*, 87:3, May-June, p. 6067.

Leibenstein, M., (1976) *Beyond Economic Man* (Cambridge, Mass.: Harvard University Press).

McCraw, Thomas K., (1986) "From Partners to Competitors: An Overview of the Period Since World War II," in Thomas K. McCraw, (ed.), *American Versus Japan* (Boston, Mass.: Harvard Business School Press).

McCraw, Thomas K., and Patricia A. O'Brien, (1986) "Production and Distribution: Competition Policy and Industry Structure," in McCraw, (ed.), *American Versus Japan* (Boston, Mass.: Harvard Business School Press).

Morici, Peter, (1984) *The Global Competitive Struggle: Challenges to the United States and Canada* (Toronto: C.D. Howe Institute).

Ohmae, K., (1987) *Beyond National Borders* (Dow Jones: Irwin).

Ouchi, William G., (1984) *The M-Form Society* (Reading, Mass.: Addison-Wesley).

Porter, Michael E., (1980) *Competitive Strategv: Techniques for Analyzing Industries and Competitors* (New York: The Free Press, Macmillan).

Rugman, Alan M., (1981) *Inside the Multinationals: The Economics of Internal Markets* (London: Croom Helm and New York: Columbia University Press).

Rugman, Alan M. (1987a) and Andrew Anderson, *Administered Protection in America* (London: Croom Helm and New York: Methuen).

Rugman, Alan M., and Andrew Anderson, (1987b) "A Fishy Business: The Abuse of American Trade Law in the Atlantic Groundfish Case of 1985-1986," *Canadian Public Policy*, 13:2, June, pp. 152-164.

Rugman, Alan M., and Alain Verbeke, (1987a) "Strategic Management and Trade Policy," Dalhousie Discussion Papers in International Business, No. 69, Dalhousie University.

Rugman, Alan M., and Alain Verbeke, (1987b) "Bilateral Trade Liberalization and the Strategic Management of Multinational Enterprises," Dalhousie Discussion Papers in International Business, No. 70, Dalhousie University.

Rugman, Alan M., and Alain Verbeke, (1988c) "American Trade Policy and Corporate Strategy," mimeo, June.

Rugman, Alan M. and Samuel Porteous, (1988) "The Softwood Lumber Decision of 1986: Broadening the Nature of U.S. Administered Protection," *Review of International Business Law* 1:4 (forthcoming).

Tyson, Laura, (1987) "Creating Advantage, an Industrial Policy Perspective" in Richard G. Lipsey and Wendy Dobson, (eds.), *Shaping Comparative Advantage* (Toronto: C.D. Howe Institute), pp. 65-82.

Yoffie, David B., (1986) "Protecting World Markets," in Thomas K. McCraw, (ed.), *American Versus Japan* (Boston, Mass.: Harvard Business School Press).

[12]

Hitotsubashi Journal of Commerce and Management 25 (1990) pp. 75–97. © The Hitotsubashi Academy

STRATEGIC TRADE POLICY IS NOT GOOD STRATEGY

ALAN M. RUGMAN and ALAIN VERBEKE

Abstract

The focus of this paper is the process by which strategic trade policy is implemented. Due to an institutional structure under which democratic government is responsive to pressure groups, strategic trade policy may include strong protectionist elements. While the objective of strategic trade policy is to promote new firm-specific advantages for chosen industries, in practice a type of corporate "shelter" results. In terms of the strategic management literature we find that there is a type of "administrative heritage" in government policy making that hinders the implementation of effective strategic trade policy. From the viewpoint of both corporate strategy and public policy, we find that the result is neither efficient nor effective.

I. Introduction

According to traditional economic theory, trade occurs due to differences in the relative factor endowments of nations. In terms of a neoclassical economics model countries trade to benefit from each other's comparative advantages, i.e. they engage in inter-industry trade. Within the stylized nature of neoclassical market-driven models, free trade can lead to efficient outcomes. However, these models become stretched when we observe today that much of the world's trade is of an intra-industry nature and is conducted by multinational enterprises (MNEs). Most trade and direct investment now occurs between countries with more or less similar factor endowments. Consequently the reasons for international trade need to be attributed to other factors and new models are required.

Intra-industry trade, which is defined as two-way trade of similar goods within an industry, is a reflection of the specialization of countries in producing certain products or product-classes. This specialization allows firms, especially MNEs, to take advantage of potential economies of scale, to reduce their production costs by moving down the learning-curve, and to improve technological know how. These are the factors now being modeled in the new international economics theories being put forward to explain international trade and investment.

In addition, the structure of world markets has changed dramatically over the last decade. The exploitation of economies of scale, the possibility of appropriating technological innovations by means of exclusive patent rights, and high barriers to entry (high capital costs; high R & D expenditures) have all contributed to reducing the number of market participants in numerous industries. If markets are becoming more oligopolistic this could imply the persistence of above-normal profits or rents.   The possibility of abnormal economic rents has provided a strong basis upon which new trade theories are built, see Krugman (1986) for an overview.

What are the implications of these new developments for the analysis of trade policies? In particular, is "strategic" trade policy justified?   The first justification for the theory of strategic trade policy relies on the existence of above-normal profits in certain industries. If this argument is correct, government trade policies could be developed to shift much of these profits to domestic firms and consequently raise national welfare at the expense of other nations.   Strategic trade policy is being based on government measures that take into account international interdependence in an oligopolistic industry structure.   We shall discuss the validity of this viewpoint in the next section.

A second alleged justification for an interventionist industrial and trade policy is the existence of external economies.   For example, the technological know how gained by supporting a high-tech industry such as the semiconductor industry may have positive effects on related industries.   One problem is that if such spill-over effects are spread internationally then the impact of such a policy on national welfare may well be much lower than initially expected.

The first and most obvious tool available to government policy makers who wish to use trade policy as a means of enlarging the market share of domestic firms in world markets is the granting of (export) subsidies to a "strategic" industry, i.e., an industry characterized by high dynamic internal and external economies.   One purpose of this article is to identify the fallacy of such strategic trade policy arguments.   It is demonstrated that strategic trade policy cannot even be considered to be good strategy.   Here, "good strategy" is defined as consistent patterns in decisions and actions which advance national economic welfare in the long run.

In the next two sections, conventional economic trade theory reasons are advanced for the probable failure of strategic trade policy.   The remainder of the article then identifies policy implementation elements as causes of strategic trade policy failure.   The definition of the "strategic" character of an industry is a very controversial issue.   Traditionally the role of international trade policy has focused on the protection of domestic firms against foreign competition.   In particular, quotas and import tariffs have been widely used to protect infant industries and old sectors in order to allow them to develop new firm specific advantages.   However, the theory of strategic trade policy suggests that these tools can also be used in an "export promoting" manner, much in the same way as with subsidies, see Krugman (1984).   We make use of this insight.

II.   *Profit-Shifting Through Strategic Trade Policy*

The profit-shifting case of the use of subsidies has been formalized by Brander and Spencer (1985).   Their reasoning is as follows: suppose the structure of an industry is duopolistic; one domestic firm and one foreign firm.   The market they are competing for is a third importing country.   This situation calls for a "strategic game" since the actions of one firm will be strongly influenced by the other firm's moves.

More precisely, in the Brander and Spencer model, Cournot-like conduct is assumed in which each firm decides on its optimal profit maximizing output level, given the output level of its rival.   If one firm were persuaded to reduce its output, the other's market share would grow and earn even greater profits.   What is then needed to induce a contraction is a credible threat, such as a cost reduction.   The main point in the Brander and Spencer model is that such a cost reduction can be substituted for by a subsidy.   The effect of this is twofold.   The first effect is really nothing more than a transfer for the amount of the subsidy from taxpayers to the firm.   The second effect—the strategic effect—allows the domestic firm to enlarge its market share at the expense of the foreign firm and hence to shift some porfits from the foreign country to the home country.

A hypothetical example may explain the concept more clearly.   Utilizing the matrix framework developed in Krugman (1987b), let us consider the market for a new high technology product.   Assume that there are two potential entrants to an export market, say a domestic firm and a foreign firm.   The export market leaves room for only one competitor, so if neither of them renounces the idea of entering the market it will be detrimental to both. Assume further that both firms are identical and face only the choice to produce (P) or not to produce (N).   In each cell of the matrix, the lower left number represents the foreign firm's profit (over and above the normal return on capital), the upper right number represents the domestic firm's profit.   The pay-off matrix in Diagram 1 shows the possible outcomes.

The strategic game will have a unique outcome if one firm has a headstart and can commit itself to produce before the other firm's decision.   Suppose this is the foreign firm: it will earn large profits, while the domestic firm will refrain from entry (Quadrant 2).   However, as suggested by strategic trade policy theory, government could easily alter the possible

DIAGRAM 1.   DUOPOLY STRATEGIC GAME WITHOUT GOVERNMENT INTERVENTION

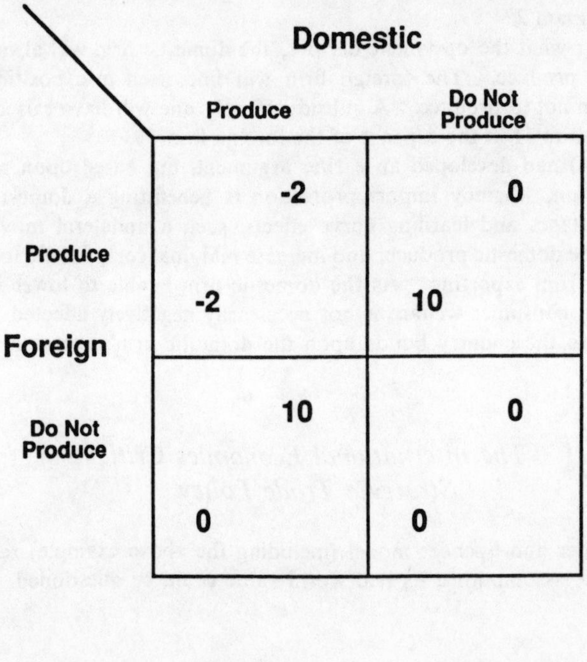

DIAGRAM 2. DUOPOLY STRATEGIC GAME WITH GOVERNMENT SUBSIDY

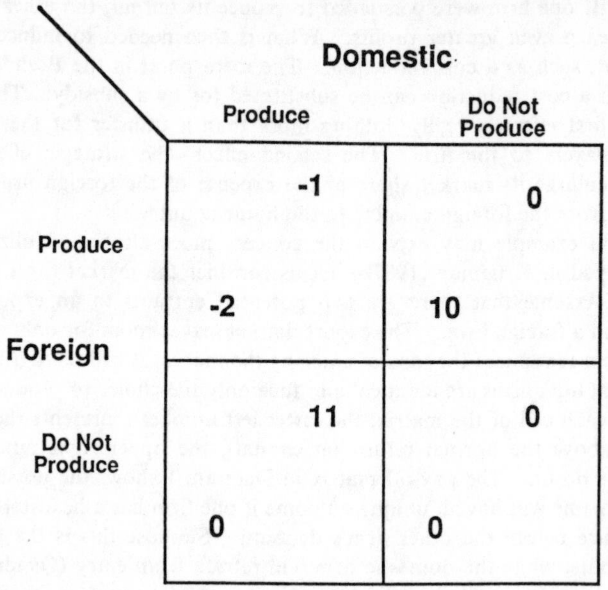

Domestic

	Produce	Do Not Produce
Produce	-1 -2	0 10
Do Not Produce	11 0	0 0

Foreign

outcomes by subsidizing the domestic firm in the early stages of the production process by an amount of, for example, one before the foreign country decides to produce. This is illustrated in Diagram 2.

Then no matter what the opponent decides, the domestic firm will always be better off with a decision to produce. The foreign firm will find itself in a position where it can decide no other than not to produce. A subsidy of only one will have raised the profits for demostic firm from 0 to 11 at the expense of the foreign firm.

Krugman (1984) had developed an earlier argument, but based upon a situation with domestic consumption, whereby import protection is benefitting a domestic firm. In the case of scale advantages and learning curve effects, such a unilateral move will decrease marginal costs for the domestic producer and increase marginal costs for the foreign producer, which is prevented from exporting. As the domestic firm is able to lower its costs by expanding production, consumer welfare is not necessarily negatively affected by import protection. The gain to the country builds upon the domestic firm's increase in profits from exporting.

III.   *The International Economics Critique of Strategic Trade Policy*

Since the Brander and Spencer model (including the above example) relies heavily on a series of restrictive assumptions, its real world value could be questioned. We now turn to these assumptions and the implications of a relaxation of them. To be of more general value, the model should also incorporate other forms of duopolistic conduct. For example, Eaton and Grossman (1986) argue that in the case of Bertrand competition, rather than Cournot-like conduct (recall that under Bertrand competition, prices are set in response to the competitor's price setting) an export tax would be more appropriate as an optimal policy. In addition, in cases with more than two firms, i.e. an oligopoly, policy conclusions may be altered drastically. With too great a number of home firms, each will compete against all others, resulting in a suboptimal level of joint profits. It should also be stressed that trade or industrial policy itself may alter the total number of competitors. As more and more firms are attracted to the industry, above-normal profits may eventually disappear, making a profit-shifting policy of little use, see Horstman and Markusen (1986). Of course this would only occur in the absence of high barriers to entry.

In the Brander and Spencer model it is assumed that there is no domestic consumption. In that case government trade policy is equivalent to government industrial policy. According to Eaton and Grossman (1986), allowing for home consumption, a subsidy as well as a tax may raise domestic welfare. Also the rent-extraction argument in the Brander and Spencer model does not take into account the scarcity of production factors. The promotion of one sector over another might draw out scarce resources from other industries, compelling these industries to cut back on their production, or to increase their factor re-numeration, making them less competitive. Thus the advantage gained in one industry is offset by losses incurred in other industries using the same (scarce) production factors, see Dixit and Grossman (1986). As a consequence of these restrictions, the possibilities of shifting profits from foreign countries to the national economy in real life situations might be much less evident than claimed by the theory.

As could be expected, it is very unlikely that any government would be able to implement a predatory policy without eliciting a response from other nations. These retaliatory measures then lead to trade wars with losses for both parties. National welfare is thus not only dependent on national trade policy but on foreign policies as well. Governments finding themselves in a strategic situation like this—often referred to as the "prisoner's dilemma"—each faces the option to cooperate (i.e. not to engage in a "begger-your-neigh-bor" policy) or to defect. As illustrated in Diagram 3, in a "prisoner's dilemma," defection is the dominant strategy because defection will lead to the greatest profits for the nation, regardless of the decision of the opponent. The pay-off matrix shows there are three possible outcomes.

The first one is that one country unilaterally tries to appropriate a gain by adopting a "begger-your-neighbor" policy. This strategy works well as long as the other country does not retaliate, which, as already mentioned is very unlikely. The second outcome is that both countries engage in protection, with the result that no firm is actually able to do well in export markets. The third and most desirable outcome from a collective point of view is that both nations agree to cooperate. In this situation, however, there always remains the temptation to defect, since this would improve profits for the defector. But as soon as the trading partner perceives the cheating, retaliation will follow and the result will be the least successful outcome of quadrant 4. Now what is needed to avoid the trap of the prisoner's dilemma is a set of rules, a set of explicit and binding agreements allowing nations to communicate, to monitor each other and to sanction cheating. Since free trade

DIAGRAM 3.   COOPERATION VERSUS DEFECTION IN A PRISONER'S DILRMMA GAME

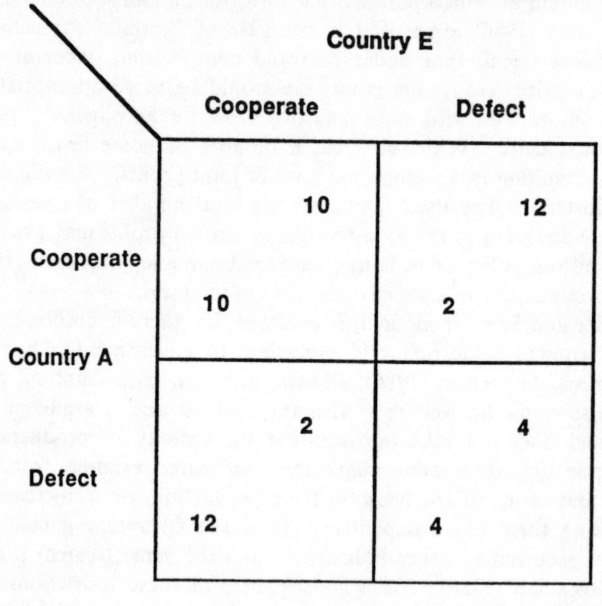

Country E

	Cooperate	Defect
Cooperate	10 / 10	12 / 2
Defect	2 / 12	4 / 4

Country A

is probably the simplest of all such rules, it may turn out to be the best way to avoid retaliation and trade wars.

An alterative solution is to take into account the impact of present behaviour on the value of expected flows of surplus in the future.   In the case of an infinitely repeated oligopoly game, implicit international cooperation may be stimulated, so as to avoid reprisal measures of trading partners, see Shapiro (1989) and Jacquemin (1989).

Finally, it should be emphasized that the strategic trade policy literature neglects the impact of foreign ownership in the industries selected for support.   Krugman (1987a) suggests that strategic trade policy measures in favour of foreign owned firms could decrease national welfare.

IV.   *Administrative Heritage and the Structure of Trade Policy*

Apart from the economic arguments against strategic trade policy, two additional elements should be taken into account.   First, international trade results fundamentally from strategic decisions made by business firms based on their firm specific advantages, (FSAs). A strong interaction exists between the strategies of business firms and government trade policies.   A firm's strategy is defined here simply as all consistent patterns in decisions and actions which significantly affect the firm's survival, profitability and market share.   Second, protectionist policies can only be successful (in terms of efficiency), from a national point of view, if they can be considered as "FSA-developing," both in their formulation *and* implementation.   The concept of "FSA-developing" policy was introduced by Rugman and Verbeke (1987) to describe active government policies aimed at *complementing* the FSAs of the firms benefitting from this support. This is in contrast to sheltering policies aimed at protecting domestic firms against market forces in the long run. Here, the main purpose of trade policy measures is to *substitute* for the existence of strong FSAs.

In practice, it is not always easy to distinguish FSA-developing and shelter-based trade and industrial policies. We have argued elsewhere, see Rugman and Verbeke (1990) that the issue of *strategic intent* is of major importance here. Is the intent of the public policy makers and business firm managers to use government support as (a) a *temporary* tool to improve the long run international competitive position of the firm involved (which is an implicit assumption of the strategic trade policy models) or (b) as an instrument to be used idenfinitely without the end goal of long run international competitiveness after elimination of all government support? In this second case, firms often engage in rent-seeking behaviour, i.e., they seek rents arising from activities with negative social value, see Tullock (1988).

However, a shelter-based policy may also be introduced when alleged strategic trade policy intentions are "captured" by pressure groups seeking protection.

Two elements are especially important when assessing the transformation of strategic trade policy intentions into shelter based policies. First, is strategic trade policy implemented by an agency (either part of the political or technical track) that is non-responsive to pressure groups, even in a dynamic sense? Second, if some sensitivity is unavoidable, is the institutional structure designed in such a way that shelter-seeking and anti-shelter firms have equal access to the agency involved?

In order to analyze a country's trade policy, two elements should always be studied. First is the nature of the political decision-making processes through which trade policy decisions are formulated and implemented. Particularly relevant is the interaction between trade policy and strategies of business firms. Second is the economic efficiency of a country's trade policy, using a comparative institutional assessment.

In terms of the political decision-making process, it is an empirical question whether public policy makers, both politicians and bureaucrats, should be regarded as individuals maximizing their own utility or as leaders pursuing the public interest. The former approach has been suggested by public choice theory, see e.g., Olson (1965) and Brock and Magee (1978). In this case, government is seen as having little independence vis-a-vis pressure groups. However, an alternative view, emphasizing the autonomy of the state, has been put forward by other authors, see Baldwin (1982).

The issue is important because of the free rider problem. Trade policy measures in favour of a particular industry or set of firms can be considered as a collective benefit generated through voluntary collective action by the different firms involved. However, an individual firm has an incentive not to engage in lobbying efforts in order to obtain only the benefits (and not the costs) of trade policy measures lobbied for by the other firms. Hence, according to Olson, higher benefits and fewer firms organizing to secure particular trade policy measures will lead to higher demands for shelter. If the size of the benefits to be gained is interpreted in terms of relative contribution to survival, profitability and growth of a firm, as in the case of companies with weak FSAs in import competing sectors, the probability of rent seeking behaviour will increase, see also McKeown (1984) on this issue.

82   HITOTSUBASHI JOURNAL OF COMMERCE AND MANAGEMENT   [December

If the independence of government vis-a-vis pressure groups is low, this implies the possible implementation of trade policy measures in favor of particular industries, at the expense of the domestic economy in general. This could include the creation of shelter against foreign firms, at the expense of society a large. However, when performing a comparative institutional assessment of the relative efficiency of a country's trade policy, the sensitivity of public policy makers to pressure groups should not be criticized. More damaging are the inefficient outcomes resulting from the free rider problem. Hence, public policy decision structures must be designed in such a way that rent seeking activities of specific groups do not have an excessive impact.

Here, the question arises as to the optimal level of centralization of trade policy. If trade policy is decentralized, this has the potential advantage of economizing on bounded rationality, as more informed decisions can be made by experts in specific fields. On the other hand, the risk of fragmentation becomes larger. Trade policy decisions made by different agencies may be inconsistent and even contradictory. Decentralization is defined as an allocation of authority over several public agencies, each with substantial decision making power on specific issues. This implies that the lobbying costs of particular pressure groups, aimed at generating specific trade policy measures, may decline. Then the focus of lobbying becomes more precise and the number of competing pressure groups is reduced.

When studying trade policy decisions, it is useful to know, from a descriptive point of view, which of the four quadrants of Diagram 4 is most characteristic of a particular country. The framework described here cannot be used directly for policy prescription.

DIAGRAM 4.   THE ADMINISTRATIVE HERITAGE OF NATIONAL TRADE POLICIES

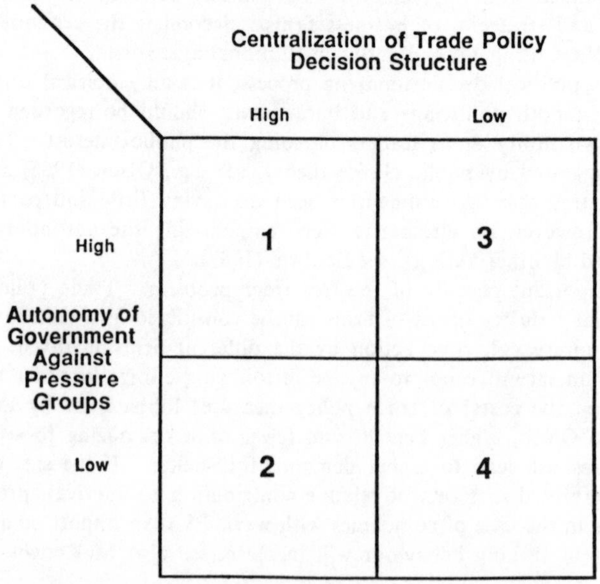

It only gives an indication of the administrative heritage of a particular country's conduct of trade policy.

Trade policy in any country can be classified in a particular guadrant of Diagram 4. In our view, the main question is whether the existing institutional structure does or does not allow the creation of long run shelter at the expense of society at large.

As trade policy is an extremely complex issue, we feel that it is very difficult to perform efficiency assessments for the whole of a nation's trade policy. Hence, it is of more relevance to study these issues in connection with specific "segments" of trade policy. Examples would be: strategic trade measures such as tariff and non-tariff barrier policies; countervail and anti-dumping actions; export promotion policy; voluntary export restriction policies, etc. Although an overall assessment of a country's trade policy may put it in one specific quadrant of Diagram 4, each separate type of measure may be located in any quadrant of the diagram. Segments of trade policy situated in any of the four quadrants can then be efficient or inefficient.

In order to assess the relative efficiency of a particular trade policy measure, the question should always be answered whether or not increased economic efficiency is actually pursued through the implementation of specific trade policy measures, or whether this goal is subverted as a result of an unadapted trade policy structure? Trade policy structure is defined here as the way in which trade policy actions are performed and coordinated by different agencies. If inefficiency is observed, structural changes may be suggested, given however, that the position of any country's trade policy in Diagram 4 is mostly fixed in the short run.

V. *Problems in the Implementation of Strategic Trade Policy*

When assessing the economic efficiency of specific trade policy measures, a comparative institutional approach should always be used in order to avoid unrealistic policy alternatives. The framework developed below provides a useful basis for such an approach.

Once it is accepted that firms can influence government trade policy, it becomes necessary to analyze the basic principles which govern these interrelations between government and firms, especially for firms with weak FSAs attempting to gain shleter. The main issue here is that democratic government will only alter its existing trade policies if it faces incentives to do so. This depends on how the incentives are structured for government. Some prior assumptions must be made concerning the goals of democratic government. Two extreme situations can be distinguished.

First, government may aim to sustain international competition based on economic theory such as the principle of comparative advantage. It may favour free trade, but be willing to help domestic firms expand, without sheltering them from foreign competition in the long run. The issue of export subsidies for profit shifting purposes is an example. Government may grant export subsidies to domestic firms to obtain such a shift in profits. As a result, these domestic firms may become subject to the countervailing protection mechanisms of foreign governments. On the other hand, the pursuit of free trade goals may in itself lead to countervailing measures against other countries that grant export subsidies. In any case, an FSA-developing trade policy is pursued.

The second possibility is the pursuit of shelter. Efficient foreign competitors are excluded from the market, while trade barriers, substituting for strong FSAs, may be created for inefficient local producers.

Apart from the "trade policy formulation" goals of government, it is important to recognize the role of "trade policy implementation." This distinction between formulation and implementation is crucial. In particular, what was decided in terms of trade policy objectives will not necessarily be achieved, as what is implemented may be different from what was originally intended. In order words, it only makes sense to speak of an FSA-developing or sheltering policy in the implementation stage.

Diagram 5 develops a new framework that takes into account the distinction made between FSA-developing versus shelter based trade policies and the formulation versus implementation of trade policies. It also links our framework with the traditional and strategic trade policy arguments for protection.

In the first quadrant of Diagram 5 a strategic trade policy is conducted and its implementation is FSA-developing. In this case, active government trade policy may be efficient vis-a-vis a situation of free trade. In quadrant 2, however, strategic trade policy is being subverted into a tool of shelter aimed at protecting domestic firms against international market forces in the long run. In quadrant 3, the infant industry and old industry arguments for government intervention are used and the implementation of trade policy measures is FSA-developing. Quadrant 4 exemplifies the cases whereby the traditional arguments for protectionism are used to create shelter for domestic firms. This creates economic inefficiency vis-a-vis a situation of free trade.

The main focus of this present article is to investigate the possibility that alleged

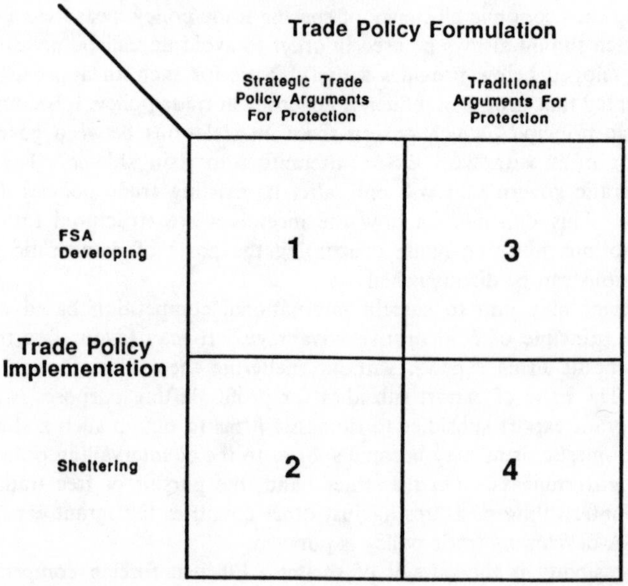

DIAGRAM 5.   THE FORMULATION AND IMPLEMENTATION OF PROTECTIONISM

strategic trade policy measures would fall in quadrant 1 or in quadrant 2 of Diagram 5. An example of quadrant 1 strategy is the rise of "Airbus Industrie" in Europe. In this case, government support complemented the FSAs of the consortium of four West-European producers, leading to the production of highly differentiated civil aircraft with life cycle costs for the customers lower than those of competing U.S. aircraft, see Majumbar (1987). Today the Japanese automobile and consumer electronics industries have used their FSA developing strategies to take themselves out of Diagram 5, i.e., Japanese protectionism is redundant for these successful industries. However shipbuilding in Japan remains in quadrant 3.

Trade policy measures could be considered as efficient because they aim at developing or refocusing the FSAs of the firms benefitting from government support. It should be recognized that import protection may sometimes be FSA developing (quadrant 1 or quadrant 3). A well known case in quadrant 3 is Harley Davidson, which filed a petition in 1982 to gain escape clause protection in the U.S. As a result, tariffs up to 40 percent were levied on non-European motorcycles in the U.S. market, to decline over 5 years. This allowed the U.S. firm to develop new FSAs; two years before expiration of the tariffs the firm itself was able to ask for their removal, see Yoffie (1989).

VI. *The Fallacy of Strategic Trade Policy*

Krugman (1986), (1987b) has developed the notion of "strategic" trade policy to include all trade policy activities aimed at stimulating the growth of selected "stragetic" industries. Factors of production either benefitting from internal economies (e.g. economies of scale, learning curve effects and innovation) or external economies (especially technological spill-overs) are generated for other sectors in the economy. Although these two arguments in favor of protectionism may seem new, as compared to the old arguments (such as the infant industry and old industry arguments) they raise exactly the same questions from a policy point of view. The two following questions are crucial in this respect:
1) Is it possible to identify strategic industries with high dynamic internal and/or external economies?
2) Is the existing institutional structure, aimed at conducting a strategic trade policy, conducive to FSA-development in the implementation of strategy?

The first question, relating to identification, is a complex one. First, strategic industries are industries characterized by high dynamic internal or external economies. In terms of efficiency the former should be identified as the result of observing (or predicting) above-normal profits. The problem is that so-called "above-normal" profits often result from investments with highly uncertain outcomes, so that they merely constitute "normal" profits when adjusted for risk. In other words apparently high profits in an industry may result from high economics based entry barriers. The latter are themselves the consequence of high costs incurred during previous periods and effective corporate strategies. This also implies that many "losers" may have exited from the market.

Furthermore, the issue of FSAs and natural country specific advantages is important. It is not because an industry in one country is characterized by high profitability that government support in another country could automatically lead to a "duplication" of this situation.

For example, in high technology industries, FSAs in the form of proprietary know-how and country specific advantages such as an attractive business environment cannot be "bought" through export subsidies. A strategic sector for one country may not be strategic at all for another one, if dynamic internal economies cannot be captured by government trade support. In fact, when identifying strategic industries, it is important to know to what extent government support will lead to shifts of foreign profits to domestic firms, per unit of government support.

Dynamic internal economies could also be given another interpretation, merely by using the concept of value added. A strategic industry is one where high value added is being created rather than one where the existence of high profits is important. Industries characterized by high value added can be more easily identified than industries with above normal profits. Value added is only partly dependent upon international competition, in contrast to the firm's profits. In addition, value added is less sensitive than profits to changes in international market structure. Even if strategic trade policy support does not drive down international prices through increased output, it should be recognized that above-normal profits will only be temporary in global industries moving toward mature product lines.

With respect to the dynamic external economies case, e.g., the diffusion of technological know-how, it should be emphasized that it will seldom be evident which sectors should be chosen. For example, the R and D intensity of a sector can hardly be used as a proxy of potential technology diffusion. If innovations in an industry require high and risky investments and are protected by economics based entry barriers in the form of patents, it is not clear how stimulating this industry will result in a diffusion of know-how. If, on the other hand, innovative know-how in an industry is not protected, no dynamic external economies will be found, for the simple reason that no innovation will occur, with or without government trade support. In terms of value added, however, sectors with high external economies may be easier to use. For example, high R and D efforts imply the development of highly skilled human capital, which will increase the added value created in the economy, irrespective of the protection of R and D results.

Spencer (1986) has analyzed the issue of strategic trade policy, focussing on the conditions that need to be fulfilled when selecting industries to be targeted in order to capture dynamic internal economies. She identified seven basic requirements that should be met by an industry so as to maximize the chances of success of an active national trade policy programme. Unfortunately, in none of these seven requirements is the issue of shelter substituting for strong FSAs dealt with. First, only those sectors should be selected where trade policy can directly (e.g. trade barriers) or indirectly (e.g. export subsidies) lead to the erection of entry barriers for foreign competitors, as this is a necessary condition for domestic producers obtaining rents exceeding the economic costs of protection.

In terms of our framework, an important element neglected here is the fact that every entry barrier is not a "good" entry barrier. If the barriers resulting from strategic trade policy merely aim at sheltering domestic producers without time limits, trade policy measures will stimulate mciro-economic inefficiency and may even reduce value added.

Second, strategic trade policy only makes sense in sectors characterized by strong international competition, whereby protectionist trade policy measures will indeed lead to profit shifting on an international scale and entry deterrence. The main element neglected by Spencer is that such a policy can only work in the absence of sheltering policies of foreign governments. However, if sheltering policies are in fact implemented, strategic trade policy measures in one country may merely increase the level of sheltering abroad and hence completely eliminate both potential rents to be captured in the industry and the expected increases in value added.

Third, seller concentration in the domestic industry should be higher than abroad. In this case, negative spill-over effects resulting from excessive capacity increases by the different domestic producers will be more limited, while entry deterrence for foreign competitors will be higher; in the case of declining marginal costs, the cost differential with the domestic firms will be greater. Two important elements are not considered by Spencer. First, the fact that high domestic concentration may generate a lower domestic incentive to engage in innovative behaviour and improve micro-economic efficiency. Second, lower concentration abroad may be an indication of focus strategies, so that alleged attempts to gain global cost leadership through strategic trade policy will not substantially affect the competitive position of foreign rivals.

Fourth, the prices of production inputs should not increase substantially as a result of strategic trade policy measures. This will be the case if bargaining power of labor is low, and labor benefits from profit-sharing reward systems and production inputs are substitutable. A major factor not taken into account by Spencer is the issue of X-inefficiency resulting from government sheltering policy. In this case, government protection may not only stimulate production workers to demand higher rewards; it may also induce management to increase overhead, to attach less importance to improving micro-economic efficiency and to use resources for rent-seeking purposes. In the short run this may not negatively affect the structure of value added created in domestic firms, but in the long run it will if the firms' performance in the market is not based on their FSAs.

Fifth, strategic trade policy has a higher probability of success if the selected domestic industrial sector has a comparative cost advantage vis-a-vis foreign rivals and potential scale economies and learning curve effects are higher. It is clear that in this case the expected return on, e.g., every export subsidy dollar, will be higher. However, we should point out again that a domestic industry's competitive advantage in the international market place may be differentiation based instead of cost based. In this case, international competitiveness is not a question of providing cheaper products, but a problem of creating FSAs with high differentiation enhancing potential (e.g., brand names).

Sixth, targeting an industry through granting R and D subsidies will be more effective if the transfer of domestic technology to foreign rivals is more difficult and/or foreign technology can easily be acquired by domestic firms. While this argument cannot be easily discarded, it should be mentioned that the technology transfer problem is double-edged: if technology transfer by domestic firms is made more difficult, this implies that domestic firms are able to avoid the dissipation of their proprietary know-how. In many industries, this may require that competition on international markets is done through FDI. However, FDI will limit exports and allow other countries to profit from domestic R and D subsidies in terms of value added. Similarly, if foreign technology can be acquired easily this implies that foreign firms do not regard this technological know-how as a key-asset; hence, in many cases the question will arise as to the actual "high-tech" nature of the acquited technology.

Seventh, R and D and investment subsidies will be more effective if R and D and capital costs constitute important cost factors and or substantial entry barriers in an industry (which is more likely to be the case if the industry is in its early development stage). Here too, the distinction between shelter based policies and FSA-developing policies is neglected. The creation of shelter based entry barriers is not beneficial to long run national efficiency.

It will now be clear that even the mere selection of strategic industries is not an easy problem to solve. Even if specific industries are "correctly" selected the important question is whether an FSA-developing strategic trade policy can be implemented. The importance of this issue will be demonstrated in the next section using the example of the United States.

VII.   *The Failure of Strategic Trade Policy in the United States*

The United States has a trade policy heritage positioned in quadrant 4 of Diagram 4 (decentralized, very sensitive to business demands), see Nelson (1989).

Reich (1982a) has advocated the development of a coherent FSA-developing industrial policy in the United States. This is to be an alternative to the existing set of uncoordinated sheltering measures in industrial and trade policy. He demonstrates that most federal expenditures for industrial development programmes in favor of specific industries are the result of political pressures exerted by established industries to get shelter. He has also shown how the U.S. government failed to support growing industries such as semiconductors as compared with major competitors, for example Japan and West Germany.

While his analysis of the existing U.S. sheltering policies is undoubtedly correct, his proposal to develop an extensive set of FSA-developing measures for selected industries seems unrealistic. His proposed measures for those businesses that can achieve competitive leadership in world markets include: helping businesses fund research; underwriting high-risk investments; aiding export sales; sharing the costs of developing foreign markets; and subsidizing education and training.

The main problem with this is the issue of implementation. Reich completely neglects the problem of administrative heritage. He states that industrial policymaking must seek "broad public consensus" on the means by which U.S. industry can improve its competitive advantages. This broad consensus should involve "consumers, small business, emerging industries and non-union workers as well as organized labor and big business" (Reich, 1982a, p. 81).

It is remarkable that Reich sets forward this proposal since his own analysis demonstrates that U.S. industry "tribunals" responsible for the development of single industries and composed of government, business and (occasionally) labor, have consistently failed. They rested on the false assumption that industries are "monolithic blocs of business with identical interests." In reality, these tribunals were dominated primarily by older and well established businesses which resisted any significant economic change. Hence, it is not clear how a much broader inter-industry forum, with an even larger diversity of interests, could produce a broad consensus on FSA-developing trade and industrial policies, creating a shift from the lower side to the upper side of Diagram 5.

Badaracco and Yoffie (1983) have argued that the administrative heritage of the existing U.S. political decision making structure eliminates all chances of successfully implementing FSA-developing trade and industrial policies. They disagree with Vogel's (1979) suggestion that government should foster competitive industries and phase out declining ones, through the establishment of a new cadre of senior-level bureaucrats with wide autonomy to implement strongly interventionist policies. Their main arguments against the successful establishment of a politically independent institution relate to many obstacles. In terms of staff they doubt that a professional government elite could be created because of a lack of financial and other incentives. Moreover the probability of being able to centralize the authority for an effective public policy is very limited. The dozens of agencies responsible for selected issues in these areas and the existing prerogatives of Congress make it extremely unlikely that sufficient power could be given to a single new agency.

The authors also reject Reich's proposal to reshape trade and industrial policies by creating a new forum for formulating policy. Reich (1982b) argues that a "single bargaining arena" would lead to the achievement of a broad-based consensus about adjustment policies whereby management, labor and government would discuss adjustment packages to shape new competitive advantages fo declining industries. Although such a bargaining arena may seem attractive at first sight, the authors argue that the incentives for potential losers to seek better results (e.g. protection) in Congress, the executive branch, and the courts, would be very high. Finally, attempting to pick out winners and to eliminate losers could lead to enormous expenses for the federal government.

Badaracco and Yoffie demonstrated that the problem of administrative heritage constitutes an important impediment for the effective implementation of centralized FSA-developing policies. Yet the authors then mistakenly argue that this same administrative heritage would also prevent the creation of sheltering policies. The decentralized nature of government policy making would moderate the possibilities of implementing inefficient sheltering policies as compared with centralized regimes. As we demonstrated earlier, however, decentralization does not guarantee the absence of sheltering policies at all. This was shown in Rugman and Anderson's (1987) account of the recent evolution in U.S. decentralized administered protection.

Moreover, sheltering policies can take many forms and are not restricted to protectionist trade measures. For example, in the U.S. defense industry, perverse incentives exist for contractors to raise costs of defense contracts. Profit rates considered appropriate by the department of defense depend upon the cost of the programme. In addition, overhead costs are expressed as a percentage of direct costs. Hence, producers have an incentive to raise production costs. This system can be maintained because of the absence of strong price competition, see Fox (1984). While this may raise the value added created in the firms benefitting fom this support, it is not evident that such policies will be beneficial to their international competitive position in the long run.

The development of a new "focal point" for conducting an interventionist trade and industrial policy in the United States has also been advocated by Scott (1982). He argues that a new department of industry, trade and commerce should be established with broad powers to promote U.S. exports and to establish a dialogue with the business community at large. However, he too neglects the issue of administrative heritage as developed within our framework. As it was noted by Safarian (1989), following Olson (1982) and Katzenstein (1985), some nations possess country specific advantages in terms of responding to important environmental changes which require intense cooperation among such actors as government, business, labour unions etc. The United States does not possess the advantages of other countries, such as Japan. For example, the interaction of business and government in Japan, especially with respect to the dynamics of industrial policy, has been described by Horvath and McMillan (1980). They have demonstrated that Japanese policy explicitly accepts the existence of "winning" and "losing" industries, and hence prevents inflexibility, protectionism and organizational inertia.

Hence, it is not surprising that several recent proposals have been formulated by legislation in the United States to introduce structural reforms in the "political architecture," in order to allow more interventionist trade and industry policies. For a partial overview, see Lodge and Crum (1985) and Scott (1989). The danger exists, however, that the "administrative heritage" of U.S. public policy may lead any new public agency to become the captive of powerful special interest groups, especially from non-competitive sectors in the economy.

Such a situation has already been characteristic of the implementation of unfair trade laws dealing with countervail and anti-dumping cases, see Rugman and Anderson (1987). Just as in the case of strategic trade policy, these unfair trade laws aim at improving national economic efficiency (in this case through the development of a level playing field). They are meant to increase the value added created in the domestic economy, as they are imposed on foreign competitors. In practice, they shelter inefficient domestic producers from international market forces.

The negative effects of sheltering policies on firm behavior are often neglected, as exemplified by Culbertson (1986) who advocates permanent protection against imports and the reservation of fixed market shares for producers located in the United States. The author argues that such measures would lead to innovative behavior by U.S. firms and prevent them from moving more production overseas. Borrus, Tyson and Zysman (1986) have also argued that Japanese strategic trade and industrial policy measures, in particular domestic market closure and the financing of generic research projects, have allowed the Japanese semiconductor industry to gain a global competitive advantage vis-a-vis its American counterpart. However, the possibility of implementing a Japanese-like industrial policy structure was not seriously dealt with. In addition, many authors have argued that Japanese FSA-developing policies in particular industrial sectors were not a major factor of success, see e.g., Saxonhouse (1983) and Trezise (1983).

Sharp (1987) has argued that industrial policy in Japan has changed substantially, toward the use of indirect measures, e.g. R and D without direct commercial application. Moreover, it appears that its success lies primarily in its efforts to persuade Japanese firms to invest resources in innovative ideas rather than in its ability to provide generous subsidies, e.g., in the electronics industry. In other words, even in the country which is often considered as the prime example of successful FSA-developing policies, there is considerable discussion as to the actual contribution of trade policy to economic efficiency and effectiveness.

Furthermore, even strategic R and D subsidies to develop high technology sectors may be a second best solution. In the post World War II period, Japan primarily purchased and adapted U.S. technologies instead of developing its own. Such a policy may have the benefits of letting other countries develop new technologies at high costs (and risks) and purchasing the successful results. In other words, R and D subsidies should only be granted for the development of technologies that cannot be easily imitated. This is the case with only a restricted number of technologies whereby information is not easily diffused through the product itself, see Boltho and Allsopp (1987).

VIII. *Strategic Trade Policy and the Fair Trade Issue*

In spite of these concerns about the development and implementation of strategic trade policies, Yoffie and Milner (1089a; 1989b) have argued in favor of strategic trade policy in sectors supported by foreign governments. In their view, strategic trade policy measures need to be used as tools to create a level playing field, ignoring both the prisoner's dilemma outcome of such behaviour and the danger of shelter during implementation.

Their work reflects an ethnocentric U.S. attitude, as they argue that internationally oriented, U.S. firms would normally be supporters of unconditional free trade except in those circumstances where foreign governments would be able to "create" competitive advantages in the U.S. In other words, their view is that a foreign firm can only be successful in the United States if helped by its home country government. Hence, this simplistic view of the world assumes that the demand for strategic trade policy in the United States mostly results from unfair trade practices by foreign governments, while the demand for government support by foreign firms would always precede U.S. government support. In reality, of course, this is not the case.

Yoffie and Milner (1989b) extend the definition of strategic trade policy to include not only government imposed programmes aimed at reaping dynamic internal and external economies, but also those measures meant to counteract the effects of auch programs abroad. These include countervail and anti-dumping measures. In addition, the authors even argue that a U.S. firm might express demands for strategic trade policy pre-emptively, when it anticipates its competitive position could be endangered. This could occur if a foreign government has a reputation for effective implementation of strategic trade policies. However, if strategic trade policy measures follow from the demands of firms instead of being decided upon by autonomous government agencies, why would U.S. firms always be engaged in this mode of "reacting" to moves or expected moves of foreign firms? Why would efficient foreign firms be more inclined to engage in first mover demands for strategic trade policy measures whereas U.S. firms would only react to such signals?

The answer is that, in reality, demands for strategic trade policy are similar in the United States and abroad. As Milner (1988) herself pointed out in her seminal work on the forces resisting protectionism in France and the United States, domestic firms in import competing sectors will usually favor protection. Firms with either exports or multinational operations will usually favour free trade, unless respectively exports are subject to erosion and specific operations of the multinational enterprise are inefficient. Finally, firms with a high degree of exports and a high degree of multinationality will usually be unconditional supporters of free trade.

If this analysis is correct, there are three possible explanations for the phenomenon observed by Yoffie and Milner (1989a, 1989b). First, U.S. firms have not been successful in their demands for strategic trade policies. Only when foreign firms have improved their competitive position as a result of these policies will the domestic demands be perceived as credible by U.S. government agencies. This in itself demonstrates that no suitable institutional structure exists in the United States, which would allow the pursuit of an FSA developing strategic trade policy.   A clear example of this situation namely in the United States machine tool industry has been described by Collis (1988).

Second, U.S. firms have actually benefited from some type of strategic trade policy measures, but these measures have taken more "subtle" forms than those used abroad, see e.g., Cohper (1988).   In addition, McNiven (1989) provides an overview of decentralized export development policies implemented by different U.S. states.   When foreign firms appear to be successful internationally, the U.S. firms initiate demands for similar types of programmes or for measures aimed at eliminating the competitive effects of foreign support programmes.

Third, U.S. firms have benefited from similar types of strategic trade policy measures, but the lower effectiveness of implementing these measures in the United States, as contrasted to foreign countries, such as Japan, has reduced the competitiveness of U.S. firms.   Hence, these firms wish to create shelter from international competition through the application of so called "fair trade" laws.   If these laws are implemented in such a way that only foreign support measures are investigated, this may lead to the creation of a shelter based advantage for U.S. firms in the domestic U.S. market.

Substantial empirical evidence in several industries, see, e.g., Rugman and Anderson (1987), and Anderson and Rugman (1989) suggests that each of the three alternatives may be valid in particular cases and that the latter explanation can certainly not be excluded. The implication of each explanation in terms of our conceptual framework remains the same.   U.S. firms are unable to compete against foreign rivals and use government shelter to substitute for strong FSAs.

In the first case, foreign firms have actually become more efficient than U.S. firms. If the dynamic internal economies argument is correct, this implies that in most cases it is too late to start supporting the U.S. firms so as to gain international competitiveness. Hence, government support, if granted will likely take the form of shelter.   In the last two cases, firms see their international competitive position being eroded in spite of strategic trade policy measures in the United States.   Hence, their demands for measures aimed at curtailing foreign policies are almost certainly shelter based.

Milner and Yoffie (1989b, p. 129; footnote 14) argue, in effect, that they are able to distinguish between strategic trade policy demands in quadrant 1 of Diagram 5 and traditional shelter based protectionism in quadrant 4 by taking into account two elements.   First, they regard an industry's demand as strategic only if the industry's demand is conditional, i.e., dependent upon foreign governments' willingness to open their markets.   In other words, trade protectionism is only demanded if the foreign market is kept closed.   Second, demands are considered as strategic only if the firms involved engage in activities to penetrate foreign markets through, e.g., "high international marketing expenditures, important foreign assembly operations or sales operations."

The first element is a very controversial issue.   For example, the problem of market penetration in Japan has been the subject of extensive academic discussion, see, e.g., Balassa and Noland (1988).   The evidence appears to be that direct government regulation is responsible for entry barriers in only a limited way.   If high entry barriers exist, this results from the nature of the Japanese economic system, including, for example, high distributor switching costs.

The second element does not appear to be very relevant either for discriminating between FSA-developing strategic trade policies and traditional shelter based protectionism. A substantial literature exists on the comparative inefficiency of certain operations of MNEs in particular locations, see Rugman (1990). In other words, the mere fact of being an MNE does not imply that no government shelter will be sought for any of the MNE's operations, especially those in the home market, where a dominant market position used to prevail or is considered as "normal", but where both national comparative advantage of the country and FSAs of the corporation may have been eroded.

The authors also argue that the probability of having strategic trade policy demands, as opposed to demands for outright trade protectionism increase if the domestic industry's international market position is eroding very slowly. While it is indeed true that strategic trade policy has a higher probability of being effective if foreign firms do not dominate world markets (in which case domestic attempts to capture dynamic internal and external economies would fail), it is not clear why this would exclude domestic demands for shelter. Here again, it is not the speed with which the erosion of a market position takes place that is important, but the intent of the firm's management. This intent may very well be to create shelter based entry barriers against foreign rivals.

The three examples given of industries with alleged demands for strategic trade policy, namely semi-conductors, commercial aircraft and telecommunications equipment demonstrate by themselves that the so called strategic trade policy arguments are seriously flawed. In the semi-conductor case, Japanese trade protectionism is seen as the main cause of the low market share of U.S. firms in Japan. Yet, no evidence whatsoever is given of such protectionism. In other words, the inability of U.S. firms to enter the semi-conductor market may be more the result of "natural" entry barriers created by Japanese competitors than the outcome of government protection (i.e., shelter based entry barriers).

The commercial aircraft case, which appears to be the only "real world case" that corresponds somewhat with the hypotheses of the Brander and Spencer (1985) strategic trade policy model, focuses on the demands of Boeing and McDonnell Douglas for "fair" competition from the part of the European firm Airbus. Yet, no analysis whatsoever is performed of the direct and indirect support granted to the U.S. firms by the U.S. government. In addition, it is argued that McDonnell Douglas only took steps against Airbus to create a level playing field, when plans to build aircraft through a joint venture with Airbus failed. This demonstrates that McDonnell Douglas was not really interested in "fair" competition, but in maintaining market share through every means possible, including government shelter.

Finally, the example of the telecommunication equipment industry is characteristic of U.S. ethnocentricity. It is recognized that the U.S. market was kept closed itself until U.S. deregulation, including the break-up of AT&T. Once this occurred and foreign competitors entered the U.S. market, U.S. firms demanded reciprocity. However, this demand was not triggered by unfair trade policies abroad, but was the result of a change in U.S. market conditions. In addition, it is argued that "the U.S. firms pushed Japan, largely because the U.S. ran a telecommunication equipment trade surplus with most other countries than Japan" (Milner and Yoffie, 1989b, p. 123).

This analysis suggests that U.S. firms consider fair trade with competitors of a particular foreign country to be the equivalent of having a trade surplus with that country. This reflects the biased view that foreigners can only be competitive in the United States if they are doing something wrong, like being subsidized or protected. In reality, foreign corporations are often efficinet producers with sustainable competitive advantages, in contrast to many U.S. firms which are comparatively inefficient. This implies, they lack cost or differentiation advantages. As a result U.S. firms pursue shelter-based strategies attempting to generate trade policy measures in quadrant 2 of Diagram 5.

In fact, Yoffie (1989) has demonstrated himself that the United States cannot at present pursue an FSA developing strategic trade policy in quadrant 1. In institutional terms, such a policy far exceeds the present capabilities of both Congress and the Executive. From a political perspective, he has argued that substantial authority on trade policy issues should be transferred from Congress to the Executive. In reality, the 1988 trade bill has accomplished the reverse. Yoffie (1989) then concludes that it would take a force similar in strength as the Great Depression to generate this transfer.

IX.   Conclusions

In this article we demonstrated that it is not easy to implement FSA developing strategic trade policies. If the government and its institutional structures are excessively responsive to the demands of specific pressure groups, then there is a high probability of having shelter-based policies. The main problem associated with shelter-seeking behaviour is that government support does not build upon the FSAs of the companies involved.

In theory the existing institutional structure within which trade policy is conducted could be changed, given a particular administrative heritage of (de)centralization and (in)sensitivity to demands of pressure groups. Yet, in reality, this is difficult to implement. For example, the case of administered protection in the United States, especially as regards countervail and anti-dumping actions, demonstrates how the technical track in trade policy administration can subvert fair trade intentions and turn them into tools of shelter. There is no managerial reason to believe that it would be any different with instruments of strategic trade policy.

The efficient implementation of an FSA developing strategic trade policy requires a competent executive bureaucracy with (a) extensive industry-specific knowledge, (b) the capacity to identify "winning" and "losing" industries and firms and (c) institutional characteristics that insulate it against pressure exerted by rent-seeking firms. Only a few countries possess such an executive bureaucracy. For all other countries, strategic trade policy is bad strategy.

UNIVERSITY OF TORONTO

REFERENCES

Anderson, A. and A.M. Rugman, "Subsidies in the U.S. Steel Industry: A New Conceptual Framework and Literature Review," *Journal of World Trade* Vol. 23, No. 6 (December 1989): 59–83.

Badaracco, J.L. and D.B. Yoffie, "Industrial Policy: It Can't Happen Here," *Harvard Business Review*, No. 6 (November–December, 1983): 96–105.

Baldwin, R.E., "The Political Economy of Protection," in J. Bhagwati (ed.) *Import Competition and Response*, (Chicago: University of Chicago ,1982): 263–286.

Balassa, B. and M. Noland, *Japan in The World Economy* (Washington, D.C.: Institute for International Economics, 1988).

Boltho, A. and C. Allsopp, "The Assessment: Trade and Trade Policy," *Oxford Review of Economic Policy*, 3: 1 (Spring 1987): 1–19.

Borrus, M., L. Tyson and J. Zysman, "Creating Advantages: How Government Policies Shape International Trade in the Semiconductor Industry," in P. Krugman (ed), *Strategic Trade Policy and the New International Economics* (Cambridge, Mass.: MIT Press, 1986): 91–114.

Brander, J.A. and B.J. Spencer, "Export Subsidies and International Market Share Rivalry," *Journal of International Economics* 18 (1985): 83–100.

Brock, W.A. and S.P. Magee, "The Economics of Special Interest Politics: The Case of Tariffs," *American Economic Review*, 68 (1978): 246–250.

Collis, B.J., "The Machine Tool Industry and Industrial Policy, 1955–82" in A.M. Spence and H.A. Hazard (eds.) *International Competitiveness*, (Cambridge, Mass.: Ballinger, 1988).

Cooper, R.N., "Industrial Policy and Trade Distortion: A Policy Perspective," in A.M. Spence and H.A. Hazard (eds.) *International Competitiveness*, (Cambridge, Mass.: Ballinger, 1988).

Culbertson, J.M., "The Folly of Free Trade," *Harvard Business Review*, No. 5 (September–October, 1986): 62–70.

Dixit, A.K. and G.M. Grossman," Targeted Export Promotion with Several Oligopolistic Industries," *Journal of International Economics* 21 (November 1986): 233–249.

Eaton, J. and G.M. Grossman, "Optimal Trade and Industrial Policy Under Oligopoly," *Quarterly Journal of Economics* 101 (1986): 383–406.

Fox, R.J., "Revamping the Business of National Defense," *Harvard Business Review*, 84: 5 (September–October 1984): 62–70.

Horvath, D. and McMillan, C., "Industrial Planning in Japan," *California Management Review*, 23: 1 (1980): 11–21.

Horstman, I. and J.R. Markusen, "Up the Average Cost Curve: Inefficient Entry and the New Protectionism," *Journal of International Economics*, 20 (May 1988): 225–247.

Jacquemin, A., "International and Multinational Strategic Behavior," *Kyklos* (Vol. 42, No. 4, 1989): 495–513.

Katzenstein, P., *Small States in World Markets* (Ithaca: Cornell University Press, 1985).

Krugman, P.R., "Import Protection or Export Promotion," in Kierzkowski, ed., *Monooilistic Competition and International Trade* (Oxford: Oxford University Press, 1984).

Krugman, P.R. (ed.), *Strategic Trade Policy and the New International Economics* (Cambridge, Mass.: MIT Press, 1986).

Krugman, P.R., "Strategic Sectors and International Competition," in R.M. Stern (ed.) *U.S. Trade Policy in a Changing World Economy* (Cambridge, Mass.: MIT Press, 1987a).

Krugman, P.R., "Is Free Trade Passe?" *Journal of Economic Perspectives*, 1: 2 (Fall 1977b): 141–144.

Lodge, G.C. and W.C. Crum, "U.S. Competitiveness: The Policy Tangle," *Harvard Business Review*, No. 1 (January–February, 1985): 34–55.

Majumbar, B.A., "Upstart or Flying Start? The Rise of Airbus Industries," *World Economy*, 10: 4 (December 1987): 497–517.

McKeown, T.J., "Firms and Tariff Regime Change: Explaining the Demand for Protection," *World Politics*, 36 (January 1984): 215–233.

McNiven, J.D., "Challenge and Response: The Rise of States Export Development Policies in the U.S.," Dalhousie Discussion Paper in International Business, No. 80, Centre for International Business Studies, Dalhousie University, (Halifax, 1989).

Milner, H.V., *Resisting Protectionism: Global Industries and the Politics of International Trade* (Princeton, N.J.: Princeton University Press, 1988).

Nelson, D., "Domestic Political Preconditions of U.S. Trade Policy: Liberal Structure and Protectionist Dynamics," *Journal of Public Policy*, 9: 1 (January–March, 1989): 82–108.

Olson, M., *The Logic of Collective Action: Public Goods and the Theory of Groups* (Cambridge, Mass.: Harvard University Press, 1965).

Olson, M., *The Rise and Decline of Nations* (New Haven: Yale University Press, 1982).

Reich, R.B., "Why the U.S. Needs an Industrial Policy," *Harvard Business Review*, No. 1 (January–February, 1982a): 74–81.

Reich, R.B., "Making Industrial Policy," *Foreign Affairs*, (Spring 1982b): 876.

Rugman, A.M., *Multinationals and Canada-United States Free Trade* (Columbia: University of South Carolina Press, 1990).

Rugman, A.M. and A. Anderson, *Administered Protection in America* (London: Croom Helm/Routledge and New York: Methuen, 1987).

Rugman, A.M. and A. Verbeke, "Trade Policy in the Asia-Pacific Region: A U.S.-Japan Comparison," *Journal of Business Administration*, 17: 1, 2 (1987): 89–108.

Rugman, A.M. and A. Verbeke, *Global Corporate Strategy and Trade Policy* (London: Routledge, 1990).

Safarian, E., "Firm and Government Strategies in the Context of Economic Integration," Working Paper No. 19, Ontario Centre for International Business Research Programme, University of Toronto, July 1989.

Saxonhouse, G.R., "What is all this about Industrial Targeting in Japan?" *The World Economy*, 6: 3 (September 1983): 253–273.

Scott, B.R., "Can Industry Survive the Welfare State?" *Harvard Business Review*, No. 5 (September–October, 1982): 70–84.

Scott, B.R., "Competitiveness: Self-help for our Worsening Problem," *Harvard Business Review*, 67: 4 (July–August, 1989): 115–121.

Shapiro, C., "Theories of Oligopoly Behaviour," in R. Schmalensee and R. Willig (eds.), *Handbook of Industrial Organization* (Amsterdam: North Holland Publishers, 1989): Chapter 6.

Sharp, M., "Europe: Collaboration in High Technology Sectors," *Oxford Review of Economic Policy*, 3: 1 (Spring, 1987): 52–65.

Spencer, B., "What Should Trade Policy Target?" in P.R. Krugman, *Strategic Trade Policy and the New International Economics* (Cambridge, Mass.: MIT Press, 1986): 69–90.

Trezise, P.H., "Industrial Policy is Not the Major Reason for Japan's Success," *The Brookings Review*, No. 1 (Spring, 1983): 13–18.

Tullock, G., "Rent Seeking and Tax Reform," *Contemporary Policy Issues*, Vol. VI (October

1988): 37–49.

Vogel, E., *Japan As Number 1: Lessons For America* (Cambridge: Harvard University Press, 1979).

Yoffie, D.B., "American Trade Policy: An Obsolete Bargain?" in J.E. Chub and P.E. Peterson (eds.), *Can the Government Govern?* (Washington: The Brookings Institution, 1989): 100–138.

Yoffie, D.B. and H.V. Milner, "Between Free Trade and Protectionism: Strategic Trade Policy and a Theory of Corporate Trade Demands," *International Organization* Vol. 43 (Spring 1989a).

Yoffie, D.B. and H.V. Milner, "Why Corporations Seek Strategic Trade Policy," *California Management Review* Vol. 31, No. 4 (Summer 1989b): 113–131.

[13]

Does the United States have a deficit with Japan in foreign direct investment?

Sidney J. Gray and Alan M. Rugman*

Several articles in this journal have examined the nature and extent of both Japanese foreign direct investment in the United States and United States foreign direct investment in Japan. This article asks a more basic question: does the United States have a deficit in its bilateral foreign-direct-investment stocks with Japan? The answer is no. Here, the methodology for the calculation of the deficit is explained and related policy literature reassessed in the light of this unconventional finding.

Introduction

Conventional wisdom has it that Japanese foreign direct investment (FDI) in the United States dramatically exceeds that of United States FDI in Japan. In the United States, there is a feeling that Japan is not sufficiently open and receptive to United States investments and that policy measures need to be taken so that Japan receives its fair share of FDI (Bergsten and Noland, 1993). In particular, C. Fred Bergsten and Marcus Noland (1993, p. 79) argue that "restrictions on FDI in the form of both oligopolies and the *keiretsu*" have impeded imports of manufactured goods into Japan. Similar arguments have been advanced by Robert Z. Lawrence (1991, 1992) and Dennis Encarnation (1992, 1993), whereas Eric Ramstetter and Willian F. James (1994) have been more careful in their analysis. This literature is discussed in the second part of this article. The next section of this article re-examines data on both annual flows and stocks of bilateral FDI between the United States and Japan and explains the methodology behind the recalculation of the stock data using conventional economic and accounting analysis. The conclusion is that there is no significant United States deficit in terms of FDI stocks with Japan.

* The authors are, respectively, Foundation for Management Education Professor of International Business, Warwick Business School, University of Warwick, Warwick, United Kingdom, and Professor of International Business, Faculty of Management, University of Toronto, Toronto, Ontario, Canada. The authors would like to thank Michael Gestrin and Walid Hejazi for comments on an earlier draft, but any errors remain the responsibility of the authors.

Data on the United States-Japan balance of FDI

In recent years, there has been a deficit in bilateral FDI *flows* between the United States and Japan (table 1). For example, in 1990, Japanese FDI in the United States was 22 times higher than United States FDI in Japan; in 1991, it was 44 times higher, and in 1992, it was five times higher.

But *stock* data are, of course, of greater relevance. The United States Department of Commerce statistics reveal that sizeable Japanese surpluses in its bilateral FDI stock with the United States have occurred only since 1989; at that time, the Japanese FDI stock was four times higher than that of the United States (table 2). Furthermore, the United States FDI stock in Japan is measured at historical book value. Since the yen has appreciated considerably during the past ten years, and much of the United States FDI stock in Japan occurred before then, it is significantly undervalued.

A more up-to-date valuation of the United States FDI stock in Japan shows that the United States and Japan are basically in balance as far as these investments are concerned. Tables 3 and 4 adjust each year's data to reflect exchange-rate changes and the index of share prices in each country to capture better market values rather than being based on historical book-value costs. The result is that the ratio of Japanese FDI in the United States to that of United States FDI in Japan falls significantly (from 3.69 to 1.44.) This is shown in table 5, which takes the restated 1992 values of FDI from tables 3 and 4 and reports the annual ratios from 1982-1992. It is only since 1988 that there has been a surplus of the adjusted stock of Japanese FDI in the United States compared to that of United States FDI in Japan. Rounded this would result in a 1:1 ratio. Clearly, this is not evidence of a significant deficit in United States FDI with Japan.

The methodology used in tables 3 and 4 to adjust the official data takes the year 1960 as the starting point. It adjusts FDI for that year and the increases or decreases in subsequent years for changes in exchange rates (from a dollar perspective) and market values to give a more accurate and comparable view of Japanese FDI relative to United States FDI as at the end of 1992.

The problem with the official FDI statistics is that they are based on historical cost estimates of investments derived from company accounting records. Over time, such historical book values become more and more misleading as market values change. Even estimates of current values based on replacement cost (using asset price indices) are limited because they measure

Table 1.   Bilateral FDI flows between the United States and Japan, 1982-1992

(Millions of dollars)

Year	United States FDI in Japan	Japanese FDI in the United States	Ratio (2)/(1)
	1	2	3
1982	243	1 977	8.14
1983	1 257	1 653	1.32
1984	−340	4 374	−12.86
1985	1 131	3 394	3.00
1986	639	7 268	11.37
1987	1 493	6 181	4.14
1988	1 313	17 205	13.10
1989	299	18 653	62.38
1990	844	18 754	22.22
1991	244	10 660	43.69
1992	867	3 960	4.57

Source: United States Department of Commerce, *Survey of Current Business*, various issues.

value changes by making reference to the value of individual assets and liabilities. What is really relevant is the value of the investor's ownership stake in the net assets or equity of the FDI taken as a whole. From this perspective, the market value of the ownership stake would seem to be a much more useful indicator. It is not easy to estimate the current market value of FDI, but an approximation can be made by using national share-price indices that reflect general trends in economic value and provide a broadly based measure of changes in the prices at which investors' ownership shares can be traded in each country. (Share-price indices for Japan and the United States are published, along with exchange-rate data, in the International Monetary Fund's *International Financial Statistics Yearbook*.)

The use of current market values is also consistent with the adjustment made to United States FDI stock in Japan to reflect changes in the exchange rate between the yen and the dollar which—in theory at least—are linked to price differentials between these countries. Before adjusting for market values, the United States FDI data (in dollars) were translated first into yen (at historical cost), then adjusted to market values in Japan and finally translated back into dollars at the current exchange rate. The United States FDI

**Table 2.   Bilateral FDI stocks between the United States and Japan,
1982-1992**

(Millions of dollars)

Year	United States FDI in Japan	Japanese FDI in the United States	Ratio (2)/(1)
	1	2	3
1982	6 407	9 677	1.51
1983	7 661	11 336	1.48
1984	7 920	16 044	2.03
1985	9 095	19 313	2.12
1986	11 472	26 824	2.34
1987	15 684	35 151	2.24
1988	18 009	51 126	2.84
1989	19 911	67 268	3.38
1990	22 511	83 091	3.69
1991	24 938	92 896	3.73
1992	26 213	96 743	3.69

Source: United States Department of Commerce, *Survey of Current Business*, various
issues.

data can, thus, be compared with the Japanese FDI data (in dollars) adjusted
to market values in the United States. In this way, the limitations of the FDI
data of the United States Department of Commerce can be overcome to
provide a more realistic picture of the relative Japan/United States FDI
positions.

The data recorded by the Japanese authorities are, however, even more
misleading than those of the United States. In Japan, there are two sets of
data on FDI. One of these is issued by the Bank of Japan and uses flow data
from the balance-of-payments accounts; these flows are aggregated to provide an estimate of stocks. These data exclude reinvested earnings—a potentially large source of FDI—and the cumulation of annual flows, to estimate
stocks is also a drawback. The other set of data (and the one most widely
used in various publications, including UNCTAD's annual *World Investment
Report*) is produced by the Ministry of Finance. These data, used by the Ministry of International Trade and Industry and most other Japanese-based trade
and investment research groups, are both on outward and inward FDI and are
based on approvals and notifications, not actual FDI.

Table 3.   United States foreign direct investment in Japan
(Millions of dollars)

Year	FDI (increase/ decrease)	Exchange rate (historic)	Market value adjusted	Exchange rate (current)	Adjusted FDI (to 1992 values)
1960	254 ×	360 ×	136.9/ 9.8	127	10 057.96
1961 +	48 ×	360 ×	136.9/ 11.2	127	1 663.13
1962 +	71 ×	360 ×	136.9/ 9.9	127	2 783.08
1963 +	99 ×	360 ×	136.9/ 10.9	127	3 524.61
1964 +	127 ×	360 ×	136.9/ 9.6	127	5 133.75
1965 +	177 ×	360 ×	136.9/ 9.2	127	7 465.99
1966 +	55 ×	360 ×	136.9/ 11.0	127	1 940.31
1967 +	103 ×	360 ×	136.9/ 11.1	127	3 600.94
1968 +	171 ×	360 ×	136.9/ 11.9	127	5 576.37
1969 +	221 ×	360 ×	136.9/ 15.2	127	5 642.23
1970 +	256 ×	360 ×	136.9/ 16.4	127	6 057.57
1971 +	431 ×	349 ×	136.9/ 18.0	127	9 008.03
1972 +	410 ×	303 ×	136.9/ 28.3	127	4 731.95
1973 +	348 ×	272 ×	136.9/ 36.4	127	2 803.15
1974 +	648 ×	292 ×	136.9/ 30.8	127	6 622.27
1975 +	20 ×	297 ×	136.9/ 31.3	127	204.57
1976 +	458 ×	297 ×	136.9/ 34.9	127	4 201.42
1977 +	346 ×	269 ×	136.9/ 37.8	127	2 654.22
1978 +	820 ×	210 ×	136.9/ 41.7	127	4 451.40
1979 −	812 ×	219 ×	136.9/ 45.2	127	4 240.93
1980 +	468 ×	226 ×	136.9/ 47.6	127	2 395.23
1981 +	564 ×	221 ×	136.9/ 55.3	127	2 429.66
1982 −	400 ×	249 ×	136.9/ 55.1	127	−1 948.53
1983 +	1 254 ×	238 ×	136.9/ 64.9	127	4 957.12
1984 +	259 ×	238 ×	136.9/ 81.9	127	811.32
1985 +	1 175 ×	239 ×	136.9/100.0	127	3 027.16
1986 +	2 377 ×	169 ×	136.9/132.9	127	3 258.30
1987 +	4 212 ×	145 ×	136.9/196.4	127	3 352.08
1988 +	2 325 ×	128 ×	136.9/213.9	127	1 499.76
1989 +	1 902 ×	138 ×	136.9/257.8	127	1 097.50
1990 +	2 600 ×	145 ×	136.9/218.8	127	1 857.35
1991 +	2 427 ×	135 ×	136.9/184.9	127	1 910.15
1992 +	1 275 ×	127 ×	136.9/136.9	127	1 275.00
Sum					**118 285.98**

Source: United States Department of Commerce, Survey of Current Business, various issues.

Table 4.   Japanese foreign direct investment in the United States
(Millions of dollars)

Year	FDI (increase/ decrease)	Market value adjusted	Adjusted FDI (to 1992 values)
1960 +	80 ×	236.1/ 28.6	660.42
1961 +	8 ×	236.1/ 33.7	56.05
1962 +	4 ×	236.1/ 31.5	29.98
1963 +	10 ×	236.1/ 35.3	66.88
1964 −	8 ×	236.1/ 41.5	−45.51
1965 −	32 ×	236.1/ 45.0	−167.89
1966 +	46 ×	236.1/ 43.8	247.96
1967 −	15 ×	236.1/ 47.7	−74.25
1968 +	5 ×	236.1/ 51.7	22.83
1969 +	75 ×	236.1/ 51.2	345.85
1970 −	5 ×	236.1/ 43.9	26.89
1971 +	53 ×	236.1/ 52.1	240.18
1972 −	456 ×	236.1/ 58.6	−1 837.23
1973 +	73 ×	236.1/ 58.0	297.16
1974 +	306 ×	236.1/ 44.7	1 616.26
1975 +	193 ×	236.1/ 46.5	979.94
1976 +	246 ×	236.1/ 55.0	1 056.01
1977 +	587 ×	236.1/ 52.2	2 654.99
1978 +	577 ×	236.1/ 51.1	2 665.94
1979 +	1 686 ×	236.1/ 55.3	7 198.27
1980 +	1 282 ×	236.1/ 64.7	4 678.21
1981 +	2 974 ×	236.1/ 69.4	10 117.60
1982 +	1 980 ×	236.1/ 64.3	7 270.26
1983 +	1 659 ×	236.1/ 86.9	4 507.36
1984 +	4 708 ×	236.1/ 87.2	12 747.23
1985 +	3 269 ×	236.1/100.0	7 718.11
1986 +	7 511 ×	236.1/126.2	14 051.88
1987 +	8 327 ×	236.1/159.2	12 349.28
1988 +	15 975 ×	236.1/147.6	25 553.51
1989 +	16 142 ×	236.1/178.2	21 386.79
1990 +	15 823 ×	236.1/188.1	19 860.77
1991 +	9 805 ×	236.1/214.6	10 787.33
1992 +	3 847 ×	236.1/236.1	3 847.00
Sum			**170 916.06**

Source: United States Department of Commerce, *Survey of Current Business*, various issues.

**Table 5.   United States and Japan foreign-direct-investment
stocks between 1982-1992, adjusted data, end 1992 values**

(Millions of dollars)

Year	United States FDI in Japan (1)	Japanese FDI in the United States (2)	Annual ratio (2)/(1) (3)
1982	95 240	38 107	0.40
1983	100 197	42 614	0.42
1984	101 009	55 361	0.55
1985	104 036	63 080	0.61
1986	107 294	77 131	0.72
1987	110 646	89 481	0.81
1988	112 146	115 034	1.03
1989	113 243	136 421	1.20
1990	115 101	156 282	1.36
1991	117 011	167 069	1.42
1992	118 286	170 916	1.44

Source: United States Department of Commerce, *Survey of Current Business*, various
issues.

According to these Japanese data, as of 31 March 1993, the stock (accumulated flows of FDI approvals/notifications over the fiscal years 1951-
1992) of Japanese FDI in the United States was $162 billion. The stock of
United States FDI in Japan, estimated in the same way, was $11 billion. The
ratio of Japanese FDI in the United States to United States FDI in Japan is
14:1. Thus, the data of the Japanese Ministry of Finance are even more misleading than the United States data in that they greatly exaggerate that ratio.
The reporting of approved, instead of actual, FDI appears to significantly
overestimate both Japanese FDI in the United States and United States FDI
in Japan compared to the actual data reported by the United States Department of Commerce.

Related literature

Robert Z. Lawrence (1993), like C. F. Bergsten and M. Noland (1993),
has accepted the premise that the low level of FDI in Japan can be attributed
to a "history of official inhibitions of FDI" (p. 86). He also argued that the
FDI data on notifications by the Ministry of Finance actually overstate

United States FDI in Japan, since there have been major withdrawals of these investments in recent years. Lawrence reported that the value of the total stock of FDI in Japan in 1989, at historical cost, was only about $9 billion (p. 86), according to balance-of-payments data from the Bank of Japan that exclude reinvested earnings. Robert Z. Lawrence also reported FDI stock data by the United States Department of Commerce (as in table 2) showing that United States FDI in Japan is about half of all FDI in Japan. Robert Z. Lawrence interpreted these data to mean that the growth of United States FDI in Japan has been dominated by the activities of United States transnational corporations (TNCs) already in Japan and that the inflow of new equity capital from the United States into Japan in the 1980s was negative. Indeed, the key point made by Lawrence is that there are significant barriers to the acquisition of Japanese firms. These obstacles mean that the preferred mode of FDI is greenfield operations, or that foreign firms are forced into licensing. In particular, Lawrence found that there are very low levels of FDI in *keiretsu* networks because the extensive cross-holdings of stocks by the network members act as a device to prevent inward FDI to Japan.

A somewhat related, but essentially different, argument to the one made here was advanced by Kenichi Ohmae (1987). Using data for 1984, Ohmae demonstrated that the "real" trade balance was close to zero. This occurs when United States exports to Japan ($26 million) are supplemented by the production and sales affiliates of United States TNCs in Japan ($43 million in 1984). The total of $70 million represents Japan's consumption of goods and services produced by United States firms. In contrast, in 1984, Japanese exports to the United States ($57 million) were supplemented by $13 million of production and sales of affiliates of Japanese TNCs in the United States, making a total of $70 million. Since 1984, the sales of Japanese affiliates in the United States must have increased, but Ohmae's data reinforce the emphasis placed here on the tremendous importance of the stock of United States FDI already in Japan, that, in 1984, led to sales in Japan being twice as high as the flow of United States exports to Japan.

Dennis Encarnation (1992, 1993) went into much greater depth than Ohmae in his analysis of bilateral intra-company trade. Encarnation found that TNCs in Japan have not contributed to the bilateral trade balance because they do not import very much from the United States. He argued that United States FDI in Japan has an above-average share of minority affiliates and that they do not purchase as many goods and services from the United States as do United States (majority-owned) affiliates in other developed countries. Thus, the United States-Japan trade deficit is worsened by the relatively small amounts of imports from the United States by United States firms in Japan. In contrast, Japanese FDI in the United States has usually been in the form of majority holdings, and majority-owned affiliates import from Japan much more than United States affiliates in Japan import from the United States.

These are interesting data, but there is no reason to assume that bilateral intra-company trade flows should balance; such an imbalance, for example, also reflects differing industrial structures. Evidence that the bilateral trade and investment imbalances are the result of different industrial structures is found in Lincoln (1990). According to Edward J. Lincoln (1990), the intra-industry trade index (theoretically, equal to 100 when imports equal exports) for Japan in 1985 was unusually low at 26, whereas that index was 61 for the United States and 67 for Germany. The latter ratios are more representative of countries with a significant transnational presence and two-way flows of FDI. Lincoln, and others, interpreted the very low number of intra-industry trade as evidence that Japan has adopted an institutional structure that limits imports of United States (and other) manufactured goods and that this structure is pervasive throughout the public administration and business. Robert Z. Lawrence (1991) further argued that the dominant role of *keiretsu* limits Japanese imports from the United States and that United States TNCs have not penetrated these network relationships to any significant degree.

The findings in this article are also consistent with those in a recent article in this journal by Ramstetter and James (1994), in particular, their statement that ''Japanese restrictions on United States transnational corporations are not a major factor'' in explaining the relatively low sales of United States affiliates in Japan compared with Japanese affiliates in the United States.

Finally, Alan Rugman (1990) provides a different perspective on Japanese FDI in the United States (in comparison to Canadian FDI in the United States). In that study, several aspects of the ''quality'' of FDI in the United States are discussed. For example, although the stock of Japanese FDI in the United States in 1987 was double that of Canada's, the Canadian affiliates in the United States employed twice as many people as did the Japanese affiliates in the United States. The reason was that nearly half of all the Canadian FDI in the United States was in manufacturing in 1987, whereas only 8 per cent of Japanese FDI in the United States was in manufacturing (with over 80 per cent of it in wholesale trade, i.e., distribution). Thus, the quality of FDI needs to be examined, as well as its stock. In this regard most United

States FDI in Japan is in manufacturing, reinforcing the quality of such FDI and again helping to "balance" the bilateral United States-Japan FDI stocks.

Conclusions

The policy implications of this article are of great importance. Once the actual data on stocks of United States-Japanese FDI are understood to be in approximate balance, rather than tremendously asymmetrical in favour of Japan, the most obvious policy implication is to have no policy! There is no need for the Government of the United States to continue applying pressure on the Government of Japan to open up its market to United States FDI, since the stock of United States FDI in Japan is not "too small" relative to the stock of Japanese FDI in the United States. The correct data on relative stocks of FDI do not provide any support for United States allegations that the Japanese market is relatively closed to United States FDI; indeed United States TNCs have obviously performed rather well in Japan during the last thirty years despite the alleged barriers to entry and transaction costs involved in penetrating the Japanese distribution system. The United States does continue to have a large bilateral trade deficit with Japan, and part of this is probably due to relative differences in intra-firm and intra-industry trade. However, United States-Japanese economic relations should not be entirely driven by their bilateral trade performances, and the apparent misunderstanding of the bilateral FDI balance should be addressed at once by policy makers and analysts. ■

References

Bergsten, C., Fred and Marcus Noland (1993). *Reconcilable Differences: United States-Japan Economic Conflict* (Washington, D.C.: Institute for International Economics).

Dunning, John H. and Rajneesh Narula (1994). *Transpacific Foreign Direct Investment and the Investment Development Path: The Record Assessed* (Columbia, South Carolina: University of South Carolina (CIBER) 10 (May)).

Encarnation, Dennis J. (1992). *Rivals Beyond Trade* (Ithaca, New York: Cornell University Press).

————— (1993). "A common evolution?: a comparison of United States and Japanese transnational corporations," *Transnational Corporations*, 2, 1 (February), pp. 7-32.

Lawrence, Robert Z. (1991). "How open is Japan?", in Paul Krugman, ed., *Trade with Japan: Has the Door Opened Wider?* (Chicago: University of Chicago Press), pp. 9-49.

————— (1992). "Japan's low levels of inward investment: the role of inhibitions on acquisitions," *Transnational Corporations*, 1, 3 (December), pp. 47-75.

————— (1993). "Japan's low levels of inward investment: the role of inhibitions on acquisitions", in Kenneth A. Froot, ed., *Foreign Direct Investment* (Chicago: University of Chicago Press), pp. 85-112.

Lincoln, Edward J. (1990). *Japan's Unequal Trade* (Washington, D.C.: The Brookings Institution).

Ohmae, Kenichi (1987). *Beyond National Borders: Reflection on Japan and the World* (Homeward: Illinois Dow Jones-Irwin).

Ramstetter, Eric D. and William E. James (1994). "Transnational corporations, Japan-United States economic relations and economic policy: the uncomfortable reality", *Transnational Corporations*, 2, 3 (December), pp. 65-96.

Rugman, Alan M. (1990). *Japanese Foreign Direct Investment in Canada* (Ottawa, Canada: Canada-Japan Trade Council).

Strange, Susan (1994). "European business in Japan: a policy crossroads" (mimeo).

United Nations Conference on Trade and Development, Division on Transnational Corporations and Investment (1994). *World Investment Report 1994: Transnational Corporations, Employment and the Workplace*. Sales No. E. 94.II.A.14.

Europe 1992 and Competitive Strategies for North American Firms

Alan M. Rugman and Alain Verbeke

> *North American firms must quickly consider and act on their European strategies before barriers to entry become too large to overcome.*

As the European Community (EC) proceeds with its plans for the completion of a single internal market by 1992, issues arise for the managers of multinational enterprises (MNEs). "Europe 1992" means the elimination of all remaining internal barriers to the free movement of goods, services, capital, and labor. The focus of this article is the probable strategic planning response by North American managers to Europe 1992. The profound changes for business arising from the implementation of the Single European Act are a typical "environmental" change that can be analyzed using modern methods of business policy, such as those popularized by Michael Porter (1980, 1985).

The public policy content of Europe 1992 targets the elimination of most non-tariff barriers to intra-EC trade through the implementation of approximately 280 measures. These directives require the elimination of technical, physical, and fiscal barriers, as well as the liberalization of capital and government procurement policies. The technical barriers refer to heterogeneous standards related to, for example, health and safety, that often serve to protect domestic producers. The physical barriers primarily relate to excessive border controls due to administrative requirements (such as differences in value added taxes).

There will be greater conformity among different national policies and governmental control systems as a result of two factors. The first is "approximation," or bringing such things as indirect tax rates in line so the range of different tax rates is diminished. The second is mutual recognition—reciprocal recognition by all national governments of economic activities (by, say, financial institutions) and professional qualifications accepted in one of the EC countries.

The concept of reciprocity involves harmonization of policies, since "home" country standards will apply in "host" countries. It involves a much greater degree of integration than "national treatment," under which host country standards are applied equally to domestic and foreign firms.

The rationale for the movement toward a single market by 1992 for the 12 members of the EC is articulated in a large and growing amount of literature. Perhaps the most influential of the studies is Paolo Cecchini's rationale for the internal market (1988). Background studies by Emerson et al. (1988) examine the economic benefits of 1992 in greater detail. The EC commissioned both of these studies, which have helped create a favorable climate of opinion in support of Europe 1992. For a more critical British analysis of 1992, the study by the Centre for Business Strategy at the London Business School, by Davis et al. (1989), is of interest. An American perspective is provided by Calingaert (1988) for the National Planning Association.

In this environment of planned internal harmony and standardized regulatory and fiscal practices, there is a natural corporate response institutionalized by the design and implementation of appropriate strategies. To a degree, European firms have an edge in adapting their strategies for 1992 because they have already anticipated pan-European production, distribution, and human resources management. Their competitive strategies already incorporate aspects of 1992. The focus here will be on the competitive strategies of non-European corporations, including multinationals from Canada and the United States. We argue that these firms need to understand the new European "mindset" to react favorably to 1992, a point also made by D'Cruz (1989). North America includes the United States and Canada, as these markets are now highly integrated as a result of the Canada-U.S. Free Trade Agreement of 1989.

CORPORATE STRATEGIES FOR EUROPE 1992

Conceptually, the impact of Europe 1992 on different industries, even on individual firms, is displayed in **Figure 1**. This is based on Bartlett's (1986) globalization/national response matrix. We have extended this framework to consider corporate strategy and reaction to changes in trade policy (Rugman and Verbeke 1990). We now adapt it to consider the issue of corporate responses to Europe 1992.

The horizontal axis measures the need for corporations to respond to sovereignty. Companies need to be "nationally responsive" to consumer tastes and government regulations in the relevant countries of Europe in which they operate. Sovereignty means that corporate activities need to be adapted to local conditions, both in content and process. This may imply a geographical dispersion of activities or a decentralization of coordination and control for individual firms. The single market of 1992 can lead to either a low or a high degree of need for awareness of sovereignty by business.

The vertical axis gives an analysis of the need for economic integration, frequently referred to as globalization. Movement up the axis results in a greater degree of economic integration, defined as economies of scale captured as a result of centralizing specific activities in the value-added chain in locations with the strongest perceived country specific advantages, or reaping benefits of increased coordination and control of geographically dispersed activities.

On the basis of the two axes of Figure 1, four cases can be distinguished. Quadrants 1 and 4 are simple cases. These are two cases where the impact of an environmental change such as 1992 clearly affects the firm's movement toward a higher required responsiveness to one variable and simultaneously decreases the required responsiveness to the other variable. In Quadrant 1, the need for globalization increases and the need for awareness of sovereignty is low. This focus

on scale economies will lead to competitive strategies based on Porter's first generic strategy of price competition. Mergers and acquisitions will result. The opposite situation is characteristic of Quadrant 4, where sovereignty matters but globalization is low. There, niche strategies must be pursued; companies will adapt products to satisfy the high demands of sovereignty and ignore scale economies, as globalization does not matter.

Quadrants 2 and 3 reflect more complex situations. Quadrant 2 refers to those cases in which both the need for integration and awareness of sovereignty is low. This implies that both the potential to obtain economies of scale and benefits of regional responsiveness decline. Typical strategies for Quadrant 2 would involve industries characterized by increased international standardization of products and services. This could lead to lower needs for centralized quality control and centralized strategic decision making, while simultaneously eliminating requirements to adapt activities to individual countries.

Finally, in Quadrant 3 the need for both integration and sovereignty increase, implying that different activities in the vertical chain are faced with opposite tendencies—for example, a higher need for integration in production along with higher requirements for regional adaptations in

Figure 1
Globalization and Sovereignty

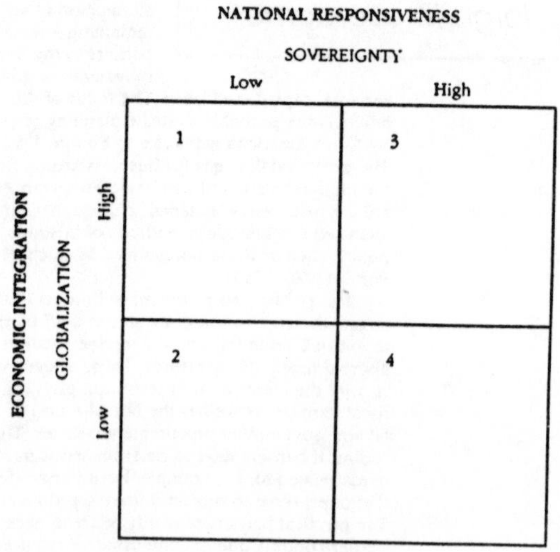

NATIONAL RESPONSIVENESS

SOVEREIGNTY

Low   High

ECONOMIC INTEGRATION

GLOBALIZATION

High

Low

1   3

2   4

marketing. This is the most challenging quadrant, and one in which many successful globally adaptive MNEs must perform. Using this framework, we can analyze the impact of 1992 on different industries and firms located both in the EC and outside of it (especially third-country exporters).

The key proposition in this article is that Europe 1992 has been designed by the Brussels bureaucrats to help European firms move into Quadrant 1. This will create a natural barrier to entry (in Porter's terms). The new entrepreneurial climate, which now exists due to the expected harmonization, is already creating a tendency towards integration. Consequently, mergers and acquisitions are occurring as larger industrial groups are formed throughout Europe. The harmonization of technical barriers and the reduction of transaction costs at physical frontiers are designed to limit sovereignty elements in production, marketing, and human resource management. It will be easier for European firms to operate with scale economies in the different national markets.

A survey of the top management of Europe's 300 largest corporations has confirmed this tendency towards integration (*Le Monde* 1988). This survey produced results entirely consistent with Quadrant 1 thinking. European managers anticipate increased integration due to perceived benefits of a large market (49 percent), strategic partnerships, mergers and takeovers (46 percent), and scale economies (25 percent). The managers also anticipate less protection and subsidization for sheltered industries such as textiles, metal manufacturing. and agriculture. They expect the development of more efficient, rationalized, modern industries.

Furthermore, the *Le Monde* survey found that European managers were confident that economic integration was a viable strategy for them, but not for rival non-European MNEs. Only 9 percent of the European managers expect U.S. firms to gain from Europe 1992, whereas 42 percent of them expect U.S. firms to lose their competitive positions. A similar viewpoint is held by European managers about the disadvantages of 1992 for Japanese and Southeast Asian firms.

In contrast, a different conceptual picture is characteristic of third-country firms (such as those from Canada and the United States) now located outside the EC Though some of their costs of doing business in Europe will decline. outside firms will be confronted with increased information costs in comparison to "insiders." In addition, as relatively larger industrial groups emerge in Europe, enjoying greater scale economies, this will increase entry barriers for non-European firms. For example, consider the issue of Porter's distribution switching costs. It can be expected that smaller non-European firms will find it more

difficult to penetrate EC markets if confronted with distribution networks that are integrated to a greater extent with large European groups. After 1992 Europe's distribution networks will act as entry barriers, more like those of Japan.

For non-European firms, this situation will put corporations dependent on exporting to the EC primarily into Quadrant 4. They will find it more difficult to export to Europe and compete on scale economies in the face of integration by rival firms in the EC Thus, non-European "outsiders" will need to be more responsive to the specific requirements of the EC market. They need to adapt their products and follow Porter's third generic strategy of focus, finding niche markets.

Exporters from the two nations of North America will be confronted with higher marketing costs when exporting to the EC market and yet need to consider moving to niche strategies. Smaller businesses will find this a major problem. They can be helped by government agencies (in Canada and the United States) acting as intermediaries to provide good marketing information. Alternatively, a switch of entry mode to foreign direct investment can secure access to EC markets. In short, outsiders (exporting to the EC) need to become insiders.

In this sense, some of the U.S. auto companies, such as Ford of Europe, are in a better position than Japanese auto makers. The restrictive auto import policies of Italy and France discriminate against Japanese-made autos; even those assembled in Britain have experienced barriers to entry into France due to arguments about the extent of value added production. If the EC imposes uniform import restrictions for a five-year period, it would force Japanese auto MNEs into switching to FDI in the EC on a broader basis. Such FDI in the EC is already being undertaken by Toyota and Nissan in anticipation of such government-imposed entry barriers. This confirms our point that the day of the insiders is here.

In this section, the impact of 1992 on EC and non-EC firms in general has been discussed. We now consider how 1992 will affect specific North American businesses and the appropriate competitive strategies for these firms. It is necessary to consider four sets of bilateral firm cases: North American firms in or out of Europe, and European firms currently in or out of North America.

THE IMPACT OF 1992 ON NORTH AMERICAN BUSINESS STRATEGY

Building upon the previous discussion of Figure 1, the impact of 1992 can now be examined in terms of the four quadrants of **Figure 2**. Figure 1 is primarily prescriptive, because it suggests how strategic planners of both European and third-country firms should attempt to analyze 1992. In contrast, Figure 2 is primarily descriptive. It allows us to classify the probable impacts of 1992 on North American business into four categories.

In Figure 2 the horizontal axis distinguishes between two types of impacts, using an inward and outward perspective. The former relates to the activities of European firms in North America, the latter to the activities of North American firms in Europe. In both cases the appropriate competitive strategy as a reaction to the type of impact can be to change existing activities or develop new activities, as identified on the vertical axis.

With respect to changes in existing activities of European firms in North America (Quadrant 1 of Figure 2), a tendency toward global rationalization is expected. This implies that the existing North American subsidiaries of European firms would become integrated in larger global networks and thus could lose part of their autonomy. Greater responsiveness to pressures for integration in Europe will undoubtedly have similar spillover effects in North America. In addition, exporting activities of European firms to North America will probably be consolidated into larger European groups, leading to increased scale economies and thus probably to stronger competition within North America.

Examples of European MNEs with Canadian subsidiaries in Quadrant 1 include Imasco (owned by British-American Tobacco), ICI, Rio Tinto Zinc, Royal-Dutch Shell, and auto makers with distribution in Canada, such as Volkswagen and BMW. For all these companies the impact of 1992 at the "head office" in Europe will have repercussions in their Canadian subsidiaries.

Quadrant 2 deals with the impact on new activities of European firms in North America. Here an increase of FDI is expected in North America, especially by medium-sized European groups who have not been operating in North America before. There is also an opportunity to use Canada as an export platform to U.S. markets. The Canada-U.S. Free Trade Agreement took place between two countries of unequal size. This leads to a relatively higher incentive for third-country foreign direct investment (FDI) in the smaller nation for reasons of political risk diversification. There is likely to be greenfield FDI in Canada rather than takeovers by these European medium-sized groups. The very largest European MNEs (such as Unilever) and those engaged in pure globalization efforts will go directly to the United States and seek to acquire U.S. firms instead of Canadian firms. This will minimize the additional costs of operating a pure globalization strategy in the large integrated North American market.

Quadrant 3 will be characterized by an increase of integration in North American firms that

Figure 2
The Impact of "1992" on North American Business

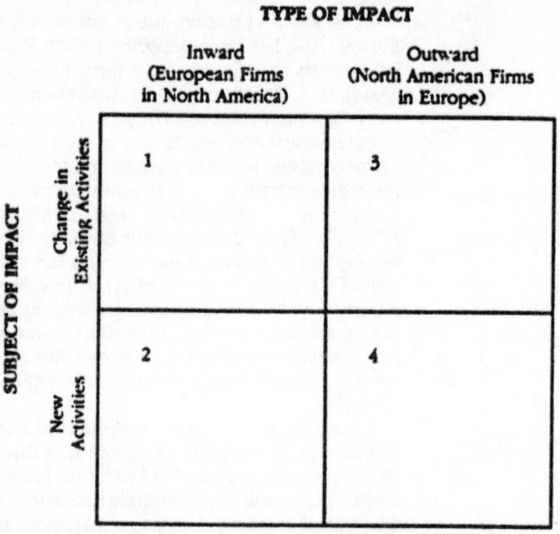

already possess facilities in the EC. They are the "insiders," and their situation is equivalent to that of European groups already analyzed in Figure 1. These North American firms can also play the game of mergers or takeovers (including the possibility of *being* taken over). This holds for both the United States and Canada. Canadian MNEs that are already insiders include Northern Telecom, Alcan, Bombardier, International Thompson, and the five large Canadian chartered banks.

In contrast, in Quadrant 4 North American exporters to the EC may see their exports jeopardized. Europe 1992 will lead to an integrated market characterized by larger European rival firms with stronger relations between production and distribution. This may force North American exporters to switch to FDI to meet the new nature of competition in Europe. Exporters need to become insiders in the European market of 1992. The main problem associated with FDI, especially for medium-sized North American firms, is the increase of entry barriers into the EC for third country corporations due to integration strategies (and resulting scale effects) by current insiders. A rational action alternative may then be to engage in strategic alliances with European groups of similar size.

A recent empirical study by Denis and Burke (1989) offers support for our analysis. In a study of 18 of the largest 30 Canadian exporters to the EC, they find that 15 firms have developed a "1992" strategy. Of these, 13 plan to have a narrower focus, with a much narrower range of products to be exported to the EC than are offered in Canada. In addition, 11 of these 15 firms plan to start up production facilities in the EC Thus, as a response to Europe 1992, the majority of affected Canadian exporters plan to switch to FDI and attempt to become insiders.

Finally, small business in North America is affected by Europe 1992. Small business usually follows a niche strategy. Essentially, Quadrant 4 is where small business operates. There are pressures on North American small business because rival firms in the EC will have better access to information. It is a fallacy to think that 1992 will reduce the costs of doing business in Europe if standards and regulations are harmonized. This is a simplistic view of the 1992 measures. Instead, a new, wealthy, vibrant, and economically integrated market is emerging, but one characterized by multiple preferences and distinctive regional tastes. This will require a greater awareness of sovereignty, as discussed earlier in Figure 1. Thus, small business in North America faces a major investment in becoming familiar with the diverse segments of Europe 1992. A successful niche strategy requires national responsiveness. Again, small business must consider local joint venture partners and other methods to become familiar with Europe.

BALANCING ECONOMIC INTEGRATION AND SOVEREIGNTY IN EUROPE 1992

The strategic impact of the Europe 1992 measures means that the benefits of integration need to be weighed against the continued importance of sovereignty. Excessive attention to integration is a simplistic strategy. This is not to deny that, even without complete harmonization, there may be important economies of scale to be captured in a more integrated market. There will be substantial effects from 1992 measures on both European and non-European firms in several industries that are now being forced to be nationally responsive and forgo benefits of integration.

Europe 1992 will lead to greater economic integration and scale economies for EC firms. This will be realized through mergers and takeovers and also through company rationalization. In the former case, non-European producers such as North American exporters will be confronted with larger, more efficient European groups and thus with higher entry barriers. In the latter case, North American firms will be facing more competition, also in non-EC markets. Yet national responsiveness and sovereignty will be as impor-

tant to corporate strategy as integration.

The telecommunications sector is a case in point. As a result of protected domestic markets with specific national standards, the average prices for telecommunications equipment are 90 percent higher than in the United States. If domestic monopolies are partly abolished as a result of opening public procurement contracts to non-domestic firms and harmonizing technical standards, the economies of scale will be gained. Similarly, in packaged goods, food processing, and the beer industries, which have many internal barriers to trade, economies of scale are often lacking due to stringent heterogeneous laws related to labeling, purity, additives, and other standards.

Yet sovereignty will not fade away as Europe 1992 unfolds. In some areas, such as telecommunications, the role of state and quasi-state monopolies may be reduced. The British government has been keen to privatize many publicly owned utilities and corporations. Other European governments, especially Italy and France, retain large public sectors where privatization seems remote. As long as major chunks of European economies remain under state control it will be necessary for private corporations to continue to design strategies that accept the reality of such state-imposed national entry barriers. Sovereignty is not about to take a back seat after 1992. The potential extension of 1992 to Eastern Europe offers a further caveat to the decline of the state. For all these reasons the issue of the appropriate corporate response to sovereignty will continue to demand as much attention as that of economic integration, especially for outsiders.

As discussed in the last section, smaller non-European exporters especially will be faced with the costs of national responsiveness. They will need to adapt to EC needs, principally through substitution of FDI for exporting or the formation of strategic partnerships with groups already located in the EC. Only through such regional responsiveness will non-European country exporters be able to maintain and strengthen niches they developed in the different protected national markets or markets characterized by strong idiosyncrasy (without integrated European manufacturers).

The changes in company strategies as a result of 1992 will lead to pan-European consolidation, but there is no reason to believe that any decrease in competition will take place. All cases with a "community dimension" will still be reviewed and controlled. Thus the establishment of new monopolies in the EC seems rather unlikely, which would tend to confirm the expectation of increased competition.

A final question is whether or not new government-imposed entry barriers will be created as a result of 1992. Will "Fortress Europe" emerge? The EC itself, and member governments, clearly reject the creation of protectionist entry barriers to be imposed on non-European firms. However, this does not imply that items such as public procurement will be opened to non-EC firms. In addition, services will not be unilaterally liberalized to give access to non-European corporations.

The competitive strategies for non-European firms after 1992 will be partly influenced by the strategies already underway by their current European rivals. They also depend critically upon the nature of market access to the EC: is it by exporting or by FDI? It is apparent from the framework developed here that non-European firms need to establish themselves in the EC before 1993 to avoid potential barriers to entry and forced changes in their desired competitive strategies.

It is also apparent that a "Fortress Europe" is emerging, vis-à-vis non-EC exporters, even without an explicit strategy by EC governments to erect protectionist barriers. Rather, Europe 1992 means an indirect entry barrier to non-European firms. As their European competitors reposition themselves in a harmonized internal market, non-European firms face the challenge of rethinking their own strategies. Even with no more government intervention, the process of firm-driven competitive strategy suggests that European firms will be able to erect "natural" barriers to entry, to which non-European firms must react just as if they were losing market access through protectionism. Ultimately a barrier to entry is just that, whether it is private or government-driven. Yet it should also be recognized that "new insiders," former exporters to the EC who have now shifted their entry mode to FDI, may be well positioned to challenge the "old insiders," who will not take up the challenge of seriously rethinking their strategies. ☐

References

Charles A. Bartlett, "Building and Managing the Transnational: The New Organizational Challenge," in M.E. Porter (ed.), *Competition in Global Industries* (Boston: Harvard Business School Press, 1986).

Michael Calingaert, *The 1992 Challenge from Europe: Development of the European Community's Internal Market* (Washington: National Planning Association, 1988).

Paolo Cecchini, *The European Challenge: 1992* (Hants, England: Wildwood House Ltd., 1988).

Evan Davis et al., *1992: Myths and Realities* (London: Centre for Business Strategy, London Business School, 1989).

Jean-Emile Denis and Wivina Burke, "Canadian Multinational: Their Strategies to Face the European Community of 1992," in R. Luostarinen (ed.), *Dynamics of International Business: Proceedings of the 15th Annual Conference of the European International Business Association*, Vol. 2, (Helsinki: Helsinki School of Economics, 1989), pp. 19-32.

Joseph D'Cruz, "The Practicing Manager's Guide to 1992," *International Business Scene*, Fall 1989.

Michael Emerson et al., *The Economics of 1992: The EC Commission's Assessment of the Economic Effects of Completing the Internal Market* (Oxford: Oxford University Press, 1988).

Le Monde, "Les entreprises européennes face un marché unique," October 15, 1988, p. 1.

Michael E. Porter, *Competitive Strategy* (New York: Macmillan, 1980).

Michael E. Porter, *Competitive Advantage* (New York, Macmillan, 1985).

Alan M. Rugman, *Trade Liberalization and International Investment*, Discussion Paper No. 347 (Ottawa: Economic Council of Canada, April 1988).

Alan M. Rugman and Alain Verbeke, *Global Corporate Strategy and Trade Policy* (London and New York: Routledge, 1990).

Alan M. Rugman is a professor of international business, and **Alain Verbeke** is a visiting professor of international business, both in the Faculty of Management, University of Toronto.

PART III

THE DOUBLE DIAMOND
FRAMEWORK

Alan M. Rugman, Professor
of International Business
Faculty of Management
University of Toronto

Diamond in the Rough

Michael Porter's blockbuster book, *The Competitive Advantage of Nations*,[1] has been elegantly summarized by Donald Thain in the Summer 1990 issue of *Business Quarterly*.[2] Unfortunately, the length and complexity of Porter's work means that it is probably doomed to be one of the most unread books on the manager's bookshelf. Therefore, Professor Thain's laudatory review may leave Canadian managers with a rather sanguine view about the relevance of Porter's book. While most of Porter's analysis would work for managers based in the U.S., the European Community or Japan, much of it is superficial and plain wrong when applied in a Canadian situation.

His work needs to be modified in order to analyze the issue of Canada's international competitiveness. These modifications are not simple extensions; rather they represent an entirely different way of conceptualizing and testing the nature of Canadian competitiveness in an integrated global economic system.

Concept of the Diamond is Brilliant

About 90% of Porter's book is accurate and potentially relevant for Canadian managers. This includes the brilliant concept of the diamond, the identification of clusters and the four stages of economic development. Yet, as is well known, Canada is only one-tenth the eco-nomic size of the U.S. Unfortunately, it is the very 10% of Porter's book that is most relevant for Canadians that is the questionable part. In particular, the sections of his book that are most debatable include Porter's treatment of inbound foreign direct investment and the role of Canadian multinationals.

In these vital areas Porter's lack of knowledge of Canada tends to devalue the application of his core model to Canada. Porter's focus on Canada's "home country" diamond cannot explain Canadian competitiveness and, whereas Canada's successful clusters are resource-based, they have value added in them. Porter's statements in his book, to the effect that Canada is a stage one "factor-driven" economy simply is inaccurate and dangerously misleading as policy advice to Canadians.

Porter's Diamond Model

The Porter model is based on four country-specific determinants and two external variables: chance and government. Porter's four determinants and two outside forces interact in the diamond of competitive advantage, with the nature of a country's international competitiveness depending upon the type and quality of these interactions. He says the four determinants for a nation " . . . shape the environment in which local firms compete and promote or impede the creation of competitive conditions." The four determinants are:

1. *Factor conditions:* the nation's factors of production, including natural resources and created factors, such as infrastructure and skilled labor.

2. *Demand conditions:* the nature of home demand for products or services.

3. *Related and supporting industries:* the presence or absence of supplier and related industries that, themselves, are internationally competitive.

4. *Firm strategy, structure and rivalry:* the domestic rivalry of firms and the conditions governing how companies are created, organized and managed.

Porter's two outside forces, chance and government, present interesting contrasts. Government is clearly of critical importance as an influence on a home nation's competitive advantage. For example, to penalize foreign firms, government can use tariffs as a direct entry barrier, or it can use subsidies as an indirect vehicle. In both cases domestic firms benefit from short-run competitive advantages. These discriminatory government actions can lead to shelter for domestic firms, where shelter actually prevents the development of sustainable (long-run) competitive advantages.

While there is a certain lack of originality in the components of Porter's diamond model, it has exactly the correct perspective by its focus on the strategies of firms rather than nations. Porter says,

Diamond in the Rough / Alan M. Rugman

Alan M. Rugman is Professor of International Business at the University of Toronto's Faculty of Management. He is also Research Director of the Ontario Centre for International Business. A professor for 20 years he has held visiting appointments at Harvard University's Center for International Affairs, the London Business School and Columbia University. He was a member of Canada's International Trade Advisory Committee during the free trade negotiations. His latest publications include *International Business in Canada* (Prentice-Hall, Canada, 1989), *Global Corporate Strategy and Trade Policy* (Routledge, 1990) and *Japanese Direct Investment In Canada* (Canada-Japan Trade Council, 1990). He is a frequent contributor to *Business Quarterly*.

" . . . firms, not nations, compete in international markets." To the extent that he brings together the firm-specific linkages between the four determinants and the two outside forces, his model is useful and, potentially, predictive. Porter's policy recommendations to restrict the nature of government industrial and strategic trade policy, and instead, to open markets and have no arbitrary restrictions applied on foreign investment, are also to be welcomed.

Porter's Testing is Conventional

To operationalize the model Porter constructs 16 industry clusters and tests the model across ten countries, although only eight are reported. The eight are: West Germany, Italy, Japan, South Korea, Sweden, Switzerland, the United Kingdom and the United States. Of these countries, in terms of its diamond, Sweden is closest to Canada and can act as a base to think about applying Porter's model to Canada.

For each of the eight countries reported, Porter divides their industries into the 16 clusters, which incorporate a conventional grouping into four upstream clusters, six clusters for industries and supporting sectors, and six clusters for final consumption of goods and services. The four upstream clusters consist of materials and metals, forest products, petroleum and chemicals, and semiconductors and computers. The six industry

and supporting sector clusters include multiple business, transportation, power generation and distribution, office, telecommunications, and defense. The six industry clusters for final consumption expenditure include food and beverages, textiles and apparel, housing and household, health care, personal, and entertainment and leisure. While these 16 clusters are quite useful for international comparisons they are probably not the set that would be used to analyze Canada's situation. For example, defense and most of the six final consumption clusters are obviously geared up for local (Canadian-based) use and will not show up in export statistics as a source of competitive advantage. We already know the reasons for this – Canada-first protectionist policies. What can Porter tell us that is new?

Finally, Porter describes four stages of national competitive development: factor driven, investment driven, innovation driven, and wealth driven. The last stage is associated with a decline in international competitiveness. At several points in the book Porter makes the classic mistake of stating that Canada is stagnating in Stage 1, due to its reliance on resource industries.

Canada's Most Successful Industry Clusters

Based on conventional statistical analysis of export shares it can already be predicted that Porter will

find that Canada's most successful industry clusters will be: materials and metals, forest products, petroleum and chemicals, and transportation. The first three of these, which are upstream, will be determined by Canada's natural resources in minerals, timber and energy. There is, however, substantial value added due to managerial and marketing skills in these areas. The transportation cluster's competitiveness will be determined by the institutional device of the Canada-U.S. autopact, since nearly one-third of Canada's exports (and imports) are in autos and auto-related products. This will drive the data on international competitiveness based on exports and world market share. While Canada's telecommunications sector should show up as a successful cluster, the particular role of Northern Telecom may be missed in Porter's national data, but may perhaps be captured by an industry study. Other clusters that might be close to inclusion but probably will not make it based on their global market shares, are power generation and distribution, and food and beverages. In the other nine clusters Canada is highly unlikely to be internationally competitive according to Porter's approach, although there may be successful segments within some of these clusters.

Porter's Diamond is Flawed

The model developed by Porter fails to explain key issues in

*"The model developed by Porter fails to explain key
issues in Canada's international competitiveness."*

Canada's international competitiveness on its own terms, for a variety of interconnected reasons. The major conceptual problem with Porter's model is due to the narrow definition that he applies to foreign direct investment (FDI). Porter defines only outward FDI as being valuable in creating competitive advantage. He then states that foreign subsidiaries are not sources of competitive advantage and that inward FDI is "not entirely healthy." He also states that foreign subsidiaries are importers, and that this is a source of competitive disadvantage.

All of these statements are questionable and have long ago been refuted by Canadian-based scholars. All have demonstrated that the research and development undertaken by foreign-owned firms is not significantly different from that of Canadian-owned firms. The largest 20 U.S. subsidiaries in Canada export virtually as much as they import. (The ratio of exports to sales is 25% while that of imports to sales is 26%).

The work by Porter actually reveals a branch plant mentality. He sees foreign firms in Canada as simply micro-replicas of their parents that only exist because of unnatural entry barriers, for example the tariff. While he states that judgment is used in examining the competitive performance and managerial autonomy of foreign-owned subsidiaries he does not specify how this is to be done and then

indicates that it does not apply to "production subsidiaries of foreign companies." This thinking then rules out the broader nature of the foreign-owned subsidiaries' contributions to the development of Canada's manufacturing base.

Foreign Direct Investment is Two-Way

The real weakness in Porter's book is its flawed understanding of the nature of two-way foreign direct investment. In the Canadian context, 70% of Canadian trade is done by 50 multinationals, with half of these being foreign owned. The methodology used by Porter permits only an examination of the exports and outward FDI of Canada's "home" industries. Yet there is as much inward FDI as outward and the imports of the foreign-owned subsidiaries are matched by their exports. Indeed, Canada runs a slight surplus on the intra-firm trade of the sum of U.S. firms in Canada plus Canadian - owned firms in the U.S., demonstrating that foreign-owned firms act and play as significant a role as do the domestic-owned Canadian corporations.[3]

The views expressed by Porter on the role of natural resources is old fashioned and misguided. He argues that reliance on natural resources is as bad as reliance on unskilled labor or simple technology. In fact, Canada has developed a number of successful megafirms

that have turned our comparative advantage in natural resources into proprietary firm-specific advantages in resource processing and further refining.[4] These are sources of sustainable competitive advantage. Canada's successful multinationals such as Alcan, Noranda and Nova, illustrate the methods by which value added has been introduced by the managers of these resource-based companies. Over time, Canada's resource-based industries do, in fact, have sustainable advantages.

True Significance of Multinational Activity Important

Almost all of Canada's large multinationals rely on sales in the U.S. and other triad markets. Indeed, it could be argued that the U.S. diamond is likely to be more relevant for Canada's industrial multinationals than is Canada's own diamond, since, on average over 70% of their sales take place there. The Canada-U.S. free trade agreement reinforces this point. It rather devalues the entire approach of Porter's book to dismiss Canada's diamond in this manner, however.

We can conclude from this, that tensions arise in Porter's model as soon as a serious effort is made to incorporate the true significance of multinational activity. It is questionable if multinational activity can actually be added into any, or all, of the four determinants, or included as a third exogenous variable.

Diamond in the Rough / Alan M. Rugman

"The work by Porter actually reveals a branch plant mentality."

This weakness in Porter's model would not only apply to Canadian-based firms but to multinationals from all small open economies, that is, over 90% of the world's nations potentially cannot be modelled by the Porter diamond. Besides Canada, other nations with their own multinational enterprises based on small home diamonds include Australia, New Zealand, Finland and most, if not all, Asian and Latin American countries, as well as a large number of other small countries. The small nations in the European Community, such as Denmark, have been able to overcome the problem of a small domestic market by gaining access to one of the triad markets – a point somewhat neglected by Porter. Perhaps "triad-based diamonds" should be constructed and analyzed.

The main point of this criticism of Porter's methodology is that a clear recognition of the need to model multinational activity correctly in a Canadian context is necessary if policy prescriptions and activities are to be properly defined and undertaken. This requires a deep and consistent understanding of the nature of the multinational enterprise in Canada, coupled with a rich empirical and practical understanding of the actual performance of multinationals in Canada. Porter's book does not demonstrate mastery of these twin requirements.

Canada Needs a North American Diamond

Canada's home country diamond does not have the answers to explain Canada's international competitiveness. Instead, as Canada is highly integrated already with the U.S., it is much more useful to conceive of a North American diamond for Canada. Once individual Canadian managers and workers perform to North American standards they can take the next step, which is to perform at a global standard.

Most Canadian manufacturing is already being forced to compete globally. Therefore the North American diamond is much more relevant for both FDI into Canada as well as Canadian FDI into the U.S. (Some small, multidomestic businesses are not globalized.) In sharp contrast, most of Canada's service sectors are not globalized; they still rely on Canada's own diamond. The few globalized service sectors include banking and business services.

Canada needs to play in the big leagues of international competition and this means having the North American diamond as the basic unit of analysis for Canadian business decisions.[5] Success in North America can then be used as a base for success in the global economic system. Thus the North American diamond must be interpreted as an intermediate step in the development of globally competitive Canadian business. With-

out success in North America, survival is unlikely for any Canadian business subject to global competition. Virtually all Canadian manufacturing firms and most service sector organizations are now in this position.

Misplaced Policy Initiatives Possible

While it is useful for Canada's business and government leaders to seek advice and ideas from all over the place, including outside of Canada, it will only compound the problems of Canada's lack of international competitiveness if the wrong framework of analysis is adopted carte blanche. Porter's original diamond model is conceptually flawed and empirically unsound when applied unchanged in a Canadian context. The thoughtless application of his book to Canada could reap a whirlwind of discontent and misplaced policy initiatives.   BQ

References
1 Porter, Michael E., *The Competitive Advantage of Nations*, New York: Free Press, and Toronto: Collier Macmillan, 1990.
2 Thain, Donald H., "The War Without Bullets," *Business Quarterly*, Summer 1990, Volume 55, Number 1, pp. 13-19.
3 Rugman, Alan M., *Multinationals and Canada-United States Free Trade*, Columbia, University of South Carolina Press, 1990.
4 Rugman, Alan M. and John McIlveen, *Megafirms: Strategies for Canada's Multinationals*, Toronto, Methuen/Nelson, 1985.
5 For discussion of this, see Rugman, Alan M. and Joseph R. D'Cruz, *Fast Forward: Improving Canada's International Competitiveness*, Toronto, Kodak Canada, 1991.

mir Special Issue 1993/2, pp. 17–39

mir
Management
International Review
© Gabler Verlag 1993

Alan M. Rugman/Joseph R. D'Cruz

The "Double Diamond" Model of International Competitiveness: The Canadian Experience

Abstract

■ Porter's home-base diamond model of international competitiveness is seriously flawed when applied to a small, open, trading economy like Canada's.

■ Porter's framework needs to be adapted to explain Canada's successful resource-based multinationals, foreign subsidiaries and access to the triad market of the United States through the Free Trade Agreement. A new "double diamond" framework is developed to achieve this.

Key words

■ Porter's single diamond model works for large triad economies but needs to be adapted for smaller countries like Canada.

Authors

Alan M. Rugman is Professor of International Business, Faculty of Management, University of Toronto, Canada.
Joseph R. D'Cruz is Associate Professor of Strategic Management, Faculty of Management, University of Toronto, Canada.

Manuscript received January 1992, revised April 1992.

Alan M. Rugman/Joseph R. D'Cruz

Introduction

The influential Porter (1990) study on the determinants of international competitiveness suggests that the home country "diamond" is the source of competitive advantage for domestic firms. The competitive advantage of a firm depends upon one, or more, of the four key determinants of the nation's international competitiveness. The successful domestic firms build upon this home base and can then export or engage in outward foreign direct investment. In short, Porter's model states that a global firm needs to have a sustainable competitive advantage based on the successful utilization of components of its home country diamond.

The thesis of this article is that Porter's diamond framework explains the success of U.S., Japanese and E.C.-based multinationals, i.e. the triad. However, Porter's model is not applicable to small, open, trading economies which are not parts of this triad. For example, Rugman and D'Cruz (1991) have demonstrated that Canada's international competitiveness is not explained by the Porter home country diamond. They show that substantial modifications of the Porter framework are required to analyze the nature of Canada's foreign-owned firms and institutional arrangements, such as the Canada-U.S. Free Trade Agreement. The latter arrangement suggest that the Canadian diamond need to be considered jointly with the U.S. diamond, i.e. that the Canadian managers needs to operate in this "double diamond" framework. Indeed, Rugman and D'Cruz propose that a "North American diamond" be used by Canadian managers and policy makers in searching for useful answers to the question of how to improve Canada's international competitiveness.

A similar insight emerges from the work of Cartwright (1991) in his assessment of the application of the Porter model in the New Zealand study. A team headed by Porter used the Porter single diamond theory as a benchmark for a study of the international competitiveness of New Zealand, see Crocombe, Enright and Porter (1991). In his critique, Cartwright demonstrates, using empirical judgemental impact scores, that a "double diamond" framework has much greater explanatory power in a New Zealand context than does Porter's home country diamond model Cartwright concludes that his results "cast serious doubt on the ability of the Porter diamond theory to account satisfactorily for the international competitiveness of land-based industries that must export a high proportion of their production" (Cartwright 1991, p. 7).

In a related, but independent, development Cho (1991) has also adapted the Porter diamond in order to better explain the role of inward foreign direct investment into Korea. Cho extends Porter's six factor model into a nine factor model and tests it to explain Japanese FDI (that by Japanese sogo-shoshas) in Korea, in relation to the performance of Japanese sogo-Shoshas in Korea, whereas the methodology of Porter (1990) would require the use of the Japanese diamond, not the Korean.

How, then, should Porter's model be modified to explain the international competitiveness of small, open, trading nations such as Canada, New Zealand, and Korea? Here it is demonstrated that each country needs to set its own home-country diamond against the relevant "triad" diamond. In general, most Asia-Pacific nations will set theirs against Japan's. Canada, Mexico, Latin America and most Carbibean countries will consider theirs against the U.S. diamond. Finally, European nations such as Finland and Poland, outside of the E.C., will set theirs against the E.C. Porter did not recognize that there was an E.C. diamond, instead treating the member states as independent nations. This is obviously a faulty viewpoint, given the interdependene of intra-industry trade and foreign direct investment, especially as the E.C. 1992 measures come into effect.

In the study for Canada, Porter (1991), put his entire focus upon the manner in which the domestic firms in home country "clusters" develop competitive advantages from relevant elements of the home country diamond and use this as a base to become successful in global business. This thinking is potentially correct for large "triad" nations or blocks like the United States, Japan, and the E.C. It also explains special cases, such as South Korea, which had a low wage, high-tech, export-led development strategy.

The home base diamond analysis, however, is incorrect for small, open economies such as Canada, Finland, and New Zealand. These countries are highly interdependent with one or more of the triad blocks. They are characterized by two way flows of trade and investment. For example, in Canada the auto sector accounts for one third of both Canada's exports and its imports. Porter's diamond is also inaccurate for smaller nations such as Denmark, which is in the E.C.; or Switzerland which is closely affiliated to it. These E.C.-related countries harbour firms who have secured access to the large "triad" market of the E.C.

Porter's Single Country Diamond

The Porter model is based on four country-specific "determinants" and two external variables, chance and government, see Porter (1990), especially Chapters 3 and 4. Porter's four determinants and two outside forces interact in the "diamond" of competitive advantage, with the nature of a country's international competitiveness depending upon the type and quality of these interactions. The four determinants for a nation ". . . shape the environment in which

Alan M. Rugman/Joseph R. D'Cruz

local firms compete and promote or impede the creation of competitive conditions", see Porter (1990), p. 71. The four determinants are:

1. Factor conditions:
   the nation's factors of production, including natural resources and created factors, such as infrastructure and skilled labour.
2. Demand conditions:
   the nature of home demand for products or services and the degree of sophistication of buyers.
3. Related and supporting industries:
   the presence or absence of supplier and related industries that, themselves, are internationally competitive.
4. Firm strategy, structure and rivalry:
   the domestic rivalry of firms and the conditions governing how companies are created, organized and managed.

None of these determinants is new or unexpected. Porter's principal contribution is to bring them together in a manner useful for business and government strategy. As an example of the lack of originality in the elements of the Porter diamond it is useful to discuss the Canadian case. There is an extensive literature in Canada on the components of the diamond.

For example, a key aspect of the first determinant, labour productivity in Canada, has been calculated for over 30 years by scholars at the Economic Council of Canada; for a survey of recent results see Daly (1990). The critical nature of Canada's natural resources as a source of value added has similarly been recognized, see Rugman and McIlveen (1985).

Determinant two is covered by extensive work by Canadian micro economists on the nature of consumer demand and by macro economists and the Department of Finance on the management of the Canadian economy.

Determinant three was explicity discussed by Rugman and D'Cruz (1990) where the critical lack of an international mindset in some of the service sectors was classified in a matrix framework. It is good to see that Porter also stresses this; most other studies have ignored the role of services in international competitiveness. The ability of firms to develop external economies through clusters and networks of suppliers has also been studied by international business scholars in relation to the Japanese system and joint venture activity, for example, see Contractor and Lorange (1988).

A rich tradition of work in Canada using industrial organization models has attempted to handle determinant four. Indeed the nature of the tariff and industrial concentration in Canada has led to the development of such theories as the Eastman and Stykolt (1967) conditions for pricing and performance of foreign-owned and domestic manufacturing companies in Canada under conditions of domestic tariffs and high concentration ratios. Further, these studies of the nature of inter-firm competition in Canada probably better reflect the reality of foreign ownership than those of most other economies, especially those of the United States.

Porter's two outside forces, chance and government, present interesting contrasts. Government is clearly of critical importance as an influence on a home nation's competitive advantage, for example, it can use tariffs as a direct entry barrier penalizing foreign firms or it can use subsidies as an indirect vehicle to penalize foreign-based firms; in both cases "domestic" firms benefit in terms of short-run competitive advantages. However, Rugman and Verbeke[9] develop models in which these types of discriminatory government actions can lead to "shelter" for domestic firms, where shelter is defined to prevent the development of sustainable (long-run) competitive advantages. In contrast, work on "chance" has been minor. It is probably confined to those economists who inject "shocks" into a model system, such as the OPEC oil crises, to forecast aggregative responses. Porter, itself, uses it to refer to events such as wars.

To conclude, while there is a certain lack of originality in the components of Porter's diamond model, it has exactly the correct perspective by its focus on the strategies of firms rather than nations. It is vital to recognize that ". . . firms, not nations, compete in international markets" (Porter 1990, p. 33). To the extent that Porter brings together the firm-specific linkages between the four determinants and the two outside forces, his model is useful and, potentially, predictive. Porter's policy recommendations to restrict the nature of government industrial and strategic trade policy, and to instead open markets and have no arbitrary restrictions applied on foreign investment, are also to be welcomed.

Porter's Empirical Analysis

To operationalize the model Porter constructs 16 industry "clusters" and tests the model across ten countries, although only eight are reported. The eight are: West Germany, Italy, Japan, South Korea, Sweden, Switzerland, the United Kingdom, and the United States. In addition, Denmark and Singapore are listed, but are not discussed in the book.

The testing is almost entirely statistical analysis which relies on aggregate data on export shares for national industry groups for 1985, as collected by the United Nations. These data are inferior to those used by Rugman and D'Cruz (1990) since their study used a cleaner data set, with 1989 data. They have already computed Canada's international competitiveness for ten manufacturing sectors in 1989, using data from the IMD's *World Competitiveness Report,* of which D'Cruz is a contributing editor.

Alan M. Rugman/Joseph R. D'Cruz

For each of the eight countries reported, Porter breaks down the analysis of their industries into 16 clusters. These incorporate a conventional grouping into four "upstream" clusters, six clusters for industries and supporting sectors, and six clusters for final consumption of goods and services. The four "upstream" clusters consist of Materials and metals, Forest products, Petroleum and chemicals, and Semiconductors and computers. The six "industry and supporting" sector clusters include Multiple business, Transportation, Power generation and distribution, Office, Telecommunications, and Defense. The six industry clusters for "final consumption expenditure" include Food and beverages, Textiles and apparel, Housing and household, Health care, Personal, and Entertainment and leisure. While these 16 clusters are quite useful for international comparisons they are probably not a set of clusters that is relevant, for small, open trading economies such as Canada's.

One of the most peculiar features of Porter's book is the "league tables" on pages 536 and 537. This is a classic case of comparing apples and oranges. A competitive industry is defined as one whose export shares are above that for the country as a whole. The United States has a world export share of 15 percent, Canada, 4 percent and Korea 1 percent. Obviously Korea ends up with more industries above 1 percent than the United States – so what? The Porter book does not have a table showing these critical cut off points. This sloppy and unprofessional scholarly reporting is a characteristic of Porter. Another absurd mistake occurs in the discussion of R and D on p. 633. In this table on R and D spending, Korea does not appear. The reason? It is not a member of the O.E.C.D. Why did Porter not send his research assistant to find Korea's R and D from another source?

Smaller nations will have weak components in their home diamonds (especially in demand conditions) when compared to large nations. But smaller nations are not condemned to a second rate status for their clusters, as the empirical measurements of competitivenes by Porter purport to reveal. This is because Porter's measure of international competitiveness is export shares. Yet much of the business of smaller countries is conducted abroad (through foreign direct investment), within the larger triad markets of the United States, E.C. and Japan – where the action is.

In his Canadian study Porter (1991) does not count the sales abroad by the foreign subsidiaries of Canadian-owned multinationals in the (Canadian) export share data, nor is any serious effort made to adjust the study for their importance. In the study Porter has "league tables" across nine countries. These show that Canada performs poorly in exports except in forest products and minerals. These tables ignore FDI. Porter also states that foreign-owned firms in Canada do not benefit Canada, although (paradoxically) his data would include any exports of such foreign-owned subsidiaries.

The Double Diamond Model: Canada's Experience

In contrast, the Porter (1991) data exaggerate the export shares and league ranking of U.S. and E.C.-based businesses because many of these have elements of foreign ownership, which are ignored in their date (it is assumed that the U.S. export data, for example, on chemicals reflect no foreign ownership, although this sector is over forty percent foreign owned). Thus the relative rankings of Canadian industries and clusters are biased downwards in the Porter league tables.

There are also four historical industry case studies described in the book. The first is on the German printing press industry, the second is on the U.S. patient monitoring equipment industry, the third is on the italian ceramic tile industry, while the fourth is on the Japanese robotics industry. In addition, there is a chapter on service industries, with several case studies. Again, none of these seems to be particularly relevant for small, open economies.

Finally, Porter describes four stages of "national competitive development": factor driven; investment driven; innovation driven; and wealth driven, see Porter 1990, p. 546. The last stage is associated with a decline in international competitiveness. At several points in the book Porter makes the classic mistake of stating that Canada is stagnating in Stage 1, due to its reliance on resource industries e.g. Porter 1990, p. 548.

Based on conventional statistical analysis of export shares Rugman (1991) already predicted that Porter will find that Canada's most successful and internationally competitive industry clusters will be:

a. Materials/metals,
b. Forest products,
c. Petroleum, chemicals, and
d. Transportation.

The first three upstream industry clusters (a), (b) and (c) for Canada will be determined by its natural resources in minerals, timber, and energy. However, it is likely that there is substantial value added due to managerial and marketing skills in these areas. The Transportation cluster's competitiveness will be determined by an institutional factor; the Canada-U.S. Autopact. Indeed, nearly one third of Canada's exports (and imports) are in autos and auto-related products. This factor alone will explain much of Porter's data on international competitiveness, as they are based on exports and world market share. While Canada's Telecommunications sector should show up as a successful cluster, the role of Northern Telecom's U.S. operations may be missed in Porter's national data for Canada, but may perhaps be captured by an industry study. Other clusters which might be close to inclusion, but probably will not make it based on their global market shares, are: Power generation and distribution; and, Food and beverages. In the other nine clusters Canada is highly unlikely to be internation-

Alan M. Rugman/Joseph R. D'Cruz

ally competitive, according to Porter's approach, although there may be successful segments within some of these clusters.

Rugman's predictions were confirmed by the Porter (1991) study, a synopsis of which was released in October 1991. Although the October synopsis did not contain much analytical detail, several drafts of the study were widely circulated throughout 1991, with little change being made in any of the statistical figures.

Porter's Diamond is Flawed

The model developed by Porter fails to explain key issues in Canada's international competitiveness, on its own terms, for a variety of interconnected reasons which we will now discuss.

A major conceptual problem with Porter's model is due to the narrow definition that he applies to foreign direct investment (FDI). Porter defines only outward FDI as being valuable in creating competitive advantage. He then states that foreign subsidiaries are not sources of competitive advantage (p. 14) and that inward FDI is "not entirely healthy" (p. 671). He also states that foreign subsidiaries are importers, and that this is a source of competitive disadvantage, p. 18.

All of these statements are questionable and have long ago been refuted by Canadian-based scholars, e.g. see Safarian (1968), Rugman (1980), and Crookell (1990). They have demonstrated that the research and development undertaken by foreign-owned firms is not significantly different from that of Canadian-owned firms. Rugman (1990) shows that the largest 20 U.S. subsidiaries in Canada export virtually as much as they import (the ratio of exports to sales is 25 percent while that of imports to sales is 26 percent).

The work by Porter actually reveals a branch plant mentality. He sees foreign firms in Canada as simply micro-replicas of their parents, which only exist because of unnatural entry barriers, for example the tariff. While he states that "judgement" is used in examining the competitive performance and "managerial autonomy" of foreign-owned subsidiaries (p. 21) he does not specify how this is to be done and then indicates that it does not apply to "production subsidiaries of foreign companies" (p. 25). This thinking then rules out the broader nature of the foreign-owned subsidiaries' contributions to the development of Canada's manufacturing base.

A real weakness in Porter's book is its flawed understanding of the nature of two way FDI. In the Canadian context, seventy percent of Canadian trade is done by fifty multinationals, with half of these being foreign-owned, see Rugman (1990). The methodology used by Porter permits only an examination of the exports and outward FDI of Canada's "home" industries. Yet there is as much inward FDI as outward and the imports of the foreign-owned subsidiaries are matched by their exports. Indeed, Canada runs a slight surplus on the intrafirm trade of the sum of U.S. firms in Canada plus Canadian-owned firms in the United States. This demonstrates that foreign-owned firms act and play as significant a role as do the domestic owned Canadian corporations.

The views expressed in Porter on the role of natural resources is old fashioned and misguided. It argues that reliance on natural resources is as bad as reliance on unskilled labor or simple technology (e.g. pp. 13, 28, 564, 740). In fact, Canada has developed a number of successful megafirms which have turned Canada's comparative advantage in natural resources into proprietary firm-specific advantages in resource processing and further refining. These are sources of sustainable competitive advantage, see Rugman and McIlveen (1985). Case studies of Canada's successful multinationals like Alcan, Noranda, Nova, etc., illustrate the methods by which value added has been introduced by the managers of these resource-based companies. Studies by D'Cruz and Fleck (1987) and by Rugman and D'Cruz (1990) demonstrate that, over time, Canada's resource based industries have developed sustainable competitive advantages.

Porter Misunderstands Foreign Ownership

In an attempt to incorporate the vital role of multinational activity and overcome some of the flaws in Porter's framework, Dunning (1990) has adapted some of Porter's model. Dunning adds multinational activity as a third outside variable (the others being chance and government). This is an ingenious idea but itself raises problems, especially in a Canadian context. The role of multinationals is so widespread in Canada that it is difficult to believe that these firms can be assigned a role equal to that of chance.

It is a serious criticism of Porter's framework when the world's leading scholar in international business finds that the role of multinationals is not covered adequately by the diamond framework. Porter's thesis is that firms in global industries are actually multinational enterprises and that nations prosper when firms in such global industries are successful. Yet if one were to accept Dunning's basic premise, namely that multinationally is missing from Porter, where else could it be put?

Perhaps the most logical place is in the determinant called "firm strategies, structure and rivalry". To some extent Porter is already trying to include it here, especially in his attempts to deal with "global" industries. Yet his diamond is

Alan M. Rugman/Joseph R. D'Cruz

also supposed to explain "multidomestic" industries. However, it does not make sense that the same rivalry determinant can both include multinationality for global industries yet exclude it for multidomestic industries. This may be an explanation as to why Dunning wants multinationality to be laid across the four determinants in the diamond in a broad and even manner, like chance and government.

> On another point Dunning may be quite correct in his insight that: ". . . there is ample evidence to suggest that MNEs are influenced in their competitiveness by the configuration of the diamond in other than their home countries, and that this, in turn, may impinge upon the competitiveness of home countries" (Dunning 1990, p. 11).

Dunning cites the example of Nestlé having 95 percent of its sales outside Switzerland; therefore the Swiss diamond of competitive advantage is less relevant than that of foreign countries in shaping the contribution of Nestlé to the home economy. If that is true for Switzerland than it is just as applicable in a Canadian context. Virtually all of Canada's large multinationals rely on sales in the United States and other triad markets. Indeed, it could be argued that the U.S. diamond is likely to be more relevant for Canada's industrial multinationals than is Canada's own diamond, since over 70 percent of their sales take place there, on average. The Canada-U.S. Free Trade Agreement reinforces this point. However, it rather devalues the entire approach of Porter's book to dismiss Canada's diamond in this manner.

What we can conclude from this, however, is that tensions arise in Porter's model as soon as a serious effort is made to incorporate the true significance of multinational activity. It is questionable that multinational activity can actually be added into any, or all, of the four determinants, nor included as a third exogenous variable.

This weakness in Porter's model would not only apply to Canadian based ones but to multinationals from all small open economies, i.e. over 90 percent of the world's nations potentially cannot be modelled by the Porter diamond. Besides Canada, other nations with their own MNEs based on small home diamonds include Australia, New Zealand, Finland, and most, if not all, Asian and Latin American countries, as well as a large number of other small countries. The small nations in the E.C., like Denmark, have been able to overcome the problem of a small domestic market by gaining access to one of the triad markets – a point somewhat neglected in Porter. Obviously "triad-based diamonds" need to be constructed and analyzed.

Porter on Autos: Out of Gas

An application of Porter's work to Canada would also have some serious methodological problems. Three of these problems, for example, can be identified in the following statement on methodology for assembling clusters.

"We also excluded a few industries from the list when their trade was almost exclusively with neighbouring nations. For example, U.S. automobile chassis exports are heavily skewed toward Canada. A preponderance of trade with neighbours indicated that the nation's competitive advantage was not significant in international terms and trade solely reflected geographic proximity, unless we had indicators of significant foreign direct investment by the nation's firms in the industry. In the latter case, the industry was left off the list," Porter 1990, p. 740.

The first of these methodological problems relates to the fact that over seventy percent of Canada's exports and FDI go to the United States, a trend recognized by the Canada-U.S. Free Trade Agreement, which is an attempt by Canada to maintain a market already developed but which has come under increasing pressure from protectionists to close out foreign competition. As the United States' largest trading partner, this has direct ramifications for continued access by Canadian businesses to their U.S. markets. Porter's model dismisses these seventy percent of Canada's exports and argues that they do not reflect a competitive advantage since they go to a neighbouring state. Canada's "diamond" is therefore not supportive of industries which are internationally competitive, i.e. Canada needs to export to somewhere else other than the nearby U.S. triad market. This ignores the fact that these U.S. sales take place in a competitive, foreign market to Canada's. This indicates that Porter's model is not particularly useful in capturing the nature of Canada's trade and investment relationships with the large U.S. market.

Second, the example chosen, of automobile chassis trade, is actually a case of the successful creation of competitive advantage. The huge economic success of the Canada-U.S. autopact over the last quarter century, with benefits to both nations in terms of output, employment and wealth creation, is precisely due to this negotiated international treaty; one which builds upon the geographical proximity of the Windsor-Detroit corridor. Canada has developed skilled human capital and satisfied industry and national requirements through the value added and local context provisions of the autopact, see Fuss and Waverman (1991). As stated earlier, trade in autos and auto-related inputs, in fact, account for about one third of all U.S.-Canadian trade. Yet Porter dismisses this based on a definition that is clearly inapplicable to the Canadian context.

Alan M. Rugman/Joseph R. D'Cruz

Third, Porter's inability to reconcile his model with all aspects of foreign direct investment appears again. As stated earlier, he only defines *outward* FDI as being valuable, Porter, pp. 55, 779. The vast bulk of Canada's auto industry (and all of it for Porter's 1986 data) is U.S. owned; the big three (General Motors, Ford and Chrysler) all have substantial FDI in Canada. They are making valuable contributions to Canada's manufacturing sector and international competitiveness. While there is no FDI by Canadian auto assemblers in the United States, there are exports of autos and auto parts to the United States by U.S. owned firms in Canada. Porter's approach would lead us to discount the latter.

The lack of internal consistency in Porter's model should now be apparent; it is not operational in a world of intra-firm and intra-industry trade. Today there are two way flows of exports and imports across national borders. These have little to do with a nation's home country diamond and cannot be measured by exports alone. Instead, multinationals operate across borders and the sources of international competitiveness stem from successful global corporate strategy.

Another example of the lack of robustness of Porter's model and its inability to describe the current Canadian situation comes from Porter's neglect of the auto-industry in his discussion of data on robots in Canada, Porter, p. 230. These are drawn from one of Porter's firm industry case success stories – robotics in Japan. Here Porter actually reports data showing that Canada has a sizeable number of robots. Many of these are in the auto industry, which, at the time of these data (1980 and 1983) were entirely foreign-owned. Yet, as noted previously, Porter suggests repeatedly that foreign-owned firms are not sources of competitive advantage. Porter cannot have it both ways.

The main point of this criticism of Porter's methodology is that a clear recognition of the need to model multinational activity correctly in a Canadian context in necessary if policy prescriptions and activities are to be properly defined and undertaken. This requires a deep and consistent understanding of the nature of the multinational enterprise in Canada, coupled with a rich empirical and practical understanding of the actual performance of multinationals in Canada. Porter's book does not demonstrate mastery of these twin requirements. This weakness of Porter would be generalizable to many other smaller, open, trading nations.

Despite these conceptual and data-based flaws, it is not impossible to modify Porter's model and test it on Canada. A new study has in fact been released by the federal government and the B.C.N.I., see Porter (1991). It was done by Porter's consulting group, the Monitor Corporation, and it examines Canada's competitiveness position using Porter's diamond. In this new work Porter made a few changes but he did not modify substantially the methodology used in his book. Indeed, he rejects the three points made here, i.e. the need to correct for the nature of foreign direct investment in Canada, the value added in Canada's resource industries, and the relevance of Canada's home country diamond in an integrated North America economic system.

The "Double Diamond" Framework in Canada

Rugman and D'Cruz (1991) have adapted Porter's model to make it relevant in diagnosing Canada's international competitiveness. Their approach should not be viewed as a substitute for Porter; instead, it builds upon his central theme of the focus on corporate strategy and process as a source of competitive advantage for a nation. Canada's home country diamond does not have the answers to explain Canada's international competitiveness. Instead, as Canada is highly integrated already with the United States, it is much more useful to conceive of a "North American" diamond for Canada. Once individual Canadian managers and workers perform to North American standards they can take the next step which is to perform at a global standard. The Technical Appendix explains and develops the conceptual framework for this North American diamond.

Most Canadian manufacturing is already being forced to compete globally. Therefore the North American diamond is much more relevant for both FDI into Canada as well as Canadian FDI into the United States. Some small, multidomestic, businesses are not globalized. In sharp contrast to manufacturing, most of Canada's service sectors are not globalized; they still rely on Canada's own diamond. The few globalized service sectors include banking and business services.

The Canada-U.S. Free Trade Agreement did not suddenly make the Canadian diamond obsolete; instead it was an institutional device which recognized the high degree of economic integration already in place. How ironic it would be if, despite the FTA, business and government leaders in Canada still attempt to apply Canada's home country diamond instead of working towards an understanding of the emerging North American diamond.

Porter will only work in a Canadian context when the North American diamond is used instead of Canada's "home" diamond. Canada needs to play in the big leagues of international competition and this means having the North American diamond as the basic unit of analysis for Canadian business decisions. Success in North America can then be used as a base for success in the global economic system. Thus the North American diamond must be interpreted as an intermediate step in the development of globally competitive Canadian business. Without success in the North American diamond, survival is unlikely for any Canadian business subject to global competition. Virtually all Canadian manufacturing firms and most service sector organizations are now subject to this form of competition. In the next section these points are illustrated.

Alan M. Rugman/Joseph R. D'Cruz

The Porter Diamond Applied to Canada

Building on Rugman and D'Cruz (1991) Figure 1 illustrates the application of
Porter's concepts. Figure 1 has Porter's four diamond components, with Canadian governments affecting these components as an overlay, although the major
impact is on customers and leading firms. For simplication, chance is left out.
In addition, the Canada-U.S. border is shown to illustrate that over 70 percent
of Canada's exports go to the United States. The Canadian market is too small
to support the development of the economies of scale that are required in many
manufacturing product lines, and in services, in modern industry. Hence, it has
been the practice in Canada to view the U.S. market as a set of export opportunities to provide the base for developing large-scale industrial businesses in
Canada. These businesses have been largely designed to exploit the base of
natural resources found in Canada. Emphasis has been placed on commodity
products that have been developed in isolation from major customers.

Figure 1. Porter's Home Country Diamond says treat the United States as an Export Market

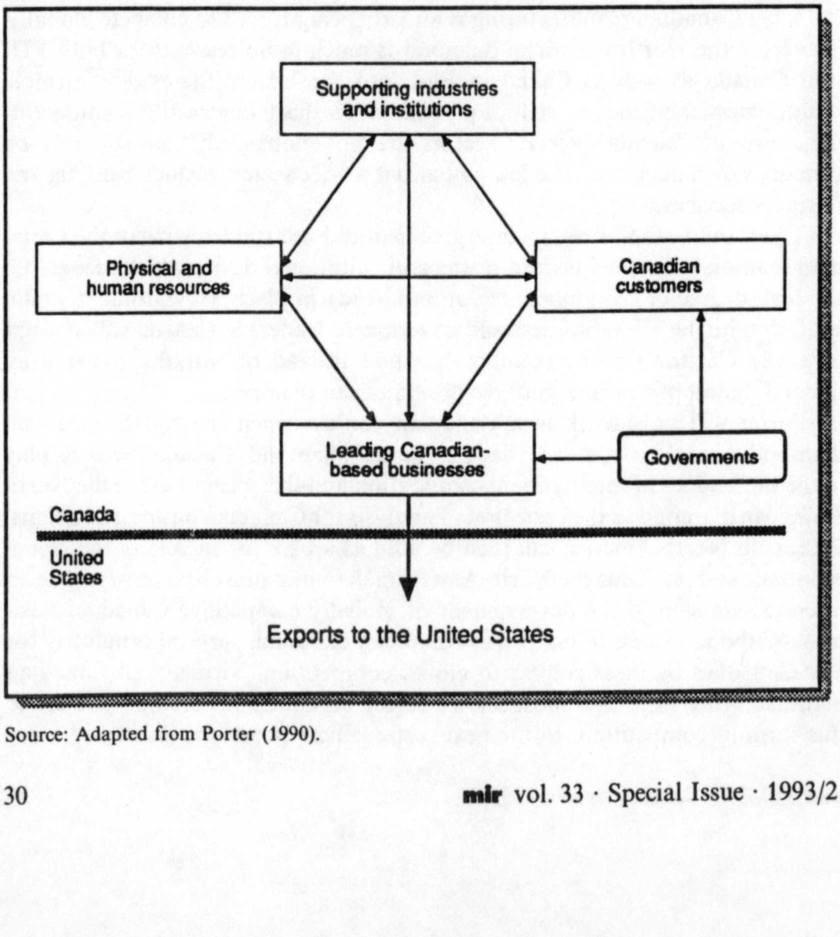

Source: Adapted from Porter (1990).

In the Porter (1991) study he states that the role of government has been protectionist. Canada has lived off its resources in an "old economic order". Government has seldom paid attention to the simultaneous development of the supporting industries and infrastructure, or to the upgrading of physical and human resources. According to Porter, policy use of the Canadian diamond has been excessively inward looking, content to rely on the extent and quality of the country's factor endowment as the base for wealth creation.

The North American Diamond

The Canada-U.S. Free Trade Agreement (FTA) marked the culmination of a long drawn-out debate to recognize that Canada's former protectionist approach was no longer viable. The border between the two countries has become less and less of a factor in the development of Canadian business strategy and industrial policy. Instead of seeing the U.S. market solely as a set of export opportunities, Canadian-based businesses now recognize that they are in direct competition with businesses operating in the U.S. diamond. These leading U.S. businesses are created in a home base where the markets are considerably larger than those of Canada, where there are more customers who are more demanding than Canadian customers, and where supporting industries and institutions are more competitive.

To survive in rivalry with the leading U.S.-based businesses, Canadian-based businesses need to develop competitive capabilities of a high order. This requires that they link the Canadian and U.S. diamonds, as illustrated in Figure 2. This diagram was first developed by Rugman and D'Cruz (1991), especially in Chapter 3. No longer can Canadians rely solely on a home country diamond and Canada's natural resource base. In particular, today, innovation and cost competitiveness are especially important, and this requires access to the U.S. diamond.

The FTA has brought about some changes in the nature of the Canadian market that have been painful in the short run. Canadian customers now have better access than ever before to products and services made in the United States. As the importance of the border as a factor in business dealings diminishes, Canadian customers are becoming more and more like U.S. customers. Canadians become spillover targets of "made-in-the-USA" strategies aimed at the domestic U.S. market. In the long run, this can be of significant benefit to Canada, because Canadian customers are learning to be as demanding as U.S. customers. Canadian-based businesses that learn to serve these customers well will be to hone their competitive skills to better serve their customers in the United States.

Alan M. Rugman/Joseph R. D'Cruz

Figure 2. The Free Trade Agreement Links the Canadian and U.S. Diamonds into a "North American Diamond"

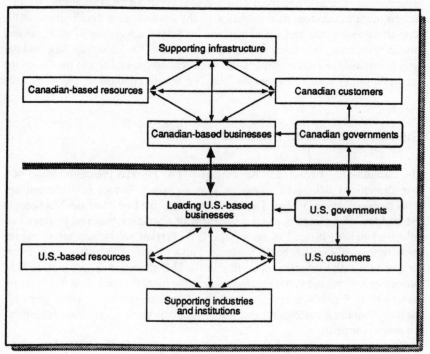

The FTA has also created a unique set of pressures on the Canadian subsidiaries of U.S. multinationals. For a few, the rationale for setting up operations in Canada was based on a desire to gain access to Canada's natural resources. However, many were based originally on the impulse to overcome the tariff barriers erected by Canadian governments to encourage the development of secondary manufacturing. The integration of the Canadian economy with that of the United States has rendered such "tariff factory" businesses unviable. If they are scaled only to serve the Canadian market, they will find themselves in direct competition with their parents' U.S.-based businesses for mandates to serve the Canadian market. Several recent plant closures have been the result of the Canadian subsidiary's losing the battle for that mandate to a business unit of the U.S. parent. This is based on the U.S. plant's ability to serve the Canadian market at a lower cost because of its superior scale, lower labour rates or other competitive advantage.

The Double Diamond Model: Canada's Experience

Rivalry for mandates is not limited to Canadian subsidiaries of U.S. multi-nationals; similar conditions apply to Canadian-owned multinationals. Their Canadian-based operations are in rivalry for mandates with their U.S.-based operations. If their U.S.-based operations are better able to mobilize the resources in the local U.S. diamond, then the mandate for development of future business will go south of the border.

It must be emphasized that while these decisions are driven by many considerations, wages are the principal determining factor in industries that are labour intensive. In those cases, the most significant threat to Canadian businesses comes, not from the United States, but from Mexico and other low-labour-cost countries. In other industries, considerations such as proximity to key customers and the depth and effectiveness of the local support network weigh more heavily. Thus, the attraction of U.S. locations for future mandates for Canadian-based businesses must not be regarded solely as an attempt to gain access to low-wage labour.

A North American Diamond is a Step Towards Becoming Globally Competitive

One way out of this dilemma is for Canadian businesses to operate with a North American mindset; managers need to lay the groundwork for becoming globally competitive (see Figure 3). This would involve treating the United States and Canada as a single market, and integrating the use of the U.S. and Canadian diamonds as a single home base for the development of their forward strategies. The four components of the Canadian diamond plus the four in the U.S. one add up to seven.

In particular, a North American diamond strategy would require:

– developing innovative new products and services that simultaneously meet the needs of U.S. and Canadian customers, recognizing that close relationships with demanding U.S. customers should be used to set the pace and style of product development;
– drawing on the support industries and infrastructure of both the U.S. and Canadian diamonds, realizing that the U.S. diamond is likely to possess deeper and more efficient markets for such industries; and
– making free and full use of the physical and human resources in both countries.

The goal of this strategic approach must be to develop businesses that are capable of competing effectively by exporting outside North America. Success in the integrated U.S. and Canadian market must be regarded only as an intermediate step for the firm, otherwise it risks making the strategic error of

Alan M. Rugman/Joseph R. D'Cruz

Figure 3. The North American Diamond helps Canadian Businesses to Become Globally Competitive

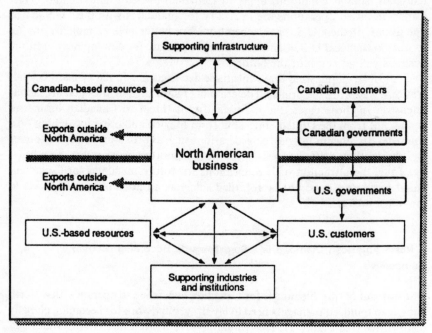

remaining content with being competitive only with its domestic rivals and ignoring the danger of being outpaced by rivals from other parts of the world. Thus, while these strategic approaches will have a North American focus at the outset, it is vital that they be executed by managers who have highly developed skills in international business. This requires managers who can anticipate the form and intensity of competition from businesses based outside North America.

Using North America as a base for developing global competitiveness is very different from the "Fortress America" mindset that is responsible for the decline of so much of U.S. industry. In this regard, Canadian managers may take some comfort from the fact that, living in a relatively small economy, they have less temptation to slip into the complacency that has led many U.S. managers to believe that their domestic market is large enough to sustain success against global rivals by using strategies which are strictly North American in their market scope. In contrast, Japanese and South Korean managers have a deep conviction that their countries must export and succeed globally to survive. It is time that Canadian managers came to the same realization. The difference is that they should now regard sales to U.S. destinations as domestic sales, not exports; and eventually focus on markets outside North America.

This approach applies both to multinationals owned by Canadians and to foreign-owned multinationals that have a significant business in Canada, with a global mandate and capability. In particular, this applies to businesses of U.S. multinationals operating with Canada as a home base. The stock of U.S. foreign direct investment is higher in Canada than in any other part of the world. Therefore, U.S. multinationals have a great deal at stake in their Canadian businesses. In order to protect their stake, U.S. multinationals need to take vigorous measures to make these businesses globally competitive.

Above all, Canadian governments, and the public at large, must show that they are willing to treat these foreign investments as if they were "domestic" to Canada. They must be willing to support these businesses in their efforts to develop new, globally competitive products and services in the same manner and to the same degree as support is provided to Canadian-owned businesses. Then it is up to Canadian managers to design and implement strategies for the firm-driven global success which is the basis of a nation's international competitive advantage.

Strategic Clusters in the North American Diamond

The advantage of using a North American diamond is that it forces business and government leaders to think about management strategy and public policy in a different way. No longer is the domestic Canadian diamond useful as the unit of analysis. Neither managers nor politicians can ignore global competition; both need to recognize that doing well in North America is the first step towards global success. The correct perspective for Canadian strategies for international competitiveness is to identify successful and potentially viable "strategic clusters" of industries within Canada, and to examine their linkages and performance across the North American diamond.

A strategic cluster is defined as a network of businesses and supporting activities located in a specific region, where the leading flagship firms compete globally and the supporting activities perform to international standards. In the case of a Canadian-based strategic cluster the flagship firms will be based in Canada, but they can be either foreign-owned or Canadian-owned. Their economic performance is of more significance then their ownership. Most of the supporting activities will be Canadian-based, but some of them can be foreign-owned. In addition, some of the critical business inputs and skills may come from outside of Canada; their relevance and usefulness is determined by the membership of the strategic cluster.

Alan M. Rugman/Joseph R. D'Cruz

For example, a successful strategic cluster, based in Canada will have one or more large multinational enterprises at its centre. Whether these are Canadian-owned, or foreign-owned is irrelevant, despite Porter who argues that the former are the only sources of competitive advantage. These large multinationals are flagships on which the strategic cluster depends. They should operate on a global basis and plan their competitive strategies within the framework of global competition. A vital component of the strategic cluster will be a group of companies with related and supporting activities. This will include both private and public sector organizations. In addition, there will be think tanks, research groups and educational institutions characterized by the excellence of their work rather than their quantity. Clearly, some parts of this network will be based outside of Canada; what is important to understand is the nature of the linkages across the border and the leadership role of the Canadian flagships. These are all world class, competitive, multinationals.

What is being described is a regionally-based strategic cluster in Canada of large multinationals with related and supporting industries and services making up a network of economic and commerical activity across North America. While the lead multinationals perform at global standards the other members of the network need to perform at least to North American ones. The reason is that there will be competing clusters at other locations across North America. Therefore, a Canadian-based and Canadian-led strategic cluster cannot afford to have any component of its network performing at "domestic" rather than international levels.

Canada's Strategic Clusters

Rugman and D'Cruz (1991) discuss the ten strategic clusters in Canada. One is the auto assembly and auto parts industry in southwestern Ontario, led by the big three U.S. auto multinationals with their related and affiliated suppliers and distributors. There are linkages to various high-tech firms and research groups; these linkages span the border, as does the auto assembly industry itself. Other strategic clusters are based on the banking and financial services in Toronto; the advanced manufacturing and telecommunications strategic cluster in Toronto; the forest products industries in Western and Eastern Canada; the energy strategic cluster in Alberta; the aerospace and electronics strategic clusters in Montreal and Ottawa and, possibly, a fisheries strategic cluster in Atlantic Canada. Some of these strategic clusters are led by flagship Canadian-owned multinationals such as Northern Telecom, Nova or Bombardier; others are led by, or include, foreign-owned firms like IBM Canada and DuPont Canada.

Many of the Canadian-based clusters will be resource based. The challenge for managers in these strategic clusters is to continue to add value and eliminate the commodity nature of Canada's resource industries. One way is to develop a global marketing strategy, building on the North American diamond, instead of remaining as the extractor or harvester of the resource. To implement such a global strategy will then require a large investment in people to develop not just marketing skills but a global intelligence network in which the different tastes and preferences of customers can be identified and serviced. Here there is a role for smaller knowledge intensive marketing research and consulting firms to participate in the resource-based strategic cluster. There is also the potential for collaborative ventures, provided that a sound governance structure for the joint ventures can be constructed.

Further research is required to investigate Canadian-based strategic clusters and their competitive advantages compared to rival clusters within North America, and also the world. This requires two types of work. First, the intra-firm competition of clusters within North America requires new data which ignores the nature of foreign ownership and whether U.S. and Canadian foreign direct investment by sector is inbound or outbound. Instead, foreign direct investment in North America must be regarded as "domestic" and be contrasted with "external" direct investment from Japan and the E.C. Similarly, trade flows between Canada and the United States must be thought of as intrafirm when they occur between components of a cluster, or even between and amongst clusters.

This approach is so radical that many existing concepts must be rethought. For example, the level and extent of subsidies available to clusters located in the United States must be related to those paid by provinces in Canada. Yet there is little or no published work on state or provincial subsidies; even the work on federal subsidies in either country is extremely thin.

Finally, the real sources of competitive advantage are to be discovered not only by statistical analysis but by interviews of managers and officials, i.e. by field work in the strategic clusters. Such "hands on" research is exceptionally time consuming and expensive. To make the task feasible a number of important strategic clusters can be selected for analysis; self audits could be made; conferences held, etc. This paper can only raise the issue and map out the route to be followed in order to improve Canadian competitiveness. It is up to business leaders and government officials to read the map and get moving.

Conclusion

There is a rich vein of Canadian scholarship dealing with the topic of international competitiveness for Canada. This theoretical and empirical research

Alan M. Rugman/Joseph R. D'Cruz

needs to be built into a greatly revised and modified version of Porter's diamond framework. A mechanical application of the methodology in Porter's book, to the Canadian situation, would result in an erroneous evaluation of the sources of Canada's international competitiveness. It would ignore the role of inbound foreign direct investment, the nature of Canada's foreign-owned autoindustry, the value added in Canada's resource industries, the Free Trade Agreement, and other key related issues.

In particular, the statistical and related empirical work identifying Canada's successful clusters would be too narrow if the logic of Porter's book were to be strictly applied. A focus on Canada's home country diamond alone is unlikely to detect the real nature of Canada's international competitiveness; this is already being determined within a North American diamond. Helped by the Free Trade Agreement, the North American diamond is already forcing Canadian managers, in services as well as manufacturing, to think globally and plan accordingly. At worst, Porter's book, and its identification of a weak home country diamond, would offer support to such closet protectionists as economic nationalists, the science and technology lobby, and advocates of industrial policy. These are people who would seek to subsidize technology and innovation, at the expense of resource industries, and thereby isolate Canada from the realities of global competition.

References

Cartwright, Wayne. "An Independent Test of the 'Diamond' Theory and Development of a Revised Model for Land-Based Industries", paper presented to the Academy of International Business, Miami, October 1991, availabe from the author at the University of Auckland, New Zealand, 1991.

Cho, Dong-Sung, and Hyeon-Deong Cho. *Comparison of Competitiveness Between Jonghap-Sangsa and Sogo-Shosha in the Korean Market*. Korea: Seoul National University, 1991.

Contractor, Farok J. and Peter Lorange, *Cooperative Strategies in International Business:* (Lexington, Mass.: D.C. Health, 1988).

Crocombe, F. T., M. J. Enright and M. E. Parker. *Upgrading New Zealand's Competitive Advantage*. (Auckland: Oxford University Press, 1991).

Crookell, Harold, *Canadian-American Trade and Investment Under the Free Trade Agreement* (Westport, Conn: Quorum Books 1990).

Daly, Donald J. "Canada's International Competitiveness", in Alan M. Rugman (ed.) *International Business in Canada: Strategic Management* (Toronto: Prentice-Hall of Canada, 1990).

D'Cruz, Joseph R. and James Fleck, *Yankee Canadians in the Global Economy* (London, Ontario: National Centre for Management Research and Development, 1987).

Dunning, John, "Dunning on Porter", Paper to the Annual Meetings of the Academy of International Business, Toronto, October, 1990, Mimeo.

Eastman, Harry C. and S. Stykolt, *The Tariff and Competition in Canada* (Toronto: Macmillan, 1967).

Fuss, Melvin and Leonard Waverman, *Costs and Productivity in the Automobile Industry:* Japan, Germany, the U.S.A. and Canada (New York: Cambridge University Press, 1991).

The Double Diamond Model: Canada's Experience

Porter, Michael G. *The Competitive Advantage of Nations.* New York: Free Press, Macmillan, 1990.
Porter, Michael G. *Canada at the Crossroads: The Reality of a New Competitive Environment* (Ottawa: Business Council on National Issues, October 1991).
Rugman, Alan M., *Multinationals in Canada: Theory, Performance and Economic Impact* (Boston: Matinus Nijhoff, 1980).
Rugman, Alan M., *Multinationals and Canada-United States Free Trade* (Columbia; University of South Carolina Press, 1990).
Rugman, Alan M. "Diamond in the Rough," *Business Quarterly* 55:3 (Winter 1991), pp. 61–64.
Rugman, Alan M., and Joseph D'Cruz. *New Visions for Canadian Business: Strategies for Competing in the Global Economy* (Toronto: Kodak Canada, 1990).
Rugman, Alan M., and Joseph D'Cruz. *Fast Forward: Improving Canada's International Competitiveness.* Toronto: Kodak Canada Inc., 1991.
Rugman, Alan M. and John McIlveen. *Megafirms: Strategies for Canada's Multinationals* (Toronto: Methuen, 1985).
Rugman, Alan M. and Alain Verbeke, *Global Corporate Strategy and Trade Policy* (London and New York: Routledge, 1980).
Safarian, A. E. *Foreign Ownership of Canadian Industry* (Toronto: McGraw Hill, 1968).

Appendix to References

Since this paper was first drafted in early 1991 the "double diamond" framework has become the subject of fierce debate, especially in connection with Porter's Canadian study (Porter 1991). In this study Porter explicitly rejected the double diamond, alleging that Canadians should only "tap into" the U.S. diamond but otherwise build global industries from the single Canadian diamond. He argues that, at best, Canadians can only achieve parity with Americans when operating in the United States, and that their locus of competitive advantage is in Canada. These ideas, and the Porter Canadian study itself, have been roundly criticized by Rugman (1992a). Armstrong and Porter (1992) have replied, leading to a further dialogue, Rugman (1992b). These recent references are now listed:

Porter, Michael G. and the Monitor Company *Canada at the Crossroads: The Reality of a New Competitive Environment* (Ottawa: Business Council on National Issues and Minister of Supply and Services of the Government of Canada, 1991).
Porter, Michael E. and John Armstrong "Canada at the Crossroads: Dialogue", *Business Quarterly* 56:4 (Spring 1992), pp. 6–10.
Rugman, Alan M. "Porter Takes the Wrong Turn," *Business Quarterly* 56:3 (Winter 1992a), pp. 59–64.
Rugman, Alan M. "Canada at the Crossroads: Dialogue" *Business Quarterly* 57:1 (Summer 1992b), pp. 7–10.

CANADA AT THE CROSSROADS

Alan M. Rugman, Professor
University of Toronto

Porter Takes the Wrong Turn

Michael Porter's Analysis of the Canadian Economy is
Seriously Flawed and Should be Viewed Circumspectly

The study described in the report, "Canada at the Crossroads: The Reality of a New Competitive Environment",[1] faithfully applies Michael Porter's "diamond" framework to Canada. It was prepared under Porter's supervision by the Canadian office of his Monitor consulting firm, using precisely the same methodology and conceptual framework as for the eight countries actually reported in his 1990 book.[2]

In an earlier *Business Quarterly* article, I outlined some of the problems with such an approach.[3] The Porter/Monitor team have missed the opportunity to amend the Porter framework to make it relevant for Canadians. Their conclusions and recommendations are inconsistent with their own analysis.

Does Canada Have a Weak Home Base Diamond?

The key result of the Porter/Monitor study is the finding that Canada's home "diamond" is weak and leads to an inability of Canadian-based businesses to develop sustainable global competitive advantages, except in resources. But Porter states that resource-based industries are an essential part of Canada's "old economic order", which Porter thinks has no future. He says, in effect, that Canada's diamond is broken and that it needs to be upgraded to improve Canada's lack of international competitiveness.

Most of Porter's policy recommendations are sound, especially his call to reduce the budget deficit, upgrade worker and management skills and improve business-labor-government relations. Yet these policy recommendations are actually incompatible with his analysis.

This incompatibility arises because Porter insists on applying his home base diamond analysis to Canada, whereas a much more relevant concept for Canadian managers is that of a North American diamond. This approach, developed by Joe D'Cruz and me in 1991,[4] suggests that to become globally competitive, Canadian managers need to design strategies across both the U.S. and Canadian dia-

monds. They need to benchmark decisions on a North American basis, not just a Canadian one. Yet Porter rejects this approach when he states that Canadian businesses can only "tap into" the U.S. diamond but not develop competitive advantages from it.

Unfortunately, Porter's focus on the home base on which to build a successful business is consistent with an economic nationalist's call for national champions. The weak home country diamond analysis suggests that Canada needs another 20 Northern Telecoms. Porter's analysis might be misinterpreted by nationalists to mean the broken Canadian diamond should be fixed by an industrial policy.[5] Porter's view that multinationals can only succeed with a strong home country base may still be true for the U.S., but it is at least 30 years out of date for Canada.

Porter's old-fashioned, naïve and politically mischievous viewpoint is inconsistent with Canada's support of the free trade agreement, tax reform, constitutional renewal and other economic, social and political measures aimed at improving the climate for doing business in a Canadian economy that is interdependent with that of the U.S. It is as if Porter/Monitor had never heard of, or participated in, the divisive free trade election in Canada in 1988. In this the forces of economic nationalism were narrowly defeated by the economic realism and sovereignty considerations underlying the free trade agreement.

Canadian Managers Should Use a North American Diamond

A better approach to Canada's public policy is that of the Rugman/D'Cruz North American diamond framework. This approach says that a Canadian manager needs to consider the U.S. diamond as well as the Canadian and should design strategies across the two diamonds. This means that Canadians should view the U.S. market as a home market, not just as an export market. This

Alan M. Rugman is Professor of International Business at the University of Toronto's Faculty of Management, and Research Director of the Ontario Centre for International Business. Professor Rugman has published 16 books and over 100 articles dealing with multinational enterprises. This scholarly work was recognized recently when Professor Rugman became the first Canadian to be elected as a Fellow of the Academy of International Business. In the last few years Professor Rugman's advice on international competitiveness has been sought by senior cabinet ministers, private sector organizations, government agencies and the media.

does not preclude consideration of elements in the Canadian diamond; it does preclude excessive reliance on it alone.

In practice, Canadian businesses already use North American benchmarks in their search for global competitive advantage. Our research indicates that most Canadian managers of large firms already use this double diamond framework. The problem is that small businesses and people in services still think in terms of the Canadian diamond, not realizing that they are often indirectly involved across the North American diamond.

The rejection of the North American diamond concept by Porter is really quite stunning, implying that the Porter/Monitor group did not fully understand the nature and role of multinational enterprises in a small, open, trading economy like Canada's.

A multinational enterprise is defined as a corporation that operates across borders in the production and distribution of its goods and services. There are various types of management control exercised by modern multinationals, some being highly centralized, that is, Porter-type home based, others being much more decentralized, some even operating as networks of virtually autonomous firms. The actual choice of management structure depends upon the strategy being pursued by the multinational enterprise. To use Porter's terms, the multinational enterprise operates across diamonds.

Contrary to Porter's thinking, there is no particular reason why a multinational needs a home base. It just so happens that U.S.-based multinationals grow up in a large domestic market where new products can be rolled out across the U.S. regions. For the U.S. manager, Canada is just another region. But this is not the case for a Canadian manager.

A Canadian multinational needs to build competitive advantages based on a foreign diamond rather than on its home diamond alone. A multinational from a smaller economy will experience greater opportunities in a larger foreign diamond. This double diamond approach is relevant to over 95% of the world's nations, that is, all those that are not in the triad of the U.S., Japan or Europe.

In practice, Canadian-owned multinationals such as Northern Telecom, Alcan, Bombardier, Inco and Seagram have competitive advantages derived from attributes of the U.S. or other foreign diamonds, rather than the Canadian diamond alone. A major characteristic of Canadian-owned multinationals is that their ratio of foreign to domestic sales is often 70% to 90%, far higher than the average of U.S.-based multinationals at 25%.

Of course, this can raise the question of whether these Canadian-owned multinationals are really Canadian. Even to ask this question shows the basic error in the approach of Porter/Monitor. It does not matter to the strategy of the multinational if it is Canadian or North American. It does matter that a Canadian manager needs to think about more than the Canadian diamond to develop a successful global strategy.

Managers of Canadian businesses today cannot base their strategies on the Canadian home-country diamond alone and tap into the U.S. diamond as Porter recommends. To do so would be totally irresponsible and a recipe for disaster. Porter's strategy would have been suitable in the 1890s, but it is wrong for the 1990s. Instead, to become globally competitive a North American mindset is required for Canadian business decisions.

Porter's Case Studies Fit the Double Diamond

The free trade agreement is the institutional device that recognizes the linkages of the Canadian and U.S. diamonds; it institutionalizes the double diamond for Canadian managers. The Monitor group, and Porter, overlooked the details of the free trade agreement. For example, the vital concept of national treatment and the five exempted service sectors are overlooked in the Porter/Monitor study.

*"Contrary to Porter's thinking, there is no
particular reason why a multinational
needs a home base."*

Since Canadian managers already operate within the framework of the free trade agreement their investment decisions are already benchmarked at North American standards and not just those of the Canadian diamond. Consequently, managerial strategy is already North American; examining the Canadian diamond alone, as Porter does, is not good enough for any Canadian business or for any firms in a cluster.

Examples of the Porter/ Monitor misunderstanding of the Rugman/ D'Cruz North American diamond abound in the study. The four detailed case studies are not fully explained, as alleged, by the Canadian diamond. They are better explained by the double diamond approach, for the following reasons:

1. The success of Northern Telecom in the U.S. is as much due to the intangible marketing skills and insights of its former CEO, Mr. Walter Light, about the need to manage within the U.S. diamond as it is to observable R and D expenditures and protection for Bell labs' research in Canada's home-country diamond. The whole organizational structure of Northern Telecom is designed around the North American diamond; it does not "tap into" the U.S. market, but is totally integrated across the border.

2. The same analysis of the validity of the double diamond is also true for Seagram in the whiskey industry, rather than the Monitor single diamond approach. The success of Seagram was due

> **PORTER'S STATES OF COMPETITIVE DEVELOPMENT**
>
> *Factor-Driven.* The nation's companies draw their advantages almost solely from basic factors of production. They compete primarily on the basis of price in industries that require either little product or process technology or technology that is inexpensive and widely available.
>
> *Investment-Driven.* National competitive advantage is based on the willingness and ability of a nation and its firms to invest aggressively. Foreign technology and methods are not just applied but improved upon.
>
> *Innovation-Driven.* Consumer demand is sophisticated because of rising personal incomes, higher levels of education, increasing desire for convenience and the invigorating role of domestic rivalry. New competitive industries emerge out of related industries. Firms not only appropriate and improve technology and methods from other nations but create them.
>
> *Wealth-Driven.* The Wealth-Driven stage ultimately leads to decline because the driving force in the economy is wealth that has already been achieved. Firms lost competitive advantage by ebbing rivalry and by influencing governments to insulate them from competitive pressures.

largely to its understanding of demand conditions in the U.S., and not just government taxes and regulations in Canada's diamond.

3. The Monitor case study of the newsprint industry is also quite banal; it appears that the Monitor team overlooked the fact that there are at least two newsprint clusters in Canada (west coast and eastern Canada), with different characteristics and strategies as they operate in the North American diamond.

4. The Monitor team took out their best example of the Canadian diamond – hockey – perhaps because they had already used rugby football as their example for the New Zealand book.[6] Except for hockey, nearly everything else in Canada is better explained by the double diamond framework.

To summarize, the "North American" diamond suggests that Canadian managers treat the U.S. market as their home market, not an export market, and that a Canadian manager needs to make strategic decisions based on as thorough an understanding of the U.S. diamond as of the Canadian diamond. Our field research has revealed that Canadian managers already do this. Why Porter wants to reject this current managerial reality is a puzzle.

Canada's Resource Industries are Wrongly Dismissed

Porter states that Canada's abundance of natural resources leads to resource-based industries that

> *"It does not matter to the strategy of the multinational if it is Canadian or North American."*

compete in commodity markets and lack the ability to achieve upgrading. He states that Canada is a resource-based economy that has not been able to move beyond his first Factor-Driven stage.(See box)

Porter's conclusion is the same as that reported in several throw-away lines in his book, that Canada (like Australia) is stuck at the Factor-Driven stage and lacks the ability to move on to the more desirable Innovation-Driven stage. Indeed, Porter implies that Canada may flip all the way to decline in the Wealth-Driven Stage, missing out the useful middle two stages of development. The argument here, and the superficial analysis of resource-based industries throughout the Monitor study, is questionable.

Many of Canada's resource-based firms have intangible firm-specific advantages in marketing and management skills.[7] In Porter's terms, these are often the source of their sustainable competitive advantages. Yet the Monitor group makes the mistake of only analyzing and measuring what they can see – output and exports of goods using the observable physical natural resources. But because you cannot measure something does not mean that the intangible firm-specific advantage is insignificant.

In short, Canada's resource-based industries already make attempts to add value through marketing and management skills; these are just as valuable as high-tech expenditures. Good case studies would reveal this; the superficial ones done by Monitor miss it.

Ironically this point is confirmed later in the study when the Monitor team makes the naïve argument that greater R and D expenditures and technological improvements will result in upgrading and productivity growth and benefits. If these intangible benefits exist for the production side of the business, why not for the marketing side?

Porter's "four stages" model is too simplistic and probably meaningless for Canadian policy makers. Specifically, there is no valid reason why clusters of resource-based industries cannot be placed in Porter's Innovation-Driven stage, rather than the Factor-Driven stage. If there is value added in a resource-based industry due to marketing or management skills, it has just as much right to be in the Innovation-Driven stage as an R and D based business. The Monitor data themselves confirm that resource-based industries are Canada's most competitive industries, accounting for the largest share of world cluster exports.

Foreign Ownership is Not Analyzed Properly

In his discussion of foreign ownership in his 1990 book, Porter repeatedly states that "inbound" foreign direct investment is not a source of competitive advantage for a nation; instead it brings the products of another country's diamond strength into the home base without adding any value. Consistent with this thinking, in the Monitor report, Porter states that a home base is superior to foreign ownership. This statement is just a simple repetition of the criticism of foreign investment built into Porter's 1990 book.

Porter states that local ownership and a local home base generate greater benefits than foreign ownership and a foreign home base. This is totally inaccurate and an insult to the Canadian managers and workers in foreign-owned firms operating in Canada in a socially useful manner. There is no serious literature in international business supporting such a nationalist bias.[8]

The "home base" approach is also wrong since it does not specify the nature of benefit. Is this to be measured by wealth generation, by jobs, by R and D, by process technology, by regional benefits or by other criteria? The sorry experience of Canada's Foreign Investment Review Agency (FIRA) from 1974-1985, until it was abolished, is a testimony to the lack of validity of a concept calling for improvements in the net economic benefits of foreign investment. Porter's limited discussion of FIRA is totally inadequate, as it does not assess its

*"To become globally competitive a
North American mindset is required
for Canadian business decisions."*

impact on managerial behavior and strategy. FIRA was supposed to find the net benefit from foreign ownership; instead it made decisions based on political grounds. See the well known work by A.E. Safarian and my book, *Multinationals in Canada*.[9]

Porter's attempt to classify foreign direct investment into three alternative types – resource based, market access based and home based – is not useful; indeed it is wrong. Multinationals exist to internalize (make proprietary) firm-specific advantages to conduct successful international business operations. In doing so managers evaluate sets of host-country factors, including availability of resources, tariffs and political risk, as well as home-country and international institutional factors, and consider these against various internal strategic factors to determine the location of their activities. Porter's three classifications are far too simplistic and are misleading.

Porter's Logic is Flawed

After Canadian managers have read Porter's study they should ask the following questions. First, does Canada need an industrial strategy to mend the broken Canadian diamond? Second, should Canada give up on its resource-based industries and replace them by innovation-driven industries? Third, does Canada need to keep out foreign-owned firms that do not develop product lines using Canada as a home base? The reason these questions are important is that Porter says that Canada's lack of international competitiveness is due to problems in these areas. Yet his analysis fails to provide logical support for his recommendations. Here is why.

First, Porter says that Canada's home country diamond is broken, but then he says that he is not in favor of an industrial strategy to fix it. This is inconsistent, as shown above; the double diamond approach overcomes this inconsistency and is a much better method to develop a global strategy for Canadian firms.

Second, Porter says that Canada's most successful export industries are resource-based, but that Canadians rely on an "old economic order" in which resources cannot be the basis for future success. He then says that more R and D is required for innovation-led growth to take place. This is neither necessary, nor feasible. Instead, the resource-based industries need to be properly evaluated and their value added recognized.[10]

Third, Porter says that most foreign-owned firms in Canada are of no use as they do not build upon a home base for their product lines. Porter says that R and D is lacking and that world product mandates are few. He invents a theory of foreign ownership to support this, which is not adequately explained in the September 1991 draft of his report, and is wrong in any case. The logical absurdities of Porter's one-way theory of multinationals were explored above. In practice, since there are two-way flows of trade and investments, a home-country model is useless for Canadian managers and policy makers.

Porter is Out of Date

Porter's book is 30 years out of date in its thinking about multinationals and in its analysis of Canadian management. Porter repeatedly states that Canada has lived well off an "old economic order" and now a new vision is required – one where upgrading of skills is a priority. This is an agreeable recommendation but it is a pity that Porter, himself, could not follow his own advice and do some new thinking in a Canadian context. Porter has presented old economic wine in a new bottle, but few Canadians are likely to become intoxicated by his conceptually flawed analysis.

The application of Porter's irrelevant single diamond model to current Canadian conditions leads to misleading analysis, which is actually inconsistent with Porter's (correct) public policy recommendations. The recommendations are familiar and

"Many of Canada's resource-based firms have intangible firm-specific advantages in marketing and management skills."

reasonable; in particular, upgrading of human resource skills is necessary. Yet the analysis itself is a mechanical application of Porter's single diamond formula. It was not worth the money. More relevant insights into Canadian strategic management and public policy issues come from the North American diamond framework. Porter's directions for the future of Canadian business are useless; he took a wrong turning when he crossed the border.   BQ

References

1 Porter, Michael E., *Canada at the Crossroads: The Reality of a New Competitive Environment*, Business Council on National Issues and Minister of Supply and Services, Ottawa, October, 1991.
2 Porter, Michael E., *The Competitive Advantage of Nations*, New York: Free Press, and Toronto: Collier MacMillan, 1990.
3 Rugman, Alan M. "Diamond in the Rough," *Business Quarterly*, Winter 1991, Volume 55, Number 3, pp.61-64.
4 Rugman, Alan M. and Joseph D'Cruz, *Fast Forward: Improving Canada's International Competitiveness*, Toronto: Kodak Canada, 1991. It should be noted that Porter does not cite this study correctly in Chapter 3 of his report; instead he cites the study referenced here as number 10.
5 Crane, David, "High Level of Foreign Ownership Hampers Our Ability to Compete," *The Toronto Star*, 19th October 1991.
6 Crocombe, F.T., M.J. Enright and M.E. Porter, *Upgrading New Zealand's Competitive Advantage*, Auckland, New Zealand: Oxford University Press, 1991.
7 Rugman, Alan M., and John McIlveen, *Megafirms: Strategies for Canada's Multinationals*, Toronto, Methuen, 1985.
8 Porter actually cites Richard Caves' *Multinational Enterprises and Economic Analysis*, New York: Cambridge University Press, 1981 incorrectly, since there are no statements in the text to support such nonsense. Rather, there is a large literature finding the opposite of Porter, namely that the performance of capital is not determined by its ownership. This literature includes Johnson, Harry G., *The Canadian Quandary: Economic Problems and Policies*, Toronto, New York: McGraw-Hill, 1963; Safarian, A.E., *Foreign Ownership of Canadian Industry*, Toronto, New York: McGraw Hill-Ryerson, 1967; and Rugman, Alan M., *Multinationals in Canada: Theory, Performance and Economic Impact*, Boston: Martinus Nijhoff/Kluwer, 1980.
9 Safarian, A.E., *FIRA and FIRB: Canadian and Australian Policies on Foreign Direct Investment*, Toronto: Ontario Economic Council, 1985, and Rugman, Alan M., *Multinationals in Canada: Theory, Performance and Economic Impact*, ibid.
10 Rugman, Alan M. and Joseph D'Cruz, *New Visions for Canadian Business: Strategies for Competing in the Global Economy*, Toronto: Kodak Canada, 1990.

[18]

How to Operationalize Porter's Diamond of International Competitiveness

Alan M. Rugman and Alain Verbeke

Michael Porter's "diamond" framework has as its focus a set of home country national determinants of international competitiveness. For applications to international business this presents analytical difficulties because Dunning's eclectic theory of the multinational enterprise demonstrates that it is the interaction between national and international determinants that leads to the competitive success of global industries. This article suggests a method of extending Porter's framework to incorporate the modern theory of the multinational enterprise; in particular, a variant of SWOT analysis is used to operationalize the Porter diamond. © 1993 John Wiley & Sons, Inc.

INTRODUCTION: THE PORTER DIAMOND

A recent contribution by Porter (1990) on the competitive advantage of nations has led to an extensive discussion among academics and practitioners on the sources of international competitiveness (Grant, 1991; Gray, 1991).

Porter's focus is on the impact of national determinants on international competitiveness. The main question answered in his work is

Alan M. Rugman is Professor of International Business at the University of Toronto, Faculty of Management, 246 Bloor Street West, Toronto, Ontario M5S 1V4.

Alain Verbeke is Professor of International Business at the University of Brussels, (V.U.B.), Solvay Business School, Pleinlaan 2, 1050, Brussels Belgium.

The International Executive, Vol. 35(4) 283–299 (July/August 1993)
© 1993 John Wiley & Sons, Inc.   CCC 0020-6652/93/040283-17

"Why does a nation become the home base for successful international competitors in an industry?" (Porter, 1990: 1) Porter measures international success as an industry's ability to export and to engage in outbound foreign direct investment.

Two important problems arise in terms of managerial applicability of the Porter diamond framework. First, it is not clear why the national level would necessarily be the best geographic indicator for an industry's "proximate environment," shaping its success over time (Dunning, 1990). Other geographic levels may be important, such as the local, regional, foreign, or global level, for particular determinants of international success. This problem is acknowledged by Porter (1990: 154–159, 606–607) but did not lead to an adaptation of his framework. Rugman (1991, 1992) has explored this issue in the context of Porter's application of his framework to Canada (Porter and the Monitor Company, 1991).

Second, six forces and their mutual interactions are recognized as determining an industry's international competitiveness: factor conditions; demand conditions; related and supporting industries; firm strategy, structure, and rivalry; government; and chance. The two latter elements are not included in the four basic determinants of the diamond but their role is important because either of them can influence the entire diamond. These six forces and their interactions were studied for 100 industry case studies (see Porter, 1990: 26–27 for a complete list). However, Porter's case studies lack a homogenous analytical tool to determine the importance and precise impact of each determinant on the industries' competitive position. In short, it is extremely difficult to "operationalize" Porter's diamond. By operationalize we mean put the diamond theory into practice, as a consultant or strategic planner would try to do.

The aim of this article is to correct these two weaknesses in Porter's seminal contribution to improve the managerial relevance of the diamond framework. More specifically, this article will extend Porter's model through explicitly introducing four additional geographic levels relevant to the analysis of international competitiveness and linking this framework with the well-known and operationally simple SWOT-analysis (strengths, weaknesses, opportunities, and threats) in strategic management theory.

OPERATIONALIZING PORTER ACROSS MULTIPLE GEOGRAPHIC LEVELS

Porter (1990) focuses his attention on the international success of a national industry based on the analysis of determinants at the national level. Two comments should be made here. First, from a managerial perspective it is not always evident that an analysis of a national industry is sought (although this was of course explicitly the case in Porter's work). A useful framework for the study of an industry's competitiveness should explicitly allow for an analysis of the competitiveness of a regionally based industry (e.g., the computer software industry in Silicon Valley) or an industry that is located across a number of nations (e.g., the consumer electronics industry in the European Community, EC). For purposes of clarity, however, the remainder of this paper will also focus on the competitiveness of an industry at the national level.

Second, whatever the chosen geographic level for the definition of an industry, it should be recognized that the six determinants could be important at other levels than the national one. In some cases an industry may be influenced by particular determinants at the local level (e.g., the impact of transportation facilities on the petrochemical industry in Rotterdam). Sometimes, some determinants in a region may be of major importance (e.g., factors of production in the French Champagne region for the sparkling wine industry). Finally, any of the determinants may influence an industry's competitiveness from outside the geographic locus of a home nation. For example, a strong influence may be exerted by demand conditions in another country. This is especially the case for small, open economies such as Austria, Canada, or New Zealand, where firms take into account demand conditions prevailing in larger foreign trading partners from the outset even when designing new products or engaging in R & D. Rugman and D'Cruz (1991, 1993) have explored the reasons for a "double diamond" across the Canadian–U.S. economic space. In some cases, such as the pharmaceutical industry, even global trends in demand or in any other determinant may stimulate firms in a particular nation to engage in specific strategic behavior (Hamel and Prahalad, 1988).

An industry's international competitiveness may then result from responding effectively to, and building on, the determining factors at any of the various geographic levels, as suggested by White and Poynter (1990). Hence, it is the successful combination by a particular firm or industry of particular determinants at the relevant geographic levels, that leads to international competitiveness, not an exclusive or primary focus on national or local determinants (Diagram 1).

In Diagram 1, the international competitive performance of a firm or industry is determined by the six elements identified by Porter (1990), but potentially at five different geographic levels.

This leads to a possible impact of 30 influences on a particular firm or industry. In practice, it may not be feasible, nor desirable, to study each of these 30 influences. A more limited number of influ-

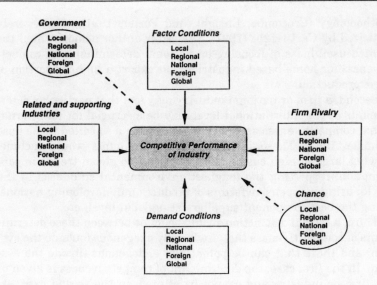

Diagram 1. An extension of Porter's international competitiveness framework.

ences considered as critical and their mutual interaction may be selected for in-depth investigation. In any case, the important conclusion of the above analysis is that a firm or industry's competitiveness
may or may not result primarily from influences at the national or
subnational level. Determinants in the international environment
may be just as important for national competitiveness as elements
inside a nation. International competitiveness depends on the ability
of a firm or industry to adequately respond to these determining
influences, at any of these geographic levels, to its own advantage.

Porter (1990: 606–607) recognizes the possibility of "tapping selective advantages in other nations," for example, when developing a
global strategy, but he does not believe that determinants in other
nations can contribute as much to the competitiveness of an industry
as determinants at the national level. This view is based on the
assumption that a firm can only have one true home base for each
distinct business or segment. "If [the firm] attempts to have several,
it will divide strategic authority, fragment technology development,
and forego the synergistic benefits of concentrating the critical
skills. Most importantly, it will sacrifice the dynamics that arise
from true integration in a national 'diamond'" (Porter, 1990: 606–
607).

Three comments should be made here. First, Porter's statements
above were not substantiated in his work with case data, nor with
relevant examples. In fact, a report on New Zealand using the same

methodology (Crocombe, Enright, and Porter, 1991), was severely criticized by Cartwright (1991). The latter author demonstrated the limited usefulness of focusing on national determinants of competitiveness for home-based industries that export a high proportion of their production.

Second, a firm or national industry may feel that particular determinants at the international level may be as crucial for its international competitiveness as determinants inside a so-called home base (Ohmae, 1987). These international determinants would include: serving large foreign customers; responding to global trends in consumption; respecting the toughest environmental standards in the world; using inexpensive factors of production in developing nations; using the best component suppliers at a global level; etc.

Third, a crucial distinction should be made between those determinants of competitiveness that are largely exogenous (outside the system) and those that can be potentially endogenous (inside the system). In the first case, the determinant of competitiveness is given to the firm or industry and cannot be altered. In the second case, attempts are made to use or transform the external factor into a proprietary, internal, firm, or industry characteristic. Porter's (1990) view implies that the second case would primarily be observed inside a country, where an industry could upgrade itself over time, whereas this would be much more difficult in the international context. In reality, numerous examples of multinational strategic management behavior demonstrate how determinants of competitiveness emanating from foreign environments may be used and appropriated by firms from particular nations, thus boosting their international competitiveness as much as national determinants (Bartlett and Ghoshal, 1989; Douglas and Craig, 1989; Bartlett and Ghoshal, 1992; Julian and Keller, 1991).

In fact, it may be precisely a synergistic combination of determinants at the national or subnational level and determinants at the foreign or global level that may generate international success. In this case, it would be sensible to attribute international competitiveness primarily to a mutual reinforcement among national and international factors leading to success, although a simultaneous response to critical factors at different geographic levels may obviously lead to tensions among competing influences (Westney, 1990).

We will need to know why international influences, whether at the level of one or more foreign nations or at the global level, would have a specific impact on a particular national industry. After all, rivals in other nations would be confronted with similar influences. The reason is that firms in a national industry may be characterized by sharing conceptual maps and ongoing interactions leading to convergent responses to international influences. Such behavior was observed by Ghoshal (1988), in the context of environmental scanning by Korean firms.

In this context, leanings toward similar strategic behavior result from country-specific organizational structures (isomorphisms). (Sub)National determinants lead to isomorphic leanings toward specific managerial behavior in an industry, in terms of using foreign building blocks for improved competitiveness; but it may be the content of these foreign elements that actually contributes to international competitiveness. For example, superior organizing principles in a national industry may lead to a comparatively more effective adoption of foreign innovations, but it is obviously the combination of the two influences, at different geographic levels, that leads to lower or higher international competitiveness. An example of a successful case is the adoption of quality management systems in Japan (Yoshida, 1989). A less successful case is the use of JIT-systems in the United States (Daniel and Reitsperger, 1991). In these cases, (sub)national and international determinants of competitiveness cannot be separated.

SWOT-ANALYSIS AND PORTER'S DIAMOND

If the view is accepted, in principle, that six determinants can influence a firm or industry's competitiveness through working at five geographic levels, then how should these 30 potentially relevant influences be studied? In Porter's (1990) work, in-depth case studies analyzing the determinants at the national level were used for the ex post rationalization of observed success in terms of exports and/or foreign direct investment. Firm managers and public policy makers, however, are primarily interested in a tool that would allow a systematic analysis of these different influences on international competitiveness, as well as their strategic implications for the firm or industry. The use of the well known SWOT-analysis allows both such a systematic analysis and a focus on strategic management implications. The conventional SWOT-analysis (Thompson and Strickland, 1989; Weihrich, 1990) provides a tool for the analysis of both the external and internal environments of firms.

The analysis of the external environment leads to the classification of critical exogenous influences on international competitiveness as opportunities and threats. In the context of the framework developed in this paper, each of the six determining factors, at any of the five geographic levels, can constitute the source of such opportunities or threats. The main characteristic of opportunities and threats is that they act as environmental constraints on business firms' operations and strategic decision making.

The study of the firm's or industry's internal environment allows the identification of strengths and weaknesses. Strengths refer to categories of skills or assets, where the firm or industry is better positioned than foreign rivals. Weaknesses imply a lack of such skills or assets, relative to foreign competition. In the context of the international competitiveness framework, each of the six determinants at any of the geographic levels may have been transformed into a firm or industry specific skill or asset, in a more or less effective way, as compared to foreign rivals.

For example, a firm or industry in a particular nation may have developed network linkages with related and supporting industries at various geographic levels. Special government relations may have been established with a variety of public agencies both nationally and internationally. A chance event such as a scientific innovation, occurring anywhere in the world, may have been turned into a distinctive competence. Trends in local or global demand conditions may have led to the creation of unique marketing skills. The perceived availability of particular factors of production, again in any nation or region, may have led to a specific choice of production process.

The analysis above is visualized in Diagram 2, suggesting that a

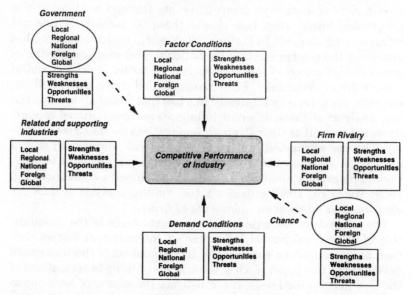

Diagram 2. A SWOT-analysis of international competitiveness determinants.

SWOT-analysis could be performed for the six determinants at five geographic levels, leading to 30 SWOT-assessments. In practice, a SWOT-analysis may only be performed for those factors considered critical. However, each determinant such as factors of production may itself be unbundled into several subdeterminants for which a SWOT-analysis may be required. In addition, the SWOT-results for some critical factors may be related to SWOT-outcomes for other determinants.

The use of a SWOT-analysis for each of the six influencing determinants at five geographic levels does not imply that national or subnational influences are less important for competitiveness than suggested in Porter's (1990) framework. It does imply, however, that the national determinants should be viewed as part of a broader spectrum of influences at a variety of geographic levels, including subnational and international ones. Hence, the competitive advantages of a firm or industry originating in a particular nation are undoubtedly largely influenced by (sub)national determinants of competitiveness, but, depending upon firm and industry characteristics, international influences may be just as important.

Porter's (1990) proposed hierarchy of influences, discriminating between primary "national diamond characteristics" and secondary determinants in other nations that can only be "tapped into selectively" should be dismissed as a general rule. It could even be argued, especially for small, open economies, that nationally and subnationally driven opportunities and strengths can often be exploited only when linked to opportunities prevailing, and strengths developed, at the international level.

The need for an outward focus for strategy operationalization is exemplified by the attempts of business firms to become "insiders" into at least one of the "triad" powers (see Burgenmeier and Mucchielli, 1991) for an analysis of outsiders' motivations to become insiders in the EC. Porter is correct that in the past a sequential exploitation of opportunities and development of strengths at the national level and international level needed to take place, whereby the latter was not possible without the former. The reality of today's international business implies, however, that firms, obviously building on national or subnational determinants, often also consider elements in the international environment such as opportunities and threats or sources of strengths and weaknesses of equal importance when engaging in strategic decision making as suggested by Reich (1991).

Firms in a national industry may be prevented from gaining a competitive advantage relative to foreign rivals. This occurs for several reasons: differences in technological and organizational capabilities and trajectories; institutional inertia; behavioral constraints on the identification and adoption of superior organizing principles; the absence of isomorphic pulls to adopt the best practice in a global industry; etc. But here it is precisely the difference in responses among nations to determinants at a foreign or global level that determines the ultimate competitiveness of these firms.

There is no scientifically grounded rationale to dismiss such international factors or classify them as less important than national determinants, although many case studies on the historical growth patterns of industries may suggest that national influences were indeed prevailing during their initial development (Dunning, 1983). Even if organizational and institutional capabilities of nations are different for long periods of time and diffuse relatively slowly to firms of another nation, specific international determinants of competitiveness may be crucial for the long-run survival and success of these firms, as suggested by the creation of the European single market (Emerson, 1998).

PRACTICAL VALUE OF SWOT-ANALYSIS FOR THE DIAMOND

We now discuss the practical use of the various SWOT-analyses performed for the influencing factors considered to be critical in the formulation and implementation of strategy. From a strategic management perspective, it is important to position the main results of each of the SWOT-analyses in a comprehensive framework that could lead to corporate or industry-wide responses to those SWOT-results perceived as most important.

Diagram 3 provides such as framework. In this matrix, the different critical influencing factors can be positioned in two ways. First, according to the extent to which they constitute an endogenized strength or weakness, vis-à-vis foreign rivals. Second, the extent to which this present internal capability could be challenged in the future as a result of environmental threats, or reinforced through capitalizing on external opportunities.

Diagram 3 is largely capability driven. To operationalize Porter requires first a positioning of the determinants on the horizontal axis as strengths or weaknesses, and second that these internal positions are linked to external (exogenous) circumstances providing threats or opportunities.

Each cell of the matrix obviously leads to different strategy implications. We shall discuss the "core" cases of cells 1, 2, 4, and 5 first and then turn to the other cases. Determinants of competitiveness in cell 1 constitute both the major positive force for present internation-

| | Internal Capabilities | | |
Attractiveness of External Environment	Strengths	Weaknesses	Neutral
Opportunities	1	4	7
Threats	2	5	8
Neutral	3	6	9

Diagram 3. The SWOT-positioning of competitiveness determinants.

al competitiveness and the source of new competencies in the future. In principle, a firm or industry would like to have as many critical competitiveness determinants as possible in this cell.

The second cell means that a company or industry built core competencies for this determinant of competitiveness but is now faced with environmental threats that may lead to a weakening of the existing strengths relative to rivals better positioned to respond to these new environmental factors. For example, the availability of government support in another nation may be a threat for an industry. The local industry may have endogenized this factor, whereas it remains largely exogenous and unavailable to outsiders, even if good business–government relations traditionally constituted a strength for these outsiders. The case of the Canadian lumber industry exporting to the United States is a case in point. This industry traditionally benefited strongly from good business–government relations in the United States, but became seriously threatened in the early eighties by the capture of U.S. trade policy by U.S. lumber producers seeking shelter (Gold and Leyton Brown, 1988). Here, the main challenge is to improve and maintain existing strengths in the face of environmental threats. Examples of this strategy are discussed, using the theory of shelter, by Rugman and Verbeke (1990).

The fourth cell refers to the case where a competitiveness determinant represents significant opportunities for improved competitiveness, but where the firm or industry has not been able to capitalize on past or present opportunities through the development and use of distinctive competencies relative to rivals. This occurs when a divergence exists between competitive opportunities with a particular geographic scope and a firm or industry's ability to build competitive advantages on the basis of critical influencing factors with the same geographic locus. For example, the world automobile industry undoubtedly is faced with a number of global opportunities, but firms from some nations may not be able to adequately respond to these opportunities as a result of their lack of internal strengths at a global level (Casson, 1987). Then we need to know the firm's or industry's capability to develop the required strengths in order to be able to respond adequately to opportunities.

The fifth cell reflects the situation whereby a firm or industry is confronted with both external threats and internal weaknesses for particular competitiveness determinants. In the best case scenario, this quadrant may reflect selective factor disadvantages, pushing firms to improve their position for other critical determinants in other cells. In the worst case, if several critical determinants are positioned in this cell, this may be an indication of declining international competitiveness, requiring actions such as mergers or even liquidation.

Cells 3, 6, 7, and 8 are cases whereby either the exogenous factors or internal capabilities are thought to have a neutral effect. For example, in the area of production factors, cells 3 and 6 could include firms with particular internal capabilities in international human resources systems, but where the environment would not lead to substantial opportunities or threats in the area of management–labor relations in the near future. Cells 7 and 8 could reflect firms with innovation strategies that constitute neither a strength nor a weakness, vis-à-vis foreign rivals, but where global technological changes may pose a threat or opportunity in terms of, for example, the required speed of innovation. Finally, cell 9 implies that the determinant in question is really not a critical factor because it constitutes neither the source of a weakness or strength, nor an external opportunity or threat relative to rivals.

The case studies described in Porter (1990) do not allow managers to clearly analyze how particular determinants can lead to improved or deteriorated competitive advantage, nor do they allow a prediction of future competitiveness based upon strategic decision making. Through using Diagram 3 in a dynamic fashion, however, these two problems can be solved.

First, a SWOT-positioning of competitiveness determinants can occur at several points in time that allows managers to clearly visualize changes in Diagram 3. Second, an analysis of the present set of SWOT-studies may result in strategic decisions to shift certain critical factors from the weakness side to the strength side of Diagram 3 (or to maintain a number of factors on the strength side). This should lead to an improved internal compatibility between strength and strategy. New trends in opportunities and threats emanating from specific competitiveness determinants may also be identified or anticipated, thus stimulating external compatibility between the firms' strategy and their environment. Hence, a set of sequential SWOT-positioning matrices may be developed, describing the dynamics of international advantage of a national industry over time.

DIAMOND SWOT-ANALYSIS AND THEORY OF MULTINATIONAL ENTERPRISE

In the case of multinational enterprises with several strategic business units (SBUs), the conceptual tools developed in this article can be applied for each SBU. If an SBU has its headquarters in a foreign nation, that country becomes the unit of analysis for the study of national or subnational influences on competitiveness. The international environment will almost invariably be of major importance, for example, if the SBU operates with a world product mandate (but is still largely influenced by the corporate home base), or if it coordinates the activities of a number of globally rationalized businesses in various nations (Etemad and Seguin Dulude, 1986). Foreign subsidiaries with strong internal capabilities and the ability to capitalize on host country opportunities may take strategic initiatives that are as important to a firm or industry as home country determinants (Morrison and Crookell, 1991).

In a more general sense, the framework described in the previous sections can be linked to the eclectic paradigm developed by Dunning (1988). According to Dunning, the international competitiveness and patterns of international production of a particular national industry are seen as the result of three elements: ownership advantages; location advantages; and internalization advantages. The ownership advantages are strengths that may derive from unique corporate attributes. They may also result from the endogenization, by a particular national industry, of environmental characteristics related to any of the six determinants recognized by Porter (1990), but not only at the national level. In fact, ownership advantages derive from acquiring or developing strategically relevant skills or assets, both tangible and intangible, at various geographic levels.

Dunning (1988) also makes a distinction between asset and transaction advantages of multinational enterprises. Whereas the former may be largely dependent on (sub)national determinants, the latter can obviously be reaped only as a result of international influences. Transactional advantages reflect the capacity of multinational enterprises to capture transactional benefits (or economize on the transactional costs) arising from the common governance of a network of assets, located in various countries. Although a national industry's administrative heritage may be an important input for realizing transactional advantages, as suggested by Bartlett (1986), it cannot be dissociated from internationally driven opportunities and strengths built up in foreign subsidiaries to realize such advantages. Porter's (1990: 60–61) view that home-based advantages are intrinsically more valuable than systemic advantages does not seem to be compatible with the Dunning framework.

Location advantages refer to external opportunities or potential sources of internal strengths, again at various geographic levels. They lead to strategic decisions on the configuration of an industry's asset base. The determinants of internal capabilities, and external attractiveness prevailing in the home country, are linked to possibilities for developing complementary capabilities and building on the attractiveness of host nations. Dunning (1988) recognized that home country and host country elements cannot be separated. For example, the formation of customs unions and regional trading blocs and the reduction of transportation costs on particular international routes have led to a strengthening of ownership advantages of multinational enterprises.

In contrast, Porter's view of foreign direct investment is out of date. In Porter, horizontal foreign direct investment would be viewed primarily as an international transfer of organizing capabilities developed in the home country. Vertical foreign direct investment would merely imply "tapping into" host nations for sourcing inputs, producing intermediate outputs, or marketing final outputs, without substantial learning. In contrast to Porter's view, the endogenization of foreign location advantages and international learning among subsidiaries have become core sources for the development of new ownership advantages or improvement of initial ones (Bartlett and Ghoshal, 1989; Johanson and Mattsson, 1988).

Finally, Porter's (1990) analysis suggests that internalization through FDI takes place to exploit tangible and intangible skills, and assets developed in the home base as the result of (sub)national determinants. This assumes the nonlocation bound nature of these skills and assets can be best exploited internationally through their use within the MNE rather than through their sale. Three important comments should be made here.

First, a large literature on the requirements for both national responsiveness and integration (Roth and Morrison, 1990) suggests that knowledge developed in a home nation cannot always be transferred abroad easily without substantial adaptation. This demonstrates the need for taking into account international determinants of competitiveness as much as national determinants.

Second, the formation of global networks and the rise in international cooperation strategies (Contractor and Lorange, 1988) suggests that determinants of competitiveness emanating from foreign environments are just as important, if not more important, as domestic ones. International cooperation may be crucial for an effective and rapid acquisition and diffusion of knowledge.

Third, the choice of entry mode in foreign markets is critical to the likely success of a foreign operation. Even at the stage of initial entry, the exploitation of home-based ownership advantages cannot be dissociated from foreign location advantages and internalization advantages. The latter may depend as much on global technological factors and perceived opportunities in foreign markets as on domestically driven internalization capabilities.

To summarize, the operational framework developed in this paper is entirely consistent with Dunning's (1988) eclectic paradigm of international production, whereas Porter's (1990) diamond cannot fully deal with the complexity of interactions among ownership advantages, location advantages, and internalization advantages in multinational strategic management.

CONCLUSIONS

Many factors may influence the competitiveness of a national industry. National determinants and their mutual interactions undoubtedly play a major role in this respect. The relative stability of international success (or lack of success) of a particular industry over a long period of time and the observation that firms from a particular nation often adopt similar competitive strategies, demonstrates the importance of Porter's national "diamond." However, the role of international determinants cannot be reduced to secondary status, as compared to the role of (sub)national ones. From Dunning's (1988) eclectic theory of the multinational enterprise we know that it is precisely the interaction among (sub)national and international determinants that leads to competitive success in global industries. The framework presented in this article can operationalize the study of the complex nature of international competitiveness by analyzing Porter's six influencing factors at five geographic levels. It also suggests that all the factors considered as critical by Porter can be operationalized through a SWOT-analysis, thus allowing a consistent and homogeneous managerial approach to each determinant.

Porter's exclusive focus on national determinants of global competitive success may turn the attention of managers and public policy makers away from the need to monitor international threats and opportunities, as well as the requirement to build up strengths and reduce weaknesses in foreign nations. Such an inward diversion of focus in the long run would serve neither the affected firms or industries nor the home nations involved.

REFERENCES

Bartlett, Christopher A. (1986) "Building and Managing the Transnational: The New Organizational Challenge," in Michael E. Porter (ed.), *Competition in Global Industries* (pp. 367–401), Boston, MA: Harvard Business School.

Bartlett, Christopher A. and Ghoshal, Sumantra (1989) *Managing Across Borders: The Transnational Solution,* Boston, MA: Harvard Business School.

Bartlett, Christopher A. and Ghoshal, Sumantra (1992) *Transnational Management,* Irwin, Boston, MA.

Burgenmeier, Beat and Mucchielli, Jean-Louis (1991) *Multinationals and Europe 1992,* London: Routledge.

Cartwright, Wayne (October 1991) "An Independent Test of the "Diamond" Theory and Development of a Revised Model for Land-Based Industries," paper presented to the Academy of International Business, Miami. Available from the author at the University of Auckland, New Zealand.

Casson, Mark (1987) *The Firm and the Market,* Oxford: Basil Blackwell.

Crocombe, F.T., Enright, M.J., and Porter, M.E. (1991) *Upgrading New Zealand's Competitive Advantage,* Auckland: Oxford University Press.

Contractor, Farok J. and Lorange, Peter (1988) *Cooperative Strategies in International Business,* Lexington, MA/Toronto: Lexington Books.

Daniel, Shirley J. and Reitsperger, Wolf D. (1991) "Management Control Systems for J.I.T.: An Empirical Comparison of Japan and the U.S.," *Journal of International Business Studies,* 22(4), 603–617.

Douglas, Susan P. and Craig, C. Samuel (Fall 1989) "Evolution of Global Marketing Strategy: Scale, Scope and Synergy," *Columbia Journal of World Business,* 24(3), 47–59.

Dunning, John H. (1983) "Changes in the Level and Structure of International Production: The Last One Hundred Years," in Mark Casson (ed.), *The Growth of International Business,* London: George Allen & Unwin.

Dunning, John H. (1988) *Explaining International Production,* London: Unwin Hyman.

Dunning, John H. (October 1990) "Dunning on Porter," paper to the Annual Meeting of the Academy of International Business, Toronto.

Emerson, Michael (1988) *The Economics of 1992,* New York: Oxford University Press.

Etemad, Hamid and Seguin Dulude, Louise (1986) *Managing the Multinational Subsidiary,* London: Croom Helm.

Ghoshal, Sumantra (Spring 1988) "Environmental Scanning in Korean Firms: Organizational Isomorphism in Action," *Journal of International Business Studies,* 14(1), 69–86.

Gold, Marc and Leyton Brown, David (1988) *Trade-Offs on Free Trade,* Vancouver: Carswell.

Grant, Robert M. (October 1991) "Porter's Competitive Advantage of Nations: An Assessment," *Strategic Management Journal,* 12(7), 535–548.

Gray, Peter H. (Spring 1991) "International Competitiveness: A Review Article," *The International Trade Journal,* V, 503–517.

Hamel, G. and Prahalad, C.K. (1988) "Creating Global Strategic Capability," in Neil Hood and Jan-Erik Vahlne (eds.), *Strategies in Global Competition,* New York: Croom Helm.

Johanson, Jon and Mattsson, Lars-Gunnar (1988) "Internationalization in Industrial Systems—A Network Approach," in Neil Hood and Jan-Erik Vahlne (eds.), *Strategies in Global Competition,* New York: Croom Helm.

Julian, Scott D. and Keller, Robert T. (Fall 1991) "Multinational R&D Siting: Corporate Strategies for Success," *Columbia Journal of World Business,* 26(3), 46–57.

Morrison, Alan and Crookell, Harold (1991) "Free Trade: The Impact on Canadian Subsidiary Strategy," in Earl H. Fry and Lee H. Radebaugh (eds.), *Investment in the North American Free Trade Area: Opportunities and Challenges,* Provo, Utah: Brigham Young University.

Ohmae, Kenichi (1987) *Beyond National Borders,* Homewood, IL: Dow Jones–Irwin.

Porter, Michael E. (1990) *The Competitive Advantage of Nations,* New York: Free Press, Macmillan.

Porter, Michael E. and the Monitor Company (1991) *Canada at the Crossroads,* Ottawa: Business Council on National Issue.

Reich, Robert B. (March–April 1991) "Who Is Them?", *Harvard Business Review,* 69(2), 77–89.

Roth, Kendall and Morrison, Allen J. (1990) "An Empirical Analysis of the Integration-Responsiveness Framework in Global Industries," *Journal of International Business Studies,* 21(4), 541–564.

Rugman, Alan M. (Winter 1991) "Diamond in the Rough," *Business Quarterly,* 55(3), 61–64.

Rugman, Alan M. (Winter 1992) "Porter Takes the Wrong Turn," *Business Quarterly,* 56(3), 59–64.

Rugman, Alan M. and D'Cruz, Joseph R. (1991) *Fast Forward: Improving Canada's International Competitiveness,* Toronto: Kodak Canada, Inc.

Rugman, Alan M. and D'Cruz, Joseph R. (Spring 1993) "The Double Diamond Model: Canada's Experience," *Management International Review,* 33.

Rugman, Alan M. and Verbeke, Alain (1990) *Global Corporate Strategy and Trade Policy,* London and New York: Routledge.

Thompson, Arthur A. and Strickland, A.J. (1989) *Strategy Formulation and Implementation: Tasks of the General Manager* (4th ed.), Boston, MA: Richard D. Irwin.

Weihrich, Heinz (1990) "The TOWS Matrix: A Tool for Situation Analysis," in Robert G. Dyson (ed.), *Strategic Planning: Models and Analytical Techniques* (pp. 17–36), Chichester: John Wiley & Sons.

Westney, D. Eleanor (1990) "Internal and External Linkages in the MNE: The Case of R&D Subsidiaries in Japan," in C.A. Bartlett (ed.), *Managing the Global Firm* (pp. 279–302), London: Routledge.

White, Roderick E. and Poynter, Thomas A. (1990) "Organizing for World Wide Advantage," in C.A. Bartlett (ed.), *Managing the Global Firm* (pp. 95–116), London: Routledge.

Yoshida, Kosaku (Fall 1989) "Deming Management Philosophy: Does It Work in the U.S. as Well as in Japan?", *Columbia Journal of World Business,* 24(3), 10–17.

[19]

Environmental Regulations and International Competitiveness: Strategies for Canada's Forest Products Industry

Alan M. Rugman

INTRODUCTION

This article describes a case study of the manner in which environmental regulations in one country can affect the competitiveness of an industry from another country. An existing analytical base (Rugman and Verbeke, 1990, 1992) will be extended and applied to assess the impact of environmental regulations on the strategic management and competitiveness of Canadian firms, especially in the forestry sector. The work is generalizable because most industries from small, open, trading economies (like Canada's) need access to a triad market, like that of the United States.

The author is on the Faculty of Management, University of Toronto, 105 St. George Street, Toronto, Ontario, M5S 3E6, Canada.

A previous version of this article was first presented at the Academy of Management Division, Social Issues in Management, Dallas, August 1994 at the session on "Trade, Technology and the Environment." The author thanks participants at the session for their helpful comments and he also acknowledges the comments of participants at a seminar at the University of Toronto's Centre for International Business. Research support for this work on competitiveness was provided as part of a strategic grant by the Social Sciences and Humanities Research Council of Canada.

The International Executive, Vol. 37(5) 451–465 (September/October 1995)
© 1995 John Wiley & Sons, Inc.   CCC 0020-6652/95/050451-15

ENVIRONMENTAL REGULATIONS AND COMPETITIVENESS STRATEGY

The thesis of this study is that environmental regulations by large triad groups such as the European Community (EC) and the United States can pose nontariff barriers to entry to firms from small, open economies like Canada. The "asymmetry" in size between the triad markets, where economies of scale and scope are possible, and small, open economies, means that access to a triad market is required for a Canadian firm to develop a global strategy (see Rugman, 1994b). Knowing this, rival firms in the EC or United States can lobby for tighter environmental regulations within their regimes, thereby forcing outsiders to incur costs in conforming to triad-based measures, because the outsiders cannot afford to lose access to these critical markets. In other words, there is a potential incentive for US and EC firms to attempt to "capture" the administration of environmental laws and use them as entry barriers.

A related issue is that international trade law, with its emphasis on national treatment, does not fully compensate for the size asymmetry problem. The North American Free Trade Agreement (NAFTA) contains environmental provisions based on the principle of national treatment (see Rugman, 1994a), meaning that Canadian-based firms have an equal opportunity to adapt to new US environmental regulations along with their US rivals. Under NAFTA and the GATT, US-based environmentalists have no international trade rights to establish the extraterritoriality of domestic US environmental laws, because the principle of national treatment means that US laws cannot be applied to the sovereign jurisdictions of Canada and Mexico. Under NAFTA an environmental commission has been set up to ensure no lowering of environmental standards in the three member countries and to monitor policies designed to increase standards, but its entire operation is subject to the national treatment principle.

From the viewpoint of a Canadian firm selling its products to the large US market (such as in the lumber, fish, pork, wheat, or even steel sectors), a domestic US environmental regulation can affect its trade strategy. If domestic US laws are enforced against Canadian imports, entry could be denied Canadian produced products that do not comply with US environmental standards. Note that it is the US regulations that matter here, not the Canadian ones.

However, if US laws are tightened it can affect the strategy of Canadian firms. Because US market access is vital for most Canadian firms to achieve basic economies of scale in a globalized industry, denial of entry to Canadian exports will require a substitution of exports from Canada toward foreign direct investment in the United

States. Thus US environmental laws could force Canadian firms to take over US rival firms, or to open up new business behind the US environmental shield. Then, of course, the Canadian multinational enterprises (MNEs) would operate according to US practices, so US environmentalists would be happy. But Canadians may be unhappy at the forced transfer of business out of Canada and consumers in both Canada and the United States would suffer due to the loss of efficiency gains as the true comparative advantages of such Canadian—US industries are distorted by new US environmental regulations.

THEORETICAL LITERATURE

To analyze the use of environmental regulations as a strategy with asymmetric differences between firms in the triad and outsiders, it is useful to build upon the mainstream literature in strategic management. According to Porter (1990), a strong "home base" diamond is required to develop successful corporate strategies for national competitiveness. Furthermore, in an analysis of Canadian competitiveness, Porter and Armstrong (1992) argue that Canadian firms can only "tap into" the US market and its diamond characteristics and, at best, achieve parity with US rivals but never beat them. The principle of national treatment does, indeed, permit parity but parity is not a competitive advantage; the latter requires the ability to beat the average competitor.

In a related article Rugman (1994b), building on Rugman and Verbeke (1993b) and Rugman and D'Cruz (1991), argued that a "double diamond" approach to corporate strategy is required for Canadian managers. They need to understand both the Canadian and US diamonds and then they need to develop a North American strategy in order to have a chance of beating their US rivals. In developing a Canadian corporate strategy to deal with US environmental regulations, it is apparent that the double diamond approach offers very useful insights and guidelines. Indeed, Canadian managers who can move quickly to respond to such change are engaging in a form of "national responsiveness" (see Rugman and Verbeke, 1993b; and Rugman, 1994b).

This viewpoint, however, is not widely accepted, and has been explicitly rejected by Porter and Armstrong (1992). Instead, Porter and Monitor (1991) have been interpreted as advocating strong environmental regulations in Canada, the home base, so that its firms can embody these strengths in their sales abroad. This is the so-called "Porter Hypothesis." To be precise, in Porter and Monitor (1991) it is stated that:

> Stringent standards and regulations for product performance and environmental impact can create and upgrade competitive advantage by pressuring firms to improve product and process quality. Further, standards that anticipate international trends often have particularly beneficial benefits.

This is not a good recommendation for the two reasons discussed above. First, there is an asymmetry of market access to a triad market for Canadian-based firms with the small size of the "domestic" market not providing a strong enough base for new environmental strategies relative to the large US "foreign" market. Second, the double diamond framework suggests that it is difficult to build a supportive institutional framework in the Canadian diamond alone and that an understanding of US economic regulations is just as important as Canadian ones. Thus environmental policies in Canada's triad customers (the United States and EC) are much more relevant benchmarks for competitiveness strategies than are purely Canadian environmental policies.

Although the Porter policy recommendation may be relevant for a triad economy, it is entirely wrong for Canada, because over 70 percent of Canadian trade and investment is with the United States and the host country environmental regulations are much more important, for strategy, than Canadian home-based ones. In other words, the Porter hypothesis of tight, home-based environmental regulations completely ignores the asymmetry trap and the related issue of the need for triad market access for companies from smaller nations.

These issues of competitiveness, home and host country diamonds, national treatment, national size asymmetry, and market access are explored in this article, all as they relate to environmental regulations. The case example taken is the West Coast Canadian forest products cluster. For discussion of the institutional differences between the British Columbia (provincially owned) forestry system and the US Pacific Northwest "market-based" system, see Hoberg (1994). The international competitiveness of Canada's West Coast Forest Products Cluster has been analyzed in Rugman and D'Cruz (1991, 1993). The concept of "clusters" is found in Porter (1990) and has been adapted in a Canadian context by Rugman and D'Cruz (1991, 1993) and Rugman and Verbeke (1993a). Indeed, a distinction has been made between the competitiveness of regions, clusters, and business networks, in the discussion of the "five partners" framework of international competitiveness (see D'Cruz and Rugman, 1992, 1993). In the next sections this work on market access and asymmetry is reviewed; then it is applied to the issue of the impact of

environmental regulations on competitiveness, using the double diamond framework.

TRIAD MARKET ACCESS STRATEGIES FOR CANADIAN FOREST PRODUCTS

The Canadian forest products industry consists of two distinct clusters. First is the West Coast forest products cluster based in the
province of British Columbia (BC) and led by large MNEs like Mac-
Millan Bloedel and Fletcher Challenge. Second is the Eastern Canada
forest product cluster, including the Atlantic provinces, Quebec, and
Ontario. This cluster is led by paper and newsprint firms like Abitibi
Price, Stone Container, and Repap. The majority of sales of the BC
cluster goes to Asia and the United States, whereas the Eastern
Canadian cluster has a much bigger proportion of sales to Europe.

The Eastern Canada forest products cluster is potentially much
more affected by EC trade and environmental regulations than is the
West Coast cluster, although some recent measures also affect the
latter. For example, for many years there has been an EC quota on
newsprint sales from Canada, as well as other nontariff barriers to
trade such as discriminatory watermark requirements for paper
products. Recently the EC has pursued a series of environmental and
health regulations to shelter European business from Canadian competitors. One example, over the 1992–1994 period, has been the pine-
wood nematode regulation. This is designed to keep out Canadian
green lumber and force it to be kiln dried, thereby increasing the relative costs of Canadian compared to Scandinavian lumber. Other environmental regulations are proposed, especially in Germany, for example, to enforce the end of chlorine bleaching for pulp and paper
products (due to chemical side affects in Canadian waterways). Another environmental barrier to trade is the proposed ban against sales of
Canadian West Coast paper products in the EC due to the adverse
environmental affects of clear cutting (which led the British subsidiaries of two firms, Scott Paper and Kimberly Clark, to terminate
contracts in 1993 with Canadian suppliers of paper products, specifically in response to threats from Greenpeace to boycott their products).

Perhaps the most important example of environmental regulations affecting Canadian firms is state level newspaper recycling
laws, especially in California. This can be considered as such a significant factor that it may require a switch from exporting to foreign
direct investment by Canadian MNEs such as MacMillan Bloedel
and Noranda Forest Products. This subnational regulation could
have a major impact on the global strategy of Canada's West Coast

forest products cluster. The competitiveness issue is that a state level requirement for 50 percent recycled fiber in newsprint runs up against the logistical impossibility for Canadian firms in transporting old newspapers and magazines back to their "home base" newsprint mills in Canada. It is a regulation that discriminates in favor of US based mills against foreign ones. Given that approximately 80 percent of all newsprint produced in Canada is exported to the United States, it is too costly to transport enough of the used newsprint back to Canada and convert it for use in the Canadian mills. Instead, Canadian firms will need to access the "urban forest" of large American cities instead of the natural forest in British Columbia. To do so in an efficient manner they will need to make major capital investments in new deinking plants in California and other states with these environmental regulations. (This actually shifts the location of environmental pollution from Canada to California, because a deinking plant is basically a huge amount of chemical sludge close to a city.)

Such state level environmental laws will have profound repercussions on the strategic management of the forest products industry and it will benefit local US firms at the expense of foreign (Canadian) firms. The state laws are discriminatory in an international context. This occurs despite NAFTA giving Canadian firms national treatment because the California type laws are applied equally to Canadian and US firms. Yet the size asymmetry effect will force Canadian firms out of their home base and destroy Canada's comparative advantage in resources. To survive in this global business, Canadian firms are forced to switch from exporting from British Columbia to foreign direct investment in California.

The legality, or illegality, of such laws is not the issue. What matters is the impact on Canadian firms of denying them market access to a triad economy. When subnational levels of government impose such indirect barriers to international trade and commerce, these laws effectively discriminate against foreign producers and protect domestic producers. This is an example of the theory of "shelter," as developed by Rugman and Verbeke (1990, 1992). Given that shelter exists, how can Canadian firms react? The next sections outline a strategic rationale for Canadian firms to be nationally responsive to US environmental regulations.

THE DOUBLE DIAMOND AND CANADIAN COMPETITIVENESS IN FOREST PRODUCTS

The relevant conceptual tool for Canadian managers to employ when developing a global competitive advantage is that of a North American double diamond. Strategies for Canadian businesses need to be designed across both the US and Canadian diamonds (see Rugman and D'Cruz, 1991, 1993). For an American business, the US market is large enough to provide rivalry, customers, and supporting infrastructure and demand conditions to the extent that the home nation diamond tests and hones the ability of its firms to compete successfully. Yet, the Canadian market has not and does not offer such rigors and opportunity. It is for this key reason of asymmetry that Canadian firms should not in theory (and do not in practice) consider the US market as an export market but as an extension of the domestic (Canadian) market. More specifically, Canadian managers look to North America as a regional home base and do not use a single Canadian home base diamond. This double diamond thinking is illustrated in Figure 1.

For US-based MNEs, Porter's (1990) single diamond model makes conceptual sense but it is made operational due to the special case of the United States as a triad market. US-based multinationals have grown up in a large domestic market that provided opportunity for product development and economies of scale (Rugman, 1992). The size and attractiveness of the US market is reflected in the fact that US-based multinationals typically garner 20–40 percent of their revenues from foreign sales versus 60–90 percent for Canadian-based multinationals (see Globerman, 1994). Another ex-

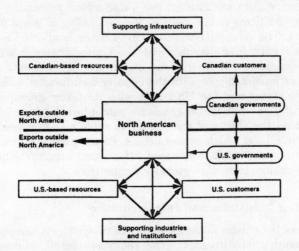

Figure 1 Double diamond framework

Source: Adapted from Alan M. Rugman and Joseph R. D'Cruz, *Fast Forward: Improving Canada's International Competitiveness* (Toronto: Kodak Canada, 1991).

ample of a Canadian-type company with too small a domestic national diamond is Nestlé, which obtains 95 percent of its revenues from outside Switzerland. (This latter point was also made by Dunning, 1993).

The relevance of the North American double diamond for Canadian strategic management has been discussed elsewhere (see Rugman, 1992; Rugman and D'Cruz, 1993; Rugman, 1994b; Rugman and Verbeke, 1993a). To build a global business, Canadian firms need access to a triad market. Companies in the forest products industry on Canada's West Coast benefit from relative nearness to two of these triad markets, the United States and Japan. Across Canada, there are clusters of industries in which firms face competition from close rivals, draw inputs from supporting industries and infrastructure, and depend upon the close availability of physical and human resources. In work by Rugman and D'Cruz (1991) building on Porter's (1990) use of strategic clusters, several such clusters of industries are readily identifiable in Canada. The competitiveness of the West Coast forest products cluster can be analyzed using Figure 1. This is a straightforward application of Porter (1990) as modified by Rugman and D'Cruz (1991, 1993).

Resource Base

The widespread forests of British Columbia and parts of western Alberta offer a close and easily accessible physical resource/input for the cluster. Within the cluster, low value-added processing or raw product opens firms to the risks of the cyclicality of world demand and prices. The competitiveness of this cluster is affected by trade sanctions arising from disputes with the United States over alleged industry subsidies (for further discussion see Governments below). The cluster must compete with the equally well-forested US Pacific Northwest states and the US South with its faster growing trees. Increasingly, environmental concerns and interest group lobbying are affecting the ability of the cluster to exploit and process/refine this resource base which impacts costs. Forest products firms have heavily unionized work forces that affects cost structures and the ability to change to remain globally competitive.

Supporting Industries and Infrastructure

This part of the cluster is not as widely developed as is necessary for international competitiveness. The relatively small economies of British Columbia and Alberta hinder the depth of this infrastructure.

Customers

The domestic market of Western Canada does not provide a large enough base of demanding customers to support the development of new, globally competitive products and services. The United States has served this purpose in some product lines and continued focus on the North American customer will improve product development. Demanding customers, like those in more competitive markets such as the United States and where consumer demands for quality are paramount such as Japan, help push firms to focus on the production of higher value-added products. This focus is necessary to reduce dependence on the depth of the resource base (the forests) and public subsidies.

Leading Firms

MacMillan Bloedel is the largest company in the cluster and has been recognized as a leader in the industry. Continued growth of competitors should enhance the ability of the cluster to develop internationally competitive products and advantages.

Governments

Both Canadian government policy (at provincial level of course) and US government policy is important. The BC government from 1990–1994 increased the taxation of BC-based forest product companies through changes in the stumpage rates and other methods. The Canadian Federal Government has helped to organize legal defense against ongoing US countervailing duty cases (see Stranks, 1994). US use of countervailing duty and the abusive use of this type of administered protection has meant that Canadian exporters have been forced to participate in legal cases before the US International Trade Commission and the US Department of Commerce on an almost continual basis since 1983 when three major countervail cases were heard (see Anderson, 1995). The direct legal costs of the 1991–1994 case and appeals has run to over Cdn $40 million for Canadian firms. Elements of a nationally responsive strategy are beginning to appear, for example when a Canadian firm persuaded the US home builders association to file an intervention on their behalf stating that a countervail duty on imports of Canadian softwood lumber would increase US house prices. But, in general, Canadian firms have been slow to adopt a full double diamond strategy and they have relied too much on the Canadian government to carry the ball instead of making a US play themselves.

Clusters

Porter (1990) also says that a nation's industries tend to cluster for synergistic purposes and that national competitiveness depends upon success in clusters of industries, not just in isolated industries. This clustering occurs in the home base single diamond and competitiveness is measured by exports or outward foreign direct investment. According to Porter, successful industries develop both vertical (buyer and supplier) and horizontal (customers, distribution channels, technology sharing) relationships that, combined with the "systemic" nature of the diamond, help to create other successful and competitive industries. Moreover, this replication of success is alleged by Porter to occur in both large and small countries, although the nature of the clusters varies according to national/regional-specific factors like legislation and industrial/union history.

Porter's view of clustering needs to be modified to take account of the double diamond. The West Coast forest products cluster will not evolve toward a more efficient and competitive system within its home base. The increase in US environmental, and other protectionist, regulations means that its cluster is now transborder. Several good examples of clustering in economies similar in nature to Canada's highlight this double diamond process. Sweden has a competitive pulp and paper industry and draws on the forest resource much like British Columbia does. However, unlike Canada, Sweden has preferential access to the EC triad market, and this helps it to be internationally competitive in related industries such as sulfur boilers, paper making machinery, paper drying machinery, wood handling machinery, etc. The reinforcing nature of a cluster in developing competitiveness in related industries is illustrated sharply by the fact that Sweden is competitive in chemicals required for pulp and paper making but not in chemicals in general (Porter, 1990: 149). But Porter fails to note that if Sweden did not have secure market access to the EC, its competitiveness and cluster development would have been slower, as is the danger in British Columbia.

While Porter's views on the single home diamond of competitiveness and the clustering of industries are necessary background (and relevant for triad-based clusters), they need to be modified and adapted in Canada for the asymmetry reasons given earlier. Canadian corporate strategy must necessarily be less nationalist and home-country oriented than Porter implies. Canadian forest products firms are competing not just against other Canadian or American or Swedish forest product firms; they are competing with US firms and clusters who can exploit US laws and environmental regulations and deny market access. If Swedish pulp and paper firms (who have secure access to the EC) benefit from equipment innovation, chemical process improvement, etc. derived from cluster relationships, then they are likely to gain cost and/or product advantages over Canadian firms (who are being denied access to the EC and the United States). In any case, Canadian firms are finding it harder to get their products into protected US and EC markets. Thus the vital amendment to Porter's home base, single diamond cluster thinking is the critical issue of market access. To achieve this requires a strategy of national responsiveness (see Rugman, 1994b).

ENVIRONMENTAL REGULATIONS AND CORPORATE STRATEGY

Figure 2 brings together these issues of firm-level strategy with and without a firm's interaction with government. This is a simple variation of the Bartlett and Ghoshal (1989) framework of globalization and national responsiveness. On the horizontal axis is depicted the firm's responsiveness to environmental regulations, low and high. (No distinction needs to be made on this axis between domestic and foreign firms, although the matrix will be used later to illustrate the arguments developed in this article.) On the vertical axis is shown the firm's commitment to pure globalization (such as increased market share and/or profitability), that is, ignoring any environmental considerations.

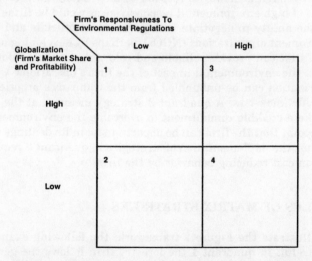

Figure 2 Environmental regulations and corporate strategy

There are some firms that are potentially concerned with both globalization and environmental responsiveness. These are in quadrant 3, and will be discussed in detail below. There are other firms who ignore environmental regulations and have a single minded focus on globalization. These are the traditional "business first" efficiency-driven firms in quadrant 1. These are the firms identified by environmentalists as ignoring environmental issues, which is quite true in quadrant 1, because a competitive advantage can be achieved by efficiency-driven strategies alone, such as price competition. In contrast, conceptually at least, there can be firms in quadrant 4 that are so highly responsive to environmental regulations that they can ignore the firm's objective of globalization. In quadrant 4 the firm can beat other firms solely on its environmental responsiveness strategy. While both quadrants 1 and 4 have potentially viable strategies, the unfortunate firms in quadrant 2 whose globalization and environmental commitment are both low, are losers. This indicates the need to change strategies in order to move out of quadrant 2.

Potentially the most interesting quadrant to consider is number 3. The significance of a quadrant 3 strategy is that it suggests that a firm can beat other firms by combining managerial skills in globalization and environmental responsiveness. This, of course, is not easy to accomplish. The firm must make a major investment in the development of green management skills, such as the ability to adapt quickly to government imposed regulations; indeed, it is the ability to anticipate such changes in policy that will give the firm a competitive edge over rivals slower to respond to environmental pressures. Examples of high environmental responsiveness would be firms that develop the ability to negotiate with government officials and with non-government organizations (NGOs), perhaps by developing a special team that can provide reliable and relevant scientific information about the environmental impact of the firm's operations, where this information can be unbundled from the company's proprietary firm-specific know-how. A quadrant 3 strategy means that the firm must make a credible commitment to overcome the environmentalists' viewpoint that the firm can be opportunistic in its dealings with them. Thus, the implementation of strategies in quadrant 3 requires transaction cost reducing behavior by the firm.

EXAMPLES OF MATRIX STRATEGIES

To help illustrate the Figure 2 framework, the following examples may be useful. In quadrant 1 the forestry firm follows the generic strategies of cost, differentiation, or finding a global niche. In the case of newsprint and paper producers the firm can be a "low cost polluter," that is, its competitive advantage is derived from price competition and it ignores environmental issues. Many environmentalists simply assume that all producers are in quadrant 1, following economic, efficiency-driven strategies that ignore environmental externalities. For example, the Canadian forest products sector has been accused of ignoring the effects of chlorine bleaching in the production of BC newsprint.

In quadrant 4 the opposite strategy is followed, that is, the firm ignores efficiency-driven globalization issues and concentrates only on being responsive to environmental regulations; indeed the firm tries to anticipate new environmental thinking. This is a "green alone" strategy. Here firms can beat the average competitor by having firm-specific advantages in responsiveness to environmental regulations. There are few firms today in quadrant 4, which is a pity from the viewpoint of Greenpeace, as it would like regulations to be stringent enough to force firms into quadrant 4. Some firms may develop environmental technologies at home due to stringent domestic environmental regulations and then export such products or services. This is a green alone export strategy, and there are a few examples of such companies doing business in Mexico since NAFTA.

Quadrant 2 deals with local products and services where environmental issues are ignored, that is, a "local polluter." Many observers allege that some of Mexico's manufacturing sector is in quadrant 2.

Quadrant 3 is theoretically attractive but practically difficult to achieve. It is desirable because both economic efficiency and environmental responsiveness is achieved but this dual focus requires a mixed (or matrix) organizational structure that few firms can develop. To implement a quadrant 3 strategy would require combining the talents of efficiency-driven accountants, economists, and production managers with the sensitivity and responsiveness skills of marketing and government relations managers.

One interesting potential difference between quadrants 3 and 4 in terms of environmental strategies is that firms in quadrant 3 could possibly succeed with *compliance* to environmental regulations whereas, in quadrant 4, a more proactive strategy is required. In other words, to beat the average competitor on environment alone requires the anticipation of new environmental regulations and the design of a firm-specific advantage.

Canadian firms that pursue quadrant 1 strategies in Figure 2 are in danger, and they need to develop quadrant 3 strategies. In the long run, perhaps Canadian firms in quadrant 3 can even beat US rivals. There is little evidence of much movement from quadrant 1 to 3 in

industries such as lumber, steel, pork, and others where the FTA and
NAFTA dispute settlement panels have been used frequently as nation to nation conflicts are pushed along by corporate rivalry.

To summarize, for sensible reasons of corporate survival, Canadian firms must adopt strategies to comply with the increased environmental regulations of larger triad countries like the United
States. The size asymmetry of the small open trading economy versus the large triad market means that the larger market's environmental standards become the norm for strategic decision making
when there are adverse repercussions in global consumer welfare.
From this perspective environmental regulations are economically
inefficient, but need to be dealt with through corporate strategy.

REFERENCES

Anderson, A. (1995) *Seeking Common Ground: An Analysis of the Canada–
U.S. Dispute Settlement Cases,* Boulder, CO: Westview Press.
Bartlett, C.A. and Ghoshal, S. (1989) *Managing Across Borders: The Trans-
national Solution,* Boston, MA: Harvard Business School Press.
D'Cruz, J.R. and Rugman, A.M. (1992) "Business Networks for Internation-
al Competitiveness," *Business Quarterly,* 56, 101–107.
D'Cruz, J.R. and Rugman, A.M. (1993) "Developing International Compet-
itiveness: The Five Partners Model," *Business Quarterly,* 58, 60–72.
Dunning, J.H. (1993) *The Globalization of Business: The Challenge of the
1990s,* London: Routledge.
Globerman, S. (Ed.) (1994) *Canadian-Based Multinationals,* Calgary: Uni-
versity of Calgary Press.
Hoberg, G. (1994) *Regulating Forestry: A Comparison of British Columbia
and the U.S. Pacific Northwest,* Discussion paper, School of Policy Studies,
Queen's University, 94–107.
Porter, M.E. (1990) *The Competitive Advantage of Nations,* New York: The
Free Press.
Porter, M.E. and Armstrong, J. (1992) "Canada at the Crossroads: Dia-
logue," *Business Quarterly,* Spring, 8–12.
Porter, M.E. and Monitor (1991) *Canada at the Crossroads,* Business Coun-
cil on National Issues, Ottawa, Canada.
Rugman, A.M. (1992) "Porter Takes the Wrong Turn," *Business Quarterly,*
56, 59–64.
Rugman, A.M. (Ed.) (1994a) *Foreign Investment and NAFTA,* Columbia SC:
University of South Carolina Press.
Rugman, A.M. (1994b) "Strategic Management and Canadian Multination-
al Enterprises," in S. Globerman (Ed.), *Canadian-Based Multinationals,*
Calgary: University of Calgary Press, 241–262.
Rugman, A.M. and D'Cruz, J.R. (1991) *Fast Forward: Improving Canada's
International Competitiveness,* Canada: Kodak Canada Inc.

Rugman, A.M. and D'Cruz, J.R. (1993) "The 'Double Diamond' Model of International Competitiveness," *Management International Review*, 33, 17–40.

Rugman, A.M. and Verbeke, A. (1990) *Global Corporate Strategy and Trade Policy*, London: Routledge.

Rugman, A.M. and Verbeke, A. (1992) "Shelter, Trade Policy and Strategies for Multinational Enterprises," in A.M. Rugman and A. Verbeke (Eds.), *Research in Global Strategic Management, Vol. 3, Corporate Response to Global Change*, Greenwich, CT: JAI Press, 3–25.

Rugman, A.M. and Verbeke, A. (1993a) "Foreign Subsidiaries and Multinational Strategic Management: An Extension and Correction of Porter's Single Diamond Framework," *Management International Review*, 33 (Special Issue 2), 71–84.

Rugman, A.M. and Verbeke, A. (1993b) "Generic Strategies in Global Competition," in *Research in Global Strategic Management, Vol. 4, Beyond the Three Generics*, Greenwich, CT: JAI Press, 3–16.

Stranks, R.T. (1994) *Pandora's Box?: Countervailing Duties and the Environment*, Department of Foreign Affairs and International Trade, Ottawa, Canada.

PART IV

FREE TRADE AND NAFTA

[20]

Corporate Strategy and the Free Trade Agreement: Adjustment by Canadian Multinational Enterprises

Alan M. Rugman, Alain Verbeke, and Stephen Luxmore
Faculty of Management
University of Toronto
Toronto, ON M5S 1V4

The strategic responses of four Canadian multinational enterprises (MNEs) to the Canada-U.S. Free Trade Agreement (FTA) are used here to examine Canadian corporate competitiveness. The predicted responses of the firms to the FTA were gathered using an analytical framework that assesses the diverging strategic needs of the firms. These predictions are then confirmed by data gathered through interviews with and questionnaire surveys of key firm personnel.

The impact of trade liberalization on the strategies of business firms has been the subject of a growing body of literature. The main contribution of Dunning and Robson (1987), a recent overview, is its analysis of the interrelationships between regional economic integration and the international expansion strategies of MNEs. Most of the managerially oriented literature on this topic is related to one of three issues: (1) the impact of free trade on the competitive position of firms vis-à-vis international rivals (see Magun, Rao, and Lodh 1987; Magun et al. 1988); (2) the effects of trade liberalization on the choice of entry mode to serve foreign markets, especially the choice between exports and foreign direct investment (FDI) and the degree of complementarity of entry modes (see, for example, Rugman 1990); and (3) the impact of the changed trading environment on the internal restructuring of MNEs, especially the transformation of subsidiaries from "miniature replicas" into globally rationalized business operations or "domestic" firms with world product mandates (see, for example, Hood and Young 1987). In each case, the regional economic implication of the restructuring process involves a shift from a Canadian national focus toward a global focus.

© Canadian Journal of Regional Science/Revue canadienne des sciences régionales, XIII:2/3 (Summer-Autumn/été-automne 1990), 307-330.
ISSN: 0705-4580   Printed in Canada/Imprimé au Canada

Little research has been done, however, on the need for strategic adaptation processes to be responsive to the diverging needs of the different strategic business units (SBUs) within one firm. Studies that have focused on strategic adjustment primarily discuss strategies at the corporate level, or perhaps at the level of a single plant or division (see Crookell 1987, 1989; D'Cruz and Fleck 1988a, 1988b; Rugman and Verbeke 1988, 1989, 1990; Rutenberg 1988; Wolf 1986, 1989).

The framework developed in this article assesses the diverging needs of the strategic business units on the basis of the perceived impact of trade liberalization on their firm-specific factors (FSFs) and country-specific factors (CSFs). These FSFs and CSFs are analogous to the Rugman et al. (1985) concept of firm-specific advantages and country-specific advantages. But whereas that work analyzed the performance of successful MNEs, we are dealing here with SBUs that might have been uncompetitive before, or perhaps after, the FTA. Thus, we have allowed for negative or non-existent country- or firm-specific factors.

The country-specific factors are interesting from a regional perspective. In spite of increased international economic integration, CSFs remain extremely important as a source of a firm's international competitiveness. But business firms can remain successful global competitors only if they build upon both FSFs and CSFs simultaneously. If locational advantages are reduced or non-existent, a corporation's success in the marketplace may be severely affected. The framework developed here—which is meant to be of direct use to corporate managers—integrates the internalization paradigm of international business from Rugman et al. (1985) with the strategic management perspective developed by Porter (1980, 1985, 1986).

This article has five sections. The first develops the framework utilized in the analysis, and section two introduces the four MNEs analyzed and presents our methodology. The third section discusses the positioning of the SBUs before the FTA. The projected impact of the FTA on the SBUs is then assessed in the fourth section. The final section summarizes the findings and presents the authors' conclusions.

Internalization Theory: Trade Liberalization and the Analytical Framework

A multinational enterprise is a firm that has production activities in at least two countries. Internalization theory, as developed by Rugman (1981), demonstrates that to be successful abroad an MNE must possess proprietary knowledge—that is, a firm-specific factor to compensate for the additional costs (for example, for information) associated with doing business abroad. The theory also holds that subsidiaries are set up to serve the foreign market if the net benefits of internalizing the FSF (that is, its use within the firm) across borders are higher than the net benefits resulting from other modes of entry—for example, through the use of exports, licencing, or joint ventures.

From a regional economic perspective, the concept of country-specific factors is also important as each internalization decision takes into consideration the context of a specific location for the production operation. The CSFs of a nation include its factor endowments, market characteristics, and government regulations. A CSF always relates to a national characteristic with the potential for either a positive or a negative impact on a firm's competitiveness. It is reflected in the firm's ability to provide cheap products (low-cost strategy) or products perceived as unique (differentiation strategy) to its customers as compared to the products of rival companies, including other MNEs. It should be recognized that CSFs can differ from one region to another—even within one country. But in the context of bilateral trade liberalization between countries, we assume, for simplicity, that the impact of free trade on nationwide CSFs is more important than interregional changes in CSFs (or location advantages) within one nation. From a national perspective, only the total net impact of free trade on the economy (including the issue of adjustment costs) is relevant.

The analysis developed in this article is primarily at the micro level. The relevance of the concepts of FSFs and CSFs will be demonstrated through their use in the strategic positioning of four MNEs. The actual unit of analysis will be the SBU. Each SBU within one MNE can be defined as a set of product market lines sharing the same FSFs, and, within one firm, there may be different SBUs that depend in part on different types of FSFs. From a regional perspective, each SBU may face a specific set of environmental parameters determining, for example, its geographic scope and therefore generating a different bundle of CSFs.

From an internalization perspective, trade liberalization can have two main effects. First, it can either strengthen or weaken the country-specific factors. In the Canadian context, "strengthening" implies that the competitive position of operations located in Canada improves (for example, because easier access to a larger market improves the possibility of obtaining scale economies). "Weakening" refers to the deterioration of a firm's competitive position. Second, because the country-specific factors and firm-specific factors are interdependent, the impact of a change in CSFs on the FSFs of each strategic business unit must be analyzed. If the CSFs are strengthened, the improvement may be internalized into the FSFs of an SBU, and there may be a corresponding change in competitive position in terms of obtaining additional benefits of scale, scope, and the exploitation of national differences. But if the CSFs are weakened, this may affect the FSFs of an SBU by eliminating one of the building blocks of the FSFs (for example, a relative cost advantage is eliminated when foreign rivals with scale economies begin serving the Canadian market). The weakening of the CSFs may also may occur when a government shelter is reduced in cases in which the shelter was used as a substitute for the existence of strong FSFs.

Depending on whether foreign direct investment (FDI) and exports are substitutes or complements, the geographical configuration of a SBU's operations may be altered after trade liberalization. This occurs in cases in which unnatural market imperfections, or trade barriers, rather than natural market imperfections, such as the public goods nature of know-how, are responsible for the choice of FDI over exports to serve a particular market.

Following the integration of the internalization model and the competitive strategy framework developed by Porter (1980, 1985, 1986), changes due to the FTA in each SBU's set of FSFs and CSFs can be analyzed in terms of their impact on the firm's potential cost-reducing or differentiation-enhancing capabilities. This will determine the MNE's capacity to pursue successfully a particular cost- or differentiation-based strategy both domestically and abroad.

The above analysis is represented in Figure 1. Each SBU of an MNE can be positioned in one of the four quadrants according to the relative strength of its FSFs and CSFs as compared with those of rival firms. The strengths of the FSFs and CSFs were determined by the authors on the basis of an ongoing cross-sectional assessment of the skills and environmental characteristics of the firms involved (for an early analysis, see Rugman and McIlveen 1985). A strong parameter implies the potential for at least average industry profitability and stabilization of market share in the relevant market.

Complementary information is represented in Figure 1 by the cost-reducing (CR) or differentiation-enhancing (DE) characteristics of strong CSFs and FSFs. Thus, quadrant 1 of Figure 1 is divided into four cells, each of which reflects the nature of the strong FSFs and CSFs. One SBU may be positioned in two or more cells of quadrant 1 simultaneously, depending on its FSFs and CSFs. Quadrants 2 and 3 each contain two cells, allowing determination of the nature of the strong CSFs and FSFs benefiting the SBU. A SBU can be positioned in both cells of either quadrant 2 or quadrant 3 simultaneously. Quadrant 4 contains SBUs with weak or non-existent FSFs and CSFs. The

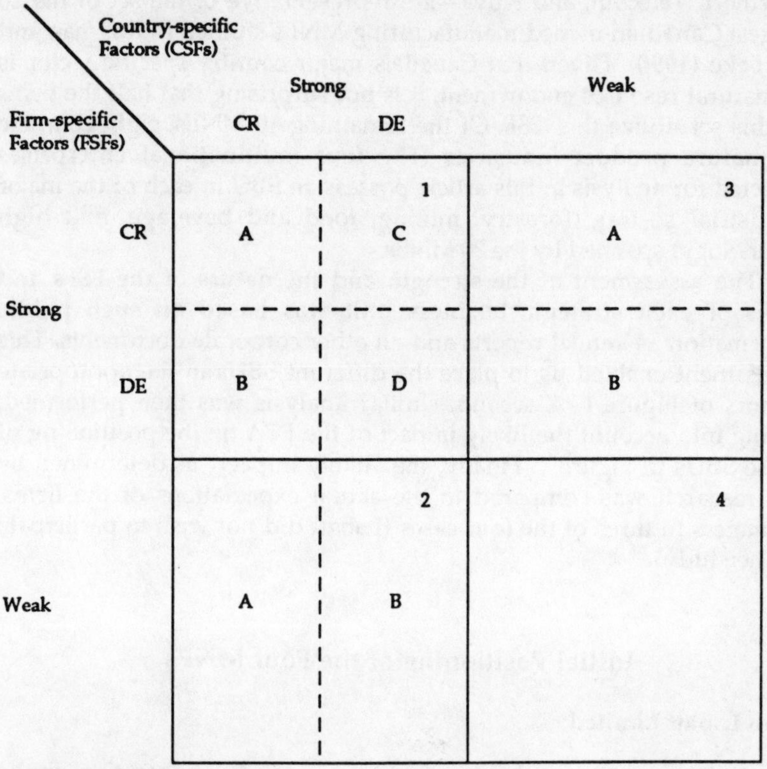
Country-specific Factors (CSFs)
Firm-specific Factors (FSFs)
Strong
Weak
CR
DE
CR
DE
1
3
A
C
A
B
D
B
2
4
A
B
Strong
Weak

CR = Cost Reducing
DE = Differentiation Enhancing

FIGURE 1 Competitive positioning of multinational strategic business units

implication is that such an SBU cannot survive over the longer term without the development of a FSF.

To assess the impact of the Free Trade Agreement on the strategic SBUs of an MNE, we examine whether the FTA will cause a shift in the positioning of the different SBUs in Figure 1. Such shifts can occur either directly, from a change in CSFs, or indirectly, through the impact of an external change on the CSFs or FSFs. For example, in the latter case a relative change in location of an SBU may affect the MNE's profitability and market share by changing its internal cost-reducing and differentiation-enhancing capabilities.

Four multinational enterprises were selected for strategic-positioning analysis at the strategic business unit level. The SBUs were then analyzed for changes in strategic positioning subsequent to the FTA. The four firms—John Labatt Limited, Noranda Incorporated, Northern Telecom, and Nova—are representative of the set of the 20 largest Canadian-owned manufacturing MNEs studied in Rugman and Verbeke (1990). Given that Canada's major country-specific factor is its natural resource endowment, it is not surprising that half the firms in this set utilize this CSF. Of the remaining 10 MNEs, eight compete in mature product industries. The four multinational enterprises selected for analysis in this article possess an SBU in each of the major industrial sectors (forestry, mining, food and beverage, and high technology) spanned by the 20 MNEs.

The assessment of the strength and the nature of the FSFs and CSFs of each strategic business unit was based on such public information as annual reports and on other corporate documents. This assessment enabled us to place the different SBUs in the appropriate sectors of Figure 1. A second, similar analysis was then performed, taking into account the likely impact of the FTA on the positioning of these SBUs in Figure 1. Finally, the "likely impact" as determined by the research was compared to the actual expectations of the firms' managers in three of the four cases (Labatt did not wish to participate in the study).

Initial Positioning of the Four MNEs

John Labatt Limited

Labatt is a management holding company comprising operations in the food and beverage industry. The firm experienced sustained growth of assets employed and revenues (an increase of 78.1 percent and 93.2 percent, respectively) between 1985 and 1989, a period during which it was expanding geographically. Labatt is 96.9 percent Canadian-held; the principal shareholder is Brascan Limited, which in 1989 had a 41 percent interest, but Brascan intends to increase this to 50 percent. Within the two operating groups of Labatt—the Brewing Group and the Food Group—12 SBUs were identified.

Brewing Group. Before the FTA, the Brewing Group dominated an industry in which three firms accounted for 95 percent of sales. Indeed, the Brewing Group's market share increased from 36.8 percent in 1979 to 42 percent in 1989. Under the FTA, Labatt has successfully maintained its status in the beer industry because of its lobbying to maintain shelter. The firm is being forced, however, to respond to a global market and its resulting pressures.

Although the Brewing Group is attempting to enter foreign markets, its activities are, for the most part, centered on the Canadian market. Currently, the Brewing Group is located in quadrant 1, cells C and D, of Figure 1. The firm enjoys the country-specific factor of a protected market—the result of interprovincial trading restrictions imposed by the provincial governments. Its dual strong firm-specific factors are found in marketing skills, which are differentiation enhancing, and in provincial scale economies in the protected markets, which are cost reducing.

The Brewing Group has strong differentiation-enhancing and weak cost-reducing CSFs. Although the interprovincial trading restrictions have made it possible for Labatt to be a low-cost brewer in Canada, they also have forced Labatt to operate smaller and more inefficient plants as compared to its global-scale competitors, thus generating a negative cost-reducing CSF. But these restrictions have also enhanced the firm's marketing skills by creating an environment conducive to responding to regional tastes with regional brands and, thus, a strong differentiation-enhancing CSF.

Indeed, the brand loyalty enjoyed by the Brewing Group, along with its distribution network, act as effective entry barriers in the domestic market and may, in fact, have implications for the smallest regional production units of Labatt and other producers facing global competition. For example, one particular brand of beer in the Maritimes enjoys such a large market share that even if its market were subject to international competition, this brand could survive, and production would most likely stay in the Maritimes because of the small market and short production runs required. Such regional barriers to entry tend to partially offset the global cost disadvantage of Labatt Brewing.

The wine-producing unit, Chateau-Gai, had successfully entered the wine-based "cooler" market in Canada, but the operation suffered from the weak CSFs of high input costs and a relatively short growing season. The cost-reducing FSFs were weak as well because of a lack of scale economies. Moreover, for the wine product lines brand loyalty was questionable since Canadian wines do not in general enjoy a good reputation, even within Canada. This business unit, positioned in quadrant 4 of Figure 1, was sold in fiscal year 1989.

Food Group. The Labatt Food Group has strong marketing skills, and it has developed the distribution channels and brand identification aspects necessary for success in a competitive market.

Retail dairy market production units operate in Canada (Ault Foods) and the United States (Johanna Dairies). Although both producers possess differentiation-enhancing firm-specific factors, they also both face a high degree of price competition, especially in the table milk market. In response to the latter, both divisions are rationalizing operations to further lower production costs. Ault Foods, which has a 35-40 percent market share in Ontario, has the capability to be the lowest-cost producer in its Canadian markets. In contrast, Johanna Dairies is faced with a cost disadvantage resulting from operating difficulties and the acquisitions of inefficient plants and emphasized by the highly competitive market in which it operates. Johanna has closed or modernized the inefficient dairies in an attempt to become a low-cost producer. The firm claims that its recently reopened Baltimore dairy is one of the most efficient in the United States. Both Johanna and Ault operate in an environment of strong differentiation-enhancing CSFs (high income, intelligent consumers, excellent media). But because of agricultural price-fixing in Canada, Ault is subject to a weak cost-reducing CSF, while Johanna enjoys a relatively strong CSF is this area. This would position Ault Foods and Johanna, respectively, in quadrant 1 CD and 1 BD of Figure 1.

Ogilvie, a grain-processing SBU, is difficult to position. Recent plant rationalizations indicate that its cost-reducing FSFs have been strengthened, and its exports to the United States have created the potential for economies of scale. Ogilvie most likely possesses dual strong FSFs, allowing it to become the largest producer of wheat starch and gluten in the world. Since domestic wheat prices exceed world wheat prices, Ogilvie is located in quadrant 1 CD of Figure 1.

Several American operations of the Labatt Foods Group derive their CSFs and FSFs from agricultural resources and marketing skills, respectively. The operations Chef Francisco, Delicious Foods, Oregon Farms, and the U.S. operations of Everfresh Juice are all located in quadrant 1 BD of Figure 1. The other American member of Labatt Foods, Pasquale, is in quadrant 1 ABCD because of its strong FSFs in distribution channels and in-store marketing skills, used particularly effectively in preparation booths and merchandising support. The cost advantage of Pasquale is a function of size and the related economies of scale. The Canadian operations of Everfresh Juice are most likely situated in quadrant 1 D because of the higher input costs in Canada relative to those in the United States. The strong differentiation-enhancing FSFs are derived from brand recognition and distribution channels.

Before its sale and subsequent breakup, the Catelli SBU was engaged in the manufacture of groceries. The unit is positioned in quadrant 1 D of Figure 1 because of its access to agricultural products and its marketing abilities. Its differentiation-enhancing FSFs were strong given the brand names—Catelli, Habitant, and Five Roses—

and the distribution network of the unit. Its cost-reducing FSFs were weak because of the high domestic wheat prices set by the Canadian government; these prices put Canadian operations at a competitive disadvantage when compared, for example, with those of European producers. Expansion into the U.S. market through foreign direct investment may have helped offset the weak cost-reducing CSFs faced by Catelli by making it more cost competitive (it had four American plants), but because of its cost disadvantage, Labatt decided to divest this SBU.

Noranda

Noranda is the stereotypical Canadian MNE—a natural resource extractor encompassing the mining, forestry, and energy sectors. But the firm engages in activities that extend far beyond extraction: Noranda is increasing its output of value-added products; it is committed to a significant marketing effort; and it has diversified into such areas as fibre optics technology. Three of its four divisions (minerals, forestry, and manufacturing) have revenues in excess of $1 billion annually, and the fourth division, energy, has grown significantly with recent acquisitions. These four divisions also constitute Noranda's core SBUs.

Minerals. In the minerals division, the most important country-specific factor is Canadian resources. Noranda's mineral deposits are close to major markets and to its downstream manufacturing facilities. The division has access to skilled labour, and it has internalized this CSF into an FSF, as illustrated by the productivity gains and cost reductions realized in many of its operations. These two factors are essential to any firm wanting to be a low-cost producer. Noranda states that cost is a function of ore grade, productivity, and technology (engineering expertise). The ore grades found in Canada—especially those employed by Noranda—are high, as are the skilled labour functions at the blue-collar level and in the engineering department.

Noranda Sales, which works closely with buyers to help them develop both new uses for Noranda's products and new markets, is moving the minerals division from a production orientation toward a customer orientation. This requires research and development and, equally important, prompt responses. The minerals division is internalizing the marketing function, and, since customer contact is essential for the firm to remain informed of market trends, brokers are now rarely used.

The weaknesses of the minerals division stem from the cyclical price structure of minerals, increased competition in the form of buyers switching to new suppliers, and the replacement of minerals with plastics, ceramics, and so forth. This SBU builds primarily on its strong cost-reducing FSFs. It has recorded numerous productivity gains, but it has encountered a very competitive market. Because the division produces industrial output, it is difficult to differentiate it physically (and its promotion of its industry goods) from the other materials used in its place. This has the disadvantage of benefiting all mineral producers. Differentiation will most likely take the form of service—of becoming more customer-responsive by participating in product development and by supplying customer-specified inputs. Although in its publications Noranda emphasizes the need for further value-added production, examples of substantial progress in this area are few. The division seems to be having difficulty in switching from a low-cost strategy to a differentiation, or dual, strategy. It is now located in quadrant 1 A of Figure 1.

Forestry. Noranda's forestry division faces increased international competition, and it too is moving toward the production of higher value-added products. The main country-specific factor of this division is its resource base, which includes the FSF of its large cutting rights. The access to skilled labour in both the woodlands operations and the production processes is a strong CSF, internalized to an FSF. The division has strived to reduce costs and increase productivity in all areas of its operations. Its marketing skills are well developed, and research into new, high value-added production should increase profit margins and strengthen the degree of vertical integration (by internalizing knowledge and marketing skills). Because the division has strong FSFs and benefits from strong cost-reducing CSFs, it can be positioned in quadrant 1 AB. Unfortunately, the move by British Columbia to increase stumpage fees and the prospect of Quebec following this lead threaten the strong cost-reducing CSFs and may move the division to quadrant 3 AB. Thus, regional policy has a major effect on this firm.

Manufacturing. The manufacturing division is resource based and marketing oriented. In any discussion of its FSFs, Canada Wire and Cable and Wire Rope Industries must be separated from the rest of the division.

Canada Wire and Cable operates in a mature industry, although the company prefers to regard itself as dynamic because of its product and marketing innovations. Customers and competitors alike consider its operations among the best in the world because of the quality of both its products and service. The high-voltage cable business has benefited from the geography of Canada—the fact that energy has to be transported across vast distances from source to user. Consequently, the firm's higher-voltage cable plants are on a world scale. The unit, specifically the higher-voltage cable operation, has dual strong FSFs, which place it in quadrant 1 ABCD of Figure 1.

Wire Rope Industries (WRI) has strong differentiation-enhancing firm-specific factors, the result of proprietary products, some of which are required exclusively by mining firms to meet their engineering needs. The firm's cost structure is higher than that of its competitors, but this is improving through plant rationalization and an expanded customer base resulting from the purchase of the wire rope assets of Greening Donald Company. WRI is located in quadrant 1 BD of Figure 1. The rest of the division (including an aluminum unit and Carol Cable) is subject to a very competitive environment. New competitors from low-wage countries are entering the market and reducing profits. These operations are positioned in quadrant 2 AB because they are faced with weak FSFs.

Energy. The energy division's Canadian Hunter Exploration Limited has been relatively successful in its explorations as demonstrated by its low exploration costs. It estimates that over the past three years its exploration cost per barrel of oil equivalent (BOE) has been $3.50 compared with an industry average of $8-$9 per BOE. The division is positioned in quadrant 1 AC of Figure 1.

Northern Telecom

Northern Telecom is the only Canadian firm with sales exceeding the $1 billion level that competes exclusively in a high-technology industry. Specializing in the design and manufacture of telecommunications equipment, this firm is the world's leading supplier of digital systems. Its expertise, coupled with a secure domestic market in Bell Canada (Northern Telecom is 52.3 percent owned by Bell Canada Enterprises), has contributed to the firm's past success.

Northern Telecom has introduced the notion of "effective use of time" in an attempt to gain a competitive edge on its competitors. This ambitious policy has produced results: manufacturing time has decreased to approximately half that required two to three years ago; both inventory and overhead have decreased; and customer satisfaction levels have improved (Merrills 1989). The reduction in manufacturing time applies not only to production time for existing products but also to development time, including that for product enhancements and new product development. To achieve this, the company formed cross-functional teams made up of R&D,

manufacturing, and marketing personnel. The team approach avoids or reduces many of the difficulties encountered in the previous approach in which R&D might have sent a prototype to manufacturing only to have it rejected or to see marketing place particular design demands on it at a later point. This new approach has implications for both types of FSFs: the reduced operating costs assist the cost-reducing FSFs, and the increased response to customer requests, as measured by customer satisfaction, enhances Northern Telecom's differentiation-enhancing FSFs.

Northern Telecom is difficult to analyze because it markets its major product lines across all of its geographic divisions. Since revenues and operating earnings are reported by geographic segment— but simply revenues are given for product lines—only the geographic operations can be placed. Four SBUs can be distinguished: Northern Telecom Canada Ltd., Northern Telecom Inc., Northern Telecom World Trade Corp., and Bell-Northern Research Ltd.

Northern Telecom Canada Ltd. Northern Telecom Canada has dual strong FSFs. Its status as a low-cost producer and price leader is sustained by its consolidation programme in North America and by the time management programme just mentioned. The differentiation-enhancing FSFs are derived from quality products and service excellence, as well as from an intense marketing programme. The latter firm-specific factor has been enhanced by the internalization of country-specific factors. The firm's excellent R&D staff partially stems from the CSF of the large skilled labour pool in Canada. But more important to the development of marketing skills has been the firm's relationship with Bell Canada, which gave Northern Telecom the foundation on which to enter world markets. Although the affiliation with Bell Canada has endowed the firm with a stable selling base, the volume of sales is still inadequate to support substantial R&D or permit economic scale production. Furthermore, government support for R&D in Canada lags behind that of other industrialized countries. Because of its lack of strong cost-reducing CSFs, the firm has maintained a niche in the narrow field of telecommunications, placing this SBU in quadrant 3 CD of Figure 1.

Northern Telecom Inc. The American operation, Northern Telecom Inc., also enjoys strong firm-specific factors, which stem from the strengths of the Canadian parent base. These FSFs are based on marketing expertise, quality products, and service excellence. The strength of the FSFs is evidenced by the fact that Northern Telecom Inc. increased its sales volume of most products despite an extremely competitive market characterized by price discounting. Given the size of the

American market, the firm can realize economies of scale. Coupled with the availability of skilled labour, this tends to ensure strong cost-reducing CSFs. But the differential treatment of indigenous versus foreign firms with respect to government procurement and R&D support has negative implications for its CSFs. Overall, Northern Telecom Inc. is located in quadrant 1 AB of Figure 1.

Northern Telecom World Trade Corp. The European and Pacific operations of Northern Telecom benefit from the same FSFs as the North American operations. Although such advantages may not have been developed in these overseas operations, they have been effectively transferred from North America. The problem for these two units lies in weak CSFs, the result of the differing government procurement policies and technical requirements of many countries. Northern Telecom tries to minimize these negative aspects by directing foreign direct investment to politically stable countries, by developing joint ventures and licencing agreements in less favourable environments, and by exporting to the riskier countries. But until government-owned systems direct procurement toward other than their traditional suppliers, Northern Telecom World Trade will remain in quadrant 3 AB of Figure 1. Northern Telecom's new relationship with STC PLC of Britain, however, may move its European position into quadrant 1 CD. The same possibility exists for its joint ventures in France and China.

Bell-Northern Research Ltd. Bell Northern Research is at a cost disadvantage because of poor R&D support in Canada and its exclusion from American programmes. In addition, its research base is smaller than those of its competitors, reducing the potential for economies of scale or scope. Its differentiation-enhancing FSFs are strong but subject to decline: the firm has maintained an excellent research department, which has kept the firm competitive. Unfortunately, the firm faces such difficulties as a small revenue base, confinement mainly to North America, maturing products, and exclusion from American government support, a factor that could affect its ability to attract qualified scientific personnel and fund R&D. Its country-specific factors are dual weak, but they could improve.

Nova

Nova represents the energy and petrochemical industry in this set of Canadian multinationals. The energy and petrochemical units of Nova are, as separate entities, billion-dollar players in their respective markets. The six SBUs identified—pipeline and gas marketing, petrochemicals, basic petrochemicals, rubber, plastics, and petroleum—have experienced a range of impacts from the FTA and thus are interesting subjects for analysis.

Pipeline and Gas Marketing. The deregulation of natural gas prices has prompted the pipeline and gas marketing division to develop marketing expertise in addition to its transportation proficiency. The unit is vigorously pursuing the American market where it is subject to intense competition. But it has not abandoned the challenge of reducing costs through better control; it recognizes that higher volumes also lower costs through scale economies. The division has strong cost-reducing and weak differentiation-enhancing FSFs. The same analysis holds for the CSFs—the cost-reducing CSFs are strong, and the differentiation-enhancing CSFs are weak. Thus, the division falls in quadrant 1 A.

Petrochemicals. The petrochemical business is best examined by product line since not all units possess the same FSFs. In particular, a distinction must be made among Nova's petrochemical operations, Polysar's basic petrochemical unit, and the polymer division.

Nova's petrochemical unit has an agreement with the Alberta government that guarantees Nova's supply of ethane at a regulated price—another demonstration of the impact of regional policy on a firm's competitiveness. This agreement was reviewed in 1988, but, despite opposition to the agreement by competitors and the Energy Resources Conservation Board which recommended elimination of Nova's special status, the government decided to continue this arrangement for existing plants.

Nova has strong cost-reducing and weak differentiation-enhancing FSFs. The petrochemical division has increased capacity and reduced costs through scale economies and productivity gains. Its marketing efforts also aim to reduce costs by striving to increase market share and maintain economic scale production.

The weakness of the polyethylene segment lies in the distance of its Alberta-based plants from major users of the product, although this weakness is countered by the unit's proximity to feedstocks. The marketing arm of the methanol operations has tried to penetrate the market for such value-added products as a blend of methanol and unleaded gasoline for automobiles, but the unit still emphasizes scale economies as a means of reducing costs. Polyethylene is sold internationally—but mainly as a commodity—so there is little emphasis on marketing. Nova attempted to improve its differentiation ability through the purchase of Polysar in 1988, a move meant to enhance its downstream, value-adding activities and differentiation-enhancing FSFs (see next section). Because the petrochemicals division benefits from strong cost-reducing CSFs, it is positioned in quadrant 1 A of Figure 1.

Basic Petrochemicals. Polysar's basic petrochemical unit is an interesting contrast to that of Nova. According to Polysar, for feedstock and feedstock transportation costs it is at a competitive disadvantage with the American Gulf Coast producers, but the firm counters this with lower electricity costs, proximity to a large American market from its southern Ontario operations, and flexibility, especially in using alternative feedstock based on current market costs (crude oil or natural gas). The elimination of tariffs and the location advantage with respect to buyers will definitely enhance its competitive position, and the fact that it is a division of Nova should help it secure feedstock at favourable prices. Its recent purchase of a catalytic distillation company gives the unit the technology for the low-cost construction of a petrochemical plant and the ability to operate it as a low-cost production facility. Polysar's FSFs are cost reducing as determined by its ability to use the least expensive feedstock source. The division is increasing its output of higher value-added products and may improve its differentiation-enhancing FSFs in so doing. Additional efforts to strengthen these FSFs involve basic petrochemical R&D, which few of its competitors undertake. Because the division has strong cost-reducing and weak differentiation-enhancing FSFs and benefits from strong cost-reducing CSFs (human resources and location advantage to buyers), it can be placed in quadrant 1 A of Figure 1, although a shift toward quadrant 1 AB is anticipated.

Rubber. The rubber operation of the polymer division is emphasizing higher value-added products. Its synthetic rubber products are sold throughout the world, with the automotive sector accounting for approximately 75 percent of sales of which 80 percent is to tire manufacturers. Global marketing expertise is improving with the production of such specialty rubbers as nitrile, an oil-resistant butyl rubber for high-performance tires. The research department has invented TORNAC, a heat and oil nitrile rubber that sells for 10-15 times the price of conventional oil-resistant rubbers. The rubber operation has strong CSFs and strong differentiation-enhancing FSFs. Its FSFs are both process oriented (R&D) and marketing based (specialty products, new applications, increased sales effort in the Asia-Pacific region). The division is moving away from commodities and is attempting to focus on specialty, high value-added products as outlined above. Part of the division's strength lies in its quality technical service, both before and after sales. Another differentiation advantage lies in its ability to innovate for commercial gain on the basis of existing products without having to purchase a new technology. The rubber unit is lower cost than its European-based competitors, equal in cost to its American competitors, but higher cost than its Japanese competitors. Its CSFs, in the form of excellent engineering personnel, are strongly differentiation enhancing, and so the operation is in quadrant 1 D of Figure 1.

The rubber division was sold to Bayer AG of West Germany in May 1990, for $1.48 billion. The acquisition gives Bayer's rubber operations, which were not globally integrated, production facilities in, as well as access to, the North American market. Nova benefits through debt reduction, which should improve profitability and enhance efforts to strengthen the competitive position of its basic petrochemical and plastics operations.

Plastics. The plastics operation has grown through acquisition and, consequently, has too many plants. It is anticipating a rationalization that will reduce the number of production facilities from seven to three or four. Concurrent with this plan is one to expand its Sarnia, Ontario, operations to take advantage of the proximity to: (1) a feedstock source (basic petrochemical plants), and (2) buyers in the northeastern United States, who have taken on new importance as a result of the elimination of tariffs on the unit's output. The plastics operation is stressing higher value-added products. The differentiation-enhancing FSFs are derived from both process technology and marketing skills, but these FSFs are relatively weak. Nonetheless, given the strengths of the rubber operation's FSFs and the transferability of these skills, the plastics division sees an opportunity to develop strong differentiation-enhancing FSFs. The division is now located in quadrant 2 AB. This positioning indicates that the firm must restructure or exit. It is now restructuring, building upon the FSFs of other divisions.

Petroleum. The petroleum division is subject to the same unstable pricing environment affecting all other petroleum producers. Recent announcements by the governments of Canada, Alberta, and Saskatchewan about financial support for a heavy oil upgrader plant for Husky (Nova has a 43 percent ownership position) have, however, tended to reduce the impact of pricing uncertainty. Because the division has strong cost-reducing and weak differentiation-enhancing FSFs and is currently benefiting from strong cost-reducing CSFs, it can be placed in quadrant 1 A.

Other Business Interests. All of Nova's other business interests depend on skilled human input, especially its consulting and research activities. Novacorp, a consulting firm, and Nova Husky, a research firm, most likely possess differentiation-enhancing FSFs. Grove, a manufacturer of valves, relies on cost-reducing FSFs (this division was sold to Grove Management in June 1990). Novacorp and Nova Husky emphasize technological expertise and attempt to differentiate themselves as innovators in this area. Both firms have strong differentiation-enhancing and weak cost-reducing FSFs, although their CSFs do not provide them with a competitive advantage. Thus, they could be positioned in quadrant 3 B of Figure 1.

Positioning the MNEs under the FTA

This section analyzes how the SBUs discussed above adjusted to the Canada-U.S. Free Trade Agreement, which became effective 1 January 1989. The FTA both eliminates tariffs and reduces non-tariff barriers (Economic Council of Canada 1988). Several economic sectors are exempted from the FTA, however, including the brewing industry. This industry is characterized by relatively small, inefficient plants—the result of interprovincial trade barriers. If it had not been exempted from the FTA, this sector would have been subject to extreme cost disadvantages or substantial adjustment costs in response to free trade. In other words, interregional impediments to trade within Canada have a substantial impact on strategies to adjust to the FTA.

John Labatt Limited

If Labatt Brewing had to face global competition, its cost-reducing firm-specific factor would be lost. Currently, Labatt and another brewery, Molson-Carling O'Keefe, operate small, inefficient plants to comply with provincial restrictions on the beer trade. Although this represents an effective entry barrier in a protected market (as demonstrated by the licencing and producing arrangements with foreign producers), in a global context such a CSF would have a large negative impact on the competitiveness of the Canadian brewing industry.

Entry barriers exist in foreign markets, of course, including distribution channels (especially the closed houses in Europe). These prevent economies of scale and cost competitiveness on a global basis. Labatt is attempting to hurdle the European entry barriers through partnerships with regional brewers in the United Kingdom, and it entered the home consumer market there in June 1989. The group also has a 70 percent interest in Birra Moretti, the third largest brewery in Italy.

The FTA has no direct effect on the brewing division and, consequently, its strategic direction. But the status quo in the Canadian brewing industry is unlikely to remain in effect because of the recent GATT findings against provincial discrimination in the pricing of foreign wines and other beverages. In addition, the merger of Molson and Carling O'Keefe increases pressure at the provincial and federal government levels to liberalize trade in the brewing industry within Canada and internationally.

Although company statements indicate Labatt prefers the current Canadian market environment, the firm is still acutely aware of the implications of global competition. As demonstrated in 1989, imports of low-priced American beer could reduce (at least temporarily) the domestic industry market share or, at the very least, dramatically reduce profit margins. Labatt would no doubt respond to such an environmental shock by reducing the number of its production facilities and becoming internationally cost-competitive.

The FTA is not completely responsible for Labatt's divestiture of Chateau-Gai. The poor positioning of the firm before the FTA indicated that the division would have to be restructured or divested. This factor, in combination with the FTA as well as the GATT decision against discriminatory wine pricing in Canada and the need to comply with the ruling, contributed to the firm's decision to sell the division rather than to restructure it to make it competitive.

The FTA will alter the position of Ault Foods since its low-cost status will disappear after the elimination of import tariffs on American dairy products. Thus, Ault Foods can be placed in quadrant 1 D. As long as the import quotas on many dairy products (as defined by the Import Control List set forth by the federal government) are maintained, however, Ault will be able to continue its current low-cost strategy vis-à-vis other Canadian competitors. Should the quotas disappear, forcing Ault to become cost-competitive relative to American producers, Labatt could import into Canada from its Johanna Dairies division, which is expected to become more cost-efficient from rationalizations. This is paradoxical as it implies that the U.S. operation, now faced with a weak cost-reducing FSF, could after developing a strong cost-reducing FSF export to the market where Labatt now benefits from a strong cost-reducing FSF that is likely to be lost after trade liberalization.

In response to the elimination of tariffs under the FTA, Ogilvie is rationalizing, although the industry remains protected because of import controls on wheat and flour (to be eliminated when producer subsidies are equalized between the United States and Canada). Ogilvie also maintains American mills so that it, like Ault Foods, could import into Canada from the United States if its Canadian plants lose their cost advantage.

All of Labatt's American-based SBUs are unaffected by the Free Trade Agreement. They benefit from low-input costs and the potential to realize economies of scale, which, when coupled with strong differentiation-enhancing FSFs, enable the firms to continue their current strategic plans.

Given the increasing investment by Everfresh Juice in the United States, its competitive position in Canada will probably remain strong based on the substitution of imports for domestic production in response to increased competition. In other words, this strategic business unit will remain competitive in spite of the weak cost-reducing CSFs and FSFs of its Canadian operations—the result of its linkage with U.S. operations. From a regional perspective, this demonstrates the ability of some multinational enterprises to benefit from the use of strong CSFs in one location to compensate for weak CSFs in another location.

Noranda

The introduction of the FTA will benefit Noranda minerals by improving the cost position in the United States of many of its alloys and augmenting its attempts to move to higher value-added products. As for those alloys that encounter high nominal tariffs (and in some instances extremely high effective tariffs such as the 300 percent effective tariff on zinc alloys), the Free Trade Agreement enables Noranda to process them in Canada as opposed to shipping the ore concentrate to the United States, remelting it, and producing the alloys. The elimination of the intermediate step lowers production costs, and the integration of production in Canada facilitates the division's move to higher value-added production and the ensuing development of marketing expertise. Thus, the FTA provides the environment for Noranda minerals to improve its potential to move from cell 1 A to cells 1 AB, with dual strong FSFs. As this was its goal before implementation of the FTA, the division was an enthusiastic supporter of the agreement.

The FTA will have little impact on the current FSFs and CSFs of Noranda's forestry division. Any positive change would require a mechanism to avoid administered trade actions such as the softwood lumber decision in which the Canadian government imposed an export tax equivalent to the countervail duty that the United States was proposing (for an analysis, see Rugman and Porteous 1988; Rugman and

Verbeke 1989). This factor will tend to preserve the strong cost-reducing CSF.

The dual strong FSFs of Canada Wire and Cable will not be altered by the FTA. Wire Rope Industries may be able to improve its cost structure through scale production, although its strong differentiation-enhancing FSFs remain intact under the agreement. The other operations of the division still face exit or restructuring after the FTA is implemented. The agreement offers them only marginal assistance in reducing costs through scale economies because these operations are already located in the United States. The development of product differentiation skills remains a priority for the aluminium unit, and Carol Cable has been divested.

The benefits of the FTA for the energy division will take the form of a positive atmosphere among its American customers, but implementation of the agreement will not change the position of the unit in Figure 1. Although there is potential for increased sales volumes to the United States, which could result in lower per-unit production costs, the division already possesses strong cost-reducing FSFs.

Northern Telecom

The FTA does not alter the position of Northern Telecom Canada in Figure 1 and thus requires no direct strategic response. The FTA could enable Northern Telecom Inc. to develop dual strong country-specific factors if it were granted equal access to government procurement and support, but because this is still uncertain any prediction of a move toward quadrant 1 ABCD would be speculative. The FTA does not affect the position of Northern Telecom World Trade. Although the dual weak CSFs of Bell Northern Research might improve under the FTA, it is unlikely that this SBU would be able to move out of quadrant 3 B of Figure 1.

Nova

The Free Trade Agreement, with its provisions for energy contracts, guarantees Nova a strong cost-reducing CSF because it allows for larger volumes and reduced unit transportation costs. But the agreement has little or no impact on the pipeline and gas marketing unit.

The FTA will not alter the cost structure of the existing facilities, but it could cause Nova petrochemicals to further emphasize global markets and leave the northeastern United States to its sister operations (Polysar) in southern Ontario and the United States (see below).

The reduction of tariffs will benefit the styrene operation of the basic petrochemicals division. It is reconsidering its target market and plans to focus on the northeastern United States. The prospect of increasing the gains arising from the FTA and becoming a dominant force in this market has impelled the operation to evaluate the construction of a low-cost production facility. Thus, the agreement will not greatly alter the position of the division, but it could strengthen the firm's FSFs if the new plant becomes reality.

The FTA has a neutral effect on the rubber division for two reasons. First, the tariffs on synthetic rubber are already zero for most products, and, second, the division is globally competitive and integrated and intends to continue exploiting its existing competitive advantage in the marketplace. The rubber division will continue operations under the ownership of Bayer AG.

The Free Trade Agreement has focused attention on the plastics division and its need to restructure. It is currently positioned in quadrant 2 AB.

The FTA will have a neutral effect on Husky, although it could encourage the development of the firm's differentiation-enhancing attributes. The FTA does not alter its position in Figure 1, nor does it encourage or require Novacorp and Nova Husky to develop new strategic initiatives. Grove will also continue its current low-cost strategy but under management ownership.

Conclusions

Although only four Canadian MNEs were examined here, the number of their strategic business units substantially increases the number of observations. As we have seen, most SBUs were well positioned before and after the FTA. The questionnaire/interview process with the management personnel (excluding Labatt) confirmed the positioning of the SBUs before the FTA, and the strategic reactions of the SBUs to the FTA confirm the predictions based on the strategic framework developed in this article. Adjustment costs have been minimal and easily absorbed by the units.

Of all the SBUs discussed above, only four were poorly positioned after (and before) the FTA: the plastics operations of Polysar, the aluminum and the American cable operations of Noranda, and the wine division of Labatt. At Nova, the plastics operation is restructuring to become cost-efficient. Noranda is attempting to reposition its aluminum business through the creation of production differentiation attributes, and it has shed its American cable segment. Finally, Chateau-Gai was divested by Labatt. These events are consistent with the model, which predicted restructuring or exit: currently, the first two SBUs are developing new FSFs, and the parent firms chose to exit from the last two operations.

The case studies presented here emphasize the need for SBUs in mature industries to be cost-competitive. The resource-based firms, building on the country-specific factors of location in Canada, experienced depressed commodity prices as a result of excess capacity on a global basis. They now perceive that to remain operational (not necessarily profitable) they must be low-cost producers. This situation is paralleled on the high-tech front by Northern Telecom's confrontation with reduced margins in the maturing digital switching industry and the subsequent development of its cost-reducing/efficiency-enhancing programmes.

The situation in the resource sector is further aggravated by the relative decline in Canada's CSFs (the choice forests have been harvested and the best ore bodies mined), which was not discussed in this article, and by the introduction of new technologies by competitors, which reduces the relative strength of FSFs (for example, the oxygen bleach process in pulp and paper technology). The long-run operations of the commodity producers are threatened, and, at best, the future of these operations is unattractive because of low margins.

This discussion has revealed the common experience of the resource-based SBUs: they have evolved from low-cost commodity producers to cost-competitive, high-margin, value-added marketers. This transformation is continual: several firms that have made advances are still striving to improve product differentiation skills in conjunction with their efforts to maintain cost-competitiveness in commodity production.

Clearly, as global competition reduces margins, cost-competitiveness is essential in mature or maturing industries. But even the lowest-cost producers in mature industries will exhibit low attractiveness in the long run, thus prompting these firms to shift to the development of differentiation-enhancing FSFs and the expansion of value-added activities. This implies that the FTA, when interpreted as an institutional adjustment to the reality of increased global rivalry, does not automatically enable multinational enterprises to improve their competitive positions based on the economic principles of regionally based comparative advantages. Only when CSFs are internalized into FSFs, which are then renewed continually at the SBU level, can global competitive success be achieved. In contrast to Porter (1980, 1985), we conclude that a dual emphasis on cost reduction and differentiation enhancement does not mean firms will become "stuck in the middle". In the long run such an emphasis leads to global competitive success.

References

Crookell, Harold. 1987. "Managing Canadian Subsidiaries in a Free Trade Environment", *Sloan Management Review,* 29(Fall):71-76.

——. 1989. "Managing Canadian Subsidiaries in a Free Trade Environment". Pp. 189-199 in Alan M. Rugman (ed.), *International Business in Canada: Strategies for Management*. Scarborough, Ont.: Prentice Hall Canada.

D'Cruz, Joseph R., and James D. Fleck. 1989a. *Yankee Canadians in the Global Economy*. London: National Centre for Management Research and Development.

——. 1989b. "Strategies for U.S. Subsidiaries after Free Trade". Pp. 51-56 in Maureen Farrow and Alan M. Rugman (eds.), *Business Strategies and Free Trade*. Policy Study No. 5. Toronto: C. D. Howe Institute.

Dunning, John H., and P. Robson. 1987. "Multinational Corporate Integration and Regional Economic Integration", *Journal of Common Market Studies,* 26(2):103-125.

Economic Council of Canada. 1988. *Venturing Forth: An Assessment of the Canada-U.S. Trade Agreement*. Ottawa: Economic Council of Canada.

Hood, Neil, and Stephen Young. 1987. "Inward Investment and the EC-UK Evidence on Corporate Integration Strategies", *Journal of Common Market Studies,* 26(2):193-206.

Magun, Sunder, Someshwar Rao, and Binal Lodh. 1987. "Impact of Canada-U.S. Free Trade on the Canadian Economy". Discussion Paper No. 331, Economic Council of Canada, Ottawa.

Magun, Sunder, et al. 1988. "Open Borders: An Assessment of the Canada-U.S. Free Trade Agreement". Discussion Paper No. 344, Economic Council of Canada, Ottawa.

Merrills, Roy. 1989. "How Northern Telecom Competes on Time", *Harvard Business Review,* (July-August):108-114.

Porter, Michael. 1980. *Competitive Strategy*. New York: Free Press.

——. 1985. *Competitive Advantage*. New York: Free Press.

Porter, Michael (ed.). 1986. *Competition in Global Industries*. Boston: Harvard Business School Press.

Rugman, Alan M. 1981. *Inside the Multinationals: The Economics of Internal Markets*. New York: Columbia University Press.

——. 1990. *Multinationals and Canada-United States Free Trade*. Columbia: University of South Carolina Press.

Rugman, Alan M. (ed.). 1989. *International Business in Canada: Strategies for Management*. Scarborough, Ont.: Prentice Hall Canada.

Rugman, Alan M., and John McIlveen. 1985. *Megafirms: Strategies for Canada's Multinationals*. Toronto: Methuen.

Rugman, Alan M., and Sam Porteous. 1988. "The Softwood Lumber Decision of 1986: Broadening the Nature of U.S. Administered Protection", *Review of International Business Law,* 2(1):35-58.

Rugman, Alan M., and Alain Verbeke. 1988. "Strategic Responses to Free Trade". Pp. 13-29 in Maureen Farrow and Alan M. Rugman (eds.), *Business Strategies and Free Trade*. Policy Study No. 5. Toronto: C. D. Howe Institute.

——. 1989. "Strategic Management and Trade Policy". Pp. 144-159 in Alan M. Rugman (ed.), *International Business in Canada: Strategies for Management*. Scarborough, Ont.: Prentice Hall Canada.

——. 1990. *Global Corporate Strategy and Trade Policy.* London: Routledge.

Rugman, Alan M., Donald J. Lecraw, and Laurence D. Booth. 1985. *International Business: Firm and Environment.* Toronto: McGraw-Hill.

Rutenberg, David. 1988. "Structural Effects of Free Trade". Pp. 31-40 in Maureen Farrow and Alan M. Rugman (eds.), *Business Strategies and Free Trade.* Policy Study No. 5. Toronto: C. D. Howe Institute

Wolf, Bernard M. 1986. "The Reaction of Multinational Enterprises to Sectoral Free Trade between Canada and the United States". Economic Analysis and Policy Evaluation Branch, Bureau of Competition Policy, Ottawa.

——. 1989. "American Subsidiaries in Canada and the Free Trade Agreement". Pp. 178-188 in Alan M. Rugman (ed.), *International Business in Canada: Strategies for Management.* Scarborough, Ont.: Prentice Hall Canada.

Reprinted from
NORTHEASTERN JOURNAL OF AGRICULTURAL AND RESOURCE ECONOMICS
Vol. 19, No. 2, October 1990

Invited Presentation

The Canada-U.S. Free Trade Agreement and Canada's Agri-Food Industries

Alan M. Rugman and Andrew Anderson

The food processing industry is Canada's second-largest manufacturing industry. It employed 226,579 people in 1986, and shipments were valued at CDN $47 billion, or 15 percent of the value of total manufactured output that year. More significantly, the food and beverage industries together ranked highest among all manufacturing industries in terms of value added, at CDN $15 billion or approximately 14 percent of total value added in Canadian manufacturing industries in 1986 (Statistics Canada). Given the high degree of competition in this industry in the United States, the history of "comfortable" competition in the food industry in Canada, and the significant contribution of this industry to the Canadian economy, it becomes important to look more carefully at how this industry has been and will be affected by the Canada-U.S. Free Trade Agreement (FTA).

During the FTA negotiations, several interest groups in Canada and the U.S. lobbied hard to be exempted from the agreement (Rugman and Anderson 1987c). Given its strength, both federally and provincially, the Canadian agricultural lobby succeeded in having marketing boards exempted. In so doing, the burden of adjustment to the FTA was placed squarely on the shoulders of Canadian-based food processors, who now need to either rationalize production in Canada or move to the U.S. This problem has been aggravated by the size asymmetry that characterizes the U.S. and Canadian markets. Although this problem has a bearing upon the effects of the FTA upon the Canadian food processing industry, the FTA is obviously not to be blamed for differences in the size of the Canadian and U.S. markets.

This article will focus upon the following sectors: dairy (milk), feathers (chicken, turkey, eggs), pork processing, fish processing, and beef and veal processing. In 1986, the total numbers of farms in Canada were grouped in the census as follows.

Cattle and small-grain farms accounted for the highest numbers, with 59,000 farms each. Wheat ranked second, with 47,000 farms, followed by dairy, with 34,000; pigs, with 12,000; and, finally, poultry with 5,000 farms. Table 1 examines the extent to which Canadian agriculture is involved in trade with the U.S. It reports the import and export percentages in 1986 as well as the importance of the U.S. to each major agricultural sector. These data do not distinguish between trade of raw versus processed products. However, it does indicate Canada's dependence on the U.S. market, since nearly 61 percent of the value of Canada's exports of agricultural products, excluding grains and oilseeds, went to the U.S. over the 1981 to 1987 period.

Supply Management and the FTA

Many of Canada's food industries are highly regulated by supply-management programs at the farm level. The most common mechanisms used are production quotas, mandatory pricing, import controls, and restrictions on interprovincial trade. In the FTA, supply management and the rest of this structure were retained, including import controls that keep out potentially cheaper U.S. products. Article XI of the General Agreement on Tariffs and Trade (GATT), which permits import controls, reinforces this aspect of the FTA but is currently being negotiated in the Uruguay Round. Certain processed products were not included in the import control list, including frozen pizzas and frozen chickens. As a result, these products are no longer economical to produce in Canada, since U.S.-produced imports are cheaper. These product lines are being lost to U.S. producers.

In addition, Canadian food processors are being forced to purchase more expensive inputs from Canadian suppliers, leading to severe adjustment costs as tariffs are reduced on processed food, leading to potential problems for future investment and plant location decisions, especially for larger firms. Companies like George Weston, Labatts, McCain

Alan M. Rugman is a professor of international business and Andrew Anderson is a research associate, both of the Ontario Centre for International Business (OCIB), University of Toronto. The authors are grateful to the research assistance provided by Michael Gestrin of the OCIB.

Table 1.   Canada-United States Agricultural Trade, 1986

Product Traded	Percentage Share of Trade by Volume		Percentage of Total Exports Going to the U.S.[a] (As a percent of value)
	Exports	Imports	
Animals and products	43.9	17.8	23 (other animal products) to 89 (live animals)
Grains and products	10.8	7.1	64 (products) to 3 (grains)
Animal feeds	4.1	2.6	49
Vegetables	3.6	16.5	36
Potatoes	2.1	1.3	49
Fruits and nuts	0.8	24.1	70
Oilseeds and products	3.9	10.7	26 (products) to 7 (oilseeds)
Other	30.8	20.0	NA
Total	100.0	100.0	60.5[b]

Source: Agriculture Canada, Communications Branch, "The Canada-U.S. Free Trade Agreement and Agriculture: An Assessment," 1988, p. 10.
[a] Where two numbers appear, this represents a range since each category contains a variety of crops.
[b] Canadian agricultural exports (excluding grains and oilseeds) to the U.S. from 1981 to June 1987 as a percent of total dollar value. With grains and oilseeds, this figure drops to 32% in 1986.

Food, and other multinational enterprises will find it more attractive to locate future production in the U.S. than in Canada. This is because the U.S. market, both for processed foods and for the industry's inputs, is ten times larger than Canada's, leading to greater economies of scale for U.S. producers over Canadian producers. Thus, even if U.S. dairy and poultry producers receive the same production subsidies as Canadian farmers, the larger multinational food processors would be more efficient in the larger U.S. market. If, in practice, U.S. subsidies in these agricultural sectors are lower than in Canada, then this economic factor is reinforced.

That this is in fact the case was suggested by a report released by the Organization for Economic Cooperation and Development (OECD). Although the Canadian federal government disputed the report's estimates of Canadian agricultural subsidization, its own revised estimates still indicated that U.S. subsidies to the agricultural sectors were lower than Canada's (Drohan).

Press reports on plant closures due to the FTA reinforce this argument. While much of the media coverage listing plant closures due to the FTA is superficial and biased (as plant openings are routinely ignored), some facts can be derived. At least five plants appear to have been shut down: St. Lawrence Starch Co., Ltd. in Mississauga; Cobi Foods in Port Williams, Nova Scotia; Gerber (Canada) International in Toronto; and two Campbell Soup plants in Montreal and Portage la Prairie. Of these, St. Lawrence Starch closed because of a Canadian-imposed countervailing duty on imports of fresh grain corn. This has absolutely nothing to do with the FTA. In addition, several other plants are alleged to have taken action to meet the chal-

lenge of heightened competition south of the border.

The most recent news highlighting the attempts by the industry to cut costs comes out of H. J. Heinz Co. of Canada Ltd. in Leavington, Ontario, where workers recently voted to accept a wage freeze over two years when faced with the real possibility of plant closure (*Globe and Mail*). Other companies that have taken measures to cut costs include Borden Inc. of Montreal, the Hunt-Wesson division of Beatrice Co., Inc. of Chicago, E.D. Smith, Cadbury Schweppes Canada, Campbell Soup, and Labatt's Ault Foods.

Several recent reports have confirmed the theoretical analysis of this paper. In February 1989 the Ontario Ministry of Agriculture and Food released a report of the Food Industry Advisory Committee on the food industry. It stated that supply-management policies would make it more difficult for food processors to compete under the FTA. The report stated that marketing boards serve to stabilize producers' income rather than achieve competitiveness. The nature of strategic management in multinational enterprises, including the food processing industry (especially multinational fish processors), has been examined by Rutenberg and by Rugman and Verbeke.

Trade Law Actions against Canadian Food Processors

The Canadian pork industry is not affected directly by the FTA. Indeed, it was doing well until the rival U.S. industry essentially imposed a prohibitive entry barrier by winning a trade-law action against Canadian producers. This countervailing duty goes back to the "live swine and pork" case of 1985 where the U.S. agencies placed a duty on imports of live swine but not on processed pork products. Accordingly, the Canadian industry switched more to processing the pork before exporting it to the U.S. However, those in the U.S. industry kept up their legal harassment of Canadian pork exporters, alleging subsidies were now going to the Canadian pork processors. In 1989, the U.S. side won an affirmative ruling from both the U.S. International Trade Commission and the U.S. Commerce Department against the Canadian processors. This has been appealed to one of the new Chapter 19 binational panels set up in the FTA, and its decision will be of great interest. For an overview of the comparison of U.S. and Canadian unfair trade laws, see Rugman and Porteous (1989).

The process by which U.S. trade law results in an administrative bias against Canadian producers is discussed in Rugman and Anderson (1987b). They show that a variety of Canadian agricultural and fish products have been harassed since the changes in the GATT Subsidies and Anti-dumping Codes were adopted by the U.S. in 1979. Table 2 shows that there were a total of sixteen U.S. countervailing duty cases and twenty-two antidumping cases over the last ten years against Canada. Of these, eight countervailing cases were against agricultural and fish products, while there were six antidumping agricultural cases. It is obvious that Canadian food producers and processors could face more trade-law-related actions in the future given the high degree of dependence on the U.S. market for certain agricultural and fish sectors. The softwood lumber industry learned how devastating the misuse of U.S. trade laws could be when it was forced to adopt a 15 percent export tax as settlement on a preliminary countervailing duty case decision made in 1986 (Rugman and Porteous 1988).

The Atlantic fish processing industry had been subject to five U.S. countervail actions before the FTA. The most significant was the 1986 fresh groundfish countervail of 6.2 percent. Many in the industry felt that without the FTA, action would be taken against exports of frozen fish (the great bulk of fish exports to the U.S.). There were two hard smoked herring fillet cases, since the first case was terminated and then restarted a month later by a new claim that the Canadian producers were subsidized. For a discussion of the trade-law fish cases, see Rugman and Anderson (1987a). The FTA will eliminate all tariffs by the end of a ten-year phase-in period. For some fish exports of prepared meals (fish sticks, etc.), these tariff cuts (of 10 to 25 percent) offer significant benefits.

Table 2. U.S. Countervailing Duty and Antidumping Duty Cases Against Canada: 1980–89

Year	Products Covered	Positive or Negative[a]
Countervailing Duty Cases		
1980	Frozen potato products	Negative
1980	Fish (fresh, chilled, or frozen)	Positive
1981	Hard smoked herring filets	Negative
1981	Hard smoked herring filets	Negative
1982	Certain rail passenger cars and parts	Positive
1982	Softwood lumber	Negative
1982	Softwood shakes and shingles	Negative
1982	Softwood fence	Negative
1984	Live swine and pork	Positive
1985	Certain raspberries	Positive
1985	Oil country tubular goods	Positive
1985	Certain fresh Atlantic groundfish	Positive
1986	Softwood lumber	Positive
1986	Certain fresh-cut flowers	Positive
1988	Thermo. cntrlld. appl. plugs/probes	Negative
1989	Fresh, chilled, and frozen pork	Positive
Antidumping Cases		
1980	Sugars, syrups	Positive
1980	Clams in airtight containers	Negative
1980	Asphalt roofing shingles	Negative
1981	Sheet piling	Positive
1982	Chlorine	Negative
1982	Frozen french-fried potatoes	Negative
1983	Certain fresh potatoes	Positive
1983	Choline chloride	Positive
1984	Certain red raspberries	Positive
1984	Certain dried salted codfish	Positive
1984	Egg filler flats	Positive
1985	Rock salt	Positive
1985	Welded carbon steel pipes/tubes	Positive
1985	Iron construction castings	Positive
1985	Oil country tubular goods	Positive
1986	Certain brass sheets and strips	Positive
1986	Certain fresh-cut flowers	Positive
1986	Color picture tubes	Positive
1987	Potassium chloride	Suspended
1987	Certain line pipes and tubes	Negative
1988	Certain fabricated structural steel	Negative
1988	Appl. plugs/probe thermostats	Positive

Source: United States International Trade Commission, *Annual Reports*, 1980–88.
[a] A positive case is one found against Canada; a negative case is one in favor of Canada.

On the West Coast, the ruling of the Chapter 18 panel on the landing of salmon and herring was a reasonable decision, reflecting the panel's independence on a very political issue. The Canadian case for landing salmon and herring for inspection was a thinly disguised protectionist device, illegal under both the GATT and the FTA. The panel found this to be so, but still ruled that 75 percent of the fish could be landed for inspection. The Canadian government was forced to accept this decision.

The FTA was of benefit to beef producers since it removed import laws and other restrictions and all U.S. tariffs on red meat. This encouraged exports of processed high-value-added Canadian meat products. We now turn to a more detailed analysis of the impact of the FTA on these key food processing sectors.

Effects of the Canada-U.S. FTA on Food Processing

The Canada-U.S. FTA has resulted in a variety of changes to the laws governing the import and export of processed and unprocessed agricultural products between Canada and the U.S. In order for a thorough examination to be made of the FTA's effects on food processing in Canada, we also need to examine other indirect effects as well as exemptions and future negotiations that are contained in the agreement. Most of the provisions contained in the FTA governing agricultural products will result in the opening of markets between the two countries in the long run. There are, however, a variety of provisions that will continue to severely restrict the import of agricultural products into Canada and exports to the U.S. These provisions will affect Canadian food processors. Before examining these effects, it is necessary to review the relevant chapters and articles contained in the FTA.

The Direct Provisions of the FTA Affecting Agriculture

The articles governing trade in agricultural products between Canada and the U.S. are contained in Chapter 7 of the FTA (Canada 1988a). The first of these articles (701) is neutral in its effect on the opening or closing of markets, but it does encourage a more even playing field by prohibiting the use of agricultural export subsidies and by eliminating the transportation subsidies previously given on shipments of grain to the U.S. under the Canadian Western Grain Transportation Act.

Four of the articles are oriented towards the opening of agricultural markets. These include Article 702 (in combination with Article 401), which will involve the phased elimination of all tariffs over a ten-year period, excluding a twenty-year snapback provision on fresh fruits and vegetables due to any depressed price conditions, combined with declining or constant acreage of the crop under cultivation. Article 704 exempts restrictions by Canada and the U.S. on imports of beef and veal. As well it provides for consultations on third coun-

tries' meat imports that are reexported to either Canada or the U.S. Canada has also been excluded from any future restrictions on products containing 10 percent or less sugar under Article 707. Article 708 will open markets by the gradual elimination of technical barriers through continuing negotiations by the two countries on the harmonization of their technical regulations on agricultural products.

Article 705 has the potential to open the markets for wheat, barley, and oats, as well as their products, through the elimination of Canadian import licenses. This may not occur for a number of years, since it requires U.S. grain support levels to become equal to Canadian grain support levels. Even then, there is a provision built into the agreement to permit the reimposition of import restraints if U.S. imports increase significantly.

Two of the articles either have the potential to restrict markets or permit the same conditions to continue as were in effect prior to the signing of the FTA. The first of these, Article 706, maintains U.S. market access to Canada for chickens, turkeys, and eggs but only at the traditional average levels of actual imports over the five years prior to the signing of the FTA. The second of these, Article 710, is probably the most important section for restricting the opening of agricultural markets between Canada and the U.S. This article maintains the restrictive trade practices negotiated under GATT Article XI(2)(c) that permit a national government to (1) restrict the quantities of agricultural products to be produced or marketed or their substitutes, (2) remove surpluses of the domestic product by restrictions on production or through giveaways or price reductions, and (3) restrict production of animal products that are directly dependent on an imported commodity for their production (i.e., reducing import dependence). These provisions permit the federal governments of Canada and the U.S., as well as the provincial and state governments, to control the pricing and supply of food products. In the case of Canada, this perpetuates the existence of agricultural marketing boards.

Indirect Provisions of the FTA Affecting Agricultural Trade

As well as the provisions contained in Chapter 7 of the FTA, there are a number of other provisions in the agreement which will also have an effect on the food processing sector in Canada. Chapter 8 contains provisions that relate strictly to the production and distribution of wine and spirits in Canada and the U.S. In general, the articles contained under Chapter 8 will eliminate the pricing differential between imported and domestic distilled spirits immediately and by 1995 for wine. Also, any blending requirements of import with domestic product will be eliminated by both countries. The chapter does, however, permit private wine outlets in the provinces of Ontario and British Columbia to continue their present levels of discrimination against imported products.

Two of the articles contained in Chapter 12 also have some impact on food processing under the FTA. The first of these, Article 1203(c), permits restrictions to be maintained on the export of unprocessed fish products as contained in the existing statutes of New Brunswick, Newfoundland, Nova Scotia, Prince Edward Island, and Quebec. The second of these, Article 1204, excludes national treatment from applying to products containing beer or malt. In effect, Canada, or the provinces in this instance, as they are responsible for the regulation on products containing alcohol, can continue to discriminate against beer or malt products from the U.S. Canada is not, however, exempt from prohibitions placed against it through any GATT rulings that find Canadian practices discriminatory (including provincial regulations) and therefore GATT illegal (Article 1205).

Dispute-Settlement Provisions in the FTA

Three other chapters in the FTA are also of importance to the opening up or closing down of trade in agricultural products. These are the two dispute-resolution chapters, Chapters 18 and 19, and the emergency-action provisions contained in Chapter 11. For a more thorough overview of the dispute-settlement mechanisms in the FTA, see Anderson and Rugman (1989a), and for a discussion of the extension of net-net to the Canada-U.S. Subsidies Code, see Anderson and Rugman (1989b).

Chapter 18 is responsible for providing the institutional structure—the Canada-United States Trade Commission—that will manage the agreement as well as settle any trade disputes that arise between Canada and the U.S. concerning the interpretation or application of any element of the agreement. Chapter 19 is responsible for settling trade disputes that pertain strictly to the use of antidumping or subsidy-countervailing duties by undertaking the final review where the parties disagree, rather than having a federal court in Canada or the U.S. do the review.

Chapter 19 is also responsible for the statutory review of any changes to the antidumping or countervailing duty laws by either country, while under

Article 1907 it is also responsible for the establishment of a working group that will develop more effective rules and disciplines concerning the use of government subsidies, including agricultural export subsidies that are banned under Article 701.

Tables 3 and 4 indicate the cases under Chapters 18 and 19 that have been handled to date. There have been a total of eight cases under Chapter 18 to date. Of these cases, six have been or are concerned with agricultural and fish products. The lobster case has already resulted in the restriction of sales of small live Canadian lobsters to the U.S. There have been twelve Chapter 19 cases to date. Four of these cases have been concerned with fish or agricultural products. As already mentioned, the countervailing duty processed pork case by the U.S. against Canada has been appealed to a Chapter 19 panel for review. A decision on this case is expected by August 1990. The red raspberries case was settled by the panel in Canada's favour, resulting in the overturning of dumping duties against British Columbia raspberries exported to the U.S.

Chapter 11 permits either country to nullify any tariff reductions that have taken place with regard to the duty reductions negotiated on goods under Chapter 4, where surges in imports cause serious injury to domestic production. Any increase in duty cannot exceed the most favoured nation (MFN) rate

Table 3. Chapter 18 Dispute Panels and Cases

Dispute Process Used To Handle the Case	Outcome[a]	Date
Handled by the Commission		
Cases initiated by the U.S.:		
1. Wine and spirits	Not completed	Unknown
2. Plywood	Not completed	June 1990
3. Cable retransmission	Not completed	July 1990
4. Wool	Not completed	Unknown
5. Fruits and vegetables	Not completed	Monitoring
Referred to an Arbitration Panel		
Cases initiated by the U.S.:		
1. Salmon and herring (CDA-01)	Positive	October 1989
Cases initiated by Canada:		
1. Lobsters (federal) (USA-01)	Negative	May 1990
2. Lobsters (state)	On hold	Unknown

Source: Binational Secretariate Canadian Section, "Status Report of Cases (Chapter 18 and 19)," Ottawa, May 14, 1990; various papers, etc.
[a] Positive if it favors the initiator(s) and negative if it does not.

Table 4.   Chapter 19 Dispute Panels and Cases

Cases	Outcome[a]	Date
Cases initiated by the U.S.		
1. Induction motors (CDA-01)	Case dropped	January 1990
Cases initiated by Canada		
1. Red raspberries (USA-01)	Positive	May 1990
2. Paving equipment 1 (USA-02)	Negative	January 1990
3. Paving equipment 2 (USA-03)	Negative	March 1990
4. Paving equipment 3 (USA-05)	Negative	March 1990
5. Salted codfish (USA-04)	Case dropped	—
6. Fresh, chilled, and frozen pork (USA-06)	Not completed	November 1990
7. New steel rails (Sydney Steel) (USA-07)	Negative	August 1990
8. New steel rails (Algoma Steel) (USA-08)	Negative	August 1990
9. New steel rails (USA-09/10)	Negative	August 1990
10. Fresh, chilled, and frozen pork (USA-11)[b]	Negative	October 1990

Source: Binational Secretariate Canadian Section, "Status Report of Cases (Chapter 18 and 19)," Ottawa, May 14, 1990; various papers, etc. (revised October 1990).
[a] Positive if it favors the initiator(s) and negative if it does not.
[b] Remanded back to ITC by panel which reaffirmed its initial ruling.

of duty in effect the day of the signing of the FTA, or in effect at the time Chapter 11 is invoked. The imposition of restraints can be for no longer than three years, and emergency action cannot be invoked beyond 1998 when Chapter 11 becomes defunct. In terms of agricultural products, Chapter 11 is extremely important since it eliminates the ability of either country to use quotas. Even when restrictions are imposed, quantitative restrictions cannot be applied below ". . . the trend of imports over a reasonable base period with allowance for growth (Article 1102(4)(b))."

A Model of the Effects of the FTA on Food Processing

In order to examine the long-run effects of the provisions of the FTA on the Canadian food processing industry, the framework outlined in Figure 1 is used. Three different effects that will occur simultaneously are examined: the price effect, the

trade-protection effect, and the import-competing effect. Two of these effects involve actual trade flows—the price and import-competing effects—while the trade-protection effect is an institutional mechanism that can enhance or reduce the effects of the other two. These effects are found on the right-hand side of Figure 1 and correspond to the "windows" of opportunity of market growth, or the loss of opportunity through increased protectionism, indicated by the opening in the "border" as permitted by the FTA.

The circular nature of the apparent flows of both goods and institutional protection, or assistance measures to producers and processors, is designed to reflect the reality that the provisions contained in the FTA have a continuing effect and are not one-time shots that adjust the trade flows of agriculturally based products between Canada and the U.S. This dynamic interpretation is extremely important since it can dramatically reverse a static interpretation of the long-run effects of changes brought about due to an FTA provision. We will now examine each of the effects.

The Price Effect

Prior to the signing of the FTA, the normal distribution, or export channel, for agricultural products from Canada to the U.S. was through producers supplying Canadian processors with the final products being exported across the border. A secondary channel was by exporting unprocessed products, or products with marginal preparation for packaging purposes, directly to the U.S. for either final consumption or further processing.

Both channels were subject to U.S. tariffs and other border measures, some of which have been changed by the FTA. These two flows can be seen at the top of Figure 1. With the FTA, agricultural exports are enhanced over the long term by the reduction of duties on agricultural products agreed to under Chapter 4. This is further aided by Chapter 11 of the FTA, which can restrict the imposition of duties should the U.S. apply for emergency relief, and for certain agricultural products by the immediate acceptance of either country's technical standards, particularly for beef and veal under Article 704. In the longer run, these standards will be harmonized across all agricultural products with the negotiations undertaken under Article 708.

However, with the maintenance of marketing boards under Article 710 and the ongoing limitations on imports of chickens, turkeys, and eggs under Article 706, there is the possibility that Canadian food processors could find themselves noncompetitive due to the higher prices imposed by

76   *October 1990*   *NJARE*

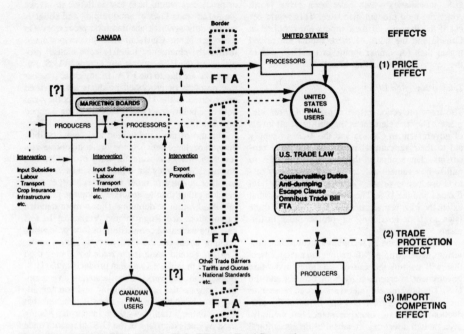

Figure 1.   Effects of the Canada-U.S. FTA on Food Processing

these marketing boards. This could lead to the scenario depicted in Figure 1.

Due to the marketing boards, the export channel from food processors in Canada shrinks, or even disappears for some types of food processing. If the Canadian food processor is producing under scale economy conditions (where price is of the utmost importance and there is extensive import competition, either presently existing or stimulated by the FTA), then the higher input costs of marketing boards could well put this type of food processor out of business. Only if the Canadian food processor is niche oriented and is primarily servicing the Canadian market, and also faces limited price competition from U.S.-based producers, could the Canadian firm be expected to survive.

Canadian producers face a number of possibilities if the scenario outlined above is correct. First, those producers already exporting directly to the U.S. as input suppliers to U.S. processors in such areas as potatoes, fresh fruit, grains, and other unprocessed crop forms may gain if the U.S. processors increase their output to supply processed food products directly to Canada. This is assuming

that first they are not already servicing the Canadian market, and second that the FTA stimulates them to now serve the Canadian market or increase their service to the Canadian market if they are presently doing so, perhaps due to tariff reductions under Chapter 4. If, on the other hand, U.S. marketing boards or programs provide the same sort of restrictive trade or pricing practices as the Canadian boards do, then the market opening generated by duty reductions under Chapter 4 will not permit the Canadian producers to increase their exports directly to the U.S.

In general, the price effect is a result of internal domestic regulations governing agricultural input prices. They segment production into either a predominantly export-oriented food processing sector that has to compete on price, or a Canadian-based sector selling mainly in the domestic market, but facing lower-cost competing products from the U.S. This includes substitutes brought about by the lowering of customs duties under Chapter 4. The price effect applies primarily to economies-of-scale producers who are price dependent to sell their product. Scope processors' operations in Canada, which sell only one or two products across North America, will be similarly affected. This could include U.S. subsidiaries which have been given North American food product mandates. This would occur if the majority of their inputs are supplied in Canada and the costs of these inputs are priced higher than for similar inputs in the U.S. due to the control of a marketing board.

Trade-Protection Effect

The trade-protection effect consists of three elements. The first element is the ability of all levels of government in Canada and the U.S. to supply aid to their agricultural producers and food processors. The second is the ability of the FTA to nullify government assistance that artificially distorts production or sales of food products in both Canada and the U.S. The third element is to what extent the FTA restricts or enhances the use of trade laws as trade-restricting or protectionist instruments.

Chapter 19 of the FTA contains institutional provisions under Article 1907 to develop an agreement that will control the use of subsidies and other government intervention by both Canada and the U.S. The government interventions can be seen in the middle of Figure 1 and can apply at the production, processing, or export stage. Interestingly, even though direct export subsidies on agricultural products are banned under the FTA (Article 701), there are still a variety of programs in both countries that encourage the export of both processed and unprocessed food products.

The eventual decrease in subsidies should permit agricultural prices of inputs to more closely reflect the real cost of their production. This will be of benefit to some products in Canada that receive lower subsidies, or none at all, as compared to their counterpart products in the U.S. Conversely, for those Canadian products that without subsidies are noncompetitive, it could mean a shift for agricultural producers in Canada away from protected crops and also the closure of any Canadian processors who were dependent on the artificially lower-priced input.

Neither Canada nor the U.S. has been exempted from the use of GATT-based Anti-dumping and Subsidy-Countervailing Duty Codes in the FTA. Therefore, while governments may subsidize, or firms price-dump, any artificial benefits received that permit the imported product to be favoured over the domestically produced one can be reduced by the imposition of antidumping or countervailing duties. If Canadian producers are primarily affected by the price effect and are subsequently reduced

in number, the level of government support may be reduced. Therefore, U.S. agricultural producers or processors would have less initiative to invoke the unfair trade laws of antidumping and countervailing duty against Canadian food processors. On the other hand, Canadian food processors could invoke the emergency relief (escape clause) provisions of the FTA against any surges in U.S. imports that are due to the FTA. In any case, whether raw products or processed products are imported or exported to the U.S. is irrelevant, as they can both face punitive actions if they are being dumped or subsidized.

The use of the antidumping and countervailing duty trade laws can become anticompetitive and result in market closure for both processors and producers when they are captured by interest groups in either country in order to reduce market competition rather than to genuinely stop the practices of subsidization or dumping. (For a more detailed explanation, see Rugman and Verbeke.) In this case, the increased competition in food processing brought about by the reductions in duties under Chapter 4 could result in the trade laws being used to restrict the sale of Canadian products in the U.S. market and vice versa. Canada sought an exemption from the use of antidumping and countervailing duty laws by the U.S. since it believed that U.S. "unfair" trade laws were increasingly being used by interest groups in the U.S. to restrict trade (Rugman and Anderson 1987; Rugman 1986 and 1988). This situation may not be entirely an American phenomenon but can also occur in Canada (Porteous and Rugman 1989).

While Canada did not obtain this exemption, it did gain somewhat by the establishment of the right to jointly review the appeals of the decisions of the national authorities on dumping and countervailing in the U.S. These Chapter 19 panels of the FTA are an important gain. The dispute panels set up under Chapter 19 to review the decisions consist of five members, with either two or three Canadians sitting on each panel. Americans can similarly sit on the dispute panels where U.S. producers appeal the decisions of Canadian antidumping and countervailing duty cases. In general, if the panels work properly, they should help to mitigate any unfair use of the trade laws by vested interests in both Canada and the U.S. (Anderson and Rugman 1989 and 1990). At this stage, it is still too early to say whether the dispute panels are working.

Import-Competing Effect

The import-competing effect can be seen in the lower part of Figure 1. This effect is due strictly to the reduction in the barriers to trade, including duties under Chapter 4 and technical-standards barriers under Chapter 7 that have been eliminated with the FTA. These reductions in barriers permit the increased import of U.S. processed and unprocessed agricultural products to Canada. This effect is somewhat mitigated by Canadian controls on raw products governed by marketing boards and by the special provisions contained in the FTA on chickens, turkeys, and eggs under Chapter 7. This is similar to the situation facing some types of Canadian exports to the U.S. where state governments directly restrict imports through their own types of market control mechanisms.

The increased imports of U.S. processed food products could have a negative impact on Canadian food processors based strictly on overall operating costs, regardless of whether there is any government assistance provided to the industry or whether the inputs are governed by a marketing board(s). Large-scale producers in the U.S. will in many cases be more efficient and be able to supply lower-priced products to the final Canadian users.

An example of a U.S. industry facing both lower operating costs as well as an advantage due to lower agricultural input costs is given by the frozen pizza industry. According to a report done for the Canadian Dairy Commission, the two largest Canadian frozen pizza manufacturers, McCain Foods and Pillsbury Foods, have stated that they will move their production facilities to the U.S. unless they can purchase their cheese requirements at competitive prices. The report argues that the Canadian industry, through investments in capital equipment, can increase the efficiency of the Canadian plants, thereby overcoming lower labor costs in the U.S. However, it cannot take corrective measures to reduce the total ingredient cost of a pizza, which is made up of approximately 50 percent mozzarella cheese. The only way the industry can be made competitive in this regard is by having the government adjust the dairy support program or by allowing the industry to purchase cheese at competitive prices so it can compete on an equal basis with imported frozen pizza.

According to the report, 75 percent of Canada's mozzarella cheese production is utilized by the pizza industry. Therefore, any loss of Canadian processing capability would also have serious implications for the dairy industry. The report indicated that Loblaw Companies Limited has already introduced a new frozen pizza, "Presidents Choice—The Decadent," which is imported from the U.S. This product, even including shipping costs, is approximately 5 percent cheaper than a similar Canadian product. Furthermore, there is the likelihood

that Loblaw's will increase its line of imported pizzas as the tariff decreases.

The above case is similar to the situation that Rugman and D'Cruz advance for Canada's service industries. While in many cases services are supplied locally, they often form an input into a larger production process that in many cases has to compete internationally. It is little solace for a Canadian manufacturer to make parts of the process globally competitive if many of the domestic inputs are uncompetitive. According to Rugman and D'Cruz, the whole system has to be made internationally competitive if the Canadian manufacturers are going to succeed.

The import-competing effect may, however, be somewhat mitigated to the extent that cheaper raw agricultural products can enter Canada. In this case, some Canadian food processors may find themselves quite competitive compared to their U.S. counterparts. In many cases it will depend on consumer demand elasticities and price elasticities. For some types of higher-priced processed food products, taste patterns can still permit market differentiation even if a strict niching strategy is not undertaken by Canadian food processors.

It is also not clear to what degree the marketing of products, rather than the consumer pricing decision, influences purchase patterns. It is not apparent that lower-priced processed food products will always have a competitive edge due to differences in taste and perceived quality by differentiating consumers. In this case, each type of food processor will have to determine its relative market positioning—whether as a low-cost price-driven processor, as a niche specialty-product player, or even as a combination player exhibiting some of the benefits of both a low-cost and niche player. In either case, it can be assumed that as barriers to trade come down between Canada and the U.S., there will be necessary adjustments in certain sectors of the Canadian food processing industry based strictly on U.S. comparative advantage in those processed food products sold in Canada.

Canadian Internal Adjustments

In addition to the direct FTA provisions governing trade in agriculture between Canada and the U.S. and the dispute-settlement procedures that may also have an effect on agricultural trade, there are other key considerations that must be taken into account. One is the decentralized nature of the political process in Canada that governs the regulation of agricultural production and processing in Canada. Overall there is no centralized strategy for agriculture. What one government in Canada does may be entirely different than the other provinces or the federal government. This can have the effect of creating market restrictions within Canada such that the FTA will encourage a north-south orientation in agricultural trade, permitting U.S. producers or processors to target the entire Canadian market with adjustments for the individual provinces.

In many cases, these U.S.-based producers or processors already have a distinct market advantage due to the larger consumer market areas in the U.S. Canadian producers, on the other hand, face restrictions on operating east-west at the same time they have to contend with smaller consumer market areas in Canada. Therefore, while the FTA is encouraging a more competitive environment in Canada-U.S. agricultural trade, agricultural market practices in Canada are restricting intra-Canadian trade. In the long run this noncompetitive market environment in Canada could be more detrimental to Canadian food processors and producers than the changes in the competitive environment that are actually due to the FTA.

In this context, agriculture is a microcosm of Canada. The decentralized nature of the Canadian federation led to many sectors being exempted from the FTA (Rugman and Anderson 1987b). The net result of this is simply to postpone economic adjustment to a later date, depending upon the suppressed degree of protectionism inherent in the exempted sector. In some cases, such as marketing boards in agriculture, the postponement was a lot shorter than anticipated. Now food processors will need to become stronger lobbyists in order to offset the protectionist farming lobby.

References

Anderson, Andrew, and Alan Rugman. "The Canada-U.S. Free Trade Agreement: A Legal and Economic Analysis of the Dispute Settlement Mechanisms." *World Competition: Law and Economics Review* 13, no. 1 (1989a):43–60.

———. "Subsidies in the U.S. Steel Industry: A New Conceptual Framework and Literature Review." *Journal of World Trade* 23, no. 6 (December 1989b):59–84.

Canada. Agriculture Canada. Communications Branch. *The Canada-U.S. Free Trade Agreement and Agriculture: An Assessment*. Ottawa, 1988a.

Canada. International Trade Communications Group. Department of External Affairs. *The Canada-U.S Free Trade Agreement*. Ottawa, 1988b.

Canada. Ministry of Agriculture and Food. Food Industry Advisory Committee. *Report of the Food Industry Advisory Committee*. Ottawa, January 1990.

Canadian Dairy Commission. Dairy Task Force. *Comparative Canada-U.S. Frozen Pizza Industry Cheese Prices*. Produced for the Canadian Dairy Commission by A.A. Hunt & Associates, 5 January 1990.

Drohan, Madelaine. "Portrayal as farm subsidy sinner irks Canada." *Globe and Mail* (Toronto), 3 April 1990, B3.

"Gloom Greets Heinz Pact." *Globe and Mail*, 12 June 1990, B4.

Organization for Economic Cooperation and Development (OECD). *Modelling the Effects of Agricultural Policies*. OECD Economic Studies, no. 13. Winter 1989–90.

Porteous, Samuel, and Alan M. Rugman. "Canadian Unfair Trade Laws and Corporate Strategy." *Review of International Business Law* 3, no. 1 (November 1989): 237–70.

Rugman, Alan M. "U.S. Protectionism and Canadian Trade Policy." *Journal of World Trade Law* 20, no. 4 (July/August 1986): 363–80.

———. "A Canadian Perspective on U.S. Administered Protection and the Free Trade Agreement." *Maine Law Review* 40, no. 2 (1988): 305–24.

Rugman, Alan M., and Andrew Anderson. "A Fishy Business: The Abuse of American Trade Law in the Atlantic Groundfish Case of 1985–1986." *Canadian Public Policy* 13, no. 2 (June 1987a): 152–64.

———. *Administered Protection in America*. London: Croom Helm, and New York: Methuen, Inc., 1987b.

———. "Business and Trade Policy: The Structure of Canada's New Private Sector Advisory System." *Canadian Journal of Administrative Sciences* 4, no. 4 (December 1987c): 367–80.

Rugman, Alan M., and Joseph R. D'Cruz. *New Visions for Canadian Business: Strategies for Competing in the Global Economy*. Toronto: Commissioned and produced by Kodak Canada Inc., 1990.

Rugman, Alan M., and Samuel D. Porteous. "The Softwood Lumber Decision of 1986: Broadening the Nature of U.S. Administered Protection." *Review of International Business Law* 2, no. 1 (May 1988): 35–58.

———. "Canadian and U.S. Unfair Trade Laws: A Comparison of Their Legal and Administrative Structures." *Canadian Business Law Journal* 16, no. 1 (December 1989): 1–20.

Rugman, Alan M., and Alain Verbeke. *Global Corporate Strategy and Trade Policy*. London: Routledge, 1990.

Rutenberg, David P. "Multinational Food and Fish Corporations." In *New Theories of Multinational Enterprises*, ed. Alan M. Rugman, 217–37. London: Croom Helm, 1982.

Statistics Canada. Minister of Supply and Services Canada. *Manufacturing Industries of Canada: National and Provincial Areas*. Ottawa, 1989.

United States International Trade Commission. *Annual Reports*. Washington, DC, 1980–89.

[22]

FOREIGN OWNERSHIP, FREE TRADE, AND THE CANADIAN ENERGY SECTOR

Alan M. Rugman and Mark Warner*

Introduction

The Canada-U.S. Free Trade Agreement signed by Prime Minister Brian Mulroney and President Ronald Reagan on January 2, 1988, signals the beginning of a new era in bilateral trade and investment relations. In no sector is this more apparent than in energy. From the date the agreement came into effect, there has been an integrated energy policy for North America. Canadian producers of energy now have secure access to the U.S. market which will enhance the future prosperity of the industry. American investors now face greater predictability in the conduct of Canadian

---

*Alan M. Rugman, Professor International Business at the University of Toronto, is Research Director of the Ontario Center for International Business. Previously, he was on the faculties of Dalhousie University and the University of Winnipeg and has also held visiting posts at Columbia Business School, London Business School, and Harvard University. Author of a dozen books and over 60 papers published in such journals as the *American Economic Review*, *Journal of World Trade Law*, and *California Management Review*, as a sampling, his more recent work has dealt with Canadian investment strategy and global trade policy. Dr. Rugman served on Canada's International Trade Advisory Committee from 1986 to 1988, during the period of negotiations for the Canada-U.S. Free Trade Agreement.

Mark Warner, currently in the law program at Osgood Hall, York University (Ontario), holds an M.A. in economics from the University of Toronto. He was a Research Assistant at the Ontario Center for International Business when this article was prepared.

The Journal of Energy and Development, Vol. 14, No. 1

1

2   THE JOURNAL OF ENERGY AND DEVELOPMENT

energy policy. No longer will potential investors be deterred by the prospect of another economic fiasco along the lines of the 1980-1981 National Energy Program (NEP). A major benefit of the bilateral trade agreement is that future flip-flops of government policy will be prevented. This is a significant consideration in an industry where long-term capital investment decisions have to be made. This will benefit Canadian-owned multinationals such as Alcan, Nova, and Gulf Canada, as well as energy developments by foreign-owned firms such as Shell Canada, Mobil Oil, and Imperial Oil.

Based on 1986 data, the energy sector accounts for over 7 percent of Canadian gross domestic product (GDP) and for over 305,000 jobs. In certain regions, such as the three prairie provinces of Alberta Saskatchewan, and Manitoba, energy accounts for over 20 percent of output. The United States is the destination for more than 80 percent of Canadian energy exports and, in turn, it supplies 36 percent of Canada's energy imports. Canada realized a bilateral balance-of-trade surplus in energy in 1986 with its $10 billion of exports being five times as much as energy imports. The importance of energy trade to the Canadian economy is further underlined by the fact that in 1986 energy exports to the United States accounted for 11 percent of merchandise exports to the United States.[1]

The main proposition of this paper is that, on efficiency grounds the Free Trade Agreement will ensure the future prosperity of the Canadian energy industry. However, there is more to the economics of energy than efficiency. For most of the last 30 years, Canada has pursued policies to safeguard Canadian sovereignty in the development of its own energy resources. These may, in economic terms, be classified as "nonefficiency," or distributional, policies. The NEP was the most extreme form of such interventionist policies. It was based on the questionable premise that the ownership of capital and resources is somehow more important than the performance and conduct of capital and corporations. In the remainder of this article Canada's interventionist attitude towards the economics of energy is reviewed and analyzed.

We find that certain of Canada's regulatory policies did succeed at "Canadianizing" the oil and gas sector. However, this was achieved at the cost of huge capital outflows from the energy sector and a deepening of the recession in Canada over the 1981-1983 period. The

FOREIGN OWNERSHIP, TRADE, CANADIAN ENERGY   3

recent experience strongly suggests that although foreign ownership restrictions have been grandfathered in the Free Trade Agreement, they have already achieved their goals and now represent a drag on the performance of this key industrial sector. As is the case in a few other areas, such as agricultural marketing boards, the provisions of the Free Trade Agreement represent an unfinished agenda.

We begin with a brief analysis of multinationals and efficiency. Second, we examine the policies of the Foreign Investment Review Agency (FIRA) and the NEP as a case study of the impacts of the regulatory regime on foreign ownership and the economic vitality of the energy sector. We conclude with a discussion of the new market-based emphasis in Canadian energy policies embodied in other sections of the Canada-U.S. Free Trade Agreement.

Multinationals and Efficiency

The global energy industry is dominated by large multinational enterprises. These firms function in a similar manner to other multinational enterprises in other global industries. Essentially these are companies which have obtained a competitive advantage through the possession of some knowledge or skill. These firms have internalized their skills in the production and retrieval of oil and gas. In order to maintain the source of their competitive advantages, they operate through the use of foreign subsidiaries. The theory of internalization argues that these skills are often difficult to value and price in a regular market system. Thus these firms utilize an internal market within the firm.[2]

Crucial to the ability of these firms to maintain their competitive advantages are the global coordination and configuration decisions that they make. These decisions allow the firm to combine the country-specific advantages of many regions with their own firm-specific advantages.[3] As a result, policies which interfere with their internal corporate strategic operations are likely to make them wary of making new investment decisions. Such policies increase the uncertainty of the environment in which they operate and, if prices are unstable, then the problem is only accentuated. One of the principal reasons for foreign direct investment is risk diversification, so

4   THE JOURNAL OF ENERGY AND DEVELOPMENT

further uncertainty will raise questions about the appropriateness of any new initiative.[4]

However, neither internalization theory nor corporate strategy finds that these firms earn monopoly rents. Previous empirical work also supports the contention that these firms do not earn excess profits.[5] Through the competition between these firms in the global marketplace, any economic rents are competed away. Both theory and empirical evidence suggest that there are strong adverse implications for countries pursuing noneconomic, antiefficiency policies in key industrial sectors. Yet even in developed resource-abundant countries such as Canada, the foreign ownership of capital is often resented, leading to mistaken regulatory policies usually based on false information and fears about the power of multinational enterprises.

The Regulatory Climate of 1980-1986

Trade and foreign direct investment have always been contentious issues of public policy in Canada. The introduction of the NEP in 1985, its abolition in 1985, and changes in the operation of FIRA between 1980 and 1985 have focused the debate between efficiency and distribution in the energy sector. A number of analysts have discussed aspects of the NEP and FIRA, and the reasons for these changes in policy administration.[6]

The major goal of the NEP was to reduce foreign ownership of the energy sector and its major tools were two types of regulations: first, regulations to increase Canadian ownership of the oil and gas industry to the 50 percent mark by 1990; and second, regulations to give discriminatory incentives to Canadian firms to engage in frontier exploration.

These regulations were implemented by a series of discriminatory policy initiatives. First was the Petroleum Incentives Program (PIP) grants to encourage exploration by Canadian-owned and controlled firms. These discriminatory grants were structured so that the highest grants went to those with 65 percent or more Canadian ownership. Second was the reservation of a 25-percent interest in the Canada Lands for the Crown. This permitted the federal government a "back-in" on successful discoveries. The third initiative was

FOREIGN OWNERSHIP, TRADE, CANADIAN ENERGY 5

the requirement that the overall average of Canadian ownership of a producing field in the Canada Lands be 50 percent. Fourth was the use of Petro Canada to acquire major foreign-owned Canadian operating companies. Fifth was the establishment of the Canadian Ownership Rate (COR) tests. These provided that if the COR was less than 50 percent, the federal government could expropriate, without compensation, to bring the COR to the requisite level. This provision applied retroactively to discoveries made before the 1982 enactment.[7]

At the same time, with Herb Gray as Minister in 1980-1981, FIRA began to monitor applications for acquisitions and new investments by foreign interests very closely. As a result, the approval rate for all new applications fell to about 70 percent in the 1980-1982 period.[8] The Foreign Investment Review Agency also began to set more stringent performance requirements on the applicants. This created a climate of uncertainty, leading to reduced inflows of foreign direct investment at a time when the recession began to bite.

Since the Progressive Conservative government came to power in 1984, many of the energy programs have been abolished or modified. Petroleum Incentives Program grants have been replaced by an exploration tax credit accessible to both foreign and Canadian firms, in effect from December 1, 1985 to December 31, 1990. Exploration licenses are now auctioned as is done in the United States, and preferential treatment is no longer maintained for Petro Canada.

Even with the signing of the Free Trade Agreement, the Canadian government is still committed to 50 percent Canadian ownership of the industry. The 50-percent ownership guideline now, however, does not apply retroactively. A company will now have to submit a plan to reach this level by reasonable commercial measures. If the company does not abide by the plan, then the energy minister may require an auction of a suitable portion of the production licence to attain the minimum level of Canadian ownership.[9]

In November 1986 the Honorable Marcel Masse, Minister of Energy, Mines and Resources, outlined government policy for the upstream oil and gas sector. Investment Canada (which replaced FIRA) is bound by this policy not to "approve the acquisition of a healthy Canadian-controlled firm valued in excess of $5 million."[10] This policy does not apply to indirect acquisitions or to those

6   THE JOURNAL OF ENERGY AND DEVELOPMENT

involving Canadian firms (such as Dome Petroleum) in clear financial difficulty.

In 1985 the Foreign Investment Review Agency was essentially abolished and its place was taken by Investment Canada. This new agency, established under the Investment Canada Act, has as its goal the promotion and attraction of foreign investment in Canada, rather than the discouragement of such capital. No longer is an investment reviewed to demonstrate "significant" benefit to Canada; there need only be a demonstration of a "net" benefit. Investment Canada decisions are based on six criteria set out in the act. These evaluate the contributions of the investment to economic activity, productivity, technological development, intra- and interindustry competition, and export potential. Under the Free Trade Agreement this screening procedure is essentially retained, although the threshold level for review will rise to $150 million in sales. This will obviously cover all major oil takeovers. Some of the performance requirements will no longer apply, but others are grandfathered.

In practical terms foreign ownership levels have not been of deep concern under the implementation of the Investment Canada Act. In fact, new foreign investments are not reviewed and no takeovers have been turned down by Investment Canada, nor have any performance requirements been imposed during the first three years of the act. Investment Canada is a welcome mat for foreign direct investment. The bilateral trade agreement now adds the principle of national treatment to the current open-door policy for foreign investment in Canada, although currently excepted sectors are grandfathered.

Foreign Control in the Energy Sector

We now analyze data on the level of foreign ownership and control and recent foreign direct investment trends in the energy sector. Most of the focus will be on the petroleum and gas industry, since the other sectors are less affected by changes in government regulations. The electrical energy industry is run mainly in the form of provincial public utilities across Canada, thus minimizing issues of foreign ownership and investment. As for the coal sector, it tends to

FOREIGN OWNERSHIP, TRADE, CANADIAN ENERGY   7

be affected by the same set of factors that affect the petroleum and gas sector, since coal production is related to the upstream segment of the petroleum and gas industry.

We use data on foreign control because it is more up to date than the foreign ownership data. For the most part, there is little divergence between the two measures except in the rail and utilities sector, which exhibit higher foreign control ratios than foreign ownership ratios.

Table 1 demonstrates that significant reductions in foreign control in the energy sector have occurred in recent years. Today, the degree of foreign control is under 1 percent in electricity, 26 percent in coal, 46 percent in natural gas, and 57 percent in crude oil. The decline in the latter two sectors can be attributed partly to the activity of NEP and FIRA. The NEP created incentives to provide a major thrust towards Canadian control. Foreign control fell from 70 percent in 1981 to 56 percent in 1985 for the petroleum sector. Similarly, in terms of natural gas, foreign control of upstream production fell from 59 percent in 1981 to stand at roughly 45 percent in 1985. Canada is now below the 50-percent target. Interestingly, in 1986 with the end of the NEP, the decline in these foreign control ratios appears to be leveling off. For the coal industry, Canadianization occurred very early in the life of the NEP. In the first year alone, the foreign control level fell by half from roughly 60 percent in 1979 to 29 percent in 1980.

These declines in foreign control are more marked than those in the manufacturing sector. Between 1978 and 1984 the foreign control ratio declined from 56 percent to 50 percent. This hints that the selective approaches of the NEP and not the broader screening by FIRA was primarily responsible for the decline in foreign control in the energy sector.

Data provided from the Balance-of-Payments (BOP) Division of Statistics Canada offer further insight into trends in foreign control. These data report the same marked decline in foreign control of Canadian industry over this period. However, the actual level of foreign control is substantially lower. Table 2 indicates that in 1986 foreign control of the petroleum and natural gas industries together was 31 percent as opposed to the Corporation and Labour Unions Relations Act (CALURA) data used by the Petroleum Monitoring

8   THE JOURNAL OF ENERGY AND DEVELOPMENT

Table 1

FOREIGN CONTROL[a] BY REVENUES, 1978-1986
(as percent of revenues)

Year	Total Manu-facturing	All Non-financial	Crude Oil	Natural Gas	Coal	Electric Utilities
1978	56.0	33.5	–	–	60.6	1.9
1979	54.0	33.6	–	–	59.0	2.2
1980	51.8	31.7	–	–	28.8	0.6
1981	49.2	29.1	70.1	58.7	27.0	0.6
1982	50.2[b]	29.2	68.8	53.6	33.4	0.6
1983	50.2	29.6	66.7	55.1	30.5	0.5
1984	50.4	29.7	65.0	51.8	26.3	0.5
1985	49.9	29.0	56.4	45.6	–	–
1986	–	–	56.9	45.5	–	–

[a]Control taken as 50 percent or more of voting shares.
[b]The 1978-1982 totals calculated by total foreign-controlled manufacturing revenues, over total manufacturing not including undistributed revenues.
Sources: Canada, Petroleum Monitoring Agency, *Annual Reports*, 1981-1986, especially 1986, p. A-17; 1985, p. A-15; 1984, p. 13-13; 1982, table 14; and Corporation and Labour Unions Relations Act, *Annual Report*, Part I, 1979-1984, and 1985 (Sales).

Agency (PMA) which was used in table 1. The discrepancy is lower for data on the manufacturing sector. The CALURA data in table 1 report foreign ownership at 49 percent in 1985 while the BOP Division data give 48 percent.

These data, shown in table 2, demonstrate that, as of 1986, foreign interests controlled only 22 percent of all nonfinancial corporations, with American control being only 16 percent. Thus, the trend in the decline of foreign control is not particular to the energy sector. These new data in table 2 call into question the view that the Canadian economy is controlled abroad. The low and falling foreign control ratios are further evidence of the need to rethink policies and institutions designed to discourage foreign investment, especially where these policies may be hindering economic growth.

FOREIGN OWNERSHIP, TRADE, CANADIAN ENERGY   9

Table 2

SECTORAL FOREIGN AND U.S. CONTROL BY CAPITAL EMPLOYED,
1978-1986
(in percent)

Year	Total Manufacturing		All Nonfinancial Corporations		Petroleum and Natural Gas	
	Total Foreign	United States	Total Foreign	United States	Total Foreign	United States
1978	53	41	28	22	54	41
1979	51	39	28	21	53	40
1980	51	40	27	21	50	38
1981	47	36	25	19	38	30
1982	49	37	24	18	38	30
1983	48	36	24	18	36	28
1984	48	36	24	18	36	28
1985	48	36	23	17	31	23
1986	47	35	22	16	31	23

Sources: 1981-1986 data obtained from Statistics Canada, Balance of Payments Division, and 1978-1979 data from Statistics Canada, *Canada's International Investment Position*, 1978 and 1979, publication no. 67-202, table 32.

The new BOP Division data demonstrate that the degree of foreign control of the Canadian economy has been overstated in recent years. These data for foreign control are based upon total capital employed in the enterprise.   Therefore, all the capital employed by a firm is placed under the country of effective control.   The CALURA data, in table 1, are based on the revenues of the firms in the industry. CALURA takes 50 percent of voting shares as indicative of control unless effective control is exercised with less.   After this determination, the revenues are allotted to either the foreign or Canadian data.

Another difference between the BOP Division and the CALURA data is the survey reporting requirements.   The BOP Division data require corporations to report any holding of 5 percent of any class of share, while CALURA's requirement is 10 percent.   Thus the data of the BOP Division are more comprehensive in determining the actual level of foreign control. One further difference between the two data bases is that the BOP Division includes the pipeline sector, which is substantially Canadian owned. So, in a sense, the CALURA data underestimate the total foreign control of the oil and gas industry.

To the extent that Canadianization has been achieved, further data from the PMA raise some important questions. The financial performance of Canadian-owned enterprises in this sector has been less satisfactory than for the foreign-controlled firms, whether this financial performance is measured by return on capital employed or return on equity. For example, in 1986 after six years of Canadian takeovers in the oil patch, the return on capital employed for foreign firms was 4 percent while on Canadian firms the rate was negative 4 percent. Canadianization of the energy sector may have been achieved at the expense of the financial health of the industry. (Table 5 will amplify this point.)

Table 3 demonstrates the success rate under FIRA for acquisition applications in the mines, mineral fuels, and incidental services sector of which energy is a component. Beginning in 1980 the success rate dropped from slightly above the all-industry rate in 1979 to well below the all-industry rate. There was only an 18-percent approval rate in the 1981-1982 period for the energy sector. This trend continued until 1984, when the success rate grew from 65 percent in the previous year to 94 percent. The most recent data available from Investment Canada demonstrate that the success rates have reached 100 percent for new establishments and 97 percent for recent acquisitions. These higher success rates, while still marginally lower than the all-industry rates, reflect the new features of the Investment Canada Act.

Table 4 shows another dimension in the decline in foreign control. Taking 5 percent of voting shares as the relevant criterion to measure foreign ownership, the PMA has combined data to reflect the fact that control of a corporation can be exercised without 50 percent of all voting shares. Essentially, the PMA has amended CALURA data with BOP Division data. This table aggregates both the upstream and downstream revenues for the oil and gas industry. Foreign ownership has declined from 73 percent in 1980 to 55 percent in 1986. Over the same period foreign control fell from 81 to

FOREIGN OWNERSHIP, TRADE, CANADIAN ENERGY   11

Table 3

FOREIGN INVESTMENT REVIEW AGENCY APPLICATIONS SUCCESS
RATES FOR MINES (M), MINERAL FUELS (MF), AND INCIDENTAL
SERVICES (IS), 1978/79-1986/87

	M, MF, IS			Total All Industries			Success M, MF, IS (%)	Success All Industry (%)
	A[a]	D[b]	W[c]	A[a]	D[b]	W[c]		
Acquisitions								
1978/79	19	-	2	296	26	91	90.5	87.8
1979/80	17	6	2	331	29	68	68.0	85.1
1980/81	5	5	3	215	36	39	38.5	73.4
1981/82	2	7	2	248	36	18	18.2	79.0
1982/83	17	5	4	469	13	65	65.4	90.5
1983/84	16	-	1	430	5	94	94.1	91.9
1984/85	23	-	2	464	4	26	92.0	93.9
1985/86	29	-	1	475	-	7	96.7	98.5
1986/87	28	-	1	642	-	10	96.6	98.5
New establishments								
1978/79	15	-	4	280	18	24	78.9	87.0
1979/80	16	2	1	356	29	25	84.2	86.8
1980/81	8	1	6	233	27	33	53.3	79.5
1981/82	21	3	6	265	45	95	70.0	65.5
1982/83	15	-	1	455	47	59	93.8	81.1
1983/84	15	-	3	428	22	43	83.3	86.8
1984/85	12	1	1	474	6	27	85.7	93.5
1985/86	13	-	-	318	-	-	100.0	100.0
1986/87	5	-	-	313	-	-	100.0	100.0

[a] A = accepted applications.
[b] D = disallowed applications.
[c] W = withdrawn applications.
Sources: Canada, Foreign Investment Review Agency, *Annual Reports*, various issues, 1979/80, 1984/85, especially tables XI and XXI, and Investment Canada, *Annual Report*, 1985/86, especially tables XIV and XII.   Data for 1986/87 obtained from Investment Canada.

12   THE JOURNAL OF ENERGY AND DEVELOPMENT

Table 4

OWNERSHIP[a] AND CONTROL[b] BY COUNTRY AND SECTOR FOR OIL AND GAS INDUSTRY, 1980-1986
(as percent of revenues)

	United States	Other Foreign	Total Upstream + Downstream	Total Upstream
Ownership				
1980	57.2	16.7	73.9	71.6
1981	52.7	14.5	67.2	62.6
1982	51.2	14.1	65.3	61.0
1983	50.4	10.7	61.1	58.7
1984	48.3	11.3	59.6	57.5
1985	40.3	11.5	51.8	51.7
1986	40.2	14.8	55.0	51.2
Control				
1980	61.6	19.7	81.3	76.9
1981	56.5	17.6	74.1	63.5
1982	56.8	17.5	74.5	81.7
1983	56.5	13.9	70.4	61.6
1984	53.8	14.2	68.0	59.5
1985	42.8	14.4	57.3	52.1
1986	42.3	17.5	59.9	52.3

[a]Ownership taken as 5 percent or more voting shares.
[b]Control taken as 50 percent or more voting shares.
Sources: Canada, Petroleum Monitoring Agency, *Annual Reports*, various issues, 1981-1986, especially table 14.

60 percent. In terms of upstream revenues alone, foreign ownership fell from 72 to 51 percent and foreign control from 77 percent to 52 percent.

These results demonstrate that Canadianization in the upstream sector outpaced the downstream effort. This is partly due to the nature of the incentives offered under the NEP. As expected, the decline in foreign control outpaced the decline in ownership; the overall decline is very significant. One interesting footnote is that in 1985 and 1986 both the ratios of control and ownership seem to be increasing due primarily to trends in the downstream parts of the

FOREIGN OWNERSHIP, TRADE, CANADIAN ENERGY 13

market. Over the same period, upstream control and ownership ratios have remained fairly constant at 52 percent and 51 percent, respectively. However, for both the upstream and downstream parts of the market, control and ownership ratios have risen slightly.

Table 4 also gives an insight into the geographic distribution of the decline by area of control. In terms of both ownership and control, the major declines have come at the expense of U.S.-based interests. Between 1980 and 1986, U.S. ownership declined from 57 percent to 40 percent (mainly in the first three years). Non-U.S. foreign ownership fell from 17 to 15 percent.

Foreign Investment and Energy Policy

Table 5 shows the direct investment flows associated with the Canadianization policy. In 1979 and 1980 the flow of foreign direct investment (FDI) in Canada was positive. However, beginning in 1981 this trend was reversed with a high outflow of just over $5 billion. If one considers similar Canadian direct investment abroad, there was already a net outflow in 1979. Net outflows from the oil and gas sector alone rose consistently from 1979 to 1982 where they represented 87 percent of total all-industry outflows from Canada. Between 1980 and 1985 net outflows from this sector totaled slightly more than $15 billion. The decline of inward foreign direct investment represented close to 80 percent of the total outflow from this sector.

These results are consistent with previous studies.[11] What is significant is that these Canadian policies also increased uncertainty about the overall health of the industry, even from the point of view of Canadian firms. Thus, even these companies shifted their investment spending abroad to the United States, which was deregulating the energy industry and providing a favorable business climate. The NEP and tightened administration of FIRA were the nails in the economic coffin that was Canada during the recession years.

In 1985 and 1986 total outflows from the oil and gas sector accounted for 53 percent and 74 percent of the total, respectively. Recent changes in the NEP and FIRA have not yet encouraged renewed foreign investment. Data from the PMA reveal that in 1986

14   THE JOURNAL OF ENERGY AND DEVELOPMENT

Table 5

FOREIGN DIRECT INVESTMENT (FDI) FLOWS FOR THE OIL AND
GAS INDUSTRY, 1979-1986
(in millions of Canadian dollars)

Year	Canadian FDI Abroad	FDI in Canada	Net Inflow/ (Outflow)
1979	-517	78	- 439
1980	-1,252	228	-1,024
1981	-1,849	-5,168	-7,017
1982	-586	-1,069	-1,655
1983	-575	-492	-1,067
1984	-231	-117	-348
1985	-335	-3,991	-4,326
1986	-49	-2,152	-2,201

Source: Statistics Canada, *Canada's Balance of International Payments,*
quarterly, 1985-1987, no. 2.

Canadian firms reduced their capital expenditure by nearly 40 percent while foreign firms reduced their own by 26 percent. Perhaps
this is, in part, due to the negative investment signals sent out by the
goal of 50-percent Canadian ownership retained even in the current
energy policy.   Possibly it is also due to persistent low world oil
prices, although there is some recent evidence that this is changing.
  Finally, it is worth noting that the regulations imposed by Canada
in the energy sector have been timed to maximize efficiency losses.
B. W. Waverman has calculated that over the 1973-1986 period there
was an inverse correlation between the price of crude oil and Canadian exports.[12]   Over these years of regulation, Canadian exports
increased in periods of low world oil prices and fell in periods of
potential profitability.   It would appear from this evidence that the
Free Trade Agreement would be a marked improvement over policies which have failed to use Canadian energy exports in an efficient
manner.

FOREIGN OWNERSHIP, TRADE, CANADIAN ENERGY   15

Energy Policy and the Free Trade Agreement

The Canada-U.S. Free Trade Agreement recognizes the importance of the energy sector in bilateral trade. It builds upon the deregulation of the energy sector that has occurred in both countries. In so doing, one of the principal objectives of the agreement is to reestablish the role of markets in economic decision making. Analysts such as Edward Carmichael show that the agreement represents a formal recommitment, by both countries, to their international obligations under the General Agreement on Tariffs and Trade and the International Energy Agreement of 1974.[13]

Even before the Free Trade Agreement there were no tariffs imposed by either country on natural gas, electricity, or uranium, except for the custom's user fee imposed by the United States. It has been estimated that the five-year phasing out of this program will result in savings of close to Canadian $17 million per year to the energy sector in Canada.[14] The United States also maintains tariffs on crude-oil and petroleum products. This has hampered the growth of the downstream energy sector in Canada. For example, in 1986 Canada exported to the United States 39 percent of its crude-oil output and 23 percent of natural-gas production but only 10 percent of its refined petroleum products. Under the agreement the downstream oil and gas industry should benefit through scale economies and productivity gains.

The Free Trade Agreement is also significant in reinforcing existing prohibitions of the General Agreement on Tariffs and Trade on the use of quantitative restrictions, taxes, and duties on energy imports and exports. In so doing, the agreement applies the national treatment standard to the energy sector. The United States thereby assures market access for Canadian coal, oil, natural gas, uranium, and even electricity. Both countries, however, retain the right to employ incentives for exploration and development. It is expected that in flagrant cases of subsidization, either party may still seek recourse to countervailing duty action, although such decisions would then be subject to appeal to the new binational dispute settlement panel. This panel will have the power, in effect, to review the economic substance of U.S. trade law decisions, an ability unfortunately lacking in current practice.[15]

16   THE JOURNAL OF ENERGY AND DEVELOPMENT

Price discrimination by governments has been eliminated under the agreement. The National Energy Board price tests will remain, as these are principally concerned with ensuring that energy exports are not underpriced. Campbell Watkins and Leonard Waverman have demonstrated that any price differentials between Canadian and U.S. users will be due to the terms and timing of contracts.[16] In times of shortage both countries have reaffirmed their commitment to proportional supply based on the previous 36-month moving average of supplies. The rationale for proportionality is to prevent a cycle of downturns in the energy sector worsening the overall economies of both countries. It is also a sound business strategy. To impose the full costs of such problems on a trading partner may encourage it to seek other sources of supply in the future.

While the national treatment principle has been extended to investment, the existing Canadian ownership restrictions have been grandfathered. Direct foreign acquisition of healthy Canadian oil and gas firms with sales over Canadian $5 million will be precluded. Unhealthy firms may be sold to foreign interests, but these may be subject to the performance requirements and the net-benefit tests of Investment Canada. New investment will not be subject to review by Investment Canada. In the "Frontier Lands" the 50-percent Canadian ownership rule will continue to be strictly applied.

The Canada-U.S. Free Trade Agreement goes some way towards reestablishing the importance of markets in energy policy, through tariff reductions, the principle of national treatment, and rules on proportional sharing in times of shortage. However, the discriminatory rules on foreign ownership remain. As the analysis of an earlier section demonstrated, it is precisely these provisions which have had such a negative effect on growth in the energy sector.

Conclusion

The Canada-U.S. Free Trade Agreement is an extension of the efficiency-based energy policy which exists today. It will help to minimize future uncertainties about Canadian energy policy and thereby improve the investment climate, leading to prosperity for Canadian energy producers. The Free Trade Agreement will save

FOREIGN OWNERSHIP, TRADE, CANADIAN ENERGY 17

Canadians from repeating such misconceived policies as the National Energy Program, which led to a $15-billion outflow from the oil and gas sector.

Yet the Free Trade Agreement has grandfathered Canadian policy in regard to foreign control of the energy sector. Thus, Canada retains the right and ability to pursue the goals of "Canadianization" to which successive governments have been committed. However, the data suggest that the goal has been achieved, for the most part at very great cost to the Canadian economy and the energy sector in particular. If such restrictive policies were to be reintroduced, growth in investment in the oil and gas industry would be slow and another recession could result. In the interests of efficiency and economic growth, Canada should consider moves to abolish all remaining inefficient foreign ownership policies in the energy sector.

NOTES

[1]Canada, Department of Energy, Mines and Resources, *The Canada-U.S. Free Trade Agreement and Energy: An Assessment* (1988).

[2]See Alan M. Rugman, *Multinationals in Canada: Theory, Performance and Economic Impact* (Boston: Martinus-Nijhoff Publishers, 1981).

[3]Alan M. Rugman, *Trade Liberalization and International Investment* (Economic Council of Canada Discussion Paper 347, 1988).

[4]See Alan M. Rugman, *International Diversification and the Multinational Enterprise* (Lexington, Massachusetts: Lexington Books, 1979).

[5]Ibid. and Rugman, *Multinationals in Canada*, chapter 5.

[6]Samuel Baker, "From FIRA to Investment Canada," in *Canada-U.S. Economic Relations*, eds. Earl Fry and Lee Radebaugh (Provo, Utah: Brigham Young University, 1985); David Burgess, "Canada/U.S. Energy Issues: A Canadian Perspective," in *Canada/United States Trade and Investment Issues*, eds. Deborah Fretz, Robert Stern, and John Whalley (Toronto: Ontario Economic Council, 1985); Edward Carmichael and Corina Herrera, "Toward More Flexible Energy Policy," in *Canada's Energy Policy, 1985 and Beyond*, eds. Edward Carmichael and Corina Herrera (Toronto: C. D. Howe Institute, 1985); Brendan Quirin, "Issues in Canada/U.S. Energy Trade and Investment: A U. S. Perspective," in *Canada/United States Trade and Investment Issues*; and Ralph Sultan, "Canada's Recent Experiment in the Repatriation of American Capital," *Canadian Public Policy*, supplement, 1982.

18   THE JOURNAL OF ENERGY AND DEVELOPMENT

[7]Details appear in Canada, Department of Energy, Mines and Resources, *National Energy Program* (1980) and *National Energy Program: Update 1982* (1982), and Edward Carmichael and James Stewart, *Lessons from the National Energy Program* (Toronto: C. D. Howe Institute, 1983).

[8]See Alan M. Rugman, "Canada: FIRA Updated," *Journal of World Trade Law*, July-August 1983.

[9]See Canada, Department of Energy, Mines and Resources, *Canada's Energy Frontier: A Framework for Investment and Jobs* (1985) and Carmichael and Herrera, "Toward More Flexible Energy Policy."

[10]Marcel Masse, Notes for an address by the Canadian Minister of Energy, Mines and Resources, Canada to the American Stock Exchange, Seventh Annual Canadian Oil and Gas Symposium, Toronto, November 6, 1986.

[11]See, for example, Sultan, op. cit.

[12]B. W. Waverman, "Canada's Energy Policy after 1985: Lessons from the Present," in *Canada's Energy Policy, 1985 and Beyond*, 1985.

[13]Edward Carmichael, "Energy and the Canadian-U.S. Free Trade Agreement," *Trade Monitor* (Toronto: C. D. Howe Institute, 1988).

[14]See Canada, Department of Energy, Mines and Resources, *The Canada-U.S. Free Trade Agreement and Energy*.

[15]Alan M. Rugman and Andrew Anderson, *Administered Protection in America* (London: Croom Helm and New York: Methuen, 1987).

[16]Campbell Watkins and Leonard Waverman, "North American Free Trade in Energy: What Might Have Happened and What May Happen," a paper presented to the International Conference of the International Association of Energy Economists, Luxembourg, July 4-7, 1988.

23

A Canadian Perspective on NAFTA

Alan M. Rugman

Although most analysis of the North American Free Trade Agreement (NAFTA) has focused on the bilateral relationship between Mexico and the United States this article concentrates on the larger trading and investment linkages of Canada and the United States. From a Canadian perspective the NAFTA is an extension of (and improvement upon) the Canada–U.S. Free Trade Agreement (FTA) of 1989. The FTA introduced new dispute settlement mechanisms that Canada views as essential to partially offset U.S. administered protection. The new rules-based system of the FTA is also the basis for the NAFTA, and it has been extended from the trade law regime to cover foreign investment disputes. All three parties in NAFTA will benefit from a rules-based system rather than the power-based system that permits U.S. producer interests to exploit the size asymmetries between the large triad market of the United States and the smaller open trading economies of Mexico and Canada. © 1994 John Wiley & Sons, Inc.

INTRODUCTION

The negotiated text of the North American Free Trade Agreement (NAFTA) raises important issues for those interested in U.S.–Canadian economic and business relationships. Assessments of NAFTA are being published elsewhere, for example see Globerman

This is a revised version of an inaugural lecture for the Ross Distinguished Visiting Professorship of Canada–U.S. Business and Economic Relations at the College of Business and Economics, Western Washington University.

Dr. Rugman is Professor of International Business in the Faculty of Management at the University of Toronto, 246 Bloor Street West, Toronto, Ontario, Canada, M5S 1V4.

The International Executive, Vol. 36(1) 33–54 (January/February 1994)
© 1994 John Wiley & Sons, Inc.   CCC 0020-6652/94/01033-22

and Walker (1993), Hufbauer and Schott (1993), Lemco and Robson (1993), Rugman (1994), etc. Here a Canadian perspective on NAFTA is presented. The key Canadian objective in the NAFTA negotiations of 1990–1992 was defensive, to avoid any dissipation of the Canada–U.S. Free Trade Agreement (FTA), which became effective on January 1, 1989. This is because there is relatively little trade, or foreign direct investment, between Canada and Mexico (trade in 1991 was $2.5 billion) compared to the predominant economic relationship between Canada and the United States (with trade of about $180 billion in 1991). These economic principles lead to three propositions.

First, a Canadian perspective on NAFTA requires a focus on U.S.–Canadian economic integration within a triad framework of global competitiveness, and the implications of this for a small open trading economy. Second, the political issue of NAFTA and Canadian sovereignty is to all intents and purposes a discussion of the U.S.–Canadian relationship. In particular, concern over Canadian cultural sovereignty is almost entirely a reflection of perceptions of U.S. domination due to the large size of the United States relative to Canada. Third, the NAFTA is not a customs union, yet it provides an opportunity for Canada to mitigate U.S. economic and political power over Canadians and replace the bilateral FTA with a new trilateral institutional framework, based on the principles of the European Community (EC).

In the next section data are presented on the extent of economic integration between Canada and the United States, all within a "triad" context. Mexico is included as a reference point and the implications for a NAFTA are drawn out. The key role of multinational enterprises (MNEs) as agents for globalization (economic integration) across the triad is discussed in the next two sections with their strategies being related to a discussion of the concepts of globalization and sovereignty in a matrix framework. The matrix is then used to analyze the actual text of the negotiated NAFTA. This framework is also used to discuss the FTA, NAFTA, and the problem of administered protection by the misuse of U.S. trade law. It is suggested that such remaining impediments to true free trade can be overcome by a potential EC type linkage. Finally, there are conclusions.

TRIAD POWER AND CANADA–U.S. ECONOMIC INTEGRATION

To understand the nature of global competition and the role of Canada's economic integration with one of the triad powers (the United States), it is necessary to review the relative positioning of Canada's

Table 1. The World's 500 Largest MNEs

Country/Block	Number of MNEs in 1992
United States	161
Japan	128
EC	125
Sweden	14
South Korea	12
Switzerland	9
Australia	9
Canada	8
Finland	4
Turkey	3
India	3
South Africa	3
Other	21
Total	500

Source: Adapted from *Fortune* (July 26, 1993) "The Fortune Global 500."

multinationals compared to those of the triad. The eight largest MNEs are drawn mainly from the triad of the United States, Japan, and the EC. Table 1 shows that 414 of the world's 500 largest MNEs come from the triad, that is, over 80 percent of the total. These large MNEs also account for well over half of the world's trade and direct investment. Indeed, another way of measuring the importance of MNEs is to look at the data on the world's stock of foreign direct investment (FDI). This is reported in Table 2.

The Triad and Foreign Direct Investment

Table 2 reports changes in the stocks of outbound FDI in the triad over the 1980s. Although the triad's percentage of the world's FDI stayed relatively consistent at just over 80 percent of the total, there were remarkable changes within the triad. The most dramatic change was not the growth of Japanese FDI (which increased from 4 to 12 percent between 1980 and 1989) but the replacement of the United States by the EC as the world's largest single source of FDI. By 1989 the EC accounted for 41 percent of the world's total, and the United States was down to 28 percent (from 40 percent in 1980). The stock of EC FDI increased by nearly $350 billion over the decade of the 1980s, whereas that of the United States rose by $160 billion and Japan's by over $130 billion.

Table 2 also demonstrates that there is relatively little FDI from

Table 2.   Outward Stocks of Triad FDI

Country/Region	1980 (U.S.$Billions)	Percent of World	1989 (U.S.$Billions)	Percent of World
United States	220	42	380	25
EC	203	39	549	41
Japan	20	4	154	12
Triad	443	85	1083	81
Canada	22	4	64	5
All Others	59	11	195	14
World	524	100	1342	100

Note: Data for the E.C.'s FDI include intra-EC FDI, and 1989's figures are based on the U.K., Germany, France, the Netherlands and Italy.

Sources: Data for 1980 are from UNCTC (August 1991) *World Investment Report 1991: The Triad in Foreign Direct Investment,* New York: United Nations. Data for 1989 are provided by the Policy and Research Division, UNCTC (September 1991). Data for Canada's FDI (1980) are based on the data from UNCTC (1988) *Transnational Corporation in World Development: Trends and Prospects,* New York: United Nations.

other countries, including third world countries. Indeed, much of the 19 percent of the nontriad stock of FDI in 1989 was from Canada (at 5 percent) and other advanced nontriad nations.

The Triad And Global Trade Patterns

The pattern of dominance of the world's FDI by the triad is repeated with data on world trade. Figure 1 reports data for 1991 on the annual flows of trade by the triad. Note that the United States could be extended to include Canada (and Mexico) as a "North American" block relevant for discussion of the NAFTA.

The largest number in Figure 1 is in the EC box, that is, trade within the 12 member countries of the EC is the largest in the world at $846 billion. Next largest is the trade between the United States and Canada at $180 billion. Indeed this is the world's largest single trading relationship. There is more trade between the United States and Canada than between the United States and Japan ($140 billion). Further, the United States runs a large deficit (of $44 billion) in its merchandise trade with Japan, whereas U.S. merchandise trade with Canada has a deficit of $10.5 billion, which is offset by a surplus in services to give the United States a current account surplus with Canada.

Figure 2 is identical to Figure 1 except that it is for global stocks of FDI. It reveals a large amount of EC FDI going to North America, more than the North American FDI in the EC. There is also a lot of Japanese FDI into North America but not nearly so much into the EC. There is a large amount of intrablock FDI; these FDI data are

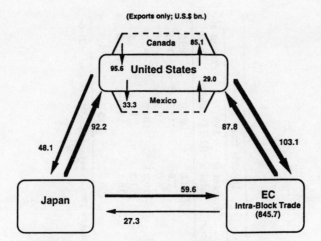

Figure 1. Global flows of trade in the triad, 1991.
Source: See Tables 1–4 sources.

part of the total EC data of Table 2, but here the internal data are broken out from the external data.

Note that the EC data on both trade and FDI should be treated with caution. Each nation publishes data on its trade and FDI, but the numbers of the trade data of Figure 1 and the FDI data of Figure 2 exclude intra-EC trade in order to show a proper triad picture. Unfortunately, the data in Table 2 cannot be constructed to exclude intra-EC data due to statistical problems.

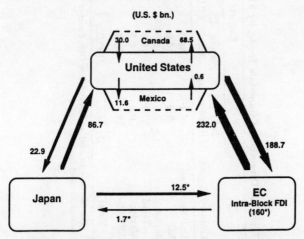

Figure 2. Global stocks of FDI in the triad, 1991.
Source: See Tables 1–4 sources.

Table 3. Direction of Canada's Trade, by Flows

Country/Region	Exports to				Imports from			
	1981 (U.S.$Billions)	Percent of Total	1990 (U.S.$Billions)	Percent of Total	1981 (U.S.$Billions)	Percent of Total	1990 (U.S.$Billions)	Percent of Total
United States	46.4	64.0	95.4	73.0	45.2	66.5	83.0	69.3
EC	7.2	10.0	10.0	8.0	5.3	7.8	13.3	11.1
Japan	3.6	5.0	7.0	5.0	3.4	5.0	8.2	6.9
Triad	57.2	79.0	112.4	86.0	53.9	79.3	104.5	87.3
Mexico	0.6	0.8	0.5	0.4	0.8	1.2	1.5	1.2
All Others	14.9	20.2	18.1	13.6	13.3	19.5	13.7	11.5
Total	72.7	100.0	131.0	100.0	68.0	100.0	119.7	100.0

Sources: Data for 1981 are adapted from IMF, *Direction of Trade Statistics Yearbook 1985*, 126–128. Data for 1990 are adapted from IMF, *Direction of Trade Statistics Yearbook 1991*, 123–125.

Table 4. Direction of Canada's FDI, by Stocks

Country/Region	Outward				Inward			
	1981 (Can.$Billions)	Percent of Total	1990 (Can.$Billions)	Percent of Total	1981 (Can.$Billions)	Percent of Total	1990 (Can.$Billions)	Percent of Total
United States	18.6	66.4	53.1	61.2	52.1	78.2	80.4	64.2
EC	4.1	14.6	16.8	19.4	10.7	16.1	30.0	23.9
Japan	0.1	0.4	0.8	0.9	1.0	1.5	4.3	3.4
Triad	22.8	81.4	70.7	81.5	63.8	95.8	114.7	91.5
Mexico	0.2	0.7	0.2	0.3	0.001		0.001	
All Others	5.0	17.9	15.8	18.2	2.8	4.2	10.6	8.5
Total	28.0	100.0	86.7	100.0	66.6	100.0	125.3	100.0

Sources: Data for 1981 are adapted from Statistics Canada (1986) *Canada's International Investment Position*, Catalogue 67-202. Data for 1990 are adapted from Statistics Canada (1991) *Canada's International Investment Position*, Catalogue 67-202.

Canada's relationship with the triad, and its dependence on the
United States in particular, can be further understood if we consider
its trade and investment with these markets. A more detailed discussion of these points and their relevance for the FTA appears in Rugman (1990). In Table 3 we report data on the direction of Canada's
trade for 1981 and 1990. For example, over this 10-year period Canada's exports to the United States increased from 64 percent to 73
percent of its total; exports to the EC declined to only 8 percent by
1990; and exports to Japan remained at nearly 5 percent. Exports to
Mexico were under half of a percentage point in 1990, and imports
were three times as large at 1.5 percent. A similar picture of Canada's overwhelming dependence on the United States appears in Table
4, except that by 1990 the stock of EC foreign direct investment in
Canada was nearly 24 percent. The U.S. stock of FDI in Canada fell
from 78 percent to 64 percent over the 10-year period.

NAFTA AND STRATEGIES OF MNEs

The major push behind the NAFTA is globalization. Globalization
means the production and distribution of products and/or services of
a homogenous type and quality on a world-wide basis. The producers
and distributors enjoy economies of scale through large volume production of standardized products and services. Most of these goods
and services are provided by MNEs operating across national borders.

To an extent, the MNEs of the triad homogenize tastes and help
spread consumerism (Ohmae, 1990). Throughout the wealthier nations of Europe, North America, and Japan there is a growing acceptance of standardized consumer electronics goods, automobiles,
computers, electric appliances, and so on. Yet, to a large degree, the
MNEs have to respond to consumer needs and tastes. So, multinational enterprises need to consider more than the single goal of efficient economic performance through globalization. They also need to
be more responsive to social needs and national interests. MNEs will
have to deal with the twin goals of globalization and national responsiveness (Bartlett and Ghoshal, 1989). By national responsiveness is
meant the need for corporations operating across national borders to
invest in understanding the different tastes of consumers in segmented regional markets, and the ability to respond to different
national standards and regulations imposed by autonomous governments and agencies. Reich (1991) now recognizes that MNEs are not
just "national champions" and that they also respond to host country
as well as home country values.

To answer the dual challenges of globalization and national responsiveness requires new thinking by managers and policy advisors. The days of simple globalization are limited. Instead, MNEs must face up to making major investments in being nationally responsive, that is, in understanding what makes people tick and why people differ across borders. Cultural understanding is becoming as important as R&D. Globalization of production and distribution feeds one desire but it also creates a hunger for more individual care and attention, requiring the response of a two-pronged corporate strategy.

Put more formally, the corporation now faces a basic challenge of transaction costs economics in dealing with the consumer on a global basis. Because there are literally millions of consumers, yet only a few hundred large MNEs, there exists a problem of asymmetry in information costs, a type of buyer uncertainty. There is no possible solution to this problem by consumers because it is not in any one individual's interest to make the investment of time and money required to achieve a solution that will satisfy everyone else (Rugman, 1981). But the relatively few large MNEs do have this incentive. The MNEs need to stay in business, so they need to be able to achieve both economic efficiency through globalization and also to keep sovereignty at bay, or at least accommodated to the extent that business does not suffer. In short, the MNEs themselves should develop management strategies to be nationally responsive as well as globally efficient. It is to the method of achieving this balance that we now turn.

THE GLOBALIZATION AND SOVEREIGNTY MATRIX

Conceptually, the twin issues of globalization and sovereignty can be analyzed through the use of Figure 3. This is adapted from Bartlett (1986), where he uses a globalization/national responsiveness matrix to analyze the strategies of large MNEs. This work was extended and tested on nine MNEs in the three triad blocks by Bartlett and Ghoshal (1989). Here this framework is adapted to consider the nature of corporate strategies in a world with an increasing amount of sovereignty being exhibited.

The vertical axis captures the concept of the need for economic integration, frequently referred to as globalization. Movement up the axis results in a greater degree of economic integration. Globalization generates economies of scale as a firm moves into worldwide markets selling a single product or service. These are captured as a result of concentrating specific activities in the value-added chain in

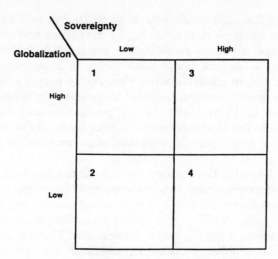

Figure 3. Globalization and sovereignty.

locations with the strongest perceived country specific advantages. They also occur by reaping the benefits of increased coordination and control of geographically dispersed activities.

The horizontal axis measures the need for corporations to respond to sovereignty. Companies need to be "nationally responsive" to consumer tastes and government regulations in the relevant countries in which they operate. Sovereignty means that corporate activities need to be adapted to local conditions, both in terms of content and process. This may imply a geographical dispersion of activities or a decentralization of coordination and control for individual firms. Corporations and financial institutions need either a low or a high degree of awareness of sovereignty.

On the basis of the two axes of Figure 3, four cases can be distinguished. Quadrants 1 and 4 are simple cases. These are two cases where the impact of an exogenous "environmental" change (such as the NAFTA or Europe 1992 measures) unambiguously affects the firm's movement toward a higher required responsiveness to one variable and simultaneously decreases the required responsiveness to the other variable. In quadrant 1, the need for globalization increases and the need for awareness of sovereignty is low. This focus on scale economies will lead to competitive strategies based on Porter's first generic strategy of price competition (Porter, 1980). Usually mergers and acquisitions will result. The opposite situation is characteristic of quadrant 4 where sovereignty matters but globalization is low. There national responsiveness must be pursued; companies will adapt products to satisfy the high demands of sovereignty and ignore scale economies because globalization does not matter very much.

Quadrants 2 and 3 of Figure 3 reflect more complex situations. Quadrant 2 refers to those cases where both the need for integration and awareness of sovereignty is low. This implies that both the potential to obtain economies of scale and benefits of being sensitive to sovereignty decline. Typical strategies for quadrant 2 would be firms and industries characterized by increased international standardization of products and services. This could lead to lower requirements for centralized quality control and centralized strategic decision making, while simultaneously eliminating requirements to adapt activities to individual countries.

Finally, in quadrant 3 of Figure 3, both the needs for integration and sovereignty increase, implying that different activities in the vertical chain are faced with opposite tendencies, for example a higher need for integration in production, along with higher requirements for regional adaptations in marketing. This is the most challenging quadrant and one where many successful globally efficient MNEs must perform.

This framework can be used to analyze the impact of various government policy shocks and trends on different industries, firms, and other private sector institutions. The globalization-only view of Ohmae (1990) is shown in quadrant 1 of Figure 3. Here the overarching commercial and economic interests of the MNE are paramount and aspects of sovereignty are ignored. In contrast, in quadrant 4, globalization pressures on the MNEs are less important than sovereignty. Quadrant 4 is one where governments dominate the MNE. Quadrant 2 is now of minimal interest (it is one where neither globalization nor sovereignty issues dominate) but quadrant 3 is the one where the current problems of globalization and sovereignty coexist. Figure 3 can also be used to reinterpret the literature of international political economy. Quadrant 1 is a case of markets in contrast to quadrant 4, which is one of states. In between, quadrant 3 is where both coexist, as pointed out by Strange (1991) and Eden (1991).

From the viewpoint of private sector corporations, the most important business decision to be made is a judgment about where the tradeoff between globalization (economic efficiency) and sovereignty (noneconomic issues) will fall. By now it should be clear why both of these two issues are of concern to business. Today a successful company can no longer afford to ignore sovereignty and just concentrate on globalization; quadrant 3 matters. Each business therefore bears the costs of making the decision about the tradeoff itself. Evidence

that sovereignty is of growing importance and that a private sector
company must understand its role in NAFTA can be found by understanding the NAFTA text using this matrix.

THE ANALYTICS OF NAFTA

The institutional complexity of the NAFTA cries out for simplifica-
tion. In order to provide some analytical insight into the mixed aspects of economics and politics reflected in the NAFTA document we
can adapt Figure 3 into Figure 4.

As explained above the vertical axis of Figure 4 represents the
degree of economic integration, however measured, increasing from
a low to a high level as we move up the axis. It captures many of the
elements of globalization, for example, the business strategy of seeking economies of scale by selling across nations to increase world
market share. Industries or business firms that are on the high sector of the axis are global ones, while those in the low sector are
predominantly domestic in their thinking and strategy. In terms of
NAFTA the argument to reduce and abolish tariffs represents a
movement up the axis. We are particularly concerned with the direction of corporate strategy; is it global or domestic? Over the last
quarter of a century there have been tremendous competitive pres-

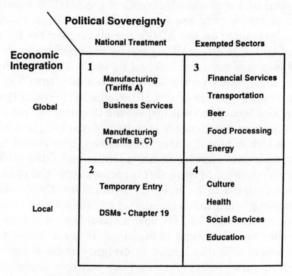

Figure 4. NAFTA: A balanced deal.

sures on most manufacturing firms forcing them to become more global. Examples include autos, consumer electronics, agriculture, high technology, and even steel and apparel. However, some small businesses may be thought of as local as may many service industries. Economists used to refer to these as "nontraded," but in reality, most services are now involved in international activity even if it is indirectly as inputs into traded goods.

The horizontal axis of Figure 4 of political sovereignty is similar in design to the vertical axis of economic globalization. The argument is that, conceptually, we can have increasing degrees of sovereignty by moving along the axis, such that we can create a dichotomy between low and high sovereignty, however it is defined or measured. It could, for example, encompass the notion of democratic institutions having the ability to pass and enforce laws and regulations. The relevant institutional provision of the NAFTA is that "national treatment" is applied to investments in certain sectors. This can be perceived as a constraint on unfettered political sovereignty, so it should appear on the "low" end of the axis. In contrast the NAFTA contains extensive lists of "reservations" from the principle of national treatment, that is, exempted sectors where sovereignty is high in the sense of the nation being able to discriminate against foreign investors in its laws and regulations.

The beauty of the matrix in Figure 4 now becomes apparent. Quadrant 1 is an economics-driven one where the forces of globalization are high and sovereignty low. Most manufacturing and business services are here. Tariffs are cut immediately (A), over five years (B), or over ten years (C) in NAFTA. The opposite case is quadrant 4, with high sovereignty and low globalization. This is where culture, health, social services, and education can be placed due to the NAFTA. The diagonal between quadrants 1 and 3 highlights the classic debate between the international economist and the economic nationalist, both of whom see trade-offs in free trade. Quadrant 4 is relatively uninteresting because these are local/domestic industries where the application of national treatment has little relevance. But the really interesting quadrant is 3 of Figure 4. Here we have the problem children of international business, those affected by globalization yet looking for protection.

There is some logic for exempting industries in quadrant 4 (as they are domestic) but none for exempting them in quadrant 3 (as these are global). Yet the NAFTA has many industries in quadrant 3 including transportation, food processing, financial services, agriculture, beer, energy, and fishing. These sectors are all exempted from the national treatment provisions of NAFTA.

THE PROBLEM OF U.S. ADMINISTERED PROTECTION

One of the unresolved problems of NAFTA is that the perceived protectionist use of U.S. trade law remains, although Chapter 19 panels are extended to cover Mexico. The problem of administered protectionism occurs because the United States experiences considerable decentralization in economic decision making. It is a country in which the political power of subnational units (including domestic producers such as the steel industry as well as state governments) continues to increase in importance. This issue of the capture of federal trade administration by domestic interests should not be confused with pluralism. A variety of political opinions and parties is a strength of democracy. It can put the United States into quadrant 3 of Figure 3. The problem comes when the institutional structure of the nation breaks down and business cannot operate in an efficient manner, especially relative to global competitors. This leads to the need for dispute settlement mechanisms (DSMS), as shown in quadrant 2 of Figure 3.

The U.S. Constitution was designed to allow Congress to be a broker for regional and special interests. On occasions the Congress works with the Executive branch and a coordinated economic and even social policy can be both formulated and implemented. The examples of social reform and government economic activity in the Kennedy–Johnson years can be contrasted with a return to more market based principles and somewhat reduced roles for government in the Reagan years.

However, in many areas affecting the private sector today the overwhelming characteristic of doing business in the United States is the responsiveness of governments to special interest groups and lobbies. The more decentralized the level of government the more responsive is the regulatory activity to the lobbyist. On occasions, businesses themselves can be lobbyists, but there are many other groups, such as environmentalists and social activists who seem to be growing in power. Examples of conflicts in business lobbying occur in the areas of administration of U.S. trade remedy laws and in the current United States debate about the possible regulation of inward FDI.

It has been demonstrated by Rugman and Anderson (1987) and others that the current administration of U.S. countervailing duty (CVD) and antidumping (AD) laws is highly responsive to domestic producer interests and biased against foreign firms. Rugman and Verbeke (1989, 1990) demonstrate that United States corporations use CVD and AD as a competitive strategy to erect entry barriers against rival firms. Even as the United States government was pursuing negotiations for free trade with Canada, individual United States corporations employed this tactic against Canadian rivals.

This was a clear example of the U.S. national interest being offset by selective producer interests. More of the same is in store in the future, although Canadian concerns about the administration of CVD and AD laws have been somewhat answered by the establishment of binational panels under the terms of the FTA.

These panels have helped to mitigate some of the worst abuses of U.S. trade law by domestic producer interests seeking shelter. For example, perhaps the most notorious example of U.S. producer interests offsetting official U.S. trade policy was the 1986 softwood lumber CVD, which led to the Canadian federal government responding by imposing an export tax of 15 percent on a major Canadian industry. (As discussed later this issue was not resolved and it led to a 1992 lumber CVD case, which resulted in a U.S. trade law decision against Canada that was overturned by the binational panels in 1993.) Other examples of United States cases against Canada over the 1986–1988 period of the FTA negotiations included fresh Atlantic Groundfish, potash from Saskatchewan, live swine and pork, and others. During the 1980–1986 period there were over 50 cases of CVD and AD brought by United States companies against Canadian exporters, and this barrage of actions did not let up during the negotiations. None of these routine company-led applications of U.S. CVD and AD law was particularly helpful to the United States or Canadian governments. In Canada especially, the FTA was nearly sabotaged by such parochial corporate interests.

The manner in which the administration of U.S. trade law can become captured by protectionists seeking shelter unfortunately finds an echo in U.S. investment policy. The previous open and market driven United States commitment to national treatment is under threat. Although certain Congressional leaders now wish to restrict inward FDI, most of the individual American states actively encourage it. Some Americans seem to be concerned with the growing amount of Japanese FDI, which is, in practice, concentrated on the West Coast. Over one quarter of all Japanese FDI in the United States is in Hawaii, another quarter is in California. Many in Congress pushed for protectionist trade bills over the 1981–1988 period, leading to the passage of the 1988 trade bill. Its super 301 provisions are restrictive and protectionist. Members of Congress have urged more screening of Japanese FDI. There is a strong "Japan bashing" stance in U.S. trade policy. Yet Tennessee, for example, and virtually all other states have officials actively seeking out Japanese FDI for their states; they want the jobs and tax base. Tennessee has attracted Nissan and Bridgestone tire plants. State officials there, like their compatriots elsewhere, are falling over themselves endorsing these Japanese owned firms as good corporate citizens. This potential clash between Washington "beltway" thinking (which is anti-Japanese) and state level activity (which is pro-Japanese) parallels Canada's experience with the regulation of FDI.

In terms of FDI, the United States seems destined in the next 10 years to repeat many of the mistakes made in Canada over the last 30 years. Canadians are experts at restricting FDI; it has not been a happy experience. In 1974 the Trudeau government introduced the Foreign Investment Review Agency (FIRA), designed to screen FDI on economic criteria to assess if there was a "net benefit" to Canada. Yet, over the 1974–1985 period FIRA responded to Ottawa's political winds, at times rejecting as much as 30 percent of applications, but at other times (especially 1982–1985) approving virtually everything (Rugman, 1980). The administrators at FIRA, and the responsible ministers, abused the economics-based tests of FIRA and made political decisions just as the U.S. International Trade Commission and Commerce Department do today in U.S. trade law cases.

In 1985 FIRA was abolished and a new agency, Investment Canada, was created with the mandate to attract rather than discourage FDI. Throughout the lifetime of FIRA, most provinces, especially those in Atlantic Canada but also in the West, still wanted FDI for jobs and taxes. The clash between the provinces who favor FDI and the central Canadian economic nationalists who want to scare it off has now led to the federal government giving up many of its powers to regulate FDI by buying into the agenda of the provinces, especially their overwhelming priority about jobs. Perhaps this is some evidence of the triumph of decentralized economic power.

But a paradox emerges. In Canada, the economic nationalists, who have used central government power, are in retreat; but it appears that in the United States economic nationalism is just beginning to take off. If Japan bashing continues then the United States proponents of restrictions on FDI should learn from Canada's unhappy experience with FIRA. In any case, the private sector corporate strategists will need to respond to a large dose of economic nationalism and the downside of sovereignty. Fortunately the NAFTA is a potential safeguard against United States protectionism and investment discrimination because it does enshrine the principle of national treatment, albeit with many exceptions and reservations embedded in it. For more detailed analysis of the investment implications of NAFTA see Rugman (1994).

A NORTH AMERICAN ECONOMIC COMMUNITY

Free trade agreements are a necessary but not sufficient condition for North American economic integration. Both the Canada–United

States FTA and the NAFTA are designed to remove tariffs, apply national treatment to investment, and address some of the pervasive nontariff barriers to trade. They also provide temporary entry for designated business people and attempt to remove some of the barriers to trade in services. However, both the FTA and NAFTA fall short of the type of economic and political integration achieved by the EC.

For North America it is probably not desirable to seek the degree of political integration as in the EC, that is, a common parliament, a powerful central bureaucracy (in Brussels), a social charter, common currency, etc. However, it would be desirable to seek a proper economic union.

Neither the FTA nor the NAFTA go far enough to be designated a common market of North America. Over 70 percent of Canadians and Americans work in the service sector, yet in the Canada–United States FTA, major service sectors were exempted from national treatment (i.e., health, social services, education, cultural industries, and transportation). More people work in these five exempted sectors than work in business services, which did receive national treatment. In any case, national treatment is a lukewarm form of economic integration because it only allows host country rules to be applied when doing business, that is, an American firm can do business in Canada, but only according to Canadian laws and regulations, not United States ones. In contrast, in the EC reciprocity now applies; a firm can do business according to its home country rules. The NAFTA is designed to be a similar type of agreement with provisions for national treatment and many exempted sectors.

The reason for this particular institutional framework of the FTA and NAFTA is twofold. First, national treatment has always been a cornerstone of U.S. "free market" policy for foreign investment. Second is the fear by both Canadians and Mexicans of United States domination of their economic and political systems. The choice of national treatment over reciprocity (both of which are General Agreements on Trade and Tariff, GATT, consistent) minimizes the extent of United States influence, from their viewpoint, because it slows down the forces of harmonization. If reciprocity were applied it would speed up harmonization, usually to United States standards and practices. Given the very open nature of the Canadian and Mexican economies it would be more difficult to justify exemptions for service sectors if an EC-type model were being adopted. In particular, the transport sector faces the forces of globalization and its exemption from the national treatment provisions of the FTA has not insulated it from these forces.

The other problem with the FTA and NAFTA is that national unfair trade laws remain. The United States, especially, is the victim of sectoral lobbies that abuse its AD and CVD laws to raise the prices of imported products, thereby penalizing intermediate processors and consumers. The welfare costs of such administered protection are usually drowned out by the chorus of industries demanding government help in erecting barriers to entry against rival producers.

As introduced in the last section one of the most appalling examples of the abuse of U.S. trade law procedure is the use of CVD actions against the Canadian software lumber industry in 1983, 1986, and 1992. The American protectionists lost the 1983 case but won in 1986, when the U.S. Commerce Department established a 15 percent duty. Instead, in 1986 the Canadian government imposed a 15 percent export tax. Subsequently the government of British Columbia (B.C.) imposed a 15 percent increase in its stumpage rates so the export tax was removed in 1991. (B.C. accounts for 80 percent of Canada's lumber exports to the United States.) Yet the United States industry pressured the United States government to launch a new CVD case in 1991. Again the ITC voted injury and the Commerce Department imposed a duty of six percent in 1992. Commerce found that the alleged stumpage subsidy was now de minimis, but applied a new duty to offset the ban on exports of raw logs imposed by B.C. (although exports of raw logs are also prohibited in the U.S. Pacific Northwest). In 1993 binational panels overturned both the ITC and Commerce decisions, stating that the ITC decision was not based on scientific evidence and Commerce got the numbers wrong.

This latest lumber case, together with the 1992 U.S. Honda Canada ruling (that an engine made in Marysville, OH is not an American engine), and the 50 previous CVD and AD cases against Canada, has led to the widespread perception in Canada that United States producers can use U.S. trade laws as a weapon to harass Canadian exporters (Rugman and Anderson, 1987). The Mexicans may not yet feel the same way because there have been fewer cases against their exports. In the FTA the Chapter 19 dispute settlement panels have worked well to offset some of the most egregious legal errors in the application of U.S. trade law. In particular, the pork case led to the reversal of a blatantly protectionist decision by the U.S. International Trade Commission; an earlier case on red raspberries reversed a technical error by the Commerce Department (Boddez and Rugman, 1991). Yet these Chapter 19 panels cannot root out the abusive use of trade laws by industry protectionists and poorly trained officials who are too responsive to political pressures (Rugman and Verbeke, 1990). Instead, the whole system of CVD and AD should be done away with, as it is within the EC.

The main benefit of an EC-type arrangement for North America would be the abolition of trade law actions against the member states. Instead, a new North American Trade Commission would only

take trade law actions against Asian and European rivals. Neither
the FTA, nor the NAFTA, was able to shift CVD and AD actions to a
new tripartite North American Trade Commission, which is logically
desirable in a world of trade power and global competition. It remains the key piece of the unfinished agenda of the economic integration of North America. Canada is already in favor of such a shift
and Mexico will soon support this move. In the United States there is
strong resistance to this step due to an old fashioned insistence that
the United States Constitution insulates the U.S. domestic judicial
system from international forces. Yet as the United States economy
becomes more internationalized, U.S. domestic institutions will need
to be modernized to take into account the realities of globalization,
regionalism, and NAFTA.

The authority for a new North American Trade Commission needs
to come from a new North American Economic Community. This
could be modeled on the EC itself. In particular, the North American
Economic Community needs to have a new trilateral parliament,
assembly, or Congress, a new centralized bureaucracy and set of commissioners with responsibility for trade policy, competition policy,
etc., and a new neutral site for its administrative offices. I would
envisage the following components:

1. The North American Economic Community (NAEC) consisting
   of the United States, Canada, and Mexico as full and equal
   member states.

2. North American Parliament (NAP), consisting of 100 elected
   parliamentarians, with 50 from the United States, 25 from
   Canada, and 25 from Mexico. The NAC would make laws and
   regulations affecting the economic life of North Americans, for
   example, in trade, investment, and competition policy, but it
   would not impose supranational laws affecting the political,
   social, or cultural lives of North Americans.

3. North American Commission (NAC), based on the model of the
   EC bureaucracy in Brussels, in which appointed Commissioners
   would have responsibility to administer economic policies for
   North America, especially in the areas of trade, investment,
   and competition policy. One of the economic agencies would be a
   North American Trade Commission (NATC) responsible for the
   administration of all trade law. This would require the abolition
   of all national trade law agencies, such as the U.S. International Trade Commission (ITC).

4. The site for the NAP and NAC should be in a neutral area, such
   as Puerto Rico or some other area remote from the three nation-

al capitals and their associated political, legal, and related in-
frastructures.

CONCLUSIONS

It is puzzling to many Americans that economic-based deals such as
the FTA and the NAFTA are opposed so passionately by so many
Canadians. After all, the FTA and NAFTA provide Canadians with
access to the world's largest and richest market; they are good for
business. Yet a majority of Canadians oppose the FTA. In the 1988
Canadian election on this issue, the Mulroney government only won
because the two opposition parties split the anti-FTA vote. Nearly 60
percent of Canadians did not vote for the government or the FTA.
The reason is simple; Canadians are afraid of U.S. economic power
and potential political, cultural, and social dominance.

To an extent, the national treatment provisions of the FTA and
NAFTA should reduce Canadian fears of United States domination.
National treatment leaves Canadian federal and provincial governments with the legal right to impose their own laws and regulations,
reflecting the interests of Canadian voters. National treatment does
not invite harmonization; rather it spotlights the economic pressures
of globalization and forces an internal Canadian debate whenever
there are economic pressures to harmonize. Thus national treatment
is a safeguard for Canadian sovereignty. Most of the opponents of the
FTA remain unaware of this institutional protection and continue to
blame the FTA for a perceived loss of sovereignty that has nothing to
do with the FTA itself.

In a similar manner, Canadian opponents of the FTA have not
acknowledged that the exemptions from the FTA serve to preserve
key aspects of Canadian sovereignty. For example, the exemption for
health services protects the Canadian medicare system. There are
economic pressures on the provinces due to the escalating costs of
delivering a universal health care system, but these pressures were
not caused by the FTA. The introduction of realistic user fees could
help reduce the excess demand for health care under a subsidized
medicare program, but this potential solution has nothing to do with
the FTA itself. Similarly, the economic problems facing Canada's
social, transport, education, and cultural services are all real and
urgent, but none of them are due to the institutional provisions of
the FTA.

The NAFTA is opposed in Canada by the same group of economic
nationalists who have still not read the FTA, nor acknowledged the
exemptions from it for cultural, social, health, education, and trans-

portation industries. There is little or no learning curve for old-fashioned nationalists; the facts of globalization and triad power are dismissed as a probusiness agenda. Many Canadian nationalists would rather have no business at all if it is American.

The business leaders, consumers, workers, educators, and others in Canada, Mexico, and the United States who would benefit from a NAFTA need to speak out. The public at large have been subjected for too long to the protectionist arguments of nationalist and protectionist lobbies in all three countries. The NAFTA, and an eventual North American Economic Union, are inevitable building blocks toward the future prosperity of North America.

REFERENCES

Bartlett, Christopher A. (1986) "Building and Managing the Transnational: The New Organizational Challenge," in M.E. Porter (Ed.), *Competition in Global Industries,* Boston: Harvard Business School Press, 367–401.

Bartlett, Christopher A. and Ghoshal, Sumantra (1989) *Managing Across Borders: The Transnational Solution.* Boston: Harvard Business School Press.

Boddez, Tom and Rugman, Alan M. (1991) "Effective Dispute Settlement: A Case Study of the Initial Panel Decisions Under Chapter Nineteen of Canada–U.S. Free Trade Agreement," in Earl H. Fry and Lee H. Radebaugh (Eds.), *Investment in the North American Free Trade Area: Opportunities and Challenges,* Provo, UT: Brigham Young University, 93–126.

Eden, Lorraine (Summer 1991) "Bringing the Firm Back In: Multinationals in International Political Economy," *Millennium* 20, 197–224.

Globerman, Steven and Walker, Michael, Editors (1993). *Assessing NAFTA: A Trinational Analysis.* Vancouver: The Fraser Institute.

Hufbauer, Gary C. and Schott, Jeffrey J. (1993) *NAFTA: An Assessment.* Washington, D.C.: Institute for International Economics.

Lemco, Jonathan and Robson, William B.P. (1993) *Ties Beyond Trade: Labor and Environmental Issues under the NAFTA.* Toronto: C.D. Howe Institute.

Ohmae, Kenichi (1990) *The Borderless World: Power and Strategy in the International Economy.* New York: Harper Business.

Porter, Michael E. (1980) *Competitive Strategy: Techniques for Analyzing Industries and Competitors.* New York: The Free Press, Macmillan.

Reich, Robert (1991) *The Work of Nations.* New York: Free Press, Macmillan.

Rugman, Alan M. (1980) *Multinationals in Canada: Theory, Impact and Economic Performance.* Boston: Martinus Nijhoff.

Rugman, Alan M. (1981) *Inside the Multinationals: The Economics of Internal Markets.* London: Croom Helm and New York: Columbia University Press.

Rugman, Alan M. (1990) *Multinationals and Canada–United States Free Trade*. Columbia SC: University of South Carolina Press.

Rugman, Alan M., Editor (1994) *Foreign Investment and North American Free Trade*. Columbia SC: University of South Carolina Press.

Rugman, Alan M. and Anderson, Andrew (1987) *Administered Protection in America*. London and New York: Routledge.

Rugman, Alan M. and Verbeke, Alain (1989) "Strategic Management and Trade Policy," *Journal of International Economic Studies,* The Institute of Comparative Economic Studies, Hosei University, 3, 139–152.

Rugman, Alan M. and Verbeke, Alain (1990) *Global Corporate Strategy and Trade Policy*. London and New York: Routledge.

Strange, Susan (Summer 1991) "Big Business and the State," *Millennium,* 20, 245–250.

United States International Trade Commission (January 1993) *Potential Impact on the U.S. Economy and Selected Industries of the North American Free-Trade Agreement*. Washington, D.C.: U.S.I.T.C. Publication No. 2596.

24

The North American Free Trade Agreement and foreign direct investment

Michael Gestrin and Alan M. Rugman*

The North American Free Trade Agreement substantially liberalizes the North American investment regimes. The Agreement establishes a clear, rules-based framework for the impartial treatment of foreign direct investment and places strict limits upon the use of performance requirements. It also establishes dispute-settlement mechanisms specifically designed to deal with investment issues. With the added clarity and security that these provisions provide to foreign investors in North America and the drastic reduction of Mexico's tariffs on regionally originating goods, transnational corporations will be encouraged to rationalize the organization of their North-American operations and to increase substantially foreign direct investment in Mexico. In addition to these rules and procedures, however, the North American Free Trade Agreement also contains significant discriminatory measures. Several industries have been exempted by the signatories from key investment provisions of the Agreement. Other industries, such as automobiles, textiles and apparel and segments of the electronics industry, will be protected from import competition by strict rules of origin.

Introduction

This article describes and analyses the provisions of the North American Free Trade Agreement (NAFTA) in terms of their impact upon the North American investment regimes.[1] The principal aims of NAFTA investment provisions[2] are to encourage foreign direct investment (FDI) in North America and to create an integrated North American market. These aims are pursued through the estab-

---

* The authors are, respectively, Lecturer and Professor of International Business at the Faculty of Management, University of Toronto, Ontario, Canada. The authors are grateful for the insightful comments and suggestions received by an anonymous referee on earlier drafts of this article.

[1] Throughout this paper, "North America" refers to Canada, Mexico and the United States.

[2] Investment provisions in this article refer to all investment-related provisions in the Agreement, including investment-related trade measures.

---

lishment of rules that reduce the scope for the adoption of discretionary and discriminatory policies with respect to FDI by the signatory Governments, as well as rules of origin that encourage North American value-added activity in several industries.[3]

While NAFTA's investment provisions are meant to contribute to a less discriminatory North American investment environment, they also reflect the protectionist demands of several powerful North American industries. Numerous exceptions to the investment provisions serve to protect regionally based producers from foreign competition through the targeted "grandfathering" of discriminatory measures that were in place before the Agreement came into effect, as well as through the establishment of a few new discriminatory measures. In addition, the rules of origin are highly restrictive in some industries and are therefore likely to result in trade and investment diversion in these cases.

The next section describes NAFTA's new investment rules. The Agreement's discriminatory measures and their potential impact upon intra- and inter-regional investment patterns for particular industries are examined in the section that follows. The last section concludes with a summary of the main findings and some observations concerning the viability of NAFTA as a model upon which investment agreements in other regional forums might be based in the post-Uruguay Round era.

Investment provisions of the North American Free Trade Agreement

The North American Free Trade Agreement can affect FDI regimes in North America through two types of provisions. The first type deals explicitly with FDI issues. These appear in chapter 11 of the Agreement (in which the basic rules for the treatment of FDI and the resolution of disputes between investors and States are outlined), chapters 12 and 14 (in which investment issues related to the provision of services and financial services are dealt with, respectively), and chapter 17 on intellectual property rights. The second type consists of investment-related trade measures. These include the rules of origin and measures related to duty drawback and deferral.[4]

The investment measures

The investment and services chapters

The national treatment provisions (articles 1102, 1202, 1405 of the

[3] For a theoretical analysis of the impact of NAFTA investment provisions on the strategic behaviour of TNCs operating in North America, see Rugman and Gestrin (1993).

[4] For an overview of the theory of TNC activity and the relationship between environmental factors and TNC behaviour, see Dunning (1993), Rugman (1981) and Rugman and Verbeke (1990b).

Agreement) stipulate that each party[5] must accord to investors and investments from the other NAFTA parties "treatment no less favorable than that it accords, in like circumstances, to its own investors" (article 1102.1). The national treatment provisions constitute the conceptual cornerstone of NAFTA. Several provisions of the Agreement, however, move beyond national treatment either by establishing common norms for the treatment of FDI among the three signatories (e.g., articles 1105 and 1110, described below), or through the adoption of measures based upon reciprocity (e.g., the so-called "tit-for-tat" reservations in the annexes, also explained below).

The most-favoured-nation treatment provisions (articles 1103, 1203, 1406) stipulate that each signatory must accord to investors from the other signatories to NAFTA "treatment no less favorable than that it accords, in like circumstances, to investors of any other Party or of a non-Party" (article 1103.1). The most-favoured-nation provisions confer upon foreign investors based in North America the best possible treatment among all foreign investors in instances where one of the parties has chosen to hold a reservation against the national treatment provisions. Under the terms of the United States-Canada Free Trade Agreement, this added security was not available.

The minimum standard of treatment provisions (article 1105) mainly reflect the concerns of United States and Canadian firms that the national treatment and most-favoured-nation provisions might not provide adequate protection in Mexico. Article 1105 attempts to commit the parties to a performance "floor", reflecting the unique concerns arising from the negotiation of an economic agreement between economies at such disparate levels of development. Similarly, the expropriation and compensation provisions (article 1110) also seek to establish a minimum North American standard. The acceptance of these articles by Mexico is historically significant in so far as these represent a weakening of the Calvo doctrine.[6]

The performance requirements provisions (article 1106) contain a list of requirements that the parties may not impose upon investors of other parties or of non-parties with respect to the establishment or operation of an investment. These include export requirements; domestic-content requirements; import requirements; trade-balancing requirements; the linking of domestic sales to export levels or foreign-exchange earnings; technology-transfer requirements (except when required to remedy violations of domestic competition laws); and

[5] The term "party" is hereafter used to refer to the signatory Governments to NAFTA.

[6] The Calvo doctrine was enunciated in 1868 by Carlos Calvo (1824-1906) of Argentina. The doctrine stipulates that foreign investors will be subject to domestic laws and that disputes can only be resolved in domestic courts (Power, 1993, p. 12).

requirements that a firm act as "the exclusive supplier . . . to a specific region or world market". In addition, article 1106 forbids the linking or the conferral of an advantage (such as a subsidy or a tax advantage) to domestic-content requirements, domestic-input requirements, trade-balancing requirements; and the linking of domestic sales to export levels and/or foreign-exchange earnings. Article 1106 does permit Government support to be linked to the location of production, the provision of particular services, the training and employment of workers, the construction or expansion of particular facilities and the conduct of research and development.

The limits of NAFTA upon the use of performance requirements are more stringent than those included in the Uruguay Round Final Act in two respects.[7]

- First, the Uruguay Round Final Act prohibits trade balancing and local-content requirements (with respect to both right of establishment and conferral of advantages). The North American Free Trade Agreement also prohibits those requirements, as well as the technology and exclusive supplier requirements, with respect to establishment.

- Second, the Final Act allows developing countries a five year phase-out period (seven years for the least developed countries), as well as several broad exceptions, such as the use of prohibited performance requirements to protect infant industries. In this respect, Mexico has committed itself to much stricter limits on the use of such measures under the terms of NAFTA than those of the developing countries under the terms of the Final Act.

The Denial of Benefits provisions (article 1113) establish the rights of non-North American investors who are established in one NAFTA country and who want to expand their operations into another NAFTA country. The key feature of the article is that it accords full NAFTA rights to outside investors as long as they have "substantial business activities in the territory of the Party under whose law (the business) is constituted or organized" (article 1113.2).

Finally, NAFTA's investment chapter expands upon the types of investment covered by the Agreement beyond the coverage offered by the United States-Canada Free Trade Agreement. Indeed, whereas the United States-Canada Free Trade Agreement covers only foreign direct investment, NAFTA also protects portfolio investments. This additional coverage is significant, albeit difficult to quantify. Of interest, however, is the lack of coverage for the

---

[7] Ratification is scheduled to take place on 15 April 1994 in Marrakesh, Morocco. The agreement must then be adopted by the signatory Governments by 1 July 1995.

growing number of strategic business alliances.[8] Given the increasingly important role of these alliances in international business and their implications for
capital movements, that omission is noteworthy.[9]

The Investor-State Dispute Settlement Mechanism

The North American Free Trade Agreement also sets out rules for the settlement of disputes between investors and signatory Governments. The
Investor-State Dispute Settlement Mechanism consists of a set of rules that
create an interface between NAFTA and either of two international arbitration
conventions, namely, the International Convention for Settlement of Investment
Disputes (ICSID) and the arbitration rules of the United Nations Commission
on International Trade Law (UNCITRAL).

The Investor-State Dispute Settlement Mechanism establishes the conditions under which an investor can take a NAFTA member-state to arbitration,
the functions of NAFTA's Commission during disputes,[10] the forms of compensation that the arbitration panels can award, enforcement mechanisms available to the disputing parties, and exclusions from the Dispute Settlement
Mechanism.

The Dispute Settlement Mechanism is important in several regards. First,
and from a historical perspective, the introduction of the Investor-State Dispute
Settlement Mechanism based upon the existing international conventions and
rules highlights the depth of the Mexican reforms that have been under way
since the mid-1980s. The Dispute Settlement Mechanism of NAFTA is binding
and based upon international law; as such it runs counter to the Calvo Doctrine
upon which Mexican (and most other Central and South American) policy
towards foreign investors has been based since the 19th century. It also reflects
the extent to which NAFTA goes beyond being based purely upon national
treatment. In effect, NAFTA has enhanced the role of supra-national rules and

[8] These are defined as medium- to long-term cooperative ventures between two or more TNCs,
in which the contractual relationships between these firms usually fall somewhere in between arm's-
length relationships that characterize market transactions and fully internalized relationships, such
as joint ventures or mergers. In other words, a part of the value of the relationship is intangible in so
far as it involves the combination and reorganization of the existing capital of the partners, without
necessarily involving changes in the ownership structures of the firms in question.

[9] For an in-depth discussion of networks and their impact upon the global economy, see OECD
(1992).

[10] The Commission consists of cabinet-level representatives from all parties whose mandate is
to oversee the Agreement's implementation and to provide interpretation of sections of the
Agreement, when required, within the context of the Dispute Settlement Mechanism (article 2001).

administrative structures in the governance of the FDI regimes of North America.[11]

Intellectual property protection

The protection of intellectual property in North America has been significantly improved with the adoption by the Mexican Government of stringent intellectual property laws in 1991. The North American Free Trade Agreement adds to this improvement in marginal ways, namely, by establishing clear rules and expectations for investors operating across borders in North America and by turning Mexico's domestic intellectual property reforms into international commitments. Furthermore, investors are able to make use of NAFTA dispute settlement mechanisms when disputes over intellectual property issues arise. Some areas are likely to continue to give rise to conflicts due to divergent domestic policy approaches among the signatories, the protected cultural industries of Mexico and Canada being a prominent example. The agreement on intellectual property rights under the Uruguay Round is comparable to NAFTA intellectual property provisions in terms of achievements. However, NAFTA provides more protection with regard to intellectual property than the Uruguay Round Final Act in several respects. For example, NAFTA protects pharmaceuticals in the process of being developed, while the Uruguay Round Final Act provides only limited protection under those circumstances.

Investment-related trade measures

The rules of origin

The rules of origin establish procedures for determining whether products traded within NAFTA are originating within the member countries and, therefore, are eligible to enjoy the benefits of NAFTA tariff reductions. These rules have been formulated to encourage production in North America and to avoid the establishment of export platforms by non-regionally based firms in any member country of NAFTA.

The rules of origin[12] contain two types of requirement that are applied in different combinations to different products. The basic requirement is for imported intermediate inputs to undergo a change in tariff classification. The second requirement (sometimes applied in addition to the change in tariff classification) is that products must contain a minimum regional value content. For those products to which the minimum regional value content applies, the exporter can

---

[11] A more detailed analysis of the dispute settlement procedures is found in Graham and Wilkie (1994).

[12] For a more detailed explanation of the rules of origin, see Johnson (1993).

choose between one of two methods to calculate that value: the first is based upon a transaction value test and the second is based upon a net cost test. The transaction value test uses the selling price of the good. The net cost test uses the producer's total cost less the cost of sales promotion, marketing, after-sale service, royalties, shipping and packaging and certain interest costs.

For several important sectors, NAFTA rules of origin are considered to be stricter than those of the United States-Canada Free Trade Agreement. The rules have been tightened in terms of the change in tariff classification requirements, the regional value content requirements and, in some cases, requirements that specific sub-assemblies be produced in North America. The potential impact of the rules of origin for investment patterns in several industries is considered in the section on discriminatory aspects of NAFTA investment provisions.

Restrictions upon duty drawback and deferral programmes

The North American Free Trade Agreement places restrictions on duty draw-back and deferral programmes. These programmes allow producers duty waivers on intermediate inputs if the final product is subsequently exported, or if pre-specified minimum levels of domestic value-added are achieved. The restrictions that NAFTA places upon these programmes have a similar impact upon FDI as the rules of origin. Indeed, these restrictions are intended to promote regional sourcing and to avoid the establishment of export platforms. As such, they affect Canada and Mexico, both of which have maintained such programmes in the past to encourage production for export to the United States market.

The elimination of duty drawback (after a transition period of seven years for Mexico-Canada and Mexico-United States trade and two years for Canada-United States trade), combined with stricter rules of origin, will potentially have dramatic effects upon the trade and investment patterns in some industries. These effects are considered together with the analysis of the impact of the rules of origin in the next section.

The exceptions to the North American Free Trade Agreement investment provisions

The previous section described the main provisions of NAFTA that form the basis for the treatment of FDI by the signatory Governments once the Agreement comes into effect. These rules centre upon the principles of national treatment, most-favoured-nation treatment, as well as upon certain supra-national norms and regulations (i.e., the minimum standard of treatment provisions and the Investor-State Dispute Settlement Mechanism). Foreign-direct-investment regimes in North America under NAFTA are also shaped by investment-related trade measures, such as the rules of origin and restrictions upon duty drawback and deferral programmes. The principal goal of the investment-related trade measures is to ensure that NAFTA benefits and promotes North American producers and production.

This section examines discriminatory measures of NAFTA that run counter to either the letter or the spirit of the investment provisions described in the previous section. These measures reflect the concerns of politically important industries in the North American economies that, for one reason or another, have sought and obtained protection from global competition. Four sections of the Agreement stand out in this regard: the annexes, the broad national security exemption (article 2102), the automotive annex, and the rules of origin.

The annexes

The Free Trade Agreement grandfathered all measures and laws that were in effect prior to its ratification and that ran counter to aspects of that Agreement. The appeal of the grandfathering instrument was its simplicity. However, given the complexity and discriminatory nature of the Mexican investment regime relative to its Canadian and United States counterparts, grandfathering all past Mexican legislation would have effectively defeated the purpose of negotiating a free trade agreement with Mexico. As a result, grandfathering was replaced with negative lists. These lists consist of reservations — existing measures and/or laws[13] that run counter to one or more provisions of the Agreement. One of the main advantages of these lists is that they have made discrimination in the investment regimes of the signatories much more transparent.

The function of the annexes[14] is to exclude "sensitive" industries in each of the signatory economies from the main investment and trade provisions of NAFTA (subject to the "existing measure" constraint). The Canadian and United States reservations do not contain many economically significant industries since the investment regimes of both countries are already very liberal. Historically sensitive sectors in both countries have been accorded reservations such that while each regime remained largely open to FDI, NAFTA negotiations did not produce any substantive advances in terms of further

[13] Formally defined, an existing measure is one that was in effect before the Agreement came into effect. However, to avoid the possibility that industry groups in any of the signatory economies might pressure their Governments to slip in new protectionist measures before 1 January 1994, an informal agreement between the three signatories established the cut-off date for the definition of an existing measure as 7 October 1992, when the draft text of the Agreement was initialled by Ministers from each of the parties.

[14] The annexes which contain reservations against investment provisions are 1, 2, 3 (unique to Mexico, encompassing that country's constitutional restrictions upon FDI) and 7 (financial services). For a detailed analysis of the annexes and the reservations they contain, refer to Gestrin and Rugman (1993).

liberalization.[15] The most important Canadian exclusion from the main NAFTA investment provisions is its cultural industries. The most important United States exclusion is its maritime industry.

The Mexican lists are much longer than those of Canada or the United States. However, most of Mexico's reservations in the manufacturing sector are subject to complete phase-out provisions. For example, although foreign ownership of an enterprise of the autoparts industry will be limited initially to 49 per cent, that restriction will be completely lifted five years after the Agreement comes into effect. Seven years after the Agreement comes into effect, the export requirements imposed upon investors under the ALTEX and PITEX decrees will be completely eliminated. On 1 July 1995, investors based in Canada and the United States will be allowed to own 100 per cent of enterprises engaged in the provision of value-added telecommunication services.

Annex 3 is unique to Mexico and covers industries whose control is reserved for the Mexican State and is enshrined in the Mexican constitution. Eleven industries are covered in that annex: petroleum and derivative products, electricity, nuclear power and materials, satellite communications, telegraph services, radiotelegraph services, postal services, railroads, the issuance of currency, control over maritime and inland ports, and control over airports and heliports. Phase-outs do not apply to any of these reservations.

One of the most important Mexican reservations consists of constraints placed upon FDI in the energy industry. While foreign participation is permitted in petrochemicals up to 49 per cent, the energy industry remains in the hands of the State. The concern raised by this particular reservation is that energy could become a bottleneck in the Mexican economy as the manufacturing sector expands in response to NAFTA liberalization measures. In the absence of an infusion of foreign capital, the inefficient State-run energy industry will probably not be able to keep up with projected increases in demand.[16]

The Agreement does contain some liberalizing measures in the energy industry. For example, it allows for increased foreign involvement in Government procurement contracts and for expanded foreign involvement in the generation of electricity for own and other non-public use. Ultimately, the impact of the Mexican energy restrictions depends upon the extent to which the Mexican Government chooses to exercise its right to exclude foreign participation.

---

[15] For a detailed discussion of the Canada-United States trade and investment relationship, refer to Rugman (1990).

[16] For a detailed examination of NAFTA energy provisions, see Plourde (1993) and Hagen *et al.* (1993).

In addition to the specific sectoral reservations, the annexes also contain "all sector" reservations. These reservations apply to particular groups, regions or procedures. They include the foreign investment review processes of Canada and Mexico. For acquisitions[17] above specified amounts ($150 million in Canada and $25 million in Mexico, subject to a "phase-up" schedule which will bring the Mexican review threshold to $150 million by the year 2003), Government approval is necessary. The most notable feature of these exclusions is that the outcomes of the review processes in both countries are not subject to challenge under the terms of NAFTA dispute settlement procedures. This being said, however, the high thresholds will ensure that most acquisitions will not be subject to review.

In sum, the annexes identify sensitive industries in each of the signatory economies and describe the measures that each of these economies has chosen to maintain in order to protect these industries. In Canada and the United States, the annexes serve to maintain the *status quo*. In Mexico, the annexes will serve to gradually open most of the manufacturing sector to full foreign participation. However, several industries of the Mexican economy (most notably, energy) will remain off-limit to FDI, largely for political reasons.

The national security exemptions

The United States also maintains investment review procedures, but these are not described in the annexes. The reason for this is that the United States review of FDI is based upon national security considerations and, therefore, falls under the terms of NAFTA's broad national security exclusion (article 2102). The review of FDI in the United States is conducted by the Committee on Foreign Direct Investment in the United States and the procedures for the conduct of the review are based upon the Exon-Florio amendment (Section 721) of the Omnibus Trade and Competitiveness Act of 1988 (Graham, 1991; Graham and Ebert, 1991).

The scope of the United States investment review process is much less clearly specified than it is in Canada and Mexico. Concern over the United States review procedures stems partially from amendments to the Exon-Florio legislation in 1992 stipulating that the need for United States technological leadership in industries related to defence should serve as a legitimate basis for blocking foreign acquisitions (greenfield investments are excluded from review by the Committee). Since most advanced technologies have military and civilian use, the discriminatory potential of the Exon-Florio legislation is considerable. While this potential has not yet been realized, the continued erosion

---

[17] Greenfield investments are not subject to review.

---

of the United States position in high-technology manufacturing[18] could give rise to calls for a more active role for the Committee on Foreign Direct Investment — and no rewriting of the Committee's mandate would be necessary.

Furthermore, it is not clear whether outcomes of the United States review process are subject to challenge under the terms of NAFTA dispute settlement procedures. The United States position is that all national-security-related decisions are not subject to dispute resolution under the terms of NAFTA. However, article 1138 of the investment chapter states that only the decision to allow or disallow an investment on the basis of national security considerations is excluded from the review process. The Canadian position is therefore that, apart from the specific exclusion of article 1138, any other matter related to article 2102, such as the question as to what constitutes a legitimate national security concern in the first place, is subject to the Agreement's dispute settlement provisions. Since Canada and the United States do not see eye to eye on this point, the issue will only be resolved if a case is brought before the NAFTA Commission.

Another exception to the principal investment rules of NAFTA that does not appear in the annexes concerns the funding by the Government of the United States of high-technology consortia that exclude participation by foreign firms. The best known example is Sematech, a consortium comprising United States computer chip producers. Again, the exclusion is omitted from the negative lists because it falls under the auspices of the national security clause (for a brief but thorough history of Sematech, refer to *The Economist*, 1994, pp. 77-79).

The strengthening of the Committee on Foreign Direct Investment in 1988, the relaxation of anti-trust policy beginning in the early 1980s and the increased financial support for high-technology consortia beginning in the late 1980s are signposts marking a shift in United States policy towards its trading partners and towards FDI in high-technology industries (Rugman and Warner, 1994). With respect to NAFTA, these developments serve to highlight the importance of the national security article (2102) to FDI in high-technology industries and the potential — as yet unrealized — of that article for allowing discriminatory treatment of FDI in the United States.

The North American Free Trade Agreement automotive provisions

The history of the North American automotive industry is one of managed

---

[18] Estimates by the Organisation for Economic Co-operation and Development, based upon the STAN database, show that the United States share of high-technology exports from OECD countries declined from 31.1 to 26.3 per cent and that import penetration for high-technology products (imports as a share of domestic consumption) increased from 4.2 to 18.4 per cent between 1970 and 1990 (OECD, 1993, p. 87, table 16).

---

trade and investment.[19] Trade and investment have been administered through the 1965 Automotive Agreement between Canada and the United States; a series of voluntary export restraint agreements[20] on Japanese automotive products beginning in 1981; five Mexican Automotive Decrees beginning in 1963; and, to a lesser extent, the Caribbean Basin Initiative of 1982 (establishing a 35 per cent local-content requirement for products entering the United States).

The main features of NAFTA automotive provisions from an investment perspective are the complete opening up of the Mexican automotive industry to North American investment over the Agreement's first ten years, the establishment of tighter rules of origin and tracing requirements to encourage more regional sourcing, and various advantages conferred upon "incumbent" producers.

In terms of opening the Mexican automotive industry to North American investment, NAFTA phases out the numerous performance requirements and investment restrictions left over from the 1989 Automotive Decree by 1 January 2004. The North American Free Trade Agreement allows for full foreign participation in the automotive parts industry, eliminates all sourcing restrictions on the five existing Mexican assemblers,[21] and completely phases out the trade-balancing requirements for parts and finished vehicles.

The opening of the Mexican automotive regime, however, has been accompanied by a tightening of the rules of origin. For automobiles and light trucks and their engines and transmissions a regional value content requirement of 62.5 per cent applies under NAFTA. Automobile producers, unlike producers in other industries, cannot choose between the transaction value and net cost tests — they must use the net cost test (the same restriction applies to the footwear sector). The reason is that the net cost test reflects better regional content when there is extensive vertical integration that largely eliminates market determined prices along the value-added chain for automobiles.[22]

The rules of origin have also been tightened through the introduction of a "tracing" requirement that is intended to deal with the problem of "roll-up". Roll-up occurs when intermediate inputs, containing materials that do not

[19] Two excellent analyses of the impact of NAFTA upon the North American automotive industry are Eden and Molot (1993) and Johnson (1993).

[20] For an analysis of the empirical record of the use of United States trade laws, see Rugman and Gestrin (1991) and Rugman and Verbeke (1990a).

[21] The Big Three automobile producers (General Motors, Ford and Chrysler), plus Nissan and Volkswagen.

[22] In 1982, intra-firm trade in the transportation-equipment industry accounted for 44, 45 and 50 per cent of total trade for that industry in the United States, Japan and the United Kingdom, respectively (OECD, 1992, p. 220).

originate within NAFTA, but that meet the regional value content and change in tariff classification requirements, are treated as if they originate within NAFTA when introduced to the next stage of assembly in another NAFTA member. Tracing seeks to overcome this problem by requiring manufacturers to keep track of materials not originating in NAFTA members that would otherwise "disappear" along the various stages of production as sub-assemblies are granted "originating" status. The ultimate effect of tracing is to raise the regional value content requirement of automotive production, since non-NAFTA originating materials that would otherwise be rolled-up in the absence of tracing now count against regional value content.

Although not explicitly discriminatory, the tightened rules of origin and the new tracing requirement constitute an attempt to promote regional sourcing in the automotive industry. As an instrument of industrial policy, however, rules of origin are extremely blunt and usually costly from an economic welfare perspective. In this case, the greatest efficiency loss to which NAFTA is likely to give rise is associated with the diversion of parts sourcing away from efficient Asian suppliers.

In terms of the effect of these rules upon investment patterns, Peter Morici (1993, p. 247) suggested that, "given the number of stages in the transformation of basic components into automobiles, the use of non-North American parts by transplants should be substantially reduced". In addition, the restrictions which NAFTA places upon duty drawback programmes for new producers suggests that future investments by these companies will be predominantly located in the United States.

Finally, NAFTA, by grandfathering the United States-Canada Auto Pact and the Free Trade Agreement revisions to it, distinguishes between Auto Pact and non-Auto Pact producers and confers specific advantages to the former. Existing producers are defined as those producing vehicles prior to model year 1992. That distinction, and the associated differences in treatment based upon it, runs counter to national treatment. Indeed, article 1 of the automotive annex (annex 300-A) stipulates that "existing" producers must be granted "treatment no less favorable than (is accorded) to any new producer" (article 1, annex 300-A). In contrast to the national treatment provision, which is intended to protect foreign producers, the "foreign treatment" provision of the automotive annex allows for the conferral of advantages on incumbent assemblers. One significant reservation in this regard can be found in Canada's extension of duty waiver programme for the Big Three and Volvo (annex I, p. C-17).

On balance, NAFTA is beneficial for the North American automotive industries. The Mexican automotive and auto-parts industries, in particular, stand to benefit as investment is expected to increase by over 16 per cent (USITC, 1993, p. x). Furthermore, the North American automotive industry will become more competitive globally as a result of the increased scope for rationalizing production and the heightened regional competition to which NAFTA will give rise. However, these efficiency gains will be partially offset by the trade and investment diversion caused by the extremely strict rules of origin. Asian parts manufacturers stand to lose the most in this regard.

The rules of origin and sectoral adjustment

The North American Free Trade Agreement's rules of origin are intended to discourage the establishment of export platforms within NAFTA and encourage regional production in industries for which the regional value content requirements are high. Although these rules are not discriminatory in the same way as the measures contained in the annexes or in the national security exclusion provisions, they do constitute a form of industrial policy aimed at reorganizing productive capacity along regional lines through administrative and, hence, arbitrary incentives (as in the case of the automotive rules of origin outlined above).[23]

In addition to automobiles, several other industries in North America have been conferred considerable competitive advantages with respect to non-regionally based producers through tighter regional-content requirements (usually in combination with restrictions upon duty drawback and related programmes). These include electronics, textiles and apparel, home appliances and measuring and testing equipment (USITC, 1993, p. 3).

The rules of origin for electronics embody the explicit strategic objective of increasing regional production of high-technology components (USITC, 1993, p. 5-4). For numerous electronic products containing non-NAFTA originating materials, the rules of origin are complex, involving change in tariff classification and regional value content requirements, as well as the requirement that certain sub-assemblies be completely produced in North America. Theses rules have been applied to encourage more regional production of parts related to the production of high-definition televisions, flat-panel displays and printed circuit sub-assemblies, among other products (USITC, 1993, p. 5-3). These products and, especially, the technologies upon which they are based have been at the centre of the current policy debate in the United States over the erosion of its competitiveness in high-technology industries.

---

[23] The rules of origin do not, strictly speaking, derogate from national treatment unless, as in the case of provisions for the automobile industry, they confer upon established producers preferential rules of origin.

In addition, the rules have also been tightened for more mature technologies. In particular, the rules of origin aim at increasing the regional production of television tubes. Televisions made in North America with regionally produced tubes will enjoy duty-free access into any NAFTA market. Televisions made with foreign tubes are subject to a 5 per cent duty in the United States. Furthermore, duty drawback restrictions increase the duties on Asian tubes that previously entered Mexican *maquiladoras* from 0 to 15 per cent. Thus, the rules of origin in the electronics industries explicitly aim at increasing regional production. The tight rules of origin will encourage an increase in productive capacity for television tubes in the United States, largely at the expense of Asian producers. The latter have been effectively shut out of the North American market. The effects of tighter rules of origin and restrictions upon duty drawback, however, are not always as clear. Indeed, in a few cases, producers might find it in their best interests to move the production of sub-assemblies completely offshore in response to the duty rate differentials created by the combination of the elimination of duty drawback and deferral benefits, tight rules of origin and the level of the external tariff (USITC, 1993, p. 3-5; Peter Morici (1993) also considers this potential problem in greater detail).

The rules of origin for textile and apparel producers are based upon the concepts of "yarn forward" and "fibre forward". To qualify for NAFTA treatment, goods must be made in North America from the yarn and fibre stages onward (the two rules apply to different types of material). These rules have been described as "ultrastrict" by Gary Hufbauer and Jeffrey Schott (1993, p. 44) and as an example of rules of origin "at their worst" by Peter Morici (1993, p. 241). Indeed, they are likely to have significant investment implications. In particular, since NAFTA substantially liberalizes trade in textiles and apparel between Mexico and its NAFTA partners, low-wage producers of apparel for export to North America stand to experience at least some investment and trade diversion to Mexico (to the extent that it is possible to talk about trade diversion at all in an industry in which trade and investment patterns are already highly administrative in nature). The Caribbean Basin Initiative economies are particularly concerned about this possibility (Hufbauer and Schott, 1993, p. 46). The increase in apparel production in Mexico that NAFTA will bring about is also likely to lead to decreases in North American imports from Asia (USITC, 1993, p. 8-2).

The Uruguay Round Agreement's proposed phase-out of the Multi-Fibre Arrangement and the gradual incorporation of the global textile and apparel industry into the GATT of most-favoured-nation-based tariff system mean that global production patterns will be shaped increasingly by market forces. Mexico stands to benefit from the Multi-Fibre Arrangement, as well as from the enhanced market access afforded by NAFTA. Apparel producers located in Mexico are likely to expand their share of the North American market significantly as a result of the Uruguay Round Agreement and NAFTA.

Machine tools is another industry in which the rules of origin have been tightened. The rules for that industry stipulate that non-NAFTA originating parts may not be used in sub-assemblies, and they impose strict limits upon the use of non-NAFTA originating motors, pumps, electrical control panels, lasers and "major castings, weldments, and fabrications" (NAFTA, article 401, section B and USITC, 1993, p. 6-2). The United States International Trade Commission estimates that the United States machine tools industry might respond to the stringent rules of origin (in combination with the relatively low external tariff on these products) by moving more production offshore (USITC, 1993, p. 6-2).

Conclusions

On balance, NAFTA treatment of FDI is impressive. New ground has been broken in terms of establishing clear rules, enforceable dispute settlement mechanisms and increased transparency in the discriminatory regimes of the signatories. The North American Free Trade Agreement is therefore likely to stimulate FDI and give rise to efficiency gains as TNCs rationalize their operations across the three signatory economies.

This being said, the Agreement is not simply an exercise in trade and investment liberalization. It establishes discriminatory measures for particular industries and practices at the national and regional level. At the national level, each member of NAFTA has chosen to exempt particular industries from various investment provisions (usually some combination of the national treatment, the most-favoured-nation and the performance requirements articles). The most notable exemptions are the energy industry in Mexico, the maritime industry in the United States and the cultural industries in Canada.

At the regional level, the extremely tight rules of origin for particular industries (although technically consistent with national treatment) will probably give rise to some trade and investment diversion and will also serve to disadvantage new producers in North America whose traditional supplier networks are located in other regions. In essence, these rules seek to reduce import competition (on an interregional basis) for automobiles, textiles and apparel, electronics (particularly, television) and certain machine tools. Provisions that distinguish between incumbent and new producers and accord preferential treatment to the former on the basis of this distinction act as protective complements to the rules of origin. While the rules of origin reduce import competition, the preferences accorded to incumbents soften transplant competition. Such use of this type of derogation from national treatment is concentrated in the automotive industry.

The numerous positive precedents set by NAFTA concerning FDI will invariably influence the negotiation of future regional trade and investment agreements (not to mention any extension of NAFTA itself) and will probably serve as benchmarks for future investment-related negotiations in the World Trade Organization. The tight rules of origin in the industries discussed above will not significantly detract from the positive contribution of NAFTA to the FDI regimes in North America, mainly because the United States external tariff on many of these products is already low (which means that the diversion effects of the rules will be low as well).

Rules of origin are necessary for the functioning of free trade agreements. However, as these agreements come to constitute an increasingly significant element in the administrative structure of global trade, especially among developing countries, their potential to serve protectionist goals and a beggar-thy-neighbour type of quest for manufacturing capital and employment should be considered more carefully. Within the context of NAFTA, the rules of origin are extremely tight only in a limited number of industries, such as automobiles, textiles and apparel and electronics. Furthermore, the pernicious diversion effects of tight rules of origin are reduced to the extent that the external tariff on the products to which these rules apply is already low in the biggest NAFTA market — the United States. The 2.5 per cent tariff for automobiles and most auto-parts into the United States, for example, is helpful in this regard (although the failure of the Uruguay Round to have this rate further reduced is a disappointment). Unfortunately, NAFTA, in addition to all of the positive precedents it establishes in the area of international investment, also sets a dangerous example for future regional trade agreements in its limited, but obvious, use of rules of origin to support particular industries. ∎

References

Dunning, John H. (1993). *Multinational Enterprises and the Global Economy* (Wokingham, United Kingdom and Reading, Mass.: Addision Wesley).

The Economist (1994). "Uncle Sam's helping hand", 331 (2 April), pp. 77-79.

Eden, Lorraine and Maureen Appel Molot (1993). "The NAFTA's automotive provisions: the next stage of managed trade", *C. D. Howe Institute Commentary*, 53, November (Toronto: C. D. Howe Institute).

Gestrin, Michael and Alan M. Rugman (1993). "The NAFTA's impact on the North American investment regime", *C. D. Howe Institute Commentary*, 42, March, (Toronto: C. D. Howe Institute).

Graham, Edward M. (1991). "Foreign direct investment in the United States and U.S. interests", *Science*, 254, 20 (December), pp. 1740-1745.

_____ and Michael Ebert (1991). "Foreign direct investment and U.S. national security: fixing Exon-Florio", *World Economy*, 14, pp. 245-268.

_____ and Christopher Wilkie (1994). "Multinationals and the investment provisions of the NAFTA", *The International Trade Journal*, 8, 3 (Spring), forthcoming.

Hagen, Daniel, Steven Henson and David Merrifield (forthcoming). "Impact of NAFTA on energy markets", in Alan M. Rugman, ed., *Foreign Investment and NAFTA* (Columbia, University of South Carolina Press), pp. 228-248.

Hufbauer, Gary Clyde and Jeffrey J. Schott (1993). *NAFTA: An Assessment* (Washington, D.C., Institute for International Economics).

Johnson, Jon R. (1993). "NAFTA and the trade in automotive goods", in Steven Globerman and Michael Walker, eds., *Assessing NAFTA: A Trinational Analysis* (Vancouver, Canada, The Fraser Institute), pp. 87-129.

Morici, Peter (1993). "NAFTA rules of origin and automotive content requirements", in Steven Globerman and Michael Walker, eds., *Assessing NAFTA: A Trinational Analysis* (Vancouver, Canada, The Fraser Institute), pp. 226-250.

Organisation for Economic Co-operation and Development (1993). *Economic Surveys: United States* (Paris, OECD).

_____ (1992). *Technology and the Economy: The Key Relationships* (Paris, The Technology/Economy Programme, OECD).

Ostry, Sylvia (1990). *Governments and Corporations in a Shrinking World: Trade and Innovation Policies in the United States, Europe, and Japan* (New York and London, Council on Foreign Relations Press).

Plourde, Andre (1993). "Energy and the NAFTA", *C. D. Howe Institute Commentary*, 46, May (Toronto: C. D. Howe Institute).

Power, Michael E. (1993). "Foreign investment protection agreements: a Canadian perspective", Working Paper Series No. 14 (April), mimeo.

_____ (1992). *The Work of Nations* (New York, Vintage).

Rugman, Alan M. (1981). *Inside the Multinationals: The Economics of Internal Markets* (New York, Columbia University Press).

_____ (1990). *Multinationals and Canada-United States Free Trade* (Columbia, University of South Carolina Press).

_____ and Michael Gestrin (1991). "U.S. trade laws as barriers to globalization", *World Economy*, 14, 3, pp. 335-352.

_____ and Alain Verbeke (1990a). *Global Corporate Strategy and Trade Policy* (London and New York, Routledge).

_____ and Alain Verbeke (1990b). "Multinational corporate strategy and the Canada-U.S. Free Trade Agreement", *Management International Review*, 30, 3, pp. 253-266.

_____ and Michael Gestrin (1993). "The strategic response of multinational corporations to NAFTA", *Columbia Journal of World Business*, 28, 4 (Winter 1993), pp. 18-29.

_____ and Mark Warner (1994). "Competitiveness: an emerging strategy of discrimination in U.S. antitrust and R&D policy?", *Law and Policy in International Business*, forthcoming.

Tyson, Laura D'Andrea (1993). *Who's Bashing Whom? Trade Conflict in High Technology Industries* (Washington, D.C., Institute for International Economics).

UNCTAD Division on Transnational Corporations and Investment (1993). *World Investment Directory 1992, Volume III, Developed Countries* (New York, United Nations), United Nations publication, Sales No. E.93.II.A.9.

United States International Trade Commission (1993). *Potential Impact on the U.S. Economy and Selected Industries of the North American Free-Trade Agreement* (Washington, D.C., United States International Trade Commission), publication 2596.

COMPETITIVENESS: AN EMERGING STRATEGY OF DISCRIMINATION IN U.S. ANTITRUST AND R&D POLICY?[1]

MARK A. A. WARNER*

ALAN M. RUGMAN**

This Article discusses the discriminatory use of performance requirements and reciprocity provisions of certain recent U.S. antitrust and research and development (R&D) policy initiatives. These initiatives, rooted in trends already existing in U.S. law, represent a significant hardening of the U.S. position in this regard. Both the economic critique of strategic trade theory and the modern theory of international investment demonstrate that these initiatives are not in the best interest of U.S.-based firms, the U.S. economy, or the global trading system.

Furthermore, certain aspects of these initiatives are inconsistent with U.S. obligations pursuant to international agreements such as the Canada-U.S. Free Trade Agreement (CFTA), the North American Free Trade Agreement (NAFTA), the General Agreement on Tariffs and Trade (GATT), and various instruments of the Organization for Economic Cooperation and Development (OECD). A strong international agreement could protect these obligations and discipline the use of these discriminatory policies, at least among the "Triad" economies of North America, Europe, and Japan. Such an agreement should establish the principles of national treatment and non-discrimination as binding obligations in the areas of domestic trade, investment, competition, and R&D laws without exception. Furthermore, such an agreement should also provide for binding arbitration of disputes between private parties and the Triad members arising out of the use of these kinds of international investment-related measures.

I. INTRODUCTION

U.S. Secretary of Labor Robert Reich recently posed the provocative question "Who is Us?" in a thoughtful article.[1] Current legislative

---

* Associate, Curtis, Mallet-Prevost, Colt & Mosle, Washington, D.C.

** Professor of International Business, Faculty of Management, University of Toronto.

An earlier draft of this paper was presented to the 1993 Annual Meeting of the Academy of International Business held in Maui, Hawaii, October 21–24, 1993. Helpful comments on earlier drafts have been received from Manuel G. Serapio, Harvey M. Applebaum, E.M. Graham, Michael Ebert, Michael Woods and Jonathan Fried. The authors are, however, solely responsible for the views expressed herein.

1. Robert B. Reich, *"Who is Us?"*, HARV. BUS. REV., Jan.–Feb. 1990, at 53.

initiatives before the U.S. Congress highlight the importance of providing the correct response. On May 19, 1993, the House of Representatives by a vote of 243 to 168[2] passed H.R. 820,[3] the National Competitiveness Act of 1993, which, if written into law, would limit foreign access to U.S. technology initiatives.[4] On June 10, 1993, President Bill Clinton signed amendments to the National Cooperative Research Act of 1984[5] (NCRA) that effectively ease antitrust review of certain U.S. production joint ventures.[6]

In this Article, we first review these legislative initiatives. Second, we answer Professor Reich's question by critiquing strategic trade theory and "shelter" strategies for multinational enterprises (MNEs). We conclude that such strategies are inefficient, welfare-reducing, and therefore not in the interest of the international trading system generally, or of the U.S. economy or U.S.-based MNEs in particular. Third, we show how certain aspects of these legislative initiatives may be inconsistent with certain of the international trade and investment obligations of the United States, in particular the Canada-U.S. Free Trade Agreement,[7] the North American Free Trade Agreement,[8] the General Agree-

---

2. 139 CONG. REC. H2562 (daily ed. May 19, 1993).

3. H.R. 820, 103d Cong., 1st Sess. (1993).

4. On March 16, 1994, the Senate passed S. 4, 103d Cong., 2d Sess. (1994), its own version of H.R. 820, by a vote of 59 to 40 with one abstention. *See* 140 CONG. REC. S3006 (daily ed. Mar. 16, 1994). For the text of S. 4, see 140 CONG. REC. S3182 (daily ed. Mar. 17, 1994). The Senate version of H.R. 820 does not contain the same protectionist provisions as the House version. Consequently, the House and Senate will go into conference to iron out the differences between the two versions of H.R. 820. At the time of writing this Article, the outcome of such a conference is uncertain. However, notwithstanding its outcome, the analysis herein remains relevant to other legislation before Congress containing similar protectionist elements. *See, e.g.*, H.R. 3626, 103d Cong., 1st Sess. § 201 (1993); S. 1822, 103d Cong., 1st Sess. (1993) (proposing to reform telecommunications law in the United States by, *inter alia*, prohibiting a manufacturing affiliate of a Bell operating company from using component parts manufactured outside the United States under certain circumstances).

5. 15 U.S.C. §§ 4301–05 (1988).

6. 139 CONG. REC. D648 (daily ed. June 14, 1993).

7. U.S.-Canada Free Trade Agreement Implementation Act of 1988, Pub. L. No. 100-449, 102 Stat. 1851–98 (1988) [hereinafter CFTA].

8. *See* North American Free Trade Agreement, H.R. DOC. NO. 159, 103d Cong., 1st Sess. (1993). Although no provision of the NAFTA provides for the repeal of the CFTA, the U.S. implementing legislation provides that by reason of the entry into force of the NAFTA on January 1, 1994, Canada and the United States have agreed to suspend the operation of certain provisions of the CFTA. *See* The North American Free Trade Agreement Implementation Act, Pub. L. No. 103–182, § 107, 107 Stat. 501 (1993) [hereinafter NAFTA]; THE NORTH AMERICAN FREE TRADE AGREEMENT IMPLEMENTATION ACT: STATEMENT OF ADMINISTRATIVE ACTION 7–8 (Nov. 4, 1993). However, as it is useful to contrast the two agreements to determine emerging regulatory trends in this area of law, the authors do so here.

COMPETITIVENESS & U.S. POLICY DISCRIMINATION

ment on Tariffs and Trade,[9] and various instruments of the Organization for Economic Cooperation and Development. Finally, we conclude that these legislative initiatives demonstrate the need for a strong international discipline against protectionist national trade, investment, and competitiveness policies.

II.   RECENT U.S. POLICY INITIATIVES

A.   *The National Cooperative Production Act, 1993*

In 1984, the U.S. Congress passed the NCRA to ease the antitrust treatment of certain research joint ventures that are notified to the Attorney General (DOJ) and the Federal Trade Commission (FTC).[10] The NCRA provides that qualifying R&D ventures would be subject to rule of reason rather per se illegal analysis.[11] Rule of reason analysis condemns only those joint ventures that, on balance, are anticompetitive.[12] If anticompetitive effects are established, a court must weigh them against any demonstrated pro-competitive effects in determining whether an antitrust violation has occurred.[13] The NCRA also attempted to change the incentives to initiate costly litigation against joint research ventures by providing that (1) certain notified ventures would not be subject to punitive treble damages[14] and that (2) the "substantially prevailing party" in an antitrust action involving a notified venture could, in certain circumstances, recover legal costs (including reasonable attorneys fees and pre-judgment interest) if the claim or the claimant's conduct during the litigation was "frivolous, unreasonable, without foundation or in bad faith."[15]

The NCRA was controversial when it passed Congress and remains so to this day.[16] Some commentators have argued that the act addresses a non-existent problem because of the few prior challenges of research

---

9. General Agreement on Tariffs and Trade, *opened for signature* Oct. 30, 1947, 61 Stat. A3, 55 U.N.T.S. 187. The current amended version of the GATT appears at 4 B.I.S.D. 1 (1969).

10. 15 U.S.C. § 4305 (1988).

11. *Id.*

12. *Id.*

13. S. Rep. No. 427, 98th Cong., 2d Sess. (1984), *reprinted in* 1984 U.S.C.C.A.N. 3114–16; H.R. Conf. Rep. No. 656, 98th Cong., 2d Sess. (1984), *reprinted in* 1984 U.S.C.C.A.N. 3133–36.

14. 15 U.S.C. § 4303 (1988).

15. 15 U.S.C. §§ 4303–04 (1988).

16. For proposals to loosen the U.S. antitrust standard with respect to joint ventures, see Walter Adams & James W. Brock, *Joint Ventures, Antitrust and Transnational Cartelization*, 11 Nw. J. Int'l. L. & Bus. 433, 434–38 (1991).

joint ventures in the absence of ancillary restraints on trade.[17] However, others note that regardless of how minimal actual enforcement has been, misapprehensions about such enforcement probably have had a dampening effect on collaborative activity.[18] Correcting these misapprehensions may thus produce tangible and important benefits: according to a House Judiciary Committee Report, in the nine years following the 1984 passage of the NCRA, 300 research joint ventures were registered, whereas between 1976 and 1979 only an estimated twenty-one research joint ventures were formed.[19] Accordingly, there have been consistent calls since the passage of the NCRA to expands its coverage to joint production ventures and joint marketing ventures.[20]

These initiatives culminated in the passage of the National Cooperative Production Amendments of 1993[21] (NCPA). The House Judiciary Committee identified two areas where exaggerated perceptions may have adverse effects on joint production activity. First, the committee reasoned that smaller firms are the most likely to be overdeterred, due to less knowledge about the intricacies of antitrust law.[22] Second, risk-averse larger firms may hesitate before collaborating in "experimental" joint production ventures.[23] Current antitrust law generally permits cooperation among firms with market power where such cooperation is "necessary" to create or sustain a new product or production process.[24] However, little judicial guidance is available to define the parameters of the term "necessary."[25]

The following quotation from the Judiciary Committee's Report on the NCPA exemplifies the House's ambivalence towards relaxing U.S. antitrust laws to spur innovation:

> In some quarters, a new theory appears to be developing which holds that cooperation between firms engaged in industries

---

17. Robert Pitofsky, *Proposals for Revised United States Merger Enforcement in a Global Economy,* 81 GEO. L.J. 195, 240–44 (1992).

18. Thomas M. Jorde & David J. Teece, *Innovation, Cooperation and Antitrust,* 4 HIGH TECH. L. J. 1, 4 (1989).

19. H.R. REP. NO. 94, 103d Cong., 1st Sess. 11 (1993) [hereinafter H.R. REP. NO. 94], *reprinted in* 64 ANTITRUST & TRADE REG. REP. (BNA) 717, 720 (1993).

20. *Id.* at 13–14.

21. H.R. 1313, 103d Cong., 1st Sess. (1993) (enacted); S. 574, 103d Cong., 1st Sess. (1993) (enacted).

22. H.R. REP. NO. 94, *supra* note 19, at 12.

23. *Id.*

24. *Id.*

25. *Id.*

COMPETITIVENESS & U.S. POLICY DISCRIMINATION

subject to rapid technological change cannot possibly injure competition, because of the diversity of sources of innovation and the new nature of global competition. Yet, at this point in time, that theory—though obviously the product of thoughtful analysis—nevertheless remains an economic hypothesis, and not a statement of empirically demonstrated fact.

Nevertheless, there is compelling argument that innovation-related joint ventures—if properly structured—can often be economically beneficial and conducive to a resurgence of U.S. leadership in high technology. The bill reported by the Committee reflects the judgement that collaborative innovation efforts should be encouraged. The permissive and facilitating approach taken by the antitrust laws for years reflects this same consensus.[26]

To be clear, the authors agree with the essential goals of the NCPA. Had Congress stopped at this point, there would be no need for criticism and, perhaps, no need for this Article. However, Congress, through two additional conditions, limited access to the new favorable antitrust treatment for joint production ventures. First, subsection 7(1) of the new National Cooperative Research and Production Act of 1993[27] (NCRPA) requires that the "principal facilities" of the venture be located in the United States or its territories. Second, subsection 7(2) of the act requires that

each person who controls any party to such venture (including such party itself) is a United States person, or a foreign person from a country whose law that accords antitrust treatment no less favorable to United States persons than to such country's domestic persons with respect to participation in joint ventures for production.[28]

In other words, to qualify under the NCRPA, a joint production venture must (1) have production take place principally within the United States and (2) be controlled by (i) a U.S. person (natural or artificial) or (ii) a person from a foreign country according national treatment to U.S. corporations with respect to the antitrust law on joint production ventures. Therefore, to qualify under the NCRPA, an MNE must also be

---

26. *Id.* at 16.
27. 15 U.S.C. § 4301 (1988).
28. *Id.* § 4301(7)(2).

LAW & POLICY IN INTERNATIONAL BUSINESS

from a country that meets what can be termed a "conditional" or "reciprocal" standard of national treatment.

Notably, the conjunction "and," not "or," links subsection 7(1) to 7(2). The language of the statute itself does not conclusively indicate whether the link is meant to be inclusive. Therefore, future plaintiffs may argue that *both* conditions must be satisfied for a foreign-based MNE to qualify for favorable antitrust treatment under the NCRPA. Both the House Report[29] and the Senate Report on the NCPA,[30] which use identical language to discuss these provisions, buttress such a view. Each refers to subsections 7(1) and 7(2) as setting forth two "additional conditions."[31] Both further describe the purpose of the specific statutory language:

> The language in the new section 7 reinforces the fact that this legislation is intended to benefit the U.S. economy by encouraging companies to enter into production joint ventures. Whether the motivation is accessing technology and capital, or obtaining production efficiencies, such collaborative efforts may speed the commercialization of new technologies and products and make them more widely available. These ventures may involve U.S. companies, companies from foreign nations, or a combination thereof.[32]

However, this statement is inconsistent with the economic analysis provided in Part III below. To the extent the United States retains the right to apply its antitrust laws extraterritorially,[33] a production joint venture with foreign principal production facilities may be denied the protection afforded to its U.S.-based competitors by the NCPRA. Such treatment is anomalous and discriminatory, regardless of whether the offshore production venture included U.S.-based MNEs. The net effect of such a rule may be to deny U.S. producers and consumers the full range of competitive choices and innovations that the NCRPA was intended to provide.

In recognition of this anomaly, the legislative history of the act offers

---

29. H.R. REP. No. 94, *supra* note 19, at 19.

30. S. REP. No. 51, 103d Cong., 1st Sess. 11 (1993) [hereinafter S. REP. No. 51], *reprinted in* 64 ANTITRUST & TRADE REG. REP. (BNA) 725, 728 (1993).

31. *Id.*; H.R. REP. No. 94, *supra* note 19, at 19.

32. H.R. REP. No. 94, *supra* note 19, at 20; S. REP. No. 51, *supra* note 30, at 12.

33. For a recent restatement of this policy, see the majority judgement of Justice Souter in *Hartford Fire Ins. Co. v. California*, 113 S.Ct. 2891 (1993).

COMPETITIVENESS & U.S. POLICY DISCRIMINATION

further clarifications to subsections 7(1) and 7(2). First, it indicates that subsection 7(1) does not preclude a venture from utilizing and placing "significant production and production support facilities" outside the United States so long as they are "ancillary in nature."[34] Unfortunately, this concession does not solve the fundamental problem discussed above. Second, the legislative history indicates that the phrase "whose law" in subsection 7(2) refers not only to a foreign country's domestic antitrust law but also to

> all international agreements and other binding obligations to which that country and the United States are parties. Accordingly, a country that is a party to an international agreement with the United States that provides national treatment satisfies the requirements of section 7(2).[35]

The House and Senate Committee reports indicate that such obligations would include treaties of friendship, commerce, and navigation; bilateral investment treaties; various OECD instruments; and the CFTA and NAFTA.[36]

On the basis of these clarifications, the House and Senate Committees posit that the NCRPA "is, and should be construed to be, consistent with the national treatment commitments of the United States set forth in such agreements."[37] Both of the relevant U.S. administrative agencies responsible for the antitrust laws, the Department of Justice and the Federal Trade Commission, have indicated their acceptance of the legislative history.[38] However, it is worth noting that the legislative history, although highly persuasive, is neither determinative of the positions that will be advocated by private plaintiffs in reliance on the statutory language nor binding on the U.S. judiciary.[39] Further, it is also worth considering whether the DOJ or FTC will accept as sufficient a party's mere membership to a treaty of the type enumerated above or whether some attempt will be made to unilaterally assess the performance of trading partners under their treaty obligations.

---

34. H.R. REP. NO. 94, *supra* note 19, at 20; S. REP. NO. 51, *supra* note 30, at 12.

35. H.R. REP. NO. 94, *supra* note 19, at 20; S. REP. NO. 51, *supra* note 30, at 12.

36. H.R. REP. NO. 94, *supra* note 19, at 20; S. REP. NO. 51, *supra* note 30, at 12.

37. H.R. REP. NO. 94, *supra* note 19, at 20; S. REP. NO. 51, *supra* note 30, at 12.

38. DEP'T OF JUSTICE & FED. TRADE COMM'N, STATEMENT ON NOTIFICATION PROCEDURES UNDER NATIONAL COOPERATIVE RESEARCH AND PRODUCTION ACT (1993), *reprinted in* 65 ANTITRUST & TRADE REG. REP. (BNA) 28 (1993).

39. 2A NORMAN J. SINGER, SUTHERLAND STATUTORY CONSTRUCTION § 48.02 (5th ed. 1992).

LAW & POLICY IN INTERNATIONAL BUSINESS

Some may object that we protest too much, given that the NCRPA effects only very minor changes to U.S. antitrust law insofar as it applies to production joint ventures.[40] However, the above cited statistics on the NCPA clearly demonstrate the potentially significant consequences of any change in policy.[41] Further, the NCRPA exemplifies an emerging trend in U.S. competitiveness legislation. To illustrate the latter point we discuss certain provisions of H.R. 820, recently passed by the House. These provisions are not contained in the Senate version.[42]

B. *H.R. 820: The National Competitiveness Act of 1993*

The House of Representative passed the comprehensive technology bill H.R. 820 in May 1993. The bill expresses the sentiment that the creation, development, and adoption of advanced technologies are significant determinants to sustainable economic growth, productivity improvement, and competitive standing.[43] Further, the bill notes that over the last decade the rate of advanced technology adoption in the United States has been about half that of some unnamed prominent foreign nations, thereby contributing to a decline in U.S. industrial competitiveness.[44] Not surprisingly, H.R. 820 seeks to promote and facilitate the creation, development, and adoption of such technology throughout the United States.[45] As a means to this end, H.R. 820 aspires to enhance the competitiveness of U.S. manufacturers, particularly small businesses, by developing a technology outreach program to improve access to information, expertise, technology, and management practices necessary to compete globally.[46]

H.R. 820 further aims to promote the development and rapid application of advanced manufacturing technologies and processes by U.S. manufacturers.[47] To accomplish this goal, H.R. 820 endeavors to stimulate long-term investment in U.S. companies engaged in the development or utilization of critical and other technologies.[48] H.R. 820 is designed to expand cooperation among the various levels of government

---

40. Eleanor M. Fox & Robert Pitofsky, *United States Country Study*, in GLOBAL COMPETITION POLICY (E.M. Graham & J.D. Richardson eds., forthcoming 1994) (manuscript at 70, on file with author).

41. *See supra* note 16 and accompanying text.

42. *See supra* note 4.

43. H.R. 820, 103d Cong., 1st Sess. § 102(1) (1993).

44. *Id.* § 102(2).

45. *Id.* § 103(1).

46. *Id.* § 103(2).

47. *Id.* § 103(3).

48. *Id.* § 103(4).

COMPETITIVENESS & U.S. POLICY DISCRIMINATION

in respect to technological policy.[49] H.R. 820 also provides a mechanism to monitor foreign technological capabilities relative to the United States, in order to identify and respond to "competitive opportunities and challenges."[50]

H.R. 820, as amended, consists of six titles. Title I contains statements of findings, purposes, and definitions. Title II, the Manufacturing Technology and Extension Act of 1993 (MTEA), sets out the role of the Department of Commerce (DOC) and the National Science Foundation (NSF) in furthering the above-referenced objectives.[51] Title III provides for "bench-marking U.S. science and technology against foreign capabilities" and establishes various assistance programs for advanced and civilian technologies.[52] Title IV manages a number of miscellaneous provisions.[53] Title V authorizes the appropriations necessary to fund H.R. 820. Title VI, added to H.R. 820 by an amendment, provides that funds made available pursuant to the bill would, for the most part, benefit only "citizen(s) or national(s)" of the United States.[54]

The attempt to define "United States company" and "United States manufacturer" to limit foreign access to the technology programs created or enhanced pursuant to H.R. 820 constitutes the most striking and controversial aspect of the bill. Currently, neither of these terms is defined in the Stevenson-Wydler Technology Innovation Act of 1980[55] (SWTIA), the primary legislation subject to amendment by H.R. 820. However, section 10a of the SWTIA authorizes federal agencies to permit the directors of their federal laboratories to enter into cooperative R&D agreements with state, local, and private parties.[56] In deciding what agreements to enter, the director is instructed to "give special advantage to small business firms, and consortia involving small business firms."[57] Additionally, the director is instructed to

> give preference to business units located in the United States which agree that products embodying inventions made under the cooperative research and development agreement or pro-

---

49. *Id.* §§ 103(5)–(6).

50. *Id.* § 103(7).

51. *Id.*

52. *Id.* § 301.

53. *Id.* § 401.

54. 139 Cong. Rec. H2561 (daily ed. May 19, 1993) (considering the National Competitiveness Act of 1993).

55. 15 U.S.C. §§ 3701–14 (1988).

56. *Id.* § 3710a(a)–(b).

57. *Id.* § 3710a(c)(4)(A).

duced through the use of such inventions will be manufactured substantially in the United States and, in the case of any industrial organization or other person subject to the control of a foreign company or government, as appropriate, take into consideration whether or not such foreign government permits United States agencies, organizations, or other persons to enter into cooperative research and development agreements and licensing agreements.[58]

The version of H.R. 820 put to the floor of the House did not contain such discriminatory language. Instead, it adopted the definitions of the National Institute of Standards and Technology Act[59] (NISTA). To receive Advanced Technology Program (ATP) financial assistance under the NISTA, a company must be, *inter alia*, (1) a "United States-owned company," defined as "a company that has majority ownership or control by individuals who are citizens of the United States,"[60] or (2) incorporated in the United States and has

a parent company which is incorporated in a country which affords to United States-owned companies opportunities, comparable to those afforded to any other company, to participate in any joint venture similar to those authorized under this chapter; affords to United States-owned companies local investment opportunities comparable to those afforded to any other company; and affords adequate and effective protection for the intellectual property rights of United States-owned companies.[61]

---

58. *Id.* § 3710a(c)(4)(B).

59. 15 U.S.C. § 278n(d)(9)(B) (1988).

60. *Id.* § 278n(d)(9)(B)(i).

61. *Id.* § 278n(d)(9)(B)(ii) (emphasis added). These definitions are part of a series of provisions that came into force pursuant to the American Technology Preeminence Act of 1991 (ATPA). Subparagraph 278n(d)(11)(A) of the NISTA, also passed pursuant to the ATPA, further provides that title to any intellectual property arising from assistance provided under the ATPA shall vest in a company or companies incorporated in the United States, and that such title shall not be transferred or passed until the expiration of the first patent, except to a company incorporated in the United States. *Id.* § 278n(d)(11)(A). However, subparagraph 28(d)(11)(C) states that paragraph 28(d)(11) shall not be construed to prohibit the licensing to any corporation of such intellectual property. *Id.* § 278n(d)(11)(C). While paragraph 28(d)(11) is clearly discriminatory, it does not impose the additional foreign ownership and control restrictions on the transferee corporation incorporated in the United States.

COMPETITIVENESS & U.S. POLICY DISCRIMINATION

In other words, to qualify for financial assistance under the NISTA, a company has to be majority-owned or controlled by U.S. citizens— meaning natural persons, not corporations—or its parent corporation country must afford conditional or reciprocal national treatment to U.S. companies. A standard of "comparable" rather than "equivalent" treatment is employed to evaluate the adequacy of national treatment accorded. As above, this provision of the NISTA is subject to the economic critique raised in Part III below regarding the NCPRA requirements of conditional or reciprocal national treatment.

In sum, the unamended version of H.R. 820 debated in the House defined "United States company" solely in terms of subparagraph 28(d)(9)(B) and paragraph 28(j)(2) of the NISTA.[62] That version of H.R. 820 defined "United States manufacturer" in the same terms, with the additional requirement that such a company be "engaged in manufacturing activities."[63] Further, the unamended H.R. 820 provided that, with respect to manufacturing companies alone, the Secretary of Commerce could make a finding under subparagraph 28(d)(9)(A) of the NISTA based on a certification by the company.[64] Subparagraph 28(d)(9)(A) of the NISTA sets out the additional criteria for financial assistance under the ATP. The Secretary of Commerce must find that the company's participation would be in the "economic interest of the United States" as evidenced by four enumerated factors discussed below.[65]

In debate on the floor of the House, Representative Manton (D-NY) successfully amended without a vote H.R. 820's definition of both "U.S. company" and "United States manufacturer."[66] The Manton amendments impose even more stringent language than the original bill submitted to the House, defining a "United States company" as an entity which, according to a finding by the Secretary of Commerce "based on demonstration" by such entity

A) maintains substantial employment in the United States;[67]
B) agrees to promote the manufacture within the United States of

---

62. H.R. 820, 103d Cong., 1st Sess. § 206(a)(20) (1993), *reprinted in* 139 CONG. REC. H2316 (daily ed. May 6, 1993).

63. *Id.* § 206(a)(21), *reprinted in* 139 CONG. REC. H2316 (daily ed. May 6, 1993).

64. *Id.*

65. 15 U.S.C. § 278n(d)(9) (1988).

66. H.R. 820, § 206(a)(20)–(21), *reprinted in* 139 CONG. REC. H2324 (daily ed. May 6, 1993).

67. *Id.* § 206(a)(20)(A).

and technology developed with assistance pursuant to H.R. 820;[68]
C) agrees to buy parts and materials from competitive U.S. suppliers;[69] and is either
D) (i) a United States-owned company;[70] or

(ii) its parent is incorporated in a foreign country that provides national treatment with respect to participating in "programs and to have access to resources and information *equivalent* to the opportunities" authorized pursuant to H.R. 820;[71]

(iii) its parent country has a transparent standards development and conformity assessment process that does not discriminate against U.S. products and production processes;[72]

(iv) its parent country provides local investment opportunities, *comparable* to those afforded its own companies, to United States-owned companies;[73]

(v) its parent country provides "adequate and effective" protection for the intellectual property rights of United States-owned companies.[74]

The Manton amendments define "United States manufacturer" as a U.S. company that "makes substantial investments in the United States in research and development and manufacturing (including the manufacture of major components and subassemblies in the United States)."[75] The company must establish this fact to the satisfaction of the Secretary of Commerce.

The Manton amendments essentially formalize the eligibility criteria to receive financial assistance under the advanced technology programs established by paragraph 28(d)(9) of the NISTA.[76] However, there are key differences between the two. For instance, the Manton amendments require that the parent's country provide national treatment with respect to participation in programs and access to resources and infor-

---

68. *Id.* § 206(a)(20)(B).

69. *Id.* § 206(a)(20)(C).

70. *Id.* § 206(a)(20)(D)(i).

71. *Id.* § 206(a)(20)(D)(ii)(I) (emphasis added).

72. *Id.* § 206(a)(20)(D)(ii)(II).

73. *Id.* § 206(a)(20)(D)(ii)(III) (emphasis added).

74. *Id.* § 206(a)(20)(D)(ii)(IV).

75. *Id.* § 206(a)(21).

76. *See* Letter from Abraham Katz, President, United States Council for International Business, to Ronald Brown, Secretary of Commerce (June 14, 1993) [hereinafter USCIB Letter] (on file with author).

COMPETITIVENESS & U.S. POLICY DISCRIMINATION

mation,[77] yet those programs and that access must be "equivalent to the opportunities" provided for in H.R. 820.[78] Thus the Manton amendments require more than the conditional or reciprocal national treatment discussed of the NCRPA; they require reciprocity.

Similarly, in defining "United States company" the Manton amendments exceed the requirements of the NISTA by mandating "substantial investment in," rather than "significant contributions to," the United States. Similarly, in defining "United States manufacturer" the Manton amendments establish a "substantial" investment test, unlike the NISTA, which merely requires the Secretary of Commerce to consider whether the company agrees to purchase parts and material from "competitive" suppliers as a factor in determining whether granting financial assistance would be in the "economic interest of the United States."[79] The Manton amendments make such an agreement a necessary condition to receipt of financial assistance. However, since the bill nowhere defines the term "competitive," only actual practice will determine the degree to which it functions as a protectionist device.

Further, the Manton amendments, unlike the NISTA, place the onus on the company to satisfy the Secretary of Commerce with respect to each of the items enumerated above. In addition, H.R. 820 empowers the Secretary of Commerce to unilaterally assess the performance of foreign states in meeting national treatment obligations pursuant to treaties with the United States. However, the bill nowhere explicitly requires the Secretary of Commerce to exhaust any applicable treaty dispute settlement provisions before reaching a decision.

The net effect of these rigid eligibility criteria and performance requirements may be to preclude many MNEs, including some traditionally viewed as U.S.-based, from participating in the technology programs pursuant to H.R. 820, a point made publicly by several industry groups and MNEs.[80] By rejecting a case-by-case or project-by-project approach

---

77. *See supra* note 64 and accompanying text.

78. *Id.*

79. *Compare* H.R. 820, § 206 (a)(20) & (21) (Manton amendments), *reprinted in* 139 CONG. REC. H2316 (daily ed. May 6, 1993), *with* 15 U.S.C. § 278n(d)(9) (NISTA).

80. *See* Letter from Thomas Patton, Chairman, Investment Committee of the Organization for International Investment, to Ronald Brown, Secretary of Commerce 2 (July 21, 1993) [hereinafter OFII Letter] (on file with author); Letter from Jerry Jasinowski, President, National Association of Manufacturers, to Ronald Brown, Secretary of Commerce 1 (July 14, 1993) [hereinafter NAM Letter] (on file with author); USCIB Letter, *supra* note 76, at 2; Letter from Leslie Simon, Office of the IBM Director of Public Affairs, to Senator Ernest Hollings 1 (July 8, 1993) [hereinafter IBM Letter] (on file with author); Letter from John Pickitt, President, Computer and Business

to determining the suitability of a given company for a given program, H.R. 820 will exclude some otherwise eligible MNEs. As we discuss in Part III of this Article, this policies may induce inefficient strategic choices by MNEs, thereby reducing the very U.S. welfare and competitiveness that H.R. 820 sought to remedy.

Representative Traficant (D-OH) voiced perhaps the clearest statement of the protectionist intent of the Manton amendments:

> If President Clinton does not sign this, I do not think we elected a Democrat. The American workers are tired of philosophical Members of Congress selling our jobs down the drain and bringing lame, half-witted protectionist debates here. If this is protectionism, I am stone cold guilty, and proud of it.[81]

In fact, Representative Traficant successfully offered a "friendly" protectionist amendment to Title IV of H.R. 820. Subsection 410(a) prohibited the fraudulent use of "Made in America" labels for use in connection with any procurement pursuant to H.R. 820. Subsection 410(b) required compliance with the "Buy American Act"[82] in connection with certain procurements made pursuant to H.R. 820. Representative Traficant added paragraph 410(c)(1), presenting the congressional view that any recipient of an H.R. 820 grant "should purchase only American made equipment and products when expending grant monies."[83] The Traficant amendment directs the Secretary of Commerce to provide each recipient notice of this Congressional viewpoint.[84]

Finally, Representative Mac Collins (R-Ga.) successfully added Title VI, which provides in part that no funds available pursuant to H.R. 820 may be used to provide "any direct Federal financial benefit to any person who is not . . . a citizen or national of the United States."[85] Since only natural persons can be citizens, the Collins amendment, which passed by a margin of 288 to 127,[86] would preclude all companies from funds under the bill if read literally.[87] Even read less broadly, Title VI

Equipment Manufacturers Association, to Senator Ernest Hollings 1 (May 24, 1993) [hereinafter CBEMA Letter] (on file with author).

81. 139 CONG. REC. H2328 (daily ed. May 6, 1993) (statement of Rep. Traficant).

82. 41 U.S.C. § 10(a)–(c) (1988).

83. H.R. 820, § 410(c)(2), *reprinted in* 139 CONG. REC. H2533 (daily ed. May 6, 1993).

84. *Id.*

85. *See supra* note 48 and accompanying text.

86. *Id.*

87. *See* OFII Letter, *supra* note 80, at 4–5.

COMPETITIVENESS & U.S. POLICY DISCRIMINATION

prohibits funding to any entity with foreign shareholders, which includes virtually every publicly traded company.[88]

What then is the status of H.R. 820? The House and Senate have each passed different versions of the bill. The Senate version, however, does not attempt to define "U.S. company" or "U.S. manufacturer."[89] Therefore, the NISTA definitions would continue to determine access to the ATP, but not to the provisions of H.R. 820. The House and Senate are appointing conferees to resolve the inconsistencies between the two versions of the bill.[90]

Secretary of Commerce Ronald Brown has publicly opposed certain of the Manton amendments and the Collins amendment, stating: "These provisions are inconsistent with our international policies and may be contrary to our international obligations, including those under Bilateral Investment Treaties and the [CFTA]."[91] However, as indicated above, the NISTA definitions are not without their own problems. Further, Secretary Brown only expressed opposition to the definition of "United States company," not "United States manufacturer."[92]

III. THE ECONOMICS OF PROTECTIONISM

In this section, we review the economic effects of the discriminatory aspects of the SWTIA, NISTA, NCPRA, and H.R. 820. First, we analyze the effects of the discriminatory performance requirements in these measures, both from the perspective of U.S.-based MNEs seeking protection and of other MNEs operating in the United States or elsewhere in the world. Second, we analyze the effects of the reciprocity or conditional national treatment aspects in these measures.

---

88. *Id.*

89. *See* S. 4, 140 CONG. REC. S3182 (daily ed. Mar. 17, 1994).

90. The Senate conferees are Senators Ernest Hollings (D-S.C.), John Rockefeller IV (D-W.Va.) and John Danforth (R-Mo.). *See* 140 CONG. REC. S3006 (daily ed. Mar. 16, 1994). At the time of publication (May 1994), the House conferees had yet to be named.

91. Letter from Ronald Brown, Secretary of Commerce, to George Brown, Chairman of the Committee on Science, Space, and Technology (Aug. 9, 1993) [hereinafter Brown Letter] (on file with author).

The U.S. Trade Representative has written similar letters to congressional leaders voicing the Clinton administration's opposition to the protectionist aspects of telecommunications legislation, referred to *supra* note 4, currently before Congress. *See also* Letter from Michael Kantor, United States Trade Representative, to John Dingell, Chairman of the Committee on Energy and Commerce, and Edward Markey, Chairman of the Energy and Commerce Subcommittee on Telecommunications and Finance (Feb. 25, 1994) (on file with author); John Maggs, *Phone Measure Becomes Clinton's First Nafta Test*, J. COM., Mar. 3, 1994, at 1A, 8A.

92. *Id.*

LAW & POLICY IN INTERNATIONAL BUSINESS

B. *Discriminatory Performance Requirements*

The competitive strategies followed by MNEs derive from the interaction of their firm-specific advantages (FSAs)[93] in such areas as technology, or managerial or marketing expertise with the natural comparative,[94] country-specific advantages (CSAs)[95] of their operational base. An MNE can pursue either a competition-based, efficiency strategy or a shelter-based, non-efficiency strategy.[96] Diagram 1 provides a useful way of conceptualizing the relationship between the relative strength of the FSAs of an MNE and its competitive strategy.[97] An MNE in quadrant 1 with strong FSAs, following an efficiency-based strategy, will support government policies that will help to develop their FSAs by lowering costs or differentiating products.[98]

An MNE in quadrant 3 following a shelter strategy will support government measures aimed at achieving survival, profit, and growth by foreclosing or excluding competition through trade and regulatory protection or other discriminatory laws and policies.[99] A quadrant 3 MNE may attempt to leverage its domestic market advantage into international markets.[100] An MNE with strong FSAs but pursuing a shelter strategy is attempting to secure extraordinary profits by way of government-supported entry barriers that give or reinforce its competitive advantages.[101] However, quadrant 4 MNEs face the risk of "X-inefficiencies"[102] that diminish once-strong FSAs, as well as the risk of increased retaliation in other markets.[103]

An MNE with weak firm-specific advantages also may choose between efficiency-based and shelter strategies. When a quadrant 2 MNE chooses an efficiency-based strategy, it may still seek short-term development

---

93. *Id.* at 8, 49.

94. *See generally* DAVID RICARDO, THE PRINCIPLES OF POLITICAL ECONOMY AND TAXATION (1817) (detailing the theory of comparative advantage).

95. ALAN RUGMAN & ALAIN VERBEKE, GLOBAL CORPORATE STRATEGY AND TRADE POLICY 49 (1990).

96. *Id.* at 9.

97. *See id.* at 15 fig. 2.2.

98. *Id.* at 9.

99. *Id.*

100. *See* Matsushita Electric Industrial Co. v. Zenith Radio Corp., 475 U.S. 574, 576, 580–81 (1986); *see generally* LAURA D'ANDREA TYSON, WHO'S BASHING WHOM?: TRADE CONFLICT IN HIGH TECHNOLOGY INDUSTRIES (1992).

101. RUGMAN & VERBEKE, *supra* note 95, at 16.

102. For a description of "X-inefficiencies," see Harvey Leibenstein, *Allocative Efficiency vs. "X-inefficiency,"* 56 AM. ECON. REV. 392 (1966).

103. Alan Rugman & Michael Gestrin, *EC Anti-Dumping Laws as a Barrier to Trade,* 9 EUR. MGMT. J. 475, 476 (1991).

COMPETITIVENESS & U.S. POLICY DISCRIMINATION

Diagram 1
Corporate Trade Policy Strategies

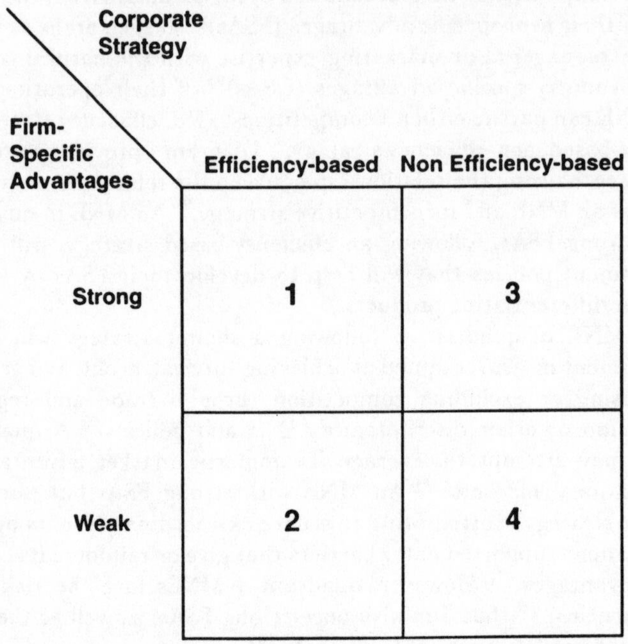

Corporate
Strategy

Firm-
Specific
Advantages   Efficiency-based   Non Efficiency-based

	Efficiency-based	Non Efficiency-based
Strong	1	3
Weak	2	4

assistance from the government,[104] but not the discriminatory treatment of its competitors. For instance, U.S.-based MNEs that support the
nondiscriminatory aspects of the SWTIA, NISTA, NCPRA, and H.R. 820
may be thought of as operating in quadrant 2 with the expectation of
moving over time into quadrant 1. If this strategy is unsuccessful, the
MNEs will fail, otherwise exit the market,[105] or pursue shelter strategies.[106] For instance, such MNEs may be contrasted with quadrant 4
MNEs, which pursue shelter strategies through the discriminatory
aspects of the SWTIA, NISTA, NCRPA, and H.R. 820.[107] In relation to

---

104. RUGMAN & VERBEKE, *supra* note 95, at 15.

105. Rugman & Gestrin, *supra* note 103, at 477.

106. *See* Alan M. Rugman & Alain Verbeke, *Strategic Trade Policy is Not Good Strategy*, 25
HITOTSUBASHI J. COM. & MGMT. 75, 84–85 (1990).

107. For a more detailed analysis of the demand for shelter strategies in the administration of
U.S. trade laws, see Alan M. Rugman & Samuel D. Porteous, *Canadian and U.S. Unfair Trade Laws: A
Comparison of Their Legal and Administrative Structures*, 15 N.C. J. INT'L. L. & COM. REG. 67, 79–84
(1990); Alan M. Rugman, *A Canadian Perspective on U.S. Administered Protection and the Free Trade
Agreement*, 40 ME. L. REV. 305 (1988); Andrew Anderson & Alan M. Rugman, *The Dispute Settlement*

quadrant 3 MNEs, quadrant 4 MNEs essentially seek to exclude competitors from their domestic market and to leverage that advantage into other international markets.

Ultimately, the success of a shelter strategy in developing the firm-specific advantages of an MNE turns on the successful implementation of governmental measures for which they lobby, known as "strategic trade policy."[108] There are essentially two versions of the strategic trade policy story. The first considers only the interests of producers[109] and assumes that by some strategic first move, such as a government-supported investment in excess capacity, an MNE can reduce the production of its competitors from other nations.[110] The first mover gains a temporary advantage until its competitors repeat the move in their respective nations, making all worse off than before the game was played.[111] The first mover will play the game only if its gains exceed any future losses caused by developments such as new entry—in other words, the industry must facilitate extraordinary profits.[112] However, empirical tests of this model generally have not demonstrated significant welfare gains to the domestic economy implementing such a trade strategy.[113] Further, the government must balance any potential gain against market structure minutiae that governments are unlikely to foresee accurately.[114] Accordingly, this view of strategic trade theory would not support the protectionist aspects of the SWTIA, NISTA, NCRPA, and H.R. 820 as FSA-developing strategic trade policies.

The second version of strategic trade theory is based on the notion that strategic support of an industry can be justified on the basis of potential "external economies" or "spillovers."[115] External economies can compensate short-term losses for an industry characterized by

---

Mechanisms' Cases in the Canada-United States Free Trade Agreement: An Economic Evaluation, 24 GEO. WASH. J. INT'L. L. & ECON. 1 (1990) (assessing the dispute settlement mechanisms of the Canada-U.S. Free Trade Agreement).

108. *See* Paul Krugman, *Does the New Trade Theory Require a New Trade Policy?,* 15 WORLD ECON. 415 (1992) [hereinafter Krugman 1992]; Paul Krugman, *The Narrow and Broad Arguments for Free Trade,* 83 AM. ECON. REV. 362 (1993) [hereinafter Krugman 1993].

109. James Brander & Barbara Spencer, *Export Subsidies and International Market Share Rivalry,* 18 J. OF INT'L. ECON. 83 (1985).

110. Krugman 1992, *supra* note 108, at 432–33.

111. *Id.*

112. Krugman 1992, *supra* note 108, at 434; *see also* J.D. Richardson, *"New" Trade Theory and Policy a Decade Old: Assessment in a Pacific Context,* NBER WORKING PAPER NO. 4042, at 21–22 (1992).

113. Krugman 1992, *supra* note 108, at 434–35.

114. Krugman 1993, *supra* note 108, at 363.

115. *See generally* GENE GROSSMAN & ELHANAN HELPMAN, INNOVATION AND GROWTH IN THE GLOBAL ECONOMY (1991).

COMPETITIVENESS & U.S. POLICY DISCRIMINATION

increasing returns to scale.[116] This second version, however, raises similar concerns of retaliation in kind.[117] Although the welfare gains from external economies may be greater than the rent-seeking approach of the first version,[118] economist Paul Krugman, the originator of strategic trade theory, has recently observed that "we will still be talking about really small stakes," perhaps resulting in less than one percent real welfare gain to the U.S. economy.[119]

Further, such gains, if any, must still be weighed against the potential for harm to other U.S.-based quadrant 1 MNEs pursuing efficiency-based competitive strategies at home or abroad. Retaliation would adversely affect such firms to the same extent as the quadrant 4 MNEs that demanded protection, and may adversely affect the quadrant 1 MNE even as the quadrant 4 firm benefits. According to the prevailing theory of foreign direct investment—internalization theory[120]—an MNE chooses a mode of entry into a foreign market from a continuum of choices ranging from trade to direct investment and licensing.[121] The MNE's decision ultimately is conditioned by the degree to which it seeks to maintain the integrity of its firm-specific advantages, which have been "internalized" within the firm.[122] If the performance requirements of the SWTIA, NISTA, NCRPA, and H.R. 820 adversely affect such MNEs, then the efficiency advantages from internalization may be lost to the MNE.[123] In such circumstances, the MNE may accept the non-optimal arrangement as a price of operation in that market or, in the extreme, may exit the market altogether.[124] For MNEs that have integrated across national borders as a result of otherwise significant trade liberalization, the efficiency losses may be even greater.[125]

---

116. Krugman 1992, *supra* note 108, at 435.

117. *Id.* at 438.

118. *Id.*

119. Krugman 1993, *supra* note 108, at 363.

120. *See generally* ALAN M. RUGMAN, INSIDE THE MULTINATIONALS (1981) [hereinafter RUGMAN, INSIDE THE MULTINATIONALS]; John H. Dunning & Alan M. Rugman, *The Influence of Hymer's Dissertation on the Theory of Foreign Direct Investment*, 75 AM. ECON. REV. 228 (1985).

121. RUGMAN, INSIDE THE MULTINATIONALS, *supra* note 120, at 53.

122. Dunning & Rugman, *supra* note 120, at 229.

123. A similar problem emerges where MNEs are following efficiency strategies that emphasize alliances and de-emphasize vertical integration (a process known as "de-internalizing"). *See* Joe R. D'Cruz & Alan M. Rugman, *Developing International Competitiveness: The Five Partners Model*, 58 BUS. Q. 60, 64–65 (1993).

124. E. M. Graham, *Japanese Control of R&D Activities in the United States: Is This Cause for Concern?*, *in* JAPAN'S GROWING TECHNOLOGICAL CAPABILITY: IMPLICATIONS FOR THE U.S. ECONOMY 189, 202–06 (T. S. Arrison et al. eds., 1992).

125. ALAN M. RUGMAN, MULTINATIONALS AND CANADA-UNITED STATES FREE TRADE 29 (1990).

LAW & POLICY IN INTERNATIONAL BUSINESS

B. *Reciprocity or Conditional National Treatment*

The above analysis also sheds light on the thorny problem of the reciprocity or conditional national treatment provisions of the SWTIA, NISTA, NCRPA, and H.R. 820. Certainly, the principles of national treatment and non-discrimination permit investors to enter new markets, thereby serving as a foundation for cooperation, coordination, and integration of multinational operations.[126] However, in certain industries, complete integration is not possible unless the same rules are applied consistently across national boundaries.[127] As a result, the demand for reciprocity strategies may be consistent with both efficient quadrant 1 behavior, and sheltering quadrant 4 behavior by MNEs. Only analysis of the industry structure and relevant policy environment will clarify the policy being pursued in a particular case. However, where reciprocity measures are combined with the more traditional protectionist policy measures discussed above, the advocates of reciprocity bear a heavy burden of persuasion. Additionally, under internalization theory, reciprocity may harm efficient quadrant 1 MNEs facing a constrained range of options, perhaps explaining the public opposition of many successful U.S.-based MNEs to the discriminatory aspects of H.R. 820.[128]

In conclusion, Part III shown that the discriminatory performance requirements of the SWTIA, NISTA, NCRPA, and H.R. 820 may serve as shelter strategies for inefficient U.S.-based MNEs and that the reciprocity or conditional national treatment provisions may also deter efficient decision-making by certain MNEs.[129] Having assessed these provisions against economic theory, this Article next discusses their consistency with existing international norms.

IV. INCOMPATIBILITY WITH EXISTING INTERNATIONAL NORMS

A. *The Canada-U.S. Free Trade Agreement*

Paragraph 102(c) of the CFTA specified that the objectives of the agreement are, *inter alia*, to (1) "eliminate barriers to trade in goods and services,"[130] (2) "facilitate conditions of fair competition within the

---

126. Alan M. Rugman et al., *Entry Barriers and Bank Strategies for the Europe 1992 Financial Directives*, 10 EU. MGMT. J. 327, 329 (1993).

127. *Id.*

128. *See supra* notes 65, 68.

129. For a useful analysis of competitiveness policies generally, see Paul Krugman, *Competitiveness: A Dangerous Obsession*, FOREIGN AFF., Mar.–Apr. 1994, at 28.

130. CFTA, *supra* note 7, § 102(a).

COMPETITIVENESS & U.S. POLICY DISCRIMINATION

free-trade area,"[131] and (3) "liberalize significantly conditions for investment within the free trade area."[132] To this end, Article 105 required that each party "shall, to the extent provided in this Agreement, accord national treatment with respect to investment and to trade in goods and services."[133] Article 501 further provided:

> (1) Each Party shall accord national treatment to the goods of the other Party in accordance with the Provisions of Article III of the [GATT], including its interpretive notes, and to this end the provisions of Article III of the GATT and its interpretive notes are incorporated and made Part of this Agreement.
> (2) For purposes of this Agreement, the provisions of this Chapter shall be applied in accordance with existing interpretations adopted by the Contracting Parties to the GATT.[134]

Paragraph 1602(1) provided that Canada and the United States shall accord national treatment to the other's investors with respect, *inter alia*, to "the establishment of new business enterprises located in its territory"[135] and (2) "the conduct and operation of business enterprises located in its territory."[136] Paragraph 1602(8) provided certain exception to this principle where, *inter alia*, the different treatment is "equivalent in effect" to the treatment accorded to a party's own investors[137] and is "necessary for . . . consumer protection reasons."[138]

To the extent aspects of H.R. 820, the SWTIA, NISTA, and NCRPA deny Canadians national treatment with respect to trade and investment, they are inconsistent with the CFTA, unless they fall within the exemptions provided in paragraph 1602(8).[139] However, nowhere do the

---

131. *Id.* § 102(b).

132. *Id.* § 102(c).

133. *Id.* § 105.

134. *Id.* § 501.

135. *Id.* § 1602(1)(a).

136. *Id.* § 1602(1)(c).

137. *Id.* § 1602(8)(b).

138. *Id.* § 1602(8)(a).

139. Subparagraph 1601(2)(b) of the CFTA and subparagraph 1108(7)(a) of the NAFTA provide that the investment provisions of the CFTA do not cover government procurement. However, it is not clear that the programs referred to herein are primarily geared towards government procurement. Similarly, paragraph 1609(2) of the CFTA provided that the investment provisions of the CFTA did not apply to any subsidy, provided that such subsidy did "not constitute a means of arbitrary or unjustifiable discrimination between investors of the Parties or a disguised restriction on the benefits accorded to investors of the Parties under this chapter." The authors submit that the subsidy provisions described herein would not have been made safe by paragraph 1609(2) of the CFTA.

legislation or their legislative histories suggest consumer protection reasons for denying Canadian traders and investors national treatment. Similarly, these acts do not indicate that the difference in treatment for foreign investors is equivalent in effect to the treatment provided U.S. investors, a fact most readily seen with respect to H.R. 820 and, to a lesser extent, the SWTIA and NISTA, which specifically define U.S. companies in order to limit access to technology programs. The NCRPA suffers from the same problem by conditioning access to favorable antitrust treatment for production joint ventures on their location.

Paragraph 1603(1) of the CFTA also prohibited the imposition of certain performance requirements as "a term or condition of permitting an investment" or in connection with "the regulation of the conduct or operation" of a business enterprise. Of particular relevance to H.R. 820, the SWTIA, and NISTA, the CFTA prohibited requirements to (1) "purchase goods or services used by the investor in the territory of such Party or from suppliers located in such territory or accord a preference to goods or services produced in such territory"[140] or (2) "substitute goods or services from the territory of such Party for imported goods or services."[141] Similarly, the CFTA banned requirements to "achieve a given level or percentage of domestic content."[142]

Some may object that the existing SWTIA and NISTA fall within the generic exception for non-conforming legislation that pre-dated the CFTA.[143] Others may argue that the NCRPA is exempted from having to comply with the terms of the CFTA because U.S. antitrust legislation was excluded from the CFTA by Article 1607. In our view, these arguments are incorrect. First, we object to the investment-related provisions of the NCRPA, not its antitrust analysis. Second, the performance requirements of H.R. 820 clearly are inconsistent with, if not contrary to, the CFTA.

B. *The North American Free Trade Agreement*

Although the NAFTA, which took effect on January 1, 1994, shares many of the objectives of the CFTA, it goes even further. For instance, the NAFTA seeks to (1) "facilitate the cross-border movement of, goods and services between"[144] parties; and (2) "increase substantially invest-

---

140. CFTA, *supra* note 7, § 1603(1)(c).

141. *Id.* § 1603(1)(b).

142. *Id.* § 1603(1)(d).

143. *Id.* § 1607.

144. NAFTA, *supra* note 8, § 102(a).

COMPETITIVENESS & U.S. POLICY DISCRIMINATION

ment opportunities in" the territories.[145] Article 301 sets out the national treatment obligations of each party in relation to goods in terms virtually identical to those found in the CFTA. Paragraph 1102(1), which specifies the national treatment obligations of the parties as they relate to investment, is more expansive than the CFTA:

> Each Party shall accord to investors of another Party treatment no less favorable than it accords, in like circumstances, to its own investors with respect to the establishment, *expansion, management*, conduct, *operation*, and sale or *other disposition of investments*.[146]

Paragraph 1102(2) repeats the same language to emphasize that national treatment also must apply to the "investments of its own investors"—in other words, both to outward and inward foreign investment. For greater certainty, subparagraph 1102(4)(a) prohibits the imposition of a requirement that a minimum level of equity in an enterprise in the territory be held by its nationals "other than nominal qualifying shares for directors or incorporators of corporations."[147] Further, subparagraph 1105(1) establishes a minimum standard of treatment for investments of investors of another party "in accordance with international law, including fair and equitable treatment and full protection and security."

Paragraph 1106(1) prohibits the imposition of performance requirements in connection with the establishment, acquisition, expansion, management, conduct, or operation of an investment. Paragraph 1106(3) proscribes the use of domestic content[148] and preferential domestic sourcing arrangements[149] as a condition to the receipt or continued receipt of an "advantage" in connection with an investment.

If the NAFTA stopped here, we could easily conclude, based on its similarity with the CFTA, its incompatibility with H.R. 820, the SWTIA, NISTA, and NCRPA. However, paragraph 1106(4) qualifies this observation:

> Nothing in paragraph 3 shall be construed to prevent a Party from conditioning the receipt or continued receipt of an advan-

---

145. *Id.* § 102(c).
146. *Id.* § 1102(1) (emphasis added to denote changes from the CFTA).
147. *Id.* § 1102(4)(a).
148. *Id.* § 1106(3)(a).
149. *Id.* § 1106(3)(b).

tage, in connection with an investment in its territory of an investor of a Party or of a non-Party, *on compliance with a requirement to locate production*, provide a service, train or employ workers, construct or expand particular facilities, *or carry out research and development* in its territory.[150]

Further, in subparagraph 1108(7)(b), the parties except "subsidies or grants provided by a Party or a state enterprise, including government supported loans, guarantees and insurance" from the national treatment provisions of Article 1102 and the performance requirements of Article 1103.[151] Accordingly, H.R. 820, the SWTIA, NISTA, and NCRPA may not be inconsistent with the NAFTA to the extent that they permit domestic content and sourcing performance requirements in the United States, regardless of any inconsistency with the CFTA. The full extent of the inconsistency between the legislation and the NAFTA depends, of course, on the scope of an "advantage," defined in paragraph 1106(3) of the NAFTA.

Unlike the CFTA, the NAFTA does specifically address competition policy. Paragraph 1501(1) of the NAFTA provides that each party shall adopt or maintain "measures to proscribe anti-competitive business conduct and take appropriate action with respect thereto, recognizing that such measures will enhance the fulfillment of the objectives" of the agreement.[152] To this end, paragraph 1501(1) obligates the parties to consult "from time to time about the effectiveness of measures" undertaken by each party.[153] Paragraph 1501(2) further provides that the parties agree to "cooperate on issues of competition law enforcement policy."[154]

Paragraph 1501(3) specifies that the NAFTA dispute settlement provisions do not apply to matters arising under Article 1501.[155] Therefore, disputes over measures taken to proscribe anti-competitive business conduct and law enforcement policy are not subject to the dispute settlement provisions of the NAFTA. Nevertheless, nothing in NAFTA Chapter 15 indicates that the parties intended it to take precedence over the other provisions of the agreement. Nowhere in NAFTA Chapter 15 is the application of the principle of national treatment expressly

---

150. *Id.* § 1106(4) (emphasis added).
151. *Id.* § 1108(7)(b).
152. *Id.* § 1501(1).
153. *Id.*
154. *Id.* § 1501(2).
155. *Id.* § 1501(3).

COMPETITIVENESS & U.S. POLICY DISCRIMINATION

rejected with respect to competition policy. Chapter 15 merely recognizes that each party may adopt its own policies to deal with anticompetitive business conduct, subject generally to its commitment to cooperation in competition law enforcement. In other words, Chapter 15 is entirely consistent with the national treatment obligations of the parties with respect to investment set out in Article 1102. Therefore, to the extent that the NCRPA is inconsistent with the national treatment obligations of Article 1102 of the NAFTA, it is not excused solely because it arises under a provision of U.S. antitrust law. Paragraph 1112(1) provides that, in the event of an inconsistency between Chapter 11 and another chapter of the NAFTA, the other chapter "shall prevail to the extent of the inconsistency."[156] However, based on the above analysis, the NCRPA, and not NAFTA Chapter 15, is inconsistent with the national treatment obligations of the United States.

C.   *GATT Obligations*

In the Punta del Este Declaration,[157] which opened the Uruguay Round of GATT negotiations, the assembled trade ministers agreed to (1) examine the operation of GATT Articles related to the trade restrictive and distorting effects of investment measures and to (2) develop, as appropriate, further provisions necessary to avoid such adverse effects.[158] On December 15, 1994, participants in the Uruguay Round negotiations reached an agreement for a new framework to govern trade relations and to establish a World Trade Organization (WTO).[159] Trade-related investment measures (TRIMs) are addressed in Part II:7 of the Final Act (TRIMs Agreement).[160] In the preamble to the TRIMs Agreement the parties recognize that "certain investment measures can cause trade restrictive and distorting effects."[161] In Article 2:1 of the TRIMs Agreement, the Members agree to limit their

---

156. *Id.* § 1112(1).

157. GATT, Ministerial Declaration on the Uruguay Round: Declaration of 20 September 1986, 33 Supp. B.I.S.D. 19 (1987).

158. *Id.* at 26.

159. Final Act Embodying the Results of the Uruguay Round of Multilateral Trade Negotiations, MTN/FA, Dec. 15, 1993, Special Distribution (UR-93-0246) [hereinafter GATT Final Act]. Before accepting the Agreement Establishing the WTO (GATT 1994) and thereby becoming Members of the WTO (Members), participants who are not contracting parties to the GATT 1947, as subsequently amended, must conclude negotiations for their accession to the GATT 1947. *See id.* MTN/FA I, art. 5; *see also id.* MTN/FA II, art. 4.

160. Agreement on Trade-Related Investment Measures, MTN/FA II-A1A-7 [hereinafter TRIMs Agreement], *in* GATT Final Act, *supra* note 159.

161. *Id.*

ability to impose trade-related investment measures: "Without prejudice to other rights and obligations under the GATT 1994, no Member shall apply any TRIM that is inconsistent with the provisions of Article III or Article XI of the GATT 1994."[162]

Article III:1 of the GATT establishes the principle of national treatment, and GATT Article XI sets out the general prohibition of quantitative restrictions. In particular, Article III:4 of the GATT provides:

> The products of the territory of any contracting party imported into the territory of any other contracting party shall be accorded treatment no less favorable than that accorded to like products of national origin *in respect of all laws, regulations and requirements affecting their internal sale, offering for sale, purchase transportation, distribution or use* . . . .[163]

Article III:5 of the GATT generally prohibits domestic sourcing requirements:

> No contracting party shall establish or maintain any internal quantitative regulation relating to the mixture, processing or use of products in specified amounts or proportions which requires, directly or indirectly, that any specified amount or proportion of any product which is the subject of the regulation must be supplied *from domestic sources*. Moreover, no contracting party shall otherwise apply internal quantitative regulations in a manner contrary to the principles set forth in paragraph 1.[164]

Articles III:4 and III:5 of the GATT, therefore, appear to proscribe the domestic sourcing requirements established in H.R. 820, the SWTIA, and NISTA. An annex to Article 2 of the TRIMs Agreement illustrates a number of TRIMs that are inconsistent with Article III:4 of the GATT. Not surprisingly, subsection 1(a) of the TRIMs Agreement indicates that domestic sourcing requirements are inconsistent with GATT Article III:4 if compliance with them is "necessary to obtain an advantage" and if they require "the purchase or use by an enterprise of products of domestic origin or from any domestic source . . . ."[165]

Furthermore, Article 5:1 of the TRIMs Agreement provides that each

---

162. *Id.* art II:1.
163. GATT, *supra* note 9, art. III:4 (emphasis added).
164. *Id.* art. III:5 (emphasis added).
165. TRIMs Agreement, *supra* note 160, art. 2.

COMPETITIVENESS & U.S. POLICY DISCRIMINATION

Member will notify the council for trade in goods, a unit of the WTO, of all non-conforming TRIMs within ninety days of the establishment of the WTO, approximately July 1, 1995.[166] Article 5:2 further provides that each developed country Member shall eliminate all notified TRIMs within two years from the establishment of the WTO.[167]

The Contracting Parties to the GATT have addressed TRIMs in one decision, which arose out of a complaint by the United States against certain aspects of the Canadian Foreign Investment Review Act (FIRA).[168] The FIRA provided that an independent review agency would consider certain factors in determining whether a proposed investment was or was likely to be of "significant benefit" to Canada.[169] Although the FIRA did not require that investors give written undertakings to demonstrate how an investment would satisfy this test, as the FIRA was administered such undertakings were routinely submitted.[170] The GATT dispute settlement panel found the following as matters of fact:

> Undertakings given by investors (dealt) with any aspect of the conduct of a business, *including employment, research and development*, participation of Canadian shareholders and managers, productivity improvements as well as practices with respect to purchasing, manufacturing and exports.[171]

The United States asked the FIRA Panel to find that undertakings that required investors to (1) purchase goods of Canadian origin in preference to imported goods or to purchase from Canadian sources, and to (2) manufacture in Canada goods that would otherwise be imported were inconsistent with, *inter alia*, GATT Articles III:4, III:5, and XI:1.[172] Holding that domestic content requirements were not covered by its terms of reference, the FIRA Panel did not examine the

---

166. *Id.* art. 5:1.

167. *Id.* art. 5:2. In the case of developing countries and less developed countries, Article 5:2 extends the time limit to five and seven years respectively. *Id.* A footnote to Article 5:1 also provides that in the case of TRIMs applied under discretionary authority, each specific application shall be notified to the Council on Trade in Goods. *Id.* art. 5:1.

168. GATT, Canada–Administration of the Foreign Investment Review Act, Report of the Panel adopted by the GATT Council on 7 February 1984 (L/5504), 30 Supp. B.I.S.D. 140 (1984) [hereinafter FIRA Panel Report].

169. Foreign Investment Review Act, 1973 S.C., C. 46, § 2(2), (*as amended*); repealed by Investment Canada Act, R.S.C. 1985, c. 28, § 46, (1st Supp.), *as amended*, Royal assent, June 20, 1985.

170. FIRA Panel Report, *supra* note 168, § 2.4.

171. *Id.* (emphasis added).

172. *Id.* § 3.1.

LAW & POLICY IN INTERNATIONAL BUSINESS

issue.[173] However, the FIRA Panel did find that the requirements to purchase Canadian goods or from Canadian sources were inconsistent with Canada's national treatment obligations set out in Article III:4 of the GATT.[174] The FIRA Panel found further that such undertakings were not saved by additional language that conditioned the performance of the undertaking on Canadian goods being "competitively available" or "reasonably available."[175] The FIRA Panel stated that

> in those cases where the imported and domestic product are offered on equivalent terms, adherence to the undertaking would entail giving preference to the domestic product. Whether or not the investor chooses to buy Canadian goods in given practical situations, is not at issue. The purpose of Article III:4 is not to protect the interests of the foreign investor but to ensure that goods originating in any Contracting Party benefit from treatment no less favorable than domestic . . . goods, in respect of the requirements that affect their purchase . . . .The Panel considered that the alternative qualification "reasonably available" . . . is *a fortiori* inconsistent with Article III:4, since the undertaking implies that preference has to be given . . . when these are not available on entirely competitive terms.[176]

Therefore, at least the purchase requirements of H.R. 820, the SWTIA, and NISTA appear inconsistent with GATT Article III:4. Due to insufficient facts, the FIRA Panel declined to make any findings with respect to the consistency of the purchase requirements with Article III:5 of the GATT.[177] In this respect, the TRIMs Agreement appears to go beyond what the Contracting Parties had stated before. Similarly, the TRIMs Agreement appears to go beyond what the Contracting Parties decided in respect of the consistency of the FIRA purchase requirements and Article XI of the GATT. With respect to import restrictions, Article XI:1 of the GATT provides:

> No prohibitions or restrictions other than duties, taxes or other charges, whether made effective through quotas, import or

---

173. *Id.* § 5.3.
174. *Id.* §§ 5.8, 5.10.
175. *Id.* §§ 5.9, 5.11.
176. *Id.* §§ 5.9, 5.11.
177. *Id.* § 5.13.

COMPETITIVENESS & U.S. POLICY DISCRIMINATION

export licenses or other measures, shall be instituted or maintained by any contracting party *on the importation* of any product of the territory of any other contracting party.[178]

However, the FIRA Panel found that as "purchase undertakings do not prevent the importation of goods, as such they are not inconsistent with Article XI:1."[179] Subsection 2(a) of the Annex to the TRIMs Agreement proscribes restrictions relating to "the importation by an enterprise of products used in or related to its local production, generally or" to obtain an advantage, as inconsistent with GATT Article XI.[180] Therefore, whether the local sourcing requirements of H.R. 820, the SWTIA, and NISTA are consistent with GATT Article XI:1 may depend on whether the TRIMs Agreement or the FIRA Panel decision is operative.

There are two caveats to the view that H.R. 820 and the existing SWTIA and NISTA are inconsistent with the GATT. First, the FIRA Panel specifically limited its findings to the undertakings that were the subject of the U.S. contention in the panel proceedings.[181] The FIRA Panel stated:

> The Panel also wishes to stress that the considerations relating to the purchase undertakings . . . remain strictly without prejudice to the status of other undertakings agreed upon in the context of the [FIRA] and referred to in paragraph 2.4 [quoted above] but pertaining to *employment, investment, research and development* and other subjects which clearly fall outside the scope of the [GATT].[182]

Accordingly, the United States may defend the SWTIA, NISTA, and H.R. 820 as being impervious to the findings of the FIRA Panel with respect to the use of purchase requirements, because each piece of legislation deals with investment and research and development. Further, the employment requirements of the NISTA and H.R. 820 arguably fall outside the scope of the GATT. However, such a reading of the GATT renders useless the principle of national treatment and suggests that, at the very least, the FIRA Panel's findings with respect to the

---

178. GATT, *supra* note 9, art. IX:1 (emphasis added).

179. FIRA Panel Report, *supra* note 168, § 5.14.

180. TRIMs Agreement, *supra* note 160, Annex § 2(a).

181. FIRA Panel Report, *supra* note 168, § 5.21.

182. *Id.* (emphasis added).

purchase requirements should apply to the SWTIA, NISTA, and H.R. 820.[183]

Second, paragraph III:8(b) of the GATT may offer some support for certain of the provisions of H.R. 820, the SWTIA, and NISTA. Paragraph III:8(b) states:

> The provisions of this article shall not prevent the payment of subsidies *exclusively to domestic producers*, including payments to domestic producers derived from the proceeds of internal tax or charges *applied consistently with the provisions of this Article* and subsidies effected through governmental purchases of domestic products.[184]

In determining whether the restriction on financial assistance under the ATP applies to U.S. companies or U.S. manufacturers, it is necessary to understand the term "domestic producers" used in paragraph III: 8(b). Annex I, which sets out the notes to the GATT Articles, provides no assistance. In fact, paragraph III:8(b) is one of the few, if not the only, distinctions made in the GATT between "domestic" and "foreign" producers, as opposed to products. However, Article 12 of the proposed Havana Charter for an International Trade Organization,[185] upon which the GATT was based, does refer to "foreign investments." Although Article 12 of the Havana Charter, dealing with international investment for reconstruction and development, was not carried over into the GATT, clause 12(2)(a)(ii) provided that members would give "due regard to the desirability of avoiding discrimination as between foreign investments" subject to certain rights of the parties set out elsewhere in Article 12 or any agreement entered into pursuant to Article 12.[186] However, that clause 12(2)(a)(ii) appears to have envis-

---

183. Canada's response to the FIRA Panel may offer something of a precedent in support of this view. Following the adoption of the report of the FIRA Panel in February 1984, Canada changed its administrative practice of requiring domestic purchase requirements. Subsequently, the FIRA was replaced by the Investment Canada Act, which took effect in June 1985, following the election of a Progressive Conservative government. Generally, the Investment Canada Act has been administered in a more liberal manner than the FIRA; hence, no such undertakings have been required under it. *See* Alan M. Rugman & Mark A. A. Warner, *Foreign Ownership, Free Trade, and the Canadian Energy Sector,* 14 J. ENERGY & DEV. 1 (1988).

184. GATT, *supra* note 9, art. III:8(b) (emphasis added).

185. Havana Charter for an International Trade Organization, Mar. 24, 1948, art. 12 (State Dept. reprint).

186. *Id.* § 12(2)(a)(ii).

COMPETITIVENESS & U.S. POLICY DISCRIMINATION

aged nondiscrimination between foreign investments, rather than national treatment as between foreign and domestic investments.

Since paragraph III:8(b) of the GATT is reproduced from subparagraph 18(8)(b) of the Havana Charter, the legislative history of subparagraph 18(8)(b) of the Havana Charter may illuminate what is meant by "domestic producer" in paragraph III:8(b) of the GATT, and the extent to which that reference overrides other GATT provisions. With respect to subparagraph 18(8)(b) of the Havana Charter, the report of the sub-committee responsible for that article stated:

> [Sub-paragraph 18(8)(b)] was redrafted in order to make it clear that nothing in Article 18[, GATT Article III,] could be construed to sanction the exemption of domestic products from internal taxes imposed on like imported products or the remission of such taxes. At the same time the Sub-Committee recorded its view that nothing in this sub-paragraph or elsewhere in Article 18 would override the provisions [of GATT Article XVI].[187]

Article XVI of the GATT does not prohibit the use of subsidies. Although the Contracting Parties recognize the harmful effects of export subsidies, their use is only proscribed in relation to non-primary products.[188] Accordingly, while the Contracting Parties have determined that domestic products should be subject to the same internal tax regime as foreign products, it is apparently permissible to discriminate between domestic and foreign producers with respect to subsidies. Neither the GATT nor the Havana Charter offers any further assistance in delineating domestic producers and foreign producers. Therefore, as currently structured, the GATT, like the NAFTA, may permit the discriminatory subsidy provisions of the SWTIA, NISTA, and H.R. 820.

Chapter Thirteen of the Final Act, which sets out the Agreement on Subsidies and Countervailing Measures, prohibits the use of subsidies conditioned upon export performance or the use of domestic rather than imported goods.[189] However, the Subsidies Agreement specifically defines as "non-actionable" those subsidies for research conducted by

---

187. GATT, Analytical Index: Third Revision–March 1970, Notes on the Drafting, Interpretation and Application of the General Agreement 28.

188. *See also* Agreement on Interpretation and Application of Articles VI, XVI and XXIII of the GATT, *done* Apr. 12, 1979, arts. 8–10, 31 U.S.T 315, 26 Supp. B.I.S.D 56.

189. Agreement on Subsidies and Countervailing Measures, MTN/FA II-13, art. 3.

firms and higher education or research establishments.[190] Therefore, the Subsidies Agreement may be useful in disciplining the local sourcing requirements of the SWTIA, NISTA, and H.R. 820. However, any other discrimination between foreign and domestic producers in the granting of subsidies may be non-actionable by other GATT Contracting Parties if it falls within the R&D exception in paragraph 8.2(a) of the Subsidies Agreement.

D. *OECD Codes and Instruments*

Two OECD instruments define the international obligations of the United States with respect to foreign direct investment: the Code of Liberalization of Capital Movements[191] and the National Treatment Declaration[192] of the OECD Council. The Code has the status of a legally binding agreement of the OECD Council of Ministers, but the Declaration expresses only a policy commitment on the part of the OECD member countries.[193] The Code concerns both inward and outward investment while the Declaration deals only with the treatment of foreign-controlled enterprises within a host country.

The Code was adopted in 1961, just after the OECD was founded. Since 1964, signatories to the Code have been under an obligation to abolish restrictions on inward and outward direct investment "to the extent necessary for effective economic cooperation."[194] In 1984, the Code was amended by an expanded definition of direct investment that included the main features of the right of establishment.[195] In remarks accompanying the definition of direct investment, the Code states that the authorities of member states shall not maintain

[r]egulations or practices applying the granting of licenses, concessions, or similar authorisations, including conditions or

---

190. *Id.* para. 8.2(a). However, such subsidies cannot cover more than "50 percent of the costs of basic industrial research or 25 percent of the costs of applied research" and would be subject to certain other use restrictions. *Id.*

191. ORGANIZATION FOR ECONOMIC CO-OPERATION AND DEVELOPMENT, THE CODE OF LIBERALIZATION OF CAPITAL MOVEMENTS (1986) [hereinafter OECD CODE].

192. ORGANIZATION FOR ECONOMIC CO-OPERATION AND DEVELOPMENT, DECLARATION ON INTERNATIONAL INVESTMENT AND MULTINATIONAL ENTERPRISES art. II (1976), *reprinted in* OECD, NATIONAL TREATMENT FOR FOREIGN-CONTROLLED ENTERPRISES 53 (1993) [hereinafter OECD 1993]; THIRD REVISED DECISION OF THE COUNCIL (Dec. 1991), *reprinted in* OECD 1993, *supra*, at 57 (1993).

193. ORGANIZATION FOR ECONOMIC CO-OPERATION AND DEVELOPMENT, INTERNATIONAL DIRECT INVESTMENT: POLICIES AND TRENDS IN THE 1980s, at 47 (1992) [hereinafter OECD 1992].

194. OECD CODE, *supra* note 191, art. 1(a); OECD 1992, *supra* note 193, at 48.

195. OECD CODE, *supra* note 191, annex A, list A, (I)(A); OECD 1992, *supra* note 193, at 48.

COMPETITIVENESS & U.S. POLICY DISCRIMINATION

requirements attaching to such authorisations and affecting the operations of enterprises, that raise special barriers or limitations with respect to non-resident (as compared to resident) investors, and that have the intent or effect of preventing or significantly impeding inward direct investment by non-residents.[196]

The question, then, becomes whether the provisions of the SWTIA, NISTA, NCRPA, or H.R. 820 (1) constitute conditions or requirements affecting the operations of foreign-based MNEs that raise special barriers and limits to such MNEs as opposed to U.S.-based MNEs *and* (2) have the intent or effect of preventing or significantly impeding foreign direct investment in the United States. That these provisions discriminate against foreign-based MNEs as opposed to U.S.-based companies and manufacturers is evident in the performance requirements set out in the legislation's definitions of these terms. U.S. companies and manufacturers are afforded favorable treatment, as opposed to those companies and manufacturers operating in the United States that do not satisfy the definitions.

Demonstrating that the Code covers the discriminatory aspects of the existing SWTIA, NISTA, and H.R. 820 does not end the necessary analysis. Paragraph 2(a) of the Code provides that members states shall grant any authorization required for the conclusion or execution of transactions listed in Annex A of the Code. Recall that direct investment is item I of List A of Annex A. However, paragraph 2(b) permits member states to lodge reservations relating to that obligation and record them in Annex B of the Code when (1) an item is added to List A of Annex A, (2) obligations relating to an item in List A are extended, or (3) obligations relating to such item begin to apply to that member state. Therefore, it follows that paragraph 2(b) of the Code provides the mechanics by which the Code achieves the progressive liberalization of restrictions on direct investment. In short, if the United States has not listed a reservation with respect to research and development, or any of the performance requirements discussed above in relation to the SWTIA, NISTA, and H.R. 820, then any such measure subsequently imposed would not be consistent with U.S. obligations pursuant to the Code. As there are no such U.S. reservations enumerated in Annex B of the Code, the discriminatory provisions of the SWTIA, NISTA, and H.R. 820 may be in violation of the Code.[197]

---

196. OECD CODE, *supra* note 191, annex A, list A, (I)(B).

197. OECD CODE, *supra* note 191, annex B.

LAW & POLICY IN INTERNATIONAL BUSINESS

However, five various exceptions could be used to support the discriminatory aspects of the SWTIA, NISTA, and H.R. 820. First, Article 3 of the Code provides a narrow exception for measures taken by member states for public order and security reasons.[198] Second, Article 7 provides a clause of derogation whereby a member state "need not take the whole of the measures of liberalization" provided for in paragraph 2(a) if (1) its "economic and financial situation justifies such a course," (2) any measures of liberalization taken or maintained in accordance with paragraph 2(a) "result in serious economic and financial disturbance" in a member state, and (3) the member state experiences balance of payments difficulties.[199] Paragraph 7(e) indicates that a member state invoking Article 7 shall do so in a way that avoids unnecessary damage to the economic and financial interests of another member state. Third, Article 10 provides an exception for special customs and monetary unions among member states. Fourth, Annex C of the Code provides that with regard to the U.S. Constitution and the federal structure of the U.S. government, the provisions of the Code do not apply to action by a state within its own jurisdiction. In such instances, the United States undertakes to bring the provisions of the Code and the circumstances notified to the attention of the state concerned.[200]

The fifth exception is provided by Annex E, which was added to the

---

198. *Id.* art. 3. The 1988 Exon-Florio Amendment, which authorizes the President to investigate and eventually block or suspend any acquisition or other foreign investment where U.S. national security is threatened, may constitute such an exception. The term "national security" is not defined and the exercise of the President's discretion is not reviewable. The President's authority is delegated to the Secretary of the Treasury, in consultation with the Committee on Foreign Investment in the United States (CFIUS), established pursuant to Exec. Order No. 11,858, 45 C.F.C. 989 (1980), *reprinted as amended in* 15 U.S.C. § 78b (1993). Despite the potential for abuse, so far only one case has resulted in a blocked transaction, although three other cases were withdrawn and one was withdrawn before a decision. *See* 50 U.S.C. App. § 2170 (1988); 53 C.F.R. 43,999 (1988), *reprinted as amended in* 50 U.S.C. App. § 2170 (1993); *see also* Fox & Pitofsky, *supra* note 40, at 66–69; Alan M. Rugman, *Investing in the U.S. After NAFTA*, Bus. Q., Summer 1993, at 26, 30–31; ALAN M. RUGMAN, OUTWARD BOUND: CANADIAN DIRECT INVESTMENT IN THE UNITED STATES 49–50 (1987). The CFTA, the NAFTA, and the GATT also provide an exception for national security.

199. OECD CODE, *supra* note 191, art. 7.

200. Subparagraph 2(a) of Annex C to the Code only states that the United States "undertakes in conformity with constitutional provisions of the United States" to do so. *Id.* annex C (2)(a). This appears to be a less onerous standard than the "federal state clause" in Article XXIV:12 of the GATT, which requires member states to take "reasonable measures as may be available to it to ensure observance" of the GATT by the states. GATT, *supra* note 9, art. XXIV:12. Article 103 of the CFTA and Article 105 of the NAFTA are even more emphatic, as each requires that the member state use all "necessary measures" to ensure state observance of the provisions of the agreements. CFTA, *supra* note 7, art. 103; NAFTA, *supra* note 8, art. 105.

COMPETITIVENESS & U.S. POLICY DISCRIMINATION

Code in 1986.[201] Article VI of Annex E provides that reciprocity measures maintained by member states should be treated as reservations to the Code obligations. To benefit from this change, Article VIII provides that the member states would have to be recorded in paragraph VIII(5) of Annex E to the Code. The United States noted no reciprocity measures in that paragraph. Accordingly, the reciprocity provisions of the SWTIA, NISTA, NCRPA, and H.R. 820 are inconsistent with the obligations of the United States pursuant to the Code. Furthermore, the United States cannot justify use of other performance requirements on the grounds that they are reciprocity provisions because they were not notified as reservations under paragraph 2 of the Code.[202]

The other relevant OECD instrument with respect to national treatment is the non-binding Declaration, which states:

> That Member countries should, consistent with their needs to maintain public order, to protect their essential security interests, and to [fulfill] commitments relating to international peace and security, accord enterprises operating in their territories and owned or controlled directly or indirectly by nationals of another Member country . . . treatment under their laws, regulations and administrative practices, consistent with international law and no less favourable than that accorded in like situations to domestic enterprises.[203]

It is important to consider the Declaration as well as the Code, although the Declaration is not binding on member states. Despite the language of the Code contained in the remark accompanying the definition of direct investment in List A,[204] proscribing measures "affect-

---

201. OECD CODE, *supra* note 191, annex E; OECD 1992, *supra* note 193, at 49.

202. Annex E to the Code represents a significant step backward from article 8 of the Code, which provides that any member lodging a reservation pursuant to paragraph 2(a) of the Code is still entitled to benefit from measures of liberalization taken by other member states. However, in article I of Annex E to the Code, the member states note that some countries "allow inward direct investment or establishment under conditions of reciprocity . . . and/or involving discrimination among investors originating in various OECD Member countries." OECD CODE, *supra* note 191, annex E, art. I. Furthermore, in article II of Annex E, the member states recognize "that reciprocity has operated with other factors, in certain cases at least until now, to broaden the effective sphere of liberalization." *Id.* annex E, art. II. Nonetheless, in articles III and IV of Annex E, the member states reaffirm their belief that reciprocity measures could lead to greater protectionism. *Id.* annex E, arts. III, IV. Hence, the principles of national treatment in Article 8 of the Code and non-discrimination in article 9 of the Code remain important.

203. OECD 1993, *supra* note 192, at 54, para. II(1).

204. *See supra* note 174 and accompanying text.

ing the operations of enterprises," its scope under OECD practice is limited to issues affecting the right of establishment.[205] The OECD Committee on International Investment and Multinational Enterprises,[206] which is responsible for the interpretation and implementation of the Declaration, has established "a clear operational dividing line" between the Declaration and the Code.[207] According to this convention, the committee is responsible for applying the Declaration to issues arising out of the post-entry treatment of foreign MNEs. However, this convention does not alter the obligations of the United States under the Code. Consequently, we submit that the discriminatory provisions of the SWTIA, NISTA, NCRPA, and H.R. 820 are not regulated by the non-binding Declaration to the exclusion of the binding Code. In any case, the United States has not designated any provision of that legislation as an exception for transparency reasons pursuant to the Declaration.[208] Furthermore, in November 1988, the member states reached a "standstill" understanding in the committee that no member state would introduce new measures contrary to the Declaration.[209]

E. *Conclusion*

In summary, we have shown that (1) the discriminatory provisions of the SWTIA, NISTA, NCRPA, and H.R. 820 are clearly inconsistent with the CFTA; (2) certain of the performance requirements associated with these measures may be inconsistent with the NAFTA; (3) the reciprocity provisions of the NCRPA may be inconsistent with the national treatment provisions of the NAFTA; (4) the local sourcing requirements of the SWTIA, NISTA, and H.R. 820 are inconsistent with the GATT national treatment provisions; (5) the domestic content requirements of the SWTIA, NISTA, NCRPA, and H.R. 820 may be inconsistent with GATT national treatment provisions; (6) the employment and R&D performance requirements and governmental support provided in H.R. 820, the NISTA, and SWTIA[210] appear to be consistent with GATT national treatment provisions; (7) the performance requirements of the

---

205. OECD 1993, *supra* note 192, at 23.

206. *See* OECD 1993, *supra* note 192, art. IV. The Committee on Capital Movements and Invisible Transactions is responsible for the interpretation and implementation of the Code. *See* OECD CODE, *supra* note 191, art. 18.

207. OECD 1993, *supra* note 192, at 23.

208. *See id.* at 127, 175.

209. OECD 1992, *supra* note 193, at 51, 55 n.8; OECD 1993, *supra* note 192, at 23–24, 37 n.1.

210. Subpara. 3710a(c)(4)(B) of the SWTIA, *supra* note 49, does not impose any employment-related performance requirements.

COMPETITIVENESS & U.S. POLICY DISCRIMINATION

SWTIA, NISTA, NCRPA, and H.R. 820 may be inconsistent with U.S. obligations under the OECD Code and Declaration; and (8) the reciprocity provisions of the SWTIA, NISTA, NCRPA, and H.R. 820 are inconsistent with U.S. obligations under the Code and the Declaration.[211]

V.   Conclusions: The Need for International Discipline

This Article has examined a disturbing emergence of protectionism in antitrust and R&D policy in the United States. These discriminatory policies are not efficient long-term strategies for MNEs. Ultimately, they may be welfare-reducing from the point of view of the nation or the global trading system. In addition, such discriminatory policies are only covered partially by existing bilateral and multilateral arrangements. Therefore, in this section, we discuss the outlines of an appropriate international discipline for protectionist investment, antitrust, and R&D policies.

We do not support the establishment of what has been termed by some commentators as a "GATT for investment" that would resemble the agenda of the "Group of 77" during the 1970s.[212] However, the Triad[213] members of North America, the European Union, and Japan may need to negotiate an agreement that would safeguard certain fundamental principles such as national treatment, non-discrimination, and the right of establishment. While the significant evidence of the distortive effects of performance requirements has been catalogued extensively elsewhere,[214] it is doubtful that their prohibition can be achieved any time soon. However, at the very least, the analysis of this Article strongly suggests that nations must commit to ensuring that performance requirements adhere to the principles of national treatment and non-discrimination. In this regard, the model should be the CFTA, not the NAFTA, since the latter appears to qualify the principle of national treatment as it applies to performance requirements. Such

---

211. This Article has not discussed whether the discriminatory terms of the existing SWTIA and NISTA, H.R. 820, and the NCRPA also may be inconsistent with various U.S. bilateral investment treaties. As many of these treaties also provide for national treatment, much of the analysis herein would be applicable to those treaties as well. *See* Kenneth J. Vandevelde, *U.S. Bilateral Investment Treaties: The Second Wave*, 14 MICH. J. INT'L L. 621, 650 (1993).

212. C. F. Bergsten & E. M. Graham, *Needed: New Rules for Foreign Direct Investment*, 7 INT'L TRADE J. 15, 33 (1992).

213. KENICHI OHMAE, TRIAD POWER: THE COMING SHAPE OF GLOBAL COMPETITION (1985).

214. *See, e.g.*, ORGANIZATION FOR ECONOMIC CO-OPERATION AND DEVELOPMENT, INTERNATIONAL INVESTMENT AND MULTINATIONAL ENTERPRISES: INVESTMENT INCENTIVES AND DISINCENTIVES: EFFECTS ON INTERNATIONAL DIRECT INVESTMENT 43–63 (1993).

LAW & POLICY IN INTERNATIONAL BUSINESS

an agreement also should apply to domestic competition,[215] trade, investment, and R&D laws without exception.

Existing international instruments do not unambiguously establish these principles. One way of furthering the adoption and adherence to these policies may be to state them in the form of binding and enforceable legal rights. Here, the investment-related dispute settlement provisions of the NAFTA may provide a useful point of departure. Section B of Chapter 11 of the NAFTA provides for the binding arbitration of certain disputes between investors and member states.[216] If a provision of this sort were included in any new international investment discipline, MNEs would have greater assurance that their substantive rights gained under such an agreement would not be bargained away on a case-by-case basis in political settlements among the member states.[217] Accordingly, investors would receive real protection from the kind of discriminatory policy measures discussed in this Article.

---

215. *See also* Mark A. A. Warner, *Efficiencies and Merger Analysis in Canada, the European Community and the United States: Implications for Harmonization/Convergence*, 26 VAND. J. TRANSNAT'L L. 1059 (1994); E.M. Graham & Mark A. A. Warner, *Multinationals and Competition Policy, in* MULTINATIONALS IN NORTH AMERICA (L. Eden ed., 1994).

216. NAFTA, *supra* note 8, arts. 1116–38.

217. For recent trends in investor to state relations in U.S. bilateral investment treaties, see Vandevelde, *supra* note 211, at 655.

Name Index